THE GOSPEL
ACCORDING TO JOHN

THE GOSPEL ACCORDING TO JOHN

A Literary and Theological Commentary

THOMAS L. BRODIE

OXFORD UNIVERSITY PRESS

New York   Oxford

Oxford University Press

Oxford   New York
Athens   Auckland   Bangkok   Bogota   Bombay   Buenos Aires
Calcutta   Cape Town   Dar es Salaam   Delhi   Florence   Hong Kong
Istanbul   Karachi   Kuala Lumpur   Madras   Madrid   Melbourne
Mexico City   Nairobi   Paris   Singapore   Taipei   Tokyo   Toronto   Warsaw

and associated companies in
Berlin   Ibadan

Copyright © 1993 by Thomas L. Brodie

First published in 1993 by Oxford University Press, Inc.
198 Madison Avenue, New York, New York 10016

First issued as an Oxford University Press paperback, 1997.

Oxford is a registered trademark of Oxford University Press, Inc.

Library of Congress Cataloging-in-Publication Data
Brodie, Thomas.
The Gospel according to John : a literary
and theological commentary / Thomas Brodie.
p. cm.   Includes author's translation of text.
Includes bibliographical references and index.
ISBN 0-19-505800-3; ISBN 0-19-511811-1 (pbk.)
1. Bible. N. T. John—Commentaries.
I. Bible. N. T. John. English. Brodie.
1993. II. Title.
BS2615.3.B74   1993   226.5'07—dc20
91-38200

1 3 5 7 9 8 6 4 2

Printed in the United States of America
on acid-free paper

*To my mother
and in memory of my father*

*and to the Clare footballers
for ending a long exile*

Preface

In recent years biblical studies have been faced with a crisis: the emphasis on the historical approach, which has prevailed during most of the modern era, is being challenged by a quite different, literary, approach. There is disagreement as to the extent of this crisis. Some regard the literary approach as a passing peculiarity. Others see it as introducing into biblical studies a fundamental change of method, a "scientific revolution."

What is certain is that biblical publications, including Johannine publications, may now largely be divided into two quite distinct and sometimes unrelated groups, one historical, the other literary. At the same time evidence is emerging of the need to develop a further and more traditional aspect of the fourth gospel—the spiritual. As a consequence, even though there are already in existence many good commentaries on John, something further is becoming necessary—a commentary which brings the different approaches together.

The present work seeks to meet that need. It does not seek to establish the gospel's historical background and sources; that is done in a separate study (Brodie, 1993). The purpose here is to glean the results of the best Johannine writers and commentators of the last century, from Westcott to Beasley-Murray, and at the same time, without becoming unduly entangled in literary theory and terminology, to take account of the essential insights of modern literary criticism. The result, so it is hoped, is to clarify the gospel, particularly its unified structure and its down-to-earth spiritual message.

Tallaght, Dublin   T.B.
November 1991

Acknowledgements

Now that the task is done there is a sense both of gratitude and of inadequacy. The gratitude is to all those, more than can be named here, who contributed to the making of this commentary. Perhaps the most decisive contributions were indirect—people who in various ways over many years have given support, criticism, confrontation—from the first unforgettable students in Trinidad and later friends in other places to the challenging colleagueship of the biblical societies.

Yet it is appropriate to mention some of those whose involvement was immediate: Diana Culbertson, of Kent State University, for invaluable advice and criticism; Everard Johnston, of the University of the West Indies, Trinidad, for reading critically certain sections of the manuscript; Yale Divinity School for granting an extended research fellowship; Harry Byrne, M. Catherine Hilkert, and Ellen Murray, all of Aquinas Institute of Theology, for diverse ideas, particularly the centrality of John's emphasis on rest; Ann Riggs of Marquette University, along with Joe O'Brien and Philip MacShane, both of the Dominican Studium, Tallaght, for guiding this rustic writer through the dark night of the computer; and Ann Cunningham, of Pietermaritzburg, South Africa, for providing, at a critical juncture, the encouragement to keep going.

It is necessary also to acknowledge inadequacy, a sense of not having given full expression to the evangelist's vision. The problem is not just that the text is difficult and the secondary literature vast, but that there is an aspect of John which almost lies beyond literary and theological commentary. The present writer hopes to have made a genuine contribution, yet the clearer the picture has become, the clearer also has become his awareness that there is much waiting to be discovered.

Contents

THE COMMENTARY
Book One • The Years of Jesus' Life
(chapters 1–12)

THE COMMENTARY
Book Two • Part 3B
The Central Mystery
Passover (chapters 13–21)

We have reached the moon and lost sight of our souls.
Elie Wiesel (1987, *paraphrased*)

INTRODUCTION

1

Johannine Studies:
The Three Ages
of Interpretation

To set the historical and literary methods in perspective, this opening chapter summarizes very briefly certain basic aspects of the history of biblical interpretation, particularly as that history impinges on Johannine studies.

To some degree the process of interpreting the Bible is easy. There are many passages which almost never fail to provide some form of meaning, whether instruction or encouragement or enjoyment.

But a more complete process of interpreting requires many competencies or skills. In interpreting the NT, for instance, it is useful to know Greek. It is also useful, given the fact that there are variants among the ancient manuscripts, if one is experienced in textual criticism.

Skills, however, need to be used in a way which is balanced, measured. Otherwise, they may be counterproductive. If, for instance, a commentary consists largely of a discussion of ancient grammar and philology, then the skill involved has become a source, not of clarification, but of distraction. Such a study may be a valuable work of research, but it is scarcely a commentary on scripture. A good commentary uses all the necessary skills and does so in an appropriate way.

To a significant degree the history of interpretation consists of the history of three basic skills—theological, historical, and literary. The theological skill dominated until the eighteenth century. Then came the historical. And the literary has just begun to emerge. Obviously to some degree all three have been present in every period, and as Meir Sternberg has warned (1985, 3–4), it is unrealistic, given the variety of approaches, ancient and modern, to refer to "*the* literary approach." But the differences of emphasis are great, so great in fact, that one may legitimately speak of three distinct ages.

The Theological Emphasis (Until the Eighteenth Century)

For many centuries the primary emphasis in the interpretation of John was on its theological meaning. There was, of course, considerable diversity, particularly between the literal and symbolic interpretations, yet there was considerable unanimity on basic presuppositions. It was taken for granted that the text was a unity, an inspired unity, and that, when properly interpreted, it provided reliable insight

3

into Christ and the ultimate meaning of life. The task of the commentator was to elaborate that insight.

In describing the biblical studies of these centuries the adjective sometimes used is "precritical"—a term which may seem to suggest that the writers of that period did not use their critical abilities, their powers of thinking. It is true that, on one level, there was a certain naivete. There were certain questions which were not asked, particularly historical questions. But to characterize the entire period as precritical is unbalanced. One can scarcely regard as lacking in critical abilities such incisive thinkers as Augustine, Aquinas, and Calvin—all of whom have written commentaries on John and all of whom, in the course of commenting on the text, have wrestled with basic and perplexing questions. It seems better, therefore, rather than characterizing the period as precritical, to refer to it as theological, or at least to refer to it in some way which brings out what it was, rather than what it was not.

The Historical Emphasis (Nineteenth and Twentieth Centuries)

Roughly at the same time that scientific discoveries, such as those of Galileo and Copernicus, were enabling science to break free of ancient views, and thus to become an independent discipline, historical studies also were breaking free of ancient restraints. By the seventeenth century, history was an independent discipline, a distinct skill or method. Just as those who learned the new science could look at the heavens and see things not seen by others, so those practiced in historical studies could look at ancient documents and arrive at new conclusions and new questions. Eventually the historical method began to be applied to the Bible (Krentz, 1975, 10–30).

There has been wide-ranging discussion about what exactly history means (Collingwood, 1946; Gardiner, 1959; Manuel, 1965), but one thing is certain: the historical method, whatever its ultimate philosophical foundations and ramifications, is a skill. It is not the totality of interpretative method; but neither is it useless.

During the nineteenth and twentieth centuries the process of theological exposition on John did not die. On the contrary, it was developed and enriched, particularly in commentaries such as those of Westcott, Hoskyns, Bultmann, and Schnackenburg. But very often the dominating interest of these years was in history. This was true of both "liberals" and "conservatives." However bitterly divided in their views, both sides, apparently without fully realizing what they were doing, agreed implicitly to put historical questions on a pedestal and to ask, not "What does it mean?" but "Did it happen?" The result was a fundamental change of focus: attention shifted from the text to its background, to the reconstructing of events and of earlier texts. The entire process of interpretation became so dominated by the single question of history that acceptable interpretative procedure came to be known as the historical-critical method, or, quite simply, the historical method. Rarely has so complex an endeavor been so governed by a single consideration, a single skill.

Hoskyns (41) saw the situation as one of profound confusion between theology and history, and he lamented the fact that "the historians had driven the theologians almost completely out of the field." It is sometimes told by R. E. Brown (for instance, when addressing the Society of Biblical Literature in New York, Dec. 20, 1982) that, when he was about to embark on his Anchor Bible commentary on John, W. F. Albright, his prestigious mentor and editor, counseled him to write a work which would deal with history rather than theology. Brown replied that in view of the way in which the gospel begins (". . . and the Word was God"), it would be difficult to write a commentary which did not deal with theology. The resulting two-volume study turned out to be uniquely comprehensive and richly theological, one to which the present writer is profoundly indebted. Yet, despite Brown's care to be thorough, the preoccupation with history still shows through. It is on that single concern that his survey of research is centered (Brown, xxi–xxii), and it is a concern which in many ways dominates his approach to the text. The same is true, for instance, of the longer survey of Haenchen (1:23–39).

The historical method's quest for history has met with mixed success. In the nineteenth century it had one central disappointment—the quest for the historical Jesus. But it also achieved a major breakthrough: it established, with considerable certainly, that both Matthew and Luke depended on Mark. In the twentieth century, as it moved even farther from the idea of full-fledged writers who composed unified texts and entered into the worlds of form criticism (based on the concept of oral tradition) and redaction criticism, historical criticism has been bedeviled by the vagueness of its central concepts—oral tradition and redaction. There has been no clear agreement, nor even a rough agreement, on how oral transmission actually works (see Kelber, 1983, 1–14); nor is there a clear understanding of the role of editors (see esp. Miles, 1981). The result has been a proliferation of complex and unverifiable reconstructions of how the various texts originated and developed.

Since the emphasis on history tended to lead people away from the final text and back into a world of reconstructions, reconstructions which at times seemed fragile or hollow, some scholars eventually began to protest against the dominance of the historical method, and even to declare the method itself to be bankrupt (Wink, 1973, 1; cf. R. E. C. Johnston, 1977, 1–23.)

But just when the historical method seemed destined to take a more modest role, in the mid-1970s, it found vigorous life within a vast new undertaking—the sociological approach. This is a method which has had considerable influence on Johannine studies, and so it is necessary to assess it briefly.

The essence of sociology is that it examines not just one aspect of society but the amalgamation of all the aspects. History by comparison has frequently been narrow—a report on, say, politics and religion—and as such it has sometimes been seen not as one of the humanities but as a subdiscipline of sociology, as one of the social sciences. History, for instance, may say that people were poor, but sociology goes further; it asks why, it seeks to trace all the underlying factors and the complex connections between those factors. If accurate history is valuable, accurate sociology is doubly so.

Accuracy, however, does not come easily. In seeking to analyze the social history of early Christianity there are two major hazards. The first is the inherent fragility of the discipline, the difficulty, even when one knows the basic facts, of analyzing a society correctly. One may live in the midst of a situation, and yet not understand it. Probably the most influential social analysis of all time was that of Karl Marx. Many of his facts were right and many of his observations astute, but the analysis as a whole was profoundly misleading.

The second problem is that, because of the time-gap of two thousand years, it is not possible to have a clear view of the initial facts. It is not just the life of Jesus which is elusive. So also is the life of the communities. Much is said, for instance, of a supposedly distinct Johannine community, but the most elementary facts about such a community are in dispute. It may seem at first that the gospels and epistles provide ample material for writing a social history, but that is debatable. If a text is primarily theological or rhetorical, then it is not easy to use it as a basis for reconstructing social conditions. The present-day endeavor to write the social history of the early church is a variation on the nineteenth century endeavor to write a life of Jesus, and it may end the same way—with a realization that the key documents are not adequate for the task.

In assessing the use of sociology, therefore, it is necessary to distinguish. When sociology is limited to social description—to telling and integrating what is known of first-century society and church—it provides a valuable service. But when it begins to reconstruct history and to base those reconstructions on theoretical social-science models, it can become misleading and can obscure the biblical text (for reviews and assessments, see esp. Harrington, 1980; Osiek, 1989; also Kee, 1989, 32–64; Holmberg, 1990).

Given the ability of historical criticism and of social analysis to lose sight both of theology and of the text, it was inevitable that some researchers would protest. One such reaction was canonical criticism (Sanders, 1984; Rendtorff, 1985; and esp. Childs, 1979, 1985). The basic point of canonical criticism was simple and central: whatever the merits of history, the essential meaning of scripture consists of the theological message which is contained in its final canonical form.

Childs has been accused of setting the Bible adrift from the people or church which produced it—an action which, in interpreting the Bible, would effectively deny the usefulness of background information, and which would tend to reinforce the unbalanced principle of relying on scripture alone (without the appropriate help of other people and of the church as a whole) (Brown, 1990, 71:74).

Yet, whatever its dangers, Childs's work was like the legitimate call of an alarmed watchman. It was a cry, in the face of advancing disintegration, to try to save the unity of the text.

Meanwhile, even as canonical criticism was beginning to develop, a further and far wider form of protest had already gathered momentum.

The Literary Emphasis (Twentieth Century)

The literary emphasis of recent decades has two basic aspects. The first, which is more innovative and which has received more publicity than the other, is based largely on a literary criticism which is relatively modern. In 1941, J. C. Ransom, in speaking of the works of several writers (especially I. A. Richards, W. Empson, T. S. Eliot and Y. Winters), brought attention to the existence of what he called the New Criticism (see Ransom, 1941).

It was not something of which Ransom particularly approved. On the contrary, his remarks were quite critical. Nor was the New Criticism of which he spoke a single, clearly defined method. But he had detected certain trends and his book helped greatly to articulate them.

The essence of these trends was the tendency to look not at the background of the text—at its author and origins—but at the text itself, the finished work—its integrity and structure, its interrelating of form and content. In other words, as a later writer would put it (Krieger, 1964, 3–4), texts are to be regarded not as windows, as ways of looking at something beyond, at distant events, but as mirrors, as surfaces which contain coherent worlds of meaning.

The impetus for this shift, from the author's world to the finished text, has not come from the New Criticism alone. It has also been informed by other literary circles, particularly the French method of *explication de textes* and the Russian formalists (cf. Wellek and Warren, 1977, 139–40; Jefferson, 1982, 16–37). It has been further underlined in some recent philosophical work, particularly that of Paul Ricoeur (see esp. R. E. C. Johnston, 1977; and Henry, 1979, 59–69). Structural criticism, though generally coming at texts from a very different, anthropologically inspired, point of view, has had the effect of strengthening the move from concentration on the author to concentration on the finished text (cf. Culler, 1975).

Recent decades have also seen the rise of deconstruction (for introductions, see Norris, 1982; Leitch, 1983). This form of criticism is as varied as its practitioners, but it is characterized by two main features. On the one hand, in the perspective of George Steiner (1989, esp. 77–127), it is a form of obscure nihilistic philosophy: words are deprived of their meaning (they refer to other words, not to any reality). In interpretation, anything goes and everything is void. On the other hand, deconstruction is a way of exposing some of the privileged misinterpretations of Western thought. Edward Said's *Orientalism* (1978), for example, shows to what extent western writers have constructed an unreal world, "the Orient." At its best, deconstruction is a wholesome philosophy of affirmation.

Partly because of the obscurantist vocabulary of postmodern literary theory and of deconstructionist writing especially, literary analysis has at times seemed to be more obviously bankrupt than the historical method.

The impact of modern literary criticism on gospel studies first began to emerge clearly about 1974. That was the year in which Paul Minear's lectures (published 1976) signaled a change of method, and in which a group from the Society of Biblical Literature embarked on what was to become a renewed approach to Luke-Acts. It was also the year of the launching of the experimental journal *Semeia*.

The entire story of literary criticism's impact on gospel interpretation has since been chronicled in detail (Moore, 1989).

Since 1974, both in *Semeia* and in other publications, a growing number of scholars have examined the biblical texts, not by regarding them as edited collections of fragments or by focusing on their origins, but by taking seriously the unity of the finished text. In an argument of great urgency and erudition, Northrop Frye (1981, esp. 40–42) appealed to biblical scholars to "relax . . . [from] their obsession with the Bible's historicity" and to give other hypotheses a chance. Fortress Press, sidestepping the quest both for the historical Jesus and for primitive communities, began publishing a series of four slim volumes on the gospels as unified narratives, as stories. In 1984 Robert Kysar brought out the volume on John, *John's Story of Jesus,* and at about the same time R. A. Culpepper (1983), published a study of John which was much more complex, *Anatomy of the Fourth Gospel. A Study in Literary Design.* Then, in 1988, came J. L. Staley's *The Print's First Kiss: A Rhetorical Investigation of the Implied Reader in the Fourth Gospel.*

What has emerged is that the Bible may usefully be approached as literature, that it has many of literature's basic qualities. This is not altogether a surprise. "No book could have had its influence on literature without itself having literary qualities, and the Bible is a work of literature as long as it is being examined by a literary critic" (Frye, 1971, 315).

The second aspect of the recent literary emphasis has to do not with modern criticism but with the ancient tradition, with rhetoric. Rhetoric was not some specialized interest, limited to one "department" of Greco-Roman schooling or politics. It pervaded the entire process of educated expression and was intimately linked with writing. As is shown, for instance, by Quintilian's review of great writers, (*Inst. Orat.* 10.1.42–131), rhetorical criticism *was* literary criticism. Promoted avidly by both the Greeks and the Romans, rhetoric "encapsulated the most ancient, central, and pervasive tradition of verbalization and of thought known to mankind at least in the West" (Ong, 1977, 214).

What is now becoming clear is that the NT has considerable affinity with ancient rhetoric, and thus with ancient (Greco-Roman) literature. For a long time such a link had not been suspected, or at least had not been emphasized. Bultmann denied such a connection; despite his immense emphasis on the relationship of the gospels, especially John, with Greco-Roman cultural elements, he did not connect the NT with Greco-Roman literature. On the contrary, he declared that the gospels, at least the synoptics, were "unliterary" [*unliterarisch*] (1963, 6; cf. 374; 1957, 7).

The basic idea of the connection between the NT and rhetoric makes sense. If the NT has influenced literature and may profitably be regarded as literature, then it must have been formed in connection with some kind of literary context; and the pervasive literary context of the first century was that of rhetoric. Besides, it had long been recognized that Luke, at least, was a writer in the Greco-Roman mold.

Unlike the emergence of the importance of *modern* literary criticism, dramatized as it was by the appearance of *Semeia,* it does not seem possible, when speaking of the emergence of the importance of ancient rhetoric, to point to a single landmark date. What has appeared is not so much one pivotal publication as a fairly steady stream of rather specialized studies. However, there are certain landmark qualities to H. D. Betz's *Galatians* (1979) and G. A. Kennedy's *New Testament Interpretation through Rhetorical Criticism* (1984). Betz showed that what might perhaps be considered as one of the less literary documents of the NT —Galatians is often regarded as a spontaneous letter expressing a rather emotional outburst—turns out, on close inspection, to involve the careful use of several rhetorical procedures. And Kennedy's work states programmatically the relevance and usefulness of rhetoric to NT studies.

Conclusion: A Triad of Strengths and Limitations

It is too soon to try to reach a clear and definitive judgement on the relative merits of the three approaches. But even at this stage one may say that each has limitations and strengths.

All three methods include some degree of incompleteness. The theological approach, intent on ultimate meaning, pays little attention to important questions of history and literary structure. Recent literary criticism occasionally gives the impression of bypassing some legitimate traditional concerns. And the history-oriented commentaries, in their preoccupation with one facet of the gospel, sometimes involve a persistent misreading of the text, a persistent lack of balance. This is true even of so comprehensive and helpful a commentary as that of Brown. Again and again the preoccupation with history prevents the commentator from seeing to what extent the focus of the text is not primarily on history at all, but on theological art. This misreading is somewhat akin to misreading a person, to being so preoccupied with one aspect of a person that the overall person is misconstrued, is never properly understood. The commentators of earlier centuries, despite all their limitations, often grasped more clearly the essence of John's focus.

The three approaches have tendencies toward certain excesses. In particular, the theological emphasis has sometimes tended towards arbitrary symbolism, the historical towards disproportionately long footnotes, and the literary towards a terminology which seems unnecessarily esoteric. Unlike the arbitrary symbolism, the long notes and complex terminology appear to have a genuine legitimacy, yet there sometimes comes a stage when, in different ways, all three excesses achieve essentially the same negative result: they obscure the view of the text. As Childs remarks at one point (1985, 548): "The danger is acute of losing the biblical text in a mountain of endless historical and philological notes."

A similar danger seems to threaten literary studies. J. Becker (1986, 13) sees some of these studies as formalistic—a reference apparently to a kind of literary scholasticism. Staley's early chapters (1988, 10–19, 28–32) suggest that there has been uncertainty with regard both to method and terminology and, at one point (p. 19), in an unwitting echo of Childs, he remarks: "We are faced with such a bewildering array of multilayered effects that the implied reader gets lost in the intratextual labyrinth, and we are left wondering whether he can ever find his way through the text.''

Another way to express some of the traits of the three methods is to say that all three have some tendencies towards a kind of "totalitarianism," in other words, towards seeing their own particular method as essentially total, complete, or at least as being *the* correct way to approach the text, a way which may not be fundamentally questioned. For centuries the theological method carried on blithely, presupposing that its emphasis was correct and comprehensive, and when historical questions were raised it often resisted fiercely. The historical emphasis, having painfully gained a hearing, has sometimes tended to regard all that preceded as *precritical,* and, in face of the rise of literary studies, to declare its own method to be *classic.* The literary method, however insightful it may be, can sometimes leave the impression that, in practice, little account need be taken of earlier approaches; as Becker comments (1986, 7), it can appear autocratic. It could even be argued, from the viewpoint of modern literary criticism, that the historical method has been precritical. The cycle of exclusivity rolls on.

There are, of course, some advantages to a certain amount of exclusivity. Very often it is only by allowing a method to develop on its own that it can reach a necessary degree of maturity.

There comes a time, however, when it is necessary to integrate the diverse kinds of emphases. Literary critics, having turned away from the preoccupation with historical origins in order to give some overdue attention to the finished text, are now accepting the need to face historical questions and "are seeking . . . a more balanced bifocal vision" (Petersen, 1978, 24).

Something similar seems to be more and more necessary in biblical studies. However limited one or another method may sometimes appear, the fact is that ultimately each represents a skill which is not only valid but valuable. As Sternberg (1985, 17) concludes about the historical and literary orientations: they "must join forces within each and every inquiry." In examining John's gospel, therefore, it is necessary to take account of all three major interpretive emphases.

2

The Approach Adopted
in This Commentary

The initial problem in developing a commentary is to find an appropriate method of approaching the text. Where does one begin? A glance at existing commentaries shows there is no agreed format, and this uncertainty is aggravated by recent discussion about exegetical method in general. The very role of commentaries is uncertain (Anderson, 1982). To some extent, of course, uncertainty is appropriate. Interpretation, in many ways, is a circular process—the proverbial "hermeneutical circle"—and in that process "we can only comprehend the details of a work by projecting a sense of the whole, just as conversely, we can only achieve a view of the whole by working through its parts" (Armstrong, 1983, 341). Thus, there is no escape from a procedure of trial and error.

Of the three basic aspects of exegetical debate—theological, historical, and literary—the best starting point seems to be the literary. From one point of view this may appear obvious. After all, the one thing that is certain is that the object of discussion is in some way literary—at least in the minimum sense of its having been written. It may seem, however, that it would be better to begin with the historical. In modern times it has become common, when writing a commentary, and when commenting on particular passages, first, to give a discussion of sources, of historical background, and of historicity. Such an approach makes a certain amount of sense. It seeks to put first things first—raw material before finished products, causes before results. Furthermore, it is arguable that in order to make any sense of a text some basic background knowledge is essential.

This is true, and it is necessary to take account of it. But there comes a point when the initial focusing of attention on an elusive background may draw attention away from the one thing that is stable, the finished text. And thus the background discussion, instead of casting light on what is obscure, may tend instead to cast confusion on what is certain. It is one of those cases in which "the historical question is posed prematurely" (Sarason, 1981, 61).

It seems better, therefore, first, to do as much as possible with what is certain, with the finished text, and only then to begin the delicate task of elaborating the background. In the words of Robert Kysar (1984, 11):

> We cannot really probe the historical setting of the Gospel . . . unless we understand the basic story of the Gospel as a whole. But once having seen how the Gospel story "works," then the interested historian can go on to the task of discovering what is behind the Gospel.

A similar idea has been promoted in a more general way by Wellek and Warren: ". . . the study of literature should, first and foremost, concentrate on the actual works of art themselves" (1977, 139).

These observations, particularly those of Sarason and Kysar, touch on something basic—the fact that there is no shortcut to history. Some historical critics, in their justifiable concern about answering historical questions, believe that the best thing they can do is press on with the historical method—and bypass the literary approach. But, to a significant extent, that is not possible. Paradoxical as it may sound, the historical method, as commonly practiced, is not the surest way of making progress in historical research. It is becoming more and more clear that literary appreciation, ancient and modern, is crucial to understanding the very nature of the NT documents—including their value as history. Any investigative method which does not adequately consider such basic data does not do justice to the cause of historical research. It is the literary aspect, therefore, which will be treated first.

It is partly because of these rather theoretical considerations that it has seemed best, in commenting on John, to concentrate on the gospel's final text, and to lay aside, in a separate volume (Brodie, 1993), questions concerning the gospel's sources and background.

Apart, however, from theoretical considerations, there have also been considerations that were more practical. At an early stage of writing this work, it seemed that it would be good, after examining each chapter or major section, to give immediately a study of its sources. This had obvious attractions. But it eventually became evident that, as the theoretical considerations suggest, it also had a major drawback: by the time one had finished with the complex discussion of sources, concentration on the final text had been lost, and, in the process, the text's delicate continuity, including its "self-referring quality" (Meeks, 1972, 68), was being obscured.

In assessing the relationship between the gospels' literary and theological aspects, it is arguable that the theological is the more essential and is, therefore, primary. Such is the implication of Hoskyns's opening line: "The Gospel according to John is a strictly 'theological' work" (17). Such also would seem to be one of the implications of the canonical approach, particularly as proposed by Childs.

But though the theological aspect is first in ultimate value (first ontologically), it is not first methodologically (or logically). The literary is what demands one's initial attention. In seeking the meaning of *Hamlet,* for instance, it is helpful at first to know the very simple literary fact that the play consists of so many acts and scenes. But in the case of John's gospel the basic divisions are not indicated, and so, before launching into theological exposition, it is first necessary to attend to the literary task of trying to discern how the gospel is organized. The same is true for other literary aspects; their detection opens the way for theological understanding.

One of the problems with the canonical approach is that, in its rush towards theology—a rush which is akin to the historical method's haste towards history —it tends to bypass adequate literary analysis. But there can be no shortcut. Failure to attend to the literary dimension impoverishes not only the historical dimension but also the theological aspect. In this commentary, therefore, the literary approach is foundational.

Yet there is no question here of trying to integrate all the aspects of recent literary research. In fact, some of the more obscure literary concepts and terminology have been deliberately avoided. In particular, even though attention has been paid to the reader, it has seemed better not to use the technical term "implied reader." This term has played a major role in recent criticism (see esp. Iser, 1974; 1978, 34–38), yet its meaning is unclear (cf. Tompkins, 1980, 201–32; Freund, 1987, 152–56; Moore, 1988, 141–59; 1989, 71–107). And insofar as it is clear it is not always convincing: "Wolfgang Iser's implied reader is a cerebral, modern construct. . . . Criticism is an institution to which real readers need not apply" (Moore, 1989, 100, 106). The danger of becoming involved in complex theory is underlined by the fact that Alter (1984) sees the rise of literary theory as contributing to "the decline and fall of literary criticism" (see also Mitchell, 1985). Rather than engage extensively in theory, the purpose here has been to take the essence of the literary approach—a respect for the unity of the finished text, as well as some of the leading literary concepts—and to attempt thereby to cast light on the gospel.

The most basic literary feature which this study seeks to discern is the text's structure—both the structure (design/plan) of the gospel as a whole and the structure of its various parts. The structure of a book is like the anatomy of a body; it gives a foundational sense of the work's organization and contents.

Analyzing the structure of the text is not always easy; in fact, such analysis may seem at times to be complex and boring—like going into the details of medicine or car engines or fine cooking. But medicine, engines, and cooking, when given sufficient time and attention, can be quite fascinating. What is necessary perhaps, to avoid frustration, is that the reader become fully aware of the two possibilities, boredom or engagement, and decide in advance whether to invest the necessary time.

A further feature of this study is its frequent reference not to what the gospel clearly states but rather to what it evokes. This may seem to be a questionable procedure but, as Clines (1980, esp. 126) indicates, one of the basic achievements of good literature is not just to make clear statements, but also, through oblique modes of communication, to evoke a world of feeling. In so doing it reaches below the surface of things and invites the reader into a deeper level of understanding and living.

Other literary features will be dealt with as they occur. But all such features are generally linked with questions of meaning, questions of theology and spirituality. And so, while the initial interest of this study is in the literary aspect of the text, the ultimate focus is on theological implication.

3

First Impressions of the Text: At the Level of Biography, Confusion; at the Level of the Spirit, Suggestions of Unity

The Problem of Confusion

At one level the gospel of John is extremely simple and straightforward. It gives an account of a God-man, Jesus, who walked the earth in the days of Pontius Pilate. Thus its most obvious focus, as a narrative, is on a sequence of events which occurred in the early part of the first century. It sounds at times like very direct reporting; "it gives the impression of 'things seen' " (Smith, 1982, 105). And it has an extraordinarily simple vocabulary.

As well as having a certain simplicity, the text also appears to have unity. The ancient manuscripts are essentially unanimous in presenting the entire gospel (chaps. 1–21) in its present form. Apart from the story of the adulteress (7:59–8:11), which is missing in the oldest manuscripts, there is no manuscript evidence which suggests the existence of any edition that was in any way shorter or longer or in a different order. And throughout most of Christian history, the idea of the gospel's unity was basic to its interpretation. It was assumed that it was written by just one person, a person who was regarded as supremely competent, even inspired.

Given this tradition, and given also the preferred starting point of recent literary criticism, it may seem best to start with the supposition that the text is a unity.

But at this point the historical-critical method intervenes and highlights a difficulty: whatever its initial aura of simplicity, John's story of Jesus seems confused. Instead of recounting events in a clear, coherent way, the gospel contains a perplexing number of breaks and contradictions; and it also contains some repetitions and changes of style (cf. Brown, xxiv–xxv). In particular, it goes against one's expectations concerning time, space, and logic. It tells, for instance, on the day the disciples stayed with Jesus, that "it was about the tenth hour" (1:39), yet the reader is left perplexed as to what exactly happened at the tenth hour, whether it was the time of the disciples' arrival or departure or some other time. In the transition between chapters 5 and 6 there is a strange geographic sequence: having been last reported in Jerusalem (chap. 5), Jesus suddenly appears in Galilee (6:1). And during the last discourse, Jesus breaks the most basic laws of logic: he says, "Arise, let us go from here," but then he does not seem to move; instead he goes on talking (chaps. 15–17).

One of the most usual ways of responding to this puzzling phenomenon, this apparent disunity, is to attempt to reconstruct some historical process which could account for it. Various reconstructions have been offered: that sections were displaced; that several sources were used but not properly integrated; that several editors were involved with it; and that it was developed through a long process of transmitting and editing (cf. Brown, xxv–xxxix; Haenchen, 1:44–51).

No agreement has been reached about which, if any, of these reconstructions is accurate. Brown disagrees with earlier theories, and Schnackenburg (1977, 23–24) regards Brown's own theory, whatever its plausibility, as difficult to verify. Thus, on this question at least, historical reconstruction has reached an impasse.

There is, however, another way of going about the problem, and that is to look again at the data. Do they really constitute disunity? Is it perhaps possible that a writer or artist would deliberately include such elements. The problem is illustrated by the case of the Polish-born Joseph Conrad:

> The paradox of a Pole and a seaman writing novels long prevented readers from seeing how serious these novels were. They interpreted as an amateur's or foreigner's clumsinesss certain experiments in structure and style which anticipated those of William Faulkner (Guerard, 1950, 7).

Further forms of apparent disunity may be found in other writers. T. S. Eliot (1957, 32), for instance, emphasizes that poetry need not follow a uniform flow and may involve a mixing of the poetic with the prosaic:

> Dissonance, even cacophany, has its place: just as in a poem of any length there must be transitions between passages of greater and less intensity, to give a rhythm of fluctuating emotion essential to the musical structure of the whole; and the passages of less intensity will be, in relation to the level on which the whole poem operates, prosaic—so that, in the sense implied by this context, it may be said that no poet can write a poem of amplitude unless he is a master of the proasaic.

If the perplexing features of Conrad and Eliot are due not to confusedness but to deliberate artistry, then perhaps something similar is true of John. In other words, is it possible, as Alter proposes (1981, 133), that "the biblical writers . . . had certain notions of unity rather different from our own"?

Unity at the Level of the Spirit

The text has another level—that of the unseen spiritual realm which surrounds the disciples. If the gospel consisted entirely of direct factual reporting then such things as breaks, contradictions, and repetitions could scarcely have a rightful place. Their presence would indeed mean that the text has become confused, that it is not a unity.

But the text is not limited to straightforward narrative about Jesus, about the "things seen" in the life of one individual. It is interested also in things unseen, and in the lives of disciples. These two factors—things unseen and the disciples—need to be looked at more closely. First, the disciples.

It is now generally accepted, particularly since Martyn's initial analysis of John 9 (1968), that John's gospel, even though its more obvious focus is on Jesus, is simultaneously telling a second story, that of the disciples, of the Christian believers in the later part of the first century. In other words, their story and experiences have been retrojected into the story of Jesus. In various ways this Jesus-disciples duality pervades the text.

Second, however much the gospel may convey a flavor of things seen, it has a profound interest in what is unseen. Though it reflects the disciples, it ignores their external appearances. In fact, it never says what anyone looked like. The decisive focus is on something deeper. Again and again it seeks to go beyond the level of the visible, the material, the superficial, and, whatever the resistance of flesh or heart or mind, it endeavors to lead a person into a further dimension, the world of reflection, of mystery, of spirit—ultimately the world of God.

This campaign—to open up the unseen—involves techniques which, to some degree, may be classed as both negative and positive.

The more negative techniques—techniques which could be termed anti-superficiality devices—consist chiefly of ambiguity, riddles, misunderstanding, and irony. The purpose of these is to challenge the mind, to stop it in its overworn tracks and to suggest that something is wrong or being missed or misunderstood. (In describing aspects of this challenge, Staley [1988, 95–118] speaks of "victimization"; the reader is being victimized. But this term, though technically correct, is unsuitable in the context of plain English; the purpose of these anti-superficiality techniques is not to victimize but to bring to life.)

Irony is especially important (cf. Clavier, 1959; McRae, 1973; Wead, 1974; Culpepper, 1983, 152–80; Granskou, 1985; Duke, 1985; O'Day, 1986; Staley, 1988, esp. 76–77). The essential idea of irony is that, in some way or other, words mean something more or other than they appear to mean. Thus when Caiaphas declares that "it is expedient that one person should die for the people" (11:50) his words say far more than he realizes. But irony is not limited to such statements. Whole scenes mean more than they appear to mean. In 4:1–42 for instance, "the reader is made aware that the narrative is not one-dimensional but multidimensional, with two contrasting narrative levels often occurring simultaneously" (O'Day, 1986, 90).

The more positive technique is that of symbolism, a technique by which various elements and events, many of them quite ordinary, are used to indicate the presence of greater realities, many of them unseen (cf. Culpepper, 1983, 180–98). Light, wind, bread, and water are among the most ordinary and obvious elements of life, but through them the gospel opens up a whole other realm.

The same is true of various events. Thus, near the beginning of the gospel, for instance, the event at Cana is referred to as a sign (2:11), and the cleansing of the temple appears to be a symbolic action (2:13–22; Brown, 121). Later, in the final stages of the gospel there is symbolism in actions such as Mary's anointing of Jesus (12:1–11; Brown, 454), and Jesus' coming to Jerusalem on a donkey (12:12–19; Brown, 463). The precise way in which actions are symbolic varies considerably from one to another. The Cana event, as already suggested, belongs to the world of signs. The other events, however—the cleansing, the anointing, the coming to Jerusalem—these constitute various kinds of prophetic actions, actions which point to further realities (cf. Brown, 121, 454, 463).

What is essential—without trying to categorize all the various forms of signs and symbols—is that symbolism is a basic aspect of the text.

The division of surface-breaking techniques into those that are more negative and those that are more positive does have some limited usefulness; but, as Culpepper (1983, 151) indicates, ultimately the gospel's techniques defy complete analysis and classification. Language, after all, is an art, not an exact science (cf. Steiner, 1975, 110–470, esp. 110–15, 220–35, 274–301, 460–62), and so it is inevitable that some of the openness of art be found in the gospel. What is reasonably clear, however, is that in a wide variety of ways the gospel keeps challenging superficial expectations and opening up a world of spirit and surprise.

The more complex levels of the gospel have not always been fully recognized or accepted. It is only in this century that the presence of the second story, that of the disciples, has been explicitly underlined and appreciated. Even more recent is the developed appreciation of the role of misunderstanding and irony. The one complex level which has long been appreciated is that of symbolism, but symbolism has often been abused, particularly in the early church, and so it came to be regarded with caution, even suspicion. This caution was greatly intensified by the Reformation insistence that scripture speaks plainly, that it has a single clear meaning (Granskou, 1985, 2; Bohlmann, 1968, 57–68). But such a doctrine, however attractive in its offer of clarity, seems inadequate in dealing with John's gospel. It is an inadequacy that is reflected, for instance, in the experience of Granskou (1985, 3): "I have heard continental Protestant bishops thunder . . . about the clarity and certainty of the word, and now I . . . see my Protestant word calling for multiple meaning, mystery, deeper and higher meaning, etc." It would seem, therefore, that there are two extremes. On the one hand, there is the rather wild symbolism of some writers in the early and medieval church; and on the other, the Reformation-based overinsistence on scripture's clarity. What is necessary is to allow for symbolism, but to do so with discretion and discipline.

The basic conclusion from this survey of surface-breaking techniques is that, however simple and direct the text may sometimes appear, it is not a single-level, straightforward report. It speaks not only of things seen in the life of Jesus but of things unseen in the lives of others. In other words, it is not only interweaving two stories, that of Jesus and the disciples, but also two worlds of perception, the easily-grasped world of what is obvious and seen, and another world, more demanding and spiritual.

The Proposal: Contradiction as a Spur to Reflection

There are a number of points in the gospel when the reader (or listener) can see that Jesus is being misunderstood, that he is spurring people to reflection and that people find it difficult to follow him into the realm of the spirit. Nicodemus and the Samaritan woman, for instance, encounter a Jesus who seems both shocking and contradictory. First there are the mild shocks—his failure to respond in kind to the flattering words of Nicodemus (3:2), and his unsolicited intrusion into the life of the woman (4:7–9). Then come the apparent contradictions—of the elementary laws for coming to birth (3:3–4), and of the elementary laws for drawing water (4:10–11). But for the reader these stories are generally not a problem. One realizes that Jesus' apparent contradictions have the purpose of inviting his hearers to move to a new level of understanding.

The proposal made here is that the gospel as a whole is doing essentially the same thing to the reader. Through its many forms of contradiction (including shocks, style changes, obscurities, riddles, and breaks) it is issuing a constant challenge, an invitation to move beyond superficiality and to enter into a new level of awareness, ultimately into the level of the holy (chap. 17).

At the end of chap. 14, for instance, when Jesus says, "Arise . . ." and then goes on talking, the reader feels like Nicodemus or the woman of Samaria: this is muddled, contradictory. But there is another possibility—that the gospel is seeking to invite the reader to become aware of a further dimension, namely that the last discourse as a whole, as well as speaking at an obvious level (concerning Jesus' departure) is speaking also at a further level (concerning a departure or movement which is spiritual, in fact, concerning the whole realm of spirit). That had been the essence of the conversations with Nicodemus and the woman: apparent contradiction had led to an awareness of the realm of spirit (3:5–8; 4:13–14,23–24). The mind-bending contradiction, instead of being merely a puzzle in the biography of Jesus, may emerge as being a clue that the focus of the last discourse (and indeed of the entire gospel) is not on biography at all but on something more—on the mind-surpassing realm of the spirit.

This thesis will need careful proof. The last discourse will have to be examined in detail, and so will other perplexing texts. But if the thesis stands then it helps to explain why, despite all the contradictions, the gospel may still be a unity. These contradictions are not alien to the text; they are part of its larger strategy of opening up the world of the unseen.

4

The Design
1. The Foundational Framework:
Time and Space

Discussion of the gospel's design (plan/structure) has centered on a variety of elements, particularly geography, chronology, liturgy, symbolism, symbolic numbers, symmetric concentric structures, chiasms, drama, journeys, and, of course theology, especially revelation (Mlakuzhyil, 1987, 17–85).

These elements are not mutually exclusive. It is frequently suggested that the gospel is structured around not just one element but around several. Giblin (1990), for instance, has compared John's interweaving structures with the way in which the water on the oceanfront sometimes reflects diverse patterns, one caused, say, by a passing ship and another by the prevailing wind.

This study does not seek to be exhaustive; it does not, for instance, attempt to trace and assess the presence of structures which are concentric or chiastic. Such elements are indeed present, but the gospel is first of all a narrative, an account in which events occur in sequence, and before discussing circular structures, it is important to clarify the more straightforward elements.

But even the straightforward-looking narrative is not easy to divide. The medieval division into chapters provides a valuable starting point. Ultimately, however, it is unreliable and may, at times, be quite misleading.

Among modern scholars it is generally agreed that an important division occurs at the beginning of chap. 13: "Now before the feast of Passover . . ." (On chaps. 13–20 as a distinct division, see Schnackenburg, 3:1–5; Bultmann, 457; and esp. Brown, cxxxvii–cxliv, 541–42).

It is also generally agreed that the beginning and end of the gospel stand out in some way; and so, for this and other reasons, the beginning and end are frequently referred to respectively as the prologue (1:1–18) and epilogue (or supplement, chap. 21).

But there the agreement ends. In particular, opinions vary as to how to divide chaps. 1–12 (cf. Brown, cxxxviii–cxliv). There are some, like Bultmann and Schnackenburg, who, in varying degrees, seek to rearrange the material in these chapters. Others (e.g., Barrett, Hoskyns, Lindars) leave it in its present order but do not attempt to make *major* divisions. And among those who do make that attempt, there is considerable diversity.

Some impression of the situation may be had by simply scanning some leading opinions.

Dividing the Main Body of the Gospel

Bultmann (1941)
    The Revelation of the *Doxa* [glory] to the World   chaps. 2–12
    The Revelation of the *Doxa* before the Community   chaps. 13–20
Dodd (1953)
    The Book of Signs   chaps. 2–12
    The Book of the Passion   chaps. 13–20
Brown (1966)
    The Book of Signs   1:19–chap. 12
    The Book of Glory   chaps. 13–20

Brown's outline blends the distinctive emphases of Bultmann (glory) and Dodd
(signs).

Dividing the Main Body of Chapters 1–12

In Bultmann's view (111), "one must regard chs. 3–6 and chs 7–12 as the main
divisions. . . . The introduction . . . for . . . ch. 3 . . . is provided by 2:23–
25." Bultmann also adds some important subdivisions. Brown (cxl) gives a double role to the Cana episodes—as conclusions and as introductions. In outline:

Bultmann (using the heading, "The Revelation of the [Glory] . . .")
    Prelude   2:1–22

    The Encounter with the Revealer   2:23–4:42
    The Revelation as *Krisis* (Judgement)   4:43–chap. 6

    The Revealer's Struggle with the World   7:1–10:39
    The Revealer's Secret Victory over the World 10:40–chap. 12
Brown (using the heading, "The Book of Signs")
    The Opening Days of the Revelation of Jesus   1:19–51
    From Cana to Cana—various responses to Jesus' ministry in the
        different sections of Palestine   chaps. 2–4
    Jesus and the Principal Feasts of the Jews   chaps. 5–10
    Jesus moves towards the Hour of Death and Glory chaps. 11–12

These views will be discussed later, near the end of Chapter 6.

The Structural Design

The hypothesis put forward here and in the succeeding chapter is that the gospel
is structured on some of the most basic elements of human reality—time, space,

and the stages of life, particularly the stages of believing. Time and space are the foundation. They are like the beams and crossbeams which, when interlocked, provide a solid base or framework for a superstructure. And the focal layer of that superstructure—the focus, in fact, of the whole gospel—is the progress of living and believing, a journeylike drama which reflects advancing stages and a conflict between revelation and rejection.

As suggested earlier, these elements of structure do not exclude others. The gospel is almost as complex as a human body, with multiple designs interweaving to form a whole, from the skeletal system to the epidermis. But the elements of time, space, and the stages of life and belief are unusually important; it is through these that one best understands how the whole functions.

This chapter will look at the foundational design—the framework of time and space. Chapter 5 will examine the central, decisive factor: the gospel as a whole is shaped to reflect human experience, especially the stages of living and believing. And chapter 6 will review a further complementary feature, the way in which the passage of human life (entry into life, life itself, death) has been depicted repeatedly as a process of descent and ascent.

The proposed structure suggests complex coherence—something quite different from the confusion implied by those theories which say that several parts of the gospel have been displaced and that it is necessary to rearrange it.

The basic idea of complex coherence, of intricate design, was not alien to the ancient world. B. H. M. Standaert has documented such a phenomenon and shown its relevance to Mark (1978, esp. 1–108). Orderly complexity has also been observed in Luke, particularly in the diptych structures of the infancy narrative (e.g., cf. Stuhlmueller, 1968, 42:24). And the gospel of Matthew has been described as "meticulous," as apparently having been put together "with the precision of a Swiss watch" (Ellis, 1974, esp. 19; cf. also Keegan, 1982, 415–30). It is of interest too that André Chouraqui (1975, 455), after a lifetime of translating the OT, came to suspect that its stories, simple though they often seem, had, in fact, been composed with as much complexity and precision as is used today in building a rocket or computer.

As for John, the preceding chapter has already suggested that the text involves a carefully ordered plurality of levels.

When inquiring about John's structure, therefore, it does not seem reasonable to rule out in advance a structure which involves complex coherence. It is such coherence that is involved in the careful interweaving of time, space, and the stages of living and believing.

The Time Structure: Basic Ideas and Arguments

It is appropriate to look first at the notion of time. Time is in some ways a rather abstract notion, yet it is a foundational element of life. Life, in fact, may be said to consist of time—a procession of passing days, circling seasons, and advancing years.

Such are some of the elements of John. In various ways he refers to the flow of days and feasts and years. The opening episodes in the gospel, from John (the Baptist) to Cana (1:19–2:11), are set on a series of successive days (cf. 1:29,35,43; 2:1: "The next day. . . . The next day. . . . The next day. . . . And on the third day . . ."). Then, just after Cana, there comes the cleansing of the temple, and at that point the gospel embarks on a series of references to various feasts:

Passover (2:13, the cleansing of the temple)

. . .

"A feast of the Jews," (5:1, at the Jerusalem pool)
Passover (6:4, the bread of life)

. . .

Tents (7:2, etc., in Jerusalem)
Dedication (10:22, in the temple)
Passover (11:55, etc., death and resurrection)

These feasts, because they include three references to Passover, imply a flow not only of seasons but also of years. Thus the text moves, imperceptibly almost, from a flow of days to a flow of feasts to a flow of years.

What is being proposed, then, is that the key to the fundamental structure of the gospel is provided not only by the general idea of time, but particularly by the Passover-centered three-year cycle. Thus the number of major parts into which the gospel falls is three. In the third year, however, Passover, to some degree, is set apart from the earlier part of the yearly cycle (cf. 13:1), and so it is appropriate that the third year be subdivided. The resulting division of the gospel is as follows:

Part 1	From the beginning to the first Passover—to the cleansing of the temple	1:1–1:22
Part 2	From one Passover to the next—to the bread of life discourse and the shadow of betrayal	2:23–chap. 6
Part 3 A	Toward death and the final Passover	chaps. 7–12
B	The final Passover, and epilogue	chaps. 13–21

At a later stage in this book, at the beginning of the introduction to Chapters 13–17, the distinctness of chaps. 13–21 will be examined more closely.

In many ways this division is not particularly new. It corresponds, in practice, with Bultmann's idea that major sections begin at 2:23 ("Now when he was in Jerusalem at the Passover feast, many believed . . ."), at 7:1 ("After this Jesus went about Galilee . . . because the Jews sought to kill him"), and at 13:1 ("Now before the feast of the Passover . . ."). It corresponds also to the emphasis which many scholars give to the feasts: Brown uses them in chaps. 5–10; Mollat (1960, 25–36, esp. 32) uses them as the key to the structure of the gospel, and Wilkens (1958, 9–24) refers to "the paschal structure" of the gospel. What is distinctive here is the emphasis on the foundational idea of time, in other words, on a category which, while it includes feasts, is more basic than feasts, more inclusive. And it is a category which covers not just chaps. 5–10 but the entire gospel.

In this hypothesis the three Passovers constitute three climactic points in the development of the gospel. In other words, the gospel builds up, first to the cleansing of the temple (Passover 1), then to the crisis surrounding the bread-of-life discourse (Passover 2), and finally to the death and resurrection (Passover 3). The climactic nature of the third Passover is generally recognized—because of its link to Jesus' death and resurrection. But the other Passovers also are linked to Jesus' death and resurrection. It is at the first Passover, during the cleansing of the temple, that the first allusions are made to death and resurrection (cf. 2:19–22, "Destroy this temple . . . when therefore he was raised from the dead . . ."). And it is at the second Passover, and at the feast mentioned in chap. 5—a feast which, as will be seen later, in some sense leads up the second Passover—that the first explicit references are made to Jesus being killed and betrayed (cf. 5:1,16–19; 6:4,71). Hence the link between Jesus' death and the Passover feast is not something which is introduced in the final chapters of the gospel. It is expressed throughout the gospel in a graded threefold pattern.

There are several arguments which help to make this hypothesis more plausible. The initial arguments are rather general and extrinsic; they are arguments from appropriateness and context.

The organizing of a narrative on the basis of time is something very common. In fact, narrative of its very nature tends to be linked to the passage of time—to a framework involving, first, a beginning, then, a sequence of events spread over various hours, days, or years, and, finally, an end. It is almost inevitable that many stories begin with "Once upon a time . . ." and conclude with ". . . ever after."

Time is particularly important in narrative which is religious. One of the basic ways in which religion brings out the presence of the sacred in things is by speaking of time and space and by sacralizing them (cf. Eliade, 1959, 20–113).

Time is an important organizing factor in texts which are in some way, directly or indirectly, related to John. The structure of the very first chapter of the OT is based on time, on the flow of days (Genesis 1). In Luke the basic organizing elements are time and space (geography) (cf. Fitzmyer, 1981, 164–79). And the importance of time and space in Mark is underlined by the subtitle of the study by W. Kelber: *The Kingdom in Mark. A New Place and a New Time* (1974).

There are other arguments which are intrinsic—based on the gospel text itself. The present gospel text (chaps. 1–21) begins and ends with the idea, implied at least, of time; it looks first to the beginning, to pre-existence before time (1:1), and finally to the future—to the deaths of Peter and the beloved disciple, and to the return of Jesus (". . . until I come," 21:18–23). Thus it sets the entire narrative within the context of time, or at least within the context of elements which surpass time. But the beginning and end of something are the most basic elements of its structure. And so, if the gospel's most basic structural elements are time-based, it makes sense that the same should be true of the structure as a whole.

The focal episode in the gospel, Jesus' death and resurrection, does not happen at a vague point in some broad period. It is repeatedly linked to a precise time, Passover, and to the coming of a particular "hour." But a text's focus—like its beginning and end—is a basic part of its structure. It is a further indication that the structure as a whole is time-based.

As already mentioned, the gospel's earliest episodes are structured according to time, according to a flow of days: "The next day. . . . The next day. . . . The next day. . . . And on the third day . . ." (1:29,35,43; 2:1). But the earliest episodes of a composition generally provide a clue about the composition as a whole. And so there is yet another indication that the structure as a whole is time-based.

As a number of writers have noted, and as shown in greater detail in the commentary, the gospel as a whole tends to be repetitious and spiralling. In other words, it repeats what was said previously but does so in an intensified form. Strong as is this general pattern of intensified repetition, it is particularly clear on the question of time. Not only does the same landmark event, Passover, occur three times, but it does so with increasing solemnity. (The first Passover is introduced on a low key, on its own [2:13]. The second, however, has another feast to herald it; the unnamed feast of 5:1 prepares, even in its phrasing, for the Passover of 6:1,4. And the third Passover has *two* feasts to herald it; in diverse ways, particularly through phrasing and through intimating Jesus' coming death, Tents [7:1,2,10] and Dedication [10:22] prepare the way for the third and final Passover. The sense of increasing solemnity is intensified yet more by the fact that it is only after repeated references to the concluding Passover [11:55; 12:1] that chap. 13 finally intones, "Now before the feast of the Passover . . ."). What is important is that one of the basic features of the gospel's structure, that of intesified repetition, is found most clearly in matters of time, and so there is yet a further indication that structure and time are connected. The rhythm of the recurring feast sets the beat for the whole gospel.

The Time Structure: Conclusion

John's time-based structure has meaning. It indicates that however high the gospel's theology may soar, the foundation for the entire narrative is the most basic element of limited human life—the reality of being placed at one point in the vast flow of time and, until the fateful hour strikes, of living out a succession of days, seasons, and years. In other words, the gospel is grounded in the most basic reality of human experience.

It also indicates that in trying to express the reality of human existence—the reality of living in time and in the shadow of one's fateful hour—the idea of a Passover has much to say. It is a complex idea, one which contains an enigmatic blend of pain and hope.

Space

The primary role of time does not rule out the complementary role of space or geography. It is basic to human life that while the passing of days and birthdays is an ever-present fundamental reality, there are times when the factor which is uppermost in one's mind is that of space—where one lives, where one is going. Even if all one's days are lived in a single neighborhood, the imagination travels far, and the passing of life is often expressed in a symbolism based on changing space or geography; life is a journey, a pilgrimage, an adventure. Thus, within human experience, time and space are interwoven.

Space is an important ingredient in the composing of narratives. A great many books and films are built largely around the describing of places and the process of getting somewhere. As for religious narratives, it has already been mentioned, when speaking of time, that religion as such tends to give considerable attention to the notion of space, the sacralizing of space (Eliade, 1959, 20–65). From Genesis 2 on, places and journeys are among the basic elements of OT narrative. However, the meaning of OT geography, its artistic dimension, has not yet been fully unraveled.

The place of geography in John is not immediately obvious. What is striking, however, is that, unlike the other gospels, he speaks of Jesus going up to Jerusalem, not just once, but several times. The first such journey occurs during *the first* (and only) *feast of Part 1* (1:1–2:22)—when Jesus goes up at Passover and cleanses the temple. The second occurs during *the first feast of Part 2* (2:23–chap. 6) —the "feast of the Jews" (5:1). And the third during *the first feast of chaps. 7–12*—the feast of Tents (7:1–14). The final journey to Jerusalem, which, unlike the others, is described not as a going up, or ascension, but as a coming (11:56, 12:12), is rather different in character and is dealt with in the commentary. The coincidence between the journeys and the first feasts of each part of the gospel tends to raise questions about the way John uses geography.

The proposal being put forward here is that John's references to places and journeys, different as they are from those of the other gospels, are highly schematic and quite symbolic. This does not necessarily mean they are unhistorical, but it highlights a dimension other than history.

This idea, that the geography of the gospels has a schematic or symbolic dimension, is not new. Though the details are disputed, it has long been recognized that Mark's use of "Galilee," including his depiction of polarity between Galilee and Jerusalem, has a symbolic aspect, that it suggests universality, the spread of the gospel "beyond the confines of Israel" (Senior, 1984, 76–78; cf. Kelber, 1974, 45–65). It is also generally recognized that, within Luke and Acts, the place of Jerusalem is highly schematic—it is used as a focal point for the gospel and as a point of departure for Acts (cf. Luke 9:51–54; Acts 1:8; Fitzmyer, 1981, 164–71).

Nor is it new to say that specifically in John the use of geography is in some way symbolic. It has already been indicated, for instance by Meeks (1966, 159–69), that John uses Jerusalem and Galilee as symbols, respectively, of rejection and acceptance.

In assessing John's use of geography, particularly of Jerusalem and Galilee, it is useful to look first at the gospel as a whole and then at its three basic parts.

When the gospel is taken as a whole there is an ambiguity about Jerusalem. At one level it comes more and more to the fore, it is the scene of more and more action. Yet at another level it appears to recede. Jerusalem is the first place mentioned in the gospel (1:19)—a curious detail considering that the action begins beyond the Jordan. And in the chapters which follow, Jerusalem is used on several occasions—twelve times altogether in chaps. 1–12. But in chaps. 13–21, even though most of the action is set in Jerusalem, the name is never again mentioned. Thus, if the use of the name is any guide, Jerusalem is being left behind. Galilee, on the other hand, though it is not mentioned so early (cf. 1:43; 2:1) eventually endures much longer. It is referred to shortly after the final reference to Jerusalem (cf. 12:12–21), and it turns out to be the last place-name in the gospel (21:2). Thus, in the use of geographic names, the gospel begins with Jerusalem and ends with Galilee.

When the gospel, instead of being taken as a whole, is taken in three (time-based) parts, the picture of the relationship of Jerusalem to Galilee is understandably more complex. Yet the essentials are coherent and clear. Geographically speaking, Part 1 (1:1–2:22) begins and ends with Jerusalem (cf. 1:19; 2:13). Part 2 (2:23–chap. 6) reflects a shift: it begins with Jerusalem and moves more and more toward Galilee (cf. esp. 2:23; 6:1). Part 3 begins and ends with Galilee (cf. 7:1; 21:2).

Without going into too much detail for the moment, it is useful to single out Part 2 (2:23–chap. 6). Here particularly one senses a shift. First, there is the systematic account of the many stages of a journey—the only such account in John—and it moves slowly from Jerusalem to Galilee (cf. 2:23; 3:22; 4:1–5,40,43–45,54). Then, in chaps. 5–6, there is a variation on that shift: instead of being slow and systematic, it is quite abrupt; the transition from Jerusalem to Galilee is sudden and unexplained (cf. 5:47–6:1). Though the lack of explanation may be disconcerting and will require later comment, there is a basic coherence: in a variety of ways, ways which contrast but may also be complementary, Part 2 is highlighting what the rest of the gospel's geographic structure suggests—that there is a basic movement away from Jerusalem and towards Galilee.

What emerges, through diverse indications, is that as far as space or geography is concerned, the gospel is focused on Galilee. This is the point towards which it is moving. In fact, the build-up in the repeated references to Galilee is rather like the build-up in the repeated references to Passover. During the first year (1:1–2:22) one may say—apart from an initial hint which alludes to what is coming (1:43)—that Galilee is mentioned in just one passage (2:1, 11). In the second year (2:23–chap. 6) Galilee is mentioned in two diverse passages (in chaps. 4 and 6: 4:3,43,46,54; 6:1). And in the third year (chaps. 7–21) the number of diverse passages in which Galilee occurs is three (chaps. 7, 12, and 21: 7:1,9,41,52; 12:21; 21:1–2). The implication is that chapter 21, with its culminating event in Galilee, is as integral to the gospel as the final Passover.

The Space Structure: Conclusion

The initial conclusion is that John's use of geography is schematic. Once account is taken both of the gospel's way of using place-names and especially of the gospel's three-part structure, the geography begins to take on an appearance not of zig-zag confusion but of complex coherence.

The further conclusion, much more tentative, is that the gospel's geography appears to be, in some way, symbolic. As already mentioned, Meeks (1966) has indicated that "Jerusalem" and "Galilee" are symbols respectively of rejection and acceptance. The carefully orchestrated series of movements from one to the other may also indicate something more specific—the movement of the gospel from rejection by the Jerusalem Jews to acceptance among the Gentiles. Luke suggests such a pattern. In his two-book work, he moves first towards Jerusalem, and then, in Acts, he moves away from Jerusalem to the Gentiles. John does not have a second book, one which will tell of the movement to the Gentiles. What he seems to have done instead is incorporate both dimensions into his single narrative. At one level the story moves more towards Jerusalem; but at another it moves steadily away—towards Galilee, and thus, by implication, towards the Gentiles.

The basic structure which emerges has three parts and involves an interweaving of time and space. Time is the foundational element, but at certain points, particularly in Part 2 (2:23–chap. 6), space or geography becomes primary.

The careful use of so basic an element as space or geography is a further indication of John's sensitivity to the reality of human life.

5

The Design
2. The Central Focus: Stages of
Living and Believing

The design (plan/structure) of the gospel is not a secondary matter, to be dealt with summarily after treating the weighty issues of history and theology. It is integral to the question of content—rather as discerning a family's structure is integral to understanding a complex household. Design and content are interwoven, design with theology, content with form; discerning one helps to discern the other. It is appropriate, therefore, when making a proposal regarding the essence of the design, to take account of views concerning content.

Recent Views on Content

As already indicated (in Chapter 3) recent decades have witnessed a growing conviction that the fourth gospel is not just a history of Jesus and an abstract theology. It is not the product of an evangelist who, while sitting in splendid isolation, recalled the life of Jesus and used it as a basis for constructing a speculative Christology. Beyond such history and theology, the gospel contains a down-to-earth reflection of people's lives.

This conviction has taken two main forms. The first is the emphasis on church or community. A generation ago, the idea that the gospels had in some way been adapted to meet the situation of the believers was already so well established that it was included in official church documents. Furthermore, since the appearance of Martyn's initial analysis of John 9 (1968) and of Meeks's examination of the idea of the man from heaven (1972), evidence has been growing that the gospel, as well as being to some degree a biography of Jesus, is in some way a reflection of the life of a community (Brown, 1979; Rensberger, 1988; Neyrey, 1988).

The second conviction has to do not so much with the community as with the individual, the conviction that somehow or other the gospel reflects the life of the individual believer. In 1986 Conrad L'Heureux showed that to a significant degree biblical narratives reflect the course of human life. More specifically, in 1987 L. W. Countryman proposed that John's gospel reflects the believer's spiritual journey. D. McGann put a similar emphasis on the idea of the journey of the individual: "This gospel . . . [is] not only . . . a story of Jesus but . . . my story. . . . It reveals to me the mystery and wonder of my own being'' (1988, 5). Something of the same idea may also be found, for instance, in Brown (730)

31

and, more clearly, in Schneiders (1975, esp. 635). Concerning the important event of seeing Jesus after the resurrection (16:16–23; cf. chap. 20), both these authors agree that, while the text may originally have focused on Jesus, as it now stands it has been reinterpreted to highlight the spiritual experience of the believer. Rissi (1983) and Staley (1986; 1988, 72–73) further highlighted the gospel's emphasis on journeys; though both were thinking of the journeys of Jesus rather than those of the believer, they helped uncover one of the gospel's central dynamics.

A Proposal: Stages of Living and Believing

The hypothesis put forward here is that the essential design of the fourth gospel reflects the journey of a human life, particularly insofar as that journey involves diverse processes and stages of believing. In thus portraying the stages of believing, the gospel speaks also of one of belief's essential results, namely community or church. Thus the text reflects both the individual and the church, and for both it presents a model.

This hypothesis therefore accepts the essence of the preceding views concerning the community and the individual, but it refines them. It also accepts that the foundational design of the gospel consists of time and space. Time and space provide the context, and within this earthbound context the drama of living and believing unfolds.

The gospel's emphasis on believing and on stages of believing is not something whimsical. Philosophers have sometimes said that the ultimate question is that of suicide, or, to put it another way, the ultimate question is whether life is worth living. To say that it is means some form of believing; and a portrayal of the stages of believing is ultimately *a portrayal of the diverse processes through which one embraces life.*

Life, however, involves death—no life is without death and without deathlike losses—and so to embrace one means embracing the other. Consequently the diverse stages of believing involve corresponding stages of embracing death. The Word in whom one believes is not only the source of life; the Word is also made into mortal flesh and ultimately into death.

Obviously the gospel is also a life of Jesus; Christology dominates. But the Christology, instead of being for its own sake, for speculation, is soteriological. In other words, it is focused on salvation, on the kind of down-to-earth salvation which enters the day-to-day journey of human life.

The other gospels may speak of the realm (or kingdom) of God, but John wants to go further—to show what this realm actually means, how it impinges on people's lives. And he does this by combining two distinct emphases: on the one hand, he places the divine realm clearly within Jesus; and on the other, he so adapts Jesus' life that it reflects the human journey.

At one level, therefore, the evangelist is speaking of God, is telling how God the Word became human and walked the earth, but at another level he is thoroughly human-centered. Somewhat like Karl Rahner's theology—Rahner's theological anthropology—this gospel approaches the divine through the human, or at least allows the divine to be portrayed through the progress of human living.

Thus, unlike the other gospels with their account of just one year of ministry, John portrays three years, and each of those years reflects a major segment of human life. The first year, as far as the first Passover (1:1–2:22), reflects the beginning of life, the youthful stage in which life seems positive, and believing is relatively easy. The second year, as far as the next Passover (2:23–chap. 6), reflects a middle-aged stage in which the awareness of sin and dividedness makes believing more difficult. And the third year, as far as the final Passover (chaps. 7–12), reflects a more advanced stage in which the shadow of death threatens to destroy both life and belief.

In the later chapters (13–21) the emphasis changes. Most of the action takes place within less than a full day, and the focus is not so much on (stages of human) time as on a certain form of space—the inner human space wherein the mystery of the Passover takes effect. In other words, in chaps. 13–21 the Passover of Jesus is so described that it involves a portrayal of how the Passover works within Jesus' disciples. Thus it is not only chap. 9 which, as Martyn (1968) indicated, refers to two levels, that of Jesus and the disciples; the same is true of the drama of the Passover. Or, as D. Harrington (1990, 79) expresses it, the last discourse has a "double focus."

One of the telling clues to the nature of chaps. 13–21 is the initial emphasis on the human heart. The last discourse mentions it several times, often in a leading position. It is the devil's invasion of Judas's heart which lends a special urgency to the washing of the feet (13:2). It is against disturbance of heart that chap. 14 is largely directed (14:1, cf.14:27). And in a later section (16:4b–33) it is again the welfare of the heart which dominates—the question of whether it will be filled with sorrow (16:6) or with joy (16:22). Thus, if chaps. 1–12 portray the Word/word as it manifests itself through the years, chaps. 13–21 focus more exactly on how the Word/word works within the human heart.

A further clue to the nature of chaps. 13–21 is the leading role given to the simple space-related idea of going out. At the beginning of all three major divisions of chaps. 13–21 it is said that Jesus "went out" (13:3; 18:1, 4; 19:17), and later the same term is used of Peter (20:3, 21:3). Without attempting to unravel the complex continuities between these images of going out, a basic observation may be made: within chaps. 13–21 there is an implication that, in Jesus, God's word goes forth and works within people. First, it works by addressing the word to the inner heart in speech (the last discourse). Then the fruit of that word is manifested in actions which are increasingly external and communitarian (19:38–chap. 21).

The precise way in which the word, the Passover mystery, works within the human heart will be seen later (in examining the last discourse). What is necessary for the moment is the central idea: the gospel gives a portrait both of the journey of life (chaps. 1–12) and of the way life's central saving mystery operates within the disciples (chaps. 13–21). Thus at its deepest level the fourth gospel is a map of spirituality and its consequences.

Supporting Arguments: Stages of Living and Believing

There are several factors which support the idea that the gospel is designed to portray the stages of life and of believing.

The Time–Space Framework

The progress of human life is so bound up with the reality of time and space that the two go well together and complement one another. In other words, given the time–space framework there is an appropriateness to employing the design of human life. Or, to view it another way, the gospel's central focus on down-to-earth human life helps explain why its broad framework should be that of time and space.

Three Stories: Three Stages of Life

In comparison with the single-year account of the synoptic gospels, John not only gives an account which lasts three years, he also gives a triple account. In other words, within each year he places the essentials of the entire story of Jesus.

In the first year (1:1–2:22), for example, brief though it is, the leading elements are there: the call of the disciples, the initial nomination of Peter, a synthesis of Christological titles, a form of Galilean ministry (at Cana and Capernaum), Passover, the ascent to Jerusalem, the cleansing of the temple, the clash with the Jerusalem Jews, and finally the references to the concluding events—Jesus' death and resurrection, and the disciples' post-resurrection faith (2:19–22).

In the second year (2:23–chap. 6) there are variations on that central story: the challenging of possible disciples (especially Nicodemus and the woman of Samaria), a gradual revelation of Jesus' identity (especially to the woman), a form of ministry in Galilee (involving Cana and Capernaum), the ascent to Jerusalem, the clash with the Jews, Passover, and a discourse which, as well as evoking Peter's confession of faith, evokes also some of the central events usually associated with the conclusion of Jesus' life—the words of the eucharist (6:52–58), rejection by the Jews (6:52, 66), the ascent of the Son of humanity (6:62), and the betrayal by Judas (6:71).

In the third year (chaps. 7–12) there is yet a further variation: initial journeying around Galilee, ascent to Jerusalem, clash with the Jews, the emergence of disciples (chaps. 9–10), Passover (11:55, 12:1), and a series of events which, in various ways, evoke aspects of Jesus' death, resurrection, and ascent (chaps. 11–12, esp. 11:45–53; 12:7,16,27–32).

Thus despite the profound variations there is a recurrence of basic elements: disciples, Galilee, ascent to Jerusalem, clash with the Jews, Passover, death, and resurrection.

What is important in the three variations is not just that they are diverse but that in their differences they correspond significantly to the three basic ages of human life—youth, midlife, and old age. The first year (1:1–2:22) suggests a mood which is essentially youthful and optimistic. The second year (2:23–chap. 6, beginning in 2:23–25) shows the kind of awareness of problems which is frequently associated with midlife. And the third year (chaps. 7–12), showing the influence of the threat of death (cf. 7:1), corresponds to old age.

Even the characters of chaps. 1–12 correspond significantly to distinct age groups. The disciples who dominate the first year (1:1–2:22) give an impression of youthful enthusiasm and vigor. And the year's most colorful event, the wedding at Cana, likewise suggests the time of young adulthood. In the second year (2:23–chap. 6), however, the characters seem full of the kind of power and preoccupation frequently associated with midlife—the prestigious leader (Nicodemus), the jaded lover (the woman of Samaria), and the worried parent (the royal official). In the third year (chaps. 7–12) it is never said that anyone is old, but for the first time in John's gospel someone dies and people cry. Thus, for each year, each stage, there is a complete story of Jesus.

This repeating of the complete story corresponds to the fact that in one's life as a believer, no matter what one's age, one knows the entire story of Jesus, or at least some version of it. Even a small child learns the complete account, from Christmas to Easter.

But the story learned in youth is not adequate in later years. As the flesh grows weak one has to rediscover again and again what it means that the life-giving God has become flesh.

What is essential is that the division of chaps. 1–12 into three diverse years seems to have a precise purpose—to reflect the three basic stages of human life.

The Commissioning of Peter

The strangely repetitive account of the commissioning of Peter (21:15–19) makes sense when it is seen as a way of saying that Peter is to care for people through the three main stages of their lives—when they are young ("Feed my lambs"), when they are grown and strong ("Shepherd my sheep"), and when, though grown, they are no longer strong ("Feed my little sheep"). Feeding of one kind or another is necessary both at the beginning and end of life. The word for "little sheep" (*probation*, following the more difficult reading; cf. Brown, 1105) is the diminutive for "sheep" (*probaton*), and therefore it suits the idea of a sheep which is grown but diminished, in this case, grown old.

The text immediately goes on (21:18) to refer explicitly to the process of aging, and it implies that there are three basic ages—youth ("when you were young . . ."), a midlife time of strength (presumably Peter's actual state as he receives heavy responsibility), and old age ("But when you grow old . . .").

Elements and Texts Reflect Stages of Living and Believing

The man born blind (chap. 9)

As the commentary on chap. 9 will indicate, the stages in the man's coming to sight and insight (belief) reflect diverse stages in human development—from babyhood to maturity. If chap. 9 is thus built around the stages of living and believing then something similar may be expected in other chapters, particularly since chap. 9 is frequently regarded as the major part of "an interpretive interlude" (Culpepper, 1983, 93), in other words, as providing a window on what is happening in the gospel as a whole.

"Believing" as a verb

The purpose of the gospel is that people might believe (19:35; 20:31). But for John, believing is not something static, not a fixed quantity; the noun "belief" never occurs, always the verb. Given such a dynamic concept of faith, it is to be expected that the evangelist should portray believing as being in motion—and therefore as going through stages.

Specific episodes imply stages of believing

Even a cursory examination of the gospel shows that some of its most striking episodes are structured on the basis of an advancing process of believing. The Samaritan woman, for instance, progresses through stages of accepting Jesus (4:1–42). There is progression also in the believing of the Samaritans (4:41–42) and of the royal official (4:50,53).

The various parts portray developing belief

Within each of the major parts of the gospel the final emphasis tends to fall not so much on the revealing of God (in Jesus) as on the reaction, the development of believing. Thus within Part 1 (1:1–2:22) there is a gradual build-up toward a final emphasis on this theme: first it is said, tentatively, that Nathanael believed (1:50); then, more clearly, that at Cana the disciples believed (2:11); and finally, at the cleansing of the temple, the believing of the disciples is set in a context (that of remembering), which gives it even greater force and clarity. Similarly in Part 2 (2:23–chap. 6): all the episodes (2:23–3:21; 3:22–36; 4:1–42, 43–54; chap. 5; chap. 6) lead ultimately to the question of believing or not believing (3:18–21, 36; 4:39–42, 53; 5:44–47; 6:64, 68). In a much more complex way, the same dynamic governs the later chapters. Thus, in the last discourse (chaps. 13–17), for example, the commentary will indicate that the decisive design consists of three advancing stages of accepting God's work.

Conclusion: Stages of Living and Believing

Whatever the further details, a conclusion may be drawn: while the structure of John's gospel may be governed by many factors, including a time–space framework and the portraying of the life of Jesus, it is a reasonable working hypothesis that the most decisive structuring factor is the gospel's focus on the progress of human life, particularly insofar as Jesus has opened new possibilities for such progress. The gospel is a map of living and believing (and of failing to live and believe). It is grounded in the day-to-day reality of time and space, but its sights are set on the steps which lead into the realm of God's Spirit.

Believing Means Involvement (Community/Church)

While the gospel is focused first on the individual, it does not stop there; it goes on to speak of people being together. It never uses the word "church," but there is a constant implication that believing leads to involvement, to community.

Even in the prologue the idea emerges. The humanizing of the Word leads not to isolated believers but to something shared: "The Word . . . among us, . . . we have seen . . . we have all received" (1:14–16).

Subsequent episodes in Part 1 (1:1–2:22) confirm this idea. When people accept the Word they go out to others. Andrew goes to his brother Peter (1:35–42), Philip goes to Nathanael (1:43–46), the servants draw water (at Cana, 2:1–11). And in the comment on the cleansing of the temple, believing the Word is again described as something shared (2:22).

Nor is this sharing something amorphous, unstructured. The implied community may be complex, involving diverse languages (Hebrew and Greek), yet there are suggestions—even in the church-evoking images of the woman (2:1,4) and the body (2:21)—of a certain cohesion. At the very center of Part 1 (in 1:40–43) there is an unusual emphasis on the name of Peter—precisely the one who will have a role which is unusually representative, ecclesial.

Part 2 (2:23–chap. 6) begins with an individual, Nicodemus, but as it advances it becomes more and more communitarian—the plurals which begin to appear in Jesus' conversation (3:7–11), the disciples' togetherness with Jesus (3:22), the imaging of the disciples as a bride (3:29), the woman's sharing with the people (4:7–42), the picture of the whole household (4:53). In chap. 5, when belief is failing, there is a corresponding absence of community. And later (6:52), when belief is rejected more explicitly, people fight among themselves. But most of chap. 6 is positive, a picture of faith which advances yet further, and there are corresponding suggestions of community—sitting together, sharing bread, the boat, the eucharistic language, and Peter's representative affirmation of living and believing.

In chaps. 7–12 much is said of failure to believe and consequently many of the pictures are not of community but of hostility, especially of increasingly hostile attacks on Jesus. Nevertheless many developments are positive. In particular, the dramatic account of the blind man's advance in believing opens the way to what is perhaps the gospel's central image of community, that of the flock (chaps. 9–10).

In chaps. 11–12 hostility increases, but so also do the suggestions of community. At this point, more clearly than before, the gospel suggests a community which is universal. The believing of Martha and the subsequent raising of Lazarus prepare the way for Jesus' community-building death (11:27,40,51–52). The blind man may have been de-synagogued as it were (*apo-synagōgos,* 9:22) but only in order to prepare the way for the bringing together (cf. *synagōgē,* 11:52, from *syn-agō,* "to bring together") of *all* people, both the Jewish nation and all the scattered children of God (11:51–52). The glorified Jesus is to draw all (12:32).

The final part (chaps. 13–21) contains at its center (the arrest and trial, 18:1–19:16a) a picture of how unbelief leads to a death-dealing alliance; the Jews and Pilate combine, under Caesar, to kill. But most of these final chapters consist of the two balancing panoramas (chaps. 13–17, and 19:16b–chap. 21) in which the opposite dynamic is at work: believing leads to community. In the last discourse (chaps. 13–17) the acceptance of God's cleansing love results in pictures of community which are developed—mutual foot-washing with love (chap. 13, esp. 13:34–35); the true vine with a yet greater love (15:1–17, esp. 15:12–13); and finally a climactic picture of the believers' God-based unity (chap. 17).

Within the death-and-resurrection account (19:16b–chap. 21) there is a similar build-up: first, the crucifixion scene with its church-evoking images of the undivided tunic and the reintegrated woman (19:16b–37); then the gathering of the disciples in faith around the risen body of Jesus (19:38–chap. 20, esp. 20:19–29); and finally the climactic picture of the believers' down-to-earth unity (chap. 21 with its many community-related images—the togetherness in the boat, the unbroken net, the shared eucharistic bread, Peter and the flock). It is essential to the design of the last discourse that it build up to the picture of (church-related) unity (chap. 17), and it is equally essential to the design of the death-and-resurrection narrative that it build up to a further picture of (church-related) unity (chap. 21). Just as the culminating "I believe, Lord" of the formerly blind man (9:38) opens the way for the image of the shepherd and the flock (chap. 10), so the culminating believing of Thomas (20:28–29, "My Lord . . .") opens the way for the image of the boat and the shepherd (chap. 21).

At one level, therefore, chap. 21 may be an epilogue, just as 1:1–18 is a prologue. The prologue is the gospel's foundation, but chap. 21 is no less integral. There is a level at which it is the gospel's ultimate focus; it highlights the gospel's persistent emphasis on the connection between believing and community.

Yet the evagelist has no illusions about the church. He places it in perspective and sometimes subjects it and its leaders to criticism. The initial call of Peter does not come from any excellence of his own; it depends on his brother's closeness to Jesus and on Jesus himself (1:35–42). The church-evoking women at Cana and Samaria take a leading role, yet they give way to the divine word of Jesus (2:4–5; 4:42). Peter's declaration of faith is followed by the chilling news that one of those for whom he speaks is a devil, "one of the twelve" (6:68–81). In chaps. 13–21 Peter is indeed a leader, but at times his attitude seems close to that of

Judas (chap. 13, esp. 13:36–38; 18:1–27, esp. 18:10), and he is dependent on the (Spirit-like) beloved disciple (13:23–24; 20:8–9; 21:7). Thus, far from being absolute, he is a sinner who depends on the Spirit and on Spirit-led disciples.

As already mentioned, John's gospel has sometimes been seen as reflecting the life of a specific community or church. Some such link is plausible. But it is extraordinarily difficult to reconstruct the history of a specific community, and, in fact, given what the gospel implies about a community open to all, it seems better to work on the hypothesis that the community which John reflects and to which he speaks is the universal Christian church. It is true, of course, that certain aspects of the community's conflicts, such as the Jews' expelling of believers from the synagogue (chap. 9), may be visualized as reflecting a specific time and place. But these conflicts, even if historical, have a broader meaning. " 'The Jews' in John represent the world that rejects the revelation of God in Jesus" (Rensberger, 1988, 95). And so the conflict which surrounds expulsion begins to represent the wider conflict between the revelation-rejecting world and believers everywhere. Neyrey (1988), for instance, has articulated the fact that John's gospel implies a revolt against certain people and values. This is an important insight. But it is not possible, at least not on the foundation of a fragile redaction theory, to reconstruct the social history of some local community. Social science may visualize John's community as a sect (see esp. Rensberger, 1988, 28), but social science has applied the term "sect" to the whole of early Christianity (Osiek, 1984, 79). If John is to be described as speaking to a sect or to a sectlike community, then it must be said that the sect consists essentially of all Christians. Furthermore this Christian community, while deeply critical of the world, is focused towards it, focused towards bringing the world to faith. What emerges primarily, therefore, is not local history but the evangelist's picture of how Christianity implies a revolt against many of the world's values—no matter when and where those values are found, even if within the community and within the individual believer.

The Gospel in Outline

The outline that follows does not focus on the gospel's details but rather on its central movement—its sense of advancing time and changing mood, particularly the Spirit-related question of whether to believe or not to believe.

Part 1 (The First Year) gives an optimistic introduction to Jesus' life and, in a series of brief episodes, it suggests that the process of believing is relatively easy.

Part 2 (The Second Year) shows Jesus' life as deepening and expanding; there is much journeying, and the episodes tend to become longer and to develop into discourses. But even as Jesus speaks, as the word seeks to take root, problems emerge. Nicodemus, for instance, exemplifies one problem, and the Samaritan woman another.

Part 3A (The Third Year) shows the way in which the ultimate problem, death, threatens to overshadow Jesus' life and to engulf his hearers in disbelief. But in three major events (at Tents, in healing the blind man, and in raising Lazarus) Jesus counters that threat.

Part 3B (The Central Mystery) looks not so much at the flow of life as at the hour of death, an hour which examplifies the larger central mystery of God's action. Death can destroy belief, but—again in three major episodes (the last discourse, the trial, the glorification)—Jesus turns death into a time of revelation.

The outline is complemented by the diagrammatic display which precedes the translation.

Book One (Chaps. 1–12) The Years of Jesus' Life

Part 1 The First Year (1:1–2:22)

As the Word Is Revealed, the Disciples Believe (Believing, as an initial assent to the basic message, is relatively easy.)

1:1–18   The prologue. A meditation on the history of the Word.

1:19–28   The initial trial: John is questioned and bears witness.

1:29–34   The initial vision: John sees Jesus coming, heavenlike.

1:35–42   The variety of calls: Jesus appears walking; the first disciples.

1:43–51   The variety of people: Philip; Nathanael begins to believe.

2:1–11   Life's sweet wine (Cana); the disciples believe.

. . .

2:12–22   The temple cleansing intimates death; remembering and believing.

Part 2 The Second Year (2:23–chap. 6)

As the Word Takes Root, Problems Emerge (Believing is difficult, blocked by human dividedness; it is accomplished only through the bridging action of the Spirit of the ascending Son of humanity.) People's quest for God, and, in answer, Jesus' journeying towards people

2:23–3:21 Nicodemus (in Jerusalem): from flesh-spirit division to God-given birth (wholeness/integration).
Believing and not believing.

3:22–36 John: further aspects of the integrating Spirit.
Believing and disbelieving.

4:1–42 The Samaritan woman: another form of dividedness and a further challenge to spirit-led renewal.
Believing and knowing.

4:43–54 The royal official (in Cana of Galilee, from Capernaum): the spectre of the ultimate dividedness—death—and the overcoming of it through the true (spiritual) seeing of signs.
Knowing and believing.
. . .

chap. 5 In Jerusalem: the creation-like giving of life. But the Jews do not accept it. "How will you believe?"

chap. 6 In Galilee and Capernaum: the complementary gift of God's providence (the bread of life)—to be accepted only through the Spirit.
Some do not believe.
Some believe and know.

Part 3A The Third Year (chaps. 7–12)

As Death Looms, Problems Intensify (The prospect of death makes believing even more difficult, but as Anointed and Son, Jesus begins to reveal a death-conquering dignity and Spirit. Reaction is often negative.)

chaps. 7–8	At Tents, in the shadow of death, Jesus (as Christ and Son) reveals life and Spirit. Reaction: division—with emphasis on disbelief.
chaps. 9–10	In contrast (to disbelief): despite intensifying division, the emphasis is placed on advancing life and revelation, both in the individual (chap. 9) and in the flock (chap. 10).
	· · ·
chaps. 11–12	Through Lazarus, the overcoming of death is shown clearly, but despite all the signs of life, some fall into unbelief.

Part 3B

At Death, the Word of Life Overcomes: The Path to Increasing Believing
(The closeness of death provokes a crisis of belief, but despite the devilish
antagonism of the world, Jesus reveals more clearly than ever that he
mediates God's Spirit, a Spirit who protects life and enriches it. Reaction is
generally positive.)

chaps. 13–17   Before Passover, in face of death, Jesus reveals advancing stages of life
                and Spirit, and also of consequent believing and knowing.

18:1–19:16a   In contrast (to preceding belief): the arrest and trials give portrayals of sin
                —of advancing godlessness (18:1–27) and of murder (18:28–19:16a).

19:16b–21:25   In Jesus' glorification (death and resurrection) the full revelation of life and
                Spirit brings into actuality the processes of believing and knowing.

Some Features of the Outline

The Distinct Final Sections

Within each major part of chap. 1–12 there is a final section which is significantly distinct. Within 1:1–2:22, the cleansing of the temple stands somewhat apart. It does not follow the steady progression of days (as found in 1:19,29,35,43; 2:1), but instead is described vaguely as taking place "After this" (2:12).

Within 2:23–chap. 6, there is a distinctness to chaps. 5 and 6. They do not fall within the steady geographic progression from Jerusalem to Galilee (as found in 2:23–chap. 4) but instead employ geographic moves which are independent, even enigmatic (5:1; 6:1).

Within chaps. 7–12, there is a form of break after chap. 10, a suggestion that, at one level, Jesus' public ministry has come to an end (Brown, 414). Thus, despite the basic unity of the text, there is a sense in which chaps. 11–12 stand apart.

The distinctness of these final sections is not an isolated phenomenon. John has a number of three-part episodes or discourses in which the third part is late or removed (e.g., within 5:1–15, see 5:14–15; within 6:1–21, see 6:16–21; within 13:1–20, see 13:12–20; within 15:18–27, see 15:26–27).

The most important common characteristic of these final sections appears to be their portrayal of various climactic life-giving interventions, interventions which break the normal structures of time and space. They suggest death and resurrection, and some future eschatology. The cleansing of the temple, which departs from the preceding time pattern, signifies Jesus' time-defeating resurrection (2:20–22). The incidents in chaps. 5 and 6, which break away in various ways from predictable space patterns (cf. the journey of 2:23–chap. 4, the non-journey of 6:21, and also perhaps the non-descent of 5:7–8), these pattern-breaking incidents tell first of all of a rising or raising (5:8, "Rise up . . ."; cf. 5:28–29; 6:39–40,54). And chaps. 11–12 deal largely with the raising of Lazarus. Thus, however much the gospel may be grounded in time and space, these final sections act as dramatic reminders that ultimately God gives life with a generosity which surpasses human patterns and expectations.

Coordination Within and Between Parts

The continuity just noted, between the various final sections, is but one element of a larger pattern of coordination. In Parts 1 and 2, for instance, there is coordination both within each part—details will be seen later—and between one part and another. And both together prepare the way for Part 3.

But it is in chaps. 7–21 that coordination most needs to be noted. First, there is the basic continuity *between* the major subdivisions: the whole of chaps. 7–12 acts both as a preparation and a foil for chaps. 13–21. Thus the discourse at Tents (chaps. 7–8), during which Jesus first begins to discuss his departure, acts as a background for the last discourse (chaps. 13–17). And the death and raising of Lazarus (chaps. 11–12) prepares for the death and resurrection of Jesus (19:16b–chap. 21). More surprisingly, chaps. 9 and 10, with their emphasis respectively on courage and care, provide a stark contrast to the spinelessness and callousness of Peter and Pilate (18:1–19:16a). The overall relationship, therefore, between chaps. 7–12 and chaps. 13–21 is one of delicate complementarity. The first (chaps. 7–12) tends to be negative, to emphasize disbelieving, but at its center (chaps. 9–10) the picture is more positive. The second (chaps. 13–21) is generally positive, but at its center (18:1–19:16a) it is largely negative.

Apart from this relationship *between* the parts, there is also coordination *within* them. This is a complex matter and would need a monograph to itself. Briefly stated, it means that the discourse at Tents (chaps. 7–8) prepares for the Lazarus chapters (11–12), and especially that the last discourse (chaps. 13–17) prepares for Jesus' glorification (19:16b–chap. 21). This latter idea is not new; it is generally agreed that the last discourse prepares for the glorification. But the full extent of the delicate correspondence between the texts has never been systematically investigated. As the texts are presented in this translation, both the last discourse and the glorification fall into five columns, and several elements of correspondence may be detected, including a relationship between chaps. 17 and 21. (See the diagrammatic display in the translation, titled Book Two, The Central Passover Mystery.) Some other aspects of correspondence will be noted in the commentary, but the full details are left to further research.

Relationship of the Present Structure to Previous Proposals

As suggested earlier, much of what is being put forward here has been proposed, implicitly at least, by others.

Brown's division of chaps. 1–12, though different in detail from the one given here, is based significantly on considerations of time and space. Three parts are discussed under time-related headings: "The *opening days* of the revelation of Jesus" (1:19–51, plus 2:1–11); "Jesus and the *principal feasts* of the Jews" (chaps. 5–10); "Jesus moves towards the *hour* of death and glory" (chaps. 11–12). A further part is described under a geography-related heading: "From Cana to Cana —various responses to Jesus' ministry in the different sections of Palestine" (chaps. 2–4). Furthermore, these headings are not limited to questions of time and space. To some degree they are also related to life; they touch on the progress of revelation, and on the movement towards death and glory, Obviously in Brown's work the emphasis on time and space is not explicit; the phrase "time and space" is never used in making these divisions, but it is real nonetheless. And it corresponds significantly not only to the fundamental role of time but also to the fact that, in one part at least—when Jesus travels to Galilee—the role of time becomes secondary to the complementary role of geography.

Brown is correct in indicating that 1:19–chap. 12 speaks of signs and chaps. 13–20 of glory. But that does not mean that the gospel should be divided on that basis. These features are part of a larger phenomenon. As Painter (1975, 51) in particular indicates, "the whole gospel is in some sense a book of signs . . . [and] the whole gospel could be called a book of glory" (cf. also Beasley-Murray, xc).

The researcher who has put most explicit emphasis on the idea of time and space is R. Kieffer (1984). Like some others, such as Mollat (1960) and Wilkens (1958), Kieffer brings out the importance of the three Passovers, and though he underestimates the full extent of the role of time—and thereby overestimates the role of space—his overall thesis is noteworthy.

Staley (1986; 1988, 50–73) also underestimates the role of time. However, following the lead of Rissi (1983), he highlights the gospel's profound emphasis on the idea of journeys, and thus, even though the details of his proposal are forced (pp. 59, 72–73), his work represents a significant advance.

The essential point is that in varying ways, and with varying degrees of explicitness, a number of writers have indicated that John's structure is linked to time and space.

Bultmann's division of chaps. 1–12 is based consistently on its central theological layer—on the notion of revelation and on various aspects of the tension between light and darkness, between the revealer and what resists the revealer. In broad terms—even though Bultmann never expresses the idea—these aspects of tension may be seen as reflecting the progression in the life of the believer. With little reference to the precise substructure of time and space, Bultmann manages, nonetheless, by theological insight to single out the major divisions—at 2:23, 7:1, and 13:1.

Bultmann's procedure highlights some of both his strengths and weaknesses. His theological interest was so great that it became the determining guide in his interpretation. At times it served him well—as it did when discerning the three basic dividing points. But it was not anchored in the gospel's literary substructure, in the carefully wrought foundations which centered on time and space. In fact, as Haenchen (1:48–51, esp. 51) indicates, he was not very interested in the gospel's literary integrity; on the contrary, he rearranged texts to suit his theological convictions. What is important, however, is that despite his theology-based rearrangements, he did highlight the text's crucial turning points.

The general conclusion which emerges is that earlier proposals concerning the structure of John's gospel are not as diverse and mutually exclusive as they may at first appear. In various ways they center on three factors—time, space, and the progress of revelation within human life—and once the interrelationship of those factors begins to be clarified, the compatibility of the proposals begins correspondingly to be visible.

The Basic Ages of the Individual: A Closer Look

However much the fourth gospel may emphasize community, it retains a strong sense of the individual. Peter, for instance, is the central church figure, leading forth the boat (chap. 21), but when he plunges into the sea he is on his own, virtually naked. And at the end, as he follows Jesus on a path which will lead to death, there is about him an aloneness (21:20–23).

Yet this aloneness does not mean sadness or emptiness. The Peter who follows Jesus has recovered from his sadness; he has "turned" from it (21:17, 19), and in this final picture there is a capsule version of what the gospel has sought to indicate: life may become more and more difficult but it also becomes richer.

The process bears reviewing.

At first (Part 1; 1:1–2:22) life looks good. In this youthful period believing is relatively easy. Though the prologue alludes to profound tensions, its overall outlook is positive, and so too is the outlook of John the Baptist as he witnesses to the light and to Jesus. Jesus himself quickly attracts disciples—people who, apart from Nathanael who is initially sceptical, appear to be receptive and harmonious. And then he presents to them at Cana the most attractive of portents—an abundance of magnificent wedding wine. When he goes on to speak of death, as he does when cleansing the temple, the impression is given that even that can be good: it is like the remaking of a temple, a process in which the accent is on resurrection. And the text emphasizes that the disciples believed this positive message, and believed it also at the end.

Life at this stage is not only good; it is almost too good. And it is the task of the evangelist, as of every incisive writer, to challenge it. In Culbertson's words, (1989b, 2):

> The literary text, like the analyst, urges the abandonment of infantile fantasies.
> . . . The elusive literary text pressures the reader to admit human limitation; in
> fact, to discover the meaning and tragic beauty of humanity precisely in limitation.

So it is in John. In the second year or period (Part 2; 2:23–chap. 6) the gospel begins to indicate that life is not so simple; people have a major problem. The matter surfaces in Jerusalem when Jesus reacts discerningly to a wave of facile enthusiasm. He did not entrust himself to them, ". . . for he knew what was in people." The problem is complex but it centers on a dividedness between flesh and spirit, and it causes difficulty in accepting the full dimensions of life. As a result, when Jesus goes through the land, revealing life in many forms, people react with varying degrees of perplexity, hesitation, and hostility. By the time the next Passover comes, in Galilee, there are indeed those who believe all the positive things Jesus has said, but there is also a growing phenomenon of disillusion, mutual hostility, and turning back. One is aware of dividedness, and one begins to sense death.

In the final period or year (Part 3; chaps. 7–21) death comes closer, and now, more clearly than before, there is a parting of the ways. In varying circumstances and degrees, some believe and others do not.

The struggle is not easy. In Part 3A (chaps. 7–12) death and darkness threaten to take over completely. Life becomes a siege. There is an increasing encroachment of scepticism, hatred, legalism, blindness, and violence. For Jesus the pressure and antagonism became intense. Once, in winter, they surrounded him. He escaped. But those he loved were not so lucky. With little warning, sickness struck down Lazarus. The negativity of death comes to the fore. Here is no simple transmutation. Instead, there are breaking hearts and a stinking body. His own violent death comes closer. In the midst of this, however, even when death and darkness are at their strongest, Jesus maintains his original message. Now more than ever he reveals the presence of spirit, light, and life. He gives sight to the man born blind, he restores Lazarus, he reflects the presence of a guiding ever-present love.

In Part 3B (chaps. 13–21) love takes over. At the very time that there is a climactic manifestation of the rotten side of life—diabolical treachery, spineless denials, corrupt authorities, barbaric violence—there is an even greater manifestation of the reality of love and the insuppressible power of life. Jesus had indeed shuddered and cried as death came close, but when the tempest is at its worst he overshadows it with his calm spirit. And as he gives himself to death, the drink which he receives is indeed bitter, yet there is no longer an atmosphere of breaking hearts and stinking bodies. Instead, those who stand by are commended to care, and his body is wrapped with perfume. When next he speaks to his disciples he imparts to them his own spirit of the wholeness of things. Finally, as a new day lights the shore, the disciples are called once more, and he restores, at a more mature level, their original sense of the nature of life.

6

The Design
3. A Complementary Aspect: Life as
Descent and Ascent

Of all the language patterns used to describe Jesus, one of the most basic is that of an enigmatic process whereby a person who has descended from heaven reascends to where he was before (3:13; 6:33–58; 20:17; cf. "lifting up," 3:14; 8:28; 12:32–34). This descent-ascent pattern, however, is not about Jesus alone. Meeks (1972, 67–70) in particular has indicated that it implies something about the community: if Jesus is someone apart, someone whom outsiders do not understand, then the community also stands apart, an enigma. This conclusion is applicable not only to a small local community but also to a community which seeks to be universal. Like Jesus, the whole church is an enigma.

The purpose here is to develop the argument further: what is said of Jesus— that his story is one of descent and ascent—applies to each individual who accepts him. The life of Jesus provides a model for believers and a fundamental part of that model is the pattern of descent and ascent. Thus it can be said that people come from God and return to God. More precisely, it may be said that people are *sent* from God. The healing of the blind man, a process which is evocative of a person's creation and birth, is described implicitly as a sending (9:1–7).

The imagery of descent and ascent, therefore, at least as used in John, is not primarily something esoteric. It refers to the fact that life in general, the whole experience of a believer, is a process of descent and ascent. The life one received from God is gradually poured out until the final descent into death, but at the same time there can be an increasing ascent to God.

The importance of this pattern is seen in the fact that it is found not only in explicit references to descending and ascending but also in the more general patterning of several key texts.

The first and most obvious example is the prologue (1:1–18). Whatever its sources, the present text is so patterned that there is a gradual transition from lofty poetry to plain prose. The transition is not simple; as will be seen in analyzing the text, it is essentially threefold and repetitious—thus giving the effect not of a straight line but of a spiral. However, the transition does occur, first soaring, then down-to-earth, and the basic effect is to communicate, through the very form of the language, what the prologue itself is all about—the implied idea of a descent, of the Word becoming flesh.

In the case of the conversation with Nicodemus (2:23–3:21) the effect is almost the opposite. The text starts on a very human note, rather negative and at night, but then, through the three increasingly long statements of Jesus, each beginning with "Amen, amen . . ." (3:3,5,11) and the third culminating in the classic "For God so loved . . ." (3:16), it suggests a process of ascent. To some degree the ascent in question is that of Jesus who, as Son of humanity, is to be lifted up (3:13), but it implies that through his ascent the way is open for Nicodemus and for others.

A further example of this dynamic may be found in chap. 10. The first part of the chapter (10:1–21) contains the parable of the good shepherd (10:7–18) and within that parable the language undergoes a steady transition from being divine and parabolic ("Amen, amen . . . I am . . .") to being human and open (v 17, ". . . I lay down my life . . ."). Again the transition is a threefold spiral, and even within each subdivision (within vv 7–10, 11–16, and 17–18) there is a gradual fading of language which is divine and parabolic.

In the second part of chapter 10 (10:22–42), however, the language tends, though less clearly, in the opposite direction. The scene begins as Jesus is in danger, in winter. But in spite of the danger, when he speaks of himself as Messiah and Son, his statements build up first to the idea of being "one" with the Father (10:30) and then to a more detailed description of that unity (10:38, ". . . the Father is in me and I am in the Father"). And it is within that general pattern of increasing build-up that he pronounces the unusually complex sentence which terminates with the clear, climactic statement, "I am God's Son/Child" (10:36).

The Lazarus story (11:1–53) follows a further variation on the pattern of descent. The Jesus who at the beginning is distant and God-like (11:1–6), at the end is doomed to die (11:53). Again the transition is threefold—from being distant (11:1–6) to being involved, communicative, and in danger (11:7–16); from being the resurrection and the life (11:17–27) to shuddering and crying (11:28–37); and from being in command of life (11:38–44) to being condemned to death (11:45–53).

The subsequent section (11:54–12:50, esp. 11:54–12:36a), however, suggests a process of ascent. The action begins on a low note, in the desert (11:54), but then there is a sense of expectation (11:55–56), and in the following scenes, as Jesus comes first to Bethany to be lavishly anointed (12:1–11) and then to Jerusalem as a new form of king (12:12–19), there is a growing sense of his impending transition through burial (12:7) to glory (12:16). Finally, when the Greeks approach (12:20–36a), the text leaves aside almost all details of time and space, and Jesus speaks as one who looks forward to being glorified, to overcoming death, to being lifted up. The unbelievers do not join in this ascent (12:36b-43), and so at the end of the chapter (12:44–50), as at the end of some previous ascentlike texts (cf. 3:20–21; 10:37–38), there is a need to choose between two ways.

Within the last discourse the pattern continues. Briefly described, the footwashing (13:1–20) suggests both descent and ascent. Jesus descends as it were to wash feet and then resumes his place. And the language changes correspondingly: from complex divinelike solemnity (13:1–3), to simplicity (13:4–5), and later back to a form of solemnity (13:12–20). The parable of the true vine (15:1–10) also suggests descent. Like the parable of the good shepherd (10:7–18) it gradually leaves aside the language of divinity and parable. The final prayer (chap. 17),

however, evokes ascent. In various ways this is suggested—from the initial raising of the eyes to heaven (17:1), through the prayer itself, as it becomes more
heaven-oriented and effective, until finally there is the majestic and climactic "*Pater
. . . thelō . . .* ," "Father . . . I will/desire . . ." (17:24).

Within the account of the death and resurrection (19:16b-chap. 20) the pattern
goes further. The crucifixion (19:16b-27), with its transition from Jesus as king
(19:19–22) to the sharing of his clothes (19:23–24) suggests a loss, a descent.
And in the death account (19:28–37) the idea of descent reaches a form which is
thoroughly human and final—the head drops (19:30) and the blood and water flow
out (19:36). The descent is complete. But then, in the resurrection narrative (19:38–
20:31), there is a climactic account of what is essentially an ascent.

Chapter 21 breaks new ground: it shows that the pattern of descent or self-
emptying, which had been seen so often in Jesus, is now reflected in Peter, the
one who in many ways represents the disciples. Within the framework of yet
another threefold text (21:1–14), Peter goes from being the clear leader (vv 2–3),
to being an attentive listener who throws himself vulnerably into the sea
(v 7), to being the one who, servantlike, obeys the command to bring in the
fish (vv 10–11).

The details of the pattern will require close scrutiny, but it is useful at this
early stage to have some overall sense of the movement of the text. The relationships between the various passages are complex but coherent. The descent accounts, for instance, become deeper and deeper: in the first case (1:1–18) the
descent is simply into flesh, but in the later ones the pattern comes closer and
closer to death—until it ends in the flow of blood and water. And the descent of
Peter in turn reflects that of Jesus. For instance, the perplexing process by which
Peter girds himself before throwing himself into the sea (21:7) is a variation on
Jesus' action of girding himself before washing the feet of the disciples (13:5).

These descent texts—perhaps there are others, not detected—though they
suggest a process of self-giving and even of self-emptying, do not end negatively.
There is always some indication of a positive result or of a turnabout, some indication of an inherent link between descent and ascent. Thus the descent into flesh
is followed by "we have seen his glory . . ." (1:14); the laying down of Jesus'
life is followed by the idea of taking it up again (10:18); and after the flow of
blood and water there is a picture of witness, faith, and fulfillment (19:34–37).

In assessing the role of Jesus it is necessary to keep the entire picture in view,
descent and ascent. Käsemann (1968, esp. 5) by focusing unduly on chap. 17,
particularly on its culminating verses, loses sight both of the repeated emphasis
on descent and also of other evidence (highlighted by Thompson, 1988) concerning the humanity of Jesus.

This pattern of descent and ascent does not take away from the main three-
part structure outlined in the preceding chapter; rather it fits into it as a kind of
substructure. Life not only consists of varying stages. It also involves a process
of descent, even unto death, and of ascent, even while on earth.

7

An Outline
of the Essence of John's Theology:
Jesus as the Spirit-Giving Healer
of Human Dividedness

John's theology is not a single coherent system. Rather it is a map of the progress of life and of faith, and such progress, by its nature, is beset with changes, setbacks, and surprises. To inquire about John's theology is like asking about the meaning of a symphony. The meaning, Beethoven would say, is not in talking about it but in listening to it. In the case of the gospel, the meaning lies in living it. What follows, therefore, is not the meaning; it is an abstraction—an abstraction, it is to be hoped, which is useful and which prepares the way for meaning.

The scholarly discussion of John's theology is vast and complex (for reviews, see esp. Giblet, 1977; Kysar, 1985, 2443–64). What is given here is an effort to trace the central thread.

The Foundational Reality

The starting point for the evangelist's theology is not human sinfulness but an ideal of abiding restful union. It is with this idea that the prologue begins and ends: the Word was "with God"; the only-begotten is "in the bosom of the Father" (1:1, 18). And it is an idea which in various forms reappears in the course of the gospel—particularly in the allusions to final togetherness (14:1–3; 17:24–27), in the picture of the beloved disciple reclining on Jesus' bosom (13:23–25), and, at the very end of the gospel, in a further and somewhat surprising reference both to reclining on the breast of Jesus and to abiding (21:20–23). In fact the images of intimate resting are so placed (in 1:18; 13:23–25; 21:20) that in varying ways they frame the gospel. Thus there is a form of restful union which exists first of all in God, but in which humans can participate both during this life and during a later life.

This union is not alien to humans or something that exists outside their being; on the contrary, it corresponds to something that is deep within them, even from their birth. The blind man of chap. 9, for instance, is a very down-to-earth character, yet his first words are *Egō eimi,* literally "I am" (9:9). At one level this expression is a prosaic self-identification ("I am he"), but at another, given the context (8:12,24,28,58; cf. 18:5–6), it is an indication that he is an image of God, of the divine "I am." As such it is in God alone that he will find complete fulfillment and rest.

55

Human Dividedness and Healing Revelation

Against this positive background the gospel reveals a deep problem: however oriented people may naturally be toward the divine realm, however deep their longing, there is within them a darkness or dividedness, with the result that they cannot immediately connect with their God. Thus, in the course of the gospel, darkness and misunderstanding are found almost from the beginning (1:5) to the end (21:23). This failure to relate to God takes two basic forms. First, in the course of their daily lives, people are so preoccupied with matters of "the flesh" —particularly with careers, love-life, and sickness (cf. Nicodemus, the Samaritan woman, and the sick man)—that they do not have the necessary "spirit" to relax and enjoy God (see esp. chaps. 3–6, particularly 3:5–8; 6:63). Second, towards the end of life, a relationship with the living God seems to be excluded: death overshadows life, and besides, one cannot cross from this life to God; people become conquered by "the world" and again, what is missing is the necessary "spirit" (cf. esp. chaps. 7–12, particularly 7:7,34,36–39; 8:21–22).

The precise origin and nature of this human dividedness is never explained in the gospel. It is connected with a desire for human glory rather than the glory of God (5:44; 12:43) and with a devil-related tendency of the will towards lies and murder (8:44). Unlike the synoptic gospels, where Jesus expels demons in dramatic actions, John implies that one's demons emerge in the course of one's life and that it is in the struggle of human living that they are driven out. Thus he does not deny the reality of demons; he simply portrays them differently.

Yet though the problem of human weakness is profound and though it evokes an evil which haunts the gospel, it is not the manifestation of an alternative god; there is no cosmological dualism; everything comes from God ("all things were made through" the Word, 1:3), and the entire phenomenon of evil, however ravaging and unexplained, ultimately forms part of the mystery of God and of the providence foretold by scripture (8:45–47, see commentary below; 13:18; 19:24,36–37).

It is this human dividedness which forms the immediate context for the coming of Jesus. Consequently, even though at one level Jesus dominates the gospel, at another his identity and role are determined by the needs of humans. In Schnackenburg's words (1:155), "his messianic and divine dignity was brought out only to disclose his function as Savior. The Johannine Christology is essentially ordained to soteriology. Everything that . . . Jesus says and does, all that he reveals and all that he accomplishes as 'signs,' takes place in view of [humans] . . . attaining salvation." Thus, as already noted in chapter 5, the shaping of his biography, into three years, is governed by the portraying of how people advance toward salvation.

The most essential function of Jesus is to communicate the divine Spirit, the very Spirit of God, and thus to bridge the dividedness between God and humans. However, the Spirit cannot be imparted immediately. What is given to people is not God's own self—to a significant degree God remains inaccessible ("no one has ever seen God," 1:18)—but rather that aspect of God which is communicable to humans—what might be called "God's human face." The purpose of the portrait of Jesus is to reveal that face. In him one sees a human shape of the divine, the Word in flesh. When he first arrives on the human stage he is not praying or preaching; he is simply living—walking and abiding (1:36–40).

It is only when he has experienced the fullness of human life, not only its wedding wine, but also its tiredness and tears and fears, even its death, that he communicates the Spirit. Thus the Spirit which is given, though it is God's own holy Spirit, is not something inhuman or alien. Rather, it comes from within a human being, from within a lived life (cf. esp. 7:37–39; 19:30; 20:21–22).

John does not say explicitly that Jesus' death was a sacrifice and that that sacrifice brought about salvation. Instead, the idea of sacrifice has been trans-formed, has been spelled out in human terms: Jesus' entire life was a sacrifice—from the moment he entered as the lamb of God (1:29) until finally, as one who had been consecrated (17:19; cf. 10:36), he died at the same hour as the Passover lambs (19:14).

The sacrifice consisted in the living of a wholesome life, and it brought sal-vation because it revealed an active healing presence. For John, revelation heals (cf. Culpepper, 1988, 422–23), and it does so precisely because, instead of being merely intellectual (indifferent knowledge), it is constituted by sacrificial self-giving (loving knowledge).

The way in which revelation heals may be seen in the well-known process of recognition. In Culbertson's words (1989a, 9):

> There is an experience in life we call recognition. It is a kind of knowledge by which we apprehend meaning in a pattern of events or realize that the meaning we had once assigned to those events has been shattered. . . . [This] experience of recognition is the central humanizing and revelatory experience, the immediate cause of psychological and spiritual change.

It is towards this process of recognition that Jesus draws people, telling them through his life and through his Spirit that in their own lives there is something more, a dimension which, slowly perhaps, gives unity and healing.

Dividedness therefore is avoidable. At every stage of life, through all its changing moods and crises, there is a Spirit, first developed within Jesus, which brings together the divine and the human, and which finds, deep within life, the human face of the divine. That is the essence of accepting Jesus—to realize, through him, that precisely what is so ordinary has a further dimension, and that in ac-cepting him one finds both one's deepest self and God.

This is the challenge which, in different ways, he places before Nicodemus and the Samaritan woman. Amid their varied forms of darkness and division they are called to awaken to the presence of the integrating Spirit.

Images and Titles

That Jesus bridges the gap between God and humanity is expressed in the gospel in a variety of ways. One, already referred to, is that, as the incarnate Word, he

is involved in the full reality of human life. Another is through the imagery and
implication of descent and ascent: Jesus has descended from the Father and to the
Father returns.

A further way of showing that Jesus acts as a bridge between God and humanity is through the use of titles, especially "Son of God" and "Son of humanity."
"Son of God" captures the divine, and "Son of humanity" the human. During
the opening drama (1:1–2:22) the two titles balance each other, one apparently
falling at the end of one day (1:34), and the other at the end of another (1:51).
Further balance is found between 1:49 and 1:51.

The term "Son of humanity/Man" is deeply controverted, but, following an
idea from M. M. Pazdan (1991, 30–75), it is appropriate to seek the evangelist's
meaning not primarily in the gospel's background but in the broad flow of John's
finished story.

John uses "Son of humanity" thirteen times, and in nine of these references
it is associated with the imagery of descending and ascending, or with variations
on that imagery (being lifted up/glorified; cf. 1:51; 3:13,14; 6:62; 8:28; 12:23,34
[twice]; 13:31). Thus it is associated with the whole flow of human life. The other
four references, which all occur towards the center of the gospel (5:27; 6:27,53;
9:35), suggest in diverse ways that Jesus is the one in whom humanity is profoundly achieved, one who has the right to judge (5:27), to communicate life
(6:27,53), and to call people to the ultimate stage of human wholeness (9:35).

"Son of humanity," therefore, is a term which is immensely variegated, but
not more variegated than human life. It reflects both the flow of life, from origin
to destiny, and life's quality. And it applies to Jesus. He is fully integrated with
life's extremes—with God and with death. For others, therefore, he is model,
judge, and mediator. And it is as such—as this multifaceted integrated human—
that he is called the Son of humanity.

Jesus is also known as the Anointed (Messiah, *Christos*). The background to
this title is complex, but its essence is simple. It indicates dignity, particularly the
dignity of someone or something close to God. In the OT, anointing was sometimes applied to kings and priests, and especially to the tabernacle of God (Exod
40:9–15). The fourth gospel never tells of Jesus' being anointed, but it reports
that the Spirit descended on him like a dove from heaven and abode on him,
causing him to be recognized as God's Son (1:31–34), and shortly afterwards he
is discovered to be the Anointed (1:35–41). His anointing therefore does not depend on other people but is a gift from God, given from the beginning.

This anointed dignity is not reserved to Jesus. In healing the blind man, Jesus
does indeed use humble clay, but he anoints (*chriō*) the man's eyes (9:6), and the
result is to evoke a process of creation in which people are sent into the world
endowed with the dignity of a Christ. It may take some time to recognize this;
chap. 9 suggests a process of maturing in which the recognition of the Christ
demands honesty and courage. But from the beginning the essential dignity is
present and it is given to everybody.

The various titles—"Anointed," "Son of God," "Son of humanity"—are
to be taken together. To the dignity implied by "Anointed," "Son" adds the idea
of personal relationship with God. The dignity, therefore, does not lie in some

cold quality; as Jesus' anointedness was recognized in connection with his role as Spirit-filled and Son, so the anointedness of others is linked particularly to the Spirit and to a personal relationship with God. Dignity, therefore, though granted initially by God, has all the vitality of a relationship and is to be developed accordingly.

This emphasis on dignity takes on added importance in view of the fact that the first-century Mediterranean world accorded a pivotal value to honor, in other words, to having a sense of one's worth and to having one's worth recognized (Malina, 1981, 25–50). Worth was established in three ways—by exercising power, by taking on one's appropriate sexual role, and by dutifulness (*religio/pietas*) towards all (towards everyone from slaves, to peers, to God).

John's gospel revolts against this system. (Neyrey's *Revolt,* 1988, whatever the merits of its reconstructions, highlights a central factor in the gospel message.) For the evangelist one's worth does not depend on power, sexual role, and dutifulness. It comes first of all from being a child of God, worthy at one's creation of being anointed by God's hands (9:6); capable, even with one's first simple words, of imaging the divine "I am" (9:9). The people who come to Jesus— especially the prestigious Nicodemus, the Samaritan woman, and the royal official —have experienced various aspects of power, sexual roles, and dutifulness. But Jesus offers them something more—a Spirit, a faith, which rejuvenates and which can set them on a stronger foundation. They may resume some of these roles and fulfil them all the more, but the roles are not the basis of their worth.

Likewise with Jesus. His worth does not depend on titles or accomplishments but rather on his relationship to the Father (Charles Giblin, in conversation, August 14, 1990). Even when he refers to his titles or works he does so in a way which evokes God. His frequent "I am," for instance, evokes the divine "I am."

In today's world the need for revolt seems to be equally great. The exposing of the dehumanizing nature of communism is an important step. But the problem is far deeper and more widespread. True human worth is obscured and measured falsely by a host of forces—from the image of humanity created by some film stars to the image of community created by shallow patriotism. "We walk on the moon, but we haven't managed to come closer to our neighbour or to ourselves. . . . In conquering space, we forget our soul" (Wiesel, 1987, 4).

Transcending Love

In describing the love which overcomes dividedness, the gospel uses imagery which is both spousal and parental. The meeting between Jesus and the people, for instance, is described in spousal language: "The one who has the bride . . ." (3:29; cf. 4:1–42). The use of parental imagery is seen above all in the fact that, more than in any other gospel, there are repeated references to God as a Father. At one level this image is narrow and therefore oppressive: like almost all language about God it is inadequate, and the inadequacy is heightened by the fact that it may reflect and reinforce arbitrary structures. At another level it is liberating: insofar as it places the fullness of divine power and love on the side of the believer—even if that power and love are expressed through a limited image—it provides the believer with a basis for questioning all images and structures, including those suggested by itself.

The image of the Father, then, expresses the idea that God's involvement includes a personal love, and as such it is at the center of the gospel message. For it is not just through exercising one's spirit that one comes to integration; it is by an active dependence on a loving God. This is the heart of the matter: following the example of Jesus and relying on the Spirit, to live one's daily life in dependence on a God who is parent, lover, and friend.

John is not glib about love. It is only in the later stages of the gospel that the word "love" (*agapē;* verb, *agapaō*) becomes frequent. In chaps. 1–12 positive love is either lacking (3:19; 5:42; 8:42; 12:43) or is present only in God (3:16,35; 10:17) and Jesus (11:5). However, from chap. 13 onwards—in other words, under the shadow of death, especially the death of Jesus—John speaks repeatedly of the disciples as being able to love. True love therefore is a gift.

The text does not say explicitly that one should pray; in fact, in marked contrast with the synoptics, the words "pray" and "prayer" never occur in this gospel. What one finds instead is the broader idea of abiding, *menō*—a verb which suggests being at rest in God, and which is exemplified by the image of reclining on the divine bosom (cf. 1:18; 13:23–25; 21:20). The result of John's procedure—avoiding explicit words for prayer while at the same time suggesting prayer in various ways—is to preserve a sense of prayer's ultimate indefinabilty.

This resting or abiding is not lazy; it is associated with love even unto death. But it involves a letting-go, including a letting-go of past and future, and even a letting-go of an overemphasis on self-development. At this point the thought of John's gospel is like that of Gerald May (1977, 6):

> The entire process [of self-development] can be very exciting and entertaining. But the problem is there's no end to it. The fantasy is that if one heads in the right direction and just works hard enough and learns enough new things and grows enough and gets actualized, one will be *there*. None of us is quite certain exactly where "there" is, but it obviously has something to do with resting.

The gospel contains the essence of this idea but brings it further: the "there," the place of wholeness or integration, is in pausing and allowing oneself to be a beloved disciple; in other words, it is in becoming one who is indeed learning but who, despite the limitations of that learning process, has abandoned oneself into a personal love.

John's central emphasis on rest helps to place him midway between the extemes of Eastern and Western thought—between the Eastern tendency to suppress the ego with all its desires and striving, and the Western tendency to exalt it, to make everything dependent on personal effort and will-power. John respects the ego, but helps it to relax and to see itself in the context of the larger divine reality (the *Egō Eimi*).

Within this place of rest there is eternal life, a sense of oneness with ultimate reality. Realized eschatology is not an abstract idea; it is a spiritual experience of knowing that the timeless God is at the door, inviting the person even now to full union. It is an attentiveness to the present, a readiness, at every moment, to receive reality, to enjoy deeply even the simplest things. In the words of poet Paul Murray (1991a, 23):

> This moment,
> the grace of this one raptureless
> moment
> is the place of pilgrimage
> to which I am a pilgrim.

Limitations of various kinds may batter the surface of such an attentive person, but deep within there is a feast, and there is no tomorrow.

The Feasts

The gospel speaks frequently of feasts—an unnamed feast (5:1), Tents (7:2), Dedication (10:22), and Passover (2:13, 6:4, 11:55; cf. chaps. 13–20)—and it is generally recognized that part of John's purpose is to show that Jesus replaces the feasts of the Jews.

But there is another factor. It is very difficult to discuss feasts in John without also discussing sabbath (see, for instance, Gail Yee, 1989), and the interwovenness of feasts with the notion of sabbath highlights a basic feature of the feasts themselves: they are an extension of sabbath, of resting in God, and thus of the gospel's central idea of abiding union. The synoptics may speak of God's realm (kingdom) as a feast, but John has something more down-to-earth—union with God which is festive, union which is linked to sabbaths and specific feasts and thus to the flow of daily life.

The connection of feasts with sabbath is seen from the way the two are interwoven. The references to sabbath occur essentially in two places—first in chap. 5 and its aftermath (5:9–10,16,18; 7:22–23; 9:14–16, a variation on 5:9–10), and later in connection with Jesus' resurrection (19:31; 20:1,19, in its plural form *sabbatōn*, lit., "week"). The first set of references speaks of a Jewish sabbath, but the later references, by using *sabbatōn* in connection with the resurrection ("the first day of the *sabbatōn*"), suggest a transition: Jewish *sabbaton* has given way to *sabbatōn*, the day of the resurrection. Resting has taken on a new meaning; it means to rest in the resurrection, in the Spirit given by Jesus.

Both of these sets of sabbath references are linked to feasts. In fact, the only thing known about the anonymous feast in 5:1 is that it was a sabbath. But that is enough; the very anonymity serves to strengthen the connection between the notion of feast and that of sabbath. (The effort to identify this feast historically obscures the theological importance of the feast-sabbath connection).

The later sabbath references, at the resurrection, are likewise linked to a feast —the climactic feast of Passover (11:55–56; 12:1,12,20; 13:1,29; 19:14,31), a feast which is the high point not only in the gospel's list of successive Passovers, but even in the list of all the gospel's feasts. It was to this final Passover that Tents and Dedication had been leading—like intimations of death leading to death itself. And so the identification of this final Passover with sabbath strengthens further the link between feast and sabbath.

The feasts therefore are not a loose appendage to John's gospel, nor are they a way simply of saying that an aspect of Judaism has been replaced. They are a way of saying that restful union with God is down-to-earth and festive.

Glory

Central to the integrating process is the idea of glory—an idea which for some (cf. esp. Käsemann, 1968; Festugière, 1974, 9–13) is the key to the gospel. Glory is a manifestation of God, particularly of God's love. For rather as love tends to show itself in sparkling ways—flowers, songs, unusual actions—so divine love tends to flow into manifestation; and that manifestation is called glory. Simoens (1981), for example, speaks of "the glory of love."

The integration occurs when one sees God's glory (cf. esp. 1:14), in other words, when, in some way, one looks at something or someone which manifests God and when one grasps the underlying divine love.

This process is inextricably linked with the action of the Spirit, and so it is necessary that the emphasis on glory be taken in conjunction with the traditional emphasis on John's gospel as spiritual.

The glory in question is not something ethereal; it is found in human realities which are down-to-earth, in situations which one may not immediately think of as manifesting the divine. The difficulty of holding the two together, the human and divine, is seen, for instance, in the diverse ways Jesus is perceived by the Samaritan woman (4:7–15) and by Peter (13:6–11). The woman, faced with the human Jesus, cannot at first perceive anything of divinity, whereas Peter, aware of Jesus' divinity, cannot reconcile it with something so human as washing feet. Shades of the same difficulty reappear in Bultmann and Käsemann. For Bultmann, Jesus was flesh; the revelation was in his humanity (1:14a). For Käsemann, Jesus was glory (1:14c); he was divine in John's gospel, but not human. The challenge—difficult for every human being, and possible only through the Spirit—is to discern the divinity precisely in what is thoroughly human. When that is done, and only when that is done, does one find authentic integration and peace.

Such integration is not something unchanging; it has to be developed as life progresses, and there is a certain dimension of it which is attainable only in the future, after death. But even now it involves eternal life, union with God, and thus one may say that eschatalogy—insofar as it means the blessings of the last days—is already present ("realized").

Believing: The Dynamics (Including Signs) and Implications

When one looks at the process of salvation from the point of view of the human participant, the most decisive factor is that of believing. Believing is not an exercise which is mechanical or intellectual. Within the gospel it is closely associated with knowing; and, in accordance with the gospel's semitic background, knowing implies a form of union.

Also associated with believing are signs. Initially the references to signs are perplexing (cf. 2:11,18,23; 3:2; 4:48,54; 6:2,14,26,30; 7:31; 9:16; 10:41; 11:47; 12:18,37; 20:30), and the scholarly debate about them is correspondingly complex (cf. Kysar, 1985, 2453–56). In the midst of this debate one of the most coherent positions seems to be that of Thompson (1988, 53–86, esp. 64): ''The signs were originally done and have now been written down in order to evoke faith.'' In other words, the evangelist views signs positively; they evoke faith and they confirm it. This does not mean that, in building faith, signs alone suffice. During his visit to Jerusalem (2:23–25) Jesus does not trust himself to those whose faith was founded exclusively on signs, not because their faith in itself was bad, but because —given the difficulties which lay ahead—Jesus knew that something more would be needed (Thompson, 1988, 65). Jesus does not condemn the signs-based faith of Nicodemus, but he challenges him to go further (3:2–3).

In the case of the royal official (4:43–54) there is a similar phenomenon: Jesus eventually allows signs to have their due role—the ascertaining of the hour (of healing) acts as a faith-confirming sign (4:51–53)—but his initial refusal (4:48) serves as a indication that ultimately the official will need a faith which is independent of signs. The official, in fact, takes the necessary step immediately; without waiting for any sign, he believes; and the sign then assumes its appropriate role, positive but limited, of confirming his faith.

The limitedness of signs is further portrayed in chap. 6. At first, when the crowd follows Jesus because of his signs (6:2), the quality of the people's response is not clear. But later there are a variety of apparently negative reactions —abusing the sign (6:14), failing to really see it (6:26), and finally, asking for one even when one has already been given (6:30). The impression is given, therefore, that signs are good, but that in various ways people can ignore or refuse them.

This impression is later confirmed. In chaps. 7 and 9 signs are associated ever more clearly with divided reactions (7:31–32 [cf. 7:43], 9:16). In chap. 10 those who believe apparently take a positive view of signs (10:19–21,41–42), but in chaps. 11 and 12, on the other hand, failure to believe is associated precisely with a refusal to pay heed to signs (11:47; 12:18–19,37). Finally, in the summary statement of 20:30, signs are viewed positively.

Signs therefore have a double role with regard to believing: they both evoke it and confirm it. But they do not guarantee it. No matter how wonderful, they may be misunderstood, ignored, or rejected.

Nor do signs constitute the full path to believing. Other factors, particularly witness and the word, indicate that in Jesus, and thus in human life, God is present. Furthermore the development of believing is frequently associated with the idea of abiding—a reference apparently to a restful process of letting the word take root (cf. esp. 1:39, 4:40–42, 10:40–42).

Believing is also associated with ethical conduct. In fact, it is precisely the implicit need for moral reform which is mentioned first as preventing people from believing (3:19–20). Later, particularly in the last discourse, the emphasis on moral conduct is made more explicit, and within the parable of the true vine the pattern of descent (as described in the preceding chapter—the introductory chap. 6) moves from "the word" (*logos,* 15:3), through "the words" (*rhēmata,* 15:7) and "the commandments" (*entolas,* 15:10), to "the commandment" (*entolē,* 15:12)— Jesus' commandment of love. The implication of the literary structure, of the linguistic descent, is that the *logos* issues in love. The Word flows into the words, into the commandments. Thus the word not only leads to believing; it keeps on flowing until it brings love into life.

Associated with conduct is the verb "to will" (*thelō*—a word which John uses with care. Human willing is important; people can be willing (5:35) or unwilling (5:40). Yet in diverse ways John's first uses of the verb (1:44; 3:8; 5:6,21) subtly place the emphasis for the process of willing on the divine. And, at the end, Peter's willing gives way to the greater divine willing of Jesus (21:18,22,23). The overall impression is that, however important human willing may be, ultimately it works beneath the umbrella of divine willing.

An example of the interweaving of human conduct with the divine occurs in the verb "to hand over" (*para-didōmi*). The handing over (or betraying) of Jesus, which is begun by the devil-related action of Judas (6:70–71; 12:4; 13:2; 18:5) and continued by the Jews and Pilate (18:30,35; 19:11,16), is the worst crime in the whole account. Yet this verb is used first and last about Jesus—about his prior knowledge that it would happen (6:64; cf. 13:11,21; 18:2), and about his own handing over of his spirit/Spirit (19:30), an action which brought the whole process of handing over to completion, deliberate completion.

The only later use of "hand over" is in the closing picture of the beloved disciple who, while leaning on Jesus' bosom, inquired about the betrayer (21:20). Treachery therefore is not some distant reality; even at the heart of love it is known.

Believing Leads to Care and Community/Church

Since believing is inseparable from love it is also inseparable from community, from church—inseparable ultimately from a concern for all people. During the final stages of chaps. 17 and 21—in the prayer that the world may believe (17:21,23), and in the image of the unbroken net of 153 fishes (21:11)—there is a concern which is universal. This includes the Jews; though at one obvious level they are depicted as symbols of unbelief, and thus even as lying murderers (cf. 8:44) there is another level, less obvious, in which, particularly through the figures of Nathanael (1:45–51), the sick man (5:1–15), and Mary Magdalene (19:25;

20:1–2,11–18), they are treated with respect and concern. The reality of this other level will be seen in the course of the commentary.

John's avoidance of the word "church" does not mean that he is opposed to the church itself—any more than his avoidance of "prayer" means that he is opposed to the reality of prayer. On the contrary, the whole thrust of the gospel is toward these realities. But they are elusive. Ultimately the spiritual link of one believer with another (the link which underlies the church) is as mystery-filled as the link between the believer and God. And ultimately it is not only prayer but also church which is indefinable. However organized, the church is simply a part of something which is bigger than itself, part of a reality which in the final analysis is founded on the divine Spirit. As the saying goes: It is not that the church has a mission, but that the mission has a church.

Nor is the evangelist opposed to Peter. On the contrary, he gives him a leading role (1:40–42; 6:68–69, and esp. chap. 21). Yet, without any hostility, he puts Peter in his place; he shows him as one who, for all his importance, is subject to the greater realities of love and spirit. This is the purpose of the healthy interplay between Peter and the beloved disciple (13:23–24; 20:1–10; 21:7,20–23); Peter is a leader, but he depends on the (Spirit-like) beloved disciple. Peter's limitations and vulnerability are underlined by the fact that in various ways he is associated or shadowed by the character of Judas (6:68–71; 13:2,6; 13:21,28; 18:2–3,10–11; cf. 18:15–16). The Peter who eventually learns from the beloved could just as easily have gone the way of Judas.

The World, Dualism, Evil

Universal concern, however, does not mean that the believers' relationship with the world is smooth. To a significant degree the world is enslaved to lies and sin and death. The divine Spirit who counters the forces of sin within the individual, counters these forces also in the outside world. In other words, the believers, by the very fact of being believers, are in tension with the outside world. It is for this reason, at least in part, that their guiding Spirit is referred to as the Paraclete and the Spirit of truth. The title "Paraclete," insofar as it means a defending counsellor, indicates that the Spirit serves as guardian and friend against the influence and attacks of the world. And "Spirit of truth" highlights the Spirit's role in bringing home to the believer the most basic of truths—that amid all of life's confusion and darkness the most decisive reality is God's power to save, to bring people to union and peace. Those who are guided by the Spirit, therefore, will have a love which is not only concerned about the world, but which also challenges it.

As well as challenging the world, the Spirit may also judge it. Jesus did not come to judge, but his presence provokes decision, and through a negative decision one brings judgement on oneself. Similarly the Spirit—which is essentially the Spirit of Jesus—brings judgement.

Following people's decision there is salvation or the lack of salvation. And it is here—in speaking of two options (rather than in speaking of the composition of the universe)—that the gospel appears to be dualistic. This impression is heightened by the fact that several texts conclude with variations on the ancient literary convention of the two ways (cf. esp. 3:18–20,36; 8:48–59; 10:37–38; 12:44–50; cf. Deut 30:15–20, Matt 7:24–27). This convention, by its nature, links dualism with making options, with choices. Thus the dualism may be seen as moral, as based on the human will.

But the will and its choices have deep-seated roots, and so opposing choices may suggest that there is a tension at the heart of reality, that there are in the world two opposing spirits. John does not exclude that; in fact, his references to Satan and darkness allow for a force which is contrary to God. But that force is in no way equal to God or even fully independent of God. Ultimately even evil, though it is clearly contrary to God, fulfills scripture and somehow fulfills God's plan.

Sending/Mission

Associated with the descent-ascent pattern there is another important concept— that of sending or mission (cf. esp. Bühner, 1977; Okure, 1988). The two ideas are like the two sides of a coin: Jesus is variously depicted as descended or as sent. He refers repeatedly to the Father as the one who sent him.

Sending in John refers primarily to human living; one is sent into this world to be a human being, to go through all of life's stages, and in the process, if one is true to one's deepest self, to reflect some of the glory of the Sender. Jesus first arrives, not as a prophet or messenger, but simply as someone who walks and responds (1:36). The blind man who is sent is not initially any kind of public figure; he just arrives, and he replies to what others say (9:1–12).

As life goes on, however, this mission of walking and responding takes on other dimensions. Jesus is drawn into dealing with the sulky Nathanael and the wine shortage (1:43–2:11). And so on. The blind man, because of his fidelity, eventually finds himself preaching to the Jewish authorities (9:24–34). Thus while John implicitly includes the idea of particular tasks and missions, all of these are simply specifications of the more fundamental mission which is given to every-body. There is no need for a specific mission to send people to teach all nations. By simply being in the world and being faithful to the God whom one images, one is inevitably drawn toward some form of involvement.

Eucharist

As indicated earlier (esp. in chap. 6) Jesus is described, not so much as he was historically, but as he now impinges on the life of the believer. A similar principle seems to govern the evangelist's treatment of the eucharist. Instead of describing its origin at the last supper, the gospel offers periodic allusions to it, some faint, some clear (cf. esp. the references to bread and wine/the vine: 2:1–11; chap. 6, esp. vv 1–13,52–58; 15:1–10; 21:9–14). The result is that *eucharistia,* the giving of thanks, is seen as something which, in varying degrees of explicitness, pervades life. Eucharistic ritual remains—reflected particularly in Jesus' sharing of bread (6:11, 21:13)—but it is set in a larger spiritual context, the context of a thankful life.

THE GOSPEL
IN ENGLISH

The Translation

The translation is based on the United Bible Societies *Greek New Testament* (3d ed., corrected). As far as possible, important individual Greek words have been rendered by a single English term. Occasionally the word order is strained to reflect the original. The oldest Greek manuscripts do not contain punctuations, quotation marks, capitalizations, or parentheses, and so the presence of these markers in translations gives the gospel text a clarity which originally it did not have. This clarity is generally an advantage, but occasionally it hides the rich ambiguity of the original—an ambiguity which is sometimes heightened by the ambivalence conveyed by specific words. In the present translation the ambiguity of certain significant words is reflected by a slash (for example, "overcome/grasped" in 1:5). Ambiguity of punctuation is indicated as far as possible by the use of italics (for example, in 1:3–4). (Italics are used in chap. 12 to highlight the arrangement of some OT quotes—in 12:13–15 and 12:38–40).

This translation uses two other features. Square brackets highlight some important Greek words (for example, *logos,* in 1:1). And the asterisk marks certain features of structure. (In 3:20–21 and 3:35b–36—texts which give variations on the idea of the two ways—the asterisks help to bring out the balance of the final phrases. In chap. 9 the asterisks mark the ten carefully arranged utterances of the healed man—five in 9:1–17 and five in 9:18–41. And in chap. 21 the asterisks indicate the division of the 9:1–14 into nine subsections).

The translation uses inclusive language. It does not change the gospel's imagery in a way that would undermine its content or its ancient character.

The most distinctive feature of the translation is its structure—the way the text is divided into sections and organized on the page. The presupposition here —a presupposition which was reached slowly in the course of writing the commentary—is that, in presenting the gospel visually, it is useful to divide the text into the following nine sections:

1:1–1:22
2:23–chapter 4
Chapters 5–6
Chapters 7–8
Chapters 9–10
Chapters 11–12
Chapters 13–17
18:1–19:16a
19:16b–chapter 21

71

Some of the reasons for this division have already been given—in the discussion concerning design—and more will emerge later. Reasons will also be given for the text's smaller divisions. The immediate problem, however, is not about theoretical reasons but about physical size: the nine major sections are too large to fit within the pages of this book. It is very helpful, for instance, when discussing the relationship between chaps. 5 and 6, if the two chapters are laid out schematically on a single sheet of paper or on two facing pages. But, unless the print is miniscule, they will not fit on two pages.

To cope with this difficulty the following pages provide an overview of the nine sections. There is, as it were, a map of each section, indicating the section's overall content and structure. And there is also an indication of how the sections are interrelated.

Like most maps, this outline has severe limitations; it captures just one aspect, not the full reality. There is much more, for instance, to John 2:23–chapter 4 than "Portraits of Lives and Their Limitations." The emphasis in this map is not on the externals of the account but on a dimension which is theological or anthropological and spiritual.

Most of these nine sections are composed of two large subsections, sometimes two of the traditional chapters (5 and 6; 7 and 8; 9 and 10). But some texts break the mold, especially the prologue, the final prayer (chap. 17), and the epilogue (chap. 21). Chaps. 17 and 21 balance one another in various ways, and individually they are the crowning pieces of the sections to which they belong.

Within this gospel, significance is frequently attached to the quantity of a text —to its physical size—and the map captures aspects of the varying quantities. The last discourse, for instance, is extremely extensive, yet as it advances, as Jesus comes closer to death, the quantity of the sections diminishes. But in the counterbalancing final text, describing the glorification (19:16b–chap. 21), the general tendency is towards a quantitive increase. The same is true in the gospel as a whole: though there are many times when the text ebbs away, as it were, the overall movement, like that of an advancing tide, is towards increasing quantity and expressiveness.

BOOK ONE (chaps. 1–12)   Parts 1, 2, 3A: The Years of Jesus' Life

Part 1   The First Year (1:1–2:22): An Introduction to Jesus' Life

| Prologue: The History of Salvation 1:1–18 | The Initiatory Trial 1:19–28 | The Initiatory Vision 1:29–34 | The Variety of Calls 1:35–42 | The Variety of Peoples 1:43–51 | Life's Sweet Wine (Cana) 2:1–11 | Intimations of Death and Home (Temple) 2:12–22 |

Part 2   The Second Year (2:23–chap. 6): From the Weight of Sin to Greater Life
(The Divided Self and the Quest for God)

Portraits of Lives and Their Limitations (2:23–chap. 4)

Nicodemus (limitations of a successful career)	John (old order fading)	The Samaritan Woman (limitations of a colorful love-life)	The Royal Official (new order emerging)
Introduction	Introduction	Introduction	Introduction
Response 1	Response 1	Scene 1	Scene 1
Response 2	Response 2	Scene 2	Scene 2
Response 3, two-part		Scene 3— with interlude	

Portraits of a Life-giving Creator and Provider (chaps. 5–6)

The Creation-like Healing	The Discourse on Ongoing Creation	The Providing, of Bread	The Discourse on the Bread of Life
Introduction	Introduction	Introduction	Introduction
Scene 1	Creation	Scene 1	Providing Bread
Scene 2	The Witness	Scene 2	The Word (Bread)
Scene 3 (later, elsewhere)	True Glory, not Sought	Scene 3 (later, elsewhere)	The Word Rejected and Accepted

Part 3A The Third Year (chaps. 7–12): From the Shadow of Death to the Light of Glory

Facing Death: The External Drama (chap. 7) and the Underlying Union (chap. 8)

Death Looms: Two Reactions	Tents: The Death-Evoking Feast		Jesus' Life-Giving Union with the Father	Judeans' Union with Their Father	The Two Ways: Life & Death
Introduction	Introduction				Reply 1
Scene 1					Reply 2
Scene 2	*Mid-Feast:*	*Final Day:*	Life-giving Union Suggested	Deathly Union Suggested	Reply 3
Scene 3	The Law	The Spirit			
	Jesus' Origin	Jesus' Origin	Life-giving Union Stated Clearly	Deathly Union Stated Clearly	
	Hostility	Hostility			

The Blind Man and The Good Shepherd (chaps. 9–10) A Drama of Creation and a Parable of Providence

The Man Born Blind		The Good Shepherd	
Scene 1	Scene 4	The Sheepfold	Winter
Scene 2	Scene 5	The Shepherd	Survival
Scene 3	Scene 6	Reactions	Reactions

Lazarus (11:1–53) and the Evoking of Resurrection (11:54–chap. 12)

Lazarus dies	Martha, Mary	Lazarus Raised	Introduction	The Greeks and the Timeless Jesus
Scene 1	Scene 3	Scene 5	Anointing at Bethany (Evoking Burial)	Unbelief and Jesus' Hiddenness
Scene 2	Scene 4	Scene 6	Entry to Jerusalem (Evoking Resurrection)	Epilogue

BOOK TWO (Part 3B, Chaps. 13–21): The Central Passover Mystery

The Last Discourse (The Word Spoken) (chaps. 13–17)

1 WASHING (chap. 13)	Human Response (chap. 14)	2 PURIFYING (15:1–16:4a)	Human Response (16:4a–33)	3 SANCTIFY-ING (chap. 17)
The Washing: Shadowed Love	The Troubled Heart	The True Vine and its Love	The Sorrowful Heart	Jesus' Ascent Sanctifies
Outcome: Love	Outcome: Peace	Outcome: Greater Love	Outcome: Confidence	Outcome: Unity
		The World and its Hatred		
		Outcome: Death		

The Arrest and Trial (The Word amid Evil) (18:1–19:16a)
Two Dramas of Sin—of Revelation Rejected

The Arrest and Interrogation		The Trial before Pilate	
Introduction	Interlude	Introduction	Interlude
Scene 1	Scene 4	Scene 1	Scene 4
Scene 2	Scene 5	Scene 2	Scene 5
Scene 3	Scene 6	Scene 3	Scene 6

Death and Resurrection (The Word in Practice) (19:16b–chap. 21)
The Working Out of the Passover Mystery in Jesus and in the Human Community

1 CRUCIFIXION Invites Love	Death	2 RESURRECTION Invites Unity	Appearances	3 ABIDING PRESENCE
Introduction		Introduction		The Sea & the "Washing" of Peter
Scene 1	Scene 1	Scene 1	Scene 1	Outcome: Love, Unity
Scene 2	Scene 2	Scene 2	Scene 2	
Scene 3	Conclusion (part 1)	Scene 3	Conclusion (part 2)	Conclusion (part 3)

Book One □ The Years of Jesus' Life

Part 1 · The First Year: an Optimistic Introduction to Jesus' Life

Prologue: The History of Salvation: A Spiralling Meditation

Origins/Creation (The Word)

1 ¹In the beginning was the Word [*logos*], and the Word was with God, and the Word was God. ²He was in the beginning with God. ³All things were made through him, and without him was not made anything that/*what was made.* ⁴*In him was life,* and the life was the light of humans. ⁵And the light shines in the darkness, and the darkness has not overcome/grasped it.

The Intermediate Stage (The Witness)

⁶There was a person sent from God, whose name was John. ⁷He came for witness —to bear witness to the light, so that all might believe through him. ⁸He was not the light, but he came to bear witness to the light. ⁹The true light which enlightens every person (was) coming into the world. ¹⁰He was in the world and the world was made through him, yet the world knew him not. ¹¹He came to what was his own, and those who were his own received him not. ¹²But to all those who did receive him, he gave power to become children of God—to those who believe in his name, ¹³who were born, not of blood nor of the will of the flesh nor of the will of a man, but of God.

The Incarnation and Its Glory

¹⁴And the Word became flesh and tented among us, and we have seen his glory, glory as of the only Son from the Father, full of grace and truth. ¹⁵John bears witness to him, crying, "This was he of whom I said, 'He who is coming after me ranks before me,' for he existed before me." ¹⁶And from his fullness we have all received grace upon grace. ¹⁷For the law was given through Moses; grace and truth came through Jesus Christ. ¹⁸No one has ever seen God; it is God the only Son, who is on the Father's bosom—he is the one who has made him known.

The Initiatory Trial

[19] And this is the witness of John, when the Judeans from Jerusalem sent priests and Levites to ask him, "Who are you?" [20] And he confessed, and did not deny; he confessed, "I am not the Anointed [*christos*]." [21] And they asked him, "Then what are you? Are you Elijah?" And he said, "I am not." "Are you the prophet?" And he answered, "No." [22] They therefore said to him, "Who are you?—that we may give an answer to those who sent us. What do you say about yourself?" [23] He said, "I am the voice of one crying in the desert make straight the way of the Lord," as said Isaiah the prophet.

[24] Now those who had been sent were from the Pharisees. [25] They asked him, "So why are you baptizing, if you are neither the Anointed nor Elijah nor the prophet?" [26] John answered them, "I baptize in water; but among you stands one whom you do not know—[27] the one coming after me, the thong of whose sandal I am not worthy to untie." [28] This took place in Bethany beyond the Jordan, where John was baptizing.

The Initiatory Vision

[29] The next day he sees Jesus coming towards him and says, "Behold, the lamb of God, who takes away the sin of the world. [30] This is he of whom I said, 'After me comes a man who ranks before me, for before me he existed.' [31] I myself did not know him; but that he might be revealed to Israel, for this I came baptizing in water."

[32] And John bore witness, saying, "I have seen the Spirit descending like a dove from heaven, and it abode on him. [33] I myself did not know him, but he who sent me to baptize in water said to me, 'He on whom you see the Spirit descending and abiding [*menō*], this is the one who baptizes in the holy Spirit.' [34] And I have seen and have borne witness that this is the Chosen One [or Son, in some mss] of God."

The Variety of Calls

[35] The next day again John was standing with two of his disciples, [36] and he looked at Jesus walking, and said, "Behold, the lamb of God". [37] The two disciples heard him speaking and they followed Jesus. [38] Jesus turned and saw them following, and said to them, "What do you seek?" And they said to him, "Rabbi (which is interpreted Teacher), where do you abide [*menō*]?" [39] He said to them, "Come and see." They came therefore and saw where he abode. And they abode with him that day. The hour was about ten.

[40] Andrew, the brother of Simon Peter, was one of the two who heard while with Jesus and followed him. [41] He finds first his own brother, Simon, and says to him, "We have found the Messiah (which is interpreted the Anointed)." [42] And he led him to Jesus. Jesus looked at him and said, "You are Simon the son of John. You shall be called Cephas (which is interpreted Peter)."

The Variety of People(s)

[43] The next day he willed to go forth to Galilee and he finds Philip. And Jesus said to him, "Follow me." [44] Now Philip was from Bethsaida, the city of Andrew and Peter.

[45] Philip finds Nathanael and says to him, "The one of whom Moses wrote in the law, and the prophets also—we have found him—Jesus, the son of Joseph, from Nazareth." [46] Nathanael said to him, "From Nazareth can there be anything good?" Philip said to him, "Come and see." [47] Jesus saw Nathanael coming to him and said of him, "Behold, a true Israelite in whom there is no guile." [48] Nathanael said to him, "From where do you know me?" Jesus answered and said to him, "Before Philip called you, when you were under the fig tree, I saw you". [49] Nathanael answered him, "Rabbi, you are the Son of God! You are the King of Israel!" [50] Jesus answered and said to him, "Because 'I said to you, I saw you under the fig tree,' (do) you believe(?). You shall see greater things than these." [51] And he said to him, "Amen, amen, I say to you [plural], you will see heaven opened, and the angels of God ascending and descending on the Son of humanity."

Life's Sweet Wine

2 ¹And on the third day there was a wedding in Cana of Galilee, and the mother of Jesus was there. ²And Jesus and his disciples had also been called to the wedding. ³When the wine failed, the mother of Jesus said to him, "They have no wine." ⁴Jesus said to her, "Woman, what does your concern have to do with me? My hour has not yet come." ⁵His mother said to the servants, "Whatever he tells you to do, do it."

⁶Now there were there, standing, six stone water jars for the Judeans' rites of purification, each holding two or three measures. ⁷Jesus said to them, "Fill the water jars with water." And they filled them to the brim. ⁸And he said to them, "Now draw some out and bring it to the steward." And they brought it. ⁹When the steward tasted the water made wine, and did not know whence it had come— though the servants knew, for they had drawn the water—the steward called the bridegroom ¹⁰and he said to him, "Everyone serves the good wine first, and when people have drunk well, then that which is inferior. But you have kept the good wine until now." ¹¹This, the beginning of his signs, Jesus did in Cana of Galilee, and he revealed his glory, and his disciples believed in him.

Intimations of Death and Home

¹²After this he descended to Capernaum, he and his mother and his brothers and his disciples, and he abode there not many days. ¹³And the Passover of the Judeans was at hand, and Jesus ascended to Jerusalem. ¹⁴And he found in the temple those selling oxen and sheep and doves, and the money-changers sitting. ¹⁵And making a whip from cords, he drove them all, with the sheep and the oxen, out of the temple. And he poured out the coins of the money-changers and turned over their tables. ¹⁶And to those selling doves he said, "Take these things out of here. Do not make the house of my Father a house of trade." ¹⁷His disciples remembered that it was written, "Zeal for your house will consume me."

¹⁸The Judeans therefore answered and said to him, "What sign do you show us because you do this?" ¹⁹Jesus answered and said to them, "Destroy this sanctuary and in three days I will raise it up." ²⁰The Judeans therefore said, "Forty-six years it has taken to build this sanctuary, and will you raise it up in three days?" ²¹But he spoke of the sanctuary of his body. ²²When therefore he was raised from the dead, his disciples remembered that he had said this, and they believed the scripture and the word [*logos*] which Jesus had spoken.

Part 2 • The Second Year: From the Weight of Sin to Greater Life (the divided self and the quest for God)

Nicodemus (the limitations of a successful career)

Introduction: The Shadow of Doubt and Withdrawal

²³When he was in Jerusalem at the Passover feast, many believed [*pisteuō*] in his name when they saw the signs which he did. ²⁴But Jesus did not trust [*pisteuō*] himself to them because he knew all people, ²⁵and because he had no need that anyone bear witness about the human person [*anthrōpos*]; for he himself knew what was in the human person.

Response 1

3 ¹Now there was a person [*anthrōpos*] of the Pharisees, named Nicodemus, a ruler of the Judeans. ²He came to Jesus by night and said to him, "Rabbi, we know that you are a teacher come from God, for no one can do these signs that you do unless God is with him." ³Jesus answered and said to him, "Amen, amen, I say to you, unless one is born from above [or anew, *anōthen*] one cannot see the realm [*basileia*] of God."

Response 2

⁴Nicodemus said to him, "How can a person be born when old? Can one enter a second time into one's mother's womb and be born?" ⁵Jesus answered, "Amen, amen, I say to you, unless one is born of water and spirit [*pneuma*], one cannot enter the realm of God. ⁶What is born of the flesh is flesh [*sarx*], and what is born of the spirit is spirit. ⁷Do not wonder that I said to you, 'It is necessary that you be born from above.' ⁸The wind [or spirit, *pneuma*] blows where it wills, and you hear its sound [or voice], but you do not know from where it comes and whereto it goes. So it is with everyone who is born of the Spirit."

Response 3—two-part

⁹Nicodemus answered and said to him, "How can this be?" ¹⁰Jesus answered and said to him, "You are the teacher of Israel, and you do not know this? ¹¹Amen, amen, I say to you, we speak of what we know and bear witness to what we have seen; but you [plural] do not receive our witness. ¹²If I have told you earthly things and you do not believe, how can you believe when I tell you heavenly things? ¹³No one has ascended into heaven except the one who descended from heaven, the Son of humanity. ¹⁴And as Moses lifted up the serpent in the desert, so it is necessary [*dei,* providential necessity] that the Son of humanity be lifted up, ¹⁵that whoever believes in him may have eternal life.

[16] For God so loved the world that he gave his only Son, so that all who believe in him may not perish but may have eternal life. [17] For God did not send the Son into the world to judge the world, but that the world might be saved through him. [18] The one who believes in him is not judged, but the one who does not believe is already judged, because of not having believed in the name of the only Son of God. [19] And this is the judgment, that the light has come into the world, and people loved darkness rather than the light, for their deeds were evil.

* [20] For all these who do evil hate the light and do not come to the light, that their works may not be exposed. * [21] But the person who does what is true comes to the light, that it may be revealed that that person's works are worked in God.

John (the old order fading)

Introduction

[22] After this Jesus and his disciples came into the land of Judea, and there he sojourned [*dia-tribō*] with them and baptized. [23] John also was baptizing at Aenon near Salim, because there was much water there; and they came and were baptized. [24] For John had not yet been thrown into prison.

Response 1

[25] Now a dispute arose between John's disciples and a Judean about purification. [26] And they came to John and said to him, "Rabbi, he who was with you beyond the Jordan, to whom you bore witness, behold he is baptizing and all are coming to him. [27] John replied and said, "A person cannot receive anything except what is given from heaven. [28] You yourselves bear me witness that I said, 'I am not the Anointed, but I have been sent before him.' [29] The one who has the bride is the bridegroom. The friend of the bridegroom, who stands and hears him, rejoices greatly at the bridegroom's voice. Such is my joy and it is now full. [30] He must [*dei*] increase, and I must decrease.

Response 2

[31] The one who comes from above is above all; the one who is of the earth is earthly and of the earth speaks. The one who comes from heaven is above all. [32] He bears witness to what he has seen and heard; but no one receives his witness. [33] Those who do receive his witness set their seal to this, that God is true. [34] For he whom God has sent speaks the words of God, for it is not by measure that he gives the Spirit. [35] The Father loves the Son, and has given all things into his hand.

* [36] Whoever believes in the Son has eternal life. * Whoever disbelieves the Son shall not see life, but the anger of God abides on that person.

The Samaritan Woman (limitations of a colorful love-life)

Introduction: Shades of Withdrawal (and Even of Death)

4 ¹When the Lord knew that the Pharisees heard that Jesus was making and baptizing more disciples than John—²although Jesus himself did not baptize, but only his disciples—³he left Judea and went away again to Galilee. ⁴And it was necessary [*edei*] that he come through Samaria. ⁵So he came to a city of Samaria, called Sychar, near the land that Jacob gave to his son Joseph. ⁶And Jacob's well was there. So Jesus, having labored [*kopiaō*] at his journey, sat as he was on the well. It was about the sixth hour.

Scene 1

⁷There came a woman of Samaria to draw water. Jesus said to her, "Give me a drink." ⁸For his disciples had gone into the city to buy food. ⁹But the Samaritan woman said to him, "How is it that you, a Judean, ask a drink of me, a woman of Samaria?" For Judeans have no dealings with Samaritans. ¹⁰Jesus answered and said to her, "If you knew the gift of God, and who it is that is saying to you, 'Give me a drink,' you would have asked him, and he would have given you living water." ¹¹The woman said to him, "Sir [*Kyrie*], you do not even have something to draw with, and the well is deep. From where do you get the living water? ¹²Are you greater than our father Jacob, who gave us the well, and drank from it himself, and his sons, and his cattle?" ¹³Jesus answered and said to her, "Everyone who drinks of this water will thirst again. ¹⁴But whoever drinks of the water that I shall give them will never thirst; for the water that I shall give them will become in them a spring of water welling up to eternal life." ¹⁵The woman said to him, "Sir [*Kyrie*], give me this water, that I may not thirst, nor come here to draw."

Scene 2

¹⁶He said to her, "Go call your husband and come here." ¹⁷The woman answered and said to him, "I have no husband." Jesus said to her, "You speak well in saying 'I have no husband.' ¹⁸For you have had five husbands, and he whom you now have is not your husband. This you have said truly." ¹⁹The woman said to him, "Sir [*Kyrie*], I see that you are a prophet. ²⁰Our fathers worshipped on this mountain, but you say that Jerusalem is the place where it is necessary [*dei*] to worship." ²¹Jesus said to her, "Believe me, woman, the hour is coming when neither on this mountain nor in Jerusalem will you worship the Father. ²²You worship what you do not know; we worship what we know, for salvation is from the Judeans. ²³But the hour is coming and now is, when the true worshippers will worship the Father in spirit and truth, for the Father seeks such to worship him. ²⁴God is spirit, and it is necessary [*dei*] that those who worship him, worship in spirit and truth." ²⁵The woman said to him, "I know that a Messiah is coming"

(that is an Anointed). "When he comes he will announce all things to us." ²⁶Jesus said to her, "I am [he] [*Egō eimi*], I who am speaking to you."

Scene 3—with Interlude

²⁷And at that his disciples came, and they wondered that he was speaking with a woman, but no one said, "What are you seeking?" or "Why are you speaking with her?" ²⁸So the woman left her water jar and went into the city and said to the people, ²⁹"Come, see a person who told me all whatsoever I have done. Can this be the Anointed?" ³⁰They went out of the city and were coming to him.

³¹In the meantime his disciples besought him saying, "Rabbi, eat." ³²But he said to them, "I have food to eat of which you do not know." ³³The disciples therefore said to one another, "Did someone bring him food?" ³⁴Jesus said to them, "My food is to do the will of the one who sent me, and to complete his work. ³⁵Do you not say, 'There are yet four months and then the harvest comes.' Behold, I say to you, lift up your eyes and see that the lands are white for harvest. ³⁶Already the reaper is receiving wages, and is gathering fruit for eternal life, so that the sower and reaper may rejoice together. ³⁷For here the saying is true, 'One sows and another reaps.' ³⁸I sent you to reap that for which you have not labored [*kopiaō*]; others have labored, and you have entered into their labor."

³⁹From that city many Samaritans believed in him because of the word of the woman witnessing, "He told me all whatsoever I have done." ⁴⁰So when the Samaritans came to him, they besought him to abide with them; and he abode there two days. ⁴¹And many more believed in him because of his word. ⁴²And they said to the woman, "It is no longer because of what you have spoken that we believe; for we have heard for ourselves, and we know that this is truly the savior of the world."

The Royal Official (a new order emerging)

Introduction

⁴³After the two days he went forth from there to Galilee; ⁴⁴for Jesus himself bore witness that a prophet has no honor in his own fatherland. ⁴⁵So when he came to Galilee, the Galileans welcomed him, having seen all whatsoever he had done in Jerusalem at the feast, for they too had gone to the feast.

Scene 1

⁴⁶So he came again to Cana of Galilee, where he had made the water wine. And there was a certain royal official whose son was sick [or weak] at Capernaum. ⁴⁷When he heard that Jesus had come from Judea to Galilee he went away to him and besought him to come down and heal his son, for he was going to die. ⁴⁸Jesus therefore said to him, "Unless you see signs and wonders you do not believe."

⁴⁹The royal offical said to him, "Lord [*Kyrie*], come down before my child dies."
⁵⁰Jesus said to him, "Go your way, your son lives." The person believed the word which Jesus spoke and went his way.

Scene 2

⁵¹As he was still going down his servants met him saying his boy lived. ⁵²So he inquired from them concerning the hour in which he improved; and they said to him, "Yesterday at the seventh hour the fever left him." ⁵³The father knew that it was at that hour that Jesus said to him, "Your son lives." And he himself believed, and his whole household. ⁵⁴This was the second sign that Jesus did on coming from Judea to Galilee.

The Creationlike Healing

Introduction

5 ¹After this there was a feast of the Judeans, and Jesus went up to Jerusalem. ²Now there is in Jerusalem, by the sheep[place], a pool, in Hebrew called Beth-zatha, which has five porticoes. ³In these lay a multitude of those who were weak [or sick], blind, lame, withered.

Scenes 1–3

The Surprising Gift of Life
⁵Now there was a certain person there—thirty-eight years he had been in his weakness. ⁶Jesus saw this person lying there and—knowing that already he had been there a long time—he said to him, "Do you will to become healthy?" ⁷The one who was weak answered him, "Sir [*Kyrie*], I have nobody so that, when the water is troubled, they may throw me into the pool. As I am coming another goes down before me." ⁸Jesus said to him, "Rise, take up your bed, and walk." ⁹And immediately the person became healthy, and he took up his bed, and walked.

Initial Reaction (legalism)
Now it was the sabbath that day. ¹⁰So the Judeans said to the one who was cured, "It is the sabbath; it is not lawful for you to carry your bed." ¹¹But he answered them, "The one who made me healthy—he it was who said to me, 'Take up your bed and walk.' " ¹²They asked him, "Who is the person who said to you, 'Take and walk'?" ¹³But the man who had been healed did not know who it was, for Jesus had withdrawn, as there was a crowd in the place.

Later, in the Temple
¹⁴After this Jesus found him in the temple and said to him, "See, you have become healthy. Sin no more, that nothing worse befalls you." ¹⁵The person went away and announced to the Judeans that it was Jesus who had made him healthy.

The Discourse on Ongoing Creation

Introduction: Reaction to Jesus as Creator

[16] And it was for this that the Judeans persecuted Jesus, because he did these things on the sabbath. [17] But Jesus answered them, ''My Father is still working, and I am working.'' [18] For this therefore the Judeans sought him all the more—to kill—because he not only broke the sabbath but also called God his Father, making himself equal to God.

Creation—Ongoing, with Judgment

[19] Jesus, therefore, replied and said to them, ''Amen, amen, I say to you, the son/ Son cannot do anything of himself, but only what he sees the father/Father doing; for whatever he does, that the Son does likewise. [20] The Father loves the Son and shows him all that he himself is doing, and greater works than these will he show him, that you may wonder. [21] For as the Father raises the dead and makes them live, so the Son also makes live whom he wills. [22] For the Father judges no one, but has given all judgment to the Son, [23] so that all may honor the Son even as they honor the Father. The one who does not honor the Son does not honor the Father who sent him.

[24] ''Amen, amen, I say to you, the one who hears my word and believes him who sent me, has eternal life, and does not come to judgment but has passed from death to life. [25] Amen, amen, I say to you, the hour is coming and now is, when the dead shall hear the voice of the Son of God and those who hear shall live. [26] For as the Father has life in himself, so he has given to the Son also to have life in himself, [27] and he has given him authority to make judgment, because he is the Son of humanity. [28] Do not wonder at this; for the hour is coming when all who are in the tombs will hear his voice, [29] and they shall come forth, those who have done good, to the resurrection of life, and those who have done evil to the resurrection of judgment.

Witness—Ongoing, Not Accepted

[30] "I can do nothing by myself; as I hear, I judge; and my judgment is just, because I do not seek my own will, but the will of him who sent me. [31] If I bear witness to myself, my witness is not true. [32] There is another who bears witness to me, and I know that the witness which he bears about me is true. [33] You sent to John, and he has borne witness to the truth. [34] Not that the witness which I receive is from humans, but I say these things that you may be saved. [35] He was the burning and shining lamp, and you were willing for a while to rejoice in his light.

[36] "But I have a witness which is greater than that of John; for the works which the Father has given me to complete—these very works which I am doing —bear witness to me that the Father has sent me. [37] And the Father who sent me has himself borne witness to me. You have never heard his voice, nor have you seen his form, [38] and you do not have his word abiding in you, for you do not believe him whom he sent. [39] You search the scriptures, because you think that in them you have eternal life; but they also bear witness to me, [40] and yet you are not willing to come to me that you may have life.

True Glory, Not Sought

[41] Glory from humans I do not receive, [42] but I know you—that you do not have the love of God in you. [43] I have come in the name of my Father, and you do not receive me. But if another comes in his own name, him you will receive. [44] How can you believe, receiving glory from one another, and you do not seek the glory which is from the only God.

[45] "Do not think that I shall accuse you to the Father. The one who accuses you is Moses, in whom you hope. [46] If you believed Moses you would believe me, for it was about me that he wrote. [47] But if you do not believe his writings, how will you believe my words?''

The Providing of Bread

Introduction

6 ¹After this Jesus went away to the other side of the sea of Galilee of Tiberias. ²And a great crowd was following him, because they saw the signs which he did on those who were weak [or sick]. ³Then Jesus went up to the mountain, and there sat down with his disciples. ⁴The Passover was at hand, the feast of the Judeans.

Scenes 1–3

The Gift of Bread
⁵Lifting up his eyes, therefore, and seeing that a great crowd was coming to him, Jesus said to Philip, "From where shall we buy bread, so that these may eat?" ⁶This he said to test him, for he himself knew what he would do. ⁷Philip answered him, "Two hundred denarii worth of bread is not sufficient for them so that each of them may receive something." ⁸One of his disciples, Andrew, the brother of Simon Peter, said to him, ⁹"There is a small boy here who has five barley loaves and two fish, but what are they among so many?" ¹⁰Jesus said, "Make the people sit down." Now there was much grass in the place, so they sat down, the men numbering about five thousand. ¹¹Jesus then took the loaves, and when he had given thanks, he distributed them to those who were seated; likewise the fish, as much as they willed. ¹²And when they were filled, he said to his disciples, "Gather up the overflowing fragments so that nothing may perish." ¹³So they gathered up, and they filled twelve baskets with fragments, from the five barley loaves, which overflowed to those who had eaten.

Initial Reaction (violent politics)
¹⁴The people then, seeing the sign which he had done, said, "This is truly the prophet who is to come into the world." ¹⁵Jesus, therefore, knowing that they were about to come and take him by force to make him king, withdrew again to the mountain, he alone.

Later, at Sea
¹⁶When it was evening his disciples went down to the sea. ¹⁷And having got into a boat, they were coming across the sea to Capernaum. Already there was darkness, and Jesus had not yet come to them. ¹⁸The sea—with a great wind blowing —was rising. ¹⁹And when they had rowed about twenty-five or thirty furlongs, they saw Jesus walking on the sea and approaching the boat, and they were afraid. ²⁰But he said to them, "It is I [*Egō eimi*], do not be afraid." ²¹Then they willed to receive him into the boat, and immediately the boat was at the land to which they were going.

The Discourse on the Bread of Life

Introduction: Reaction to Jesus the Provider

[22] The next day the crowd which stood on the other side of the sea saw that there was no other boat there but one, and that Jesus had not entered the boat with his disciples, but that his disciples had gone away alone. [23] But boats from Tiberias came near the place where they ate the bread after the Lord had given thanks. [24] So when the crowd saw that Jesus was not there, nor his disciples, they got into the boats and came to Capernaum seeking Jesus.

Providing Bread Eternal

[25] When they found him on the other side of the sea, they said to him, "Rabbi, when have you come [lit., been] here?" [26] Jesus answered them and said, "Amen, amen, I say to you, you seek me not because you saw signs, but because you ate of the loaves and were filled. [27] Do not work for the food which perishes, but for the food which abides to eternal life, which the Son of humanity will give to you, for on him has the Father, God, set his seal." [28] They therefore said to him, "What do we do that we may work the works of God?" [29] Jesus answered and said to them, "This is the work of God, that you believe in him whom he has sent." [30] So they said to him, "Then what sign do you do, that we may see and believe you? What work do you do? [31] Our fathers ate the manna in the desert, as it is written, 'He gave them bread from heaven to eat.' " [32] Jesus said to them, "Amen, amen, I say to you, it was not Moses who gave you the bread from heaven, but my Father gives you the true bread from heaven. [33] For the bread of God is that which comes down from heaven and gives life to the world."

[34] They then said to him, "Sir [*Kyrie*], give us this bread always." [35] Jesus said to them, "I am the bread of life. The one who comes to me shall not hunger, and the one who believes in me shall never thirst. [36] But I said to you that you have seen me and yet you do not believe. [37] All that the Father gives me will come to me; and the one who comes to me I will not cast out; [38] for I have come down from heaven not to do my own will, but the will of him who sent me. [39] Now this is the will of him who sent me: that I should let nothing perish of all that he has given me, but should raise it up on the last day. [40] For this is the will of my Father, that everyone who sees the Son and believes in him should have eternal life, and I will raise them up on the last day."

The Bread (Word) Is to Be Eaten Fully

[41] The Judeans then murmured at him, because he said, "I am the bread which came down from heaven"; [42] and they said, "Is this not Jesus, the son of Joseph, whose father and mother we know? How does he now say. 'I have come down from heaven'?" [43] Jesus answered and said to them, "Do not murmur among yourselves. [44] No one can come to me unless the Father who sent me draws them; and I will raise them up on the last day. [45] It is written in the prophets, 'And they shall all be taught by God.' All who have heard and learned from the Father come to me. [46] Not that anyone has seen the Father except the one who is from God; he has seen the Father. [47] Amen, amen, I say to you, the one who believes has eternal life. [48] I am the bread of life. [49] Your fathers ate the manna in the desert, and they died. [50] This is the bread which comes down from heaven, that whoever eats of it may not die. [51] I am the living bread which came down from heaven; whoever eats of this bread will live for ever. And the bread that I shall give is my flesh for the life of the world."

[52] The Judeans then fought among themselves, saying, "How can this [person] give us his flesh to eat?" [53] Jesus therefore said to them, "Amen, amen, I say to you, unless you eat the flesh of the Son of humanity and drink his blood, you do not have life in you. [54] Those who feed on my flesh and drink my blood have eternal life, and I will raise them up on the last day. [55] For my flesh is true food, and my blood is true drink. [56] Those who feed on my flesh and drink my blood abide in me and I in them. [57] As the living Father sent me, and I live through the Father, so the one who feeds on me shall live through me. [58] This is the bread which came down from heaven, not such as the fathers ate and died; the one who feeds on this bread will live for ever." [59] He said this in a synagogue, teaching in Capernaum.

The Word Rejected and Accepted

[60] Many of his disciples, hearing it, said, "This word is hard; who can hear it?" [61] But Jesus, knowing in himself that his disciples murmured about this, said to them, "Does this offend you? [62] Then what if you were to see the Son of humanity ascending to where he was before. [63] It is the spirit [*pneuma*] that gives life; the flesh [*sarx*] accomplishes nothing. The words that I have spoken to you are spirit and life. [64] But there are some of you who do not believe." For Jesus knew from the beginning who they were who would not believe and who it was who would hand him over. [65] And he said, "This is why I told you that no one can come to me unless it be given by the Father."

[66] From this point on many of his disciples went back and no longer walked with him. [67] Jesus therefore said to the twelve, "Do you also want to go away?" [68] Simon Peter answered him, "Lord, to whom shall we go? You have the words of eternal life; [69] and we have believed and have come to know that you are the Holy One of God." [70] Jesus answered them, "Did I not choose you, the twelve, and one of you is a devil." [71] He was speaking of Judas, the son of Simon Isca-
for it was he who was to hand him over [*para-didōmi*]—one of the twelve.

Part 3A · The Third Year: From the Shadow of Death to the Light of Glory

With Death Looming, Two Reactions: The Disbelievers Act Compulsively, but Jesus Keeps His Freedom

Introduction

7 ¹ After this Jesus walked about in Galilee. He was not willing to walk about in Judea, because the Judeans sought to kill him. ² And there was at hand the Judeans' feast of Tents.

Scenes 1–3

³ His brothers, therefore, said to him, "Depart from here and go into Judea, that your disciples may see the works which you do. ⁴ For no one works in secret [*en kryptō*] while seeking to be known openly. If you do these things, reveal yourself to the world." ⁵ For even his brothers did not believe in him.

⁶ Jesus therefore said to them, "My time [*kairos*] has not yet come, but your time is always ready. ⁷ The world cannot hate you, but it hates me because I witness about it that its works are evil. ⁸ Ascend yourselves to the feast; I am not ascending to the feast because my time is not yet fulfilled." ⁹ And so saying he abode in Galilee.

¹⁰ But when his brothers had ascended to the feast, then he also ascended, not publicly but in secret [*en kryptō*].

Tents: The Death-evoking Feast of Discourse and Discussion Concerning Jesus' Nature

Introduction: Contrasting Reactions to Jesus

¹¹ The Judeans therefore sought him at the feast and said, "Where is he?" ¹² And there was much murmuring about him among the crowd. Some said, "He is good"; but others said, "No, he is leading the crowd astray." ¹³ However, no one spoke openly about him for fear of the Judeans.

The Middle of the Feast

Jesus Teaches the Law

[14] When it was already the middle of the feast, Jesus ascended into the temple and taught.

[15] And the Judeans were in wonder, saying, "How does this person know letters, having never learned?" [16] So Jesus answered them and said, "My teaching is not mine, but his who sent me. [17] If anyone wills to do his will, they shall know whether the teaching is from God or whether I speak of myself. [18] Those who speak on their own seek their own glory; but those who seek the glory of the one who sent them, they are true and there is no injustice in them. [19] Did not Moses give you the law? Yet none of you keeps the law. Why do you seek to kill me?"

[20] The crowd answered, "You have a demon. Who is seeking to kill you?" [21] Jesus answered and said to them, "One work have I done, and you all wonder [22] because of it. Moses gave you circumcision—not that it is from Moses, but from the fathers—and on the sabbath you circumcise a person. [23] If a person receives circumcision [literally, *cutting* around] on the sabbath so that the law of Moses may not be broken, are you angry with me because on the sabbath I made a whole person healthy? [24] Do not judge by appearances, but judge with just judgement."

Discussion of Jesus' Identity and Origin—The Anointed?

[25] Some of the Jerusalemites therefore said, "Is not this the one they seek to kill? [26] And see, he is speaking openly, and they say nothing to him. Can it be that the rulers have recognized that this is the Anointed? [27] But we know where this person is from. Whereas when the Anointed comes, no one will know where he is from." [28] Jesus therefore cried out in the temple, teaching and saying, "You know both me and where I am from. But I have not come of my own accord. There is one who sent me, [someone] true, and him you do not know. [29] I know him, because I came from him and he sent me." [30] They sought then to arrest him; but no one laid hands on him, because his hour had not yet come.

Authorities' Hostility—Intimations of Jesus' Destiny and Death

[31] Now many of the crowd believed in him and said, "When the Anointed comes will he do more signs than this person has done?" [32] The Pharisees heard the crowd murmuring these things about him, and the chief priests and Pharisees sent officials to arrest him. [33] Jesus therefore said, "Yet a little while I am with you, and then I go to the one who sent me. [34] You will seek me and will not find me; and where I am you cannot come." [35] The Judeans said to one another, "Where does he intend to travel that we shall not find him? Does he intend to travel to the Dispersion among the Greeks and teach the Greeks? [36] What is this word of his, 'You will seek me, and will not find me,' and 'Where I am you cannot come'?"

The Last Great Day of the Feast

Jesus Reveals the Spirit

[37] On the last day, the great day of the feast, Jesus stood and cried out saying, "Whoever thirsts, let them come to me, and let them drink— [38] whoever believes in me—as the scripture said, 'Out of his heart shall flow rivers of living water.' " [39] This he said about the Spirit which those who believed in him were to receive. For as yet there was no Spirit, because Jesus had not yet been glorified.

Discussion of Jesus' Identity and Origin—The Anointed?

[40] When they heard these words, some of the crowd said, "This is truly the prophet." [41] Others said, "This is the Anointed." But some said, "Is the Anointed to come from Galilee? [42] Did not the scripture say that the Anointed is to come from the descent [lit., seed] of David, and from Bethlehem, the village where David was?" [43] So there was a division in the crowd because of him. [44] Some of them were wanting [lit., willed] to arrest him, but no one laid hands on him.

Authorities' Hostility and Insensitivity to Life

[45] The officials therefore came back to the chief priests and Pharisees, and these said to them, "Why did you not lead him [here]?" [46] The officials replied, "Never has a human being spoken like this." [47] The Pharisees answered them, "Have you also been led astray? [48] Have any of the rulers believed in him, or of the Pharisees? [49] But this crowd, which does not know the law, is accursed." [50] Nicodemus, who had come to him before, and who was one of them, said to them, [51] "Does our law judge people without first hearing them and knowing what they do?" [52] They answered and said to him, "Are you also from Galilee? Search [the scriptures] and you will see that from Galilee a prophet does not arise."[1]

---

1. For the text of 7:53–8:11, see after chap. 21.

Jesus' Life-Giving Union with the Father

Life-Giving Union Is Suggested

8 [12] Again therefore Jesus spoke to them, saying, "I am the light of the world. The one who follows me will not walk in darkness, but will have the light of life."

[13] The Pharisees then said to him, "You are bearing witness about yourself; your witness is not true." [14] Jesus anwered and said to them, "Even if I do bear witness about myself, my witness is true, because I know from where I come and whereto I am going; but you do not know from where I come or whereto I am going. [15] You judge according to the flesh; I judge no one. [16] And if I do judge, my judgment is true, because I am not alone, but with me is the one who sent me. [17] In your law it is written that the witness of two persons is true. [18] I am one who bears witness about myself, and witness about me is also borne by the one who sent me, the Father."

[19] So they said to him, "Where is your Father?" Jesus answered, "You do not know either me or my Father. If you knew me, you would know my Father also." [20] These words he spoke in the treasury, teaching in the temple. And no one arrested him, because his hour had not yet come.

Life-Giving Union Is Stated More Clearly

[21] Again therefore he said to them, "I am going away and you will seek me and you will die in your sin; where I am going you cannot come."

[22] The Judeans therefore said, "Will he kill himself, since he says, 'Where I am going you cannot come'?" [23] He said to them, "You are from below, I am from above. You are of this world, I am not of this world. [24] So I said to you that you will die in your sins. For if you do not believe that I am, you will die in your sins."

[25] So they said to him, "Who are you?" Jesus said to them, "Why from the beginning [*tēn archēn*] I speak to you. [26] I have many things to say about you, and many things to judge. But the one who sent me is true, and what I have heard from him, these things I speak to the world." [27] They did not know that he was speaking to them about the Father. [28] Jesus therefore said, "When you have lifted up the Son of humanity, then you will know that I do nothing on my own, but as the Father taught me, these things I speak. [29] And he who sent me is with me; he has not left me alone, for I do always the things that please him." [30] As he spoke these things many believed in him.

Superficial Believers' Union with Their Father

Deathly Union Is Suggested

[31] Then Jesus said to the Judeans who had believed in him, "If you abide in my word, you are truly my disciples, [32] and you will know the truth, and the truth will make you free."

[33] They answered him, "We are the descent [lit., seed] of Abraham, and have never been in slavery to anyone. How can you say, 'You will be made free'?" [34] Jesus answered them, "Amen, amen, I say to you, everyone who does what is sinful is a slave. [35] The slave does not abide in the house forever, but the son does abide forever. [36] So if the son makes you free, you will be free indeed. [37] I know you are the descent of Abraham. But you seek to kill me, because my word has no place in you. [38] What I speak is what I have seen with the Father, and what you do is what you have heard from [your] father."

Deathly Union Is Stated Clearly

[39] They answered and said to him, "Our father is Abraham." Jesus said to them, "If you are children of Abraham, you would do the works of Abraham. [40] But now you seek to kill me, a person who has spoken to you the truth which I heard from God. This is not what Abraham did. [41] You do the works of your father."

They said to him, "We were not born of infidelity. We have one father— God." [42] Jesus said to them, "If God were your father, you would love me, for from God I came forth and am here. And I did not come of my own accord, but he sent me. [43] Why do you not understand what I say? It is because you cannot hear my word. [44] You are of your father the devil, and the desires of your father you will to do. He was a murderer from the beginning [*ap' archēs*], and he did not take his stand on the truth because there is no truth in him. When he speaks a lie, he speaks from his inner self, because he is a liar and the father of lies. [45] But because I tell the truth, you do not believe me. [46] Which of you will convict me of sin? If I tell the truth, why do you not believe me? [47] The one who is of God hears God's words. The reason you do not hear is because you are not of God."

The Two Ways: Jesus Looks to Life; the Disbelievers, to Death

Reply 1: Jesus Challenges Death

[48] The Judeans answered and said to him, "Do we not speak well in saying that you are a Samaritan and have a demon." [49] Jesus answered, "I do not have a demon, but I honor my Father, and you dishonor me. [50] Not that I seek my own glory; there is one who seeks it, and it is he who is judge. [51] Amen, amen, I say to you, whoever keeps my word, will not see death forever."

Reply 2: Jesus Affirms Joy

[52] The Judeans then said to him, "Now we know that you have a demon. Abraham is dead, and the prophets also. Yet you say, 'Whoever keeps my word will not taste death forever.' [53] Are you greater than our father Abraham who died? And the prophets who are dead? Who do you make yourself to be?" [54] Jesus answered, "If I glorify myself my glory is nothing. It is my Father who glorifies me, he of whom you say, 'He is our God,' [55] though you have not known him. But I know him; and if I said, 'I do not know him,' I should be like you—a liar. But I do know him and I keep his word. [56] Abraham your father was overjoyed that he was to see my day. He saw it and rejoiced."

Reply 3: Jesus Reveals the Indwelling of Time-Surpassing Divinity

[57] The Judeans then said to him, "You are not yet fifty years old, and you have seen Abraham?" [58] Jesus said to them, "Amen, amen, I say to you, before Abraham came to be, I am [*Egō eimi*]."

[59] They then took up stones to throw at him. But Jesus hid [*ekrybē*] himself and went out of the temple.

The Man Born Blind: A Story of Creation
and of Human Growth

Scenes 1–3

The Birth, and the Creationlike Healing

9 [1] As he passed by he saw a person blind from birth. [2] And his disciples asked him, "Rabbi, who sinned, this man or his parents, that he was born blind?" [3] Jesus answered, "It was not that this man or his parents sinned, but that the works of God might be revealed in him. [4] It is necessary [*dei*] for us to work the works of him who sent me while it is day; night comes when no one can work. [5] As long as I am in the world, I am the light of the world." [6] As he said this he spat on the ground and made clay from the spittle, and he anointed [*chriō*] the man's eyes with the clay, [7] and he said to him, "Go wash in the pool of Siloam" (which is interpreted Sent). So he went and he washed, and he came out seeing.

Reactions: As to a Child, as by a Child

[8] Now the neighbors and those who had seen earlier that he was a beggar said, "Is not this the one who used to sit and beg?" [9] Some said, "This is he." Others said, "No, but he is like him." He himself said, * "I am [he] [*Egō eimi*]." [10] So they said to him, "Then how were your eyes opened?" He answered, ** [11] "The person called Jesus made clay and anointed my eyes and said to me, 'Go to Siloam and wash.' So I went, and when I washed I received my sight." [12] They said to him, "Where is he?" He said, *** "I do not know."

Among the Pharisees: Learning to Summarize and Judge

[13] They led him to the Pharisees—the one who had been blind. [14] Now it was a sabbath the day Jesus made clay and opened his eyes. [15] So the Pharisees also in their turn asked him how he received his sight. He said to them, * "He put clay on my eyes, and I washed, and I see." [16] Some of the Pharisees therefore said, "This person is not from God, for he does not keep the sabbath." But others said, "How can a person who is a sinner do such signs?" And there was a division among them. [17] So they said to the blind man again, "What do you say about him, since he opened your eyes?" He said, ** "He is a prophet."

Scenes 4–6

Away from Fearful Parents, the Person Comes of Age
[18] The Judeans therefore did not believe that he had been blind and had received his sight—until they called the parents of the man who had received his sight. [19] And they asked them, saying, "Is this your son, who you say was born blind? How then does he now see?" [20] His parents answered and said, "We know that this is our son, and that he was born blind. [21] But how he now sees, we do not know; or who opened his eyes, we do not know. Ask him; he is of age, he will speak for himself." [22] His parents said this because they feared the Judeans; for the Judeans had already agreed that if anyone should confess him to be the Anointed [*christos*], they should be put out of the synagogue. [23] That is why his parents said, "He is of age; ask him."

Back among the Leaders: Intellectual and Moral Maturity
[24] So for the second time they called the person who had been blind, and they said to him, "Give glory to God. We know that this person is a sinner." [25] He replied, * "Whether he is a sinner, I do not know. One thing I know—that though I was blind, now I see." [26] So they said to him, "What did he do to you? How did he open your eyes?" [27] He answered them, ** "I told you already, and you did not hear. Why do you wish [lit., will] to hear again? Do you also wish [= will] to become his disciples?" [28] They reviled him and said, "You are his disciple, but we are disciples of Moses. [29] We know that God spoke to Moses, but as for him, we do not know where he is from." [30] The man answered and said to them, *** "Why, this a marvel! You do not know where he is from, and yet he opened my eyes. [31] We know that God does not hear sinners, but if someone worships God, and does his will, God hears that person. [32] Never since the world began has it been heard that anyone opened the eyes of one who had been born blind. [33] If this person were not from God, he could do nothing." [34] They answered and said to him. "You were born wholly in sin, and would you teach us?" And they threw him out [*ek-ballō exō*].

Final Maturity: Full Acceptance of Humanity and Divinity
[35] Hearing that they had thrown him out, Jesus found him and said, "Do you believe in the Son of humanity?" [36] He answered and said, * "And who is he, Sir [*Kyrie*], that I may believe in him?" [37] Jesus said to him, "You have seen him, and it is he who speaks with you." [38] He said, ** "I believe, Lord [*Kyrie*]," and he worshipped him. [39] Jesus said, "For judgment I came into this world, that those who do not see may see, and that those who see may become blind." [40] Hearing this some of the Pharisees who were with him said to him, "Are we also blind?" [41] Jesus said to them, "If you were blind, you would not have sin. But now that you say, 'We see,' your sin abides."

The Good Shepherd and Winter: A Parable of Providence and an Episode of Survival

Evoking the Divine Voice/Action: The Parable of the Sheepfold

10   [1] "Amen, amen, I say to you, the one who does not enter the sheepfold through the door but climbs in another way, that is a thief and a robber. [2] The one who enters through the door is a shepherd of the sheep. [3] To him the doorkeeper opens; and the sheep hear his voice, and he calls his own sheep by name and leads them out [*ex-*]. [4] When he has put out [lit., thrown out, *ek-ballō*] all his own, he goes before them. and the sheep follow him, because they know his voice. [5] A stranger they will not follow but they will flee from him, because they do not know the voice of strangers." [6] This parable Jesus told them, but they did not know what he was saying to them.

The Divine Shepherd Enters Life, Including Death

[7] Jesus therefore again said, "Amen, amen, I say to you, I am the door of the sheep. [8] All who came before me are thieves and robbers, but the sheep did not hear them. [9] I am the door. Whoever enters through me, will be saved, and will go in and will go out and will find pasture. [10] The thief comes only to steal and kill and destroy. I have come that they may have life, and have it to the full.

[11] I am the good [*kalos*] shepherd. The good shepherd lays down his life for the sheep. [12] The one who is a mercenary and not a shepherd, whose own the sheep are not, sees the wolf coming, and leaves the sheep, and flees, and the wolf seizes them and scatters them—[13] because he is a mercenary and does not care for the sheep. [14] I am the good shepherd, and I know mine and mine know me, [15] as the Father knows me and I know the Father; and I lay down my life for my sheep. [16] And I have other sheep that are not of this fold, and it is necessary [*dei*] that I bring these also, and they will listen to my voice. And they shall become one flock, one shepherd.

[17] Because of this the Father loves me—that I lay down my life, in order that I may take it up again. [18] No one takes it away from me, but I lay it down of my own accord. I have power to lay it down, and I have power to take it up again. This command I have received from my Father."

Divided Reactions

[19] Again there was a division among the Judeans because of these words. [20] Many of them said, "He has a demon and is mad. Why listen to him?" [21] Others said, "These are not the words of one who has a demon. Can a demon open the eyes of the blind?"

Rededication: In Winter, Death Comes Closer . . .

[22] It was the [feast of the] Dedication [lit., renewal] in Jerusalem. It was winter, [23] and Jesus was walking about in the temple, in the portico of Solomon. [24] The Judeans therefore surrounded him and said to him, "How long will you hold our life [in suspense]? If you are the Anointed, tell us openly." [25] Jesus answered them, "I told you and you do not believe. The works that I do in my Father's name, they bear witness to me; [26] but you do not believe because you are not of my sheep. [27] My sheep hear my voice, and I know them, and they follow me. [28] I give them eternal life, and they shall never perish, and no one shall snatch them out of my hand. [29] My Father, what he has given me, is greater then all, and no one can snatch them from the hand of my Father. [30] I and the Father are one."

. . . and Closer—but Jesus, a Consecrated Son, Is with the Father and Survives

[31] The Judeans again took up stones to stone him. [32] Jesus answered them, "Many good [*kalos*] works have I shown you from the Father. For which of these do you stone me?" [33] The Judeans answered him, "It is not for a good work that we stone you, but for blasphemy, and because you, being a human, make yourself God."

[34] Jesus answered them, "Is it not written in your law, 'I said "You are gods" '? [35] If he called them gods, those to whom the word of God came—and scripture cannot be undone—[36] do you say of him whom the Father made holy [or consecrated] and sent into the world, 'You are blapheming,' because I said , 'I am a son [or the Son] of God?' [37] If I do not do the works of my Father, do not believe me. [38] But if I do, even if you do not believe me, believe the works, that you may know and understand that the Father is in me and I in the Father." [39] They sought therefore to arrest him, but he went out of their hands.

Jesus Crosses the Jordan: A Reaction of Faith

[40] And he went away again across the Jordan to the place where John was first baptizing, and he abode there. [41] And many came to him; and they said, "John did no sign, but all whatsoever that John said about this man was true." [42] And many believed in him there.

To Raise Lazarus, Jesus Descends towards Death

Lazarus Dies

The Apparently Distant Lord Hears of Suffering . . .

11 ¹Now there was a certain man sick [or weak], Lazarus of Bethany—the village of Mary and of Martha, her sister. ²Now Mary was the one who anointed [*aleiphō*] the Lord with perfume and wiped his feet with her hair, whose brother Lazarus was sick. ³The sisters therefore sent to him, saying, "Lord, the one whom you love is sick." ⁴But when Jesus heard he said, "This sickness is not to end in death; it is for the glory of God, so that through it the Son of God may be glorified." ⁵For Jesus loved Martha and her sister and Lazarus. ⁶So when he heard that he was sick, he abode two days longer in the place where he was.

. . . and Finally Sets out to the Place of Death

⁷Then, after this, he said to the disciples, "Let us go to Judea again." ⁸The disciples said to him, "Rabbi, just now the Judeans were seeking to stone you, and you are going back there again?" ⁹Jesus answered, "Are there not twelve hours of day? Those who walk in the day do not stumble because they see the light of this world. ¹⁰But those who walk in the night do stumble, because the light is not in them." ¹¹Thus he spoke, and after that he said to them, "Lazarus our friend has fallen asleep, but I go to awaken him from sleep." ¹²The disciples therefore said to him, "Lord, if he has fallen asleep he will recover [lit., be saved]." ¹³But while Jesus had spoken of his death, they thought that he was talking about sleep in the sense of rest. ¹⁴So then Jesus said to them openly, "Lazarus is dead ¹⁵and I rejoice for your sake that I was not there so that you may believe. But let us go to him." ¹⁶Thomas, who is called the twin, said to his co-disciples, "Let us also go, that we may die with him."

The Diverse Reactions of Martha and Mary

Jesus, the Resurrection and the Life . . .

¹⁷Coming therefore, Jesus found him already four days in the tomb. ¹⁸Now Bethany was near Jerusalem—about fifteen furlongs away—¹⁹and many of the Judeans had come to Martha and Mary to console them over their brother. ²⁰When Martha therefore heard that Jesus was coming, she went to meet him. Mary, however, sat in the house. ²¹And Martha said to Jesus, "Lord, if you had been here, my brother would not have died. ²²And even now, I know that whatever you ask of God, God will give you." ²³Jesus said to her, "Your brother will rise again." ²⁴Martha said to him, "I know that he will rise again, in the resurrection on the last day." ²⁵Jesus said to her, "I am the resurrection and the life; the one who believes in me, even if that person die, shall live, ²⁶and all who live and believe in me shall never die. Do you believe this?" ²⁷She said to him, "Yes, Lord; I believe that you are the Anointed, the Son of God, the one who is coming into the world."

. . . Comes Closer to Tearful Death

[28] And having said this she went away and called Mary her sister, and said to her secretly, "The Teacher is present and is calling you." [29] And she, when she heard this, rose quickly and came to him. [30] Now Jesus had not yet come to the village, but was still in the place where Martha had met him. [31] And when the Judeans who were with her in the house, consoling her, saw Mary rise up quickly and go out, they followed her, thinking that she was going to the tomb to weep there. [32] Mary, therefore, when she came where Jesus was, seeing him, fell at his feet, saying to him, "Lord, if you had been here my brother would not have died." [33] Jesus then, when he saw her weeping and the Judeans who had come with her weeping, breathed angrily and was shaking. [34] And he said, "Where have you laid him?" They said to him, "Lord, come and see." [35] Jesus broke into tears. [36] The Judeans therefore said, "See how he loved him." [37] But some of them said, "Could not he who opened the eyes of the blind man have done something so that this man should not die?"

The Deaths of Lazarus and Jesus Inaugurate New Life

Jesus Is Able to Raise Lazarus to Life . . .

[38] Then Jesus, again angry within himself, came to the tomb. It was a cave, and a stone lay over it. [39] Jesus said, "Take away the stone." The sister of the dead man, Martha, said to him. "Lord, by now he will be giving off a stench, for it is four days." [40] Jesus said to her, "Did I not say to you that if you believed, you would see the glory of God." [41] So they lifted away the stone. And Jesus lifted up his eyes and said, "Father, I thank you that you have heard me. [42] I know that you hear me always, but I have said this because of the crowd standing around, that they may believe that you sent me." [43] And saying this he cried out in a great voice, "Lazarus, come out." [44] The dead man came out, his feet and hands bound with linen bands, and his face wrapped with a cloth. Jesus said to them, "Loose him, and let him go."

. . . but Is Himself Condemned to Death

[45] Many of the Judeans, therefore, who had come to Mary and had seen what he had done, believed in him. [46] But some of them went to the Pharisees and told them what Jesus had done. [47] So the chief priests and the Pharisees gathered the council and said, "What are we to do? For this person is doing many signs. [48] If we let him go on like this, everyone will believe in him, and the Romans will come and will take away our place and nation." [49] But one of them, Caiaphas, being the high priest of that year, said to them, "You know nothing. [50] You do not understand that it is expedient for you that one person die for the people, and that the whole nation not perish." [51] He did not say this of his own accord, but being the high priest of that year, he prophesied that Jesus would die for the nation, [52] and not for the nation only but that the scattered children of God may be gathered into one. [53] So from that day they planned that they might kill him.

The Journey's End: Symbolically Jesus Passes from Death to Glory

Jesus' Day-to-day Path to Death in Jerusalem

Introduction: From the Desert to the Feast

⁵⁴Jesus therefore no longer walked about openly among the Judeans, but went away from there into the country near the desert, to a city called Ephraim, and there he sojourned with the disciples.

⁵⁵Now the Passover of the Judeans was at hand, and many from the country went up to Jerusalem before the Passover to purify themselves. ⁵⁶They therefore sought Jesus, and they said to one another standing in the temple, "What do you think? That he will not come to the feast?" ⁵⁷For the chief priests and the Pharisees had given a command that if anyone knew where he was, they should report it, so that they might arrest him.

The Bethany Anointing . . . Evoking Burial

12 ¹Jesus, therefore, six days before Passover, came to Bethany where Lazarus was, whom Jesus had raised from the dead. ²They made him a supper there, and Martha served. Lazarus was one of those reclining at table with him. ³So Mary took a pound of expensive perfume—oil of pure nard—and anointed [*aleiphō*] the feet of Jesus, and she wiped his feet with her hair. And the house was filled with the fragrance of the perfume.

⁴But Judas Iscariot, one of his disciples—the one who was going to hand him over—said, ⁵"Why was this perfume not sold for three hundred denarii and given to the poor?" ⁶He said this however not because he cared for the poor, but because he was a thief, and as he had the money box he used to take what was put in it. ⁷Jesus therefore said, "Let her be—that she may keep it for the day of my burial. ⁸For the poor you have always with you, but you do not always have me."

Reactions. ⁹The great crowd from the Judeans, therefore, knew that he was there, and they came not only on account of Jesus, but also to see Lazarus whom he had raised from the dead. ¹⁰So the chief priests planned to kill Lazarus also, ¹¹because on account of him many of the Judeans had gone away and believed in Jesus.

The Entry to Jerusalem . . . Evoking Resurrection

[12] The next day the great crowd that had come to the feast, hearing that Jesus was coming to Jerusalem, [13] took branches of palm and went out to meet him. And they cried, *"Hosanna! Blessed is he who comes in the name of the Lord—the King of Israel!"*

[14] But Jesus found a little donkey and sat upon it—as it is written: [15] *"Do not fear, daughter of Zion! Behold, your king is coming, sitting on a donkey's colt."* [16] These things his disciples did not understand at first; but when Jesus was glorified, then they remembered that these things had been written of him and that they had done these things to him.

Reactions.   [17] The crowd which had been with him when he called Lazarus out of the tomb and raised him from the dead kept bearing witness. [18] And it was because of this also that the crowd met him—because they heard that he had done this sign. [19] The Pharisees therefore said to one another, "You see that you accomplish nothing. Behold, the world has gone after him."

As if Beyond Death, the Timeless Jesus Appeals to All

The Coming of All Peoples ("the Greeks") . . . Evoking Jesus' Glorification

[20] Now among those who went up to worship at the feast were some Greeks. [21] So they came to Philip, who was from Bethsaida of Galilee, and they told him their request: "Sir [*Kyrie*], we will [or wish] to see Jesus." [22] Philip came and told Andrew. Andrew came and Philip and told Jesus.

[23] Jesus answered them, saying, "The hour has come for the Son of humanity to be glorified. [24] Amen, amen, I say to you, unless the grain of wheat falls to the earth and dies, it abides [or remains] alone; but if it dies, it bears much fruit. [25] Those who love their life, lose it; but those who hate their life in this world will keep it for eternal life. [26] If anyone would serve me, let that person follow me, and where I am there shall my servant also be. If anyone serves me, the Father will honor that person.

[27] "Now is my soul troubled. And what shall I say—'Father, save me from this hour'? But it was for this that I came to this hour. [28] Father, glorify your name." Then a voice came from heaven, "I have glorified it and I will glorify it again."

Reactions.   [29] The crowd, therefore, which was standing there and heard, said that it had thundered. Others said, "An angel has spoken to him." [30] Jesus answered and said, "This voice was not for my sake, but for yours. [31] Now is the judgment of this world, now shall the ruler of this world be driven out; [32] and I, when I am lifted up from the earth, will draw all to myself." [33] In saying this he was signifying by what kind of death he was going to die.

[34] The crowd therefore answered him, "We have heard from the law that the Anointed abides forever. How can you say that it is necessary [*dei*] that the Son of humanity be lifted up? Who is this Son of humanity?" [35] Jesus therefore said to them, "For a short while more the light is with you. Walk while you have the

light, that the darkness may not overcome you. Those who walk in the darkness do not know where they are going. [36] While you have the light believe in the light, that you may become children [lit., sons] of light.''

The Departure into Hiding . . . Evoking Unbelievers' Blindness
Thus spoke Jesus, and going away he hid from them. [37] Though he had done so many signs before them, they did not believe in him—[38] that the word said by Isaiah the prophet might be fulfilled: *"Lord, who has believed what we have heard, and to whom has the power of the Lord been revealed?''* [39] The reason they could not believe was that, as Isaiah said again, [40] *"He has blinded their eyes and hardened their hearts, lest they see with their eyes and understand with their hearts, and should turn, and I should heal them.''* [41] Thus spoke Isaiah, because he saw his glory and spoke of him.

Reactions. [42] Nevertheless, many of the rulers believed in him, but because of the Pharisees, they did not confess it, that they might not be put out of the synagogue. [43] For they loved human glory more than the glory of God.

Epilogue: The Divine Word and the Two Ways

[44] Jesus cried out and said,

''Whoever believes in me, believes not in me, but in the one who sent me. [45] And whoever sees me, sees the one who sent me. [46] I have come as light into the world so that anyone who believes in me may not abide in darkness. [47] And if anyone hears my words and does not keep them, I do not judge that person, for I did not come to judge the world but to save the world.

[48] ''Whoever rejects me and does not receive my words has a judge: the word which I have spoken will judge that person on the last day. [49] For I have not spoken on my own, but the Father who sent me has given me a commandment [about] what to say and what to speak. [50] And I know that his commandment is eternal life. What I speak therefore, I speak just as the Father has told me.

Book Two □ Part 3B:
The Central Passover Mystery

The Last Discourse (The Word Spoken) CHAPTERS 13–17

*Jesus' Departure and Return: A Story of Loss and Gain Which
Portrays the Drama of God's Spiritual Action within the Disciple*

THE WASHING: CONFRONTING THE MIXTURE OF
GOOD AND EVIL

Shadowed Love: Amid Evil, Jesus' Descent into Service

vv 1–3: The ultimate context: from God and to God. cf. 14:1–3; 17:24–26

13 ¹Before the feast of the Passover, Jesus, knowing that his hour had come to depart from this world to the Father, having loved his own who were in the world, he loved them to the end. ²And during supper, when the devil had already put [lit., thrown, *ballō*] it into the heart [*kardia*] that Judas, son of Simon the Iscariot, should hand him over, ³knowing that the Father had given all things into his hands, and that he had come from God and was going to God, ⁴he rose from the supper, and laid down his garments, and taking a towel girded himself. ⁵Then he put [lit., threw, *ballō*] water into a basin and began to wash the disciples' feet and to wipe them with the towel with which he was girded.

Jesus Comes to Peter
⁶So he came to Simon Peter. He said to him, "Lord, do you wash my feet?" ⁷Jesus answered and said to him, "What I am doing you do not know now, but you will understand later." ⁸Peter said to him, "You shall not wash my feet— not forever." Jesus answered him, "If I do not wash you, you have no part [or inheritance] with me." ⁹Simon Peter said to him, "Lord, not only my feet but also my hands and my head." ¹⁰Jesus said to him, "Whoever has bathed has no need to wash, but is clean [*katharos*] all over. And you are clean, but not all of you." ¹¹For he knew who was to hand him over; that was why he said, "You are not all clean [*katharos*]."

The Implications
¹²So when he had washed their feet, and taken his garments, and reclined again, he said to them, "Do you know what I have done to you? ¹³You call me Teacher

and Lord, and you speak well, for so I am. [14]If I then, the Lord and Teacher, have washed your feet, you also ought to wash one another's feet. [15]I have given you an example, that as I have done to you, you also should do. [16]Amen, amen, I say to you, a servant is not greater than the master, nor is the one who is sent greater than the sender. [17]If you know these things, blessed are you if you do them. [18]I do not say this about all; I know whom I have chosen; but that the scripture may be fulfilled, 'The one who feeds on my bread has raised up his heel against me.' [19]I say it to you now before it happens, so that when it does happen you may believe that I am. [20]Amen, amen, I say to you, whoever receives anyone whom I send receives me; and whoever receives me receives the one who sent me.''

Practical Outcome: Love

Amid the Shadow, Love

The Emergence of a Betrayer (and of a Beloved)
[21]Having said this, Jesus was shaken in spirit, and he bore witness and said, "Amen, amen, I say to you, one of you will hand me over.'' [22]The disciples looked at one another, in confusion as to whom he was talking about. [23]Reclining there next to Jesus' bosom was one of his disciples, one whom Jesus loved. [24]So Simon Peter nodded to him, to ask about whom he was talking. [25]He, lying down on Jesus' breast, said to him, "Lord, who is it?'' [26]Jesus replied, "He it is to whom I shall give this morsel when I have dipped it.'' So he dipped the morsel and gave it to Judas, son of Simon the Iscariot. [27]And after the morsel, then Satan entered him [. . . *Satanas*].

The Action of the Betrayer (with Allusions to Love)
Jesus therefore said to him, "What you are going to do, do quickly.'' [28]Now no one reclining there knew why he said this to him. [29]For some thought, because Judas had the money box, that Jesus was saying to him, "Buy what we need for the feast,'' or that he should give something to the poor. [30]So taking the morsel, he went out immediately. It was night.

Amid Glorious Love, a Shadow

The (Glory-related Commandment of) Love
[31]Then, when he had gone out, Jesus said, "Now is the Son of humanity glorified, and in him God is glorified. [32]If God is glorified in him, God will also glorify him in himself, and will glorify him immediately. [33]Little children, yet a short while I am with you. You will seek me, and as I said to the Judeans, 'Where I am going, you cannot come,' so I say it to you now. [34]A new commandment I give to you, that you love one another. As I have loved you, that you also love one another. [35]By this will all know that you are my disciples, if you have love for one another.''

The Shadow: The Spectre of Peter's Denial

[36] Simon Peter said to him, "Lord, where are you going?" Jesus answered, "Where I am going, you cannot follow me now; but you will follow later." [37] Peter said to him, "Lord, why cannot I follow you now? I will lay down my life for you." [38] Jesus answered, "Will you lay down your life for me? Amen, amen, I say to you, the rooster will not call till you have denied me three times."

The Human Response: The Shaken Heart Finds God in Jesus, the Way

Introduction: The Ultimate Finding of God, in a Future Abode

14 [1] "Let not your heart [*kardia*] be shaken; [you] believe in God[?], believe also in me. [2] In my Father's house there are many abodes [*monē*]; if not, I would have told you, for I am going away to prepare a place for you. [3] And if I go away and prepare a place for you, I will come again and take you to myself, that where I am you also may be."

Finding God Now, in the Human Jesus, the Way . . .

[4] "And where I am going, you know the way."

[5] Thomas said to him, "Lord, we do not know where you are going; how can we know the way?" [6] Jesus said to him, "I am the way and the truth and the life. No one comes to the Father except through me. [7] If you had known me, you would have known my Father also.

. . . A Way Which Is Very near to You

"And now already you know him, and you have seen him."

[8] Philip said to him, "Lord, show us the Father; and that will be enough for us." [9] Jesus said to him, "So long a time I am with you, and you do not know me, Philip? Whoever has seen me has seen the Father. How can you say, 'Show us the Father.' [10] Do you not believe that I am in the Father and the Father in me? The words that I speak to you I do not speak of my own accord. It is the Father abiding [*menō*] in me who does the works. [11] Believe me that I am in the Father and the Father in me. Or else believe because of the works."

Finding God's Abode in Oneself, Spirit-Led

[12] "Amen, amen, I say to you, the one who believes in me will do the works that I do and will do greater things than these, because I am going to the Father. [13] Whatever you ask in my name, I will do it, that the Father may be glorified in the Son. [14] If you ask me anything in my name, that I will do. [15] If you love me you will keep my commandments; [16] and I will ask the Father, and he will give you another Companion [*paraklētos*] to be with you forever— [17] the Spirit of truth whom the world cannot receive because it neither sees it nor knows it. But you know it, because it abides with you, and is in you.

[18] "I will not leave you orphans: I will come to you. [19] Yet a short while and the world will see me no more, but you will see me; and because I live, you also will live. [20] On that day you will know that I am in my Father, and you in me, and I in you.

²¹"The one who has my commandments and keeps them, that is the one who loves me. And the one who loves me will be loved by my Father, and I will love that person, and to that person I will make myself known.'' ²²Judas, not the Iscariot, said to him, "Lord, how is it that you are going to make yourself known to us and not to the world?'' ²³Jesus answered and said to him, "Those who love me, will keep my word, and my Father will love them, and we shall come to them and shall make our abode with them. ²⁴The one who does not love me does not keep my words. And the word which you hear is not mine but the Father's who sent me.

Practical Outcome: Peace

Spirit-Based Peace, Even in Face of (Jesus') Departure and Death

Jesus' Spirit-Based Peace . . .

²⁵"These things I have spoken to you while abiding with you. ²⁶But the Companion, the holy Spirit whom the Father will send in my name, that is the one who will teach you all things and recall to mind all that I have said to you. ²⁷Peace I leave to you; my peace I give you; not as the world gives do I give to you.''

. . . Even in Face of Loss and Death

"Let not your heart be shaken, nor let it be afraid. ²⁸You have heard me say to you, 'I am going away and I will be coming to you.' If you loved me you would be joyful that I am going to the Father; for the Father is greater than I. ²⁹And now I have told you before it happens, so that when it does happen you may believe. ³⁰I will no longer talk much with you, for the ruler of the world is coming. He has no hold over me, ³¹but in order that the world may know that I love the Father, as the Father has commanded me, so I do. Arise, let us go from here.''

THE PURIFYING: SEPARATING LOVE FROM HATRED, THE VINE FROM "THE WORLD"

The True Vine and Its Love

Increasing Descent into Purification Brings forth Increasing Vitality and Communion

Jesus as "the True Vine"

15 [1]"I am the true vine and my Father is the vinedresser. [2]Every branch in me not bearing fruit, he takes away [*airei*], and every branch bearing fruit he cleanses [*kathairei*] that it may bear more fruit. [3]Now you are clean [*katharos*] because of the word which I have spoken to you. [4]Abide in me, and I in you. As the branch cannot bear fruit by itself, unless it abides in the vine, so neither can you unless you abide in me."

Jesus as Simply "the Vine"

[5]"I am the vine, you are the branches. Those who abide in me and I in them, they bear much fruit, for without me you can do nothing. [6]Those who do not abide in me are thrown [*ballō*] out as a branch and they wither; and they are gathered, thrown [*ballō*] into the fire, and burned. [7]If you abide in me, and my words abide in you, you shall ask for whatever you will and it shall be done for you."

And in Place of the Vine, the Fruit

[8]"In this is my Father glorified—that you bear much fruit and become my disciples. [9]As the Father has loved me, so have I loved you. Abide in my love. [10]If you keep my commandments you will abide in my love, just as I have kept my Father's commandments and abide in his love."

Practical Outcome: Greater Love

Joyful Love (Including Friendship)

[11]"These things I have spoken to you that my joy may be in you, and that your joy may be fulfilled. [12]This is my commandment, that you love one another as I have loved you. [13]Greater love than this no one has, than that people lay down their lives for their friends. [14]You are my friends if you do what I command you."

. . . And, Finally, Friendship (Including Love)

[15]"I no longer call you servants, for the servant does not know what the master is doing. But I have called you friends, because all that I have heard from the Father I have made known to you. [16]You did not choose me, but I chose you and appointed you so that you should go and bear fruit and that your fruit should abide —so that whatever you ask the Father in my name, he may give it to you. [17]This I command you that you love one another."

The World and Its Hatred

The Deep-seated Antipathy

[18]"If the world hates you, know that it has hated me before you. [19]If you were of the world, the world would love its own; but because you are not of the world, but I have chosen you out of the world, therefore the world hates you. [20]Remember the word which I said to you, 'A servant is not greater then his lord.' If they persecuted me, they will persecute you also; if they kept my word, they will keep yours also. [21]But all these things they will do to you because of my name, because they do not know the one who sent me."

The Subsequent Sinfulness

[22]"If I had not come and spoken to them, they would not have sin; but now they have no excuse for their sin. [23]Whoever hates me hates my Father also. [24]If I had not done among them the works which no one else has done, they would not have sin. But now they have both seen and hated both me and my Father. [25]However, this is to fulfil the word which is written in their law: 'They hated me without cause.' "

Yet, Spirit-Led, You Will Witness

[26]"When the Companion comes, whom I will send you from the Father, the Spirit of truth, who proceeds from the Father, he will bear witness to me. [27]And you also bear witness, because from the beginning you are with me."

Practical Outcome: Death

Expulsion and Death

16 [1]"These things I have spoken to you that you may not fall away. [2]They will put you out of the synagogue. Indeed the hour is coming when all who kill you will think that they are paying service to God. [3]And they will do these things because they have not known either the Father or me."

Yet You Will Remember

[4]"But these things I have said to you, so that when their hour comes you may remember that I told you of them."

The Human Response: The Sorrowful Heart Lets Go
and Finds God, in Joy — the Spirit Shows the Way

Introduction: The Crisis of Sorrow
"These things I did not say to you from the beginning, because I was with you.
[5] But now I am going to the one who sent me, and none of you asks me, 'Where
are you going?' [6] Instead, because I have said these things to you, sorrow has
filled your heart."

But Sorrow Can Prepare for the Spirit—to Challenge . . .
[7] "But I tell you the truth: it is better for you that I go away. For if I do not go
away, the Companion will not come to you; but if I go, I will send him to you.
[8] And when he comes he will confront the world about sin, and about justice, and
about judgment. [9] About sin because they do not believe in me. [10] About justice,
because I am going to the Father, and you will see me no longer. [11] And about
judgment, because the ruler of this world has been judged."

. . . And to Show the Way
[12] "I have yet many things to tell you, but you cannot bear them now. [13] But when
he comes, the Spirit of truth, he will show you the way into all the truth. For he
will not speak on his own, but whatsoever he will hear he will speak, and the
things that are to come he will announce to you. [14] He will glorify me, for he will
take what is mine and announce it to you. [15] All whatsoever the Father has is
mine; that is why I said he will take what is mine and announce it to you."

The Birthlike Finding of Sight and Joy
[16] "A short while, and you will not see me any more, and again a short while and
you will see me." [17] Some of his disciples therefore said to one another, "What
is this that he says to us, 'A short while, and you will not see me, and again a
short while and you will see me,' and 'I am going to the Father'?" [18] They said
therefore, "What is this 'short while'? We do not know what he is saying."
[19] Jesus knew that they wanted [lit., willed] to question him, so he said to them,
"About this you are seeking among yourselves—because I said, 'A short while
and you will not see me, and again a short while and you will see me.' "
   [20] "Amen, amen, I say to you, you will weep and lament, but the world will
rejoice. You will be sorrowful, but your sorrow will be turned into joy. [21] A
woman when she is giving birth is sorrowful because her hour has come. But
when she has brought forth the child, she remembers no more the distress, for joy
that a person is born into the world. [22] So you are sorrowful now; but I will see
you again, and your heart shall rejoice, and your joy no one shall take from you.
[23] And on that day you will not question me any more.
   "Amen, amen, I say to you, whatever you ask the Father in my name he will
give it to you. [24] Until now you have not asked for anything in my name. Ask and
you shall receive, that your joy may be full."

Practical Outcome: Confidence

Within: A Sense of God's Friendship

[25] "These things I have said to you in parables. An hour is coming when I will speak to you no more in parables, but will announce to you plainly about the Father. [26] On that day, you will ask in my name, and I do not say that I will ask the Father for you; [27] for the Father himself loves you, because you have loved me and have believed that I came forth from God. [28] I came forth from the Father and have come into the world. I am leaving the world again and journeying to the Father.''

Without: Even amid Distress, Confidence

[29] His disciples said, ''Behold, now you are speaking plainly, and not in any parable. [30] Now we know that you know all things and that you do not need that anyone question you. Through this we believe that you came forth from God.'' [31] Jesus answered them, ''You now believe[?]. [32] Behold, an hour is coming. and has already come, when you will be scattered, each one [of you] to your own house, and will leave me alone. Yet I am not alone, because the Father is with me. [33] These things I have said to you that in me you may have peace. In the world you have distress; but have confidence; I have conquered the world.''

THE SANCTIFYING, AND CONSEQUENT UNITY

While Reviewing God's Work, Including the Disciples' Return to the World, Jesus Ascends Spiritually to God

The Glory-Based Incarnation

17 ¹When Jesus had spoken these things, he raised his eyes to heaven and said, "Father, the hour has come; glorify your Son, that your Son may glorify you; ²as you have given him power over all people [lit., flesh], that he may give eternal life to all whom you have given him. ³And this is eternal life—that they may know you, the one true God, and Jesus Christ whom you have sent. ⁴I have glorified you on earth, having completed the work which you gave me to do. ⁵And now, you glorify me, Father, in your presence, with the glory which I had, before the world was, with you."

The Going Away

⁶"I have revealed your name to the persons whom you have given me out of the world. They were yours, and you gave them to me, and they have kept your word. ⁷Now they know that all whatsoever you have given me is from you; ⁸for the words which you gave to me, I have given to them, and they have received them; and they truly know [lit., know in truth] that I came forth from you, and they have believed that you sent me. ⁹I ask for them. I do not ask for the world but for those whom you have given me, for they are yours; ¹⁰all mine are yours, and all yours are mine, and I am glorified in them.

¹¹"I am no longer in the world, but they are in the world, and I am coming to you. Holy [*hagios*] Father, keep them in your name which you have given to me, that they may be one as we are. ¹²When I was with them, I kept them in your name which you have given to me; I guarded them, and not one of them perished, except the son of perdition, that the scripture might be fulfilled.

¹³"And now I am coming to you, and these things I speak in the world, that they may have my joy fulfilled in themselves. ¹⁴I have given them your word, and the world has hated them because they are not of the world, as I am not of the world. ¹⁵I do not pray that you take them out of the world but that you keep them from [the] evil [one]. ¹⁶They are not of the world, as I am not of the world. ¹⁷Make them holy [or sanctify/consecrate, *hagiazō*] in the truth; your word is truth. ¹⁸As you sent me into the world, so have I sent them into the world. ¹⁹And for their sake I make myself holy, that they also may be made holy in truth."

The Final Outcome: Unity (Including Church Unity)

[20]"Not for these only do I ask, but also for those who believe in me through their word, [21]that they all may be one, as you Father in me and I in you, that they also may be in us, that the world may belive that you have sent me. [22]And the glory which you have given to me I have given to them, that they may be one as we are one. [23]I in them and you in me, that they may be brought to completion in one, that the world may know that you have sent me and that you have loved them as you have loved me."

Conclusion: The Ultimate Union

[24]"Father, I will that where I am those whom you have given to me may be with me, that they may see my glory which you have given to me because you loved me before the foundation of the world. [25]Just Father, the world has not known you, but I have known you, and these have known that you have sent me. [26]I have made known to them your name, and I will make it known, that the love with which you loved me may be in them, and I in them."

The Arrest and Trial (The Word amid Evil):
Two Dramas of Sin—of Revelation Rejected

Drama 1: The Arrest and Interrogation (18:1–27):
Jesus' Open/External Revelation Is Rejected by Those with
Special Inside Knowledge or Position

Introduction: Judas and His (Inside) Knowledge

18 ¹Having said these things, Jesus went out with his disciples across the winter-flowing Kedron, where there was a garden into which he entered along with his disciples. ²And Judas, who handed him over [*para-didōmi*], also knew the place, for Jesus had often gathered there with his disciples. ³So Judas, taking the cohort [of soldiers], as well as officers from the chief priests and Pharisees, went there with lanterns and torches and weapons.

Scenes 1–3

⁴Jesus therefore, knowing all that was going to happen to him, went out and said to them, "Whom do you seek?" ⁵They answered him, "Jesus the Nazorean." He said to them, "I am [he]" [*Egō eimi*]. Now Judas also, who handed him over, was standing with them. ⁶So when he said to them, "I am [he]" [*Egō eimi*], they went back and fell to the ground.

⁷Again therefore, he asked them, "Whom do you seek?" They said, "Jesus the Nazorean." ⁸Jesus answered, "I said to you that I am [he][*Egō eimi*]. So, if you seek me, let these go away"—⁹that the word might be fulfilled which he had spoken, "Of those whom you have given me, I have not lost one."

¹⁰Then Simon Peter, having a sword, drew it and struck the high priest's servant and cut off his right ear. The name of the servant was Malchus. ¹¹But Jesus said to Peter, "Put the sword into its sheath. The cup which the Father has given me, shall I not drink it?"

116

Interlude

¹² Then the cohort and the commander and the officers of the Judeans took hold of Jesus and bound him. ¹³ And they led him to Annas first, for he was the father-in-law of Caiaphas, who was the high priest that year. ¹⁴ It was Caiaphas who had counselled the Judeans that it was expedient that one person should die for the people.

Scenes 4–6

¹⁵ Now Simon Peter followed Jesus, along with another disciple. This disciple was known to the high priest, and so he went in with Jesus into the court [or fold] of the high priest. ¹⁶ Peter however stood outside at the door [or gate]. So the other disciple, who was known to the high priest, went out and spoke to the doorkeeper [or gatekeeper] and led Peter in. ¹⁷ The maid who was doorkeeper therefore said to Peter, "Are not you also among the disciples of this person?" He said, "I am not" [*ouk eimi*]. ¹⁸ The servants and officers stood there, having made a charcoal fire, for it was cold; and they warmed themselves. And Peter also was with them, standing and warming himself.

¹⁹ The high priest therefore asked Jesus about his disciples and about his teaching. ²⁰ Jesus answered him, "I have spoken openly to the world. I have always taught in the synagogue and in the temple, where all the Judeans gather, and in secret I have said nothing. ²¹ Why do you ask me? Ask those who have heard me what I said to them. Behold, they know what I said." ²² When he said this, one of the officials standing by gave Jesus a slap in the face, saying, "Is that how you answer the high priest?" ²³ Jesus answered him, "If I have spoken wrongly, bear witness to the wrong. But if I have spoken well, why do you strike me?" ²⁴ Then Annas sent him bound to Caiphas the high priest.

²⁵ Now Simon Peter was standing and warming himself. So they said to him, "Are not you also from among his disciples?" He denied it and said, "I am not" [*ouk eimi*]. ²⁶ One of the servants of the high priest, a relative of the man whose ear Peter had cut off, said to him, "Did I not [*ouk egō*] see you in the garden with him?" ²⁷ Again therefore Peter denied it. And immediately the rooster called.

Drama 2: The Trial Before Pilate (18:28–19:16a): Jesus' Inside Revelation (Concerning God's Kingdom/Realm) Is Rejected by Those Who Are Outside

Introduction: The Judeans Stay Outside

[28] Then they led Jesus from Caiaphas to the praetorium. It was dawn. They themselves did not enter the praetorium, that they might not be [ritually] defiled, but might eat the Passover.

Scenes 1–3

[29] So Pilate went out to them and said, "What accusation do you bring against this person?" [30] They replied and said to him, "If he were not an evildoer, we would not have handed him over to you." [31] Pilate therefore said to them, "Take him you, and judge him according to your own law." The Judeans said to him, "It is unlawful for us to put anyone to death." [32] This was to fulfil the word which Jesus had spoken to signify by what death he was to die.

[33] So Pilate entered the praetorium again and called Jesus and said to him, "Are you the King of the Judeans?" [34] Jesus answered, "Do you say this of your own accord, or have others said it to you about me?" [35] Pilate answered, "Am I a Judean? Your own nation and the chief priests have handed you over to me. What have you done?" Jesus answered, [36] "My realm is not of this world. If my realm were of this world, my officers would fight that I might not be handed over to the Judeans. But now my realm is not from here." [37] Pilate said to him, "So you are a king?" Jesus answered, "You say that I am a king. For this I was born, and for this I have come into the world, to bear witness to the truth. Everyone who is of the truth hears my voice." [38] Pilate said to him, "What is truth?"

And saying this, he again went out to the Judeans and said to them, "I find no case against him. [39] Now you have a custom that I should release one person to you at Passover. Do you wish then that I should release to you the King of the Judeans?" [40] They shouted again, saying, "Not him, but Barabbas." Barabbas was a robber.

Interlude

19 ¹Then Pilate took Jesus and scourged him. ²And the soldiers plaited a crown of thorns and laid it on his head, and they put around him a purple garment. ³And they kept coming up to him, saying, "Hail, King of the Judeans," and they slapped him in the face.

Scenes 4–6

⁴And yet again Pilate went out and said to them, "Behold I am leading him out to you, that you may know that I find no cause in him." ⁵So Jesus came forth, wearing the thorn crown and the purple garment. And he said to them, "Behold a human being." ⁶When the chief priests and the officers saw him, they shouted saying, "Crucify him! Crucify him!" Pilate said to them, "Take him you and crucify him, for I find no case against him." ⁷The Judeans answered him, "We have a law, and according to that law he ought to die, because he made himself a son of God."

⁸When Pilate heard this word, he was more afraid; ⁹and he entered into the praetorium again and said to Jesus, "Where are you from?" But Jesus gave him no answer. ¹⁰So Pilate said to him, "Will you not speak to me? Do you not know that I have authority to release you and authority to crucify you?" ¹¹Jesus answered him, "You would have no authority whatever over me if it had not been given to you from above. Because of this, he who handed me over to you has the greater sin." ¹²From then on Pilate sought to release him. But the Judeans shouted saying, "If you release him, you are not a friend of Caesar's. Everyone who makes himself a king defies Caesar."

¹³When Pilate heard these words he led Jesus out, and he sat [him/himself] down on the judgment seat at the place called Stone-pavement, and in Hebrew, Gabbatha. ¹⁴It was Preparation [day] for the Passover; it was about the sixth hour. And he said to the Judeans, "Behold your king!" ¹⁵But they shouted out, "Take him away, take him away! Crucify him!" Pilate said to them, "Shall I crucify your king?" The chief priests replied, "We have no king but Caesar." ¹⁶Then he handed him over [*para-didōmi*] to them to be crucified.

Death and Resurrection (The Word in Practice):
The Working Out of the Passover Mystery in Jesus and
in the Human Community

The Crucifixion

Introduction

So they took Jesus, [17] and bearing the cross himself he went out to what is called the Place of a Skull, which in Hebrew is called Golgotha, [18] where they crucified him, and with him two others, one on either side, with Jesus in the middle.

Scenes 1–3

The Inscription

[19] Pilate also wrote an inscription and placed it on the cross. What was written was "Jesus the Nazorean, the King of the Judeans." [20] And many of the Judeans read this inscription, because it was near the city—the place where Jesus was crucified. And it was written in Hebrew, Latin, and Greek. [21] So the high priests of the Judeans said to Pilate, "Do not write, 'The King of the Judeans,' but 'This man said: I am King of the Judeans.' " [22] Pilate answered, "What I have written, I have written."

The Clothes

[23] Now the soldiers, when they had crucified Jesus, took his garments, and they made four shares, to each soldier a share; and also the tunic. But the tunic was seamless, woven from above [*anōthen*] through its entirety. [24] So they said to one another, "Do not let us divide it, but let us cast lots about whose it shall be"— that the scripture might be fulfilled which says, "They shared my garments among them, and for my clothing they cast lots." And that is what the soldiers did.

The Woman/Women and the Beloved

[25] But standing by the cross of Jesus were his mother, and the sister of his mother, Mary [the wife] of Klopas, and Mary Magdalene. [26] Jesus therefore seeing his mother and the disciple standing whom he loved, said to his mother, "Woman, behold your son." [27] Then he said to the disciple, "Behold your mother." And from that hour the disciple took her to his own home.

Jesus Hands Over

Scenes 1–2

The Bitter End

[28] After this, Jesus, knowing that all was now complete [or ended, *teleō*], that the scripture might be completely fulfilled [or finished/ended, *teleioō*], said, "I thirst." [29] A jar stood there full of vinegarish [wine] [lit., sharp, bitter, *oxos*]; so putting a sponge full of the vinegar [*oxos*] on hyssop, they carried it to his mouth. [30] And when Jesus took the vinegar [*oxos*] he said, "It is complete" [or ended, *teleō*]; and bowing his head he handed over [*para-didōmi*] *the spirit.*

The Final Emptying

[31] The Judeans therefore, since it was Preparation—in order that the bodies might not remain on the cross on the sabbath, for that sabbath was a great day—asked Pilate that their legs might be broken and that they be taken away. [32] So the soldiers came and they broke the legs of the first and of the other who had been crucified with him; [33] but when they came to Jesus and saw that he was already dead they did not break his legs. [34] But one of the soldiers pierced his side with a spear; and immediately there came out blood and water.

Conclusion, Part 1: The Witnessing and Its Purpose (the Writing)

[35] And he who saw it has borne witness, and his witness is true, and he [lit., that one, *ekeinos*] knows that he speaks the truth, that you also may believe.

[36] For these things happened that the scripture [lit., writing] might be fulfilled, "Not a bone of him shall be broken." [37] And again another scripture [writing] says, "They shall look on him whom they have pierced."

The Ascent (Initiating Unity)

Introduction: The Body

[38] After these things, however, Joseph of Arimathea—a disciple of Jesus, but secretly, for fear of the Judeans—asked Pilate that he might take away the body of Jesus. And Pilate granted it. So he came and took away his body.

Scenes 1–3

The Initial Pregnant Descent: The Auspicious Burial,
in the New Garden Tomb, on Preparation
[39] And Nicodemus also came—who had come to him first by night—carrying a mixture of myrrh and aloes, weighing about a hundred pounds. [40] So they took the body of Jesus and bound it in linen cloths with the aromatic oils, as the custom is among the Judeans for burial. [41] And in the place where he was crucified there was a garden, and in the garden a new tomb where no one had ever yet been laid. [42] There, therefore, because of the Preparation of the Judeans, because the tomb was near, they placed Jesus.

Running to the Tomb (Peter and the Beloved)
20   [1] Now on the first day of the week [*sabbatōn*], Mary Magdalene came early, while it was still dark, to the tomb; and she saw that the stone had been taken away from the tomb. [2] So she ran and came to Simon Peter and to the other disciple whom Jesus loved, and said to them, "They have taken away the Lord from the tomb, and we do not know where they have placed him." [3] So Peter went out, and the other disciple, and they were coming to the tomb. [4] They both ran together, but the other disciple ran ahead, faster then Peter, and came first to the tomb. [5] And bending down he saw the linen cloths lying there. Yet he did not go in. [6] Then Simon Peter came, following him; and he went into the tomb; and he saw the linen cloths lying there, [7] and the cloth which had been on his head not lying with the linen cloths but apart, wrapped up into one place. [8] Then the other disciple, who had come to the tomb first, also went in, and he saw and believed; [9] for as yet they did not know the scripture, that it was necessary [*dei*] that he rise from the dead. [10] Then the disciples went back again to their home.

Turning at the Tomb (Jesus Appears to Mary Magdalene)
[11] But Mary stood at the tomb, outside, crying. As she wept she bent down into the tomb, [12] and she saw two angels in white, sitting one at the head and the other at the feet where the body of Jesus had lain. [13] And they said to her, "Woman, why are you crying?" She said to them, "They have taken away my Lord and I

do not know where they have laid him." [14] Saying this she turned back and saw Jesus standing, but she did not know that it was Jesus. [15] Jesus said to her, "Woman why are you weeping? Whom do you seek?" She, thinking he was the gardener, said to him, "Sir [*Kyrie*], if you have removed him, tell me where you have laid him, and I will take him away." [16] Jesus said to her, "Mary." She, turning, said to him in Hebrew, "Rabbouni," which means "Teacher." [17] Jesus said to her, "Touch me no more, for I have not yet ascended to the Father. But go to my brothers and say to them, "I am ascending to my Father and to your Father, to my God and to your God." [18] So Mary Magdalene went and announced to the disciples, "I have seen the Lord," and that he had told these things to her.

The Ascent to God Is Completed (Bringing Greater Unity)

Scenes 1–2

Jesus Appears to the Disciples
[19] On the evening of that day, the first of the week [*sabbatōn*], when the doors were closed where the disciples were for fear of the Judeans, Jesus came and stood in their midst and said to them, "Peace to you." [20] And saying this he showed them his hands and his side. The disciples were joyful when they saw the Lord. [21] Then he said to them again, "Peace to you. As the Father has sent me, so I send you." [22] And saying this he breathed on them and said, "Receive the Holy Spirit. [23] Whose sins you forgive, they are forgiven them; whose sins you retain, they are retained."

Jesus and Thomas
[24] Now Thomas, one of the twelve, called the twin, was not with them when Jesus came. [25] So the other disciples said to him, "We have seen the Lord." But he said to them, "Unless I see in his hands the mark of the nails, and put [lit., throw] my finger into the place of the nails, and put my hand into his side, I will not believe." [26] And after eight days the disciples were again within and Thomas with them. The doors were closed, but Jesus came and stood in their midst and said, "Peace to you." [27] Then he said to Thomas, "Bring your finger here and see my hands, and bring your hand here and put it into my side, and do not be unbelieving, but believing." [28] Thomas answered and said to him, "My Lord and my God." [29] Jesus said to him, "Because you have seen me, you have believed. Blessed are those who have not seen and yet believe."

Conclusion, Part 2: The Writing and Its Purpose
[30] There were many other signs that Jesus did in the presence of his disciples which are not written in this book. [31] But these are written, that you may believe that Jesus is the Anointed, the Son of God, and that believing you may have life in his name.

Epilogue: The Word Becomes Community in the World

Scenes 1–3

Fishing: The Failure

21 ¹After these things Jesus revealed himself again to the disciples at the sea of Tiberias; and he revealed himself as follows. ²There were together Simon Peter, and Thomas called the Twin, Nathanael from Cana of Galilee, the sons of Zebedee, and two others of his disciples. ³Simon Peter said to them, "I am going fishing." They said to him, "We will come with you." They went out and got up into the boat. And in that night they caught nothing. * ⁴But as it was dawn Jesus stood on the shore. The disciples however did not know that it was Jesus. ⁵So Jesus said to them, "Children, do you have any bite of fish?" They answered him, "No." * ⁶Then he said to them, "Throw the net over the right side [lit., part, *meros*] of the boat, and you will find some." So they threw it, and then they could not draw it in because of the number of the fish.

The Recognition

⁷Then the disciple whom Jesus loved said to Peter, "It is the Lord." * Simon Peter, hearing that it was the Lord, girded his apron about him, for he was stripped down, and threw himself into the sea. * ⁸The other disciples came in the little boat—for they were not far from the land (but about two hundred cubits)—dragging the net with the fish.

The Meal Pepared

⁹When they climbed out on the land they saw a charcoal fire lying there with the fish lying on it, and bread. ¹⁰Jesus said to them, "Bring some of the fish which you have just caught." ¹¹So Simon Peter went up and drew the net to land, full of great fish—one hundred and fifty three. And though there were so many, the net was not broken [lit., divided]. * ¹²Jesus said to them, "Come and have breakfast." And none of the disciples dared ask him, "Who are you?"; for they knew it was the Lord. * ¹³Jesus came and took the bread and gave it to them, and likewise the fish. ¹⁴This was now the third time that Jesus was revealed to the disciples after being raised from the dead.

Practical Outcome: Starting Over

Peter is Rehabilitated . . .

[15] So when they had breakfasted, Jesus said to Simon Peter, "Simon, son of John, do you love me more than these?" He said to him, "Yes, Lord, you know that I love you." He said to him, "Feed my lambs." [16] He said to him again a second time, "Simon, son of John, do you love me?" He said to him, "Yes, Lord, you know that I love you." He said to him, "Shepherd my sheep." [17] He said to him the third time, "Simon, son of John, do you love me?" Peter became sad because he asked him the third time, "Do you love me?" And he said to him, "Lord, you know all; you know that I love you." He said to him, "Feed my little sheep."

. . . And Commissioned

[18] "Amen, amen, I say to you, when you were young you girded yourself and walked about where you willed [*thelō*]. But when you are old you will stretch out your hands, and another will gird you and bring you where you do not will" [*thelō*]. [19] This he said signifying by what kind of death he would glorify God. And having said this he said to him, "Follow me."

Peter's Vision of the Beloved Abiding

[20] Peter turned and saw, following, the disciple whom Jesus loved, who at the supper had lain down on his breast and had said , "Lord, who is it that is going to betray you?" [21] So seeing him, Peter said to Jesus, "Lord, *for him what?*" [22] Jesus said to him, "If I will [*thelō*] that he abide until I come, *what to you?* You follow me."

And the Misunderstanding

[23] So this word [*logos*] went out among the brothers that that disciple would not die. But Jesus did not say to him that he would not die, but, "If I will that he abide until I come."

Conclusion, Part 3: The Witnessing and the Writing (Both Evoking Larger Worlds, of Knowing and of Being)

[24] This is the disciple who bears witness to these things and has written these things, and we know that his witness is true.

[25] But there are also many other things which Jesus did, which, if they were to be written down one by one, I suppose that not even the world could contain the books that would be written [lit., the written books, *ta graphomena biblia*].

The Story of the Adulteress (7:53–8:11)[1]

[53] Then each went away home; [1] but Jesus went to the Mountain of Olives. [2] Early in the morning he was there again in the temple, and all the people came to him. And he sat and taught them. [3] But the scribes and Pharisees brought a woman who had been caught in adultery, and standing her in the middle, [4] they said to him, "Teacher, this woman was caught in the very act of adultery. [5] Now in the law, Moses commanded us to stone such women. And you—what do you say?" [6] This they said tempting him, that they might have something with which to accuse him. But Jesus bent down and with his finger began writing on the ground. [7] When they continued asking him, he straightened himself up and said to them, "Let the one who is without sin among you be the first to throw a stone at her." [8] And again bending down he wrote on the ground. [9] But they hearing this went away one by one, beginning with the elders. And he was left alone with the woman still before him. [10] Then straightening himself up Jesus said to her, "Woman, where are they? Has no one condemned you?" [11] She said, "No one, Lord." Then Jesus said to her, "Neither do I condemn you. Go your way, and do not sin again."

1. *This remarkable passage was not part of the original gospel. It is not in the oldest manuscripts, and apparently was inserted into John's text about the year 200. Its origin remains elusive.*

THE COMMENTARY: BOOK ONE
THE YEARS OF JESUS' LIFE

Part 1 □ The First Year

AN OPTIMISTIC INTRODUCTION TO JESUS' LIFE

A Portrait Both from the Beginning Year and from the Positive Side of Life

Part 1 constitutes an initial synthesis of the entire gospel. First there is the striking overture, the prologue, which introduces both Part 1 and the gospel as a whole (1:1–18). Then there is a week-long drama of revelation-and-response—a summary both of the work of God (in John the Baptizer, Jesus, and the disciples), and of the disciples' advance towards believing (1:19–2:11). And finally, through a Passover in which Jesus cleanses the temple and speaks cryptically of his own death and resurrection, there is an intimation of the decisive event which will form the body of believers (2:12–22).

The dominant part of the text, lengthwise at least, consists of the large central section, the week-long revelatory drama, but it is the opening prologue and the culminating Passover which provide much of the context and meaning.

There is not much conflict in this initial synthesis. There are indeed some suggestions of tension with the Jews. But overall, the sense of conflict is muted. As was said earlier (in chap. 5) in this section, life looks good.

The emphasis, therefore, is not on conflict but on cooperation. God created and revealed; humans heard and believed. John the Baptist bore witness, and Jesus did something even greater: he took away sin ("the sin of the world," 1:29), and he brought in spirit. The disciples, despite some skepticism and slowness, perceived the reality and grew in understanding. Though life is shadowed by sin and death ("Destroy this sanctuary, . . ." 2:19) there is an abundance of fine wedding wine (at Cana) and an intimation that destruction is not supreme (". . . and in three days I will raise it up"). Conflict, though present, is swallowed up in a greater world of harmonious order and restoration.

And over all these elements there hovers a sense of mystery, a suggestion of an encompassing divine knowledge. Chapter 1 begins by telling that it was through the Word that "all things" (*panta,* 1:3) were made, and at various stages there are indications that Jesus has immense resources of knowledge and power. For instance, he knows and sees Nathanael even before they have met, and he promises that there are far greater revelations yet to come (1:47–51). Thus in 1:1–2:22 there is an atmosphere not only of basic cooperation and order but also, to some degree, of divine providence and mystery.

Reflecting Creation . . .

As mentioned in discussing the structure of the gospel as a whole, the episodes between the prologue and the first Passover are set on a series of consecutive or near-consecutive days: "The next day. . . . The next day. . . . The next day. . . . And on the third day . . ." (1:29,35,43; 2:1). The significance of these phrases is disputed. Some scholars downplay them. Others regard them as highly significant, as echoing the seven days of creation; and occasionally, partly to assure a total of seven, researchers tend to inject an extra day—to see the call of the first two disciples as being on one day ("they abode with him that day," 1:39) and the call of Peter, which immediately follows (1:40–42), as on another. (For references and discussion, see Brown, 105–06.)

In assessing these conflicting opinions, two things need to be said. On the one hand, the succession of days must, indeed, be of some significance. One could scarcely ask for a clearer literary clue to the text's structure, and also, in some degree, to its meaning. The repetitive phrases ("The next day . . .") are placed in the most conspicuous positions possible—at the very beginning of a series of successive episodes. To ignore or dismiss them is like driving along the highway and trying to find one's bearings on the basis of everything except the road signs. At the same time, to claim that there is an extra day, one which breaks the pattern, threatens to undermine the pattern itself. One may invoke a pattern-breaking sign only if an explanation is given of why the pattern should be broken.

It would seem that the best way to resolve the issue is to look at the text of Genesis. The essential structure of the first account of creation (Genesis 1:1–2:4a) is extremely simple: six days, followed by a seventh day which breaks the pattern. In most editions of the Hebrew and Greek, and also in some translations (e.g., RSV, NEB), this pattern is clear. The text begins "In the beginning," and then there are six sections, each of which concludes with a reference to the emerging days: ". . . one day . . . a second day . . . a sixth day" (cf. Genesis 1). The seventh day, however, is different. It breaks the pattern so badly that in later centuries it was assigned to a different chapter (cf. Gen 1:1–2:4a). The most obvious aspect of this pattern breaking is that even though the phrase "seventh day" is used three times, none of the instances occur in the usual position, at the section's conclusion, but rather all three are gathered in and around the section's center (cf. Gen 2:2–3). The essential point is that the seven-day pattern has a clear exception.

Given such a context, such a literary background, it becomes more plausible to speak not only of a succession of days, totaling six, but also of a further day which breaks the pattern.

The relationship between the two pattern-breaking days appears to be quite complex. In Genesis it is the day when *God rested* (*kata-pauō*, "pause/rest"). In John it is the day when *the disciples rested with Jesus* (*menō*, "remain/stay/rest/ abide"). The two are quite different, yet the differences are like two sides of the same coin. There is in both a sense of standing outside the flow of things, of resting in a time-surpassing dimension.

The overall impression—without pursuing the complex details—is that John has indeed used the seven-day structure of Genesis, but in doing so has made important adaptations. The literary indicators for the series of successive days are placed not (as in Gen 1) at the conclusion of the various sections (". . . one day . . . a second day"), but at the beginning ("The next day. . . . The next day . . ."). And the exceptional day, the day of rest, is placed not at the conclusion of the entire series, but at the center. In other words, while Genesis highlighted the succession of days by means of one rhetorical technique (by placing them at the end of the various passages) John uses a technique which is complementary (placing them at the beginning). And while Genesis, breaking its own pattern, places the references to the seventh day not at the end of its final passage but at its center (cf. Gen 2:2–3), John again provides a variation: he places the day of rest at the center of the entire text. Thus the ancient sense of harmony, as found in Gen 1:1–2:4a, is maintained in varied form.

. . . And Evoking the Resurrection

But in John there is something new. By culminating the series with "And on the third day . . ." the gospel manages, while building carefully on the OT, to make way for a series of allusions to a specifically NT idea—resurrection in three days. The evoking of the resurrection is seen more clearly when one looks at the outline of 1:1–2:22 as a whole:

"*In the beginning* was the Word . . ." (vv 1–18);

. . .

"And this is the witness of John . . ." (19–28);

"*The next day* he saw Jesus coming . . ." (29–34);

"*The next day* again John was standing with two . . . disciples . . ." (35–42)

". . . and they abode with him *that day*" (39);

"*The next day* he willed to go forth to Galilee . . ." (43–51);

" *And on the third day* there was a wedding . . ." (2:1–11);

. . .

"*After this* he descended to Capernaum . . . and he abode there not many days. The Passover was at hand . . . and Jesus ascended to Jerusalem . . . 'and *in three days* I will raise it up' . . . '*in three days*' . . . When therefore he was raised from the dead. . . ." (2:12–22).

The continuity between "third day" (2:1) and "three days" (2:19) is hardly an accident. In no other text does John use "three" or "third" concerning days. Hence, rather than invoke an unlikely coincidence, it seems more reasonable to conclude that this is part of a reasoned strategy, a technique for building narrative continuity. Thus the final day of the week ("the third day") is linked to the day of the resurrection.

To some degree, then, the timing of the concluding episode (concerning Capernaum and Jerusalem) is rather like the timing of the opening verse of the prologue ("In the beginning"): it is quite distinct from the week-long drama, yet it maintains a certain continuity with it. "In the beginning" looks to a remote past. "After this" looks to the way ahead, and it brings up the first of three Passovers, those Passovers which, when taken together, form a fateful unity and open the way to a new future. Thus the beginning and conclusion balance each other, at least to some degree, and the successive days fill up the intervening time. There is sharp development, but there is also careful coherence.

The essential point is that, beginning with the prologue, the various chronological references in 1:1–2:22 help to weave the entire text into a unity, a unity which in various ways, including the evoking of the resurrection, both reflects and surpasses the harmonious seven-day unity of the first account of creation.

The Prologue

The voice of the mystical eagle
   sounds in . . . [our] ears.
Let our exterior sense
   catch the sound that passes;
let our mind within
   penetrate the meaning that abides.

Eriugena, introducing John's Prologue,
ca. A.D. 860 (trans. by O'Meara, 1988, 158)

The prologue is a summary of history and reality. It is "a description of the history of salvation" (Brown, 23–24), and through that description it imparts a sense of reality.

Its basic impact is immensely positive. To some degree, of course, it is perplexing, particularly since it alludes, first and last (vv 1 and 18), to the fact that, in one way, God is immensely distant and other. And it is also quite sobering, for it indicates that life is surrounded by darkness. Thus it brings out the fact that at a certain point vision gives way to darkness or mystery. But amid the encircling darkness it has a keen sense of the reality of light, a sense of the way in which the distant God has entered into the flow of human history and has enabled people, regardless of the circumstances of their birth, to become, in one way or another, children of God.

Scholarly discussion of the prologue has centered on three factors—its origin, structure, and meaning. In this study attention centers largely on its structure and meaning.

Structure

It is sometimes said that the prologue does not form a clear unity with the gospel as a whole, that it stands out, particularly by the sublimity of some of its poetry and the uniqueness, within the fourth gospel, of some of its vocabulary (cf. especially, "the Word," "grace and truth," and "fullness," 1:1,14,17 [Brown, 19]). These basic observations, concerning sublimity of poetry and uniqueness of vocabulary, are essentially correct, but such features are not reliable indicators of disunity. It is altogether appropriate that a text should begin on a note that is particularly striking and memorable. Examples range from the opening lines of Genesis and of the epistle to the Hebrews, to John Bunyan's "As I walked through the wilderness of this world . . ." and Charles Dickens's "It was the best of times, it was the worst of times. . . ." John has done the same, and has done it exceptionally well. As for the terms which occur in the prologue only, it is very risky logic to jump from the unusualness of a few terms to the conclusion that the passage in question is in some way alien. (For discussion of this procedure—"the Hapax Legomenon Fallacy"—see M. Goulder, 1985, esp. 14–16.) For instance, one of the first major titles used of Jesus—"lamb of God" (1:29,36)—is never again used in the gospel. But that does not indicate that the lamb-of-God texts had an earlier independent existence. Rather than make such a leap into the dark, it may be more profitable to ask whether the terms in question function well in their present position. And it would seem that they do. The term "Word," for instance, evokes the transcendent creative God, but once that has been done, once the setting has been established, there is no need to go on repeating it. This is all the more true because in v 14 the Word becomes flesh. Thus, the Word has not disappeared from the gospel, but rather has become something else. Similarly with the terms "fullness" and "grace and truth." They are broad background terms which function well in the role they have been given—as broad background to the rest of the gospel. There is no need, therefore, to see disunity between the prologue and what follows.

In recent research, dominated as it has been by the general idea of oral tradition and the more specific idea of the influence of various liturgies, the idea has gained ground that the prologue consists largely of a pre-existing hymn, a hymn which has been edited and to which other more prosaic material has been added. There are good reasons for this view, particularly the fact that at various points the rhythm of the text changes from that of soaring poetry to straightforward prose. The references to John (the baptizer; vv 6–8,15) tend to be seen as especially obtrusive, and they are frequently referred to as patent interpolations (cf. Bultmann, 16–18; Schnackenburg, 1:225; Brown, 3–4; Haenchen, 1:108–9). As a result of this approach, discussion of the structure of the prologue has frequently been overshadowed by the effort to isolate and reconstruct the hypothetical hymn.

But no hymn has emerged, at least not one on which scholars agree. Even parts of vv 1–5 are in dispute. (For opinions, see Brown, 22.) Nor has the church ever used it as a hymn—unlike, say, Mary's canticle (Luke 1:46–55)—even though it has employed it greatly, particularly as a blessing over the sick and over newly baptized children (Brown, 18). It is not surprising, then, that Giblin (1985, 94), having noted a number of important discrepancies between the content of hymns and that of the prologue, concludes that, as it stands, it is not primarily a hymn.

The hypothesis of a half-hidden hymn is not only unworkable, it is unnecessary. There is another way of accounting for the changing style, for this interweaving of soaring poetry with simple prose. The interweaving is a way of expressing, through the very form of the language, one of the prologue's central ideas—the descent of the (soaring, poetic) Word into the (prosaic) reality of human life. In other words, the increasing mixing of Word with flesh is reflected in the increasing mixing of poetry with prose, and the persistent failure of scholars to disentangle the poetry is a reflection of something more basic: God—insofar as God is known—cannot be disentangled from humanity.

As indicated in the introduction (chap. 6), this gradual departure from the (divine) language of poetry is not an isolated phenomenon. Again and again, in diverse ways, John's gospel leaves aside language which suggests divinity and takes on a form which is much simpler, much closer to prosaic humanity.

One may proceed therefore—as several scholars have been doing in any case (see review articles by Ramaroson [1976] and Culpepper, [1981])—by concentrating on the final form of the text.

In reviewing the prologue and the variety of opinions, it may be observed that there is considerable agreement on two fundamental points. First, in comparison with the opening verses, v 6 ("There was a person . . .") involves a basic change of content and rhythm. Furthermore, in v 14 ("And the Word became flesh . . .") the text reaches a new level; it states its message in a way quite distinct from all that precedes. In other words, the first explicit references to John and the incarnation represent significant moments of change or development. It is for that reason that a number of editions and translations use vv 6 and 14 as guides or partial guides in subdividing the text (e.g., UBSGNT, RSV).

The hypothesis put forward here is that it is these first explicit references to John and the incarnation which provide the basic divisions of the text. Thus, the prologue is to be divided into three parts: vv 1–5, 6–13, and 14–18. However, this threefold structure cannot be fully understood except within the context of the prologue's overall meaning, for it is the carefully unified meaning which provides the basic clues to the most perplexing aspects of the structure.

The meaning centers on the fact, mentioned earlier, that the prologue is largely a description of salvation history. In simplified Christian terms, salvation history may be said to involve three elements: the revealing God who creates and makes it all possible; the OT (from the prophets to John the Baptist); and the NT, or incarnation. In the hypothesis being proposed here, it is these three elements which underlie the three basic parts of the prologue. The first part (vv 1–5) provides basic background —the existence of the Word with God and the general implications of that existence. Next, on a very different rhythm, comes a summary of the OT as embodied in the culminating prophetic figure of John the Baptist and as foreshadowing the coming of the incarnation (vv 6–13). Finally (vv 14–18), there is a description of the incarnation which sets it in the context of all who believe, and particularly, through the figures of John the Baptist and Moses, in the context of the OT. Thus there is a threefold division which, to some degree at least, is time-based: the beginning, the OT, the NT.

This division seems clear, yet when the three sections are examined, it is found that there is great overlapping in their contents. Such overlapping may at first suggest that the analysis is wrong, yet on reflection it makes sense. There is no way that the old prophetic era can be separated from the Creator-Word who is at the beginning, nor that the era of the incarnation can be separated from all that precedes it. The NT lies hidden in the OT, the OT is revealed in the NT, and the Word is in both. Or, to put it another way, what we are dealing with is not a straight line but a spiral or staircase, a literary structure which simultaneously repeats and intensifies; it recalls what is past, but it also moves on to something new.

The basic structure which will emerge, therefore, is that of a carefully built threefold spiral. This idea is not new. It has already been proposed, with some variation, by de la Potterie (1984).[1] These matters must now be examined in greater detail.

---

[1] In recent years some of the most notable contributions to the debate on the structure of the prologue have been those of I. de la Potterie ("Structure du Prologue," 1984) and C. H. Giblin ("Two Complementary . . . Structures," 1985). De la Potterie takes up the idea of the spiral or staircase— it is found already in others, but not fully developed—and he applies it, verse by verse, to the entire

Meaning

When the prologue is read aloud, and read well, it has unity and power. Its three-part summary of salvation history contains three increasingly clear views of the presence of God, and amid widespread darkness it suggests a spreading vision of light.

[1:1–5] Salvation History: The Origin and Basic Dynamics.   At first the divine presence is pictured as something awesomely ethereal. To set the mood it opens with "In the beginning. . . ." In reading those three words a public reader does well to lower the voice and pause momentarily—as one might in reading "Once upon a time. . . ." For just as "Once upon a time" suggests a world which is wonderfully distant, so "In the beginning" evokes a sense of something distant and awesome. In such an atmosphere, and only in such an atmosphere, is it appropriate to begin speaking of the Word.

As a human word may be intimate and yet distinct (it is intimate insofar as it reflects a person—proceeds from a person's body and spirit—yet, because it goes out from the person, it is distinct), so the Word, in relationship to God, is intimate yet distinct. It is the distinctness which is first emphasized: "In the beginning *was the Word.*" Like a lone star far beyond the edge of time, the Word at first seems

---

prologue. In retrospect he seems to have made one significant mistake: partly because he does not force himself, at the beginning, to lay down clearly the basis on which his division rests, and partly because of the way he reads the similarity between the two references to John the Baptist (vv 6–8, 15), he sets John not only at the beginning of part two, but also at the beginning of part three. In other words, he divides the text at 1, 6, and 15 (not 14). But that is not John's place. He may indeed have inaugurated the intermediate stage, but in the final verses, when the incarnation has explicitly arrived, John's role is no longer a leading one. The spiral has not just gone around; it has moved forward. John to some degree is still present—his witness is integral to understanding the incarnation and to the prologue's description of it—but he is now in the incarnation's shadow. It is with v 14, not 15, that the prologue reaches its final and climactic level.

Apart however from misplacing v 14, de la Potterie's analysis represents a major advance. His description of the entire prologue as a triple spiral ("*trois mouvements . . . en spirale,*" 374), and particularly his perception of the text's repetitiveness as something positive, as something which expresses a deliberate literary procedure ("*répétition progressive*" 359), opens the way toward appreciating the text's unity and meaning.

Giblin, working independently (1985, esp. 93–95, 99–101), does not come as close as does de la Potterie to unraveling the threefold spiral, and he obscures his own discussion of the structure by injecting into it a debatable thesis about the text's origin. But he brings out something which de la Potterie underestimates: the likelihood that the prologue, as well as having a progressive structure, has also a further complementary structure which is chiastic or concentric. He notes, for instance, that there is a balance between the opening and closing references to God (vv 1–2, 18), and between the references to John (vv 6–8, 15); and he indicates that the whole structure centers around the idea of becoming a child of God and on the contrast between those who do and do not believe in such a God (vv 10–13). What is particularly significant in Giblin's position, however, is not so much the basic idea of a chiasm—many others had had essentially the same idea—as his refusal to choose one kind of structure at the expense of the other. The acceptance of two structures, one complementing the other, seems amply justified. It corresponds to the delicately complex structural data and also to the text's general tendency towards ambiguity and richness of meaning. The three-part structure puts the emphasis on the unfolding of God's purpose—on the revelation. The chiastic structure, however, puts the emphasis on the response—on those central verses (10–13) which highlight the idea of becoming children of God. Together they form a balanced picture of what the gospel is all about.

Staley, working independently of Giblin, confirms the perception of a delicately wrought chiasm.

eerily remote. For a brief moment even the mention of God is withheld. There is no explanation, no explicit speculation, just a simple statement of existence: the Word was.

But in that remoteness there is intimacy: "and the Word was with (*pros*) God." The Greek expression is sufficiently ambiguous to suggest both presence and relationship. Then the text continues: "and the Word was God." This does not destroy the distinction, which is subtly indicated by the Greek wording and implicitly borne out by the remainder of the gospel, between the Word and the full meaning of God. But it indicates clearly, as background to understanding Jesus, that between the Word and God there is the closest possible personal union, an actual identity. And, partly in case the prologue's opening phrase may have left any lingering idea that this personal union did not exist from the beginning, the text then adds (v 2): "He was in the beginning with God," (*pros ton theon*). After the circling parallelism of the opening phrases (v 1), the effect of v 2, with its slightly different rhythm, is to bring the pieces together and draw a line: In the beginning the Word was with God.

Part of the overall effect of the spiralling phrases and of the line drawn under them is to evoke a variety of cultural backgrounds—Hellenistic and Jewish— which deal with the notion of the Word (cf. Brown, 519–24; Haenchen, 1:143– 49). The central effect, however, is not to crowd the mind with background cultural details, even religious ones, but to focus it, with contemplative simplicity, on an elusive essence, on a reality which seems overwhelmingly distant, but which contains within itself a personal union, and which, despite all its distance, is the first reality of all, the beginning.

Having established a distant still point, the text goes on, with smooth rapidity, to speak first of creation (v 3), then of God's life-giving presence among people (v 4), and finally of something that is neither distant nor still—the tension between light and darkness (v 5).

The image of creation ("All things were made through him . . .") as something which proceeded from God's *Word* suggests the idea that creation speaks, that it reveals something of God.

It is not only through creation, however, that the Word speaks. It is also through life: "In him was life, and the life was the light of humans." In other words, the Word gives life, and life speaks to people; it becomes a light for them. "When Life is recognized and accepted it is Light" (Hoskyns, 137). It is often debated, frequently as an either/or question, whether such life-giving refers to the life given at and after creation or, rather, to the life given through Jesus, in the incarnation (cf. Brown, 26–27). This either/or approach is questionable. As the immediate context suggests, the life-giving process refers first of all to God's initial giving of life, at and after creation. But within the larger context of the gospel as a whole and the NT as a whole—a context where "life" and "light" are frequently used as central concepts to describe Jesus and his mission—within that larger context such a reference to the giving of life and light must also evoke the incarnation. Thus the diverse literary contexts (the gospel and the NT), both of which are pertinent, give the text a certain ambiguity, and they stretch it all the way across history, from the time of creation to that of the incarnation. It is understandable therefore that the verse which follows the text is no longer speaking of the past but rather of the present: "And the light shines. . . ." With a minimum of words, and some subtle transitions or ambiguities, the focus has moved from a remote beginning to the present.

The rich ambiguity of v 4, its reference to both creation and the incarnation, may, perhaps, be a clue to a notorious ambiguity in v 3—the fact that the conclusion of the verse, a verse dealing with creation, may also be read, depending on the punctuation, as the beginning of the sentence in verse 4—the verse which moves away from creation towards the incarnation. The RSV, through a note, takes account of both possibilities, and, beginning with the manuscripts, opinion on the matter has always been deeply divided (see esp. Wescott, 4, 18–31; Schnackenburg, 1:239–40; Haenchen, 1:113). The question raised by v 4, where the ambiguity appears to be deliberate, is whether the ambiguity of v 3 is also deliberate. More specifically, should the conclusion's ambiguity—its ability to fit either with the preceding reference to the original creation or to the subsequent allusion to life-giving and the incarnation—should that ambiguity be read as part of the larger pattern of subtle moves and transitions by which the text descends from its soaring beginning right into the present? The original text, as far as is known, had no punctuation. Therefore, while the ambiguity may indeed have been exploited doctrinally (the Arians put the conclusion of v 3 with v 4 and then used it for their purposes) it was not bad copying or doctrinal tendentiousness which first brought it into being. It was always in the text. It is possible therefore to see it not as a problem to be solved, a carelessness to be corrected, but as part of a careful literary strategy, a sophisticated way of teasing the mind and helping it to focus on one of the gospel's basic ideas—the continuity between creation and the incarnation, between creation and redemption (cf. Bultmann, 46; Kysar, 1984, 16).

The idea of deliberate ambiguity finds corroboration not only in later texts such as the conversation with Nicodemus (3:1–21), but in the very next verse: "The light shines in the darkness, and the darkness has not *katelaben*. . . ." The Greek, *kata-lambanō,* is ambiguous. Like "to master" in English, it can mean either overcome or understand. To say that the darkness did not master the light is an appropriately positive way to conclude the first part of the prologue. It closes the scene around a shining light. But it has also an undercurrent of tragedy, an allusion to a terrible failure to accept or understand the light. Granskou (1985, 7–10), has argued strongly that in the context of ancient writing practices, particularly the practices of constructing literary riddles and of using irony, it is a mistake to attempt to regard one meaning as right and the other as wrong. Both have their place.

Part of the initial impression, then, of these early verses, is not only of soaring poetry and theology, but of a correspondingly elevated literary sophistication. The final effect, however, goes beyond mere technique. In a way that analysis and commentary cannot articulate, these opening lines draw into one all reality—everything from the eternal Word to the shadow of tragedy—and they impart to that reality a pervasive sense of wholeness.

[1:6–13] Salvation History: The Preparatory Stage. These verses, which begin with a sharp change of rhythm, tell of John and of his witness to the light which was coming into the world. The text does not state clearly to what period they refer. They do not go back explicitly to the beginning (as did v 1), but neither is it stated with explicit clarity (as it is in v 14) that the period in question is that of the incarnation. Instead they are set, rather vaguely, in between.

Modern scholarly discussion has tended to fragment the text, first, by saying that the verses dealing with John the Baptist (6–8) are alien to the basic rhythm and message of the prologue, and, further, by setting up an either/or debate in which most of the verses dealing with the coming of the light (9–12) are seen by some researchers as referring to the period of the OT (Westcott, Bernard, and in a modified way, Schnackenburg; cf. Brown, 29); and by others as referring to the incarnation, or to the ministry of Jesus (Bauer, Käsemann, Brown; cf. Brown, 30).

This debate is an expanded variation of that which surrounds v 4—the question of whether the process of granting life and light refers to the period after creation or, rather, to the time of the incarnation.

In this later debate, as in the case of v 4, and, indeed, as also in the case of the ambiguities in vv 3 and 5, it seems better, as Dodd (1953, 284) suggests, to avoid an either/or approach.

There is significant evidence that the entire section (vv 6–13) refers first of all to the OT period. Its immediate context, which has to be regarded as a basic clue to its meaning, sets it very clearly in an intermediate position—after "the beginning" but before the basic statement of the incarnation (v 14). Furthermore, the figure of John (vv 6–8) is not an alien intrusion with no bearing on the OT/NT debate. He embodies the OT and, set as he is at the beginning of vv 6–13, he acts as a basic clue to its first meaning. As has often been noticed, he is introduced in a style which is "reminiscent of . . . the OT" (Haenchen, 1:116; cf. Bultmann, 50). And he epitomized the OT. "As the last prophet, the last interpreter of the Law, he brought the preparatory discipline to its final application" (Westcott, 5–6, esp. 6). Or, in the words of the first evangelist: "It was towards John that all the prophecies of the prophets and of the Law were leading" (Matt 11:13, JB). Furthermore, when the text moves away from John and begins (v 9) to speak of the coming of the light into the world, it does so in a way which is eminently appropriate to the OT: "The true light was coming." The two words, which in Greek are separated, "was . . . coming," are clearly open to the idea of a process which was gradual, progressive—in other words, a process like the OT (Westcott, 7). It is true, of course, that the phrase is ambiguous. Grammatically, "was . . . coming" may also be taken as a complex unit, a periphrasis, and as such the emphasis on a gradual process is less pronounced. In fact, the whole of v 9 is ambiguous. Part of this ambiguity consists of the fact that it may refer not only to the coming of the light (RSV), but also to the coming of people (KJV: "the Light which lighteth *every man that cometh* into the world"). In other words there is a faint suggestion not so much of the light coming to people as of people coming to the light. At a later stage (3:21) such an idea will be stated clearly. The essential point for the moment, however, is not the detail of the ambiguity, but the ambiguity itself, the fact that the text may be read legitimately in two quite distinct ways. Given such an atmosphere of ambiguity it does not seem reasonable to deprive "was . . . coming" of one of the first things it suggests—a gradual process such as that found in the OT.

The same applies, to some extent at least, to the verses which follow. As Schnackenburg (1:256–58) indicates the failure of the world to recognize the light (v 10) is perfectly capable of being seen as referring to the time before the incarnation, and was so interpreted, with virtual unanimity, for eighteen centuries. And the account of how he came to what was his own (*ta idia,* "his own place/domain/ home") and of how his own (*hoi idioi*) did not receive him (v 11) is like a repetitious intensification of v 10 and may be applied equally well both to humans in general, because of their pre-incarnation failure to respond to their Creator (cf. Rom 1:18–32), or to the Jews because they rejected Jesus (Schnackenburg, 1:258–61).

As for the main idea of vv 12–13—belief generates birth, a supernatural birth —such an idea also is not alien to the OT. When Paul, for instance, speaks of the way in which sheer faith generates birth, the model he uses is from the OT— the case of the children of Abraham (cf. esp. Rom 4:18–25, Gal 4:23). And when the infancy narratives (Matt 1–2, Luke 1–2) tell of the supernatural birth of Jesus, they do so in a way which is thoroughly grounded in the thought and birth narratives of the OT (Brown, 1977, 156–57, 184–96, 318–28; Fitzmyer, 1981, 309, 318). Thus, as far as the NT writers are concerned, God's granting of supernatural birth was already present in the OT.

The basic point is clear: The central section of the prologue, set as it is in an intermediate position between "the beginning" and the incarnation (v 14), may reasonably be read as referring first of all to the intermediate section of history— the OT.

It is also true, however, as Brown (29) observes, that "most of the phrases used in vv 10–12 appear in the gospel as a description of the ministry of Jesus," and there is something to be said for the further observation that vv 11–12 may be seen as a summary of the gospel. Furthermore, in the final verses, when the emphasis is on the idea of becoming God's children (vv 12–13), the text shows a very close affinity with Johannine thought about the incarnation (Brown, 29).

What emerges, therefore, is that the text as a whole is ambiguous. As an intermediate text, one which begins with the embodiment of the OT (John), it refers first of all to the OT period. But as it advances, as it draws closer to the statement of the incarnation (v 14), it begins to express itself more and more through the words and concepts of the NT.

Lurking behind this ambiguity is a major theological issue which has never been satisfactorily resolved—the relevance of the OT to the Christian church. (For discussion and bibliography, see Mayo, 1982.) Ultimately, it is within that larger debate that the ambiguity of vv 6–13 needs to be discussed. If the two testaments are fundamentally different, then they should be kept clearly apart. But if there is between them a profound continuity, then it is altogether appropriate that a summary of the essence of the OT period, such as that found in vv 6–13, should have a certain ambiguity—that it should present the OT in a way which shows it as being a preparation for the NT, shows it as already containing within itself some of the basic elements of the later dispensation.

Some commentaries lack appreciation for the role of literary ambiguity. This is particularly conspicuous in Bultmann (17) and Schnackenburg (1:253–54). Both realize that the central part of the prologue, especially vv 9–12, is capable of referring either to the pre-incarnation period or to the actual incarnation. But instead of accepting the ambiguity, as Dodd (1953, 284) does, they attribute the pre-incarnation meaning to one author (the composer of the hypothetical hymn) and the other meaning to another (the evangelist who is said to have edited the hymn). In this way they seem to open up a historical background, which in many ways is plausible and fascinating, but which is quite out of control, and which is achieved by implicitly denying the theological and literary sophistication of the finished text—the possibility that a single author is grappling with the transition from one testament or order to another, and that, in so doing, he makes use, very appropriately, of literary ambiguity.

At a more general level, ambiguity is occasionally regarded not as a sophisticated literary technique but as an unfortunate confusion, a problem to be solved. The implication of such a view is that one of the world's greatest verbal composers was incapable of saying something clearly. Such a view does not really make sense, nor does it appreciate what the ambiguity frequently offers—a challenge to the mind and a richness of theological meaning.

What is also lacking is an appreciation of the fact that the text is a spiral or staircase. The principle is mentioned repeatedly (e.g. Brown, 6, 7, 19), but in practice it is not sufficiently applied, and so the repetitiousness of the text—perfectly understandable in a spiral—becomes a problem. The spiral principle is particularly important in dealing with the references to the incarnation. The first such reference—the giving of life and light (v 4)—is brief, cryptic, and ambiguous. The second—the light gave power to become children of God (vv 9–13)—is much more developed, yet it remains somewhat clouded. It is not explicit. Thus through a graded spiral technique the way is prepared for a third refrence, for one which is indeed explicit, resoundingly so: "And the Word became flesh."

[1:14–18] Salvation History: The Incarnation. The third part of the prologue brings its summarizing of salvation history to a climactic conclusion. In a single verse (14) it synthesizes the basic event of the incarnation, and at the same time it begins something equally important—to set the incarnation in the context of history as a whole, the context of the OT and the context of the history of subsequent believers.

The summary of the incarnation, as written in Greek, consists of three consecutive phrases: "And the Word became flesh, and tented among us, and we have seen his glory. . . ." The explicit reference to the Word, when taken in conjunction with the three phrases, is reminiscent of the triple rhythm of v 1 (Brown, 30–31; cf. Schnackenburg, 1:266), and in both cases the three phrases constitute a certain completeness. But instead of a serene completeness within the stillness of God (v 1), a stillness reflected in ". . . was the Word . . . the Word was, . . . the Word was, . . ." the completeness described in v 14 involves three actions which are quite distinct from one another.

"The Word became flesh" describes the inauguration of the incarnation, and it implies that God, or at least God's revelation (the Word) is to be seen in flesh, in other words, in sheer humanity. This humanity, this flesh, *sarx,* may at times be muscular and hot-blooded, but it is also fragile and mortal. In Schnackenburg's words: "*Sarx* [for John] . . . expresses that which is earth-bound (3:6), transient and perishable (6:63)." Schnackenburg goes on immediately to characterize this transient and perishable mode of being as "typically human . . . in contrast to all that is divine and spiritual." The preceding verse (1:13) had suggested something similar: it uses "flesh" as the central term in a list of human elements ("blood . . . will of the flesh . . . will of man") which are contrasted with God (". . . but of God"). Thus the incarnation involves a union of contrasts, a union which is underlined by the fact that in Greek the contrasting terms are juxtaposed: *kai ho logos sarx egeneto.*

When and where is this union to be found? As the text describes it, it is found first of all in a particular moment, in the emergence of the climactic and exemplary figure of Jesus. The *egeneto* (became) in v 14, is the third in a series of three positive uses of the term: "All things *egeneto* (v 3). . . . *Egeneto* a man (John, v 6). . . . And the Word *sarx egeneto* (v 14)." Thus the becoming process in v 14 is the third in a time-based sequence, and as such it has a newness and finality. "The *egeneto* announces a change in the mode of being of the Logos: hitherto he was in glory with his Father (cf. 17:5,24); now he takes on the lowliness of human earthly existence" (Schnackenburg, 1:267; cf. Hoskyns, 138–39).

The union of Word and flesh, however, is not limited to the case of Jesus. It is found also at a much broader level—among all humans. The text suggests that there were intimations of this union in the pre-incarnation period (vv 6–13) and that "we all" have received from it (v 16). It is a union which has implications for everyone. In E. Käsemann's view, as summarized and presented by Brown (35), "the Word became flesh" means that "God is present in the human sphere." It would seem to be this same thought which is also expressed by E. C. Johnson (1983, 210): "The world is full of God. We recognize God's features in one another's faces. That is no less true of the hustlers, hookers, and johns. Compassion and understanding, not condemnation and opprobrium, is what they deserve." Johnson, of course, is speaking from searching experience, not on the basis of v 14, but, given that experience is a valid ingredient in doing theology, his observation provides theological corrobration for the view of Käsemann.

As well as positively affirming God's presence in ordinary human existence, "the Word became flesh" also has a negative purpose—to counter either pretentiousness or shame when these are based on human lineage. As Meister Eckhart comments (1981, 167):

> In this he strikes at the pride of all those who when asked about their relatives respond by pointing to one who holds an important position, but are silent about their own descent. When asked, they say they are the nephews of such and such a bishop, prelate, dean, or the like. There is the story [from Aesop] of the mule who

when asked who his father was answered that his uncle was a thoroughbred, but out of shame hid the fact that his father was an ass.

In the light of this gospel there is no need to hide one's human origin. No matter how humble or shameful, it is in some sense the sanctuary of God.

However, apart from this broad presence, the text, in its primary level as a narrative of events, refers to one particular event, to the incarnation of the Word in Jesus. And as far as describing that event is concerned, what the first phrase of v 14 does is to describe its inauguration: "the Word became flesh."

Then come the two complementary phrases—concerning the tent and the glory.

The image of dwelling among us in a tent seems to refer not so much to the inauguration of the incarnation, and still less to its culmination, but rather to its duration, to the prolonged reality of living among people. The fact that the dwelling is associated with a tent suggests a profound ambiguity. On the one hand it evokes the presence and revelation of God—the fact that, in the OT, God and Wisdom are visualized as being present in a tent (cf. Brown, 32–34). Thus, the tent is sublime, divine. On the other hand, because a tent is like a fragile shell, easily knocked or folded, it is sometimes used as a symbol of the human body and of the vulnerability of the life within that body (cf. Westcott, 11; Jer 10:20; and esp. 2 Cor 5:1–5). The text gives no explicit indication of either connotation but, in the context, both seem to apply. Thus, through the ambiguity of the tent, the Word-flesh paradox is followed by the equal paradox of divinity-fragility.

"And we saw his glory" would seem, in the context of the gospel as a whole, to refer to the wonders or miracles, and especially to the glory surrounding Jesus' death and resurrection. Thus the three phrases—becoming flesh, dwelling in a tent, and seeing the glory—cover the full span of the life of Jesus.

Though the text does not specify explicitly which event(s) manifested glory, it does emphasize a more basic, general, point—that the glory in question is not human self-glorification but rather the glory which an only son receives from the Father. The atmosphere suggested by this parent–child interchange is one of light and affection, so it is not surprising that the text goes on to add, as a culminating factor in its account of the incarnation, that it was "full of grace and truth." The two-fold expression "grace and truth" seems, almost certainly, to reflect *hesed* and *'emet,* two OT words which together mean "merciful love," "loving-kindness," or "covenant love." It is, as Brown (14) remarks, a "famous OT pairing."

And at this point, at the utterance of this famous OT pairing, John breaks in. He "bears witness to him crying, 'This was he . . .' " (v 15). In some recent commentaries John's cry is regarded as an illogical interpolation, a sure sign of editing. But crying connotes inspiration, prophecy (Bultmann, 75; Schnackenburg, 1:174), and so, here again, as earlier, John appears to be "the final testimony of prophecy" (Westcott, 13), the embodiment of the OT. And it is in such a context, the context of the OT and especially of its prophecies, that the NT almost invariably presents the incarnation. John's crying, therefore, far from being an illogical interpolation, is altogether appropriate. It is as though, when the incarnation finally arrived, full of covenant love, the OT stood up and cheered. It said a solemn "Amen" (Lindars, 96). Or again it is like that moment in televised sports when the camera, after a climactic moment, swings suddenly from the scene of play to the jubilant coach.

The incarnation therefore is set in a double context—that of those who saw it and would later bear witness to it ("we have seen his glory," 1:14; cf. 21:24), and that of those who had seen it in advance. Together they form a compact unit.

As the text continues there is an ambiguity: "For [*hoti,* better attested and more probable than *kai,* "and"] from his fullness we have all received . . . ." (v 16). Since there are no quotation marks in Greek, it is not altogether clear who is speaking—the "we" who have seen his glory (the opinion of most modern commentators) or John (the "opinion of many Fathers"—Schnackenburg, 1:275). The problem is not unique. In chapter 3 there are two instances when doubts arise about the closing of a quotation and the identity of a speaker, and in both instances the ambiguity involves a deliberate strategy. Here too the ambiguity has its purpose. Since the "we all" (v 16) maintains continuity with both kinds of witnesses—with the "we" who saw his glory and also, to some extent at least, with the witness of John—what it effectively does is draw both elements, the authentic heritage of the OT as well as the witnesses of the NT, into a unit. In other words the compact unity of the two elements (vv 14–15) is reflected in the ambiguity which follows them, reflected in the fact that both are held together, so to speak, within that ambiguity. It is an indication of the richness wrought by the incarnation, an indication that it blends something old with something new. Once again, therefore, ambiguity is a sign not of poor writing or editing but rather of sophisticated literary technique and of theological meaning.

The idea that the text is concerned with the transition and continuity between the old order and the new is confirmed by what follows: ". . . we have all received *charin anti charitos,*" "grace upon/in place of grace," a phrase which suggests the abundance of *charis* ("grace/love") brought by the incarnation, and which more specifically—and this is the opinion of the Greek Fathers and of some modern scholars (cf. Brown 16; note Loisy, 109)—suggests that the grace of the incarnation replaces or surpasses the grace (*hesed*) of the OT.

In v 17 the fact that the text is highly concerned with the relationship of the two testaments finally becomes explicit: "For the law was given by Moses; grace and truth came through Jesus Christ." This is often seen as suggesting a strong contrast, but, as Brown (16) indicates, it need not be. The law, despite being misused by many of Jesus' contemporaries, was originally and essentially a revelation of God's love, of covenant *hesed.* Given the fact that the incarnation apparently is expressed in terms of OT covenant love, it is doubtful if a strong contrast should be understood. Rather, as v 16 had suggested, one form of grace or *hesed* surpasses the other.

The surpassing grace brings revelation to a level that had not been reached under the law of Moses, a level where, as never before, God has spoken (v 18). The text, according to the more difficult and probable reading, speaks of this revelation as coming from "God the only [Son] (*monogenēs theos*) who is on the Father's bosom." Thus, just as v 1 distinguishes God-the-Word from God, so the final verse distinguishes the revelatory God from the Father. The essence of both distinctions is between the revelatory God and the Godhead, but while v 1 does little more than hint at the fact of a personal relationship (". . . and the Word was with God"), the final verse is much more developed: being "on the bosom" of the Father is a clear expression of intimacy.

As well as coming back to the idea of an internal relationship, the prologue also comes back to the idea of the distant still point. There is a reminder that "no one has ever seen God." And the picture of the revelatory God as "*being (ōn,* present participle) in the bosom of the Father," would seem, despite some grammatical ambiguity (cf. Brown, 17), to be a way of saying that the primary home of the revealer is always within God. In other words, v 18 refers, as does v 1, to the fact that the source of that revelation is beyond time. The implication is that even while Jesus is on earth there is a certain aspect of him which is with God, beyond time. It is not surprising, therefore, that occasionally during the gospel he will refer to unity with the Father, or say, quite simply, "I am."

Conclusion

The prologue is a closeknit unity. When seen as a spiralling three-part summary of the history of salvation and of the descent of the Word, its many elements blend together. The figure of John, often regarded as alien to the prologue, culminates and embodies the OT, and as such has an integral role in this unique summary.

The author's regard for the OT period is further seen in the interweaving of language from the OT and NT. The summary description of the OT period (vv 6–13) culminates in a central Christian concept—that of becoming children of God. And the summary account of the incarnation (vv 14–18, esp. 14) culminates in a central OT concept—"grace and truth," *hesed* and *'emet.* Given such an approach it is easy to envisage the Christian church as the new Israel, and, despite the sense of newness which surrounds the statement of the incarnation (v 14), it is easier also to understand those who speak of Christ as being in the OT.

What emerges therefore is that the prologue is not just a description of salvation history. Though it has some resemblance to the form of factual narrative, it is also "a doctrinal meditation" (Giblin, 1985, 94). It goes behind the external phases of salvation history and seeks, amid a major upheaval in a centuries-old tradition, to wrestle with the reality of God and to show how that same reality is revealed, as never before, in the figure of Jesus Christ.

The ultimate God of whom it speaks is greatly distant, at the beginning of things, never seen. But at the center of that God there is a personal relationship, an intimacy, and despite the great distance, despite also the surrounding darkness of life, that central essence has entered into humanity. It is found primarily in Jesus, but it is given also to all who will accept it. The prologue, therefore, through its summary of history, indicates that, ever since creation, in every time and place, God has been with humans and, even amidst colossal ignorance, has invited them to knowledge and intimacy. It is an invitation which finds new strength in Jesus. The result is a picture of human life which may indeed be surrounded by darkness but at the heart of which lies an unquenchable fire.

The Week-Long Drama of Revelation and Response

As already indicated, in the general introduction to Part 1 (1:1–2:22), the text of 1:19–2:11 consists of five episodes which are spread over successive or near-successive days, and which, from a literary and theological point of view, may be said to occupy a week, a week which echoes the week of creation.

From one point of view the description of these days appears to be matter-of-fact. It tells things as they happened. As Lindars (100) says concerning the account of the first four days—an account which tells of John the Baptist, the appearance of Jesus, and the call of the first disciples (1:19–51)—"The narrative can be viewed quite simply in historical terms, as a record of what happened when Jesus began his public ministry." It is because of this matter-of-fact, historylike, aspect of the text that much of the scholarly discussion of 1:19–51 is taken up with questions of history, particularly the differences between the fourth gospel and the other three (cf. esp. Dodd, 1963, 248–312; Brown, 45, 52–54; Haenchen, 1:147–49, 160, 166–167).

It is generally recognized, however, that there is more to the text than history. As Lindars (100) adds: "But John is never content with simple historical reporting. He is much more concerned with the fact that the appearance of Jesus constitutes the manifestation of divine glory." Schnackenburg (1:284) expresses a similar view. Thus while the text may appear to be matter-of-fact, it is generally agreed that it is profoundly theological. Furthermore, as Dodd (1963, 249) observes, it reflects "a certain schematism."

The purpose in this study is to lay aside the historical question and to concentrate on the schematic form of the text and on its theological message.

What emerges, after further research, is that the schematic aspect is considerable. For instance, on Day 1 it describes John; on Day 2, Jesus; on Day 3, the first disciples; and on the later days, "the theme of evolving discipleship" (Brown, 105). In other words, there is a steady, schematic, progression. By the time one gets to Cana, on the final day (2:1–11), John has been left behind and the communication between Jesus and his disciples has reached an initial fullness: "Jesus . . . revealed his glory, and his disciples believed in him" (2:11). There is therefore a basic unity of content in these days, a graded picture of revelation and response.

As well as unity of content, these days show also a basic unity of form. They all consist of narration in the past interspersed with pieces of dialogue which are frequent but short. There is, for instance, no unbroken narration such as one finds in the center of the prologue (vv 6–13), nor is there, to any significant extent, unbroken direct discourse such as occurs at many points in the gospel. (Where there is something like a discourse [1:29–34, Day 2] it is broken up by flashbacks to earlier dialogue.) Even the quantity of text is roughly the same for each day. At least there is no day which, either by its brevity or length, stands out from all the others.

Basic unity of content and form does not mean that the flow of these days is monotonous. As already suggested, the content is graded, and even though the action in the opening days is rather low-key, it slowly becomes more vivid until, with the call of Philip and Nathanael (1:43–51, Day 4) and, much more so with the miracle at Cana (2:1–11), the action reaches a striking finale. The Cana incident, in fact, though built carefully on the previous days, nonetheless breaks out of their world. It is fractionally longer than any of them. It also gives far greater centrality to the notion of a miraculous sign. In previous days (cf. especially Days 2 and 4; cf. 1:32–33, 48–51) the notion of a miraculous intervention or at least of an intervention from heaven had indeed been present, but not so clearly. At Cana, however, it is clear indeed. And, in the case of most readers, the Cana incident seems to hold the imagination in a way that the previous days do not.

What begins to emerge, therefore, is that while the account of the opening week may appear to be quite matter-of-fact, it is, in reality, a carefully constructed drama of revelation and response. Drama does not necessarily exclude historicity, but it means that John's account, whatever its historicity, has been shaped to a significant extent by considerations that are dramatic and theological. In many ways such a conclusion is not saying anything new. Commentators through the ages have recognized that John is interested not so much in undigested facts as in their spiritual or theological meaning. But it spells out some of the aspects of his artistry.

Day 1 □ The Initiatory Trial

John's Testimony about Himself and about
the Coming of an Elusive Presence

The opening episode is a dramatic confrontation: Jewish priests and Levites approach John and subject him to a probing process of interrogation. First they ask his identity ("Who are you?" vv 19–23), and then, in a second scene (vv 24–28), they inquire about his motives ("Then why are you baptizing?").

The distinction between the two scenes is confirmed by the use of repetition: The first begins with a *sending . . . from Jerusalem's Jews . . . to ask him*; the second with the fact that those *sent . . . from the Pharisees . . . asked him.* Here, as in the carefully woven drama of the blind man (9:13,18), the terms "Jews" and "Pharisees" are used interchangeably. Other terms also ("priests," "Levites") are used dramatically; in other words, they are used for the purpose of building a dramatic contrast: on the one hand, the assembled ranks of the Jews; on the other, John.

The word for "Jews," *Ioudaioi,* may also be translated "Judeans," a term which has certain advantages: it omits any modern overtones of the word "Jews;" it helps partly to save modern Jews from the negativity of the gospel usage; it is closer in sound to the original *Ioudaioi;* it has an appropritate suggestion of provincialism; and, like *Ioudaioi,* it is closer to the name "Judas" (*Ioudas*). The confrontation, therefore, may be described as being between John and the assembled Judeans.

This is no ordinary confrontation. As Bultmann (86) and Brown (45) have indicated, it is something more—a trial. John is being forced to give an account of himself and, as in a trial scene, to bear witness.

Furthermore, the trial is of a particular kind—initiatory. In other words, the episode follows a well-known literary convention, that of placing near the beginning of a narrative an account of how a leading figure was tested. Such episodes have a certain pattern or predictability, and as such they are called *set scenes,* or *type scenes.* In the words of Robert Alter (1981, 51):

> There is a series of recurrent narrative episodes attached to the careers of biblical heroes that are . . . dependent on the manipulation of a fixed constellation of predetermined motifs. . . . Some of the most commonly repeated biblical scenes . . . are the following: . . . the initiatory trial; . . . the encounter with the future betrothed at a well; . . . [and] the testment of the dying hero.

At later stages the fourth gospel will provide variations on the encounter at the well (4:1–42) and on the last testament (chaps. 13–17). And so it is not surprising that it should also give a variation on the idea of an initiatory trial. Some form of initiatory trial is found in all the other gospels—in the diverse dramatizations of the temptation of Jesus.

The Revealing of Character

One of the basic purposes of a trial, and particularly of an initiatory trial, is to reveal the character of the person being investigated, to uncover what it is that lies beneath the person's surface. In a world where the emphasis on looks is paramount, and at times even enslaving, such a hidden dimension receives relatively little attention. But in a gospel where looks are never mentioned, the unseen dynamics are crucial. Furthermore, the unveiling of this unseen world gives the reader a sense of what is to come. John may soon fade from the gospel, but it is with John that discipleship of Jesus begins—Jesus' first disciples will come from John (1:35–39)—and so the revealing of the Baptist's character provides an intimation of the dispositions needed for discipleship, for learning the path to life.

As the trial begins, the first question goes to the heart of the matter: "Who are you?" At one level this is a simple inquiry. At another it is perhaps the most difficult question of all, and it is significant that it should be the very first question in the gospel. It is asked of John, and it is asked also of the reader.

John's reply is not something glib. It is introduced as a *martyria,* "witness/testimony," something which, within the prologue, is like a down-to-earth variation on the *logos,* the Word. (The prologue had begun with a triple use of "Word" and had then gone on, at the beginning of its second part, to give a triple use of "witness" [1:1, 7–8]. Thus the Word was expressed in witness.) John's reply, therefore, while telling who he is, has echoes of something greater than himself.

The concept of witness was also important in the world of rhetoric. It was central to making a persuasive presentation (Kennedy, 1984, 14). Hence, the weight of John's reply is all the greater.

The first part of this reply (1:19–23, scene 1) involves two phases—a negative phase in which John says who he is not (1:19–21), and a positive phase in which he says who he is (1:22–23).

The negative phase begins with a triple description: "And he confessed and did not deny; and he confessed . . ." (1:20). Then come three negatives: John declares that he is not the Christ, and not Elijah, and not the prophet (1:21). This repetitious structure (esp. in 1:20) may seem perplexing. It has been said, for instance, that it is cumbersome (Bultmann, 87), that it may be a sign of editing (Brown, 43), and that it cannot be explained as a peculiarity of style (Schnackenburg, 1:288). Yet Bultmann (87–88) acknowledges that it gives solemnity, and Haenchen (1:143) sees the triple repetition in 1:21 as reflecting an idealized scene. Furthermore, when judging John's disavowal it is necessary to note that one of the most famous and imitated disavowals in antiquity, that of Demosthenes regarding his involvement with the Thebans (*On the Crown,* orat. 18, 179), involves a structure which is triple and repetitious. It was found in virtually every rhetorical work of the first century (cf. Fischel, 1973, 145). The repetition in 1:20–21 involves much more variety than does the classic Demosthenes text—the gospel text swings from positive ("confess") to negative ("deny") and back again, and the negatives in 1:21 become increasingly brief—but it fits the broad pattern of triple repetition and negation.

Given the solemnity surrounding John's reply, one might have expected him to begin by making some pretentious claim. But he does the opposite. He responds to "Who are you?" by first saying who he is not. At one level this is a way of putting distance between himself and contemporary Jewish expectations (Brown, 46–50). At another broader level it is a way of saying that, in telling who he is, the first task is to empty himself of false identities. Even in the wording of his answers there is a faint evoking of a process of self-emptying: As he speaks, his replies diminish in quantity: "I am not the Anointed"; "I am not"; "No." (This pattern of diminishing language is a very small part of a larger phenomenon, one in which, through diverse procedures, the gospel text diminishes and expands; see esp. the pattern of descents and ascents, chap. 6 of the introduction.)

But then, having reduced himself to the monosyllabic "No," John begins, in a second phase, to speak of himself more positively: "I am the voice of one crying in the desert make straight the way of the Lord. . . ." This is still not claiming much. In fact, the suggestion of self-emptying, of being reduced to nothingness, is continued in the lonely image of a *"voice crying in the desert."* But John's statement can be read in another manner: *"in the desert make straight the way . . . ";* and this ambiguity in the phrasing reflects the ambiguity of the desert —it is empty, but it is ready to be filled with the Lord. The road is waiting.

In the second scene (1:24–28) the road is no longer empty; someone is coming. The questioners have now moved from asking John who he is to asking about his motives in baptizing. Previously there had been no reference to the fact that he baptized. He was simply "John." But in this scene "to baptize" is used three times, and the repetition builds a sense of expectation. As the baptizer explains what he is doing, attention moves away from him and towards an elusive presence: "I baptize in water; but among you stands one whom you do not know. . . ." And with humble words he announces the impending arrival of someone awesome.

John's character emerges as one of uncluttered receptivity. The shedding of false identities has meant not that his life is empty but that, as he goes about his work, there is an increasing fullness. He has given himself away, so to speak, but he is finding something far greater.

The Character of the Jewish Interrogators

Trial scenes frequently reveal the character not only of the defendant but also of the judge or interrogators. So it is here, at least implicitly. (Not until much later will the character of the interrogators be made fully explicit.)

When the priests and Levites first approach John, nothing derogatory is said about them. And their straightforward question, "Who are you?" may seem to reflect an open-minded quest for the truth. One detail, however, is faintly disquieting; unlike John, who was "sent from God" (1:6), these interrogators were "sent" by "the Jews" (1:19). In other words, there is a hint of contrast, as though the forces behind the interrogators are quite different from the force behind John.

It is only during the second phase of the questioning, when they repeat "Who are you?" (1:22), that there is some indication of their disposition. They give their motive: ". . . that we may give an answer to those who sent us."

It is at this stage that John's witness becomes positively prophetic, that instead of giving increasingly short negative replies, he suddenly renders the (prophetic) word into resounding form: "I am the voice of one crying . . . make straight. . . ." By any standard this is a statement of arresting poetry and striking power, one that can scarcely fail to touch the questioners.

There is no reaction. Not for a moment do they show the slightest interest in the positive testimony. There is not even a vaguely curious "Really?" This was what their motive had suggested: they did not genuinely care who John was, or what he had to say. Their preoccupation was with a demand that was political, bureaucratic—to have some kind of manageable answer for some people back in Jerusalem. They live in a world which has concerns other than those of making straight the way of the Lord.

Then comes the second scene and, as if to explain the lack of response from the questioners, there is a further detail about them—they were "from the Pharisees," in other words from those who, in the gospels' tradition, generally rejected God's word in Jesus. The reference to the Pharisees is sufficiently ambiguous that, while it can indeed refer to the senders, it may also be read, grammatically at least, as referring to those who were sent.

Thus the reference to the Pharisees need not be seen as the result of some kind of secondary "editing." When taken with the questioners' motivation and their unresponsiveness, it forms the clinching element in a subtly drawn picture of deafness. The witness cries out, but, despite all their energy and persistence, the Pharisees-related questioners are not listening.

A Surpassing Drama

The trial episode has a pervasive ambiguity. At one level it reads almost like a historical report, but as such it has many problems. For instance, the phrasing is sometimes ambiguous, the relationship of the Pharisees to other Jewish groups seems confused, and the location (Bethany beyond the Jordan) has never been found. (Not even Origen could find it, around A.D. 220).

At another level it is a theological drama, and as such it is quite coherent. Through the form of an initiatory trial it shows a character who first prepares the road (scene 1) and who then works and waits for the one who comes (scene 2). One scene builds carefully on the other, and even details which at first appear confused—such as the reference to the Pharisees—fall into place when seen as part of this intensifying drama. Thus it is indeed related to history but its primary focus is on a dimension of reality which surpasses history, surpasses the details of time and space.

It is also a careful continuation of the prologue. While the prologue had interwoven the two ideas of Word and witness (cf. 1:1, 6–8, 14–15), the trial scene now focuses on witness. In fact, the entire episode is introduced on that note: "And this is the witness. . . ." Thus the episode which tests John is not something trivial. In the details of his life, in the unfolding of his character, there is a reflection of the larger drama of the Word. The action seems earthbound, but it has a dimension which surpasses the earth.

Day 2 □ The Initiatory Vision

John Sees the Coming of Jesus and the Descending of the Spirit

On the next day John sees Jesus, first as the lamb of God (vv 29–31), and then in a flashback, as the one on whom the dovelike Spirit descends and abides (vv 32–34). Thus the structure is twofold, and, as in the previous episode, the distinction between the two parts is linked to various elements of repetition (Brown, 58).

The descent of the dove tends to recall the synoptic account of how the dove descended on Jesus at his baptism (Matt 3:13–17 and parr.), and discussion of the Johannine episode generally involves comparison with the synoptic account (e.g. cf. Brown, 65–67; Lindars, 108). But the fourth gospel does not say explicitly that Jesus was baptized. It seems better therefore not to entitle this episode "The Baptism of Jesus," but to seek a designation which does justice to the distinctiveness of the text.

Vision and Mission

A basic feature of the text is its visionlike quality. That the scene is like a vision of the divine, or at least like a down-to-earth vision, is indicated by a number of factors. The preceding context, with which it is in careful continuity, had been building progressively towards the idea of the inbreaking of the divine. Furthermore, the text itself has visionlike features. Negatively, it lacks many of the externals of more ordinary scenes. As Bultmann (94) notes, in its opening verses it "abandons altogether the realm of historical narrative." No place is mentioned, and no audience. To say that John is speaking to the people is to interject into the scene what is conspicuously absent. Even when it is said that John bore witness (v 32), there is still no mention of the people or of disciples. Nothing is inserted which can take away from John's concentration on Jesus.

More decisive, however, than these negative features, are the visionlike features which are positive. The Jesus who appears is a heavenly figure: he is described, first and last, as being "of God" ("the lamb of God," v 29; "the Son of God," v 34). And he is also described as "coming" (*erchomenos*) toward John, a word previously not used except in reference to the true light "coming" into the world (1:9), and in reference to the transcendent presence which was "coming" after John (1:27). As Hoskyns (175) notes, the "purpose is to emphasize the heavenly . . . origin of Jesus." The sense of witnessing a heavenly intervention is emphasized also by the opening exclamation: "Behold, the lamb of God, who takes away the sin of the world." It is a saying which seems to have a complex background—a background which, among other things, includes possible allusions to the apocalyptic lamb who dried tears and fought evil (Rev 7:17, 17:14), to the Suffering Servant who died like a lamb for the sins of others (Isaiah 53), and especially to the Passover lamb, a lamb which in much Christian thought was regarded as having been sacrificed (cf. 1 Cor 5:7, 1 Pet 1:18–19). (For details, see Brown, 58–63.) What is crucial, however, apart from the complex background, is the simplicity and power of the actual exclamation, its implication of God's intervention on a worldwide scale. And the fact that John should refer to Jesus' pre-existence (". . . for he was before me"), a reference which many commentators find strange or unlikely, is more understandable when seen in the context of a visionary experience, an experience similar to those through which the OT prophets apprehended the transcendent God. Hoskyns (178) suggests something visionlike when he describes what happens in this scene as a "prophetic apprehension" which "rests upon revelation."

The idea of something visionlike is even more explicit in the second part of the episode when John talks of having seen the Spirit descend like a dove from heaven (vv 32–33). In other words, both images, of the lamb and of the dove, occur in a visionlike context. Furthermore, the reaction of John, in which, after each image, he states his native inadequacy ("I myself did not know him . . . I myself did not know him") has a general similarity to the sense of inadequacy or limitation which was felt, during their visionary calls, by Moses, Isaiah, Jeremiah, and Ezekiel (cf. Exod 3:1–4:17, Isaiah 6, Jeremiah 1, Ezek 1:1–3:21).

A further feature of the text is its emphasis on mission. Both "scenes" of the episode speak of John's mission to baptize. In the first scene (vv 29–31) this mission is placed in a climactic position—at the very end: ". . . for this I came baptizing in water" (1:31). In the second scene, however, John's mission is moved to a subordinate position ("but he who sent me to baptize in water said to me . . ."), and the emphasis falls instead on the mission of Jesus: "This is he who baptizes in the holy Spirit" (1:33).

An Initiatory Vision

Given that the episode is visionlike and mission oriented, it would seem that it is a variation on a well-known type scene—that of the inaugural vision. As mentioned earlier, the term *type scene* refers to a literary convention according to which certain kinds of scenes always employ "a fixed constellation of predetermined motifs" (Alter, 1981, 47–62, esp. 51). In the case of the prophets' initiatory vision or call there are six motifs: divine confrontation, introductory word, commission, objection, reassurance, sign (cf. Habel, 1965). In one form or another, all six motifs appear to be present in the initiatory vision of John the Baptist.

- Divine confrontation: the coming of Jesus, lamb of God, in a context which emphasizes the inbreaking of God (v 29); and the descent of the Spirit from heaven (v 32).

- Introductory word: John recalls his earlier introduction to the coming of Jesus—"After me comes a man who . . . was before me" (v 30; cf. v 15).

- Commission: John recalls his own coming and his being sent to baptize in water (vv 31b, 33b). As already noted, the text refers also to the mission of Jesus (33c).

- Objection: "I myself did not know him . . . I myself did not know him . . . ." (vv 31a, 33a).
- Reassurance: "But the one who sent me . . . said to me, 'He on whom you see the Spirit descend . . . this is he . . . .' " (v 33bc).
- Sign: the descent of the Spirit, like a dove (vv 32, 34a).

Thus the six motifs are in the text, but in a way which is unusual and complex. Many factors are present in duplicate. Such variation, however, is not unique. In the account of the Samaritan woman it will be observed that, in following a type scene, the writer has introduced a radical alteration. Furthermore, radical variation of a type scene was acceptable from a literary viewpoint (cf. Alter, 1981, 48–49, 58–62).

Basic Variations in the Type Scene

The full details of how the author has altered the type scene are best left to further research. Of the several variations, however, there are two which deserve immediate mention.

The first is duplication, which is found in both concepts and language, and it goes far beyond a few structure-related elements of repetition. In itself duplication of a motif is not a problem. In the call or vision of Moses, for instance, the objection motif occurs four or five times (Exod 3:11,13; 4:1,10,13). The question is, why the duplication and how far does it go? Is the text dealing with one visionlike experience, that of John, or is it suggesting that Jesus too had some kind of inaugural vision?

The basic reason for the duplication consists of the fact that the incarnation involved two missions—the preparatory mission of John and the decisive mission of Jesus. In other words, it is appropriate, at least in dealing with the mission motif, that the inaugural call or vision should be in duplicate form. When Luke is inaugurating the incarnation by means of angelic annunciation—and an annunciation is a type scene which is akin to that of the initiatory vision (the call of Gideon seems to pertain to both; cf. Habel, 1965, 296–305; for a review of research, cf. Tucker, 1985, 340–42)—he gives not one annunciation but two, one for John (Luke 1:5–25) and the other for Jesus (Luke 1:26–38). Thus, while Luke gives two initiatory visions, the fourth gospel gives a single initiatory vision which is twofold. The essential point is that the incarnation's involvement of two heaven-sent agents helps to explain the twofold complexity of the lamb-of-God episode.

This does not, however, mean that an inaugural vision is being attributed to both John and Jesus. It is John, and John alone, who sees various forms of heavenly intervention—first the coming of the lamb of God and then the dovelike descending of the Spirit on Jesus. Jesus, far from needing a vision from heaven, is himself the heavenly figure, the one on whom the Spirit abides permanently. The impression given by the scene's final verse—"And I have seen and borne witness that this is the Son of God"—is that the dovelike descent was not so much for the sake of Jesus as for the sake of John, to help him identify Jesus as the heavenly figure which he was. Thus there are not two visions, one for John and one for Jesus; rather, John has a complex vision which tells something of his own work, but which also looks beyond it and puts it in the context of the work to be accomplished in Jesus.

Incidentally, in doing further research it may be worthwhile to ask whether the twofold complexity of John's vision—he first sees the lamb of God and, within that context, recalls having seen the Spirit—corresponds, at least in part, to a further literary convention—that of the vision within a vision (cf. Acts 9:10–16, esp. 9:12). Given the fourth gospel's tendency to synthesize, a fusing of related literary conventions is quite possible.

The second variation concerns the fact that the type scene of heavenly intervention has been brought down to earth. The usual emphasis on spectacular drama has been reduced. There is indeed a reference to the Spirit's dramatic descent from heaven, but it is a drama which, instead of being described directly, is filtered through John's remembrance of it. The emphasis has shifted considerably from what is being seen to the actual act of seeing it; in other words, from the view to the viewer, to what is going on within John. It is like a prophetic vision which has been demythologized. Even the animal references are tame—a lamb and a dove.

The fact that the heavenly vision is thus brought down to earth fits well with the context—with the idea of the Word becoming flesh. Thus the two most basic variations in the traditional type scene—its twofold form and its down-to-earthness—correspond to basic features of what the context is all about, the incarnation.

Meaning

The foregoing literary observation—that the lamb of God episode appears to be a variation on the standardized initiatory vision—is of considerable theological importance. Such visions generally capture the essence of a complex career or narrative. They are compact sources of thought. The account of the call of Moses, for instance, is "amazing[ly] . . . seminal" (Childs, 1974, 88).

The lamb-of-God episode may not be as captivating as the Exodus vision, yet its opening verse supplies the key line for one of the most solemn moments in some Christian liturgies. Furthermore, as a whole it provides a certain synthesis of Christology and of Christianity.

It speaks first of taking away what is negative —"the sin of the world." The meaning of this is not immediately clear, but the context—especially the context of the prologue with which the scene's opening verses have so much continuity (1:29–31a; cf.1:6–11,15)—the context suggests that the sin of the world is connected with the world's ignorance of the Creator ("and the world knew him not," 1:10). The text itself, because of its image of the sacrificial lamb, appears to be referring to guilt, guilt which is removed by sacrifice. It is "the whole collective burden of sin which weighs" on humankind (Schnackenburg, 1:298; cf. Bultmann, 96–97). Thus the sin of the world refers to humanity's weighty burden of ignorance and guilt, and it is taken away by a process, based ultimately on the Word, of revelation and self-giving (sacrifice).

In discussing the image of the lamb of God there is a danger that concentration on the possible background of that image—the lamblike Suffering Servant, the apocalyptic lamb, the Passover lamb, etc.—will obscure the image itself, obscure the fact that a lamb, whatever its background, suggests first and foremost a picture of playful innocence. It is true, of course, that in the world of art, animals at times convey an acquired meaning, a meaning imposed by cultural background. But it is also true that animals tend to have an inherent suggestiveness, that they tend by their very nature to evoke a certain ethos or atmosphere. It is largely for this reason that they have a considerable role in such popular art as greeting cards and national symbols. In principle at least, interpretation is open to both levels of meaning, acquired and inherent. This is particularly so in a text which employs ambiguity. In the text under discussion the lamb and the dove constitute an unusual concentration of animal imagery—apart from the cleansing of the temple (2:13–22) Part 1 of the gospel does not otherwise refer to animals—and this concentration would appear to constitute a frame of reference which is independent of background references. It is necessary, therefore, having spoken of the background to the lamb image, to give due attention to the image itself—to its suggestion, already mentioned, of playful innocence.

There is something profoundly enigmatic about saying that a lamb of any kind takes away the sin of the world. How can something so breezily light take away such a massive burden? It is somewhat like saying that a bush is burning but is not being burned up. The image is like a koan or riddle. One aspect of the answer seems to be found in the realm of the spirit: the action of beholding the lamb brings the beholder into such a realm of God-made beauty, innocence, and playfulness that, *within one's spirit and in one's relation to God's Spirit,* the killing weight of sin is no longer at center stage. The burden, though present, is relegated to its place within the larger reality of God's creative and redemptive presence, within the unutterable world which is evoked by the wonder of the lamb.

Hence, while there is much to be said for speaking of sin as being taken away by sacrifice, it is also necessary to see sin as being confronted by an overpowering transcendence which has entered into human life.

As well as referring to taking away what is negative, the scene speaks also of the coming (literally, the "descending," *katabainon*) of what is positive, the Spirit. The fact that the Spirit is described as "descending like a dove from heaven" may be explained through certain background data, particularly through the fact that after the deluge had cleansed the world of sin, it was the dove, with an olive branch in its beak, which effectively announced to Noah the possibility of an era of peace (Gen 8:10–22; see also Brown, 57). However, as with the image of the lamb, there is a meaning other than that provided by the background. There is the image itself, the fact that "descending like a dove from heaven" evokes a world of grace, both the tangible grace of a bird in easy downward flight and the ultimate grace of heaven. It is an image which is all the more suggestive of what is free and flowing because it is in contrast with the idea of sin and with the implied image of a weighty burden.

Thus, as the lamblike figure evokes one aspect of God and God's action, the dovelike descent evokes another. The two processes—of removing the burden of sin and of granting the free-flowing Spirit—are complementary. A heavy burden gives way to a presence which is light and graceful.

John's insight that Jesus removes sin and receives the Spirit, leads (v 34) to a culminating realization: that Jesus is the Chosen One (or Son) of God. (The manuscripts disagree, and judgment between them is difficult, but Chosen One seems more likely [cf. Brown, 57], and it also prepares subtly for Jesus' role in the following episode as the one who in turn chooses others [cf. Brown, 78].) In any case, John's down-to-earth vision highlights the fact that Jesus, whether as Son or Chosen One, is in an intensely personal relationship with God. It is noteworthy that in Romans and Ephesians, for instance, freedom from sin and the granting of the Spirit are associated with becoming the chosen children of God (Rom 7:14– 8:15, 8:34; Eph 1:3–5). It is not very surprising, therefore, that Jesus, who is the primary example, and more than an example, of freedom from sin and reception of the Spirit, should finally be described by John as being, more or less, the chosen child of God. In other words, if the removal of sin and the granting of the Spirit make a person into a chosen child of God, it is fitting that Jesus, above all, should be described as the Chosen/Son of God.

Conclusion

The scene as a whole offers a synthesis of what God's revelatory action is all about. The lamb, whatever its background, introduces into the world of sin an aura of playful innocence. The dovelike Spirit, which remains on Jesus, adds to that aura the suggestion of something light, flowing, graceful—ultimately of something holy (v 33: ". . . *holy* Spirit"), and of someone who is of God (v 36: ". . . the Chosen One of God"). It alludes to an inner transformation which, at one level, is akin to that sought by certain forms of yoga—a transformation from feeling overwhelmingly burdened to feeling light and holy. Thus, having begun with a reference to the stark reality of sin, the text builds an positive picture of someone who brings innocence, grace and closeness to God.

But it is not easy to see this positive presence. In the opening trial scene (vv 19–28) the Jews, in part because of their lack of genuine interest, were not aware of the awesome presence which was at hand. And in this scene John admits that, at first, he too had not known Jesus. But then, partly, it would seem, because of his receptive disposition, and especially because of God's revelatory action, he became aware, even amid the sin of the world, of the presence of innocence and grace and God.

Day 3 □ Basic Aspects of Discipleship

The Call without Names and the Call of Peter

Introduction and Structure

As on Days 1 and 2, the episode on Day 3 falls into two basic parts or scenes. First, two of John's disciples, unnamed at the time, follow Jesus and stay with him (vv 35–39). Then, in the later part (vv 40–42), there is the call and renaming of Peter.

Here, as in the previous passages, the division into two parts is accompanied by a certain amount of exact repetition—the reference, given twice (vv 35–37, 40), to two of the disciples hearing and following.

This episode is quite different from the synoptics' account both of the call of the first disciples at the Sea of Galilee (Matt: 4:18–22, and parr.) and of the later renaming of Peter at Caesarea Philippi (Matt 16:13–20), and it is better, in this work, to concentrate on the text of the fourth gospel. Here there is no mention of the Sea of Galilee, nor indeed of any specific location. As Bultmann notes (99), this episode, like the one which precedes it, is "again . . . told without any attention to historical detail. Neither the place nor the situation is described." The continuity with the preceding episode is further underlined by John's repetition of the memorable exclamation "Behold, the lamb of God!"

Despite this continuity, however, the two episodes are quite different. The visionlike drama of the preceding day had had a certain simplicity and stillness— just two characters, and no motion (except, of course, motion which in one way or another originated from heaven). But in this scene there is both multiplicity of characters (five altogether: John, two disciples, Jesus, and Peter), and there is a conspicuous amount of movement. As a foil to this sense of movement there is an opening picture of stillness, a stillness which appears as a carry-over from the preceding scene: "The next day *again* John *was standing* with two of his disciples." Then comes all the movement: Jesus was *walking;* the disciples *followed* him; Jesus *turned* and saw them *following;* he told them "*come* and see" [where he abode]; they *came* and saw; then one "of those who *followed*" *found* Peter and *led him* to Jesus. What emerges is a series of motions almost all of which converge on one place—the place where Jesus abides. It is to that place that John's two disciples are invited. And apparently it is to that place also that Peter is led.

Given so much movement, it is all the more puzzling that no locations are mentioned, particularly that the place where Jesus abode is not named. It is a puzzle that has caused a good deal of discussion (cf. Haenchen, 1:159).

At this point the continuity with the preceding scene is helpful. There the word "abide" (*menō*, "remain, rest, stay, abide") was used twice (1:32–33) to refer not to someone staying in some inn or town but to describe the abiding presence of the Spirit on Jesus. In other words "abiding" was associated with the Spirit's presence. So when the word "abide" is again used in the following scene (1:38–39), it is inevitable, given the continuity of the scenes, that it evoke the presence of the Spirit. The absence of a specific location is thus explained: the evangelist

158

leaves it out in order to suggest that, regardless of where Jesus may have been lodged physically, his primary abode was spiritual, or Spirit-related. The Spirit abode on him, the lamb of God, and he, being the lamb of God, abode in the Spirit. It is an intimation of a theme, that of mutual indwelling, which at a later part of the gospel will become more explicit. Thus the ultimate focus of all the movement in the scene is not simply Jesus' lodging place but rather Jesus himself insofar as he embodies the Spirit and God. For Boismard (1956, 79) the search for Jesus' abode is like the search for Wisdom. Or as Brown (78) expresses it, the disciples' quest touches on humanity's basic quest for God.

Two of John's Disciples Come to Jesus' Abode (1:35–39)

In this scene Jesus is still regarded as the lamb of God, but the title is now associated not with the general idea of removing the sin of the world but with the practical process of holistic teaching. In other words the gospel maintains the sacrifice-related idea of the lamb of God but transforms the self-giving of sacrifice into the self-giving of total teaching.

The word "teaching" is not used. What is given instead is a multifaceted picture of people learning. These verses provide what the preceding scene conspicuously lacks, an audience for John's words and a reaction: "The two disciples heard (*akouō*) him say this ['lamb of God,'] and they followed (*akoloutheō*) Jesus." This is the first time that the gospel uses either of these verbs, and taken together they express the foundation of discipleship. This is also the first scene to use the word *mathētēs*, "disciple." Such a sudden concentration of key words is a clue that the text is beginning to sum up basic aspects of what it is to be a Christian. As Brown (77) says of John 1:35–2:11, "Even if historical information underlies John's account, it has been reorganized under theological orientation. In [this text] . . . John presents a conspectus of Christian vocation."

It may seem, as the "learners" hear John and follow Jesus, that this discipleship comes from their own initiative. After all, as the text portrays it, while John had indeed provided witness, he did not tell them that they must go, and, so far in the gospel, Jesus has not said anything. They really do make a free decision. Yet it is hardly insignificant that in this scene of interwoven movements—this series of movements in "chain reaction" (Brown, 76; Kysar, 1984, 19)—the first movement is that of Jesus as he walks (*peripateō*). It is a movement which is highlighted not only by the preceding stillness of John and his disciples—a "picture . . . of silent waiting" (Westcott, 23)—but also by the fact that John focuses on Jesus precisely as he is walking: "he looked insightfully (*em-blepō*, to look with penetration or insight) at Jesus walking" (*tō Iesou peripatounti*). The fact that both "Jesus" and the participle "walking" are in the same case (dative), a case governed by *em-blepō*, is a grammatical clue that the gaze is not just on Jesus, but on *Jesus walking*. There are preliminary indications, therefore, that the movement of discipleship begins not with the disciples themselves, but with Jesus, and ultimately with God. The Jesus who is walking is called "the lamb *of God.*"

The initiative of Jesus is further emphasized by the fact that as the disciples follow him, he turns and begins to speak to them—his first words. Yet at this very moment there is a reminder, which in Greek is in the form of a subordinate clause, that the disciples are not inactive: "Jesus turned, and *saw them following, and said to them. . . .*"

His first words are a question: "What do you seek?" Not whom, notes Westcott (24), but what? It is an extremely basic question; one which in its probing simplicity recalls the gospel's first question of all: "Who are you?" (1:19). It may indeed be read as little more than a trivial inquiry, but it may also be seen as a far-ranging question of universal application: "What is it that you want out of life?"

Their answer has a similar ambiguity. "Rabbi (Teacher), where do you abide?" This may be read simply as an inquiry about Jesus' location, but, as explained earlier, it may also be seen as reflecting a quest for God. It is disputed, of course, whether the title "Rabbi" was so used in the time of Jesus (cf. Brown, 74), but concerning its place in the text there is no question. It was a respectful title, usually addressed to a religious teacher and, in the fourth gospel "is put . . . on the lips of imperfect or mistaken disciples" (Barrett, 180; cf. 1:39, 42; 3:2; 4:31; 6:25; 9:2; 11:8; cf. 20:16). In this case it indicates that even though the disciples are receptive, ready to be taught, their appreciation of Jesus is still quite limited.

Then Jesus said "Come and see." "And they abode (*menō*) with him that day." The richness of the word "abide" has passed from the Spirit (1:32–33), to Jesus (1:38–39), to the disciples (1:39): "they abode." It is an everyday picture, but it is a further intimation of the process of mutual indwelling of which future chapters will speak.

Then, enigmatically, the text adds: "It was about the tenth hour," and in Greek the final, climactic word is "tenth." Taken in isolation, "the tenth hour" would normally be a straightforward time-designation—a reference to 4 P.M. (cf. Brown, 75; Lindars, 114). But, as such, the text fails. Given the phrasing of the Greek, it is not clear what happened at 4 p.m.: "They came and saw where he was staying and they stayed with him that day. It was about the tenth hour." (The Greek does not contain a "for"—"*for* it was about the tenth hour"—such as put in by the RSV and Haenchen, 1:158.) What happened at the tenth hour—did they come or did they leave? The phrase ("that day") which precedes the references to the tenth hour is such that it subverts its possible function as a reference to a particular hour of the day. The implication is that that is not its function. To insist that it is means implying that the evangelist could not tell the time of day. It is better therefore, despite the demurrals of Schnackenburg (1:309) and Brown (75), to take Bultmann's suggestion (100) that, because "ten" in the OT and ancient world was a symbol of something perfect—in many ways it still is today—the reference is primarily symbolic. In Bultmann's words: "the tenth hour is the hour of fulfillment." In later texts (e.g. 13:1; 17:1) "hour" has a clearly symbolic meaning, and it refers, among other things, to a time of intimacy between Jesus and the disciples, and between Jesus and the Father. It is used in the context of the foot-washing and the final prayer (chaps. 13 and 17). Thus "ten" and "hour" both have symbolic meanings in themselves. Placed together, as they are here, they connote a perfect indwelling of the disciples with Jesus. It is hardly an accident that the phrase "that day," which is largely responsible for subverting the possible chronological function of the "tenth hour," and thus for indicating its symbolic meaning, is used in the last discourse to refer to a time of Spirit-based mutual indwelling (cf. 14:20; 16:23,26; cf. 20:19).

As already seen, in introducing 1:1–2:22 ("The First Year"), the day which the disciples spend with Jesus does not fit the general pattern of the days in Part 1. But that does not make it less important. Rather, like the pattern-breaking seventh day of creation, it is a day which may indeed break away from the normal flow of things, from the usual sense of time, but which does so in order that it may suggest a time which is special or perfect—a time of abiding with Jesus, and ultimately with God.

The conclusion which emerges is that the first part of this episode (vv 35–39) provides an initial synthesis of what is meant by discipleship; it is an attentive journey which culminates in abiding with God. It is not primarily a picture of particular disciples, but rather of discipleship as such. No names are used. It could be a picture of anybody or everybody. To some degree, it is like a capsule image of the essence of the Christian community or church.

The Call of Peter (1:40–42)

Suddenly, in v 40, the scene changes. The anonymity, and the universalism which it tends to evoke, gives way to specific names—to the picture of Andrew finding his brother Peter.

There are three striking factors about the call of Peter: First, he is extremely prominent. He is named not just once, but three times, and the names are over-loaded:

"One of the two . . . was Andrew, Simon Peter's brother."

"He finds first his own brother Simon. . . ."

"You are Simon son of John. You shall be called Cephas (which is interpreted Peter)."

The reference to Andrew puts him (Andrew) first, yet he is named, not independently, but in the context of his relationship to his brother, Simon Peter—thus accentuating the relative importance of Simon. The phrase, "He finds first . . ." (*proton* rather than the weakly attested *protos*) has a well-recognized ambiguity, part of which is an apparent intimation or suggestion that Simon is in some sense first (cf. Schnackenburg, 1:310–11; Brown, 75). And the final reference to Simon involves a total of four names. Given the fact that the first part of the scene used no names at all concerning the disciples, such emphasis and overloading is all the more striking. Against the background of the capsule picture of disciples—of the church—Peter is indeed extremely prominent.

Second, he is completely passive. He is found, he is led, he is renamed. Here, unlike the first part of the scene, the text tells of no action on his part—no hearing, following, questioning, coming, seeing, or abiding. He does nothing, and says nothing. Jesus looks discerningly (again *em-blepō*—as when John looked at Jesus, 1:36) at him, calls him son of John and renames him. Probably the best way to characterize this passive aspect of the call of Peter is to say that it is like the call of David, the outsider who, by sheer choice on the Lord's part, was brought in and given a position of leadership (cf. 1 Sam 16:1–13).

Third, his leadership is limited. There is no suggestion here that Simon Peter has an outstanding sense of the sacred. It is not Simon Peter who discerns the (sacred) presence of the Anointed. It is the two disciples, those who abode namelessly with Jesus. Peter has to be found and told, "We have found the Anointed." The repetition of the verb "to find" highlights the lateness of Peter. The finding is already over before Peter is found. It is Andrew who "finds first"—taking "first" not as an adjective modifying Peter, but as an adverb modifying the action of Andrew. Thus the ambiguity of "first" fits well with the fact that even though at one level Peter is indeed foremost, at another he is late.

This initial picture of Peter is quite revealing, an example of what Sternberg (1985, 321–41) calls proleptic portraits. It is not the only time Peter will be late.

The Text as a Whole: Unity and Diversity

The scene as a whole is a literary unit. It is held together by the triple use of transitional phrases which bridge the gap from Hebrew or Aramaic (Rabbi, Messiah, Cephas) to Greek (Teacher, Anointed, Peter). Such transitional phrases, employing either *hermēneuō* or *met-hermēneuō,* "explain/interpret/translate," are rare. Only in 9:7 ("Siloam which is interpreted Sent") is either verb otherwise used in the fourth gospel.

It is also held together by the use, first and last, of *em-blepō,* "look discerningly." It is in this way that John looks at Jesus (1:36) and that Jesus in turn looks at Simon son of John (1:42). The word is not otherwise used in the fourth gospel. There can be little doubt then: the text is a well-wrought unity.

One thing which is difficult to judge, however, is whether, despite all its unity, the episode is suggesting some process of transition. Does the highly unusual triple movement from words which are Semitic to words which are Greek intimate an aspect of the history of the disciples—the transition from the Semitic heritage to the Greek-speaking world? And is there a similar intimation of transition in the move from John (at the beginning of the scene) to Simon, son of John (at the end)? Such subtle intimations may seem far-fetched, but, as Lacan (1957, 97) indicates, the ideas of the fourth gospel develop in a way which is ever so gradual—like waves advancing on the shore.

Be that as it may, the text is certainly a unit, and it is within that unity that the diversity of its scenes should be interpreted. What the text is talking about is the emergence of something like the church—not of some local community, denomination, or sect, but of all those who are called by Jesus.

It is a church which, as here presented, has two faces. There is, first of all, a hidden face, the face of nameless discipleship, the face made up of all those who, in whatever way, hear, follow, and abide. It is no accident that of the two who follow Jesus, one is never named. It is a way of saying that there is an aspect of the church which is known only to Jesus, to God. It also helps explain why in the fourth gospel, the word *ekklēsia,* "church," is never used. To do so would imply that the reality of God's presence among people could be named, and by implication, could be understood, or controlled, or reduced to human terms.

There is another face which is highly conspicuous—that of Peter, the person who, despite limitations, is discerningly chosen by Jesus, the person whose name can be spelled out in detail.

The two faces are not unrelated. In the figure of Andrew they are shown to be linked like brothers. Peter is "his own brother." It may be significant too that when an effort is made to name the nameless disciple—a questionable procedure, perhaps, but an interesting one, one usually done with the help of the synoptics and some other data in the fourth gospel (cf. Brown, 72–73)—the answer usually given is John, a name which, at some level at least, is related to that of Simon, son of John. It seems better, however, not to rely on so tenuous a connection. What is more solid is the link of brotherhood. The other solid element is the fact, already mentioned, that the scene as a whole forms a literary unity. It is a unity which suggests that the matter of which it speaks—the church in its two faces— also forms a unity.

Day 4 □ Further Aspects of Discipleship

The Calls of Philip and Nathanael

Structure and Continuity

As on the preceding days, the episode consists of two parts, in this case two very uneven parts. First there is the finding of Philip (vv 43–44) and then there is Philip's finding of Nathanael (vv 45–51). Once again, the repetition of the phrasing, especially in Greek ("finds Philip/Nathanael, and . . . says to him") helps to indicate the distinction of the uneven parts.

This episode has affinities not only with the call of the first disciples (1:35–42; for some details, see Brown, 84–85), but also with the account of John's vision of Jesus (1:29–34; cf. Brown, 91). To some degree the idea of vision recurs in the call of Nathanael. But instead of John having a visionlike perception of Jesus, it is rather God-in-Jesus who, with a type of knowledge which surpasses that of the visionary, sees Nathanael, even before he is called, and draws him to the light.

The Call of Philip (1:43–44)

The call of Philip involves two moments. First he is found, and then, as the account tells it, "Jesus said to him, 'Follow me.' "

One of the puzzling aspects of this call is that it is encased in references to geography. The sentence which leads into it is a wish for geographical change: "He willed to go forth to Galilee and he finds Philip." And the only subsequent information given about Philip in the call account itself is again geographical: "Now Philip was from Bethsaida, the city of Andrew and Peter." Such a sudden supply of geographical information, and of little else, is all the more startling because of the fact that in the two previous scenes (1:29–42, Days 2 and 3), where one would have expected geographical references, none was forthcoming. The puzzle is not made easier by the fact that the information given does not fit easily with other data. If Jesus is still in Transjordanian Bethany (cf. 1:28), and if he is to be in Cana of Galilee in two days (cf. 2:1, "And on the third day . . .") then how, in so short a time, is he to accomplish such a journey (about seventy miles)? And the impression given by Mark 1:21,29 is that the home of Andrew and Peter was Capernaum—not Bethsaida. As Lindars (116), for instance, sees it: "It must be confessed that John's topographical care deserts him at this point."

There is a further puzzle. In this scene as a whole (1:43–51, Day 4), as in the previous scene, there is something of a chain reaction of movements, but—and this is the problem—it is not clear who is the first mover. In the Greek text, the opening sentence (in v 43) is tantalizingly vague: "On the next day *he willed* (*thelō*) to go forth to Galilee and he finds Philip. And Jesus said to him, 'Follow me.' " Who willed or wished? Many commentators and translators suggest that it was Jesus. Bultmann (98, 102) holds that in reworking his source the evangelist obscured it, and he too suggests that it was Jesus.

Thus the call of Philip, brief though it is, appears to be shrouded in obscurity and geographical confusion. If, however, the text is seen not just as historical but as predominantly theological, then the difficulties begin to fade considerably. As Westcott (23) suggests, the Philip who is portrayed here is not just an historical individual. He is representative of the Greeks. Westcott comes to this conclusion because "the very mixture of Hebrew (Simon, Nathanael) and Greek (Andrew, Philip) names seems to indicate the representative character of this first group of disciples." Haenchen (1:158) suggests something similar, but not so specific: "The way in which these disciples address Jesus shows that they proleptically represent the believing community." The idea that Philip represents the Greeks is corroborated by several factors: first, by the fact that his name is not just Greek, but—largely because it was borne by so many Greek kings (in Macedonia)—is the quintessential example of a Greek name; second, by the fact that it was Philip who in Acts 8 led the church in evangelizing the Greeks (or Gentiles); and, finally, because within the fourth gospel, it is through Philip that the Greeks come to Jesus (12:20–21). The call of Philip, therefore, is in some sense proleptic of, or representative of, the call of the Greeks.

Given that the call of the Gentiles meant that the message of Jesus went to a new place, it is appropriate that the call of their representative, Philip, be associated with a plan to go to a new place: "He willed to go forth to Galilee, and he finds Philip." In other words, the move to Galilee, "Galilee of the nations" (Matt 4:15; cf. Isa 9:1), is an intimation of the move away from Judaism and into the Gentile world. It may seem careless if seen as a simple geographic reference—rather as "the tenth hour" (1:39) seems careless—but it is its failure as simple geography that is capable of alerting the reader to the fact that it is saying something else.

The description of Philip as "from Bethsaida" may not give personal details, but it appears to achieve one basic purpose: by putting the name which is so Greek beside a name which is so Semitic or Jewish, it suggests, in a miniscule literary way, the union of what is Greek and Jewish. This union is to be achieved within the context of the unity of the church, a unity which in the preceding scene was portrayed through the brotherhood of Andrew and Peter, and so the text goes on to refer to Bethsaida as "the city of Andrew and Peter." It may make for confusing history and geography, but theologically it is coherent and concise.

Thus while the geographical reference which precedes the call of Philip alludes to the process of departing to a new Gentile world, the geographical reference which follows it takes that departure and puts it in context—the context of an all-embracing church unity.

It is hardly an accident that the call of Philip ends with the same word as did the preceding scene of church unity—"Peter." The preceding scene had incorporated the unity of the contemplative and the conspicuous. The Philip-centered verses incorporate the unity of diverse ethnic groups. Thus there are different forms of diversity, but they are brought together in a single unity—a unity symbolized in Peter. The concluding of both passages with the same crucial word is a further indication that this text is not confused, but that it has been chiseled with great precision.

As for the opening enigma—the mystery of who it was who wished to go forth to Galilee (v 43)—the reference almost certainly is to God. This interpretation is borne out by a number of factors. As Brown (85) indicates, there is "a balance" between the initiative which Jesus takes in calling Philip and that which he had taken earlier, within the preceding scene, in calling the two disciples. But that initiative was not the initiative of Jesus alone. The Jesus who called the two disciples was introduced as the lamb of God and thus there was an implication, a reminder, that ultimately the initiative went back to God.

Similarly, when the text goes on in chapter 4 to refer to Jesus' other journey to Galilee, it begins (4:1) with an enigmatic reference to "the Lord," a reference so enigmatic that some copyists and commentators prefer, as with 1:43, to change the subject of the sentence to "Jesus." But the text is saying something important: however ordinary Jesus may look, however much the divine may seem hidden or absent, it is nonetheless present. As was pointed out by Nils Dahl (1975), one of the anomalies of modern NT studies has been the virtual omission of the subject of God. To some degree this is understandable. Concentration on the history of the human Jesus and the human church tends, almost inevitably, to marginalize such a concern. But the subject, far from being marginal, is central, and that is where the fourth gospel tries to keep it. When the "he willed" is taken in context —in other words, in the light of the related texts which precede it and follow it (in 1:36 and 4:1–4)—the implication is that the initiatives of Jesus are not his own, they are from God. The two work together. Thus, in calling Philip, the first action is taken by God, and the second, as a kind of intensified parallel, is taken by Jesus.

The reason for referring to God in so elusive a way is partly because God's presence, in general, is so elusive, and partly because in the particular matter of calling the Gentiles, God's will or willing was regarded as especially mysterious (e.g. see the use of *thelō*, "to will," in Rom 9:16, 18, and of *thelēma*, "will," in Eph 1:1,5 and esp. 1:9).

Incidentally, with regard to John's usage of *thelēma* and *thelō*, the noun is used at an early stage in John (1:13, *thelēma sarkos* . . . *thelēma andros*, "will of the flesh . . . will of a man"), but this is the first usage of *thelō*, the verb— a procedure which seems to ground the entire process of actively willing in the willing of God. In other words, of all the positive willing that is done, the roots in some sense go back to God.

What emerges, therefore, is that in reading the call of Philip, the interpreter ultimately has to make a choice—between a predominantly historical account which is obscure and confused, and a predominantly theological account which is coherent and meaningful.

If taken as predominantly theological, the account is a capsule version of the call of the Greeks or Gentiles. It shows that call to be a departure, yet it sets its departure within the context of church unity, and above all, within the context of the mysterious, surprising, willing of God.

Jesus' Vision of the Man under the Fig Tree (1:45–51)

The account of the calls could well have concluded with Philip. Through him the text had achieved a certain completion—a capsule intimation of how some of the most basic diversities of the church are brought together in unity, with Peter.

But the text goes on: "Philip finds Nathanael. . . ." And then, curiously, comes the most elaborate call account of all. It is made doubly curious by the fact that, apart from a passing reference at the end of John (21:2), Nathanael is never again mentioned—not in John and not anywhere else in the NT.

As a way out of this problem, attempts have sometimes been made, and still are, to identify Nathanael with some other disciple, but as early as Augustine (*In Jo.* 7.17) such attempts were seen as forced (cf. Schnackenberg, 1:314). Consequently, as Brown (82) notes, following the research of Holzmeister (1940), "it is better to accept the early patristic suggestions that he was not one of the Twelve."

Nathanael therefore seems in every sense an outsider. His call is last, and it is not clear how he belongs with the others.

The account's only topographical detail concerns Nathanael's initial location —under a fig tree. Such trees were quite tall, and as well as providing fruit, they also provided cover. They had "spreading branches and broad thick leaves" (J. L. McKenzie, 1968, 276). Under them there was a place of shade or shelter. And there was Nathanael.

His mood seems to have been rather negative. When Philip finds him and tells him of a long-awaited discovery ("The one of whom Moses wrote in the law, and the prophets also—we have found him—Jesus, the son of Joseph, from Nazareth") his reaction is to sieze on what appears to be the last and weakest detail in the news: "From Nazareth can there be anything good?" In the Greek of Philip's statement, the phrase "we have found" comes immediately before "Jesus . . . of Nazareth" and so Nathanael's reaction is like a misreading—a way of perceiving which sees "we have found Jesus . . . of Nazareth" and ignores Moses and the prophets. The final part of his reply, which is where the emphasis tends to fall, is almost totally bleak: ". . . can there be anything good?" His negativity and doubt is emphasized by Jesus' later statement: "Because I said to you, 'I saw you under the fig tree,' you believe." The implication is that at the actual moment of being under the fig tree, he did not believe. According to Westcott (27), the variation in the prepositions used for "under" (*hypo* and *hypokatō*, vv 48, 50) "implies that Nathanael had withdrawn under the fig tree. . . ." This, perhaps is debatable, as are many of the suggestions which have been made concerning the background to the tree (cf. Brown, 83; Westcott, 27). What is reasonably certain, however, on the basis of the text as a whole, is that, underneath the shade or shelter of the fig tree, the mood was not good. It was one of alienation, of "disparaging doubt" (Brown, 86).

But the negative mood does not last. A combination of factors intervene— Philip's finding and inviting ("Come and see"), Nathanael's own guilelessness and willingness to reconsider, and the effect on Nathanael of Jesus' extraordinary vision and knowledge—all of these lead Nathanael to come and accept Jesus.

"Rabbi," he said, as he seems both to jump from one level of acceptance to another, and, within the gospel as a whole, to bring the recognition of Jesus to a new level, "You are the Son of God! You are the King of Israel!" "Son of God" probably involves a recognition of Jesus' divinity (cf. Brown, 87–88); it expresses Jesus' union with what is "above." "King of Israel," on the other hand, refers to Jesus' union with what is "below," his heavenly (not political) rule over people. Thus the two titles together imply that in Jesus there is to be some form of reunion between the divine and the human, between God and Israel. In him there is the possibility of harmony, of integration.

At this point, as the prospect of integration is implied, there is a reference to Nathanael's developing belief ("[do] you believe [?]"), and the dynamic of believing seems to spur the idea of integration: Jesus tells Nathanael (v 51) that there is yet more to come—the sight of heaven opened and of God's angels moving in two directions ("ascending and descending") upon the Son of humanity, in other words, upon Jesus as utterly human, particularly as undergoing the whole cycle of life, including death and all that death entails. For someone who had problems accepting that a person from so human a place as Nazareth could signify anything good, it must have seemed extraordinary to begin envisaging that the most human of people, the Son of humanity, could be in splendid two-way communication with heaven. From having been covered by the thickness of a fig tree, he had come to a place where he could not only look upwards in faith but could also entertain the prospect of the opening of heaven, in other words, the prospect of intimate communication with God.

It is possible, even probable, that the final verse concerning the Son of humanity was adapted by the author from some other part of the gospel tradition (Bultmann, 105; Barrett, 186; Schnackenburg, 1:319–20; Brown, 88–89). But it is not out of place. As Schnackenburg (1:320) notes, "No better context can be found for it." Its image of someone who is completely open to heaven forms a carefully contrasting balance with the image of someone who is under a (dark) fig tree. Thus it is an integral part of the story of Nathanael.

The story is one of faith, of someone who from his sheltered and rather sulky place came forth to a new presence and to a new awareness of possibilities. In Johannine terms, it is a story of moving from darkness to light.

Nathanael as a Representative Character

Apart from his role as an individual, Nathanael seems also to have a representative character. As Westcott (23) indicated, his very name (*nathana-El,* "God has given"), when taken in the context of the other disciples' names, suggests that he represents what is Hebrew or Jewish. Bultmann (98) notes that the entire Nathanael narrative is Semitic in tone. Furthermore, Philip's announcement to him emphasizes continuity with the Hebrew scriptures ("Moses and the prophets"). He himself is addressed as "a true Israelite," and he in turn addresses Jesus as "Rabbi" and "King of Israel." As Brown (82) concludes, he is "a symbol of Israel coming to God."

Two further details suggest a connection between Nathanael and the Jews. He is the first person in the gospel who is described as believing (1:50)—a distinction which suits someone who represents those who were the first to believe. And he is without guile (*dolos*, 1:47)—a word which, apart from a list of vices (Mark 7:21–22), is used in the NT only of the Jews (Matt 26:4, Mark 14:1, Acts 13:10). The Jews acted out of guile and so Nathanael, being without guile, could be a representative of a renewed Judaism.

There are elements of continuity between the figures of Nathanael and Nicodemus (John 3:1–21). Apart from their Jewishness, they both begin in situations of some form of darkness (under the fig tree; at night) and both are offered the prospect of seeing the light ("you will see heaven opened," 1:51; cf. 3:19–21, coming to the light). Furthermore, in both texts, the conversations are partly in the plural. The Nathanael scene begins and ends with a plural: ". . . *we* have found," and "Amen, Amen . . . you [plural] will see. . . ." And with Nicodemus, "Amen, Amen . . . *we* speak . . . but you [plural] do not receive" (cf. 3:11–12). The usual interpretation of the plurals in the Nicodemus conversation is that they reflect the dialogue of the church and synagogue, and something similar would seem to be true of the Nathanael scene. Judaism as a whole is involved.

But while Nicodemus reappears actively in the gospel and comes to a growing acceptance of Jesus (7:50–52, 19:39), Nathanael does not. In the final scene at the seashore he is an enigmatic background figure (21:2). If he really is a representative figure, a symbol of Israel coming to God, then what element of Israel does he represent?

There is reason to suspect that the coming of Nathanael to Jesus is a symbol —from the Christian point of view—of the eventual return of the Jews to Jesus and God, the return of which Paul speaks in Romans 9–11. It is true, of course, that parts of the fourth gospel battle bitterly with the Jews. But so at times did Paul. Yet Paul was able to try to understand what was happening with the Jews, to analyze their "fall" (Rom 11:11–12), and to envisage their eventual return. If Paul was able to do that, there is no reason why the evangelist, presumably writing years later, would not be able to do something similar. So, having used the earliest calls to give a proleptic representation of the church (the two disciples, Peter, and Philip, 1:35–44), he then goes on to give a proleptic representation of the coming of those who did not belong to the church, and he does so through the figure of Nathanael, the one who did not belong to the twelve.

A complete examination of the relationship of the Nathanael story to the thought of Romans 9–11 is outside the range of this study, but it is useful to make some preliminary observations.

As Brown (86–87) suggests, the reference to Nathanael as a "true Israelite" implies a distinction between different kinds of Israelites, a distinction which "may be close to the distinction that Paul makes in Rom 9:6: 'Not all who are descended from Israel [Jacob] belong to Israel'; the true Israelite believes in Jesus." Paul applies the idea of the genuine Israelite to those Jews who, like himself, have already accepted Jesus. The fourth gospel, in accordance with the proleptic nature of the context, appears to be applying it in a different way—to those Jews who will accept Jesus at some stage in the future. What is essential is that the basic distinction with which Paul opens the discussion (cf. Rom 9:6–13) seems to appear in another form in the Nathanael story.

The center of Paul's concern is the Jews' "fall." (He uses "fall" as both a verb and a noun, Rom 11:11–12.) Nathanael too is like someone who has fallen. The enigmatic picture of an alienated person under a *fig tree* recaptures the moment after the original fall when the couple, in their disillusion, put on *fig leaves* and hid among the *trees* (Gen 3:7–8). In other words, while there was one paradigmatic fall, that of Genesis 3, both the Jews and Nathanael are visualized as being in a position analogous to the fallen.

In Romans 9–11, the return of the Jews is preceded and occasioned by the call of the Gentiles (cf. Rom 11:25–26), and the coming of Nathanael is preceded and occasioned by the call of the Gentiles' representative, Philip (1:43–46).

There is another factor, more fundamental than the call of the Gentiles, which leads the Jews and Nathanael to accept Jesus—and that is divine foreknowledge. At various points in Romans 9–11, but especially in the final verses (cf. 11:25–36), Paul emphasizes the mystery of God's will and knowledge, and that too is found in the Nathanael story—in the mysterious willing which sets the call of Philip in motion (1:43), and in the supernatural knowledge by which Jesus knows Nathanael even before Philip calls him (1:47–48). In other words, the call of Nathanael is surrounded by a down-to-earth form of the mysterious, divine will and knowledge of which Paul speaks.

What is essential is that there are some important points of contact with Romans 9–11, and, therefore, it is reasonable to suggest, at least as a working hypothesis, that Nathanael under the fig tree is a representative of alienated Israel.

Day 6 □ Discipleship and Wine

The Wedding at Cana

The setting is an extraordinarily festive one—a wedding. But then, disaster—the wine fails. The crisis, however, instead of leading to bitter disappointment, opens the way for Jesus and for a delightful surprise—over a hundred gallons of fine wine. It is a brief miracle-drama, and its purpose, above all, is to reveal the glory of Jesus, in other words to reveal a kind of creative light (cf. Schnackenburg, 1:335–37) which transforms even the darkest of moments.

Structure

It has been suggested by Schnackenburg (1:334) that this brief drama contains three scenes: the mother and Jesus, Jesus and the servants, and the steward and the bridegroom. In other words, Schnackenburg proposes a division based on the changing roles of the characters, on the variations in the *dramatis personae*.

However plausible this may seem at first, it turns out, on closer examination, to be highly questionable. While based on the variation of characters, it omits completely the characters who enfold the entire episode—the disciples (*mathētai*). And it does not do justice to those characters who, in various ways, figure at every stage of the drama—the servants (*diakonoi*). In other words, even by its own (implied) criteria, it is inadequate.

To give a reliable division of the text, it is necessary, if possible, to find literary indicators, specific details which suggest a transition from one scene or part to the next. In the preceding scenes (1:19–51), initial clues to the divisions were provided, particularly by repetitions. In most of these cases, some phraseology from the beginning of the scene was reproduced at the point where a new part began. In the Cana scene such an initial clue is provided by the beginning of v 6: "Now there were there . . ." (*ēsan de ekei*). It is a phrase which takes up and repeats, in varied form, the end of v 1: "and the mother of Jesus was there" (*ēn . . . ekei*). The use of so small a word as *ekei*, "there," may at first seem insignificant, but it had not been used in all of chapter 1, and its sudden repetition, particularly when preceded by the verb to be, acts as an initial indicator that perhaps the scene should be divided accordingly.

Upon further examination such a division would seem to make sense. The overall drama, which deals with the revelation through the wine, contains two subdramas or scenes. The first (vv 1–5) emphasizes the idea of time. When Jesus says to his mother that his hour has not yet come, and when she nonetheless speaks to the servants as if something is about to happen, the focus shifts momentarily from the wine to the timing. And when the wine actually appears (vv 6–10) there is a further subdrama which centers on the idea of a secret or mystery. Unlike the servants, the steward does not know whence the wine has come, and as he calls the bridegroom to express his surprise, the focus again shifts—this time from the wine to the secret, and to the timing of the secret—"you have kept the good wine until now."

These two ideas, the time and the secrecy, are not peripheral to the basic drama. Rather they are important aspects of what that drama is all about—the process of revelation. Revelation, the unveiling of the secret, must await a particular time. By dividing the text in two, just when the mother has said "Whatever he tells you, . . ." there is created a sense of waiting and of expectation, a sense of pregnant time. And that sense, far from being alien to the drama, corresponds to some of its most basic elements.

The Meaning of the Wine

The Cana scene is central. What preceded consisted largely of beginnings and of various views of the nature and composition of the church. What follows—the cleansing of the temple (2:12–22)—will evoke the reality of death. In the center, however, like a parable on the space of life between, stands the wedding scene. It is a summary of life, a summary of something basic in the life of the church and of the disciple.

The text is extraordinarily dense and is open to almost endless comment. It is important, therefore, not to lose sight of the decisive elements.

The essence of the story is that Jesus gives an abundant gift of wedding wine. He releases on the world an extraordinary *joie de vivre*. If Galilee in 2:1 suggests the wide world of the Gentiles, as it does in the call of Philip (1:43), then the wedding wine is for everybody. He is not, of course, the first to offer some form of re-freshment. The six stone jars which he uses had once been used for another form of re-freshment—Jewish purification. In other words, for the cleansing of faults and impurities (2:6). Cleansing is no mean achievement, but it tends to focus on the negative. Jesus, is offering something that is overwhelmingly positive. As for the meaning of what he does, it is not terribly important that, as seems likely, the primary background for the image of the wine is to be found in the OT, and that, as Bultmann (118–20) suggested, a role was also played by the wine motif of the Dionysius legend. (For discussion, cf. Hoskyns, 190–92; Lindars, 127; Schnackenburg, 1:338–40.) What is crucial, however, is an appreciation of what is explicitly present in the text itself—a wedding with wine. To discuss the wine in a way which concentrates on its origin in the OT and in culture is to lose sight of the actual wine—of this wonderful reality which is at the center of the account. Equally misleading is the view which relegates the wedding to the status of incidental background. Jesus did not multiply vinegar at a funeral. The setting and central ingredient are crucial to what is being portrayed. There is in this account an extraordinary sense of a joy which is very human—the joy of a wedding, of an indefinite number of people being invited, and of fine wine. It is an experience which is reflected, obliquely but vividly, in the brief picture of the steward who tastes the wine and wonders at its quality. Such is the gift that Jesus offers.

This does not mean that life is being portrayed as a superficial joyride. The wine which is so abundant is given "on the third day" (2:1), in other words, on a day which, within the context of the early church, cannot but evoke the resurrection (cf. Lightfoot, 108; Lindars, 124). As Fitzmyer (1981, 781) notes: "It is

. . . likely that 'on the third day' had become a very frequently used expression in Greek pre-synoptic tradition for dating the resurrection of Jesus in the early church." The fact that, as well as being given "on the third day," the wine is also associated with Jesus' "hour" and with his "glory" means that it is an outflow of that final hour when Jesus will be glorified, when he will pass from this world to the Father (cf. 13:1, 17:1; Schnackenburg, 1:329–31). In other words, the wine in question has to do with togetherness, the ultimate togetherness of Jesus with his Father. The idea that togetherness, being in communion with someone, is like drinking wine, is not unique to this gospel. Even at a very popular level such a connection is made: "Drink to me only with thine eyes, and I won't ask for wine." As Schnackenburg (1:338) indicates, it is no accident that the miracle of the wine is preceded by a picture of exuberant two-way communication with God—angels ascending and descending upon the Son of humanity (1:51). (If the descent of just one angel indicated divine communication, how much more the descent and ascent of several?) Nor is it an accident that it is set in a context which evokes intimacy. In other words, the wine is presented in the context of a wedding, which in various ways suggests intimate two-way communication. What is in question, ultimately, is the union to which the prologue alluded, the personal union which the Word has with God, and which through Jesus and his death is filtered like fine wine into the human community. It is a union which may indeed take on an extra dimension with death, but it is already present, and, however divine its ultimate roots, it issues in a very human experience of intimacy and joy.

This intimacy, however, this fine wine, is not to be taken for granted. In the first part of the scene, when Jesus says that his hour has not yet come, there is, as already mentioned, a hint that the wine is somehow connected with death, especially with the death of Jesus.

As well as a process of death, the wine also presupposes a process of labor or service. In the second part of the drama it is the servants, and not the steward, who know the origin of the wine. Well they might. They have listened and obeyed. "Whatever he tells you, do it," Jesus' mother had said, and they did. When he said to fill the jars, they filled them "to the brim"—something not to be taken for granted in the circumstances. And when he told them to draw some out and take it to the steward, they did so—again something not to be taken for granted. Filling huge jars is hard work. And taking what had been water to a steward is not without risks.

Thus the miracle is not in any juggling which Jesus does with the water, but in the acceptance of his word by the servants. It is in them, and in the fact that they have listened sufficiently well to know the origin of the wine, that the miracle really happens. And it is because the miracle is so related to what is going on inside the disciples that it is called not a miracle but a sign, *sēmeion* (2:11). A *sēmeion* is any significant action, not necessarily a miracle. As Lindars (132) emphasizes, the fact that the gospel refers to the Cana incident as a sign rather than a miracle "indicates that it is the *meaning . . .* that is really important."

This openness to meaning is a basic factor. In the analysis of the Cana scene which is offered by Schnackenburg (1:334–39, esp. 335) there is a highlighting of the idea of revelation, of the fact that at Cana Christ's power brings into the world a manifestation of glory, a kind of creative light. It is necessary, however, to complement that emphasis by another one which is equally important: it is through and in the attentive servants and disciples that the miracle happens. It is through their grasping of his word and of its meaning—in other words, through their response—that the revelation is fulfilled. Their attitude is one of contemplative alertness, and it is through that attitude, through that disposition of heart and mind, that the wine flows. The *joie de vivre* is rooted in God.

The Woman as a Representative Figure

One of the striking features of the Cana story is that the initiative is taken by Jesus' mother. This is no minor matter. The scenes involving the call of the disciples had laid careful emphasis on the fact that, under God, the initiative came from Jesus. Now, however, it lies with Jesus' mother. It is she who is first mentioned in the text —a significant detail since the introductory verses could have been written in any of a hundred different ways. And it is she who first speaks to Jesus and the servants. Jesus' mode of addressing her (''Woman'') may sound harsh, but in its time it was polite and respectful (Brown, 99). And when he says to her *ti emoi kai soi,* literally ''What [is there] to me and to you?'' he uses a rather enigmatic phrase which may indeed suggest a clashing or confusing of roles (cf. Brown, 99; Lindars, 129) but which is ambiguous enough to bring to the fore the question of her relationship to him—exactly the question that is raised by the fact that it is she, and not he, who is taking the initiative. In other words, the enigmatic phrase, by the fact that it suggests obscurely that there is some problem about roles, helps to alert the reader to the fact the role of initiator is passing from Jesus to the woman. Jesus, however, retains a role that is all-important. The miracle must wait on his hour and his word. Thus, just as he, when the initiative was his, depended on God (cf. 1:36, 43), so his mother, when the initiative is hers, depends on him.

In scholarly discussion of the role of the mother of Jesus—the fourth gospel never refers to her as Mary—one of the key points is that, apart from her role as an individual, she seems to play a role that is representative of the people. That a woman should be a symbol or representative of the people finds considerable backing in other scripture texts, particularly those which speak of Israel as a woman, and of the church as a bride (cf. esp. Gen 3:15, Ezekiel 16, Hosea 1–3, Eph 5:21–33, Rev 12:1–6; for discussion, see Brown, 107–9).

Such a role is suggested also by the context and text. The context is that of the call of the disciples, a call which acts as a summary of the origin and nature of the church. Having thus used the various calls of the disciples to bring out different aspects of the church, it is appropriate that the narrative should then go on to speak of the disciples as a whole, in other words, to speak of the church.

The text itself confirms that there is a link between the woman and the disciples. The opening verses (2:1–2) contain two phrases which link Jesus first with his mother and then with his disciples: ''. . . the mother of Jesus . . . Jesus and his disciples. . . .'' The literary structure in these verses is such that it suggests a balance between ''mother'' and ''his disciples.'' A further balance is found in the scene as a whole: it begins with "the mother of Jesus" (2:1) and ends with "his disciples" (2:11). And in 1:5 (in Greek) the two terms are juxtaposed: "Says his mother [to] the servants."

Such details of literary structure may seem insignificant, yet it is precisely the significance of such details which recent literary studies have helped to articulate. (See, for instance, Trible, 1978, 79–105; Alter, 1981, esp. 114–15.) The essential conclusion is that, for several reasons, the woman does indeed seem to be connected with the disciples and thus with the church.

Yet it does not seem that her identification with the church is complete. Her role is preparatory—unlike the disciples, she does not appear in the second scene (vv 6–11) —and so it seems better to regard her not as the church but as the people which preceded the church, the faithful people of Israel. At the crucifixion she will reappear, again not as the church, but as someone who is absorbed into the church (19:27, "And he took her to his own home").

Conclusion

Within the gospel as a whole the wedding at Cana represents a considerable development. It indicates, more clearly than any of the preceding episodes, that the ministry of Jesus has become quite public. It also indicates explicitly that his disciples have come to believe in him. Thus it represents a dramatic advance in the narrative.

At the same time it gives an idealized summary of God's gift to the world and of life in the church. It is a church which is sensitive to need and ready to take initiative, but it is also a church which, in its directives and in its service, draws upon Jesus' decisive hour and listens eagerly to his word. As a result there flows through it and through its servants, like a rich and abundant wine, a sense of union with Jesus and, through Jesus, with God. Here there is no dichotomy between spiritual depth and external service. Rather it is spiritual depth—attentiveness to the Word—which fuels external service.

It needs to be emphasized again that this picture is idealized and that the gospel does not use the word "church." Thus it is not being said that this flow of divine union and external service is coterminus with "the church." It seems significant too that, at the wedding, the person who is supposed to be in charge, the steward, has only a limited idea of what is going on. But the servants know —those who had listened so attentively to Jesus. There is here a variation on the theme of Day 3 (1:35–42): that it is the nameless disciples, and not the prominent Peter, who discover the Anointed. Thus, while painting a magnificent portrait of the divine presence among people, the text does not glorify either "the church" or its officials.

However, despite its reservation about using the word "church," the gospel does provide a framework or context for discussing the church. The church may be narrow and its officials limited, but it partakes of the mysterious realities of which the gospel speaks. Its sacraments, likewise, despite all their limitations, are to be understood against this profound background of union with the divine. Any discussion of the eucharist and eucharistic wine, for instance, cannot but be influenced by the fact that, at Cana, wine is portrayed as depending on, or flowing from, Jesus' ''hour,'' and as something which is associated with two-way communication and a wedding. The question of marriage also cannot but be enlightened and dignified by the fact that a wedding is a way of revealing God's glory. It suggests, as does Eph 5:21–33, that there is some continuity between divine forms of union and the union of marriage. And perhaps there is some instruction in the fact that even this ''exemplary'' wedding is not without its moments of crisis, confusion, waiting, hard work, ignorance, surprise, and puzzlement.

The Cleansing and Replacing of the Temple

Evocations of Life, Death, Resurrection, and Belief

In scholarly discussion of the temple incident much attention is given to the contrast with the synoptics (cf. esp. Hoskyns, 197–99; Schnackenburg, 1:353–55; Brown, 116–20). According to these other gospels the episode occurred towards the end of the ministry, and their account of it is very short—just two or three verses (cf. Matt 21:12–13 and parr.). In John the account is not only much earlier but also much longer. The cleansing itself is recounted in greater detail (cf. 2:12–17, esp. vv 14–17), and it is then followed by an important discussion, not found in the synoptics, about destroying and raising the temple—in other words, about rebuilding or replacing it (2:18–22).

In accordance with the nature of this study, however, comparison with the synoptics is left aside, and full attention is given to John's present text—to his account of the cleansing and replacing of the temple, and to the place of that account within John's context.

While the Cana scene suggested a *joie de vivre*, the temple scene which follows it gives intimations of limitation, tension, and death. The cleansing of the temple, therefore, is quite different in mood from the Cana scene. Yet the continuity between the two scenes is considerable. For instance, the Cana scene's faint references to Jesus' death and resurrection ("On the third day"; "my hour"; "revealed his glory") are echoed in clearer references to Jesus' death and resurrection "in three days." The idea of a sign reappears in varied form. And the emphasis on the disciples is maintained—though again in varied form.

There are textual variants in 2:12, but the version given in the present writer's translation seems reasonably assured (cf. Schnackenburg, 1:343).

Structure

The text concerning the temple episode begins, not with the ascent to Jerusalem ("he ascended," 2:13), but with the preceding verse—the descent to Capernaum ("he descended," 2:12). The Capernaum verse has been seen by commentators in diverse ways. Some regard it as pertaining in some way to the Cana episode (Lindars, 132). Others, some of whom group it with the Cana scene, regard it as some kind of free-floating element—a transition or interlude (Westcott, 39; Lagrange, 62–64; Barrett, 194; Brown, 112–13; Strathmann, 58; Morris, 186–88; Schulz, 47; Haenchen, 1:175). And yet others group it in some way or other with the temple episode (Loisy, 146–47; Hoskyns, 192; Lightfoot, 111; Schnackenburg, 1:342–43; Sanders, 115).

Discussion of this puzzlingly placed verse is frequently dominated by issues of history and background, particularly by comparison with the synoptic references to a Capernaum ministry (cf. Mark 1:21–2:12 and parr.). In examining its place within the text, however, it is necessary to look at the text itself, for it is there, rather than in the background, that the necessary clues appear to be present.

And these clues, literary details, indicate that the verse belongs to the temple episode.

One clue consists of the balance between "he descended" (to Capernaum) and "he ascended" (to Jerusalem). The two phrases seem to be carefully linked, making the going down an introduction to the going up, an introduction to the ascent to Jerusalem. A further clue consists of the balance between the opening reference to his mother (". . . he descended to Capernaum, he and his mother . . .") and the closing reference to his disciples (". . . his disciples . . . believed," 2:22). At Cana "mother" and "disciples" were related. In other words, if the Capernaum verse is read as the beginning of the entire temple episode, there is a double balance—first between its two opening verses (12 and 13), and also between its two enclosing verses (12 and 22). A similar phenomenon was noticed in discussing the Cana scene and the role of the woman as representative. There was a double balance—first between its opening verses (1 and 2) and also between its enclosing verses (1 and 11).

The idea that the episode begins with v 12 finds further backing from the manner in which chap. 7 begins. There too, just as in 2:12–13, there is first an "After this . . ." (7:1; cf. 2:12), and then the introducing of a Jewish feast ("There was at hand, . . ." 7:2; cf. 2:13).

It may seem strange that the account of a simple incident, the cleansing of the temple, should reach back, so to speak, to include the descent to Capernaum. But the incident is not simple. In its later part, particularly in its final verse (2:22), it reaches far forward to include the resurrection and a summary of the disciples' post-resurrectional belief. In speaking of the temple the text wishes to speak of a much broader subject—life in the body—and part of that life is the brief sojourn at Capernaum.

The second clue concerning structure is that the text falls into two basic parts —first, the actual cleansing of the temple, and then, beginning with the Jews' demand for a sign in v 18, the discussion about the temple being destroyed and raised. That the text thus divides at v 18 is agreed to by a number of writers (e.g. Westcott, 40; Hoskyns, 192–96; Brown, 122; Morris, 188–96), and Schnackenburg (1:344) sees the narrative as "strikingly in the nature of a diptych." Whether Schnackenburg's diptych is accurate seems debatable—at some points his analysis seems forced and he does not take due account of 2:12—but he is certainly right in emphasizing that both parts of the narrative conclude with "his disciples remembered . . ." (vv 17, 22). It is this kind of repetition which in all the preceding episodes (1:19–2:11) indicates the division of the text into two parts.

The Significance of Jesus' Actions: A Protest against Abusive Commerce . . .

At first sight the cleansing of the temple may seem to be a rather restricted affair: at a given moment Jesus encountered the commercialization of temple worship and, in a protest reminiscent of the prophets, effectively halted the abuse (cf. Brown, 121).

But in John's finished text much more is at stake. The most obvious clue comes in the later part of the scene, when it is said explicitly that the word "temple" refers to a body. The body immediately in question is the risen body of Jesus, and there is an implication that the Jewish temple is to be replaced, as a center of worship, by the risen Jesus (cf. Schnackenburg, 1:356; Brown, 124–25). Thus the apparently restricted incident has a universal dimension—it involves dimly the perspective of a time when the narrowly based worship of the Jerusalem temple will be replaced by a center of worship which is open to all. It is this universal dimension which allows the whole incident to be understood more thoroughly.

Center stage consists of the *hieron* (2:14, 15), in other words, the "temple precincts . . . the outer court of the temple, the Court of the Gentiles" (Brown, 115). The area in question was vast. With a perimeter of nearly half a mile, it was almost a town unto itself. Within it was the *naos,* the sanctuary or temple proper (2:20) which had taken decades to build and which was accessible to Jews only. The outer court, however, was open to everyone, and it would seem that business was booming. It is at this point, more than in any preceding text, that the gospel describes in some detail the traffic of human transactions. These transactions centered first of all on a considerable variety of animals; they were selling oxen and sheep and doves. The transactions also centered on money and varieties of money-changers—the *kermatistai* (v 14), which refers properly to those who changed large coins into small, and the *kollubistai* (v 15) a word which is used apparently as an interchangeable term and which "is derived from the fee paid for the exchange" (Westcott, 41). It would seem to be because of a subtle satiric touch rather than coincidence that the money-changers are described in these rather obscure interchangeable terms. The various transactions may be explained in relation to the temple—in relation to the need to give animals and suitable money-offerings, coins that were Jewish rather than those that bore any heathen symbol —but the transactions also evoke the whole world of commerce, everything from animal markets to money markets. In an earlier scene, when John first saw Jesus, the gospel spoke of a lamb and a dove as animals which in some way reflected something of God. But the only thing explicitly associated with the oxen, sheep, and doves in this scene is the making of money—they were being sold.

As the text describes what happened, there is a suggestion of Jesus coming suddenly into that world of commerce. He "found" them, and then in a triad of strong verbs, it is said that "he drove out . . . and poured out . . . and turned over." There seem to be a number of ironic touches. The "driving out" (or "throwing out"), a term that could be used of animals (as it is in 10:4), is used of the animal-sellers. The "pouring out" and "turning over" has a terrible appropriateness in the context of money-changing. And the harsh way of addressing the dove-sellers—"Take these things out of here"—involves a satire on what they are selling. As they figure in the text, these are not doves that fly. Rather, in contradiction to what a dove is supposed to be and do, they are objects that have to be moved. Jesus' intervention, therefore, constitutes a severe critique of this whole world of commerce.

Such a sweeping interruption might seem to belittle human industry, to put it down in the name of religion. But Jesus, however much he wants true worship, is not discouraging human industry or work. These people are not making or producing anything, except in a highly negative sense—they are making (verb *poieō*) the Father's house into a house of trade. Ironically, the only one who is actually making anything, producing something, is Jesus—he makes (*poieō*) a whip from cords. To imply that he took some rushes and used them as though they were a whip does not do justice to what the text says—from *cords* he *made* a *whip*. It indicates a human industriousness which is in sharp contrast to those about him. Of them the only active verbs used indicate two things—they *sold* and they *sat*.

It may be seen, therefore, that, in face of negative abusive commerce, Jesus protests, and he does so both by his own human industriousness and by emphasizing that the temple is supposed to be like the house of a parent—"my Father's house."

. . . And an Implicit Reminder of a Forgotten Dimension

There are other aspects of protest too, and the first would seem to be found in the scene's opening verses—in the enigmatic account of his brief sojourn at Capernaum and of his ascent to Jerusalem.

Given that Capernaum is below sea level it may seem at first sight to make sense to speak of "going down" to Capernaum and "going up" to Jerusalem. But if Jesus wanted to go from Cana to Jerusalem a visit to Capernaum would constitute a major detour. Detours are often necessary, but they require explanations, and the account does not give one. Thus at the level of history, the text as it stands does not quite make sense. This need not indicate that it is confused or incomplete but rather that whatever its historical value, it has another meaning. Such in fact is what is perceived by Schnackenburg (1:343): "When in the fourth gospel Jesus stays at a given place, or leaves it and avoids it, there is always something more than a merely historical record." So what does the text mean when it says, literally translated, "and they abode (verb *menō*) there not many days?" What is the connotation of this brief abiding? And why the emphasis on the negative "not many"? Again, Schnackenburg (1:343): "Jesus is not tied to home or family or friends, but presses on to the self-revelation which is to be made in the city of God." In other words, home and family and friends, however pleasant, do not provide an abiding place, and it is necessary that the fundamental focus be on God. It is a thought somewhat akin to that found in Hebrews—that "we have here no abiding city" (*menousa polis,* Hebr 13:14). It is in this context of having no abiding city that Jesus' reference to his Father's house takes on greater meaning. Amid the complexities of human relationships, cities, and commerce, Jesus focuses on the ultimate reality—on God, and on the idea of dwelling with God. The idea is not explicit, but by referring to the temple as "my Father's house" there is an implication not only that God has a house but that Jesus belongs there, as a child belongs in the house of a parent. And it is towards that house—a house which in the later part of the scene is replaced by the idea of the risen body—it is towards that house rather than towards the brief abode of not many days that he directs his ultimate energy and attention.

This does not imply any neglect of down-to-earth matters. The Cana scene had shown him as profoundly immersed in human cares and joys. And in the temple precinct he is the only one actually working. But there is also a level or point at which affiliation with the divine becomes all-absorbing, and it is that which breaks to the surface in the cleansing scene. It is hardly an accident that this happens at the approach of Passover, the time of the year when Jesus will eventually die, or that the scene goes on to allude to his death and resurrection. For it is particularly death and the prospect of death which brings out the full reality of affiliation with the divine.

Thus, in face of commercialized worship and crass money-making there is, basically, a twofold protest—there is an example of work which stops the empty show, and there is a series of reminders that life on earth is brief and that one's ultimate home is with God.

Reactions: Incipient Diversity and Division

At this early stage of the gospel there are no harsh divisions between people. Where there are indications of negativity—as in the interrogators' apparent failure to appreciate John (1:19–28) or in the initial skepticism of Nathanael (1:46)—the sense of refusal is muted. So, even when Jesus does something so radical as clearing the temple, the reactions are primarily positive.

But not completely.

The first faint hint of dissonance comes with the mention of his brothers: "After this he went down to Capernaum, with his mother and his brothers and his disciples. . . ." The reference may seem absolutely innocuous, yet as Schnack-enburg (1:343) notes, something is missing. In a context which emphasizes the faith of his mother and his disciples (cf. 2:1–5,11,22), there is no indication of anything similar on the part of his brothers. The overall gospel narrative is so graded that there is no question, at this early stage, of saying openly that anybody did not believe, but the intimation is there, and at the beginning of chapter 7, when his brothers are next mentioned, their disbelief is explicit (7:3–5).

The second part of the scene begins, as did the first, with a further hint of dissonance: "the Jews" ask for a sign. It is a dissonance which is much more noticeable than the silent non-reaction of the brothers (2:12), but, as in the case of the brothers, what makes it stand out is the implied contrast with "his disciples." The brothers had been grouped with the disciples, but unlike them, were never said to have believed. And the Jews also, though in a different way, are grouped with the disciples, but, unlike the disciples, who "remembered" the scripture (2:17, cf. 2:22), the Jews apparently did not. The remembering of the scripture is related to believing (cf. 2:17, 22) and so the Jewish failure is significant; it is an early intimation of the Jewish failure to believe.

When Jesus tells them to "destroy this temple" and that he will raise it up in three days, they are so preoccupied with the superficialities of history ("It has taken forty-six years . . .") that, even though they are correct, or perhaps precisely because they are so correct, they miss the deeper theological meaning, they miss the fact that "temple" refers to his body.

The disciples, however, are more capable of seeing beyond superficialities and of setting things in their appropriate context. When Jesus first cleansed the temple and mentioned his Father's house they were able, on the basis of memory and implied earlier belief, to relate his actions and words to Psalm 69: "Zeal for your house will consume me" (Ps 69:9). Nothing similar is recorded of the brothers or the Jews. They seem withdrawn or distant, and it is interesting, following Brown (124), to quote the psalm's preceding verse (69:8): "*I have become a stranger to my brothers. . . .*"

When Jesus is raised from the dead the disciples were sufficiently alert and receptive to remember what he had said about raising the temple in three days— just as they had earlier remembered the scripture. In this episode, therefore, as also at Cana, the disciples are pictured as attentive to the word, whether the word be that of scripture or Jesus. And it is on that positive note that the narrative concludes: the disciples believed in both scripture and Jesus' word.

The Body as Representative

The positive reaction of the disciples—their believing—is not a purely individual experience. It is something shared: as if in solidarity with one another "they remembered" (2:17), and "they remembered . . . and believed" (2:22). Such apparent solidarity adds plausibility to the view that the text on the raising of Jesus' body (2:20–21), as well as referring to the resurrection, contains an implicit reference to "the body of Christ"—the church (cf. 1 Corinthians 12, Col 1:15, Eph 5:25–33) (cf. Lightfoot, 113–14; Dodd, 1953, 302). Schnackenburg (1:356–57) rejects this, but his main reason for doing so is that in this text—as earlier in the Cana episode—he is so focused on Christological revelation that he does not allow adequate emphasis on the complementary idea of the church's response.

While the matter is not easy to judge, it seems difficult to rule out the idea that "body" has a corporate dimension. The image of the church as a body would form a suitable complement to the earlier image (at Cana) of the people as a woman; in Eph 5:25–33 "woman" (or wife, *gynē*) and "body" are grouped together in speaking of the church. (It would also be seen as complementing the image of the wine; both act as signs [2:11, 18].) And it may be of significance that in some phrases of the temple episode, Jesus is almost like a corporate personality: there are two verbs ("he descended . . . he ascended") which, though used in the singular about Jesus, refer in fact to the movement not just of Jesus but also of his disciples.

Thus the cleansing of the temple, however disturbing initially, ultimately opens the prospect of a truer home and of a deeper solidarity.

The Temple Cleansing as the Culmination of 1:1–2:22

What was begun in the prologue finds a culmination in the cleansing of the temple. The *logos,* for instance, which is set at the beginning of the prologue (1:1; cf. 1:14), and which is absent in subsequent episodes, reappears in varied form at the end of the temple episode: "They believed the *logos . . .*" (2:22). The sense of someone coming, which is found in diverse forms in the opening texts (1:9,14,27,29) is counterbalanced at the end not only by faint evocations of departure (Jesus' hour, his few days, and his being consumed, 2:4,12,17), but also by ever clearer references to his death and resurrection (2:19–22). And the picture of the disciples as believing—a picture which begins implicitly with the two people who sought Jesus' abode (1:35–29)—also becomes clearer:

To Nathanael
> "Because I said to you, I saw you . . . (do) you believe(?)."

At Cana
> "His disciples believed in him."

At Jerusalem
> "His disciples remembered that it was written. . . ."
> "His disciples remembered that he had said this, and they believed the scripture and the word which Jesus spoke."

Thus the entire text (1:1–2:22) has a certain completeness.

It has been suggested in Chapter 5 of the introduction that this initial synthesis (1:1–2:22) is meant, among other things, to reflect the Jesus of a particular stage of belief, especially the belief of young adulthood. Certainly the Jesus in the temple scene is vigorous and courageous. He not only protests against crass money-making and commercialized religion, he also faces the prospect, still rather dim, of his own death and resurrection. It is as though he has a terrible clarity about his true home and destiny. From one point of view this death seems easy: what was destroyed will be raised in three days. There is no mention of anguish or pain. Yet the cleansing involves a radical disturbance, a violence almost, and that disturbance is associated with the idea of Jesus' being consumed (2:15–17). In other words, as the text now stands, the allusions to death are shadowed by the spectre of a certain form of upheaval. That spectre, however, does not conquer, for by the time the narrative is finished the emphasis has moved to the idea of resurrection.

Excursus 1: Continuity, Gradualness, and Repetition in the Narrative of 1:1–2:22

Before examining Part 2, it is useful to look more closely at the way in which John 1:1–2:22 maintains narrative continuity. Obviously all narratives, unless they are insanely incoherent, maintain continuity; every story has a beginning, development, and conclusion. But the techniques for building continuity vary enormously.

In films, for instance, whether the plot is simple or complex, the sense of continuity is heightened by the imaginative use of a musical theme, or song, which occurs again and again in a variety of ways. It may be further reinforced by the repetition of some action or phrase. In *Silverstreak*, for instance—an account of a dramatic train journey from Los Angeles to Chicago—one of the elements of continuity consists of having the hero repeatedly thrown or forced from the train. In each instance the circumstances are quite different, yet there is enough repetition both to build a sense of continuity and to heighten the viewer's amusement. However, a sense of continuity may also be heightened by a technique as simple as the word-for-word repetition of some small phrase. Thus, in the popular conception of *Casablanca,* a considerable effect is achieved by the repeated exhortation, "Play it again, Sam."

In written narrative there is equal scope for various forms of repetition (cf. Kawin, 1972), and as a number of authors have shown (cf. Gros Louis, 1982, 58; Culpepper, 1983, 74, 200; Tannehill, 1984, 237–40; and esp. Alter, 1981, 88–113; and Sternberg, 1985, 365–440), repetition forms an integral part of biblical story telling. Alter (95) sums up:

> What we find, then, in biblical narrative is an elaborately integrated system of repetitions, some dependent on the actual recurrence of individual phonemes, words, or short phrases, others linked to the actions, images, and ideas that are part of the world of the narrative we "reconstruct" as readers but that are not necessarily woven into the verbal structure of the narrative. The two kinds of repetition, of course, [the verbal or "material" kind, and the more dramatic or conceptual kind], are somewhat different in their effect, but they are often used together by the Hebrew writers to reinforce each other and to produce a concerted whole.

Both kinds of repetitions are found in John 1:1–2:22. To some degree the presence of these repetitions has already been suggested. Reference was made to the repetitions which are found within the prologue, and the work of de la Potterie (1984, 354–81) provides a partial idea of the way in which these repetitions involve order, complexity, and delicacy. It was noted too that the actions of one day are sometimes found in repeated or varied form on the following days. In particular, it was remarked that the heavenly descent on the Son of humanity involves a variation of the Spirit's descent on Jesus, and that some of the actions and ideas surrounding the wedding feast repeat aspects of the actions and ideas of the previous days.

But other aspects of continuity and repetition, particularly repetition of the more verbal or material kind, have scarcely been mentioned, and it is necessary to give at least a slightly more complete idea of this phenomenon as it occurs in John 1:1–2:22.

The phenomenon of narrative continuity is seen first of all in the relation of the prologue to the drama which follows. Apart from providing "the beginning" which precedes the succession of days, it introduces the relationship basic to the first two of those days—that of John the Baptist to Jesus. Thus, the prologue's first reference to that relationship—John was *not* the light but simply a God-sent witness to it (1:6–8)—is developed in various forms in the early days, particularly on the first (1:19–28). And the second reference—John's recognizing the grace-filled figure who came after him but who also existed before him (1:14–15; note 1:16–18)—is developed in various forms both on the first day and especially on the second (1:27,29–34). Thus, apart from the continuity between the prologue and the gospel as a whole, there is a particular continuity between the prologue and the passages which immediately follow it.

When the events of the successive days (1:19–51) are examined, one finds a similar phenomenon of literary continuity. (For some of the details, cf. Brown 67, 84–85.) Each day brings something that is quite new, but to some degree it also repeats and develops the episodes and words of the preceding days. Thus, John's concluding declarations of the first day ("I baptize in water [but] among you stands one whom you do *not know*—the one coming after me," 1:26–27) are all taken up and elaborated on the second day ("Behold the lamb of God. . . . This is he of whom I said, '*After* me comes . . .' and I did not know him, but for this I came baptizing in water," 1:29–31). And the third day, though it breaks much new ground by introducing the first disciples, nonetheless begins by repeating the opening declaration of the second day: "Behold the lamb of God" (1:36). Furthermore, while the account of the third day goes on to say that Andrew "*finds* . . . Simon *and says to him, 'We have found* . . .'" (1:41), the account of the fourth day tells that Philip "*finds* Nathanael *and says to him,* . . . '*We have found* . . .'"(1:45). And there are other elements of the fourth day which repeat and develop aspects of the preceding days (cf. esp. "Come and see" [1:39, 46]; seeing a descent from heaven [1:33, 51; cf. Brown, 91]).

Within the synthesizing drama (1:19–2:11), the wedding at Cana (2:1–11) constitutes a colorful final flourish. It is dramatically different from the earlier episodes, yet it too maintains a significant degree of continuity with the preceding text. The time ("on the third day") both sets it apart from the preceding days and builds, climactically, on them. As a striking miracle it is a partial fulfillment of Jesus' promise to Nathanael: "You shall see greater things" (1:50). As an event in which Jewish purification jars are given a new content (2:6), it corresponds to the fact that in 1:19–2:11 as a whole, the explicit Jewish presence fades away (the Jews and their leaders are mentioned on the first day [1:19, 24] but not any more). As a story in which the better wine comes later (2:10), it evokes the relationship of John and Jesus; Jesus was better, but came later (1:15, 27,30). As an event in which the disciples came to believe (2:11), it develops the process of discipleship which had been described on Days 3 and 4 (1:35–51). Brown (77, cf. 105) summarizes: "In 1:35–51 and 2:1–11 John presents a conspectus of Christian vocation. On each day there is a gradual deepening of insight and a profounder realization of who it is the disciples are following." And as a "beginning" of signs, in which Jesus revealed "his glory" (2:11), it develops the process of revelation alluded to the prologue (1:14).

Some indication has also been given of the continuity between the account of the cleansing of the temple (2:12–22) and the text which precedes it, in particular between its reference to the disciples believing and the somewhat similar references in the preceding two episodes (cf. 1:50; 2:11,22).

The essential point is that, apart from the coherence that is to be expected in any well-told account, the description of the successive days and of the temple cleansing contains a strong emphasis on narrative continuity. As the story moves forward, earlier phrases and elements reappear in repeated or varied form, and to a considerable degree, it is through these processes of repetition and variation that the narrative is forged into a unity.

One of the basic features of repetition in John is that it is carefully graded. The text moves slowly from suggestion or intimation to a narrative which is more and more explicit. To some degree this is fairly obvious. With regard to the disciples, the evangelist first gives suggestions or implications of belief (when Andrew calls Simon, and when Philip calls Nathanael) and then gives three belief statements which are not only explicit but increasingly elaborate (1:50; 2:11,22). And by referring somewhat obscurely to the destruction of "this temple" he has begun to intimate Jesus' coming death.

This technique of gradualness is not unique to John. It is found for instance in Hebrews and in various parts of the OT. Thus Job's first soliloquy "contains a skillfully graded transition from the patient Job of the prologue to the impatient Job of the dialogue" (R. A. F. MacKenzie, 1968, 31:18). And it has been noted by Reese (1983, 83) that in the Book of Wisdom the author "frequently . . . edges into his . . . subject." Von Rad (1972, 170), in a similar context, speaks of "the fine gradations of ideas from one sentence to the next." Examples could be multiplied.

It is important to note this phenomenon of gradualness because very often it is only when account is taken of it that the continuity between texts may be noticed.

Furthermore, elements which at first seem almost hopelessly obscure make more sense when viewed as a first intimation in the gradual process of developing a major idea. Thus the calling of the Greek-sounding Philip and Jewish-sounding Nathanael may seem quite unrelated to the later idea of Jesus' encounter with both Jews and Greeks, but when viewed as a first intimation of that later process it becomes somewhat more credible.

The conclusion, therefore, with regard to the literary composition of 1:1–2:22, is that it is a well-wrought unit in which, by various processes of repetition and variation, each episode maintains continuity with what precedes.

The phenomenon of continuity has been emphasized because it is one which will be noted again and again, and it is useful at this early stage to try to see it for what it is—part of a well-known literary practice, one which makes particular use of various techniques of repetition.

A further reason for emphasizing this literary practice is that it has sometimes been misunderstood. The repetitions have been interpreted as "doublets" or "imperfections"—elements which reflect a complex and rather confused process of editing (for references, see Von Wahlde, 1983, 544–45). Such an hypothesis is not only complex and unclear, it is also unnecessary. All the data in the text may be accounted for on the basis of the simplest of hypotheses—that it was composed by a competent author who knew how to use literary techniques.

One of the effects of the evangelist's pervasive use of repetitive techniques is that at times the gospel story may seem boring. Such an impression is partly valid. Similar ideas and words do indeed occur over and over and over. The repetitive technique, however, would appear also to have an immensely positive purpose. Like a repetitive mantra it helps to focus the mind, to bring it to a creative stillness in which superficial distractions fall away and in which it is possible to reach a greater sense of what is real. Thus in dealing with the idea of abiding union, the evangelist places it at the center of the gospel's spirituality. He also uses a fundamental literary technique which, insofar as it concentrates the mind in a positive way, disposes the reader for the actual achievement of union.

Part 2 □ The Second Year

From the Weight of Sin to Greater Life

The Journey, and the Tension between the
Divided Self and God's Offer of Intimate Union

The basic plot of Part 2 is relatively simple: beginning at Jerusalem, and with Nicodemus, Jesus goes through the land offering life. The action takes about a year—from one Passover to another (2:23, 6:4)—and it culminates in the contrasting reactions of Peter and Judas (6:66–71).

The first part of the plot centers on a geographic movement from Jerusalem to Galilee, particularly on a journey from Judea to Cana, and during that process significant roles are played by four peoples—Nicodemus, John the baptizer, the woman of Samaria, and the Capernaum official whose son was sick (*astheneō*, "to be weak/sick") (2:23–chap. 4).

The later part of the story (chaps. 5 and 6) consists of two complementary episodes, the first set in Jerusalem, the other in Galilee. Both episodes occur at feasts (5:1, 6:4), and–uniquely in the fourth gospel—both involve crowds of people who are either sick or intent on the sick (*astheneō*) (5:3; 6:2). To these, in diverse ways, Jesus offers life. In chapter 5 the offer of life is exemplified in the poolside curing of the man who had been impaired for 38 years; in chapter 6 it is seen in the multiplication of bread and in the discourse on the bread of life.

As well as describing Jesus' offer, the text also speaks of various responses. Some are positive, but there is doubt too, and hostility. It is the hint of the hostility of the Pharisees which first impels Jesus to journey from Judea to Galilee (4:1–3). And in chapters 5 and 6 there are reactions which are even more negative—the Jews' death-oriented persecution (5:16–18) and the spectre of Judas' diabolical treachery (6:70–71). Thus, while the text does speak of the offer of life, it also begins to evoke the shadows of death.

Apart from the plot, however, is the basic theme. To some degree it has already been indicated—the giving of new life. But the process of giving new life to human beings is not an easy one. Resistance may be offered for several reasons, whether because of a tenacious clinging to something such as prestige, power, or a way of life; because of fear; or simply because of lethargy, plain laziness. There is an internal conflict, a conflict which in some ways may be described as one of flesh versus spirit, and it is with this conflict, this picture of a divided self, that Part 2 is largely preoccupied. The use of *astheneō* (4:46; 5:3; 6:2) not only indicates sickness, it also evokes a deep-rooted weakness.

The flesh-Spirit contrast is stated most explicitly at the beginning and at the conclusion of the text. At the beginning, it occurs in the early stages of the conversation with Nicodemus: "What is born of the flesh is flesh, and what is born of the spirit is spirit" (3:6). At the conclusion, it occurs after the bread of life discourse: "It is the spirit that gives life; the flesh accomplishes nothing" (6:63). It is, as Brown (300) notes, "the same contrast." And between these clear statements (in 3:6, 6:63) this contrast is seen in a variety of ways, particularly in the conduct of the characters. There is a flesh-Spirit conflict of one kind, for instance, in the energetic Samaritan woman, and a different form of that conflict in the lethargic man at the poolside. The characters in John's narrative turn out, in fact, to be strikingly diverse, yet in various ways they all bring out aspects of this basic conflict, this struggle for or against the perceiving and receiving of life.

This part of the gospel, Part 2, insofar as it emphasizes a basic conflict, is quite distinct from Part 1. There the emphasis had been on a relatively harmonious process of revelation and response, and the entire text, centered on the week-long drama, had implied a certain harmony of creation. But now, as the flesh-Spirit drama develops, there is an implication that, whatever be creation's fundamental harmony, it contains some kind of incompleteness or wound, and that that wound runs through the entire human makeup.

Among the other NT texts which deal with the flesh-Spirit struggle one of the most notable is Romans 1–8. But while Romans conducts its debate in rather abstract terms, John 2:23–chap. 6 provides a lifelike narrative.

As well as speaking of division, Part 2 speaks also of love and union. At various stages, beginning with the explicit statement, "For God so loved the world . . . ." (3:16), there are indications that the life which is offered through Jesus is not just some kind of abstract revelation, whether gnostic or otherwise, but above all a life which involves a quality of love or intimacy. Thus the text not only uncovers the pervasive human maladies of dividedness and weakness, but it indicates also how these maladies are remedied—with a gift of life which incorporates a unifying love.

As indicated in Chapter 5 of the introduction, these chapters seem to reflect in a special way the middle part of life. The youthfulness of earlier days has been left behind and, almost without realizing it, one has embarked on a journey. (In chap. 4 the idea of a journey is clear. But it had already begun, almost imperceptibly, in the preceding episodes, in the transition from Jerusalem to the Judean countryside [2:23; 3:22].)

Structure: The Broad Pattern

There is considerable agreement that an important subdivision occurs at the end of chapter 4—in other words, at the end of Jesus' journey from Judea to Galilee (e.g. cf. Westcott, 80; Brown, cxli, 199; Schnackenburg, 2:1).

What is not so clear is the remainder of the structure. With regard to chapters 5 and 6 it will be seen that there is a dispute about how these chapters should be arranged. And the structure of the account of the movement from Jerusalem to Galilee (2:23–chap. 4) also presents some problems. For instance, because of the way the chapters have been divided, there is a tendency, especially in some translations (e.g., JB, NAB), to regard the brief account of Jesus' ministry in Jerusalem (2:23–25) as consisting primarily of a conclusion or sequel to the cleansing of the temple. Yet when these verses are examined closely they are generally seen not so much as a conclusion to chapter 2 but rather as an introduction to the Nicodemus episode (cf. Hoskyns, 201; Bultmann, 130; Dodd, 1963, 235; Schnackenburg, 1:358; Brown, 126; Haenchen, 1:192; Beasley-Murray, 43). In other words, the reference to Jesus knowing what is in a person (*anthrōpos,* 2:25) prepares the way for the next statement: "There was an *anthrōpos . . .* named Nicodemus. . . ."

Further examination of the text (2:23–chap. 4) shows that it falls into four episodes:

- The coming of Nicodemus (2:23–3:21);
- The coming of "all" ("the bride") to baptism and the fading of John (3:22–36);
- The coming of the Samaritan woman (4:1–42);
- The coming of the Capernaum official (4:43–54).

The idea of "coming" (*erchomai*) to Jesus is mentioned explicitly in all four cases (cf. 3:2,26; 4:7,47). Taken together these references build a sense of concerted movement, of people coming to Jesus from all sides.

In all four episodes there is an introduction. The coming of Nicodemus, as already mentioned, is introduced by the brief account of Jesus' Jerusalem ministry —the reaction to his signs and his knowledge of the human person (2:23–25). The account of people coming to John and Jesus is introduced by a picture of various baptisms (of Jesus and John) and by a reference to the impending demise (through imprisonment) of John (3:22–24). The coming of the Samaritan woman is introduced by an enigmatic picture of various administrators (Jesus and the disciples) of baptism and by a cryptic reference (through the image of exhaustion) to the ultimate departure of Jesus (4:1–6). Finally, the coming of the Capernaum official is introduced by a summary of the Galileans' reactions to Jesus—a reaction which is explicitly connected with Jesus' earlier brief ministry in Jerusalem (4:43–45, cf. 2:23–25). Thus the fourth introduction obliquely reflects the first, and the third reflects the second.

Taken together all four introductions constitute a progressive unity. Part of this unity is seen in details so small that they seem almost insignificant—for instance in the revolving pattern of the introductions' opening words: "When. . . . After. . . . When. . . . After. . . ." (*Hōs. . . . Meta. . . . Hōs. . . . Meta . . .* ; 2:23; 3:22; 4:1,43). Other facets of unity are more subtle or significant. For instance, the introduction to the Samaria episode—with its motifs of baptism, water (the well), journeying, latent hostility, and intimation of departure (4:1–6)—this introduction involves a complex but coherent advance on the motifs of the introduction to the John episode (3:22–24). From one introduction to the next there is a progressive geographic movement: Jerusalem, Judea (or the Judean countryside), Samaria, Galilee. And there is unified progression, too, in the picture of ministry-and-response. Introductions two and three imply dimly a progression among those who actively minister—the text suggests a shift from John to Jesus to the disciples (3:22–24, 4:1–6). And introductions one and four indicate a shift among those who respond—a shift from the inadequate sign-centered reaction in Jerusalem to the more receptive and all-embracing reaction in Galilee (2:23–25, 4:43–45).

What is being given, therefore, in these four texts is an introductory framework, a summary of the basic process of ministry-and-response and of the way in which that process moves from one place and stage to the next. It is within that framework, in the course of the various episodes, that the main theme is developed.

Structure: The Leading Role of a Neglected Text (2:23–25, the Entry of Doubt)

The preceding analysis implies that a major new section begins with Jesus' refusal at Passover to entrust himself to people (2:23–25). At first sight this may seem unlikely. The text appears to move smoothly from the cleansing of the temple (2:12–22) to the subsequent verses concerning Jesus' hesitancy; there is no change of time or place (one is still "in Jerusalem, at Passover," 2:23). It is understandable therefore that the medieval division assigned it to the end of chapter 2 and that modern students of structure have paid little attention to it.

Yet in Bultmann's judgment (111, 130) the major section which concludes in chapter 6 begins in 2:23–25, and this judgment appears to be correct. There are several reasons. The preceding text (1:1–2:22) is a close-knit unity which culminates with the resurrection-related faith of the disciples (in 2:22). The account of Jesus' hesitancy is seen increasingly by researchers as an introduction to chapter 3 (see earlier references to Hoskyns, Dodd, etc., esp. Beasley-Murray, 43, 47). And the presence of a division between 2:22 and 2:23 is confirmed by the criterion of repetition: the concluding role of believing in the scripture and in Jesus' word (2:22) is repeated, in varied form, in the threefold conclusion of the gospel as a whole (cf. comments on 19:35–37, 20:30–31, 21:24–25); and, as already indicated, the opening word in the account of Jesus' hesitancy (*hōs*, "when," 2:23) is repeated at the beginning of the account of Jesus' withdrawal (4:1).

Furthermore, the essential content of 2:23–25 represents an important turning point. Thus far, from the appearance of the first disciples (1:35–29) to the reference to post-resurrection faith (2:19–22), the gospel has given a drama of progressive believing (*pisteuō*). But in the aftermath of the cleansing of the temple, just when Jesus' signs generate an enthusiasm for believing, there is a new dynamic: "*Iēsous ouk episteuen, . . .*" "Jesus did not entrust, . . ." the same verb, *pisteuō*, as is used for believing.

This text signifies the entry of doubt. At one level, of course, the incident seems almost insignificant, an obscure reference to a moment of hesitation. And the subsequent comment that Jesus knew what was in people seems even more brief and cryptic. But *pisteuō* is the heartbeat of the gospel, and the negating of that verb—for the first time in the gospel, and by Jesus!—means that in some sense the heart has missed a beat. In the subsequent episodes there are increasing indications that life is difficult and fragile, and that it is possible to cease believing. The fact that this doubt begins so inconspicuously, in the same time and place as the temple episode, would seem to be a way of saying that that is how doubt often develops—inconspicuously.

Structure: From Sevenfold to Fourfold—Exploratory Observations

The foregoing proposal means that, while Part 1 of the gospel was fundamentally sevenfold in its structure, much of Part 2 (from 2:23 to chap. 4) is fundamentally fourfold.

Obviously, in both cases the basic structure is shadowed (or challenged?) by complexities, complexities which require further research. The basic sevenfold structure of Part 1 centers on the passing of seven days (cf. 1:1–2:11), but at the end there is the cleansing of the temple, a subdivision of Part 1, which does not fit the pattern of seven days, but which has the effect, curiously, of giving Part 1 a total of seven episodes. In other words, the major concluding subdivision (2:12–22) has the effect of both moving beyond the pattern at one level and restoring it at another.

Within Part 2 something similar seems to be at work. The initial structure is fourfold, but then there is a major concluding subdivision, chaps. 5 and 6, which moves beyond that pattern at one level and restores it at another. It moves beyond it insofar as it comes after it and thus does not fit within it. But it seems also, at another level, to restore it: by adding chaps. 5 and 6, it constitutes, along with chapters 3 and 4 (2:23–chap. 3, and chap. 4 to be exact) a different kind of fourfold structure—the structure which contributed to the traditional division into four chapters (3, 4, 5, and 6). In other words, once 2:23–25 is included with chapter 3, the traditional division into four chapters reflects a genuine fourfold structure in the text. The exact basis for this division needs further research, but its genuineness seems reasonably assured. Thus, at one level at least, the entirety of Part 2—and not just its initial phase—consists of four sections.

These matters may, perhaps, seem both trivial and debatable, yet they are worthy of further research for there appears to be at stake in them a fundamental theological idea—the idea that basic patterns of time (Part 1) and space (Part 2) may be transcended, but transcended in such a way that while something is indeed left behind, yet, in another sense, nothing is lost. It is hardly a coincidence that it is in these final pattern-transcending sections that the clearest allusions are first made to Jesus' death (cf. 2:12–22, esp. 2:19–22; and 5:18, 6:71). What is implied apparently is that the transcending of the patterns of time and space—and with it the process of leaving things and yet not really losing them—is to be connected, in some way, with death.

While the first creation story (Gen 1:1–2:4a), with its emphasis on time, is fundamentally sevenfold in structure, the second story (Gen 2:4b-25), which places greater emphasis on space or geography, does so especially through a fourfold image—that of the four primordial streams or rivers (Gen 2:10–15). Thus the fourfold structure of Part 2, like the sevenfold structure of Part 1, has at least a partial precedent in Genesis.

The Coming of Nicodemus to Jesus, and
the Difficult Process of Coming to God

Nicodemus is a striking figure, one of society's leading lights. Even among the Pharisees he stands out: he is *archōn tōn Ioudaiōn*, literally, "a ruler of the Jews." As Brown (130) indicates, this would seem to imply that, historically, he was a member of the Sanhedrin, the seventy-member governing body of Jewish society. But Nicodemus is not introduced as one of the seventy, and to translate "ruler of the Jews" by "member of the Jewish Sanhedrin" is to allow historical reconstruction and clarification to have the paradoxical effect of narrowing and thus obscuring what is actually written, the canonical text. "Ruler of the Jews," while it does indeed seem to imply membership in the Sanhedrin, has first of all a ring of political power, an evocation of the whole broad world of "kings and rulers." Nicodemus then evokes that world. More than power, however, he evokes learning, especially religious learning. Jesus addresses him not just as one teacher among many, but as a teacher who is preeminent: *ho didaskalos tou Israēl*, "the teacher of Israel" (3:10). The NEB, taking due account of the definite article, "the teacher," translates it as "this famous teacher of Israel." (For some further details on the implication of the article, especially as indicative of a representative role, see Schnackenburg, 1:375.) Nicodemus, therefore, in many ways, is a representative of human achievement and learning.

The paradox presented by the gospel is that when it comes to the basic question of God and the whole realm (or kingdom) of God, this preeminent figure is quite ignorant. He comes to Jesus "by night," a detail which—apart from its possible historical value—has the effect, within the context of the gospel's symbolism, of indicating that, when all is said and done, the enlightened Nicodemus is in the dark.

The purpose of the text is not to deride human achievement and religious leadership—ultimately the portrait of Nicodemus is quite sympathetic—but to underline the difficulty of seeing and entering the realm of God. This difficulty is generally recognized in the case of those who are obvious "sinners," and, in due time, the fast-moving woman of Samaria will exemplify such people. But the problem is much more pervasive, and the evangelist depicts it, first of all, among those who by some standards are doing very well.

When Jesus speaks to Nicodemus he does not dwell exclusively on difficulties. He gives some positive indications both of how people can reach God, and of God's eagerness to reach people. Thus while one of the text's first images is that of someone coming in the dark, its final image is of someone who "comes to the light" (3:21). Hence, despite the emphasis on human inadequacy and difficulty, the text holds out the hope of the human ascent to God.

Structure

The Basic Pattern

The episode is composed of an introduction (2:23–25) and a threefold pattern of question and reply. The questions, the first of which is merely implicit, are posed by Nicodemus. Each of Jesus' replies contains an introductory "Amen, amen, I say. . . ." Even though Nicodemus' questions, especially when taken with their introductions, become shorter (cf. 3:1–2,4,9), the replies of Jesus, as Brown (136) indicates, become longer (cf. 3:3,5–8,10–21). As a result, the three exchanges are increasingly long—three verses (1–3), five verses (4–8), and thirteen verses (9–21).

The third reply is particularly prolonged and is generally regarded as consisting of two rather distinct parts: (A) the summary account of the need for the raising of (the Son of) humanity up to heaven (10–15); (B) the summary account of God's love and of the response of faith (16–21).

Within these three increasingly long sections, the text is arranged in a repetitive spiralling manner (cf. Kysar, 1984, 27–28).

Further Details

This division, three increasingly long spirals, the third of which is divided in two, is essentially the same as that of the gospel as a whole when it is divided according to the three Passovers. Even the proportions in the Nicodemus text (3:5:13) are not unlike those in the larger gospel (2:4:15).

It is also of interest, though the details are a matter for further research, that the third part of the Nicodemus text, and its subdivision into A and B, has several items of affinity with the point at which the third part of the gospel as a whole is divided in two (cf. 3:10–21 and 12:37–13:1; for initial data, see Brown, 147–48). It is particularly noticeable that, in both cases, Part 3B begins with a solemn emphasis on love (3:16; 13:1).

One of the features of the Nicodemus conversation is that, as it progresses, the emphasis on the two individual participants tends to fade. After Nicodemus' third brief question he is heard from no more, and even the voice of Jesus, as he replies, begins to sound more like that of Jesus' followers (cf. esp. 3:11) and like that of someone reflecting on all that God had done in Jesus (cf. esp. 3:16–21). There is therefore in the text, in the voice of Jesus, a definite suggestion of a process of distancing. This distancing phenomenon will be seen again later.

[2:23–25] Introduction: Jesus in Jerusalem and his knowledge of human beings. The text refers to the distance between Jesus and the believers in Jerusalem. The belief involved may have been rather superficial. It is associated with signs, and with nothing else.

But the sense of inadequacy is not limited to the people of Jerusalem. Almost imperceptibly the text begins to refer to an inadequacy which is more general, one found among all humans: "Jesus did not trust himself to them because he knew all people . . . for he . . . knew what was in the human person." The implication seems to be that humans as such have a basic lack.

Thus while the text begins by referring to a form of inadequacy which is primarily Jewish—overreliance on signs—it concludes by referring to an inadequacy which is found among all. In other words—and this is the introduction for chaps. 3–6 in general and for the Nicodemus story in particular—both Jews and Gentiles are inadequate. They all have a problem.

[3:1–3] First exchange: The confident Nicodemus and the challenging Jesus. In the first brief exchange with Jesus, Nicodemus is brought to an abrupt halt. "Rabbi," he says, unwittingly echoing the novice disciples (cf. 1:38), "we know that you are a teacher come from God." And he adds: "No one can do these signs that you do unless God is with him." Nicodemus is himself both ruler and teacher, and as one teacher to another, he seems to feel that he can speak to Jesus with some assurance of the things of God. There is therefore in his approach a certain tone of confidence. But, Nicodemus, despite all his prestige, had been described first of all as an ordinary human person, *anthrōpos* (cf. 3:1, "Now there was an *anthrōpos* of the Pharisees . . ."), and the introduction (cf. 2:25) had intimated that human beings—all of them—have difficulties. Jesus, therefore, does not go along with this confidence. Instead he stops Nicodemus short with a mixture of challenge and vision, what Bultmann (138) calls a riddle: "Unless one is born *anōthen* [an ambiguous word, "again" or "from above"], one cannot see the realm [or kingdom] of God."

There is no question then of simply drifting from darkness to light. There is no easy intellectual path. To see the realm of God is like nothing less than a birth, a rebirth from above.

[3:4–8] Second exchange: The basic need for rebirth by water and spirit. Nicodemus, leader and teacher, misunderstands. He takes what Jesus said about birth as a reference to a physical process. It does not even cross his well-educated mind that there is another kind of regenerating process of which he is quite unaware. And his misunderstanding seems to give him even greater confidence and to add a touch of mockery. In the second exchange between the two, his questions reduce Jesus' statements to absurdity—to the idea of an old man reentering his mother's womb.

Then Jesus begins, to some small degree, to clarify: the birth of which he speaks is "of water and spirit."

Several modern writers, particularly Bultmann (138–39), have suggested that the reference to water (3:5) is in some way secondary. There is no manuscript evidence for this claim and it is usually made on the basis of an oversimplified view of the gospel's theology or literary structure. In particular, it does not appreciate fully the fact that the text of 2:23–3:21 is a rapidly ascending spiral in which, in varying degrees, several elements, including water, and even to some extent, the Spirit, are mentioned rapidly but not developed fully. (For discussion, see esp. Schnackenburg, 1:369–70; Brown, 142.)

Looking at the text more closely, the first idea to be examined is that of water. In the context of the preceding chapters, water has a preparatory role. It is used by John to baptize (1:16,33); and at Cana, where it prepares the way for the wine, it is associated with purification (2:6–7). In other words, the rebirth involves a preparatory process which is related to cleansing (baptizing) or purifying. Given the fact that Jesus had been pictured not only as receiving and imparting the Spirit (1:32–33), but, first of all, as taking away the sin of the world (1:29), it is altogether appropriate that the rebirth which he offers should involve, first of all, a process related to sin, a process of cleansing or purifying. Thus there is no short-cut to rebirth in the Spirit. It involves a preliminary process of cleansing, of dealing with accumulated sickness of heart and soul. Apart from this primary meaning, the water seems to refer also, at least secondarily, to baptism. The preceding context, with its references to baptizing (1:26,33–34), suggests such a meaning. (For discussion, see Brown, 141–44). Thus the water suggests both the whole process of moral cleansing and also the brief sacramental ritual which at times helps to articulate and further that process.

However much a preparatory cleansing may be necessary, the crucial factor in the process of rebirth is that of spirit, and it is on the notion of spirit that Jesus dwells.

As is frequent in the fourth gospel, Jesus is depicted as edging into his subject. He begins by speaking of "spirit" (*pneuma*—without any article). Then, more elaborately, he refers to "the Spirit" (*to pneuma*). The RSV seeks consistency and translates on both occasions with "the Spirit." It is better, however, to respect the graded structure of the text. (A somewhat similar grading of *pneuma* may be found in Wis 1:5–7.)

In an effort to reach the rather stiff mind of Nicodemus, Jesus speaks of spirit through both a contrast and a comparison. The contrast is between spirit and flesh (3:6) and as such seems to be aimed at the point at which Nicodemus is in a form of mental paralysis—his preoccupation with flesh, with purely physical forms of birth. The comparison with the wind—*pneuma* means both "spirit" and "wind"—is brief, but it is a magnificently poetic vision (3:8), and it seeks to open up for Nicodemus some idea of the possibilities offered by the world of spirit. It "blows where it wills, and you hear its sound, but you do not know from where it comes or whereto it goes."

This contrast of flesh and spirit is part of a recurrent theme, one which occurs especially in chapters 3 and 6, and it is expressed also, to some extent at least, in terms of the difference between what is earthly and heavenly, between what is below and above.

It is a contrast which touches the core of human life. On the one hand, the flesh, including that which is earthly/below, is very restricted: "What is born of the flesh is flesh . . ." (3:6); "The one who is of the earth is earthly, and of the earth speaks" (3:31). What is referred to here is "the radical inability of the natural to raise itself" (Brown, 160), the inability, for instance, of Lady Macbeth to break out of her cycle of guilt ("All the perfumes of Arabia will not sweeten this little hand"). In Rom 1:16–2:20, Paul speaks of the whole world as being in such a dilemma. Bultmann (141), using existentialist terminology, puts the matter strikingly: the mention of flesh in John 3:6 "refers to the nothingness of man's whole existence; to the fact that man is ultimately a stranger to his own acts; that, as he now is, he does not enjoy authentic existence, whether he makes himself aware of the fact or whether he conceals it from himself." On the other hand, the Spirit, and that which is heavenly/above, opens up new possibilities. It offers a whole new realm, a realm as mysterious as the wind. And it is with this poetic evocation of the mysterious world of the Spirit that Jesus concludes his second reply.

[3:9–15] Third exchange: A further need—to be raised up.   In the course of the discussion with Jesus, Nicodemus goes through significant changes of mind and attitude. At first he had been calmly confident. Then, as he faced something which was new and perhaps even threatening, he had entered a phase of misunderstanding and subtle mockery. And now, when Jesus has explained the basic idea of rising above the world of the flesh and entering that of the spirit, he responds by asking, "How can this be?" His reply is sometimes seen as an expression of incredulity and obtuseness (Schnackenburg, 1:374), yet it has something of Mary's, "How shall this be? . . ." as the angel declared to her the whole mystery of the incarnation (Luke 1:34). Nicodemus is indeed out of his depth intellectually and spiritually, but, to some extent at least, he is interested and ready to learn.

When Jesus answers, he speaks in the plural ("we speak . . . we know . . . we bear witness . . . you [plural] do not receive our witness"), and, as many commentators note, the conversation seems to reflect not just the meeting of Jesus and Nicodemus, but also the dialogue of the church with Judaism. A similar phenomenon, on a lower key, had been noted in the Nathanael scene (1:45,51). It is a dialogue which, to some degree, consists of a clash between law and experience. Nicodemus sees himself as well versed in God's revealed law. Jesus, however, appeals to "what we know . . . and what we have seen." In other words, the flesh-spirit distinction and the analogy of the mysterious wind come from basic spiritual observation.

Jesus realizes that if Nicodemus is having problems with basic spiritual matters ("earthly things") he will have even greater difficulty in accepting more advanced teaching ("heavenly things," 3:12).

Still, Jesus launches forth. His basic theme is that of the ascent to God. In three brief climactic verses (3:13–15) there are three references to ascending or lifting up: "No one has *ascended* into heaven except. . . . And as Moses *lifted up* . . . so it is necessary [*dei* = providentially necessary] that the Son of humanity be *lifted up*. . . ." As so often in the fourth gospel, with its pattern like that of advancing waves, the first reference to the ascent is extremely low-key, negative in fact: "No one has ascended. . . ." The second is ancient and enigmatic, but at least it is positive: ". . . as Moses lifted up. . . ." And the third, though hidden in the mystery of God's providence, is more tangible and predictable ("it is necessary that the Son of humanity . . . .").

A somewhat similar pattern may be observed in the various references to believing: they go from one which is negative (3:12a), to one which is a question (3:12b), to one which is positive (3:15).

The central idea which emerges dimly is that the ascent to God is indeed possible, but only through the ascent of the Son of humanity, the one who first descended from heaven (3:13b) and the one in whom the believer has eternal life (3:15). The title "Son of humanity" is paradoxical. It brings out the very human aspects of Jesus, living on earth and then going to his death. Yet it is used, especially in the fourth gospel "in connection with the thought of ascent (6:62), 'exaltation' (3:14; 12:34) and 'glorification' (12:23; 13:31)" (Schnackenburg, 1:393). In other words, Jesus' death, something which at this stage is not mentioned explicitly, is viewed in a way which is primarily positive. It is an exaltation, an ascent. And it is through that ascent, an ascent which involves death, that the believer comes to life eternal.

Death, therefore, the process of being lifted up, is not something to be run away from. It may indeed be destructive at one level, as were the fiery serpents, yet, paradoxically, it is by facing the thing which most terrifies—by putting the fiery serpent on a standard and looking straight at it (Num 21:8–9)—that greater life is achieved.

In these verses concerning the ascent to God the emphasis is on difficulty. Ascending to God is not something that one can do alone—it requires the prior initiative of the one who descended—and it involves the spectre of death. To Nicodemus, insofar as he is still listening, the challenge has perhaps become too great.

[3:16–21] The allure of love and the spectre of judgement. Just at the point that the ascent to God may seem overwhelmingly difficult, the gospel offers both strong encouragement and a grim warning. The strong encouragement is the classic, "For God so loved. . . ." To a weary world or faltering pilgrims it is a way of saying that God is coming to meet them, coming to them with unfathomable love. And if the ascent to God demands a form of death, the One who is being approached is not simply a bemused spectator. On God's part too there is a form of death—the giving of an only child so that the world may be saved. Thus what is demanded of the one who would approach God, however difficult it may be, is made possible when seen in the context of God's self-giving.

The grim warning is the picture of condemnatory judgment, a picture of so refusing life and love that one becomes swallowed up in darkness. As with other ideas, it is introduced gradually, first through negative references, as something which God does not want and believers do not incur (3:17b, 18a), then through a positive reference, as something which disbelievers do to themselves: "but the one who does not believe is already judged" (3:18b). And finally (3:19), there is a picture of judgement which refers to the full dimensions of human perversity: "the light has come into the world, and people (*anthrōpoi*) loved the darkness rather than the light, for their deeds were evil." This image of loving the darkness, to be followed in the next verse by that of hating the light and executing evil, indicates not just a tendency to perversity, but perversity in action, "radical evil" (Brown, 149, summarizing S. Lyonnet). Thus the final section of the Nicodemus episode swings slowly but steadily from the attraction of healing love to the threat of engulfing darkness.

This emphasis on human evil, coming at the virtual conclusion of the episode, forms a literary balance or *inclusio* with the episode's opening emphasis on human untrustworthiness (2:23–25). But while the opening text, in alluding to human evil, seemed to see it, in large measure, merely as a tendency, the closing verses speak of something further—of the actual practicing of evil.

The swing from love to loving the darkness (vv 16–19) sets the scene for the final contrast, a contrast between those who do evil (v 20) and those who do what is true (v 21), between those who "hate the light" and those who "come to the light." It is a contrast which in some ways "has remarkable resemblances [with the dualism] in the Dead Sea Scrolls" (Brown, 148), but it seems also to echo a sense of dividedness which is at least as old as Deuteronomy. At the conclusion of some of the discourses of Moses (cf. Deut 11:26–28, and esp. 30:15–20) there are references to what may be called the two ways, the ways of good and evil, life and death. A variation on the idea (or literary convention?) of the two ways may be found also at the conclusion of the Sermon on the Mount (Matt 7:13–27). Given that the idea of the two ways is found in the canonical literature, and, that within that literature, it is found at the conclusion of discourses, it seems likely that it is the same phenomenon, or rather, a variation on the same phenomenon, which occurs in 3:20–21. After all, 3:20–21, as well as having the basic idea of two possibilities, is a text which is both canonical and concluding. Hence, while granting its affinity with extracanonical materials such as the Dead Sea Scrolls, it would seem that it also involves a variation on the idea of the two ways. Thus, as the episode closes, there is placed before Nicodemus, or at least before the reader, an implicit challenge: "I set before you . . . darkness . . . and light. . . ."

The Coming of All to Jesus: The Fading of John

This episode has a dual focus. At center stage, which is set in the land or countryside of Judea, there is a dominating picture of Jesus and his disciples, of his being with them and of his baptizing. But it is at the side of the stage, set in an elusive place called "Aenon near Salim," that the dialogue takes place. There John also is baptizing, and it is through the action and words which surround John that the dominating picture is known. Thus while the ultimate focus is on Jesus and his disciples, the more immediate focus is on Aenon near Salim.

The entire episode provides a perfect complement to the Nicodemus scene. There, in speaking of coming to God, the primary emphasis was on difficulty, and only in its final stages, especially in 3:16, did attention begin to move towards God's eager love. But here the primary emphasis is on love and joy. When John is told of the coming of all the people to Jesus, he sees their journey, not as a harsh pilgrimage, but as a wedding procession (3:26,29). And having alluded to the love of groom and bride, and to the joy which surrounds it, he then goes on, in referring to the one who comes from heaven, to speak more explicitly of a further love—that of the intimate love of Father and Son, and of their total communication in the Spirit (3:31–36, esp. 3:32–35; for an analysis which brings out this emphasis on intimate parent-child love, see Schnackenburg, 1:384–88).

The love which is brought by Jesus (and the fulfillment which it implies) means that the preparatory role of John is over. Far from being resentful, however, he is overjoyed, as happy as a best man who relishes the joy of his friend, the groom.

In this context it is useful, even in the course of introducing the episode, to focus on one leading detail—the location: "Aenon near Salim."

From the point of view of geography, the location of Aenon is quite a puzzle. It is never mentioned in the OT or in any other document of the NT era, and it is simply not known to what place the gospel is referring. In the fourth century, Eusebius speaks of it as being just west of the Jordan, near Scythopolis (ancient Bethshan). The Madeba map, sixth century, gives a further Aenon, just east of the Jordan, but further south. And the only actual town with a name like "Aenon" is Ainun—and that is in Samaria. Similar uncertainty surrounds the location of Salim. (For details, cf. Schnackenburg, 1:412–13; Brown, 151.) Schnackenburg opts, fairly firmly, for the Bethshan location, but Brown tends towards Samaria. Bultmann (170) contends that "the uncertain attempts to identify the places named here geographically have no importance for the exegesis of the passage."

Yet the uncertainty itself may be significant. As noted before, for instance, in dealing with the elusive location of Jesus' place of abode (1:39) and with the rather perplexing use of place names in the call of Philip (1:43–44), the fourth gospel's geographic puzzles—like many of its other puzzles—appear to be a way of challenging the mind and of seeking to raise it to another level of perception. In the case of "Aenon near Salim" the puzzle would seem to be resolved through the fact that "the name [Aenon] is from the Aramaic plural of the word for 'spring,' while 'Salim' reflects the Semitic root for 'peace' " (Brown 151. *Shalom* = "peace" or "salvation"). In other words, "Aenon near Salim" means "Springs near Peace." This suits the context and makes theological sense. The passage as a whole (3:22–36) is largely concerned with aspects of the peace which is brought by Jesus, particularly with the ideas of love and joy (cf. esp. 3:29–36). It is also concerned with John, the representative of the old dispensation who baptized with water, and with John's relationship to Jesus (3:26–30). The picture of John as being at "Springs near Peace" fits his theological role. His is a world of springs, of cleansing water, of preparatory baptism. But nearby is Jesus, the one who, as well as cleansing what is negative, brings a positive peace. The distinctness of the two, as well as their nearness to one another, is further reflected in the image of the bridegroom and his friend, the best man (3:29).

Bultmann (170) believes that this meaning is possible. Brown (151), however, rejects it on the contention that, for such a meaning, Jesus should be placed at Salim and not in Judea. But the locating of Jesus in Judea is necessary—it is part of the carefully graded picture, built up through the four introductions (2:23–25; 3:22–24; 4:1–6,43–45), of movement from Jerusalem to the Judean countryside and on into Samaria and Galilee. Besides, as already suggested, if the text is taken as it is, it has its own coherence: John, with his cleansing baptism, is close to the coming of the dispensation of peace; he is the friend of the bridegroom.

Thus in this geographic text, as in some others, the interpreter has to choose between superficial confusion and theological coherence.

Rather than presume that the writer was incapable of giving a clear geographic designation—something which should have been very easy—it seems more appropriate, given the theological depth of the gospel, and given also its tendency towards ambiguity, to interpret "Aenon near Salim" as being primarily theological. This need not mean that there was no such place as Aenon or that John was not there. But in the present text these matters are secondary; they have been integrated in a way which makes them serve a higher theological purpose. This principle will become much clearer in dealing with Pilate. He is undoubtedly historical, yet the presentation of him in the fourth gospel is one which is heavily influenced by theology. It is not said of Aenon that it was so many stadia from, say, the well-known Samaritan city of Shechem. Rather it is given a designation, "near Salim," which perplexes the flesh-bound mind and challenges it to think on another level.

Structure

As the RSV, for instance, suggests, the text, apart from its scene-setting introduction (3:22–24), consists of two parts. The first tells of John's initial response to an obscure crisis which concerns both Jewish purification and, above all, the encounter between all the people and Jesus (3:25–30). It is a response which is joyful: he sees Jesus' action as something given "from heaven," and he is glad because of the love it brings. The second part, which, to some degree, appears to be a continuation of the response of John, goes more profoundly into variations on the ideas of "from heaven" and love (3:31–36).

One of the features of John's response (3:27–36) is that it has a certain formal or external similarity to Jesus' third reply in the Nicodemus scene (3:11–21). Just as Jesus' voice seems to give way to some extent to that of Christians as a whole, so the testifying of John is replaced by a picture of the testifying of his disciples (3:28: "you yourselves bear witness to me . . ."). Furthermore, just as in the final paragraph of Jesus' reply (3:16–21: "For God so loved . . ."), Jesus' voice has often been regarded as becoming even more distant, so a similar observation has often been made about the final paragraph of John's discourse (3:31–36: "The one who comes from above . . ."). At a later stage this phenomenon of the fading voice will be examined more closely.

Apart from these formal links with the conclusion of the Nicodemus scene, there are other more substantive connections—so much so that the second part of the episode (3:31–36) is sometimes rearranged and placed next to or even within the Nicodemus scene (e.g. cf. Bernard, 1:xxiii–xxiv; Bultmann, 160; Schnackenburg, 1:380–92).

But these rearrangements, however plausible, do not do justice to the delicate artistry of the text. As will be seen later, the affinity of the final part of this episode with the later part of the Nicodemus episode is to be seen within the context of a larger phenomenon—the fact that the two episodes, taken in their entirety, form a well-balanced diptych.

It is better, therefore, to regard the text as consisting of an introduction and two parts.

[3:22–24] Introduction: The move to Judea—the intimation of a baptism that is new, and the impending demise of a baptism that is old.

The text describes Jesus as breaking new ground—both insofar as he moves to the land or countryside of Judea, and insofar as, for the first time, he is described as actually baptizing. The nature of this baptizing is not described explicitly. In all this, both in moving and baptizing, Jesus is associated with "his disciples." It is said that "he sojourned (*diatribō*) with them," a verb which suggests a stay of limited time, a process which is passing; but, as with the baptizing, the nature of the relationship with his disciples is not described explicitly. Thus there are low-key references both to baptizing and to communing with the disciples.

John also is baptizing, at Aenon near Salim, but, unlike Jesus, the baptizing done by John is explicitly linked with water: he was at Aenon "because there was much water there." Furthermore, even though there are those who come to John for baptizing, the reference to his impending imprisonment (3:24) means that his activity is set to come to an end.

Thus, while the enigmatic baptizing activity of Jesus is coming to the fore, that of John, which is certainly with water, is coming to termination. The picture is carefully balanced, and there is no need to say that part of the text is an editorial insertion.

The major problem in this passage—apart from the location of Aenon—concerns the nature of Jesus' baptism. Was it a baptism like that of John, or was it baptism in the Spirit? Augustine and many later commentators held that it was baptism in the Spirit, but other writers, ancient and modern, including Brown (151) and Haenchen (1:210), have said that the baptizing of Jesus was like that of John, a baptism of water. (For further details, see Schnackenburg, 1:411.) The main objection to saying that Jesus baptized in the Spirit is the fact that within the fourth gospel the Spirit is not given until Jesus is glorified (cf. 7:39).

This is a formidable objection, but it does not decide the issue. When the fourth gospel speaks of John and Jesus it clearly distinguishes their roles. The episode as a whole (3:22–36) emphasizes that distinction, and at an earlier stage the distinction was expressed primarily in terms of baptism—John baptized in water, but Jesus would baptize in the Holy Spirit (1:33). Given the general context it seems reasonable—unless there is evidence to the contrary—to presuppose that in this text also their roles, and therefore their baptisms, are to be distinguished: John's is in water, but that of Jesus is in the Spirit.

The text itself (2:22–25), far from providing evidence to the contrary, has indications which confirm this. Of the two baptisms, only one, that of John, is explicitly linked with water (". . . because there was much water there"). This detail is hardly to be regarded as merely of historical value. Rather, it is part of a literary pattern in which all the passages concerning John's baptizing are accompanied by explicit references to water (1:25–27,31–33; 3:22–24). As such it would appear to be a literary clue which marks the character of John's baptism and distinguishes it from that of Jesus. In the references to Jesus' baptizing, however, water is never mentioned. The emphasis, instead of being on water, is on some form of communion—either with the Spirit (1:33) or with the disciples (cf. 3:22,26; 4:1–2). It is never said of Jesus, as it is of John, that "they came and were baptized," *pareginonto kai ebaptizonto* (3:23)—a mode of expression which, particularly in Greek, omits all emphasis on the identity of those involved and on John's relationship with them. (A similar lack of emphasis is found in 1:25–27, 31–33.) Most translations try to compensate for this rather jarring underemphasis by saying that "*people* came, . . ." but the underemphasis has its purpose: it highlights the fact that the baptizing activity of Jesus, by contrast, always involves some element of relationship, of communion.

Thus there are two persistent patterns. One emphasizes water, but never relationship or communion. The other emphasizes communion, but never mentions water. It is not possible, therefore, to regard them as the same.

The account of Jesus' baptizing (3:22), though it does not mention the Spirit, forms part of the pattern which does. Its reference to Jesus "sojourning with" (*diatribō meta*) his disciples, far from indicating any absence of the Spirit, suggests its presence. (The only preceding reference to Jesus and the disciples being "with" one another—1:39, they "abode with" him [*menō para*]—occurs in continuity with a reference to the abiding of the Spirit, 1:33.) It seems better, therefore, that Jesus' baptism be considered as being, in some way at least, a baptism in the Spirit.

But, if the Spirit depends on Jesus' glorification, how is it possible to refer to the Spirit at this stage? The answer would seem to hinge on the fact that in various ways, the fourth gospel, even in its early chapters, offers several intimations and indications of what is to come later. The prologue is an obvious example. Somewhat similarly, all of Part 1 (1:1–2:22) acts as an initial synthesis of the gospel as a whole. The wine at Cana, though seemingly dependent on Jesus' (final) hour (2:4), was given in abundance. And the early disciples represented something which was still in the future: they "proleptically represent the believing community" (Haenchen, 1:158). If the early disciples do, in fact, represent the later body of believers, then it is not inappropriate that, even as early as chapter 3, they be referred to in the context of baptism in the Spirit. In fact, the conjunction of the two ideas—the believers and baptism in the Spirit—is quite fitting.

This means, of course, that once again, as in the case of "Aenon near Salim," the primary emphasis of the text is theological. What it is giving, above all, is a capsule version of the emergence of one order, that in which Jesus offers a new baptism, and the fading of another, that in which John, the representative of the old order, baptized in water.

[3:25–30] John's witness as he gives way to the new order from heaven. Tension with the old and the nuptial joy of the new.

The text begins with a well-known puzzle—the picture of John's disciples being involved in a double tension. On the one hand, they are in dispute with some Jew (or Jews—the text is uncertain) on the subject of purification (3:25). On the other, they complain to John about Jesus' practice of baptism and about the fact that "all" are coming to him (3:26). As an account of individual historical facts, the text is rather illogical: the dispute is with the Jew(s), but the complaint is against Jesus. In other words, as an account of a particular sequence of events it does not seem to make sense. Haenchen (1:210) calls it a riddle.

However, as a representation of John's theological situation it is quite coherent. In general, John was in a rather tense position with regard both to the Jews and Jesus. On the one hand, his practice of baptism meant that he was touching a very sensitive Jewish subject—purification, the whole world of the clean and unclean, a subject already alluded to at Cana (2:6). On the other hand, his particular kind of baptism was simply a preparation for that of Jesus and would eventually have to give way to it. Thus his practice of baptism salvaged something of the Jewish concern for cleansing, but it subjected that concern to the acceptance of a more thorough form of cleansing, cleansing in the Holy Spirit. John, therefore, theologically, was in the middle, and it is that sense of being in the middle which is conveyed by the illogical-sounding account of the dispute and the complaint.

What remains puzzling, to some degree, is why the narrative is made to sound illogical. Yet this procedure seems to have a studied purpose. It suggests that John and Jesus are involved in a process which goes beyond mere logic, that a certain break is occurring, a break with the old order and fixed ways of thinking, and that something new is being inaugurated, something which, on its way toward spiritual renewal, unsettles the mind, jolts it. It was already seen that the Nicodemus episode involves wordplay and a jolting of set thought patterns, especially the thought patterns of Nicodemus. This episode involves a further teasing and jolting of the mind, especially that of the reader.

In any case, John's position, midway between the Jew(s) and the emergence of Jesus, corresponds broadly to the way in which he was earlier depicted: in his first major scene he had had to answer Jewish questions and at the same time explain that he is only a forerunner to Jesus (cf. 1:19–28).

Despite the tension, perhaps because of it, something very positive and peaceful is emerging. First, there is a sense here, as never previously in this gospel, of a major growth in the number of the disciples. "All" are coming to Jesus. Something of the same idea is reflected obliquely in the later statements that the one from above is "above all" (3:31) and that the Son has been given "all things" into his hand (3:35). Thus in contrast to the Nicodemus episode, which seemed to be focused primarily on the Jews, this episode evokes the emergence of a community which is universal.

Furthermore, John seems quite at peace. As already noted, it seems to be of some significance that his enigmatic location, "Aenon near Salim," means *springs near peace*. And as he speaks of his exit, his mood is essentially gracious and joyful, comparable perhaps to the gracious exit of Simeon when he beheld the Christchild (Luke 2:25–32).

He begins by identifying Jesus. When he is told that all are coming to him, he interprets that fact as an indication that Jesus has been given something special, something from heaven: "A person cannot receive anything except what is given from heaven" (3:27). It is this latter idea, of something or someone "from heaven," which dominates the remainder of his address.

The identifying or recognizing of Jesus was not, in itself, something new for John. On Days 1 and 2 of the opening drama (1:19–34) he had contrasted his own limited role with the more Spirit-filled role of Jesus. But now he heightens that contrast. He sees his own role not only as merely preparatory but also as almost over. In fact, he is no longer visualized as actively bearing witness. Witnessing was something which he did in the past (3:26) or something which is now being done, not by him, but by his disciples (3:28). Jesus, on the other hand, far from fading, seems to be coming more and more into focus.

In expressing the relationship of the heavenly one to the people, John uses a bold image: that of groom and bride. The idea of Christ as the groom of the baptized church is found in Ephesians (5:25–27) but John's idea is somewhat more developed: he compares his own role to that of the best man, the groom's friend whose duty it was "to lead the bride to the bridegroom and to keep watch outside the bridal chamber" (Schnackenburg, 1:416). Through this image he reinforces the idea that his own role is humble, yet from this humble position he has a unique closeness to the couple: he is with them at the blissful moments of getting together as husband and wife. More than anyone else he can hear the *phonē* ("voice/sound") of the groom. There is no description of the groom's voice or sound—whether it be cheerful greetings or gentle whisperings or startling squeals—but, whatever it is, it fills the nearby friend with joy. Thus, while the harmony of this episode (3:22–36) may be somewhat disrupted by a dispute with the Jew(s), the one who is the true representative of the old order, of the OT, is filled with a fulfilling joy.

[3:31–36] The witness concludes: the one from heaven reflects God's love.   In this second part the idea of accepting what comes from heaven is continued and

developed. And since no change of speaker is indicated, it would seem that the words are those of John.

The tone, however, is rather different from what precedes and so, while earlier commentators held that the words are indeed those of John, many recent writers see the speaker either as Jesus or the evangelist. (For opinions and discussions, see Schnackenburg, 1:383; Brown, 159.)

The difference in tone, particularly the sense of distance, is probably best seen in the context of a larger phenomenon within 2:23–chap. 4—the sense of the distancing of Jesus and John. The idea of Jesus going away, and thus, in one sense at least, becoming distant, is quite prominent in the later part of the gospel, particularly in the last discourse (chaps. 13–17). But already within Part 2, even though the major emphasis is on Jesus' increasing role, there is an undercurrent which intimates his going away. As will be seen later, the picture of the exhaustion of Jesus (4:6) is used to suggest that eventually his presence also will fade. And in the conversation with Nicodemus, the voice of Jesus seems to become more distant, and at times to become more like the voice of the disciples (cf. 3:11–21, esp. 3:11). Given this context of the distancing or fading of Jesus, it is appropriate—particularly because of the allusion to John's demise (by imprisonment), and because John's role in itself is more distant, more preparatory, than that of Jesus—that John's voice also be depicted as fading.

And so it fades. As if on cue, when the last verse of part one of this episode says that John must decrease (3:30), his voice becomes more faint, it loses its immediacy. Jesus, on the other hand, the one associated so clearly with heaven and of whom it was said that he must increase, looms larger than ever.

While it seems better, therefore, in accordance with the traditional view and the view of some modern writers (e.g. Hoskyns, 229–30; Barrett, 219, 224; Haenchen, 1:210), to accept that, as the text now stands, the voice which speaks is that of John, it also seems necessary to say that that voice has taken on a quality which is rather general and impersonal.

What is said by John in this distant-sounding swan song is momentous. His words, in content if not in form, are somewhat like those of one who is having a heavenly vision, an echo to some extent of his first visionlike perception of Jesus (1:29–34). It is as though John, bearer of the old dispensation, reaches a climactic degree of joyful fulfillment and prophetic insight, and yet, in that very moment of closeness to the divine, realizes the distance between the heavenly and the earthly, particularly as the earthly is reflected in himself. Thus the distinction between the one who is "from above" and the one who is "from the earth" refers first of all, as some earlier exegetes suggested, to John, to the distinction between Jesus and John (cf. Brown, 160). This does not involve any belittling of John and his prophetic preaching. Even the greatest of the OT prophets, when they were in the presence of the divine, experienced a great sense of unworthiness (cf. Isaiah 6; Jeremiah 1; Ezek 1:1–3:21). However, as Schnackenburg (1:382) indicates, the distinction refers also to humankind in general and to humankind's distance from the divine revealer. Thus it is a variation on the earlier contrast, given in the Nicodemus scene (3:6) on the rather formidable distinction between flesh and spirit (cf. Brown, 160). And the text goes on to mention a further element of division or alienation—the fact that even when the heavenly revealer bears witness—in other words, even when the voice of God bridges the gap—people are not receptive (3:32).

But for those who are receptive—and this is the central emphasis of these verses—the news is resoundingly positive. They can certify—literally, they have stamped with a seal—that God is true (3:33). This truth is not merely intellectual; it is based on partaking of the revealer's boundless ("not by measure") gift of the Spirit, a Spirit which reflects the intimate Father-Son love which is within God (3:34–35). In other words, for those who are receptive, the way is open to boundless Spirit and intimate love.

The episode's opening verse, with its veiled allusions to Jesus' communing with the disciples and to the baptism in the Spirit (3:22), had, from the beginning, intimated the ideas of love and Spirit. Now, virtually at the end, in a way that forms a literary balance or *inclusio,* it is to those two ideas—love and spirit—that the text returns.

The final verse (3:36), as with the final verse of the Nicodemus episode (3:20–21), is a miniature picture of the two ways: the believer has eternal life, but not the disbeliever; on such a one "the wrath of God abides [*menō*]."

This brief but startlingly dread picture—the anger of God abiding on the disbeliever (3:36)—occurs exactly at the structural midpoint of the four episodes which form the basis of Part 2; it comes after the episodes of Nicodemus and John and before the episodes of Samaria and the Capernaum official. Furthermore it provides a precise contrast to the center of Part 1: at the structural midpoint of the seven episodes or texts of Part 1, in other words, at the center of the central episode, there is a picture which is opposite but complementary—that of the receptive disciples abiding with the Spirit-baptizing Jesus (1:39).

The episode as a whole (3:22–36) is extremely positive. If it speaks of God's anger, it does so because anger is the inevitable reverse side of God's eagerness and personal love. Having faintly intimated in its opening verse (3:22) the idea of some kind of communion or love, it then goes on to build up, first to the idea of wedding love, and then to the idea of parental love. It is these two ideas which counter the sense of difficulty that is found in much of the Nicodemus episode, and it is also these two ideas which are central to the two episodes in chap. 4.

Excursus 2: Further Literary Aspects of 2:23–Chapter 3

2:23–Chap. 3 And Its Continuity with 1:1–34

It has often been noticed that the episode concerning John the baptizer (3:22–36), insofar as it shows the precursor identifying Jesus and acknowledging his own limited role, is rather like a variation on the earlier picture, given on Days 1 and 2 (1:19–34), of John's witnessing concerning Jesus. As Brown (154) comments: "Some scholars like Wellhausen and Goguel have thought that 3:22–30 is a doublet of the scene in chapter 1 where John the Baptist identified Jesus as the one to come after him. Certainly the themes are much the same."

This similarity, however, is but a small part of a much larger phenomenon: 2:23–chap. 3 has been so written that it contains careful echoes not only of John's first witnessing to Jesus but of all of the early part of chapter 1, including the prologue. The Nicodemus episode echoes the prologue (1:1–18), and the John episode echoes days 1 and 2 (1:19–34).

The Nicodemus Episode (2:23–3:21) and the Prologue (1:1–18)

That there is some similarity of form between the Nicodemus eposide and the prologue has already been implied. It was suggested by the fact that in different ways both texts have a form which is threefold and spiralling.

Apart from any similarity of form, there is continuity of content. The prologue had started with the divine and, as it depicted aspects of the divine intervention, gradually led to the idea of a special birth, birth as God's children. The Nicodemus text takes a complementary approach: it starts with the idea of a special form of birth and then traces it back to the divine intervention.

In fact, most elements of the prologue find some variation in the Nicodemus text: Jesus' closeness to God (1:1–2; 3:1–2); life and light, light and darkness (1:4–5,9; 3:2,19–21); some of the wording referring to John and Nicodemus (1:6–7; 3:1–2); the divine involvement with the world and the idea of rejection (1:9–11; 3:17–18); the special form of birth (1:12–13; 3:3–8); the coming into the world of the only Son (1:14; 3:16); witnessing to the divine intervention (1:7,14–15; 3:11–12); and the preparatory role of Moses (1:17; 3:14). With a more detailed analysis, one could probably argue for further elements of continuity.

The essential point is that the extraordinary density of thought found in the prologue is mirrored to a considerable extent in the Nicodemus episode. In fact, what Schnackenburg (1:380) says of some of the Nicodemus text (3:13–21, along with 3:31–36) could also be said of the prologue: it is "a condensation of the principal assertions of . . . Johannine theology . . . [It] contains in brief all that the evangelist had at heart in the composition of his gospel."

But however much continuity there may be, the Nicodemus text is quite distinct. It gives a more elaborate exposition of the idea of a special birth, and its depiction of the underlying divine intervention is considerably more complex. Furthermore, its view of those who participate in the divine process is more sharply drawn. The prologue had hinted at tension between "his own" ("those who were

209

his own received him not'') and an elusive ''we'' (''we have seen his glory''). In 2:23–3:21 that tension is much more pronounced. It is a tension which is seen first of all in Nicodemus's opening questions, in his rather painful struggle to understand. Most of all it is seen in the tension between ''we'' and ''you'' (plural), expecially in 3:11: ''. . . we speak of what we know . . . but you do not receive our testimony.'' In other words, in comparison with the prologue, the Nicodemus text shows a greater sense of division, and since Nicodemus is so identified with Judaism (3:1,10), the division which it most evokes is that between the Christian community and the Jewish community. However, the final verses of the Nicodemus text, with their explicit emphasis on the idea of judgment, not only underline further the sense of division; they also give it a new twist: they suggest a division not so much between God and the Jews as between God and humankind in general.

It was with God that the prologue had started, and that is probably part of the reason why the texts which immediately follow it are holistic and relatively free of conflict. The Nicodemus text, however, starts with unredeemed humans (2:23–3:1) and so tends to bring out more the perception of reality as limited and divided. It is in one sense a sad development, but it does justice to the situation, and it moves beyond the general statements proposed by the prologue.

Thus the Nicodemus text may be viewed as a second prologue, but it is a prologue in which the problems have begun to come to the surface and in which the drama is already quite developed.

The John Episode (3:22–36) and Days 1 and 2

As already mentioned, it seems that Days 1 and 2 are echoed not only in the first part of the John episode (3:22–30) but, to some slight degree at least, throughout all of it—up to 3:36. However, the most obvious area of continuity is between the first part of the episode (3:22–30) and Day 1 (1:19–28). The following elements of continuity may be mentioned:

- Discussion with the Jew(s) and the bearing of witness that John is not Christ (1:19–21; 3:25,28a)

- John's emphasis on his own limited role as forerunner (1:22–24,27a; cf. 1:30; 3:28b)

- John's special awareness and revelation of a wondrous presence (of Christ as an apocalypticlike figure who stands unknown among the people, 1:25–27; cf. 1:31; of Christ as a groom who is with his bride, the people, 3:29)

- The naming of the place and general location where ''John . . . was . . . baptizing'' (in Bethany, beyond the Jordan, 1:28; in Aenon, near Salim, 3:23)

Some of the details need further research, but it is reasonably clear that all the main elements of the early scene are echoed in some way in the later scene.

Yet, as with the prologue and the Nicodemus scene, there are also major differences between the texts. Jesus is no longer an unknown figure. It is he who is mentioned first, and all are coming to him. John, on the other hand, is no longer at center stage. He has become a kind of sideshow and is declining. John's mission, as announced in the early scene, has been largely fulfilled in the later scene. Furthermore, unlike 1:19–28, which makes no mention of disciples, 3:22–30 takes it for granted that both Jesus and John have disciples. As mentioned earlier, it is noteworthy that in the later episode John is not mentioned as actually bearing witness. Bearing witness is referred to rather, either as something which he had done in the past, or which, at the moment, is being done, not by him, but by his disciples (3:26,28).

Thus instead of a lone John heralding an unknown Jesus, the later episode is peopled with diverse kinds of disciples, and Jesus is already quite well known.

As regards the final part of the John episode (3:31–36, "He who comes from above . . . from heaven . . ."), there seems to be at least some limited continuity with the scene (on Day 2) in which John identified Jesus as one on whom the Spirit had descended from heaven (1:29–34). Though the exact relationship of the texts is not immediately obvious, the following elements of continuity may be noted—at least as tentative suggestions for further research:

- The coming of Jesus in a way which sets him apart from the world or above all (1:29; 3:31)

- The contrast between Jesus and another character (John the forerunner, 1:30; the one who is of the earth, 3:31)

- Aspects of revelation and testifying concerning Jesus' extraordinary role (1:31, 32a, 34a; 3:32–33)

- The granting of the Spirit to/through Jesus (1:32; 3:34)

- The special role of Jesus as the chosen or beloved Son (1:34; 3:35)

- Use of the phrases "from heaven" and "remain upon him" (1:32–33; 3:31, 36)

The continuity, between 1:29–34 and 3:31–36, does not seem to be as strong as the continuity between 1:1–28 and 3:1–30. But it is not negligible, and it means that echoes of 1:1–34 are found throughout all of 2:23–chap. 3.

Conclusion

The simplest and most coherent explanation of this phenomenon of continuity is that it is part of a deliberate literary process, a process which involves repetition and variation. It is not some vague or rarified procedure, unknown to other writers or unknown in other parts of John; it is a well-known literary technique, and there is ample evidence for it within John 1:1–2:22. To account for the data, there is no need to invoke some oral process, or some doubling of traditions. All that needs to be said is that the text was written by a competent author who, in accordance with a well-established procedure, built a careful continuity between the beginning of Part 1 (1:1–34) and the beginning of Part 2 (2:23–chap. 3).

2:23–Chap. 3 as Diptychlike

One of the puzzles which plagues the study of 2:23–chap. 3 is the paragraph which closes the second episode: "The one who comes from above . . ." (3:31–36). It has just been suggested, in examining the continuity of 2:23–chap. 3 with 1:1–34, that this final paragraph, particularly insofar as it identifies Jesus as heavenly, echoes something of the early scene in which John first identified Jesus as being in some way heavenly—as having received the Spirit from heaven and so on (1:29–34). While this indeed appears to be true, it has long been noticed that this closing paragraph also has links, links which are much more obvious, with another text—Jesus' closing statement to Nicodemus (3:16–21). The similarities are so strong that, as mentioned earlier, it has sometimes been regarded as the earlier text's variant (e.g. cf. Brown, 159–60) or continuation (e.g. Bultmann, 160).

These latter observations are essentially true and what they do is open the way to a more general observation: the John episode (3:22–36) varies and continues certain basic aspects of the Nicodemus episode (2:23–3:21). In other words, despite the major differences between the two episodes, they have been so constructed that they form a kind of diptych.

The idea of a diptych, of two complementary scenes, is not unlikely. Luke 1–2, for instance, with its two annunciation accounts and its two birth accounts, is built largely on the diptych principle (cf. Laurentin, 1957, 33; Stuhlmueller, 1968, 24). And within John 1–2 also there is a certain balancing of scenes: between the two initiatory texts (1:29–28 and 1:29–34), between the two days which describe the calling of the first disciples (1:35–42 and 1:43–51), and between the belief-engendering episodes at Cana and Jerusalem (2:1–11 and 2:12–22).

With regard to the balance between 2:23–3:21 and 3:22–36, Dodd (1953, 308–11) pointed out that both texts deal with some form of baptizing—one implicitly (3:5), the other explicitly (3:22–26). And J. Wilson (1981) has indicated further elements of balance.

The detailed unraveling of the complementarity of the two episodes is a matter for further research. For the moment, a few central points may be noted.

Though the structure of one episode is essentially threefold and that of the other twofold, there is some complementarity of form. Both begin with brief introductions—introductions which, at least within the pattern of the four introductions, are carefully interrelated. Both have the element of an *inclusio*—one *inclusio* which highlights, with increasingly clarity, what is negative (2:23–25; 3:19), the other which, again with increasing clarity, highlights what is positive (communion/love and the Spirit: 3:22, 33–35). And both conclude with variations on the two ways (3:20–21,36).

Apart from complementarity of form, there is also some complementarity or correspondence of content. First, there is the basic idea of a fresh beginning, of inaugurating something new. To Nicodemus, Jesus speaks of someone coming to life—through *water* and the *Spirit,* thus apparently implying a reference to *baptism* (3:3,5). In the later episode, where there is a suggestion of an old order being replaced by a new—John is to be put in prison and all the people are coming to

Jesus—there is a clear emphasis on *baptism* and *water* and there is an implied involvement of the *Spirit* (3:22–24,26; as was seen earlier, Jesus' baptizing implies a low-key reference to the Spirit).

The essential point is that in very different ways both episodes indicate that there is an inbreaking of something new into a previous mind-set or order, and that this inbreaking is brought about, in varying degrees, by water, baptism, and the Spirit.

Second, in response to the new phenomenon, to the new form of life, there is a struggle by the mind. Nicodemus cannot immediately cope with what Jesus is offering and goes through a process of misunderstanding (3:4,9). And in the John episode there is an equal sense of the mind being baffled, baffled by the seeming illogicality surrounding the dispute involving the Jew(s) (3:25–26). In both cases there is a kind of riddle. "Riddle" (*Rätsel*), in fact, is the word which Bultmann (138) uses of the Nicodemus text and which Haenchen (1:210) uses of the later text. But in the later scene the mind which is puzzled is that of the reader, who struggles, as Nicodemus had, to cope with what is being offered. In the final stages of the gospel it is, of course, explicit that the reader is visualized as a potential believer and not as a detached observer (20:31, cf. 19:35). But even now, in chap. 3, it would appear that the reader is being challenged to reflect, to unravel, to get below the surface of things.

Third, both scenes give rather long culminating statements: Jesus speaks to Nicodemus about receiving testimony concerning heavenly things (3:11–21), and John speaks to his disciples about his having testified concerning the one who comes from heaven (3:27–36). These statements do not give clear answers to the puzzles or riddles. Rather they seem to draw the mind to a new stage of perception, to an awareness of another dimension, a dimension which is referred to as heavenly, as above that of earth.

As already suggested there appear to be several links between the closing paragraphs of the two episodes. (For a partial list, see Brown, 159–60.)

A further feature of both episodes, one which to some degree has already been mentioned, is that in the course of the spoken statements which close the episodes, the speaker seems to fade from the picture, and though the statement continues, it takes on a rather distant tone. Thus, in Jesus' concluding statement to Nicodemus (3:11–21) the voice which speaks in the final paragraph ("For God so loved the world, . . ." 3:16–21) seems to be not so much that of Jesus as that of his disciples reflecting on Jesus' work (cf. Brown, 149). And in the baptizing scene, the brief discourse of John concludes with a paragraph ("The one who comes from above, . . ." 3:31–36) which again seems to be not so much the voice of John as that of someone else reflecting on the work of Jesus (cf. Brown, 159; Beasley-Murray, 53). Thus the RSV, for instance, by its quotation marks, excludes the final paragraphs from both closing speeches and then it adds two identical footnotes to say that in both cases "some authorities hold that the quotation continues through [the final paragraph]." There is no further instance of such a note in the RSV. It is attached to these two scenes and to these two alone.

In various ways then there is a balance between 2:23–3:21 and 3:22–36.

The Woman of Samaria

The Down-to-Earth Setting

The scene at the well does not at first seem very uplifting. In some ways it suggests a mood, not of dynamism, but of inertia, a mood that moves between the earthly and the earthy. Even Jesus does not appear particularly heroic. As the chapter begins, he seems, if anything, to be yielding to pressure, to be giving in to the Pharisees. By the time he reaches the well, his mood seems even less heroic. He is tired, thirsty, and presumably hot ("It was about the sixth hour"—noon). He also appears to have been hungry—his disciples had gone into the city to buy food. And he was alone. Then a woman came.

According to usual social behavior he should not have spoken to her—both because she was a Samaritan and because she was a woman. In fact, when the disciples, on their return, found him speaking to her, they seem to have been so embarrassed and suspicious that they avoided asking what he wanted with her.

The woman's words add further to the earthbound atmosphere. She is engrossed by the practicalities of the well—by the need for a bucket, by its depth, by the fact that it had once been used not only by Jacob himself but also to provide water for his sons and cattle, by her own need to come and draw. In the context of the contrast set up by chapter 3, the contrast between focusing on earth and focusing on heaven, this woman with her mind on the well seems very much focused toward earth. She is also focused on a form of "flesh"—on short-term marriages and affairs with men. She had had a whole slew of them. The situation, therefore, is not promising.

Yet it is within this situation that Jesus speaks to her. Starting from the things that are most on her mind—the water and the men—he leads her to an awareness of higher things and to a desire to communicate that awareness to others.

It turns out, of course, as the conversation advances, that the woman has far more on her mind than water and men. Though initially she falls into misunderstanding (v 11) and irony (v 12), she shows both some knowledge of tradition (concerning Jacob, Jerusalem, and a Messiah) and considerable openness and perceptiveness. The scene at the well, therefore, however languid-looking at first, emerges as one of considerable liveliness. The woman who came to draw water ends up by receiving a whole new revelation.

Furthermore, she becomes, for the whole people, an instrument leading to salvation. Her turnabout is not as dramatic as that of St. Paul. It is perhaps more like the case of Moses—someone who in the course of an ordinary day's work is made powerfully aware of the way in which slavery is challenged and broken by the divine; someone who sets out to bring that message to the people.

"Come," she said, "see a person who told me all whatsoever I have done. Can this be the Anointed?" (4:28–29). Her credibility should have been nonexistent, but her attitude to her negative background was so forthright and healthy that the people knew that she had indeed received a message.

Interwoven with the story of the woman is that of "the disciples." In many ways they are like her—intent on the practicalities of life (on buying food), and with little understanding of Jesus (they call him "Rabbi," 4:31). But when Jesus has a conversation with them, as he had with the woman, they too emerge as evangelizers (4:31–38).

Thus the episode as a whole has a pervasive ambiguity. It is centered on people who seem preoccupied with such daily chores as drawing water and buying food, yet it is precisely among these people and through their chores that God is working and that revelation begins to be spoken.

Structure

It has sometimes been suggested that the episode at the well should be divided, on the basis of varying characters or *dramatis personae,* into just two scenes— one of Jesus' conversation with the woman (4:4–26) and the second of his conversation with the disciples (4:27–38) (cf. Brown, 176–85). In its basis for division this is akin to Schnackenburg's structuring of the Cana episode (1:334) and, while it possesses an initial plausibility and is, in fact, partly true, it has drawbacks similar to those of the Schnackenburg proposal. It does not do justice to its professed basis for division—to the variety in the *dramatis personae.* Both the woman and the disciples are found in diverse parts of the episode (cf. esp. 4:8,28–29). And it allows no adequate place to the characters who climax the story—the believers from the city (cf. 4:28–29,39–42). It is necessary, therefore, to look again at the text.

One of the striking features of the episode as a whole is the varying length of Jesus' utterances. Altogether he speaks nine times. The first three utterances, concerning different meanings of water, occur in the first division of the conversation with the woman (4:7b, 10, 13–15). The next three, which deal largely with the woman's history and with the move to a more spiritual worship, occur in the later division of the conversation with the woman (4:16, 17b–18, 21–24). The final three all begin with "I" or "My" ("I . . . am he"; "I have food . . ."; "My food is to do . . ."). They deal with Jesus, his mission and the initial commissioning of the disciples, and they go from the very end of the conversation with the woman, the precise point at which the disciples return, to the end of the conversation with the disciples themselves (4:26, 32, 34–38). In other words, the final three are all said in the disciples' presence or near them, and Jesus' words manage also to bridge the gap between the woman and the disciples.

Within each group of three, Jesus' utterances become progressively longer. Thus the phenomenon found in the Nicodemus scene—"the three answers of Jesus are progressively longer in their development" (Brown, 136)—is found in triple form in the Samaria scene.

Among the three longest utterances (numbers 3, 6 and 9, i.e., 4:13–14, 21–24, 34–38), there is a similar gradation in length. Thus the final utterance, concerning the food (4:34–38), is the longest of all. And the very first utterance, "Give me a drink" (4:7) is the shortest.

This unified threefold structure in Jesus' utterances provides an initial indication that the episode as a whole, apart from the introduction (4:1–6), is to be divided, not so much into two scenes, as into three. The idea of a division into three is corroborated by another factor, that of movement, in other words, by references to people entering and leaving the drama. The most obvious are the clear references to the arrival of the woman (4:7) and the later arrival of the disciples (4:27). But it would seem that the same function is exercised by the rather perplexing command: "*Go,* call your husband, and *come here*" (4:16). It is perplexing because the woman does not move, and because Jesus could have referred to her husband without suggesting that she exit and reenter, but it makes sense as a kind of stage direction, as indicating, especially to the reader, that, to some degree at least, a new scene is beginning. (In other texts movement is also used to divide episodes into scenes, especially in chap. 9 and in the trial before Pilate.)

The third scene is different to the extent that, in recounting the basic story of the woman and the believers, it contains an interlude ("In the meantime . . .") with the disciples (4:31–38). As Lindars (193) notes, the device is a variation on Mark's "sandwich" construction—his practice of enfolding one incident within another (e.g., the woman with the flow of blood within the account of the raising of the daughter of Jairus, Mark 5:21–43). Thus the third section, in which one scene enfolds another, is twofold.

The resulting structure is an elaborate variation on the structure already seen in the Nicodemus episode—an introduction, followed by three scenes or divisions, the third of which is twofold in character. It is also a variation on the structure which has been proposed for the gospel as a whole.

And just as the conversation with Nicodemus suggested the possibility of an ascent to God, so also here, but in a more developed and down-to-earth form, the threefold episode suggests a form of ascent—"the drama of a soul struggling to rise from the things of this world to belief in Jesus" (Brown, 178). As the story unfolds she gains more and more insight into Jesus, and with that insight a new awareness of her own situation. At the end of the first scene she expresses some initial interest: "Give me this water . . ." (4:15). At the end of the second scene she implies that she is receptive to everything: she knows of the coming of a Messiah who will announce all things (4:25). And in the twofold third scene there are, appropriately, two final statements—that of the woman, who has now accepted the revelation of everything, particularly concerning herself (4:29), and the corresponding openness of the people (4:42).

The Woman as Representative of the Disciples/People

It has been indicated by a number of commentators that the woman, apart from her individual role, represents the people of Samaria (cf. esp. Hirsch, 1936, 146). Her only name is "woman of Samaria," and the reference to five husbands has sometimes been seen as a veiled reference to Samaria itself and to its complex five fold background (cf. the five national groups mentioned in 2 Kgs 17:29–31; Schnackenburg, 1:433; Lindars, 186–87; Lenglet, 1985, 494). In fact, there is a form of feminist hermeneutic which sees the five husbands in a way which is purely symbolic or representative and which effectively denies the literal meaning. But, as a general principle, the representative level does not exclude the literal level, and to say that in this case it does is ultimately a disservice to feminism. The woman has had five husbands, and, even in her many marriages, she is also representative.

The text, however, has yet another dimension. It shows the woman as representing the whole body of believers. Aquinas (*Commentary* 253) speaks of her as "a symbol of the Church of the Gentiles."

The basic clue to this corporate role is the fact that in the narrative the role of the woman is intertwined with that of the disciples. As already seen, the systematic ninefold gradation of Jesus' words bridges the gap between his two conversations, that with the woman and that with disciples. Furthermore, while the conversation with the woman begins with a reference to the disciples (4:7–8), the conversation with the disciples is introduced by a reference to the woman (4:27–31). In addition, as Brown (181) notes, there are similarities between the two conversations, between the woman's misunderstanding about water (4:7–11) and the disciples' misunderstanding about food (4:31–33). And, more striking even than the interweaving of the conversations, is the interweaving of the missions: the woman's mission to the city provides the framework for Jesus' address to the disciples about their mission to the waiting "harvest." The deliberateness of this interweaving is brought out by the fact that the woman's mission to the city is summarized not just once but twice, in slightly repetitive form (4:29–30,38), and it is in the "Meanwhile . . ." between these summaries that the disciples are tentatively commissioned. Thus their mission is encased in hers—a further indication that she is in some way representative of them, identified with them.

It is a mistake, therefore, to try to disentangle the two (the woman and the disciples) as the NEB does when it rearranges vv 7 and 8, or to refer to v 27, with its references to the disciples, as something which "spoils the connection between [the references to the woman in] vv 26 and 28" (Lindars, 192). The interweaving of the two missions, while puzzling at a superficial level, is not something muddled or spoiled; it demonstrates rather a deliberate and coherent theological purpose.

The identification of the woman with the disciples is not unique to 4:1–42. It was seen earlier in the Cana story when the mother of Jesus was introduced in the context of Jesus' disciples (2:1–11, esp. 2:1–2,11; cf. 2:12,17,22). Thus it is part of a larger pattern in John. It is a pattern in which the woman, whatever her individual or historical role, plays also a role which is representative either of the people or of the church.

The Woman as the Betrothed

Jesus' encounter with the woman follows the literary conventions of a specific type-scene, that of the encounter with the bethrothed at a well. Alter writes (1981, 52):

The betrothal type-scene . . . must take place when the future bridegroom, or his surrogate, have journeyed to a foreign land. There he encounters a girl . . . or girls at a well. Someone, either the man or the girl, then draws water from the well; afterward the girl or girls rush home to bring the news of the stranger's arrival; . . . finally, a betrothal is concluded between the stranger and the girl, in the majority of instances, only after he has been invited to a meal.

Examples of this type-scene may be found, for instance, in the stories of Isaac and Rebecca (Gen 24:11–20), Jacob and Rachel (Gen 29:1–14), and Moses and Zipporah (Exod 2:15–22).

John 4 produces this type-scene with scrupulous care, but with a glaring omission—the final elements of a meal and betrothal.

Such a startling variation on a type-scene was not unknown in biblical narrative. In fact, variations on type-scenes were ways of catching attention, of saying something. As Alter (1981, 52) comments, "If some of those circumstances [of the type-scene] were altered or suppressed . . . that communicated something to the audience." Thus, if in the repetitive Hollywood westerns about sheriff-heroes with lightning gun-hands, there is one sheriff-hero whose gun-hand is withered, it is not because the producers have forgotten. On the contrary, it is a way of focusing attention on what is absent and of telling the audience to look out for something else, for something equally effective. In this example, drawn from Alter (1981, 48–49), it turns out that the sheriff-hero, overcoming even greater odds than usual, walks with a rifle slung over his shoulder, and has trained his left arm "to whip his rifle into firing position with a swiftness that makes it a match for the quickest draw in the West."

Similarly, in John 4:1–42. If the crucial elements of the meal and betrothal are absent, it is not because they have been forgotten, but because they appear in another form. Instead of the ordinary meal there is a kind of spiritual meal. When the disciples buy food and offer it to Jesus, he replies: "My food is to do the will of him who sent me, and to accomplish his work" (4:8,31–34). In other words, at this stage of the gospel, the idea of a meal is replaced by an insistence on the priority of the spiritual, the priority of doing God's will.

And the idea of a betrothal has been replaced by two factors, by what may be called an "unbetrothal"—the liberating of a woman who had been over-betrothed physically—and, more positively, by a betrothal of a more spiritual nature, a betrothal of belief. The woman, as the text implies, comes to believe, and so do the people—the people whom she in some way represents. The text does not say explicitly that Jesus was involved in any process of betrothal, but at the end of the scene at the well, exactly where the type-scene would usually require the actual betrothal, the story tells that the believers invited Jesus to abide with them. And for two days he did so. It is in this idea, of abiding with the believers, of staying with them, that the reality of betrothal finds new expression.

The idea that Jesus' sojourn with the woman and the people represents a process of betrothal finds confirmation in the context. The preceding scene, that of the baptizing (3:22–36), gave interrelated images of Jesus "sojourning" with the disciples (3:22), of a whole people ("all") coming to Jesus (3:26), and of Jesus' relationship to the disciples or people as that of a groom to a bride (3:29). Thus what was suggested at Cana becomes somewhat clearer: Jesus communicates a presence which is better than wedding wine.

[4:1–6] Introduction: Jesus' exhausting journey and the statement that he did not baptize.

At first sight the narrative may seem straightforward: as the Pharisees' hostility began to emerge, Jesus moved to Galilee, pausing on his way at a Samaritan city, Sychar.

On closer inspection, however—and even apart from the fact that the episode as a whole is a betrothal type-scene—there are problems with regarding the text as primarily historical. It is true, of course, that the text seems close to historical reality. As Brown (175) expresses it: "The *mise en scène* is one of the most detailed in John, and the evangelist betrays a knowledge of local color and Samaritan belief that is impressive." But in the midst of this impressive knowledge there is a "tantalizing problem" (Lindars, 178): Sychar, the city around which the action revolves, is completely unknown in history. (For discussion, see Lindars, 178–79; and see also the mutually cancelling arguments of Schnackenburg, 1:423 and Brown, 169.) At an earlier stage it was noted that Bethany beyond the Jordan (1:28) and Aenon near Salim (3:23) were similarly unknown. The evangelist, therefore, seems simultaneously to set up a scene and subvert it, to paint it carefully and yet indicate that something else is going on. Furthermore, to say that "it was necessary" to pass through Samaria is not accurate geographically; there was an alternate route through the Jordan valley. Brown (169), having mentioned the problem, provides the clue to its solution by noting that "elsewhere in the gospel (3:14) the expression of necessity means that God's will or plan is involved." This reference to God's will or plan casts a new light on the scene; it suggests that the text, whatever its detailed knowledge of a historical setting, is seeking to give a picture which is theological, a picture which tells of God's plan. Such an idea is corroborated by the opening words: "When the *Lord* knew that the Pharisees had heard that *Jesus*. . . ." At first sight this looks so awkward that many ancient copyists and modern commentators have changed it to read "When *Jesus* knew that the Pharisees had heard that he. . . ." But the awkward-looking text, like the puzzle which Jesus put to Nicodemus, has a purpose—to engage the mind of the reader and alert it to a further dimension of the story, in this case the involvement of the Lord, the fact that the events reflect God's will or plan.

It is within this context of allusions to God's plan that a further problem must be considered—the notorious statement that Jesus did not baptize (4:2).

The statement that Jesus did not baptize (4:2). In 3:22 it is said that Jesus baptized (cf. also 3:26). There is no ambiguity: the verb is singular and refers to Jesus. At the beginning of chapter 4 the same idea is clearly repeated: "When . . . the Pharisees . . . heard that Jesus was . . . baptizing . . ." (4:1). But then, immediately, there is a further comment: "Although Jesus himself did not baptize, but only his disciples" (4:2).

Did he or did he not? The contradiction seems so glaring that some commentators have regarded 4:2 as an insertion, as reflecting an editorial process. In fact, Dodd and Brown see 4:2 as one of the gospel's best examples of the whole phenomenon of editing. For Brown (164) it "serves as almost indisputable evidence of the presence of several hands in the composition of John." Dodd (1953, 311) regards 4:2 as "a parenthesis which ruins the sentence, and perhaps has a better claim to be regarded as an 'editorial note' by a 'redactor' than anything else in the gospel except the colophon, xxi. 24–25."

If 4:2 is to be so regarded—as a prime example of the best evidence of an editorial process—then it is worth examining more closely. This is a test case.

The first thing to be said about the editorial hypothesis is that it does not solve the problem satisfactorily. It may sound plausible at first, but on reflection it does not really explain why 4:2 is as it is. If an editor wanted to correct the text, to remove the impression that Jesus baptized, then why not simply do so, particularly since it would have been quite easy. Thus Bultmann (176), while going along with the idea that 4:2 is an editorial gloss, nonetheless expresses a doubt: "It is hard to see why the editor did not make the correction at 3:22." To leave standing a statement of fact and then bluntly to state its opposite is not a very good method of communicating one's view. More importantly, it does not correspond to any known process of editing. As Brown (286) says with regard to some of the alleged editorializing in chap. 6: "Any editor who would add these verses would naturally make an effort to bring them into harmony with their new context." This touches the essence of the question: "editing" is generally understood, even in John, as involving at least a minimal process of harmonizing the text. In 4:2 it is exactly such basic harmony which is missing. Thus, however the text is to be accounted for, it is not by an appeal to an undefined process of "editing." Editing, insofar as it has any coherent meaning, would remove this kind of problem, not cause it.

The proposal made here is that the apparently contradictory statement has a purpose: to alert the reader to the fact that within God's plan, particularly as portrayed in chaps. 3–4, Jesus is changing roles. He no longer does all the things he used to do. There comes a time when his role gives way to that of the disciples. Hence the puzzling account: "Jesus . . . baptized;" "Jesus himself did not baptize, but only his disciples."

Thus far (in John 1–3) there had been little indication that Jesus would yield to the disciples. The disciples had indeed become more conspicuous, and his voice at one point seemed to fade (3:16–21). But he was still in charge. Now, however, there is a fading which is much more explicit: Jesus is exhausted, literally, labored out (4:6, *kekopiakōs*, from *kopiaō*, "to labor"), and it is the task of the disciples to take over, to labor where others have labored (4:38, *kopiaō . . . kopiaō*, the same rare verb, otherwise not used in John).

This picture of yielding to the disciples tells of Jesus as an individual experiencing limitation, and of his realizing, in some way, that others will replace him. It evokes an intimation of mortality.

Previous texts had hinted at some such change. Jesus' hesitancy in Jerusalem, his sudden caution (2:23–25), implied an element of withdrawal. Even when he was with his disciples, precisely when he was described as baptizing (3:22), his togetherness with them was described as "sojourning" (*dia-tribō*), in other words, as a process of just passing through, living like an alien, living on limited time. (John's only other use of *dia-tribō* is in 11:54—when Jesus is about to die; cf.

11:53.) Now, in 4:1–3, immediately before and after the reference to not baptizing, the shadow of withdrawal darkens: in the face of pressure, Jesus decides to leave. The overall effect of these allusions is to suggest that, at a level which is not felt clearly either by Jesus or by the reader, something fundamental is changing. Jesus is doing well, very well; but he is also moving away, moving on. Beneath the surface of his world the plates are shifting.

Such dimensions of the story are easy to miss. The colorful narrative, with its overtones of impending bethrothal, can lull a person into a relaxed enjoyment of the whole encounter. But the opening contradiction sounds an alert. It prefaces the evoking of love (the betrothal) with an evoking of death.

This interpretation—that the jarring text is evoking death—is confirmed by a subsequent detail: the fact that the encounter with the woman took place at the (death-evoking) sixth hour (4:6). It is unlikely, historically speaking, that the woman would come to the well "about the sixth hour," in other words, about noon. "Such a chore was done in the morning and evening" (Brown, 169). But it makes theological sense: as some poets and writers have noted, it was at such an hour that Jesus was condemned to death: "When Pilate heard . . . he brought Jesus out and sat down on the judgment seat; . . . it was about the sixth hour" (19:13–14; cf. Brown, 169). In other words, the scene is deliberately being related to the crucifixion. Something similar is found in John 9 where the symbolism "has as its background Jesus' approaching death" (Brown, 382). Obviously if one's reading of the gospel puts the primary emphasis on the historical, such a reference to the crucifixion is highly unlikely. But if it is seen that the entire Samaria episode is governed by a literary convention, and particularly that the exhaustion of Jesus alludes to his final giving way to the disciples, then it is appropriate that the hour also should allude to that final process. Furthermore, since Jesus, in speaking to the woman, will be referring in various ways to the giving of the Spirit, and since the giving of the Spirit is associated with Jesus' death and glorification, it is appropriate, before he starts to talk, that there be an evoking of that final hour.

Ultimately there are two basic ways of reading these introductory verses (4:1–6)—either as muddled history or as coherent theology.

[4:7–15] The unrecognized stranger arouses interest in living water. Whatever may be the introduction's allusions to tiredness and crucifixion (cf. 4:1–6), there is no suggestion, as the discussion with the woman develops, that Jesus is lifeless. On the contrary, just as Jesus' death would be eminently life-giving, so too is the scene at the well.

At first the woman is quite unaware of what she has encountered. As a Samaritan and a woman—a formidable double handicap—she does not regard herself as rating highly in the eyes of a Jew. Jews, because of their preoccupation with purity, had no dealings with the Samaritans, especially it would seem in the realm of sharing vessels—including water jars (Daube, 1956, 373–82). And Samaritan women were particularly suspect. As the Mishnah (Nid. 4.1) put it: "the daughters of the Samaritans are deemed unclean as menstruants from their cradle."

On the other hand, whatever she may have thought of Jesus' regard for her,

her regard for him cannot have been very high. Here was somebody who when it suited him would not keep even his own wretched rules.

The scene is striking, comparable in its dramatic irony to the famous Homeric scene in which the still-powerful Odysseus, after twenty years of wandering, stands ragged and unrecognized before his wife and nurse (*Odyssey,* Bk 19).

The Samaritan woman has no idea, in her world of mutual near-contempt, that she is in the presence of one who, in a sense, has come to betroth her, no idea that at this hour, on a day yet to come, the one to whom she is speaking will face death in order to bring life and salvation to her world.

Even when Jesus begins to reveal who he is, she does not understand. He speaks of his ability to give her "living water," something which for him apparently refers to God's gift of revelation and the Spirit (cf. Schnackenburg, 1:425–32; Brown, 178–80), but which for her refers to spring water, water which is fresh, "alive"—unlike flat cistern water. Living water, of course, is what she wants, but the stranger seems quite incapable of delivering it—he has no equipment and the well is deep—and she asks him teasingly if he is greater than Jacob, the patriarch who first gave the well. As in Nicodemus's reference to the old man reentering the womb (3:4), there is here a hint of mockery. Who does he think he is? He has indeed won a minimum respect: she calls him *"Kyrie,"* meaning "Sir." But the word also means "Lord" and "husband" (cf. Duke, 1985, 102), and of these aspects she seems quite unaware. Then Jesus speaks more solemnly and at greater length: he is not referring to ordinary spring water, something which satisfies thirst for a time only; what he is offering rather is like a perpetual fountain, "a spring of water welling up to eternal life."

She still does not recognize or understand him, but something in his words has sparked an interest. The level of that interest is not great—it is still within the realm of her previous concerns—but she begins to take him seriously. *"Kyrie,"* she said, "give me this water that I may not thirst, nor come hither to draw."

Genuine contact has been made. Now the conversation can really develop.

[4:16–26] Revelation of the disoriented plight of the woman and her people, and an intimation of God's resposiveness through the Spirit.

At first sight the conversation may seem somewhat erratic. Jesus suddenly refers to the woman's love life, and the woman, with equal suddenness, refers to her people's worship life. Whatever psychological motives may be suggested for these changes—for instance, the woman's wish to change the subject—the present text has considerable theological coherence. Love and worship are connected to the idea of living water, the water of life. They touch the core of the human heart.

It may seem strange, when so much attention is directed at the unrecognized divine Revealer and when the conversation is about to look even more closely at God and the revealing Messiah ("God is spirit . . . a Messiah comes, . . ." 4:24–25), that the spotlight at this point should focus not on the divine spirit but on the human heart, particularly insofar as that heart is fundamentally confused and disoriented—disoriented in love and in worship.

But such a change of focus makes sense. One cannot gain an increased sense of the presence of God without becoming increasingly aware of being, or of having been, without God in the depth of one's heart, in other words in the area of the heart that loves and worships. It is somewhat like studying physical health—it cannot be done seriously without becoming aware of the extent to which one may lack such health. Thus the revelation of God involves a revelation of self. The point is made forcefully by Bultmann (188):

> The revelation [of the divine] is for man the disclosure of his own life. Man is made aware of the unrest in his life, which drives him from one supposed satisfaction to another, never letting him attain the final fulfillment until he finds the water of life, of which "one drink for ever stills the thirst." This unrest is portrayed by the woman's disturbed past and her unsatisfied present state. Perhaps one may go as far as to say that the married life of the woman "who reels from desire to pleasure" portrays not only the unrest, but the aberrations of the desire for life. This leads on naturally to the next point. The fact that Jesus has shown the woman the truth of her own situation, leads her to suspect that he is the Revealer. Only by man's becoming aware of his true nature, can the Revealer be recognized. The attainment of the knowledge of God and knowledge of self are part of the same process.

On both topics, love and worship, the woman makes a partial statement, and in both cases Jesus cuts through the camouflage and, with amusing irony and considerable deference ("You speak well. . . . Believe me, woman . . ."), clarifies the true state of things: her love life is bankrupt, and the worship of her people is empty ("You worship what you do not know"). Thus, while it may indeed be disputed whether the exact number of the woman's husbands is meant to correspond to the exact number of Samaritan tribes and false gods, there can be little doubt but that the woman's marital disorder is of a piece with the spiritual disorder of her people. And it is to this interwoven disorder, this confused spiritual plight, that Jesus responds.

"The hour is coming," he says ". . . the hour is coming, and now is, when the true worshippers will worship the Father in spirit and in truth." The hour in question is that of Jesus' death and resurrection. As at Cana it is an hour which, in one sense has not yet come, but in another sense is already present and effective (2:4–10). This tension, between the "not yet" and the "already," has been described by saying that "the eschatological reign of God was [already] present and operative in the ministry of Jesus, but in a provisional way" (Brown, cxvii). Thus, at the time Jesus is speaking to the woman the Spirit has not yet been given —not fully and formally. But the hour is coming, and, as at Cana, as far as the woman is concerned, is already here. Thus, in cryptic and proleptic language, Jesus lays before the woman the richness of life in the Spirit, life in the presence of the Father. The term "Father" is used rather indirectly, and the primary emphasis, as Duke (1985, 101–3) suggests, is on a process of betrothal; but this indirect reference to the Father is given three times (4:21–23), and the eagerness of the Father to meet the woman and her people is underlined by the final references: "for such the Father seeks to adore him." Thus Jesus reveals to the woman, on the one hand, the disorientation of herself and her people, and, on the other, the nearness of a parental spouselike God who offers spiritual integration.

The woman's reply is her final statement to Jesus and it is a high point in all she has said. To appreciate it, it is necessary to look first at her previous statements. She had started with a retort ("How is it that you? . . ."), then a mocking question ("*Kyrie*, you do not even have? . . ."), and thirdly a request which despite some superficiality, is real ("*Kyrie*, give me this water . . ."). Then in the second part of the conversation she had begun with an ironically well-spoken statement ("I have no husband"), and had gone on to a perceptive observation ("*Kyrie*, I perceive that you are a prophet"). But now in her final statement to Jesus she is not only truthful about herself and perceptive about him; she also reveals a knowledge of what is yet to come: "I know that a Messiah is coming. . . . When he comes he will announce all things to us." As a person with a complicated past she might well have been afraid of a Messiah who would tell all. But her attitude is open, and thus she sets the stage for a final revelation: Jesus replies, *Egō eimi*.

When Jesus says *Egō eimi*, literally "I am," his words may indeed be read as "I am he," but they contain also an evocation of the central revelation of God to Moses (Exod 3:14, *Egō eimi* . . . "I am . . ."). In other words, Jesus' self-identification as the expected Messiah is so formulated that it indicates the presence of God. And that God is calling for a reply: "I am, *I who am speaking to you*." In Bultmann's words (192): "Whoever hears these words spoken by the Revealer is faced with the ultimate decision: the *Egō eimi* lays absolute claim to faith." But just then there is an interruption; the disciples return. The scene closes and the decision is left hanging in the balance.

[4:27–42] A culmination of revelation and response, and an explanatory interlude.

Like the woman, the disciples at first are at a very mundane level of understanding. Their minds are on buying bread, as hers had been on drawing water, and when they walk into a scene which is extraordinarily revelatory and challenging—just as Jesus is saying "I am . . ."—what they perceive in their "wonder" (verb, *thaumazō*) is not God but the whiff of scandal. The allusion to the fact that Jesus was "seeking" something (4:27) contains an evoking of the Father's "seeking" of true worshippers (4:23). But the disciples' hearts and minds are at another level.

And at that the woman left her water jar and went into the city to tell the people. The leaving of the water jar corresponds to the motif, taken from the conventional betrothal scene, of hurrying; but it indicates also the depth of her response to the Revealer's call: having found a new form of living water, she leaves behind her the symbol of her former preoccupation. She has met someone who tells all about her, and the discovery is positive. And the people went out and came to him.

And in the interlude, before the people reach Jesus (4:31–38), the disciples remain for a while on the same misunderstanding level as the woman once had been. But as Jesus speaks and explains to them their missionary role, the emphasis on their slowness fades and the focus turns to the waiting harvest. At the beginning of the episode, there had been a reference to a single field or plot of land (*chorion*), the land given by Jacob (4:5). Now, in a more ambiguous phrase, the *chōrai* ("fields" or "lands") are ready for harvest. Thus, the former land or mission gives way to one that is greater. And the former laborer makes room for others.

The interlude, therefore, serves to explain that the mission of the woman to the city has to do with the mission of the disciples to the waiting lands.

The general purpose of that mission is that Jesus should abide with those who accept him—as he abode for two days with the Samaritan believers (4:39–42). And while the woman had indeed been helpful to the believers, their acceptance of the abiding presence of Jesus brought them to such a new level of believing that they no longer depended on her.

The idea that those who abide with Jesus have an knowledge of Christ which is independent of the woman would seem to be a variation on the earlier implication that those who abide with Jesus have a knowledge of Christ which is independent of Peter (1:35–42). The fact that there is a connection between the two texts is indicated not only by the similarity of theme, but also by the fact that in both cases, and not just in the first, the term "Messiah" is explained as meaning "Christ" or "Anointed" (1:41, 4:25). As some writers have noted (cf. Lindars, 191), the repetition of the explanation is quite unnecessary. As such it is rather puzzling, but, once it is seen as a literary detail which indicates a link between the texts, its presence makes sense. Thus, a certain independence from Peter in chap. 1 is followed in chap. 4 by a certain independence from the woman. And the woman, like the woman at Cana, would seem, in some way at least, to represent the church.

This independence from Peter and the church is not peevish, arrogant, or schismatic. Rather it is a kinship with God—similar to that which is spoken of in Jeremiah's new covenant (Jer 31:31–34) and in Galatians (cf. esp. Gal 1:11–15; 5:13–15)—a kinship with God which, as well as generating independence, generates an equal measure of patience and love.

The Healing of the Son of the Royal Official

A Failing of Life and a Reaction of Belief

This is both a story of faith and a powerful father-son story. Furthermore, whatever its sources and its relationship to the synoptic story of the centurion's servant (Matt 8:5–13, Luke 7:1–10), as the text now stands it is carefully integrated with the narrative as a whole. Its emphasis on life builds on the theme of life which was announced in chap. 3 (cf. esp. 3:3,16,36) and developed in chap. 4, particularly in the discussion on "living water" (4:10–15). And, insofar as there is an inevitable suspicion that this man, an official from a border town, was a Gentile (cf. Barrett, 245; Brown, 191), the conversion of his household brings to a new stage the major movement which was described in 4:1–42: Jesus' move away from Judea, through Samaria, to being Savior of the world. In addition, the father-son emphasis brings to the fore a motif which had been present in various ways from the beginning of the gospel (cf. esp. 1:14,18; 3:16,36; and the father motif in 4:21–23), and which from chap. 5 onward, will be even more prominent. And the idea—repeated at the end of the Samaria story—of "believing because of the word" (4:39,41), gives way in the story of the official to the more direct idea of "believing the word" (4:50). Even the rare phrase "all whatsoever I have done" (*panta hosa epoiēsa,* 4:29,39)—a phrase which is found twice near the end of the Samaria story but which does not occur elsewhere in the gospel—recurs with a minor variation in the introduction to the story of the official: "the Galileans welcomed him having seen all whatsoever he had done" (*panta . . . hosa epoiēsen,* 4:45). It is hardly coincidence that even the hour at which the child receives life ("the seventh hour," 4:52) is just one hour beyond the time at which the woman asked for living water ("the sixth hour," 4:6). Such a progression, from one number to the next, is frequent in biblical poetry and, as such, would seem to be applicable also, in some degree at least, to biblical narrative (cf. Alter, 1985, 11, 6–7).

The general impression which emerges is that, while the story of the Capernaum official has its own newness and integrity, it is described in such a way that it constitutes a carefully crafted progression from the preceding narrative.

4:43–54 in Continuity with the First Cana Miracle (2:1–11)

Apart from the rather general continuity between 4:53–54 and the preceding texts, an even more pervasive aspect of continuity is explicitly indicated by the text itself —its continuity with the first Cana incident (4:46,54; cf. 2:1–11). To a remarkable extent the pattern of the two miracles is the same (cf. Brown, 194). In both cases Jesus arrives in Galilee on the third day and at first refuses a request. But when the petitioner persists, Jesus relents and the result is that another group of people (the disciples, the whole household) comes to believe (or to believe more strongly) in him. Neither story tells how the miracle is accomplished. Furthermore, these are the only two signs that do not lead to a discourse. Instead, after each, Jesus goes up to Jerusalem and the temple. Further details of similarity will be seen later in this discussion.

The similarity of the two Cana stories is not a coincidence. It emerges rather as part of what seems to be a much larger pattern, a pattern in which the text of Part 1 (1:1–2:22) is variously echoed, elaborated, and complemented in Part 2 (2:23–chap. 6). The details of this pattern are best left to further research, but for the fact of its existence there is some significant evidence. Indications have already been seen that the first part of chap. 1 (1:1–34) is carefully echoed and complemented in 2:23–chap. 3. And while the later part of chap. 1 (1:35–51) depicts the disciples' call, the Samaria story (4:1–42) contains an emphasis on something complementary—the disciples' responsibility.

Then come the Cana stories (2:1–11; 4:43–54). Both texts represent a certain culmination. The first Cana miracle comes at the end of a week-long drama; the second comes at the end of the journey to Judea (cf. 4:54)

The Cana Texts: Details of a Time-Space Complementarity

At this point it is worth pausing, so to speak, to look more closely at the careful interrelationship of the Cana texts. The first, as a culmination, is primarily a culmination of time, of a week; the second is primarily one of space, a journey. Yet both have secondary aspects. To some small degree, the first Cana miracle completes a journey, the journey to Galilee which is referred to in the preceding episode, the episode concerning the call of Philip (1:43). And, to some small degree, the second Cana miracle completes a passing of time, the two days which Jesus had spent with the people in the preceding episode, in other words with the Samaritans (4:40,43). The (secondary) time element of the second Cana miracle, insofar as it speaks of two days and suggests that Jesus arrived in Galilee on the third day, corresponds to some of the (primary) time element of the first Cana miracle—to the fact that, at the end of the week, it occurred "on the third day" (2:1). And the (secondary) journey element of the first Cana miracle, insofar as it suggests a journey to Galilee, corresponds to some of the (primary) journey elements of the second Cana miracle—the journey which, having ultimately begun in Jerusalem, went from Judea to Galilee. In other words what is primary in one finds a precise secondary balance in the other. This balance describes a complementarity between the texts, a complementarity which is both complex and delicately coherent.

There is also progression. The first, both insofar as it places the culminating miracle so far away from Jerusalem—in the actual text the very names "Jerusalem" and "Cana of Galilee" are placed at opposite ends of the drama (1:19; 2:11) —and insofar as Jesus' first move to Galilee is associated with the call of the Greek-sounding Philip (1:43), had given a faint debatable hint of a movement to the Gentiles. In the second, however, this suggestion is much more audible. The journey through Samaria leaves an unmistakable impression of movement towards non-Jews, towards the world.

The Structure of 4:43–54

As Brown's layout (190) implies, and as Schnackenburg (1:468) more clearly indicates, the episode—apart from its introduction (4:43–45)—consists of two scenes. The first, which tells of impending death and of a stark belief which is based on Jesus' word, occurs when Jesus returns to Galilee and Cana "after the two days." The second scene occurs on the following day when the servants come with the news that the son was alive, and it tells of a belief based on the living confirmation of Jesus' word.

[4:43–45] Introduction: No honor in his own country . . . welcomed in Galilee. At first sight the verses which lead into the second Cana scene may seem contradictory. Jesus testifies that in his own country (*patris*, "fatherland," "country") a prophet is not honored. Yet in Galilee, presumably his own country (cf. Matt 13:57, Luke 4:24, and esp. John 7:41,52), he is welcomed. Even as far back as Origen, the apparent contradiction led to considerable debate, and it has been suggested that responsibility lies with an editor (cf. Brown, 186–87).

But, as a number of writers have variously indicated (e.g., Hoskyns, 252; and Barrett, 246), when John speaks of Jesus' own *patris* he seems to be referring not to Galilee but to Judea, the focal point of Judaism and of Jesus' own Jewish heritage, the center of his cultural and spiritual patrimony. In other words he is taking *patris* not in a purely physical sense, the sense of the flesh, but in a more spiritual sense. In so doing he is building consistently on the various other ambiguities of chaps. 3 and 4, especially the flesh-Spirit ambiguities which had been put before Nicodemus and the woman of Samaria—concerning different forms of birth and of living water (3:3–8, 4:10–15). Bultmann (204–5) does not accept this explanation; yet, as Barrett (246) insists, it makes sense. Furthermore, it accords with the idea mentioned in discussing the gospel's space-based structure (Introduction, chapter 4) that "Galilee" is not just a geographic term; it symbolizes acceptance.

That the place which rejects Jesus is Judea and not Galilee is borne out by the larger text concerning Jesus' arrival in Galilee. Apart from saying that the Galileans welcomed him, it sets his Galilee arrival in the context of a journey from Judea, a journey which was occasioned by some form of rejection by Judaism's leaders, the Pharisees (4:1–3,43–45,54).

The actual phrasing of the Greek text (4:43–44) appears to confirm this: ". . . *he went . . . to Galilee; for Jesus himself bore witness* that a prophet has no honor in his own fatherland." Jesus' statement is not some awkward reactional intrusion which is to be placed in parentheses. Bultmann (204) notwithstanding, it is like an explanation of his move to Galilee, an explanation which resumes and develops the rather vague explanation given earlier concerning the Pharisees (4:1–3).

The essential point is that once account is taken of the text's context—the context both of the whole journey and of John's tendency, particularly in these chapters, to use words in a way which tease the mind to see beyond the purely physical—once that context is seen, the gospel account does not have to be seen as contradictory. Jesus' Judaic compatriots showed him no honor; but the Galileans—intimating the reaction of the Gentiles—welcomed him.

[4:46–50] The failure of life and the initial stage of believing. The text tells of a brief but vivid scene. When Jesus came to Cana, "where he made the water wine," a royal official (*basilikos,* a royal figure or royal official) from the border town of Capernaum came and asked him to heal his dying son. At first Jesus seemed to refuse: he complained, rather surprisingly, that people's faith—the "you" is plural (4:48)—was dependent on "signs and wonders." The official, however, was in no mood for theological discussions. "*Kyrie,*" he said, "come down before my child dies." His persistence won the day. Jesus told him that his son would live, and the man believed Jesus' word, and he went his way.

Concerning 4:48 ("Unless you see signs . . . you will not believe"), Fortna (1988, 64) indicates that "it conflicts sharply with the context." At one level this is true, but the fact that a text appears to conflict with its context does not necessarily mean that it is a redactional insertion. What needs to be asked is not whether the text involves conflict but whether the conflict has any meaning—a meaning which, from a different point of view, does accord with the context.

In this case the conflict has meaning: it is a way of indicating that the process of believing—the focus of the episode—is conflictual. In other words, believing is not a smooth development, one which follows the normal flow of feelings and logic. On the contrary, it cuts across one's accustomed patterns.

The fact that believing involves a certain disruption has already been seen in the three preceding episodes. Jesus did not respond in kind to the orderly thoughts of Nicodemus. Instead he sent a shot across the famous teacher's bows, thus challenging the now-confused Nicodemus to enter a new realm of thought and reality (3:3–4). In the episode involving John the baptizer and his disciples there is conflict or disruption of another kind—the "dispute" with the old (Jewish) order (3:25–27). And when the Samaritan woman enters, she finds Jesus' words to be extremely perplexing—at odds with her established expectations and perceptions (4:9,11–12). Thus the association of believing with conflict or disruption is part of a fourfold pattern. It is a mode of composition in which the content (faith's positive disruptiveness) is reflected in the form.

Within this fourfold pattern, two of the thought-provoking patterns are issued primarily to characters in the narrative, to Nicodemus and the woman. And in these cases the reader (or hearer) can sit back, as it were, and enjoy the scene. But in the two briefer episodes (in 3:22–36 and 4:43–54) the one who is left grappling with the message is the reader. In the case of 3:25–27 this has already been seen (see comment on 3:25–30). Now, as Jesus refers surprisingly to signs and wonders (4:48), the reader is being challenged once again. One reads on, and the story of the official and his household comes to its positive conclusion, but the ill-fitting sentence, "Unless you see, . . ." lingers in the reader's memory, and the result is a pregnant tension: on the one hand a sense of God's giving of life, on the other a reminder that such belief does not rest on signs and wonders.

The scene is typical of a situation that is very common—an acutely painful sense of the ebbing of life. Nicodemus, of course, if he could only see it, had also been in dire need of new life, and so, in a different way, had the Samaritan woman. But here the need is stark and frightening, an example of humanity's vulnerability to the devouring forces of weakness and death, especially of premature death. It is not without reason that the evangelist has placed this story in a kind of tandem relationship with the Cana wedding. The failure of the wine, threatening to throw a pall over the festivities, is roughly analogous to the failure of life, especially of young life. After such a failure it is difficult to go on celebrating. Life seems cold and bleak.

In face of this impending failure the royal official does as the mother had done —he appeals directly to Jesus. But, as at the wedding, the reaction is something of a refusal. There, by saying his hour had not yet come, Jesus effectively said, "I am not ready." Here, by saying that the people are looking first for signs and wonders, he effectively says, "You are not ready." But it turned out that Jesus was in fact ready at the wedding feast, and the same was true of the episode with the royal official. What the scene shows, therefore, is first a dread crisis, and then, after what looks like an initial stumble, a rallying and an assertion of belief.

[4:51–54] The renewal of life and a further stage of believing.   The setting moves from Cana to the Cana-Capernaum road, and this second scene, even more explicitly than the first, consists of a meeting, a coming together of complementary journeys. The royal official had come to meet the journeying Jesus. Now as he himself is journeying, his servants come to meet him. But while the first scene had begun with the story of the ebbing of life, the second tells of its renewal: "his servants met him saying his boy lived." Altogether the verb "to live" (*zaō*), which was first employed by Jesus, is used three times: ". . . your son lives . . . his boy lived. . . . Your son lives" (4:50,51,53). It is like a gentle crescendo: ". . . *zē* . . . *zē* . . . *zē*."

The life in question is not the result of some freak turnabout in the illness. By checking the hour of the improvement, the royal official is able to verify that it is from Jesus' word that the life has come. And it is not insignificant that the news, when it comes, is brought by "the servants" (*douloi*), those who, like "the servants" (*diakonoi*) at the wedding feast (2:4–9), had been closest to the miracle and, who, in some way at least, had known of it ahead of their master. Given the deliberateness with which the second Cana incident is related to the first, the reference to the servants evokes the earlier emphasis on the servants' responsiveness to Jesus' word (2:4–9). Thus the renewal of life depends on both word and response. To some degree of course, the royal official himself had already responded, and it was precisely his initial responsiveness which was crucial to the renewal of life. But now, as he realizes what the word has done, and as the presence of the servants evokes a more complete attentiveness, his own responsiveness increases: "and he himself believed, and his whole household." Unlike his first act of believing (He ". . . believed the word," *pisteuō* with the dative, an expression which suggests a belief the firmness of which is not obvious (cf. Brown, 191, 513); his later believing is stronger ("He believed, . . ." *pisteuō*, used absolutely; cf. Brown, 192, 512–14; Schnackenburg, 1:468).

What the scenes suggest, therefore, is a process of growth, an intertwining of word and response. Faced with the failure of life, the royal official, rather than sit and moan, had decided to try to do something about it. He had "heard" of Jesus (4:47)—an indication of initial responsiveness—and had come to him. His attitude at that stage could scarcely have been described as one of belief, but he was ready to listen, and by stages came to believing strongly, he and his whole household.

Obviously, in one sense life was beyond his power. People do get sick and die and the process cannot be reversed. It is a reality which is emphasized repeatedly in later chapters. Only God can give life. But human energy and faith make an immense difference, and, in a certain sense, such faith does save life. The focus of the story in the end is not on the child, but on the royal official and his household. Apart from what had happened to the boy, something had happened to them. They had become aware, amid the fragility of existence, of a greater reality of life, and of the role which belief has in bringing that life into effective contact with one's own circumstances.

The "Beginning of Signs" (2:11), "the Signs" (2:23), and the "Second Sign" (4:54)

At the end of the story of the official coming to believe, there is a puzzling statement: the healing is described as a "second sign." This fits with the fact that the wedding miracle had been called the "beginning of signs" (2:11), but it takes no account of the intervening reference to "the signs" which Jesus did in Jerusalem (2:23, cf. 3:2).

This puzzling detail has sometimes been seen as further evidence that the text is rather confused; that it is the result of complex uncoordinated editing.

It has also been used as basic evidence for the idea that originally the two Cana miracles were grouped together in a distinct source which recounted several of Jesus' miracles but which did not refer to those performed in Jerusalem. This hypothetical document is generally referred to as the Signs Source and is sometimes envisaged as one of the sources used by John (see Martyn, 1979, 164–68; Fortna, 1988; Von Wahlde, 1989).

There is reason, however, for suspecting that the present gospel text is quite coherent. The heart of the puzzle seems to lie in the fact that the word "sign" is used in different senses. It is used first of all in a positive way, as something which is not the basis of faith, but which, after faith is established, plays a secondary, confirming, role. Thus "the beginning of signs" at the wedding feast was a confirming sign for those who already believed—for the disciples (2:1–4,11). And the "second sign" likewise was not the basis for the royal official's faith; it was rather something which confirmed it. The same sense apparently applies to the famous phrase ". . . but these [signs] are written that you may believe" (20:30–31). The signs are not to initiate belief, but to strengthen it (Schnackenburg, 3:338; Brown, 1056).

The word "sign" is also used in a negative way—as the basis for a superficial belief. It is in this sense that it is used of those in Jerusalem (2:23–24), including, to some degree, Nicodemus (3:2), and it is this sense which Jesus warns against in Galilee (4:48, "Unless you see signs and wonders . . ."). But the warning does not mean that the Galileans had fallen prey to the same misunderstandings. It is never said of the Galileans or of the royal official that they had a signs-induced superficial belief. The description of the Galileans' reaction to what Jesus had done in Jerusalem omits the two crucial words "signs" and "believe." The effect of Jesus' actions on them was not superficial belief, but a welcoming attitude, in other words, not faith, but a predisposition for it. And it is that same predisposition which is manifested dramatically in the royal official who had heard of Jesus. Thus, Jesus' warning to the Galileans ("Unless you see signs . . . you will not believe"), however much it recalls the reaction of those in Jerusalem ("Many believed . . . seeing the signs," 2:23), has the ultimate effect, not of saying that the two reactions are similar, but of contrasting them with each other.

The essential point is that, like other basic elements in these chapters—being born anew, living water, food—"signs" has a profound ambiguity, and one meaning often does not take account of the other. "Being born anew" does not include the physical idea of reentering a womb (3:3–8). "Living water" does not include the earthly reality of living water (4:10–15). And "food" does not include the reality of physical food (4:31–34).

In a somewhat similar vein, the recounting of signs, signs in the true sense, does not include the debased idea of signs. The text goes from the beginning of signs to the second, and omits the others. The result is that the reader is startled —somewhat as Nicodemus, and the Samaritan woman, and the disciples were startled. But the evangelist is not confused. Rather, in a creative but faithful mirroring of Jesus, the evangelist is inviting the reader to reflect. Pay attention to signs, is what the text is saying. Count them carefully, as one counts something precious. But do not confuse them with the basis of your faith, for a signs-induced faith is superficial.

Ultimately the contrast between the two kinds of signs is part of a larger contrast or tension—the contrast between the geographic poles of this entire section of the gospel, between Jerusalem at one end and Galilee at the other (2:23 and 4:54). Jerusalem seems to evoke Jerusalem-based Judaism. Galilee however, evokes the world of the Gentiles. It is a tension which is reflected in the various ways in which the narrative, with more and more transparency, moves slowly but steadily from Jerusalem to Galilee, a tension which is expressed in what looks like a climactic disjuncture at the beginning of the final episode—in the statement that, while his fatherland rejected Jesus, the Galileans welcomed him. And it is precisely at the opposite poles of that entire text, in 2:23 and 4:54, that one finds the contrasting references to "the signs" and the "second sign." The implication would seem to be that the false idea of sign is to be associated with Jerusalem— and with Jerusalem-based Judaism. Or as St. Paul put it, "The Jews seek signs" (1 Cor 1:22). Among the Gentiles, however, it is possible to have an approach to signs which is more mature.

The Royal Official as a Representative Figure

As a final note it should be emphasized that, however much the official is an individual, the text also ascribes to him a representative role. As Brown (191) remarks concerning the plural "you" ("Unless you see, . . ." 4:48), the official "is looked upon as representing the Galileans." Furthermore, both Boismard (1962, 196–97) and Dodd (1963, 193) see the conversion of the official with "his whole household" as alluding to the mission of Christianity among the Gentiles, particularly as that mission is recounted in Acts (see, for instance, Acts 10:2, 11:14; in John 8:35 and 14:2, "household" suggests God's household). Thus, a coherent picture emerges: the account of Jesus' withdrawal from a superficial and hostile Judaism (2:23, 4:1–3), a Judaism which gives him no honor (4:44), is followed with increasing clarity by allusions to his orientation toward the Gentiles—the coming, bridelike, of "all" (3:26), the coming, in a betrothal scene, of the Samaritan woman and her people, and finally, from a border town, the coming of the royal official and his whole household. There is considerable evidence, therefore, for regarding the journey to the welcoming Galileans as indeed reflecting a journey to the Gentiles.

The Creationlike Healing at the Pool

The Limits and Structure of the Story

While it is generally agreed that chap. 5 consists of a controversial healing story and a discourse, it is not immediately clear where one ends and the other begins. Does the healing story conclude with v 15, when the man tells the Jews that it was Jesus who had healed him? (So Schnackenburg, 2:92–99; and Brown, 212.) Or does it go on to include the Jews' murderous reaction to Jesus' idea of creation (vv 16–18)? (So Hoskyns, 250–67; Bultmann, 240–47; Barrett, 249–51; Lindars, 52, 209–19; the RSV.)

What seems necessary, to get a handle on the structure of the text, is to try to identify the literary clues to the way it is divided. In many of the episodes of Part 1 (1:1–2:22), for instance, division seemed to be indicated by the repetition or partial repetition of some phrase, particularly phrases related to time and movement (or location). In Part 2 something similar seems to operate, but with a slightly greater emphasis on the importance of movement. Even in the uninterrupted part of the scene at the well, the major division in the conversation is accompanied by the idea of movement: "*Go,* call your husband and *come here*" (4:16). There is reason, then, for suspecting that in discerning the division of chap. 5, one of the clues consists of various elements of time and movement.

This suspicion is confirmed by the fact that the healing story in chap. 5 has a close literary relationship to the healing of the blind man (chap. 9; cf. esp. Culpepper, 1983, 139–40) and, as will be seen later, the basic clue to the division of chap. 9 is that of movement.

On the basis of these observations it would seem, first of all, that the healing story itself, apart from its introduction (5:1–3), consists of three scenes: Jesus' healing of the man (5:4–9a); the man's encounter with the indignant Jews (5:9b–18); and finally, Jesus' finding of the man in the temple and the man's identifying of Jesus to the Jews (5:14–15). In all of these scenes, either as they begin or conclude, there is some indication of location or movement. And the various divisions begin with phrases which are both time-related and rather repetitious:

1: "After that was a feast . . . ." (*meta tauta ēn* . . .);
5: "Now there was a person . . . thirty eight years . . . ." (*ēn de* . . .);
9b: "Now it was the sabbath . . . ." (*ēn de* . . .);
14: "After that . . . ." (*meta tauta* . . .).

But once mention is made of the Jews' hostility to the creation statement (5:17) there are no further references to changes in space and time; and so it remains, right through to the end of the discourse. In other words, both the creation-related hostility (vv 16–18) and the subsequent discourse are expressed in a way which sets them apart from the distinctive elements of the structure of the healing account. Therefore, as Schnackenburg and Brown indicated, they should be taken together, and the creation-related hostility is to be seen as an introduction to the discourse. Thus the healing account should be regarded as concluding with Jesus' finding of the man and with the man's identifying Jesus (5:14–15).

The idea that the healing account concludes with Jesus' finding of the man in the temple receives some corroboration from the fact that the healing of chap. 9 concludes with a somewhat similar scene—Jesus' finds the man and identifies himself, and, though there is no temple, the man worships (9:35–41).

Some further details may be noted. As already implied, it seems warranted to speak of a distinct introduction—the verses which set the scene (5:1–3). The subsequent phrase—"Now there was a certain person there . . ." (5:5)—is of the same general kind as that which opens the Nicodemus story—"Now there was a person . . ." (3:1). Thus the presence of introductions, noted in the earlier episodes of Part 2 (cf. 2:23–25; 3:22–24; 4:1–6; 4:43–45), continues in 5:1–3.

Scenes 1 and 2, the healing and the Jewish reaction, are closer to one each other, as regards time and space, than they are to Scene 3. This latter scene, Jesus' finding of the man, is explicitly assigned to a distinct time ("After that . . .") and to a distinct location (the temple). Thus, while it seems appropriate, as in the episode at the well (4:7–42), to distinguish three scenes, it is also true, here as well as there, that the first two share a certain unity, and the third is somewhat apart.

It has sometimes been suggested, particularly because the healing story proper (5:1–9a, Scene 1) is somewhat like a complete-looking healing story in Mark (Mark 2:1–12 and parr.), that the sabbath controversy (Scene 2) is secondary and that the episode as a whole is not a unit. (For aspects of the discussion, see Schnackenburg, 2:96–98; Lindars, 52; Bultmann, 240–42; Brown, 210.) This view is partly accurate: apparently the text is composed from multiple sources. But neither multiplicity of sources nor the presence of puzzling aspects determines automatically whether a text has unity. In chap. 9, for instance, the sabbath question is equally "secondary"—it is not introduced until Scene 3 of that drama— yet it is generally accepted that chap. 9 is a tightly woven unit. It seems better, therefore, before breaking up the three-scene episode, to ask whether the present text may reasonably be seen as a unity. To do this, it is necessary to examine the story more closely.

[5:1–3] Introduction. In Jerusalem, a multitude of the weak. The story opens on a low and rather familiar key: at the time of a Jewish feast Jesus went up to Jerusalem. The simply described journey recalls his earlier visit to Jerusalem (cf. 2:12–13), and the feast, which is unnamed, keeps continuity with the other introductory texts in which a feast is mentioned (cf. 2:23; 4:45).

But the easy familiarity suddenly gives way to a scene of swarming suffering. In the colonnaded porticoes around a Jerusalem pool lay "a multitude of those who were weak" (*plēthos tōn asthenountōn*). John's simple declarative language increases the scene's vividness: "Now there is in Jerusalem . . . a pool." This touch of vividness is understandable: the pool, as uncovered by modern archaeology, was phenomenal—big as a football field and more than twenty feet deep, a virtual lake. On its sides were four porticoes, and a fifth, which ran across its middle, divided it in two. (For details, cf. Schnackenburg, 2:94; Brown, 207.) In

a land which treasured water, such a pool, a resevoir apparently, would have a
been well-known landmark. In the porticoes lay the multitude—"blind, lame,
withered." It is perhaps not without significance that John recalled that the pool
(or its location—the mss. are obscure; cf. Brown, 206) was in some way associated with sheep. At least there is something in the mention of sheep which seems
appropriate to the sight of the pathetic multitude. It is also noticeable that, in
contrast to the preceding episode, the flavor of the text is heavily Jewish. In just
a few verses it refers to "the Jews," to Jerusalem (twice), to Hebrew, and to the
name which, regardless of which manuscript tradition is correct (Bethzatha, Bel-
zatha, Bethsaida, or Bethesda), is thoroughly semitic. To some extent, the text
evokes an image of the Jews as a suffering flock. Such is the setting—pathetic
and vivid.

There is in this situation, as indeed in the entire chapter, a kind of stony
silence. With the exception of a single confused reply, nobody ever talks to Jesus.
And despite earlier indications that Jesus was well known in the Jerusalem area
(2:23; 3:26), nothing is said of any reaction to him by anyone in the sick multitude. In the preceding episode, at Cana of Galilee, the sickness of a single boy in
a distant town meant that Jesus was besought, insistently, for help (4:46–47).
Now, as he goes up to the city which has a whole multitude of the sick, nobody
seems to move. Obviously the mood in Galilee is quite different from that in
Jerusalem. The initiative is depicted as coming not from them but from him.

The final word of the introduction would seem, with virtual certainty, to be
xērōn, the genitive plural of *xēros*, meaning "dry" or "dried up," and which can
also mean "withered" or "paralyzed." (The following reference to the moving
of the water, including v 4, is missing in many manuscripts and would seem to
be a late insertion; only in v 7 does such a reference appear authentic.) In the
context of all that has been said about water in the previous chapters, and in the
context of the pool, there is a special irony in this final emphasis on dryness. This
crowd, no less than Nicodemus and the Samaritan woman, is in dire need of
water. But, unlike those other two, they make no move to come to Jesus.

[5:5–9a] Scene 1: The Creatorlike Healing. "Now there was a certain person
there—thirty-eight years he had been in his weakness." The phrasing, as Bultmann (241) notes, is strained. Its main effect is to suggest that the man in question
was embedded "in his weakness." All the initiative comes from Jesus; it is he
who sees the man, who knows the time he has been there, and who then asks a
simple but incisive question: "Do you will (*thelō*) to become healthy?" Despite
Haenchen's assertion (1:255) to the contrary, the word *thelō*, "to will/want/wish,"
is used very deliberately and is one of the clues to the unity of chapter 5. But
instead of responding to what was being offered to him and saying a simple "Yes,"
the man gave a complaint: he had "no one" to help him into the pool when he
felt he needed that help. And "another" was always keeping him from being
cured. This man had problems. Nobody was for him! And there was always someone against him, getting in his way! In fact, he was so lost in his problems that
he no longer knew what he wanted.

The exact nature of his sickness is vague. He is simply one of the Jerusalem multitude who were variously "blind, lame, withered." This vagueness, high-lighted by the vivid background, is appropriate; it corresponds to the man's con-fusion. In other words, not only is it unclear what the man wanted, it is unclear even what is wrong with him. The whole picture is one of a confusion which is profound.

Without further discussion, Jesus tells him to rise, take up his bed, and walk. "And immediately the person became healthy, and he took up his bed and walked." So had God once said to the chaos, " 'Let there be . . .' and there was . . ." (Genesis 1).

In this healing Jesus acts with a Creator-like knowledge and authority. It is he who first sees the man, who knows the long time that he has been there, and who, by simple word of command, gives the man health, strength, and motion.

The idea that the healing is creationlike is corroborated by the fact that the healing in chapter 9—a healing for which this one prepares—is also creationlike. (Note the opinion of Irenaeus, *Adv. Haer.* v 15:2; cf. Brown, 372). It is further corroborated by the subsequent discourse. As Brown (205) indicates, the healing is "The Gift of Life."

[5:9b-13] Scene 2: The Jews' failure to recognize the lifegiver. No details are given as to what it felt like, after thirty-eight years, to be healthy again. Normally, even after just a week or two of sickness, the moment of realizing that health is returning is strikingly memorable. Elsewhere the NT speaks of enthusiastic reac-tions—of a blind man shouting at Jesus and, when cured, following him along the road (Mark 10:46–52); of a formerly lame man walking and jumping and praising God, attracting everybody to the healing (Acts 3:1–11); of an entire crowd, led by their priests, wanting to offer sacrifice to the apostles, and to acclaim them as Zeus and Hermes (Acts 14:9–13).

But in the case of the man at the poolside the main reaction is a Jewish legal objection: that day was a sabbath, and Jewish law forbade carrying anything, much less a bed, on a sabbath (cf. Mishnah, Sabb. 7.2).

That the text at this point should refer to the sabbath makes sense: according to Genesis, creation culminates in sabbath (Gen 1:1–2:4a), and so it is fitting that a Creator-like healing should be followed by a reference to the sabbath.

But the Jews, in their preoccupation with restrictive law do not see a reality that is far greater—a healing which is like creation itself. Their blindness is underlined by the phrasing: while the man who was healed speaks of Jesus in two ways—first as a healer, and second as the one who gave the (infringing) com-mand—they, in their reaction, fasten on to the second aspect:

> He answered them, "The one who healed me, he it was who said to me, 'Take up your bed and walk.' " They asked him, "Who is this person who said to you, 'Take up and walk'?"

They even managed, with some strained phraseology, and with a degree of blind-ness which was not present in their first reaction (v 10), to omit explicit reference to the bed. The entire phenomenon of the giving of health or life is being blocked out of their minds.

The man who was healed seems no better. At the beginning of this scene be could at least give an ambiguous description of Jesus—"the one who made me healthy . . . [and] who said. . . ." But, at the end, it is his ignorance which is stressed: when asked about Jesus' identity he simply did not know.

Thus, the phenomenon of advancing ignorance or blindness, so conspicuous in chapter 9 (cf. Brown, 377), is intimated in this brief scene. The Jews are shutting themselves off from life and the life-giver.

Then, in a curious detail, Jesus seems to partake in some way in this process of ignorance and alienation: he withdraws. The withdrawal is connected to the presence of "a crowd" (*ochlos*), the first use of this word in the gospel, and while it is not clear at this stage what, if any, is the significance of the crowd, it seems certain, that, in some sense, Jesus has withdrawn from the Jews.

[5:14–15] Scene 3: At a later time—an opportunity for recognition and repentance.   At some later stage, Jesus again finds the man. As in Scene 1 the initiative comes from Jesus, yet the fact that the man is in the place of worship, the temple, would seem to suggest that, like the worshipping man in the final scene of chap. 9 (9:35–41), he has a receptivity toward God. The encounter is not without humor: "See," Jesus said, "you have become healthy." It is as though the man, after so many years, is finding it difficult to adjust to the idea of health.

Jesus' next words—"Sin no more, that nothing worse befall you"—may seem strange since the story had not previously referred to sin. But the idea of sin, though not mentioned explicitly, had been implied by the man's failure in both willing (Scene 1) and recognizing (Scene 2). The sinfulness comes out more clearly in the subsequent discourse when similar failures by the Jews are clearly regarded as sinful. As Schnackenburg (2:128) says of the Jews' failure to respond (5:44): "Behind their inability to recognize the one who really speaks for God . . . lies moral guilt." And it is with the idea of the Jews' sin that chap. 9 terminates (9:40–41).

But in this third scene these fundamental failures of will and mind seem to be overcome. As already noted, the man's presence in the temple indicates good will. And in this encounter, unlike the first, he does identify or recognize Jesus. The final picture, of the man going away to announce to the Jews about Jesus, while it does indeed have a possible negative interpretation—that the man is an ungrateful informer—is also sufficiently ambiguous to be open to a positive interpretation: the man has finally come to mature (repentant) recognition of Jesus, and he is announcing the good news to the Jews.

Such also is the implication of the phrasing. Jesus is no longer referred to ambiguously or negatively, but rather in a way that is positive: "He told the Jews that it was Jesus who had made him healthy." In Greek, as in English, "healthy" is the last word.

The Man as Representative

The fact that the man had been sick for thirty-eight years—the number of years during which Israel languished in the desert at Kadesh (cf. Deut 1:45–46; 2:14)

—has led some commentators, particularly in the patristic period, to see him as a symbol of the Jewish people (cf. Schnackenburg, 2:95). This interpretation is not to be dismissed lightly. In the present text the man emerges against the background of references to large groups—the Jews and the multitude (5:3)—and he seems to blend back into such a group—the Jews (5:15–16). Thus there is some narrative support for the patristic idea that he is in some way symbolic of the Jewish people. The fact that his counterpart, the healed man of chap. 9, ends up as being clearly distinct from the Jewish community—he was cast out (9:34)—makes his own blending with the Jews all the more noticeable and provides grounds for suspecting that the two men are in deliberate contrast.

If he is indeed in some way representative of the Jewish people, then his slowness in approaching and knowing Jesus is probably meant as a reflection of the Jewish attitude in general. (Whether the ineffective pool, with its five porticoes, is in some way a symbol of the Torah, the law which Christ surpasses, is a matter which is left to further research. See Bultmann, 241; and esp. Dodd, 1953, 319–20.)

The fact that the man has a representative role does not exclude his role as an individual. In a text that makes widespread use of ambiguity and of plurality of levels of reference (cf. Barrett, 250), one role does not exclude the other. Nor, for instance, contrary to what Barrett (253) implies, does the fact that the pool with its five porticoes has been excavated by modern archaeology automatically decide the issue of whether the pool has a symbolic value. What is historical may also be symbolic.

It would seem, in fact, that the three-scene drama (5:5–15) has three levels of meaning. The first and most obvious meaning (and the one which seems primary in Scene 1) revolves largely around a colorful but limited drama—the timebound localized encounter between Jesus and the sick man. The next level of meaning (primary in Scene 2), and one which is related to the representative role of the woman of Samaria, is indeed still rather time-bound, but it is much less individual and localized: it revolves around the fact that the entire encounter, apart from being a drama between two individuals, is also a drama concerning Jesus' relationship to the Jews as a whole. It is at this level that Scene 2, with its emphasis on "the Jews," is most clearly seen as integral to the whole episode. A further level (primary in Scene 3) seems also to merit consideration. The picture of the man announcing to the Jews that it was Jesus who had given him healing, *insofar as it is open to a positive interpretation,* accords with the idea that at some later stage the alienated Jews will hear the good news of Jesus. Thus, the three-stage drama accords with the overall history of the Jews as understood elsewhere in the NT, especially in Romans 9–11: there is an initial stage in which divine power builds up Israel (Scene 1); then there is an intermediate period, in which the Jews flounder in their sinful ignorance of Jesus and in which the divine, taking account of the Gentiles ("the crowd"), withdraws (Scene 2; cf. Rom 11:25–29); and finally, the divine initiative in favor of the Jews will reassert itself and the role of Jesus as life-giver will be recognized and announced (Scene 3; cf. the "conversion of the Jews," Rom 11:30–36).

It is better for the moment not to belabor this final level of meaning. Its plausibility depends considerably on how one views other elements in the gospel.

Besides, it is not the level on which the evangelist dwells. The text goes on to focus not on the individual who was cured (level one) and not on the ultimate prospect of Jewish conversion (level three), but on the breakdown of communication between Jesus and the Jews.

"Jews" refers not only to believers in Judaism but to all those who, despite their commitment to a religious tradition, have in fact lost faith. They may seek to protect some ancient institution, such as the sabbath, but they have forgotten what the sabbath means—that it was once linked with the vitality of creation. Through their attachment to a limited heritage they develop a kind of spiritual paralysis, and become like the dissatisfied man by the poolside, unaware that they are living in sin.

The Discourse on Ongoing Person-Oriented Creation

It Is a Feast, and It Calls, but the Jews Will Not Come

The nature of this discourse is indicated by the opening comments of Brown and Schnackenburg. Brown (216) refers to it as "one of the most exalted" in John; Schnackenburg (2:99) as "one of the most profound." However one describes it, it certainly is a mind-stretching portrait, a panorama of a person-centered creation process which breaks the barriers of time.

The theme of creation had been suggested by the power with which Jesus cured the sick man (vv 5–9a). It is announced more clearly in the introduction (vv 16–18). What was once done by God is now being done by Jesus. Even in this introduction, there is some straining of the sense of time: what one might tend to regard as past, the process of creation, is present, ongoing. And that it is person-centered is indicated initially through the role being played by Jesus.

Before discussing the meaning further, however, the related question of structure must first be examined.

Structure

With regard to the discourse proper (vv 19–47), most scholars, though not all, indicate three major divisions:

Westcott	19–29[1]	31–40	41–47
Bernard, J. H.	20–29	30–40	41–47
Hoskyns	19–29	30–40	41–47
Bultmann	19–30	31–47	
Lightfoot	19–29	30–47	
Schnackenburg	19–30	31–40	41–47
Brown	19–30	31–40	41–47
Strathmann	19–30	31–40	41–47
Barrett	19–30	31–40	41–47
Morris	19–29	30–47	
Lindars	19–29	30–47	
Bernard, J., 1979	19–30	31–47	
Neyrey, 1988	19–29	30–47	
RSV	19–29	30–47	
UBSGNT	19–29	30–40	41–47

1. 30 is transitional.

Those who divide the text into just two sections do not deny the distinctness of vv 41–47; they simply want to assert that a fundamental division occurs after the description of ongoing creation (vv 19–29).

A considerable difficulty—one which is highlighted by the opinion of Westcott—concerns v 30: this verse can be seen either as a conclusion or as a beginning. Insofar as it repeats elements of v 19 it may appear to form an *inclusio* and therefore to be a conclusion. But there are indications too that it should be regarded as a beginning. In 5:1–15 repetition is used to indicate beginnings. Furthermore, the use of the first person (in v 30) links it with what follows, not with what precedes. So does the double use of *theléma,* ''will'' (the notion of willing or not willing is basic to what follows; cf. vv 35, 40). Besides, what precedes (vv 19–29) seems to have its own unity—it goes all the way from the inner creative dynamics of God to the climactic expression of that dynamism in the ultimate fate of humans. It seems better, then, to regard v 30 as a beginning. There are, therefore, three major divisions: 19–29, 30–40, and 41–47.

The discourse as a whole, with its three basic divisions, is a variation on the prologue:

The prologue (1:1–18)	*The creation discourse (5:16–47)*
	Introduction: ongoing creator rejected (16–18)
Origins/creation (1–5)	Creation, ongoing, with judgement (19–29)
Intermediate witness (6–13)	Witness, ongoing, not accepted (30–40)
Incarnation glory (14–18)	True glory, not sought (41–47)

In comparison with the prologue, the creation discourse is simultaneously more developed and more negative. It is more developed insofar as it elaborates what was said in the prologue and brings it into the present. It is more negative because it emphasizes the reaction of the Jews, their unwillingness to accept the ongoing process. Thus the discourse develops the prologue's underlying optimism, its sense of the goodness of creation and of people, but it also begins to indicate how this goodness can be rejected.

Each of the three divisions of the discourse contains two sections or subdivisions, subdivisions which in varying ways and degrees repeat one another. (The dividing of 19–29 is simultaneously the easiest and most difficult. It is the easiest because so many authors agree that it is repetitive and should be divided. It is difficult because it is so hard to be sure where exactly to make the division. Specifically, should the second section begin at 24 or at 25? As will be seen later, in discussing 5:19–29, there is a delicate coherence in the text which indicates strongly that it begins at 24.) In outline:

Introduction: as ongoing Creator, Jesus is rejected	16–18
The Creator's parent-child essence	19–23
The Creator's Son-mediated effusion of life and judgment	24–29
The witnesses and the implied call (OT): Jewish willingness	30–35
The witnesses and the clearer call (NT): Jewish unwillingness	36–40

Initial Summary Comment

First of all (vv 19–29) there is a description of ongoing creation. It is a fascinating process, the very hub of which consists of the dynamics between a loving parent and a child. From this, everything else flows—particularly the giving and cherishing ("judging") of life.

In the initial section of this text, vv 19–23, the emphasis falls on creation's inner nature, on the interaction between parent and child, Father and Son, and on the central role of the Son. In the later section, however, vv 24–29, the emphasis moves to creation's external expression, to the way in which, through the word, the parent-child dynamics give life to human beings—life for the present and life also for the future.

The portrait suggests an extraordinary process of life giving, an exuberance which, if people will accept it, goes out to everybody, for all time. It is hardly without significance that the first noun in this chapter is *heortē*, "feast," an unspecified feast of the Jews (5:1), and a word which, by its very indefiniteness suggests feast without qualification—something appropriate to the magnificence of what God is doing. The idea of a feast has often been emphasized in explaining Johannine thought (see, for instance, Braun, 1964, 120–123). In chap. 5 the imagery of eating and drinking is not emphasized as it is in chap. 6, but, in a low-key way, the idea of a feast is already present.

Then (vv 30–40), in the next major division of the text, the focus changes, and the emphasis falls not so much on the whole work of creation as on a list of witnesses who testify to the Creator. In this portion of the text, creation and the role of the Son are no longer described in the third person. Jesus is now using the first and second persons—"I-you." Thus, creation may no longer be regarded as something distant or indifferent; it is addressing people; it is calling. The Jews are being invited to the feast.

Again the text falls into two sections. The first (vv 30–35) refers to the OT period. Here the voices of the witnesses are not very clear, yet their message is significant. During this period the Jews responded to the call ("You were willing . . ."). In the later section (36–40, the NT period) the witnesses are clearer and stronger. But now the Jews refuse to come ("You are not willing . . .").

In depicting the OT as witnessing to Jesus, the evangelist "presupposes that the OT in general refers to Christ" (Kysar, 88). In other words, there reappears here the problem which haunts the prologue—and which, for that matter, despite its waning in modern times, haunts much of the history of biblical interpretation —namely, the presence of Christ in the OT. It is connected, obviously, to the question of the relationship between the two testaments, and it raises a difficult problem: how can a steadfast God, having solemnly established what seems to be a permanent covenant, inaugurate an order that is quite new? Is God fickle, or is this some other God? The questions are basic. What the text is implying is that, despite the newness, it is one and the same Creator God, and that even in the old order there was already present the creative work of God's ultimate mediator.

The discourse suggests an eternal present, a breaking of the limits of time. The very form of the discourse has a certain timelessness: apart from the fact that no time is given for the feast, the discourse itself contains no reference to time, space, or audience. (Something similar will be seen in chap. 8.) This suggestion of an eternal present is heightened by the God-related present tenses which, in the introduction and at the beginning of each major division, Jesus uses about himself (vv 17, 19, 30 41: ". . . I am working"; "the Son cannot . . ."; "I cannot . . ."; and finally, in a subtle variation, ". . . I do not receive").

This sense of an eternal present accords with another factor: in the final analysis there is not a diversity of witnesses; they all blend into a unity. The point is emphasized by Brown (227) and Schnackenburg (2:120). Whatever the variety in the form of witness—whether of external wonders ("works"), or the internal whispering of the heart, or the evidence of scripture, whether in the old order or in the new—ultimately there is just one source, namely the voice of the only God talking parent-like to beloved children. As Brown (227) says of the high point in the list of witnesses (vv 37–38): "It is . . . probable that we have here a reference to the Father's internal testimony within the human heart." Such indeed is the ultimate concern of the entire list of witnesses. They indicate, through Jesus, that creation is person-oriented. In various ways there is a single God who calls lovingly to people. Admittedly, the voice was not always clear—in v 32, when alluding to God's voice in the OT, the text is obscure—but it is the same God.

The role of Jesus now is to clarify the voice. He appeals to the Jews to listen to the wonder of creation and to the life-giving voice which, from within so much diversity, calls to them.

But they will not come. The voice of God has been blocked out (vv 37–38). Though they are embedded in the study of scripture, they cannot hear what it is saying (v 39).

Finally (vv 41–47), the concluding division of the discourse (vv 41–47) asks, first, what has gone wrong (41–44), and then, what will be the consequence (45–47). What has gone wrong is that the web of prestige, of human glory, has shut out the greater glory of the one God. The consequence is that, on the basis of their own Mosaic tradition, they face condemnation and failure of faith. They are in the shadow of being eclipsed.

In comparison with the first major division (vv 19–29), this final portion of the text (vv 41–47) has a dismal narrowness. In that earlier section (vv 19–29) the creativity of God's inner love seemed to spread out endlessly. Here that same love is simply not present (v 42). It is hardly an accident that the text at this point, though it proliferates with references to the Jews ("you . . . you . . . you . . ."), also shrinks. The penultimate section (vv 41–44) is smaller than anything that precedes it. And the final section (vv 45–47) is the shortest of all. A similar phenomenon has been noticed concerning John the Baptist: as he fades, the references to him become shorter and shorter (Brown, 415). Likewise in the healing account, the narrowness of the Jewish reaction is matched by the progressive shrinking of the scenes (cf. vv 9b–14 and vv 15–16). In comparison with the glory of the one God, human glory is very small.

Detailed Comment

[5:16–18] Introduction: The Jews' increasing rejection of God's Jesus-mediated creation. Though Genesis speaks of the Creator as resting on the sabbath (Gen 2:2–3), it was recognized by the Jews, in principle at least, that, even on sabbath days, the work of creation continued. This work of creation was particularly visible in such life-giving phenomena as birth and rain. It was also spoken of in relation to death and the raising of the dead. (See Brown, 216–17; Lindars, 218–19).

When the Jews object to Jesus' sabbath-breaking work, he justifies it as a further manifestation of the work of the Creator: "My Father is still working, and I am working." In other words he is trying to show them and tell them, in a way they had not fully realized, that creation is not over, but is still going on, and going on in him.

In the face of this awesome possibility, they do not even pause. What Jesus was saying seemed to imply a new mode of the divine presence, a mode in which the human was perceived to have a certain equality with God, and such a divine-human proximity was in tension with their own way of thinking (v 28; cf. Brown, 213–14, 217). They are so entrenched in a limited formulation of the divine, and so indifferent to the ultimate meaning even of their own formulation that, instead of accepting Jesus, they react with a desire to persecute, to kill.

The wording of the text—first the notion of persecution, and then, in a balancing phrase, the more negative idea of killing—summarizes dramatically what was suggested in the healing story: that, in the face of God's development of creation, they are becoming more and more negative, more destructive.

The account has an echo of tragedy, yet its final emphasis, as indicated by its closing phrase, is on the positive message of Jesus—the startling idea of a certain equality with God. It is on such a positive note also that the discourse begins.

[5:19–29] The interweaving, parent-like and lifegiving, of the Creator with creation. This opening part of the discourse is like a summary of God's involvement with Jesus and through Jesus with humanity. It concerns a loving, revealing, Father-Son relationship and the way in which the kind of vitality found in that relationship enters the human sphere and gives it various forms of life, including life eternal. In other words, it goes all the way from the inner Father-Son dynamics of God to the climatic expression of those dynamics in the idea that the dead will come out of their tombs. Earlier statements, especially those involving Nicodemus and the Samaritan woman, have already spoken of the granting of some such form of life (cf. 3:15–21, 35–36; 4:14), but the present statement goes considerably further.

The text falls into two parts. The first—as Giblin (1985, 96–99) and Kysar (84) have helped to indicate—consists of five verses (19–23), and in these the primary emphasis is on *the relationship of the Father and Son.* It is with that emphasis that the passage begins and ends: "The Son cannot do anything of his own accord but only what he sees the Father doing. . . . The one who does not honor the Son does not honor the Father who sent him." At its center (vv 21–22) there is a secondary emphasis—concerning the resulting role of *the Son in relation to humans:* to give life, including the giving of life to "the dead," and to give judgment. In other words, the text is concerned not only with the Father-Son relationship but also, secondarily, with the Son-humans relationship.

In the second part of the text (vv 24–29) the Son-humans relationship is primary. It is with this emphasis, the idea of humans receiving life and judgement from the Son, that the text begins and ends. And at the center (vv 26–27), as a secondary theme, there is the idea that had been primary in the earlier part (vv 19–23) of the statement: the relationship of Father and Son. But this relationship is expressed in a way which reflects the fact that the text's primary emphasis is on the Son-humans relationship: it refers to Jesus not just as Son but also as Son of humanity, a title which underlines his solidarity with humanity and with the fullness of human experience.

Thus when the two parts of the statement are compared (vv 19–23 and 24–29), what is primary in one is secondary in the other. Essentially the same phenomenon was seen in the texts leading up to the Cana signs. With regard to the emphasis on time and space (geography), what was primary in one was secondary in the other. In this case (5:19–29), the initial emphasis on the Father-Son relationship has given way to an emphasis on the Son-humans relationship and on Jesus' role as Son of humanity. What the text shows is not confusion but carefully balanced complementarity.

The lay-out of the two parts (vv 19–23 and 24–29), with its alterations of emphasis on the divine (Father-Son) and the human, suggests a process of intertwining. In other words, the very fabric of the narrative, its intertwining literary structure, suggests a theological message—the blending of the divine with the human. The same basic principle would seem to be found in the quite different structure of the prologue: its increasing blending of soaring poetry and down-to-earth prose provides a literary basis for the theological message of the Word becoming flesh. At a later stage in the gospel, in Jesus' prayer of unity, the idea of the divine-human intertwining becomes more explicit (17:21–24, ". . . I in them and you in me"). Thus the phenomenon of intertwining fits with other elements of the gospel as a whole, but in chap. 5 it is achieved through the balancing of two parts. Each part may now be examined separately.

[5:19–23] The Creator's activity in its inner dynamics: the granting of life and judgement to the Son. In this passage it is as though the veil were pulled back from the beginning of the prologue and it became possible to see the inner workings of God, at least insofar as God is a Creator who works through the Son. The scene revealed is of a Father and Son. The interaction between these two is described through the delightful image of a child imitating a parent (5:19–20). The child is all eyes, mind completely set on doing just what the parent is doing. And the parent, loving the child, is unstinting and shows the child everything it does.

More specifically, some see the Father-Son relationship as involving the kind of interaction which is found between a master craftsman and an apprentice (Giblin, 1985, 97). Such an image is well-suited to the theme of creation. A single Greek word, *technitēs,* can indicate either a craftsman or the Creator (e.g., cf. Acts 19:24,38; Rev 18:22; Hebr 11:10; Wis 13:2). The parent–child picture is one of total communication, and the result is that, at least as far as doing things is concerned, the child becomes equal to the parent and is entrusted with all the parent's activities. As Kysar (1984, 35) expresses it, there is functional unity. From now on the child does everything: "For as the Father . . . makes [the dead] live, so the Son also makes live . . ." (5:21).

The interaction of the Father and Son is not a private operation. Rather, it is being done "that you may wonder" (5:20). In other words, they are putting on a show, something that will make people pause and admire. What particularly causes people thus to wonder are certain "greater things" (*meizōna,* 5:20)—a rather obscure designation which may perhaps refer to the way the Creatorlike Son works in the new dispensation. (In the only other uses of "greater" in the surrounding chapters, the reference is always to a comparison between Jesus and a character from the old dispensation—Jacob [4:12], John [5:36], Abraham [8:53].) Thus, while the Creator may indeed have worked from the beginning, and worked through the Son, there is now coming a "greater" process of working. This greater process, this new dispensation consists particularly in focusing on the Revealer, on the Son. In these five verses (5:19–23) the word "Son" is used seven times—a higher frequency than in any other brief passage of the NT. As Bultmann (253) comments, all these son-related phrases "give expression to the same idea, namely, that he is *the Revealer in whom we encounter God himself speaking and acting.*" Thus, while this text may indeed unveil an aspect of God, its effect is to direct the mind, not to the stars or to something eerily distant, but to a revealer who is human. It is to the Son that attention is being directed. In other words, even in a discussion of the inner workings of God, the way is being prepared for an emphasis on humanity. It is person-oriented.

As if to further highlight the role of the Son, the text now describes him as involved in a process of "willing"—he "makes live whom he wills" (*thelō-*)—a verb previously not used positively in the gospel except to designate the action of the unnamed God (". . . he willed to go forth to Galilee," 1:44) and the Spirit-related wind ("The wind blows where it wills . . .", 3:8). Thus it is through the Son that there operates the whole process of life-giving.

Closely associated with the process of giving life is that of judging, particularly that of judging in an affirmative, salvific way—"the common OT sense of vindicating the good (Deut 32:36, Ps 43:1)" (Brown, 219). Thus, one of the first things a mother generally wishes to do after giving birth to a child is to judge it positively, to see it, and to affirm and cherish it by holding it close. And the first thing God did while making the world was to judge it affirmatively: "And God saw that it was good . . . good . . . very good" (Gen 1:10,12,18,21,25,31). At times, of course, judgement calls for challenge—for improvement, correction, or even condemnation.

Associated with genuine judgement is the concept of honor or respect: judgement has been "given to the Son, so that all may honor the Son, even as they honor the Father" (5:22–23). Honor, *timē,* means valuing something or someone highly—with respect or reverence. It was particularly important in the first century (Malina, 1981, 25–50). As in ordinary human relations, say, between two people or two nations, honor is more basic than love, and without it genuine love is not possible. It is something that is due above all to God, but now that same honor is to be accorded to the Son, to a revealer in human form. This may seem blasphemous, but the text is insistent: failure to honor the Son, far from being commendable, is, in fact, a failure to honor the Father, for it was the Father who sent him (5:23).

What emerges from these verses (5:19–23) is a glimpse of something alluring: that behind human existence and activity there is the creative activity of God. This creative presence is seen first of all in Jesus, but it is illustrated through the elementary interaction between parent and child, and thus it implies something about every person. In particular, it implies that the honor due to God is inseparable from the honor due to people.

[5:24–29] The effect of the Creatorlike Son in the human sphere.   Here the focus shifts more clearly from the Son to the hearers, to the human sphere. Those who hear receive eternal life, and this life—this ultimate or eschatological gift— is twofold; it is present (or "realized"—realized eschatology), and it is future. In other words, it gives life now—including an inner renewal which rescues from moral death—and it has implications for the future, for the time when the physically dead will rise from their tombs.

This twofold dimension is expressed in a way which involves considerable repetition, and the repetition, along with a perceived tension between present and future, has sometimes led to the conclusion that the text is rather confused and that it is the product of diverse writers or editors (cf. Bultmann, 260–61; Brown, 219–21; Schnackenburg, 2:114–19; Haenchen, 1:253–54). However, as Boismard (1961, 524) and Brown (220) suggest, and as Schnackenburg (2:116–17) agrees, the dichotomy between the present and future is not as sharp as is sometimes stated. In Kysar's words (84), the evangelist "intends a kind of both-and emphasis." That there is a certain tension is, in fact, implied by the text itself: it declares that "the hour is coming and now is"—a phrase which by its combining of future and present is "apparently contradictory" (Barrett, 237), and there is no way that it can be divided in two, to eliminate the perceived contradiction. If such a tension is deliberate, then the larger tension may also be quite deliberate.

To provide a perspective to this twofold view, this emphasis on both present and future, on both the moral and the physical, it is necessary to consider the broader context.

For almost three chapters Jesus has been portrayed as offering not just life in some narrow form but a wide variety of forms of life. With Nicodemus and the Samaritan woman he spoke primarily of spirit-based moral life, and it is appropriate therefore that such should be the first emphasis (vv 24–25). But in the cases of the official's son and the poolside man, the emphasis was very much on the physical. It is appropriate, therefore, that in the later verses (28–29) Jesus should speak of physical life, of a physical rising.

The grading of the text is worth noting. The fact that Jesus speaks of raising the dead who are "in the tombs" is indeed a step forward in John's narrative. It is something new. But it is not, as Bultmann (261) would have it, something alien, something introduced by a questionable editor. Rather, it is something for which the previous references to physical recovery had prepared the way. During most of four chapters the gospel had made no mention of anyone who was physically ill. Then in three successive texts it develops the idea rapidly. First it gave an image of a relatively brief, isolated sickness (the official's son was a child— in other words the picture is of a single sickness of limited duration). Then comes a picture of a multitude of the sick and of a sickness lasting thirty-eight years. (It might perhaps be argued, in view of the OT link between thirty-eight years and the passing away of an entire generation [Deut. 1:45–46, 2:14], that it evokes a full lifetime.) In any case, the text leaps from a single stark case of the danger of sudden death to a picture of debilitation that is multitudinous and prolonged. These cases do not speak of anyone rising physically from the dead, but such an idea is not far away: the child had been about to die; the man, whose mind had been set on going down, was told to rise physically ("Rise, . . ." *egeirō*). It required but one more similar leap to speak of the rising of the physically dead, of those "in the tombs." In chapter 6 there will be yet a further leap: the image of raising the dead "on the last day" (6:30, 40, 44).

What is essential is that, once account is taken of the way in which the text is graded, the twofold emphasis is quite appropriate.

A further factor in evaluating this tension of present and future is to be found in the elevated tone of this discourse, a discourse which, on occasion (beginning with "My Father is still working, and I am working," 5:17), bends or breaks the barriers of time. Working through the Son is the eternal God. A similar point is made by Kysar (84): "The key to John's dual eschatology lies in his concept of the work of the Spirit and in his concept of time, i.e., the convergence of past, present, and future in the revelation in Christ."

One of the features of creation is that it is possible that the Son's life-giving word not be heard and that, as a result, the life itself not be communicated. In this case judgement takes on a different meaning. It is a recognition not of the presence of life and goodness, but of their absence. It is a judgement which is negative, the judgement of condemnation (5:28–29).

According to the text, the role of making this condemnatory judgment on those who will not hear the word falls not so much to the Father as to the Son in his role as Son of humanity (5:26–27). This seems to be a way of putting distance between God the Father and the process of condemnation. Whatever the OT background to the title "Son of humanity"—Brown, 220, links it with Dan 7:13 and a process of final divine judgment—its use here serves, in part at least, to underline a basic idea: condemnation is not so much something that God the Father does to people; rather, to a significant degree, it is a human thing, it is something people do to themselves. When Jesus speaks as a condemning judge—and he does so for the remainder of the discourse (5:30–47)—he speaks primarily as the Son of humanity, as one who is in solidarity with humanity.

The overall impression of the Father-Son statement (5:19–29) is immensely positive. Beginning with a picture of a parent-child process of learning and love, it tells of an outpouring which gives life to all that is dead. But there are some who do not want to hear about this life, and these are judged accordingly.

[5:30–40] Creation's call: the witnesses who speak increasingly of Jesus and of a parent-child essence in creation, Diverse Jewish responses.   While the opening sections of the discourse (vv 19–29) speak of a parent-child creation which seeks to spread life unboundedly through human existence, the following two sections (30–35 and 36–40) emphasize that what God has done does not just lie there. In various ways it witnesses more and more to what it is, to what lies at its heart: a parent-child love which is manifested in Jesus. In that sense it calls and asks for a response. In this text, therefore, there is a shift of emphasis from the idea of creation to that of witness-and-response, specifically Jewish response.

However, the idea of creation and of Jesus' involvement in it is not forgotten; it still constitutes the framework for the discussion of the process of witnessing. In fact, v 30, with which it begins, is a variation on the very first verse of the discourse—concerning the basic dynamics of creation and particularly concerning Jesus' role (v 29). Both verses suggest union, but v 30, with its emphasis on willing and sending, is more immediately directed to outward action. And it is with outward action, with mission, that the text which follows is concerned.

The passage may be laid out as follows:

vv 30–35

Jesus' union with the will of the Sender	30
Three possible kinds of witnesses	
• Witness to myself	31
• "Another"	32
• John	33
Implications for the Jews. Jewish willingness	34–35

vv 36–40

Jesus' task of "completing" the works	cf.36
Three kinds of witnesses	
• The works I do	36
• The Father and his indwelling	
("abiding") word	37–38
• The scriptures	39
Jewish unwillingness	40

There is considerable continuity between the two sections of the text. First are the opening references to *the mission of Jesus* (vv 30, 36). Then there are *three possible kinds of witnesses:* what Jesus himself does, what God does ("Another" is generally seen as an obscure way of referring to the Father or the Father-related Spirit; cf. Schnackenburg, 2:121), and what is scripture-related (John, who epitomizes the OT, especially the prophets, and "the scriptures"). Finally, there is *the effect on the Jews.*

The basic relationship is not so much built on repetition as on complementarity. While the first section, in speaking of Jesus' mission, seems to refer to its foundation, to the fact that it is grounded in the will of God (v 30), the second refers to its finality, to the task of completion (v 36). In other words, the second refers to a phase which is later or more developed. Similarly in the list of witnesses. The second list is more developed than the first: Jesus' works are more effective than a useless testimony to himself; the reference to the Father is clearer than that to "Another;" and the Jewish "searching" of the scriptures—a technical term for rabbinical study (StrB 2:467)—indicates a period that is later than that of the basic witness-bearing of the scriptures themselves as epitomized by John. Finally, while the first section refers to the initial Jewish willingness with regard to John, the second section refers to a later phenomenon—their unwillingness with regard to Jesus.

Even in the quantity of the text there is complementarity. In the first section, the text on witness is short (vv 31–33), and that on Jewish involvement is relatively long (vv 34–35). In the second it is the reverse: the text on witness is quite long (vv 36–39), and that on Jewish involvement is minimal (v 40).

The complementarity found here (between vv 30–35 and vv 36–40) is not unrelated to that noted earlier between vv 19–23 and 24–29. What is essential, however, is the basic pattern. The text moves from an undeveloped stage with heavy Jewish involvement to a stage which is more developed but where Jewish involvement seems finished.

The most reasonable interpretation to put on these two phases is that the first refers to the period of the OT and the second to that of the incarnation. Such an interpretation accords with the data and accords also with the principle governing the structure of the prologue.

[5:30–35] The initial testimony (the OT); the temporary willingness of the Jews.

The section opens (v 30) by speaking of Jesus' unity with the Sender: "I can do nothing by myself; as I hear, I judge. . . ." This unity reflects not only the unity of the Son and Father (v 19), but also that of the divine Logos with God (1:1; Schnackenburg, 2:103, 118). There is here, therefore, an echo of a level of union which is beyond time.

But it is no more than an echo. For while the prologue had spoken of primordial unity (1:1), and v 19 of general unity of action (and of life-giving, v 21), this opening verse (30) refers to the way that unity is expressed in the further and more specific action of judging—an action which, while it may be one of positive affirmation, may also be one of negative condemnation. Judging also is a basic part of his mission.

What Jesus emphasizes is that the rightness of his judgement rests on a quality of the will. Obviously there is also an intellectual component, a careful gathering of data so to speak ("as I hear, I judge"), but the decisive factor is the will—"because I do not seek my own will but the will of him who sent me."

Thus, as the list of witnesses is about to be mentioned, and as the question arises why some believe and others do not, there is an initial indication that, in course of assessing the evidence, the problem identified is not primarily an intellectual one.

Then comes the first list of witnesses—three brief verses, the central one being somewhat longer than the first and third (vv 31–33).

The first (v 31) may seem to contribute nothing: Jesus says that if he testifies to himself his testimony is not true. However, in saying this he is adopting the viewpoint of the OT (Deut 19:15), and by so doing he is moving ever so gradually into the connection between the OT and himself. (In 8:14, where Jesus seems to say the opposite about the value of testifying to himself, he does so because his perspective is from outside the OT—in contradiction of the Jews.)

The central verse (32), the one which is slightly longer, speaks of the testimony of "another"—a designation which most interpreters take as a reference to the Father (cf. Brown, 224; Schnackenburg, 2:121; Lindars, 228). As noted earlier, its obscurity makes it appropriate to a period of incomplete revelation, and hence to the OT. But despite the obscurity there is already an indication of response: "another" testifies and Jesus "knows that the witness which he bears is true." In other words, what has gone forth from the witness has been received in some way by Jesus. What is given here, therefore, is a miniature picture of dialogue.

The third verse (31) refers to the testimony of John—the one who, as in the prologue, would seem to culminate and epitomise the OT.

Thus, in various ways there are suggestions of Jesus' compatibility with the OT, of his being inside it. It is hardly an accident that when Jesus first looked at the sick man—the man who, by his thirty-eight years of languishing, recalled the ancient history of Israel (Deut 1:45–46, 2:14)—Jesus knew that he had been there a long time (5:6). Jesus knew of the history, and in a sense, had been there.

But these three testimonies (vv 31–33) are not all on the same level. The first speaks of a testimony that "is not true," the second of a testimony that "is true," and the third of testimony to "the truth." Such a sequence—not true, true, the truth—indicates progression. And there is further evidence of progression in the fact that the third of these references uses the perfect tense ("You have sent to John, and he has borne witness . . .") and by so doing suggests a process that is over.

Thus, while the background verse, concerning Jesus' mission, had an echo of primordial union with God (v 30), the subsequent verses move rapidly forward, and they intimate the passing of the period of the OT.

There then follow two concluding verses (34–35), which seem to stand back and assess what that history means for the Jews. First, in an extremely obscure saying (v 34), Jesus would appear to look to the future. He regards things from a viewpoint which does not depend on human testimony, and from that elevated position he speaks (prophetlike?) to the Jews: "that you may be saved." As Barrett (258) indicates in a general way, this message of salvation is reminiscent of the prophetic hope which is found in Romans 9–11, the hope that the salvific promises of the OT will eventually culminate in the saving of the Jews (Rom 9:27; 10:1,9–13; 11:11,14,26; compare Rom 9:1 and John 5:33b-34). As already noted, the final scene in the healing story (5:14–15) appears to allude to the same hope. Thus, in assessing the OT prophecies, Jesus seems to refer to their salvific implications for the future.

He also looks to the past—to John, representative of the prophets, and to the Jewish reaction to John (v 35). He may not have been the light, but he was nonetheless a lamp burning brightly, and for a time at least ("an hour"), the Jews "were willing" to rejoice in the light. It is with this image, of rejoicing in the lamplight, that the evangelist bids a certain farewell to the old order.

[5:36–40] The greater testimony which now surrounds Jesus; the Jews' unwillingness. However much Jesus may already have been present in the old order, however much John may have borne witness to him, the incarnation brings something that is quite different. Jesus now has a testimony that is "greater." His task is "to complete" (v 36).

The testimony is indeed greater. As already noted, the text is much longer than the earlier list of witnesses (vv 36–39, cf. 31–33). Yet its arrangement is essentially similar: three kinds of witness, of which the central one (vv 37–38) receives more space than the first and third.

The first (v 36) speaks of Jesus' "works"—works given to him by the Father to complete. Such an idea, of somehow completing God's work, provides a variation and complement to earlier verses (17 and 30). For Bultmann (265), "works" refers to "the whole of Jesus' activity as the Revealer." But the word "revealer," however intended, tends to communicate something rather narrow, and it seems better (following Brown, 224; Schnackenburg, 2:123, and Lindars, 229) to emphasize that the works are connected not only with revelation but also with healing, with salvation. Schnackenburg (2:123) would widen the concept of works yet further to have it refer to Jesus' signs and thus to such bountiful gestures as the granting of wine at Cana, and indeed to the whole range of the Creator's gifts. It would seem, therefore, that the primary "work" is the whole phenomenon of the richness of life—all that is connoted by fine wedding wine and by the overtones of renewing creation. On this basis even a flower can be a witness. What is essential is that "the works show every thoughtful person that the Father is at work in them" (Schnackenburg, 2:123).

The central witness is the Father (vv 37–38). As already indicated, this probably refers to the way in which God speaks internally to the human heart. "The testimony of God would then consist in the self-authenticating quality of [God's] truth, a truth immediately recognizable to those called to believe" (Brown, 227–28).

This testimony of God had been alluded to obscurely in the discussion of the testimony provided by the old dispensation (5:32), but here it is stated more clearly. In other words, since the coming of Jesus, God's parentlike calling to the human heart has been clearer.

What is involved here is not positively described. The text tells rather of what happens when God's testimony is absent—there is no sense of God's voice or form, nor, for the unbeliever, does God's word abide within. As Brown (225) notes, the implication is that, within the believer, God's word does abide. This implied idea, of God's abiding word, is the high point in the list of witnesses, and indeed in the whole discourse.

The final testimony (v 39) comes from the scriptures—the source wherein the Jews think to find "eternal life." Jesus does not say they are wrong—though his later comments (45–47) do imply a criticism. But while he lets stand the idea that there is eternal life in the scriptures, he connects that reality with himself: "they also bear witness about me." In other words, as in the preceding text, there is an implication that the scriptures contain eternal life precisely because they speak of Jesus, or, more simply, that Jesus is the source of eternal life. And that, of course, is what the discourse is about.

The three witnesses complement one another. The first, "the works," is external, and to some extent at least, reaches out to all of creation. The second, the testimony of the Father, is internal, the world of the heart. And the third is written and reaches into the past, into tradition. Together they form a powerful appeal to the Jews.

But the Jews do not will to come (v 40). They do not want life. Here, as earlier (vv 30, 35), the emphasis on the will indicates the essence of the problem. It also prepares the way for a closer look at the Jews' negative reaction.

[5:41–44] The cause of the negative reaction—seeking of human glory, rather than the glory of God. The Jewish rejection of creation and of the Creator's witness is not based on intellectual grounds. As Brown (228) notes, "if it were an intellectual problem, it could be met by explanation." There is, for instance, no reason to suppose that the Samaritans were intellectually superior, yet they had been able, when faced with a witness, to receive Jesus (4:39–40). What emerges then is that the rejection is based on grounds that are moral, on moral guilt (cf. Schnackenburg, 2:128; Brown, 228).

The nature of this guilt is fairly clear: while Jesus takes his orientation from God, those who reject him have an orientation based on human glory. That Jesus partakes in a higher God-related world is indicated in several ways. The fact that he knows what is innermost in the Jews—their lack of the love of God (v 42)—suggests a superhuman knowledge, a knowledge which is in continuity with his Godlike knowledge of the duration of the sick man's illness (5:6). And he explicitly presents himself as having come, not to make a name for himself, but in his Father's name (5:43). He does not receive human glory (5:41). As the introduction indicated (5:16–18), he is, in some way, at one with God.

But those who reject him are in another world morally. Most basic of all, they do not have "the love of God" in them (5:42). The lack, as Schnackenburg (2:127) indicates, apparently has to do not only with their lack of "love for God" but also with lack of the love which is *from* God. In other words, they lack that love of God which is a mode of God's presence, of God's indwelling. Their orientation, instead of being from God and towards God, is toward the purely human, toward receiving glory from each other. They form a "mutual admiration society" with a vested interest in maintaining their own traditions (Lindars, 232). And the root of the disorientation is in the will.

The problem, of course—of preoccupation with human glory—is not confined to an ancient audience. As Bultmann (272) and Schnackenburg (2:128) emphasize, the problems of pride and prestige apply to human life in general. They are powerful factors, often blinding. In Dante's perception of many of the writers of his day, for instance, it is the seeking of human glory, *fama,* which destroys them within (*Inferno* 15 and 16; cf. Culbertson, 1983, 16–22). It is this which twists the judgement, which blocks out God and life.

As for the unwillingness to seek health and life, that too is not a prerogative only of an ancient Jewish audience. It is a far wider problem. Even at the level of psychology, "psychotherapists are familiar with the fact that people are routinely terrified by mental health" (Peck, 1978, 296–306, esp. 303).

One of the key words in this text is *lambanō-,* "to take," or "receive." It is used four times, and though the ways in which it is used vary, its repeated occurrence helps to emphasize a single idea—receptivity. If one's receptivity is open to nothing higher than human glory, then what one receives is narrow. But if one's receptivity goes beyond the human, beyond people speaking in their own name, then the way is open for encountering something far greater.

The idea of something greater becomes clearer when, in its final line, the text refers to "the glory which is from the only God" (v 44).[1] Thus, just as this section began by emphasizing a fundamental lack, that of the *love* of God (v 42), so now, in a balancing statement, it concludes by speaking of a further lack, that of interest in the *glory* of God. The two are closely related, complementary aspects of the highest form of communication between God and humans. More and more, at a later stage, the gospel will speak of love, and there will also be a highlighting of the idea of glory—particularly as that glory is manifested in the resurrection. (On glory and the resurrection, see Brown, 503–4.)

But concerning true life and true glory, the Jews do "not will" and do "not seek" (cf. 40, 44). And so, though previous chapters have spoken so much of the process of coming to believe, there now arises, with a new urgency, the possibility of the opposite process—of not believing (see previously, 3:12,18,36). It is no more than a question ("How will you believe? . . ."), and it is set somewhat in the background, at the beginning of the verse (44). But, like a looming shadow, it is there.

[5:45–47] The consequence of the negative reaction—condemnation by Moses, and the spectre of the Jews lapsing into unbelief. Those who rejected Jesus may have felt secure in their proud attachment to Moses, particularly because, in Jewish tradition, Moses was regarded as an intercessor or advocate (cf. StrB, 2:561; Schnackenburg, 2:129). But Jesus, building on his earlier appeal to scripture (5:39), indicates that Moses, far from being their advocate, will be their accuser.

Previously, in speaking of the Jewish searching of the scripture, he had said,

---

1. In some important mss. the word "God" is absent—thus giving a difficult text in which "glory" is combined rather enigmatically with "only," a text which could be seen as a way of deliberately highlighting, by association, that what is being spoken of is the only glory, the glory of the implied God, and that human glory is not real. (The idea that "God" was omitted by the scribal error of homoeoteleuton does not seem plausible.)

"You think (*dokeite*) that in them . . ." (v 39). Now, as he reapproaches the question of the scriptures, the phrase is turned: "Do not think (*mē dokeite*) . . ." (v 45). The precise reversal of the scripture-related phrase is a symptom of the extent to which the Jewish understanding of scripture and Moses needs to be reversed.

But having disbelieved the Moses tradition, they are unlikely to believe its development in Jesus. And so again—but now with more insistence than ever—the question is restated: "How will you believe my words?" And it is with the word *pisteusete,* "will you believe?", that the chapter ends.

The spectre which is thus raised, though not yet stated explicitly, is momentous—that the Jews, the bearers of the tradition, will lapse into unbelief.

Chapter 5: Conclusion

Chapter 5 is a carefully wrought unit. The initial story (vv 1–15) depicts both the divine initiative which offers the totality of life and the human reluctance, Jewish and non-Jewish, in seeking and appreciating that gift. The subsequent discourse (vv 16–47) spells out both the gift and the reluctance. The gift is one of intimate knowledge, integral life, and salutary judgment. And, of course, it may be rejected—thus inevitably inducing a lack of life and a different form of judgement. The reluctance is deep-seated. It is unmoved by the credibility which accompanies the gift, and it clings to its fixed world of petty prestige and revered legalities.

It is a chapter which contains an intimation of the ultimate fate of the Jews. They reject Jesus and life—and so are marginalized. Yet they carry within them, somewhere, the healed man—a man whose healthiness is an indication that eventually they, as a people, will achieve healing and restoration (cf. Romans 9–11).

The Provision of Bread

Day 1 — Bread, Violence, and Reverence

In comparison with what precedes it, chap. 6 is complex. In chaps. 3–5 Jesus had been dealing with groups that were fairly clearly defined either as Jewish (cf. 3:1–21, chap. 5) or non-Jewish (or at least non-Judean, chap. 4). And there had been similar clarity about attitudes. Those who encountered Jesus were either undecided (3:1–21), or generally favorable (3:22–chap. 4), or quite unfavorable (chap. 5). But in chap. 6 the stage makes room for everybody, and sometimes all are on simultaneously—Jews and non-Jews (or non-Judeans), favorable and unfavorable. It is, therefore, a chapter which brings things together, and, in veiled, parabolic, form, it both summarizes the message of Jesus and gives some idea of the drama to come.

The action is spread over two days. The first is dominated by the story of the multiplication of bread (6:1–21), and the second by the discourse on the bread of life (6:22–71).

Geographic Disruption and the Order of the Chapters

At the beginning of chap. 6 there is a disruption of geography: the Jesus who had been in Jerusalem is portrayed, without explanation, as crossing the sea of Galilee. This disruption, along with lesser factors, has led some commentators, notably Bernard, Bultmann, and Schnackenburg, to say that the text has been moved around by some editor(s) and to claim that originally chap. 4 (which concludes in Galilee) was followed by chap. 6 (which begins beyond the sea of Galilee). And so they rearrange chaps. 5 and 6. (For discussion, see Bernard, xvii–xix, 171; Bultmann, 209–10; and especially Schnackenburg, 2:5–9.) However, as Brown (235–36) points out, the rearrangement does not solve all the alleged problems, and besides, "there are indications that favor the present order."

The most important such indication is that the geographic disruption in 6:1–4 is not an isolated phenomenon. It is part of a larger pattern of geography-related disruptions which occur in chap. 6. Thus the chapter's narrative introduction (6:1–21) comes to an end with a space-surpassing movement of the boat: "they willed (*thelō*) to receive him into the boat, and *immediately the boat was at the land* to which they were going" (*hypagō*, "to go, go away"). Furthermore, the introduction to the subsequent discourse (6:22–24) is equally puzzling: among other things it includes a movement of boats (from Tiberias) which Wellhausen (30) and Bultmann (217) describe as a *deus ex machina*.

A hint of what is going on is supplied at the end of the chapter when the disciples decide to enter the realm of the holy, in other words, a realm which is beyond the normal limitation of space (Jesus asks if they will [*thelō*] to go away [*hypagō*], and Peter, who is associated with the boat [cf. 21:1–14], expresses a commitment to Jesus as holy [6:67–69]).

Hence—without going into detail at this point—the chapter's initial disruption of geography has a purpose: it provides a geographic contradiction which challenges the reader to rise above the level of what is space-bound and to enter into another realm, ultimately into the realm of God, the realm which in this chapter is symbolized particularly by the bread.

Chapter 5 had already suggested a surpassing of time (for instance, the feast which it mentions is not specified, not bound to time, 5:1; and the text implies an eternal present, 5:17). Chapter 6, therefore, with its surpassing of space, plays a complementary role. Together they build toward a sense of what is holy.

Structure of 6:1–21

The events of Day 1 are frequently divided into two sections, one dealing with the multiplication of the loaves (6:1–15) and the other with the walking on the sea (6:16–21). This division is not without solid foundation, yet it needs to be put within the context of a structure which is more complete.

The text begins with a brief introduction—the account of Jesus among the weak (*asthenountes*, "to be weak/sick," 6:1–4; cf. Bultmann, 211). This introduction has some affinities with other introductions of Part 2 (cf. 2:23–25; 3:22–24; 4:1–6; 4:44–45), but its closest links are with the introduction of chap. 5—the account of Jesus going up to the weak (*asthenountes*) in Jerusalem (5:1–3). Apart from 4:46 and the Lazarus story, the words for weakness (*astheneia*) or being weak (*astheneō*) do not otherwise occur in John's gospel. And it is only at the beginning of chaps. 5 and 6 that weakness is associated in some way with great crowds.

In chap. 6, of course, the action occurs not in Jerusalem, but on a far wider stage—"across the sea of Galilee of Tiberias"—and the time seems even more auspicious—not just an unnamed feast (as in 5:1), but Passover (6:4). This introduction, therefore, is like an elaboration or intensification of that found in chap. 5.

The subsequent action falls into three scenes: the multiplication (6:4–13), the violent effort to make Jesus king (6:14–15), and the sea-scene (6:16–21). Though Jesus is present in all three, the emphasis in Scenes 2 and 3 is not so much on him as on contrasting reactions to him—the violently negative reaction of those people (*anthrōpoi*) who wanted to force him to be king (Scene 2), and the reveringly positive reaction of the disciples (*mathētai*) who were willing to receive him (Scene 3).

That the effort to make Jesus king (vv 14–15) should be regarded as a separate scene is suggested by several factors. First, it is not part of the multiplication scene proper; it is rather a consequence, something which is in some way distinct (cf. Bultmann, 213; Lindars, 243–44; Kysar, 92). Second, as already indicated, its violence forms a powerful contrast with the receptivity of the sea-scene (cf. Brown, 255)—and that particular scene is definitely distinct. Finally, as so often in this gospel when it is a question of distinguishing scenes—there is an element of repetition at the point of division. Scene 1 began with: "Jesus, therefore, lifting up his eyes and seeing . . . said. . . ." Scene 2 begins: "The people, therefore, seeing . . . said. . . ." Though the Greek uses diverse words for "seeing," the repetition is sufficient to confirm the distinctness of the scenes.

The structure which thus emerges is essentially the same as that found at the beginning of the preceding episode in Jerusalem (5:1–15). In that case also there was, first, an introduction which placed Jesus among the weak (5:1–3, cf. 6:1–4), then, a striking miracle (5:5–9a, cf. 6:5–13); next, a narrow-minded reaction (5:9b-13, cf. 6:1–15); and finally, at a distinct time and place, a reaction which is more positive, or at least is more open to a positive interpretation (5:14–15, later, in the temple; cf. 6:16–21, evening, at sea).

Though the scenes in 6:1–21 are indeed distinct from one another, they nonetheless form a unity. The phrase which follows them, "The next day . . ." (6:22), had been used previously in the gospel to divide the text into units (cf. 1:29,35,43), and, as Brown (257) suggests, it now serves a similar function: to divide all of 6:1–21 from the rest of chapter 6, and thus to indicate its unity. Furthermore, even though scenes 1 and 2 are set on "the mountain" (6:3,15), it is with references to crossing the sea that the entire text begins and ends (6:1,16–21), and such references bind the scenes together. However, it is, above all, in its content, its meaning, that the unity of 6:1–21 will be seen.

[6:1–4] Introduction: Across the sea to the mountain—the weak and the great crowd.   More than any preceding section of John's gospel, these verses suggest immense space. Never before was mention made of "the sea," still less of Jesus going across it. Nor is the stage limited to the sea. On the contrary, it is simply the foreground for a space so great that a great crowd may be visualized as persistently following Jesus (imperfect tense). The very phrase "great crowd" emphasizes the expanding of the stage. The preceding episode had indeed alluded to "a crowd" (5:13), but this is the gospel's first reference to "a great crowd" (*ochlos polys*).

The great crowd followed, not for frivolity, but out of a sense of need: "because they saw the signs which he did on those who were weak." There is an implication that what was done for the weak was important also for them, that they too suffered from some form of weakness.

This implication, that the entire "great crowd" experienced a form of weakness, accords with what was suggested in other introductory texts—in 5:1–3, where the afflicted multitude evoked the Jews as a whole, and in 2:23–25 where Jesus had reacted to a failing which was universal ("in the human person"). Thus the great crowd, as it now follows Jesus, reflects a universal human need. The picture, therefore, worthy of a great painter, is a panorama of pathos.

Into this picture the evangelist suddenly introduces a new image—that of Jesus as an uplifting companion: he went up to "the mountain" and there "sat with his disciples." Like "the sea" and "the great crowd," this is the gospel's first reference to Jesus being on a mountain, and it develops further the unique landscape of chap. 6. It has been connected at times with the mountain that introduces the Sermon on the Mount (cf. Brown, 232; Lindars 240), and such an idea is partly true, yet the verb "to teach" is not used, and Schnackenburg (2:14) appears to be correct in emphasizing that at this point Jesus is being portrayed "not as law-giver and teacher . . . [but] as the leader of the people, acting in the name of God and showing himself to be God's messenger." In other words, against a background of universal human need, Jesus is first introduced not so much as a teacher—that will come later—but as someone who shares with people, who "sits with them," and raises them to an awareness of something higher. One of the earlier introductory sections (3:22–24, esp. 3:22) had already alluded faintly to such a similarly uplifting companionship.

Then, just when the severe painting has taken on a certain glow, the evangelist adds an element which chills and challenges—the approach of "Passover, the feast of the Jews." At one level this is a simple chronological detail, but within the context of the gospel as a whole, a gospel which is built around three Passovers and which links Passover with death, the addition of such a detail cannot but be significant (cf. esp. Hoskyns, 281–82). It is a faint reminder, even in a moment of companionship, that ultimately one must reckon with death. It is an idea which will cast an increasing shadow over the remainder of the gospel.

There has been considerable scholarly discussion concerning the geographical setting of the scene, and, as most authors suggest, it seems reasonable, in the context, to visualize Jesus as crossing from what would generally be regarded as the nearest side, the western shore, to the farther, eastern, side (cf., for example, Schnackenburg, 2:13; Lindars, 239; Kysar, 90). Yet, the text is puzzling: it simultaneously over-informs and under-informs. It over-informs because it speaks of "the sea *of Galilee of Tiberias*"—a designation which many regard as both awkward and redundant. And it under-informs because, concerning the voyage itself, it is vague: it gives names neither for the place of departure nor for that of arrival.

It is possible, as Schnackenburg (2:13) does, to try to explain some of this situation by invoking the work of an editor. Such an explanation, however, whatever its initial plausibility and attractiveness, implies a certain degree of bungling and suggests that the writer(s) who produced the gospel, and who sought to describe the most profound aspects of life, could not adequately describe a simple voyage.

As with other texts, including the introductory passage which tells of Jesus being in Judea with his disciples (3:22–24)—a passage which, as already noted, has some affinity with the present test—the answer may lie in the fact that the evangelist's primary interest is not in geography but in theology. The reference to Tiberias, precisely because it seems so puzzling, causes the reader, Nicodemus-like, to pause and think. And it can be seen to make sense. Since "Tiberias" was a variant of "Tiberius," the name of an emperor (A.D. 14–37) and one of the most prestigious names of the Roman Empire, it serves as a way of evoking that empire, as a way of setting the scene in the context of the whole world. Such a context fits the theme—that of universal human need, of a great crowd across the sea following Jesus. (As already suggested, the muddled-looking geographical references in chap. 6 have a purpose.)

But balancing this evoking of the Gentiles there is also an evoking of the Jews. Without needing to say so—it was already clear at the first Passover (2:13)—the gospel says that Passover was a feast "of the Jews" (6:4).

Thus, two details which at first sight may seem awkward or redundant—"of Tiberias" and "of the Jews"—may also be seen as sophisticated indications of what this complex chapter is all about: a worldwide drama involving Gentiles and Jews, a drama of universal human need and of God's care for that need.

[6:5–13] Scene 1. The feeding of the five thousand. Having suggested a great human need and having evoked a divine solidarity and companionship, the evangelist proceeds to tell how that need was met.

As the introduction intimates, the need in question is not primarily, or at least not exclusively, one of physical hunger. The text never says explicitly that the great crowd was hungry. And the initial mistake of Philip and Andrew, when Jesus asks about buying bread, is to think exclusively in physical, measuring, terms: with two hundred denarii, everyone could not receive even a little, and what is the use of five loaves and two fish among so many? Shades of Nicodemus and the woman at the well.

The fundamental relationship in this narrative, therefore, is not that of money to food, nor of food to population, but, as will be seen, of human willingness to divine providence. The evangelist is not naive; this entire episode will conclude by referring to the reality of diabolical treachery (6:70–71). But, evil notwithstanding, the interaction of the divine and the human is capable of producing something that is of surpassing goodness.

The narrative begins when "Jesus takes the initiative . . . the initiative of God" (Kysar, 91). The lifting of the eyes (6:5), as in 4:35 and especially as in 17:1, indicates a mode of vision which goes beyond the surface of things. Before the great crowd has said anything, Jesus sees, knows their need, and proposes action: he asks Philip about buying bread. The idea that he said this to test Philip and that "he himself knew what he would do" (6:6) is not an editorial addition as has sometimes been asserted. The testing of Philip helps to make the disciple conscious of his own limited awareness and thus more receptive to what Jesus is offering. Nicodemus and the Samaritan woman had been through an analogous process. Nor is the reference to Jesus "knowing" in any way alien to the text. Like the similar reference to Jesus' knowledge, when he saw the need of the man at the poolside (5:6), a reference with which it is in precise continuity, it belongs to the essence of the account. It alludes ultimately to God's provident foreknowledge.

The sense of divine providence is heightened by what follows: the ease of being made to recline, the surprising luxuriousness of the location (as a "place" of "much grass" it tends to recall the famous "verdant pastures" of Psalm 23; cf. Psalm 23:2, Greek version: "place of green grass"), the positive atmosphere of thanksgiving (*eucharisteō*), the abundance of the food. It is a providence which overflows and which takes care "that nothing may perish" (6:12).

But in all this the people have not been passive. Having been first referred to as "following" Jesus (6:2), they are depicted in this scene as "coming to" him (6:5), a phrase which, as Brown suggests (233), seems to have a theological meaning and an overtone of the coming to Jesus of the first disciples (1:35–39; Brown, 79).

Furthermore, while at one level everything depends on Jesus' God-like providence, at another the crucial step is taken by the diminutive figure who comes forward with a little food (6:8–9). Everything seems unpromising about this person. He is a *paidarion*—not just a diminutive, but a double diminutive of *pais* (a boy, slave, or child). His five loaves are of barley—poor quality apparently. And the two fish are described as *opsaria*—another double diminutive. Even his name is omitted, and, like the nameless disciple of the early call, he is hidden behind the figure of Andrew, "one of the" disciples (6:8–9, cf. 1:40). Yet like the nameless but energetic servants of the Cana miracles (2:5–9; 4:51–53) it is he who is ahead of the action. Regardless of his social and economic poverty, he does all he can—and his role is decisive.

Finally, the fact that the people will (*thelō*) to receive the food (6:11) is not without significance. A central part of the problem in chapter 5 had been a lack of willingness to receive life (5:6,40). And in Scene 3 (6:16–21) it will be important that the disciples *will* to receive Jesus (6:21). Given this context, the reference to willing indicates a crucial human contribution.

It would also seem to be significant that, in the final stage of the meal, at the gathering of the overflow, it is the disciples, rather than Jesus, who do the work. Thus, while it was Jesus who had distributed the bread, there comes a time when the responsibility for the bread falls to the disciples.

The overall picture is of a magnificent providence which, when encountered by human willingness, overflows to fulfillment. It involves the granting of bread, ordinary bread to reclining people, but it is set in the context of the larger world of human need, the whole sphere of human life and human weakness, and it cannot but suggest that toward that larger need also Jesus' providence is directed.

As well as being directed to the depth of human need, it is directed also to the breadth of human diversity. What was enigmatically suggested in the introduction (6:1–4)—that the text is evoking both Gentiles and Jews—finds confirmation in the account of the actual multiplication. This is particularly noticeable when John's text is compared with the other gospels. Unlike Mark and Matthew, both of whom depict two distinct crowds, one to symbolize the Jews (the *five* thousand, with *twelve* baskets: Mark 6:30–44, Matt 14:13–21) and the other to symbolize all peoples (the *four* thousand, with *seven* baskets: Mark 8:1–10, Matt 15:31–39; four and seven suggest universality), John depicts only one crowd, one multiplication scene. But within that one scene there are suggestions of both groups. On the one hand, there are details that suit Judaism—the references to *five* thousand and *twelve* baskets (6:4,10,13). On the other hand, there are details which in different ways evoke the non-Judean/Gentile world. The scene is set somewhere "on the other side of the sea of Galilee"—well distant from Judea. And the disciples who are named in this account, Philip and Andrew, not only include the disciple whose name is quintessentially Greek (Philip) and who had been involved in the very first move toward Galilee (John 1:43), but they are the two, who, at a later stage in John's gospel, are explicitly involved in communicating with the Greeks (12:20–22). Thus, by evocative details, John manages, in a single multiplication account, to suggest that in the event concerning the bread there are both Jews and non-Judeans/Gentiles, the full complexity of Jesus' followers.

A number of details link this text with the synoptic accounts of the eucharist —particularly the reference to Passover, the giving of thanks (*eucharisteō*), the picture of Jesus himself taking and distributing bread, and the fact that the bread was given "to those who were seated." Consequently, "the eucharistic coloring of the . . . account . . . seems beyond doubt" (Brown, 249; cf. Schnackenburg, 2:16–17; Lindars, 242–43). This does not mean that the feeding was a eucharistic meal. It indicates rather that meals such as these, and the providence manifested in these meals, provide the background to the eucharist and give it meaning. Unless one has experienced such providence there can be no genuine thanksgiving. The link between the two is essential.

[6:14–15] Scene 2: The attempt to narrow the scope of providence. Like the awesome life-giving at the poolside (5:5–13), the feeding of the five thousand is followed by a reaction that is extraordinarily narrow. Instead of seeing in Jesus a providence which responds to the totality of the human situation, to all human needs and weaknesses, the people (*anthropoi*) see nothing more than a biblically based king. They reduce providence to violent political success. This reduction or narrowing is all the more striking because of the wide, overflowing nature of the preceding miracle and of the providence it signifies.

The precise interpretation which the people put on Jesus may, at first, seem quite plausible and acceptable: they regarded him as "the prophet who is to come"— a reference apparently to the expectation, based partly on Deut 18:15–18, of a Moses-like prophetical king. (For discussion and references, see esp. Schnackenburg, 2:19.) But just as Jesus in the preceding Jerusalem episode was doing something which surpassed the law of the Jewish sabbath (cf. 5:1–15), so now in this text Jewish expectation is surpassed. And it also surpasses much human expectation. (The phrasing is such—"the people," with no explicit mention of the Jews or Moses—that it can apply to all human beings.) Thus, however wonderfully wise regimes may be, they do not embody the fullness of providence. Something greater than Solomon is here.

A puzzling detail of this text is the fact that the people are regarded as having seen a sign (or signs—the mss. vary), yet on the next day, when the crowd finds Jesus, he says that they have not seen signs (6:26). The contradiction is glaring. Yet there is no need to say that the text is confused. As earlier in the gospel, when the numeration of the Cana signs (2:11, 4:54) seemed to take no account of those that intervened (2:23, 3:2), the answer would seem to lie in the fact that "sign" is being used in diverse senses—in a negative sense wherein an alleged sign is, in fact, not a true sign, and therefore not really a sign at all (so 6:14; cf. 2:23, 3:2); and in a positive sense wherein a sign goes beyond the surface of things and presupposes genuine faith (so 6:26; cf. 2:11; 4:54). Just as 4:54 takes no account of the superficial signs of 2:23, so 6:26 takes no account of the superficial idea of the sign in 6:14.

Incidentally, the first reference to signs in chap. 6—the great crowd followed Jesus because they saw the signs (6:2)—would seem to be deliberately ambiguous. This ambiguity prepares the way for the diversity of responses which characterizes this chapter.

The text concludes with Jesus' reaction to the people: knowing (*gnous*) that they are going to come to seize him and make him king he withdraws again to the mountain alone (*monos,* 6:15; cf. *monos,* "only," 5:44). His knowing, like his knowing (*gnous*) at the poolside (5:6), reflects divine knowledge. The first was knowledge of the past, this other, like his knowledge of what he himself would do (6:6), is of the future (contrast 5:6 and 6:15). His withdrawal to the mountain is not a piece of muddled geography which, in the words of one commentator, needs to be "coordinated" with the fact that he is not described as ever having left the mountain. It is rather a way of stating a theological message: on the one hand, providence knows in advance the workings of the lesser "providence" of the political order; on the other, preoccupation with violent-minded politics leads to a withdrawal of the divine. The picture of Jesus alone on the mountain is, in fact, very carefully coordinated with the earlier picture of his being on the mountain (6:3). There, against the background of those who had some sense of their weakness, he was in solidarity with people, he "sat with his disciples" (6:2–3). But later, when faced with those who were in the business of strong-arm king-making, his position on the mountain was quite alone. Thus for those who think they can narrow and manipulate providence, providence is gone. But for those who in their weakness follow providence, providence is present and sits with them. It is this contrast which sets the stage for the following scene.

[6:16–21] Scene 3: The storm-tossed acceptance of the divine Jesus.   The narrative is brief and vivid. On the evening of the miracle of bread, as the disciples were going by sea to Capernaum, they were overtaken by darkness and a great wind. As people who had spent the day in the atmosphere of an extraordinary picnic, this development would have been particularly chilling. The providence which seemed so enjoyable amid the luxuriant grass appears now to be terribly distant: "It was already darkness, and Jesus had not yet come to them." The phrasing is indicative of both loneliness and hope.

Then, when the sea was getting worse and when they had rowed a painful twenty-five or thirty stadia—three or four miles (probably more than halfway across)—Jesus appeared in a way that has to be described as a theophany—walking on the threatening sea, evoking (reverential) fear, and pronouncing *Egō eimi.* When taken in isolation this phrase may simply mean "It is I," but in the context of something so related to the divine as walking on water it has also a clear resonance of the divine name "I am" (cf. Hoskyns, 291; Brown, 533–38; Schnackenburg, 2:79–89).

Faced with this divine presence, the disciples did not turn away. Instead "*they willed* to *receive* him in the boat." This attitude is in sharp contrast to that of the "unwilling" Jews in Jerusalem (5:6,40–44), but it is in continuity with that of those who willed to receive the bread (6:6,11).

Their willingness to receive Jesus into the boat is followed by a startling development: "immediately the boat was at the land to which they were going." In other words, instead of telling of the coming together of the boat and Jesus it tells of the coming together of the boat and *the land to which they were going.* The text is not only miraculous—something which is not surprising in the presence of a theophany—it is also extremely puzzling, another challenge to the reader to rise above a Nicodemus-like frame of mind. It would seem, above all, to indicate that while the disciples were indeed going to Capernaum, they were also going somewhere else—to union with the divine Jesus. He was their "land," their ultimate goal, and once they had accepted the theophany, they had, in a sense, already arrived. Or, to put it in terms of realized eschatology, they had already attained eternal life. In Lindars's cautious words (248): "We cannot exclude the possibility that John had an eye to the symbolism of arrival at the haven and the attainment of eternal life through faith in Jesus."

The boat-scene maintains continuity with the scenes which precede. This has already been partly indicated—in speaking of the overall unity of 6:1–21 and in noting that the disciples' willingness to receive Jesus (6:21) builds on the people's willingness to receive food (6:11). Furthermore, the picture of impending encounter, as given in Scene 3 ("They saw Jesus walking on the sea and approaching the boat, and they were afraid") plays off various aspects of the other pictures of impending encounter—the moment in Scene 1 when Jesus lifted his eyes and saw a great crowd coming to him (6:5) and the later moment, in Scene 2, when Jesus knew that they were going to come and seize him (6:15). In particular, while the first encounter promises to be positive, and the second to be violent, the third—in stark contrast to the second—turns out to be even more positive, in fact, to be reverential. Thus the text advances by contrast and intensification. What is essential, however, is that the elements of continuity are considerable. Yet, despite all the continuity, there is a difference. The boat scene is more focused. It is as though, while 6:1–15 fills a vast stage, the boat scene is played under a spotlight.

The question which arises is whether, within the wide world suggested by the larger stage, the boat has some particular significance. In other words, whatever may have been the historical details of the voyage, has it been so described in the gospel that it is meant to refer to a further reality? Specifically, is it in some way a symbol of the church? In dealing with the overall meaning of 6:1–21, one certainly has to reckon with a contrast between a wide stage and a smaller, more luminous, stage. If the wide stage is the world, then the smaller stage, with its boat, would seem to have something to do with the more limited sphere of the church. Furthermore, while in the stage as a whole there is a basic providence—a providence which, given a certain human willingness, yields bread—among those who together have rowed through the stormy darkness, there is a special sense of the fuller meaning of providence. At the least, one may say that these features—a certain limitedness in relation to the world and a greater awareness of a fuller providence—are appropriate to the church.

Day 2 — The Bread of Life Discourse

Jesus' Call for "a Surrender . . . to the Glory of Existence"

In simplified terms, the narrative consists, first, of a rather dramatic account of "the crowd" crossing the sea in search of Jesus (vv 22–24), then of the long discourse on the bread of life (vv 25–59), and finally of an account of the diverse reactions (vv 60–71).

Discussion of this text has centered on two basic questions: First, what is its structure? Second, what is its meaning? In other words, what is Jesus talking about? Above all, what is meant by bread?

The two questions are interrelated, but to a limited extent they may be treated separately.

Structure

The entire narrative (vv 22–71) begins with "The next day, . . ." a time designation which, as in chap. 1 (cf. 1:29,35,43), relates the text to what precedes (6:1–21), yet separates it and gives to all that follows a slender framework of unity.

Looking at the text in more detail, there is considerable agreement that the initial picture of the crowd seeking Jesus (vv 22–24) forms a small segment which serves as a transition or introduction to the discourse (e.g., cf. Brown, 257–59; Kysar, 96–97). The unity of this segment is confirmed by the fact that it is followed by ". . . on the other side of the sea" (v 25), a detail which at first may indeed seem "superfluous and awkward" (Schnackenburg, 2:33) but which, when taken in conjuction with the beginning of the segment (v 21, "The next day the crowd which stood *on the other side of the sea* . . .") forms exactly the kind of repetition by which the evangelist often distinguishes the beginning of a new unit.

Bultmann (216–18), Schnackenburg (2:31–35), and Lindars (248–49) include with this initial segment an extra verse or two, but that is partly because they are working on the basis of undefined hypothetical sources rather than with the present text, and partly because they do not take account of the technique of repetition by which the evangelist divides the narrative.

It seems reasonable, therefore, to work on the hypothesis that the account of the crowd seeking Jesus forms some kind of introduction.

It also seems reasonable to work on the hypothesis that the aftermath of the discourse, the account of the diverse reactions (vv 60–71), is not only distinct — as is generally agreed — but is also twofold in structure. The first section deals with the general difficulty of receiving the message (vv 60–65), the second with more specific reactions (vv 66–71). Such, for instance, among the few who raise the question, is the opinion of Schnackenburg (2:70–74) and Lindars (272–74). And like many of the evangelist's divisions, it is confirmed by the presence of repetition (cf. vv 60 and 66, "many . . . of his disciples").

With relative ease, therefore, one may distinguish a brief introduction and a twofold aftermath. But concerning the central corpus of the text, the discourse proper (vv 25–59), there is widespread disagreement. (For a review of research, see esp. Roberge, 1984. See also Brown, 293–94; Schnackenburg, 2:31; Lindars, 249–53.)

In approaching the problem once more, it is useful to list certain basic data, data which, in some way or other, must be taken into account in any proposed solution.

1. The early stage of Jesus' encounter with the crowd, at "Capernaum . . . on the other side of the sea," is strikingly similar to the early stage of his encounter with the woman at the well of Samaria (4:7–15). The woman, with her mind set on the earthly, misunderstood Jesus' statements about living water (4:7–15); and the people likewise misunderstood Jesus' early references to a bread which was higher (6:25–33). Furthermore, the question and answer format of the Capernaum scene has "a perfect parallel" (Brown, 267; cf. Strathmann, 118) in the beginning stage of the Samaria scene. But the beginning stage of the Samaria scene is a carefully wrought unit—the first segment of a two-part conversation with the woman, and of a three-part series of statements by Jesus—and so the same would seem to be true of the misunderstanding scene at Capernaum (vv 25–33). It occupies about a quarter of the discourse.

Incidentally, it is difficult to say at the outset whether this opening scene concludes with v 33 or with the request of v 34 ("*Kyrie,* give us this bread always"). The parallel with the Samaria scene suggests that it conclude with v 34 (cf. 4:15; Brown, 267), but in the Capernaum scene the request is given a different function —not to close the discussion (concerning water/bread), but to open it up to a new stage. There is some likelihood, then, that the opening scene concludes at v 33 and that it is with the request for bread, bread of a higher kind (v 34), that the next section begins.

2. There is virtual unanimity that some kind of division begins at v 41, just about halfway through the discourse proper: "The Jews then murmured at him. . . . 'Is this not Jesus, the son of Joseph. . . .' " For some researchers this division is minor, no more than the beginning of a new paragraph or rhythm, but for others it is quite major. The presence of such a division is particularly noticeable in the work of those who have the task not only of analyzing the text theoretically but also of editing or translating it. Brown (268), for instance, is one of those who would not speak of any major division at the mention of the Jews' murmuring, yet his translation acknowledges that at this point there is some kind of break in the text, at least at the level of rhythm. Examination of a considerable variety of texts and translations shows virtual agreement on this matter. (One notable exception is the KJV, but that is accounted for by the fact that it gives no discourse division at all.)

3. There is unanimity that somewhere around the second reference to the Jews' reaction (v 52, about three quarters of the way through the discourse proper) the text seems to "change gears": it develops an emphasis on eating, especially an emphasis on eating and drinking Jesus' body and blood, which was not there before. The number of those who believe that this shift takes place right at v 52 itself is considerable: B. F. Westcott, H. Strathmann, E. Hoskyns, J. Schneider, J. Marsh, R. Schnackenburg, L. Morris. (For details, see Roberge, 1984, 93–

95.) But a still greater number would put it either just before v 52 (especially at 48–51) or just afterward (at 53).

If these data alone were considered then the discourse would be divided at three points (vv 34, 41, and 52), and would fall into four fairly even sections. Such, in fact, is essentially the division contained in such standard texts as the UBSGNT and the RSV.

There are, however, other factors which must be taken into account.

1. There is evidence that the text contains some chiastic structures (cf. Brown, 276; Roberge, 1984, 107).

2. There are resemblances between the way this discourse uses two scripture quotations (vv 31 and 45) and the way scripture was used in Jewish homilies. A case can, therefore, be made that the pattern or structure of the discourse follows that of Jewish homiletic technique (see esp. Borgen, 1965). In varying degrees, this view is adopted by Brown (277–78), Schnackenburg (2:31–31), and Lindars (234–36, 249–53).

3. Brown has pointed out (288–89) that, to a significant extent, what is said in the central half of the discourse (vv 35–50) is repeated in the final section (51–58); and largely on this basis he divides the text in three: a prefatory dialogue (25–34), the discourse proper (35–50), and a (eucharistic) variation on the discourse (51–58) (Brown, 286–387, 294).

The question which needs to be answered is whether any or all of these three phenomena require the abandonment of the fourfold division which was first proposed.

It would appear that they do not.

Chiasms do not exclude other structures. As in the case of the prologue, they can be woven through them and can complement them.

Similarly with regard to homiletic technique. That it has been incorporated to some degree seems reasonably assured. It is, however, but one component in the text. The leading quotation, for instance (v 31, "He gave them bread . . ."), while it may perhaps be built upon as in a homily, receives its surrounding structure, the introductory dialogue, not primarily from a relatively remote preaching technique, but from the pattern established just two chapters earlier in the introductory dialogue with the Samaritan woman. As mentioned earlier, Brown (267) speaks of a perfect parallel. Even the meaning and phrasing of 6:31 are in careful continuity with what was said in chap. 4. The Samaritan woman had asked: "Are you greater than our father (*patēr*) Jacob who gave us (*edōken hymin*) the well, and drank? . . . (4:12). And in chap. 6 also Jesus is effectively asked if he can match and surpass the ancient tradition—that of "our fathers" (*pateres hēmōn*), of whom it was written "He gave (*edōken*) them bread . . . to eat" (6:31). In other words—without attempting a complete analysis—the challenge to Jesus to provide tradition-equalling bread to eat is a carefully crafted variation on the earlier challenge to provide tradition-equalling water to drink. Even the wording of the scripture quotation—"He gave . . ."—is brought into line with the earlier scene. (Note also, "[He] gave," in 3:16 and "given" in 3:27; 6:65.) Thus the homiletic technique, while it may indeed be present, is not the governing principle. The evangelist "has adapted it for his book" (Lindars, 253). But Lindars, having made that acute observation, does not follow it through. He does not ask, "And what is the structure of his book? What is this structure to which the homiletic technique has been adapted?" Instead, like Schnackenburg (2:31), he allows one component, a subordinate one, to act as the governing principle. The result is considerable confusion. The essential point is that the presence of homiletic technique does not require the denying of other structures.

With regard to the repetition which occurs between vv 35–50 and 51–58, Brown is essentially correct. There really is some repetition. What is noted by Brown, however, is but a small part of a much larger phenomenon: the entire discourse (vv 25–58) is crafted along highly repetitive lines. Thus Kysar (1984, 42), for instance, indicates that even within vv 35–50 there is considerable duplication. At one point he notes: "6:43 . . . spirals through some of the themes introduced in 6:36–40 but moves beyond them." However, as indicated in Excursus 3, it is through the dividing of the discourse into the four suggested sections that the full extent of the repetition can begin to be seen. Section 2 repeats elements of section 1, often in varied form; section 3 repeats elements of both 1 and 2; and section 4 repeats elements from 1, 2, and 3. Consequently, the repetition between 51–58 and 35–50 (i.e. roughly between section 4 and sections 2 and 3) does not negate the fourfold division, nor does it justify regarding 51–58 as an editorial addition. The discourse may be fourfold, but it is also a tightly woven unit.

It is one thing to say that the proposed division is not negated—whether by chiasms, homiletic technique, or repetition. It is another to say that it can be confirmed. It seems, however, that it can.

First, if the proposed division is accepted, the opening lines of the various sections, including those of 6:60–71, show an orderly pattern:

25–33, "They said to him, 'Rabbi . . .' "
34–40, "They then said to him, '*Kyrie* . . .' "

41–51, "The Jews then murmured . . ."
52–59, "The Jews then fought among themselves . . ."

60–65, "Many of his disciples . . . murmured . . ."
66–71, "From this on many of his disciples went back . . ."

The opening line of vv 25–33, as given here, does not include the scene-setting words at the very beginning of v 25 ("And finding him on the other side of the sea"). Like the scene-setting note in v 59 ("in a synagogue . . . in Capernaum"), these words pertain to the framework of the discourse rather than to the discourse itself.

The degree of correspondence between the various opening lines is considerable. "Rabbi" and "*Kyrie*"—the only such forms of address used in the discourse—follow one another in sequence. So do the only two references to "the Jews." And so do the only two references to "many of his disciples." It may also be seen that what occurs among the Jews (murmuring and internal division) occurs also, in varied form, among the disciples. As Kysar (112) notes, "the four instances [concerning the Jews and disciples] form a set of pairs."

What is important in assessing the significance of this orderly pattern is that it contains the ingredient which the evangelist so often uses in dividing the text— that of repetition. It would seem, therefore, that these various phrases do indeed divide the text, and that while the discourse is fourfold, the text as a whole is divided into six parts.

A further confirmation of the appropriateness of the proposed division may be found in the fact that it corresponds to the division of the discourse in chap. 5. There too there was an introduction (5:16–18) and then a sixfold division (5:19– 47 was divided as vv 19, 24, 30, 36, 41, 45). Such a correspondence is not surprising. It was seen earlier that the first part of chap. 6, with its introduction and three scenes (6:1–21) presents the same kind of structure as the first part of chap. 5 (5:1–15). It is appropriate that a similar correspondence be found between the later parts of the respective chapters.

This affinity with chap. 5 indicates a further element—that, like 5:16–47, the text of 6:22–71 is ultimately a complex variation on the prologue. In tentative outline:

1:1–18	5:16–47	6:22–71
	Introduction (16–18)	Introduction (22–24)
Origins: the Word, life, creation (1–5)	Ongoing creation (19–29)	The bread which sustains to the end (25–40)
Intermediate witness (6–13)	Full witness, esp. of the Father in the heart (30–40)	The bread (Word/witness) which is to be eaten (taken fully into the heart) (41–59)
Incarnation: the Word's glory (14–18)	True glory rejected (41–47)	The word rejected and accepted (60–71)

A full analysis of the relationship between these texts would require a special study. Rather than embark on such an undertaking, it seems better simply to note what is essential: the creative outpouring of God's word, as depicted in the prologue (1:1–18) and in the discourse on ongoing creation (chap. 5), finds further expression in God's outpouring of bread (''the bread of life''). In contrast to the prologue and chap. 5, the language in chap. 6 is heavily parabolic—the image of bread pervades the text—and therefore, despite the thematic continuity between all three texts, chap. 6 appears to be very different. Yet the connection is real.

This connection, between the bread and the Word/word, brings the discussion of structure to the critical point where it must inquire about meaning.

Meaning

From ancient times to the present there have been essentially two views with regard to the meaning of the bread of life discourse (cf. Brown, 272; Schnackenburg, 2:65–67).

The most basic view—the view most commentators would regard as primary, at least in most of the discourse—is that the bread refers to much or all of what was done in Christ, particularly to Christ's mediating of revelation. His word sustains people and gives them eternal life. Insofar as such *an outpouring of the word* has significant resemblances to the OT idea of *the outpouring of God's wisdom,* this view has become known in modern times as *the sapiential interpretation.*

The further interpretation, which is usually seen as secondary to the more basic meaning, or secondary at least in most of the text—though some have made it primary throughout—is that the bread in question is that of the eucharist. This view is particularly associated with the final section of the discourse (vv 52–58).

As far as this study is concerned, both of these views are essentially correct: the text is a unity, and while it is primarily sapiential, it is also, to an important degree, eucharistic. The two levels are, in fact, closely related. Before the relationship of the two levels can be discussed, however, it is necessary that the more basic level, the sapiential, be reexamined.

The proposal put forward here is that the word *sapiential* needs to be understood more broadly. It refers not only to knowledge, to revelation (the term so emphasized by Bultmann), but to the embodied form of revelation—God's down-to-earth providence, a providence which complements creation. It is to this that the bread refers—God's loving providence in Jesus, a loving providence which is remembered in the eucharist. In other words, as the bread which a parent prepares for a small child is in some way a symbol of the entire loving process of providing for that child, so "the bread of God" refers to all that God does for humans.

This proposed shift of emphasis—from the word "sapiential" to the idea of God's providence—is somewhat similar to the proposal, made in the introductory chapters of this study, that the gospel is organized on the basis of time and space. These latter categories, of time and space, did not take away from the observations that others had made about the gospel's emphasis on days, feasts, and places. Rather they went behind those observations and set them on a more basic footing.

The purpose of the discourse is not only to confirm the existence of such a providence, but above all to describe the way in which it may be received by humans. The child may kick away the meal, and the grown human may kick against life, against the flesh-and-blood reality of a crucifixion-related providence. But for those who will receive it—through believing in it and through full acceptance of its flesh and blood—there is an increasing awareness of something that is loving, and thus an increasing growth in intimacy.

It is true, of course, that the discourse never speaks explicitly of a loving providence. The clear emphasis on a loving Christ-centered providence and on a response of love does not gain much prominence until the later stages of the gospel. (It is with such an idea that chaps. 13–21 open and close—cf. 13:1, 21:15–17.) But is is towards establishing that central thesis that the gospel is building, and it is appropriate, given the gradualness with which the text generally unfolds, that at this stage Jesus speaks in a way that is somewhat veiled or parabolic.

That the text really is speaking of such a providence and of the response to it is indicated by several factors: (1) the context of the preceding day, (2) the context of the preceding chapters, (3) the context of the meaning of wisdom, and above all, (4) the text itself and its structure.

1. *The context of the preceding day (6:1–21).* The essential meaning of 6:1–21 is that, through Jesus, God provides. This does not mean that God must cater to one's political plans, but it does mean that in the basic moments of life, whether on the grassy mountain or in the buffeting darkness, there is, for those who will to receive it, generous provision from God.

But the two parts of the chapter (vv 1–21 and 22–71) form a literary unity (Crossan, 1983). Just as the discourse in chap. 5 (5:16–47) consisted to some degree of a commentary on the preceding narrative concerning the sick man (5:1–15), so in chap. 6, the later part of the chapter involves an elaboration of certain elements of the narrative which precedes.

Without attempting to be exhaustive, one may note the following points of continuity between 6:1–21 and the subsequent discourse.

The introduction to the multiplication account, with its references to crossing the sea and to the great crowd following Jesus (6:1–4), is echoed in the introductory picture of the crowd which crosses the sea seeking Jesus (6:22–24). As noted earlier, both texts are geographic puzzles.

The early part of the multiplication account, in which Jesus encounters the very limited outlook of Philip and Andrew (6:5–9), is echoed by the way in which, during the dialogue at the beginning of the discourse, Jesus encounters and reveals other limited preoccupations (6:25–33).

The later part of the multiplication account, in which Jesus takes charge and, having given thanks (*eucharistēsas*), feeds everyone with such care (6:10–13: has them sit down in plentiful grass; feeds them well; makes sure nothing perishes) is reflected in various ways in what Jesus says about himself and the bread of life — he feeds people, makes sure they do not perish, and does so in a way which evokes something of the eucharist (cf. 6:35–58, esp. vv 35, 39, 51–58).

The reaction of those who crudely misinterpret the multiplication (6:14–15) is echoed in various negative reactions to the discourse (cf. 6:26,41,52,60,66; see, for instance, the tone of violence in vv 15 and 52, and the use of *houtos,* "this person," in vv 14, 42, 53).

The picture of the buffeted disciples receiving Jesus in his awesome identity (6:16–21) is echoed in the final tense scene in which the twelve accept Jesus as the Holy One of God (6:60–71, esp. v 69).

The essential point is that, if the discourse is built on 6:1–21, then the providence theme which pervades 6:1–21 is bound to be important to the discourse.

2. *The context of the preceding chapters.* At various stages in chaps. 2–5 Jesus is shown not only as meeting people and providing for them, but as doing so in an atmosphere or way which suggests care or love. The wine is provided at a wedding (2:1–11). The discourse to Nicodemus, in explaining God's plan, begins its climactic section by speaking explicitly of God's parentlike love in his son Jesus (3:16). The suggestion of a weddinglike love is taken up in varied form both in the baptizing scene which tells of all the people coming, bridelike, to

Jesus (3:22–36, esp. 3:26–29) and in the betrothal-like scene at the well (4:1–42). Furthermore, the suggestion of a parent-child love is taken up both in the healing of the official's son (4:43–54, esp. 4:49) and in the imagery used to describe God working through Jesus (5:19–20). In other words, there is a message of a constant reaching out of love to those who will to receive. The problem in chap. 5 is the refusal of willingness and the refusal of God's love (5:40, 42).

Given such a context, and given that chap. 6 is in close literary unity with this context—the discourse has strong echoes of Nicodemus and the Samaritan woman, and its structure follows that of chap. 5—it seems likely that the same themes should be found in the bread of life discourse.

3. *The context of the wisdom literature.* The notion of a caring providence may at first seem far from the sapiential interpretation, but it is precisely in the sapiential background, in what is sometimes called the wisdom literature, that such an idea is highlighted. Von Rad (1972, 166–76) emphasizes this at length, and at one point (169) expresses it as follows:

> If there was, somewhere in Israel, a surrender, verging on the mystical, of man to the glory of existence, then it is to be found in these texts which can speak of such a sublime bond of love between man and the divine mystery of creation. Here man throws himself with delight on a meaning which rushes towards him; he uncovers a mystery which was already on its way to him in order to give itself to him.

There is a sense, therefore, in which what is being proposed here is not new. Rather it is bringing out the full implications of the sapiential interpretation. Jesus' discourse is a call to receive all that God is doing for people, a call to surrender to the God-given glory of existence.

4. *The text.* When the text is divided according to the fourfold structure proposed earlier (i.e., at vv 25, 34, 41, and 52), then a reasonable case can be made that this is a unified discourse in which Jesus is talking parabolically about the giving and receiving of God's caring providence, and in which the four sections reflect four advancing stages of union or intimacy.

Before commenting on the text in detail it is useful to give a summary of the main points. In section 1 (vv 25–33), in the opening dialogue which is rather like that with the Samaritan woman (4:7–15), Jesus tries to break through certain human barriers and to propose the basic ideas of giving (giving bread) and believing. At this point, which is one of initial contact, ideas and images of union are minimal.

It is in section 2 (vv 34–40), when the question of human barriers has already been dealt with, that Jesus makes his foundational statement about God's providence. He speaks of God as one who wills to save and give life, and as one who for that purpose has invited people to come to Jesus. The implied image is that of a feast which is sponsored by God and presented by Jesus who is the bread of life.

At this point in the discourse the idea of union is present, but it is tentative and is expressed negatively—the one who comes shall not hunger, shall not be cast out, shall not perish. The implied image is rather like that of a person who has become interested in another and who takes the tentative but crucial step of coming to the other's house for a meal. And there the person is not rejected. Not too much is said about the degree of unity which is achieved within the house, but at least the visitor is not thrown out. Furthermore, Jesus goes on to say that the believer, the visitor so to speak, will never be thrown out. It is the Father's will that such a believer be raised up on the last day (6:38–40).

In section 3 (vv 41–51), against the background of Jews preoccupied by the question of human descent and relationship, Jesus moves from discussing the foundational aspects of God's providence to summarizing its central ingredient: the way in which God draws people, teaches them, and thus builds with them the one relationship which is really crucial.

At this point the idea of union is quite developed—it involves drawing and hearing, teaching and learning. The union or communication which is pictured in these words is profoundly spiritual and there is nothing quite equal to it in the preceding parts of the discourse. It is a distinct step forward. The visitor has, so to speak, not only been admitted to the house but has also been drawn to share in the spirit of the host.

In section 4 (vv 52–59), against the background of Jews who reject one another—they are pictured as fighting—Jesus speaks of the final and most difficult ingredient of God's providence: the total acceptance (eating and drinking) of Jesus' full humanity (flesh and blood)—including his death. What makes this really hard to take is that it implies the full acceptance of one's own humanity and death. It comes, however, as the final stage of a providence which seeks, above all, to give life, and which, even in death, continues to do so.

At this point the imagery of union reaches a high point: The acceptance of the final aspect of God's Jesus-centered providence leads to nothing less than mutual indwelling (6:56–57).

When the discourse is over, the first reaction is to say that it is difficult to accept. Like Paul's emphasis on the crucifixion, it is a scandal (6:60–61, 1 Cor 1:23). But, in a message which echoes that which was once given to Nicodemus, Jesus effectively says that with the help of the Spirit it can be done (6:63,65; 3:5–8; cf. 3:16–21), and even though Judas' impending treachery heralds the coming of the cross (6:64,70–71), and thus darkens further the shadow of approaching death, still, even while standing in that shadow, Peter manages in the name of the twelve to perceive in Jesus the holiness of God. In other words, even when death looms so does God.

This is the essence, the perception, even in the darkest moments of life, of the presence of a life-giving providence.

Insofar as the entire discourse (including the disciples' acceptance of the holy) portrays a picture of advancing union between the divine and the human, it develops the prologue's initial idea of the increasing intertwining of the (poetic) Word with (prosaic) flesh.

Linked to the essence of the discourse, to its emphasis on the perceiving of providence, there appears to be another factor—the church. Obviously, as elsewhere in the gospel, the actual word is not used, but it is striking, within chap. 6, that the two climactic moments of perceiving the divine occur in situations which evoke the church—in the boat (6:16–21), and when Peter acts as representative of the twelve (6:67–69). Hence, while one can hardly say that the bread of God is the society of the church—St. Augustine's idea (cf. Schnackenburg, 2:66) —it would appear that it is particularly through the church, despite all its failings (one of the twelve is a devil and Peter too will fail), that the providence of God becomes known to people and thus becomes for them sustaining bread.

In any case, the essential conclusion seems warranted. On the basis of the text and the various contexts, a reasonable case can be made that the discourse is primarily concerned with the idea of a caring providence which culminates in physical death and which seeks at every stage, but particularly as death approaches, to impart life and evoke love.

The text is also eucharistic. It is set in the context of a multiplication account which has a eucharistic coloring and—regardless of how one interprets the variations in the manuscripts—it is with a reference to that multiplication account that the introduction to the discourse begins (". . . where they ate the bread," 6:23). It is likewise with a eucharistic coloring that the discourse concludes (cf. esp. 6:51c, 53, "give[n] . . . for the life of the world. . . . Unless you eat . . . drink . . .'').

In view of the unity of the text, carefully crafted as it is around the central idea of God's providence, it does not make sense to say that one part of the text is eucharistic and that another is not. Obviously, in some parts eucharistic language is more in evidence, but this language, even though localized, pertains to the whole. When decorating a house, for instance, one cannot put a particular color on the end windows at either end of the front of the house without affecting the overall appearance. Such is the case with the discourse, and the effect is heightened by intermittent references, in every section of the discourse, to the primary eucharistic ingredient—bread. The entire text, therefore, has a eucharistic flavor.

This literary phenomenon makes theological sense. The idea of eucharist—of giving thanks—is inherently bound to that of the entirety of God's providence. It is because of all that God has done and provided that one gives thanks. Quite apart from an explicit faith in church dogma, the experience of life can lead people to a state where they feel the need to thank someone for life. Eucharist without a sense of providence is meaningless. And providence without eucharist is incomplete. The evangelist, in speaking parabolically of God's providence, has added the element which rounds it off.

The eucharistic coloring helps also to bridge a time gap. When Jesus, the embodiment of God's providence, is no longer physically present, the eucharist is one of the ways which helps to bring to mind the ever present reality of that providence. It is appropriate, therefore, that the evangelist, in speaking of providence, should give to it a coloring of the ceremony through which it is often brought to mind.

Detailed Comment

[6:22–24] Introduction: The eager crowd and the enigmatic appearing of the boat. The initial picture here is that of a stranded crowd. On the day after the multiplication and the disciples' sea-crossing, the crowd stood at the other side of the sea and saw that there was only one boat and that it had already been taken by the disciples. As many writers have noted, the text seems illogical: how could they see a boat that had departed the previous day? One thing is clear: they were marooned.

At this point, however, just when the situation may have seemed hopeless, something extraordinary happened: "Boats came." It is not said how many, but there seems to have been no shortage, for without any further problems they got into them and came to Capernaum seeking Jesus.

As mentioned earlier, the sudden appearance of so many boats has led Wellhausen (30) and Bultmann (217) to speak of a *deus ex machina*. While such a comment may not be deserved, it has an advantage—it helps to alert the reader to the startling nature of what is being said.

Concerning the nature and origin of these boats the text says only that they came "from Tiberias," and—following the better-attested and more difficult reading—that they came "near the place where they ate the bread." This reference to Tiberias, however, instead of solving the problem, adds to it. Tiberias (on the southwest of the sea) was well removed both from Capernaum (on the northwest) and from the location usually associated with the multiplication (on the east). In other words, the mysterious boats came from a place which, in the present shape of the narrative, is quite unrelated. Besides, how could boats be supplied for so many people—for thousands apparently? It has already been noted also, both that there is an apparent illogicality in the opening verse—the crowd, with strange perception, saw the boat that was gone (v 22)—and that there is an apparent contradiction in Jesus' later statement to the crowd that they had not seen signs (6:26, cf. 6:14). Hence, Kysar (96), for instance, refers to the text as "this extraordinarily confusing passage." The variations in the manuscripts suggest that the copyists also were perplexed by it.

Diverse attempts have been made to reshape the passage into coherent history. It has been said that the extraordinary perception of the one boat (6:22) is badly stated, that "what is meant is that on the next day they remembered that on the day before they had observed only one boat there" (Brown, 257). The introduction of Tiberias has been accounted for by saying, despite the apparent reference (6:1) to the east coast, that the multiplication actually occurred near Tiberias, on the west coast. And the description of the crowd crossing has been accounted for in various ways, particularly by suggesting that "the crowd" does not refer to the entire five thousand but only to a small number, and by saying that many of the crowd could have come to Capernaum by walking, by journeying around the shore. As for the request for a sign—so strange if it comes from the crowd which had seen the multiplication—that can be seen as coming from some natives of Capernaum who had gathered, along with the previous day's crowd, to hear Jesus, but who had not themselves been at the multiplication (cf. Brown, 258–59).

In itself, such a reconstruction is eminently coherent and plausible. But—apart from implying that the writing was bungled—it breaks the foundational laws of interpretation: it builds on hypothetical data rather than the data supplied by the text.

The interpretative method which seeks to refashion the text forcibly into coherent history is particularly emphasized by Brown, but it is Brown also who supplies the initial data for an alternative approach. He indicates that the text's opening phrase, "The next day" (v 22), however historical it may seem at first, "need not be a real chronological indication" (Brown, 257); on the contrary, its purpose may be artistic—"to give the chapter a unified literary structure." More significantly, Brown (259) also notes that to a significant degree the character of the text is theological. As he expresses it: "In vv 22–24 there is a deepening of the theological motifs that were found in the multiplication scene."

It is this basic insight which begins to make sense of the text. The plight of the crowd, stranded at the other side of the sea, takes up the theme, found in the multiplication scene, of the great crowd's need—its need of healing and of food (6:1–9). More importantly, the unexplained appearance of so many boats is a variation on the supplying of bread (6:10–13). The astonishment of Wellhausen and Bultmann is well justified: the supplying of boats, no less than the supplying of bread, is a considerable miracle.

Nor is this connection—of the boats with the bread—one that is simply being imposed. The text itself explicitly links the two. It describes the boats as being "near the place where they ate the bread"—a designation which, geographically speaking, is quite obscure, but which, precisely through its geographical obscurity, highlights what is clear—that there is some connection between the boats and the bread.

The further clue, that the boats were "from Tiberias," likewise make sense if "Tiberias" is seen, not primarily from a geographic viewpoint, but—in a way similar to its use in the multiplication story (6:1)—as a way of evoking the empire, the world. Thus the boats are to be connected both with the bread and with the world at large.

It is now possible to attempt a more systematic unraveling of the entire passage. If justice is to be done both to the text's enigmatic character and also to its theology, then it seems that it should be regarded primarily, not as a narrative which is factual or historical, but as one which is parabolic. For it is precisely in a parable that one generally finds a combination of enigmatic narrative and theology. Nor is it novel to suggest that a gospel text which does not present itself explicitly as a parable should, in fact, be regarded as parabolic. With regard to Mark at least, scholars have noted that, quite apart from the obvious parable stories, the text is significantly parabolic. (E.g., cf. Kelber, 1983, 214–20.)

However, it is one thing to indicate that a narrative is to be treated as a parable. It is another to interpret that parable correctly. The interpretation which follows may not be altogether correct, and it is certainly incomplete, but its general approach seems valid and its basic interpretation reasonably accurate.

The boat is the church or some (Jewish?) aspect of it. The plausibility of a reference to the church is strengthened by the fact that chap. 6 emphasizes the role of the disciples, including the role of the twelve and of Peter (6:1–21,60–70). The other boats, the boats from Tiberias, are those which come from elsewhere to form or join the church. (Incidentally, the phrase *alla . . . ploia* is ambiguous. It may mean either "But boats . . ." or "Other boats. . . ." Ac-

cording to Haenchen (1:280), "the word *alla* is not to be taken to mean 'but';
rather it is to be understood as 'other.' " However, even if it does not, the text is
actually talking about other boats.) The combined references, to "a boat" and to
other "boats." prepares the way, within John's narrative, for the references to
"the sheep" and the "other sheep" which together are to form one flock (John
10:14–16). In other words, an allusion to the Gentiles, which most commentators
see in the reference to the other sheep, is already found, in a more veiled form,
in the reference to the boats from Tiberias.

The bread refers in some way (secondarily at least) to the eucharistic bread—
a fact writers have often noted—and it is associated with the boats from Tiberias
because the eucharistic bread is a sign of the unity of the church, of the gathering
of many into one (cf. 1 Cor 10:16–17: "The bread which we break, it is not a
sharing in the body of Christ. Because there is one loaf, we who are many form
one body . . ."). In other words the relationship between the bread and the boat(s)
is a variation on the relationship between the eucharistic bread and the body of
Christ.

The apparent illogicality of perceiving something which ordinarily could not
be perceived (v 22, "they saw that there was no other boat there but one"), may,
perhaps, have something to do with the extraordinary perception which should
surround the eucharistic bread and the one body which it signifies. St. Paul in this
context speaks of the need for perceptiveness and memory (1 Cor 10:15–17; 11:24–
25, 28–29) and it is precisely these elements, particularly that of memory, which
the text suggests. As Brown (257) notes, "what is meant is that on the next day
they remembered. . . ."

The picture of "the crowd" which crosses to Capernaum seeking Jesus (6:24)
—a picture which has some echoes of the approach of the first disciples (1:36–
38)—refers to the coming of the Gentiles. The same divine providence which had
supplied the bread now supplies the boats which will enable them to join with
"the Jews" in becoming "disciples."

They will no longer be mentioned as "crowd"—the word does not occur
again in chap. 6. With mathematical precision and balance, the text gives just two
instances of the words "crowd" and "Jews" (cf. 6:22,24,41,52). After that the
references are to "disciples" and, finally, to "the twelve" (cf. 6:60, 61, 66, 67,
70, 71). This transition in language—from "the crowd" and "the Jews" to "the
disciples" and "the twelve"—is not due to confusion. It is a way of suggesting,
even through the fabric of the text, that Gentiles (the crowd) and Jews are absorbed into discipleship and into the unity that is implied in "the twelve." Thus,
even in what at first may appear as confused details, there are indications of what
the narrative is all about—the divine providence which brings Gentiles and Jews
into unity with one another and into union with God.

It is useful to note that the structure and thought of this three-verse introduction is like an obscure counterpoint to the corresponding three-verse introduction
in chap. 5 (5:16–18). In that text it was said first and last (vv 16 and 18), and in
rather repetitious language, that the Jews "persecuted" and "sought" Jesus. In
6:22–24 also, again in rather repetitious language, it is said first and last (vv 22
and 24) that the crowd missed and sought Jesus. In both cases the repetitious

phrase (5:19, 6:24) involves an intensification of what was said earlier (in 5:17, 6:22). But while the seeking of the Jews is to kill, that of the crowd (the Gentiles apparently) is more open-minded. The conclusion which thus emerges is that while 5:17–19 showed the Jews as becoming more and more antagonistic toward Jesus, 6:22–24 shows the crowd (the Gentiles) as becoming more perceptive and interested.

Why exactly this particular text (vv 22–24) should be so unusually enigmatic, so parablelike, is not clear. It seems probable, however, that, to some degree, it is due to its context—to the fact that it is introducing and summarizing one of the most enigmatic of all realities—the mysterious providence which guides the world, which calls the diverse groups into union (cf. Romans 9–11, esp. 11:33–35; Eph 1:1–4:16). The parabolic language is also due in part to the fact that the text which is being introduced (6:25–59—unlike most of 5:19–47) is itself heavily parabolic.

It is within the context of this universal call to divine union that the discourse develops.

[6:25–33] The discourse—Section 1: The barrier-breaking conversation and the prospect of believing. At the beginning and end of the discourse there are two stage-setting details: "on the other side of the sea" (v 25a), and "in a synagogue teaching in Capernaum" (v 59). "In a synagogue" suggests the Jews. And Capernaum, being a border town, and having been used in chaps. 2–4 as the extremity of the journey from Jerusalem (cf. 4:43–54), suggests the nearby presence of the Gentiles. But the concrete reference to a Capernaum synagogue is withheld, and so it is the other, rather haunting, detail which sets the mood: "on the other side of the sea."

The sense of something haunting is increased by the opening question: "When have you been here?" The unusual phrasing manages both to ask a very ordinary question ("When did you come here?"), and at the same time to evoke something of the distant origin of Jesus ("How long have you been here?"; cf. Kysar, 97). In a context where Jesus was last seen in a theophany (6:19–20) and where it will soon be said that "he knew *from the beginning*" (6:64), such a haunting evocation is appropriate. There is present, therefore, something greater than what is immediate. Those who speak to Jesus, however, are unaware of that. Their minds are set on their stomachs.

During this dialogue the speakers (i.e. Jesus' interlocutors) are not explicitly named. In the early part of the conversation, the language, concerning food and work, is of a kind suitable to a Gentile audience and, in fact, recalls the food-and-work text in which Jesus alludes to the Gentile mission (4:31–38, esp. 4:31–34). In the later part of the dialogue, however, when reference is made to "our fathers" and "Moses," the conversation is more suited to Jews. Thus, concerning the speakers, as concerning Jesus, there is a certain ambiguity.

As mentioned earlier, the question-and-answer structure of this scene is strongly reminiscent of that involving the Samaritan woman (Brown, 267). Furthermore, in both texts, the three utterances of the opening speaker(s) become longer—those of Jesus in chap. 4 (4:7,10,13–14), and those of Jesus' interlocutors in this scene (6:25,28,30–31).

As for Jesus himself in this scene, his balancing "Gentile" and "Jewish" statements (vv 26–27 and 32–33) are of virtually equal length (46 words and 42); and both begin with "Amen, amen, I say to you. . . ." But between these two statements there is a further brief reply which, is central both in position and content (v 29): "This is the work of God, that you believe in him whom he has sent."

The resemblance of the people to the Samaritan woman emerges in their attitude. As she, with her mind bent on drawing water, approached a pattern-breaking spouse, so do they, all preoccupied with bread, approach a mystery of providential love.

The first reality which Jesus helps them to face is that of themselves. With a solemn, "Amen, amen, I say to you"—a phrase which "signals a declaration of divine authority" (Kysar, 97)—he tells them the nature and motives of their actions. Though they come to him, their lives are superficial. They may have regarded the multiplication of loaves as a sign (6:14), but their idea of sign is so empty that it simply does not count. And so Jesus tells them that they have not, in fact, seen signs. For them, all that really counts is bread.

Having said that, however, Jesus proceeds to build on it. These people are preoccupied with working for food. Very well then, he will talk about working for food. But he gives the idea a radical development: "Do not work for the food which perishes, but for the food which abides to eternal life. . . ."

Thus in a single stroke he challenges them to set their sights on a higher goal. The verb "to work" (*ergazomai*), as well as referring to physical work, is also used of moral effort (cf. Acts 10:35; Rom 2:10, 13:10; Gal 6:10), a moral effort which, in this text, continues the work of creation (it continues the creation "work" of chap. 5, esp. 5:17).

Lest the goal seem too loftly, however, and the required effort too great, Jesus immediately adds an important qualification: in a real sense the food in question is sheer gift. It is something that is given by the Son of humanity, the one on whom God has set the divine seal (v 27b). The text is striking in its emphasis on the basic ideas of humanity and God. (The use of "God" as the last word of the Greek sentence is highly unusual; cf. Schnackenburg, 2:38.) Part at least of what the passage seems to be talking about is a built-in connection between humanity (or human beings) and God. To bear God's seal is to bear something of God, to be in some way God-like, particularly to carry within oneself something of God's communicative (witnessing) Spirit. (For discussion, cf. Schnackenburg, 2:38. Note also, Brown, 261.) That is the seal which Jesus as Son of humanity bears, and it is that also which is given to those who accept the Son of humanity and all that that God-based humanity entails. Thus, however far away people may sometimes feel—far from God and far from eternal life—they are closer to God than they realize. The task may seem daunting, yet they are made for it. It has been sealed into them; it is in the genes of their souls.

So what do they need to do? What is this work (v 28)? When the speakers respond to Jesus they seem to be still thinking on a superficial level—that of external work. Jesus retains the word "work" but gives it a new meaning: "The work of God . . . is . . . that you believe in him whom he has sent." Thus instead of making a dichotomy between working and believing (a dichotomy between "works" and "faith" such as one finds in the epistles of Paul and James), the evangelist blends the two concepts: believing is working, indeed a high form of working—particularly because it opens the way for the working of God (Brown, 265).

At this point in the dialogue, therefore, the basic dynamics have been described: to those preoccupied with eating to the full, God offers a higher possibility; and on their part there is required a process of believing in the one whom God has sent.

Before the discourse can develop, however, a further unbalanced preoccupation is brought to the fore—the need for a sign (v 30). Such a demand was familiar among the Jews (cf. 1 Cor 1:11; Schnackenburg, 2:39) and had already been made of Jesus when he cleansed the temple (2:18). Now, as Jesus speaks of believing, they insist on something they can see (". . . that we may see, and believe you"). After all, they already have a spectacular bread-related tradition— that of the manna eaten by their fathers. And they quote scripture to back it: "He gave them bread from heaven . . ." (v 31).

This is formidable opposition. In a few sentences they have brought together from their established tradition a range of elements which could not be surpassed easily. Thus, just as the Samaritan woman asked Jesus if he was "greater than our father Jacob who gave us the well" (4:12), so once again he is being challenged by the tradition. What can he do to match the manna?

As at the beginning of the dialogue when he responded to the preoccupation with eating, so now, in responding to the preoccupation with tradition, Jesus' reaction is not so much to deny his listeners' viewpoint as to seek to bring them beyond it, to raise them to a new level. He accepts what they say but gives it a radical development. The once-upon-a-time bread of Moses has given way to the here-and-now true bread (v 32). And then, as they may be wondering what that means, he gives them a description of the bread of God which goes far beyond their desert-bound tradition: "For the bread of God is that which comes down from heaven and gives life to the world."

With this final phrase, "life to the world," the dialogue touches a new level. Jesus has been found by those who are engrossed in their diverse preoccupations. He listens to them and invites them to become aware of more. He speaks to them of opening out to God, the God whose seal is on (the Son of) humanity. And finally he lays before them an alluring reality: that of God giving life to the world.

[6:34–40] The discourse—Section 2: Jesus brings from heaven the feast of God's life-saving will; the need to believe, and some tentative images of union. As soon as the initial dialogue has helped to identify some major mental barriers, the discourse goes on, in its second part, to set forth more clearly the essence of its positive message. To some degree this scene is an elaboration of the previous scene's central statement about "the work of God" (6:29). The present text may be placed under two complementary headings—concerning God's feast and concerning people's response.

1. *God's feast.* Among modern commentators, it appears to be Lindars (258–62, esp. 261) who has best indicated—though in a low-key way—the fundamental nature of this scene. What Jesus is talking about here is "the universality of God's plan of salvation" and "the purpose of his Incarnation" (Linders, 261). Thus just as the dialogue with Nicodemus soon turned into a discourse on the basic truths of God's plan of salvation, so also here.

Three times Jesus speaks of *"the will"* of the Father or of the one who sent him, and that will is always focused, whether directly or through Jesus, toward some aspect of salvation, of life-giving (vv 37–40). It is a salvation which is here and now ("realized eschatology"), but it is also directed to the future ("future eschatology"), and it is at this point that there begins the refrain about raising people "on the last day" (vv 39–40; cf. vv 44, 54). What emerges is a picture of a God who actively wills to endow people with life and who carries out that life-giving providence through Jesus—through the one who, as he says, has "come down from heaven not to do my own will, but the will of him who sent me" (v 38).

This extraordinary life-giving process is envisaged, implicitly at least, as a meal, as a feast presented by Jesus. He is divine, but he is also like bread: "I am (*Egō eimi*) the bread of life" (v 35; cf. Schnackenburg, 2:43). And then, in "beautifully balanced clauses" (Lindars, 259), he promises those who come to him that he will take away their hunger and thirst. Later, when he says concerning those who come to him that he will not cast them out, "the best explanation of this vivid phrase [about casting out] . . . is . . . the metaphor of the banquet" (Lindars, 261). Those who come to Jesus, therefore, will not be cast out from his feast, from God's feast.

2. *The response.* But there is, of course, a problem. Not everyone wants to come to this feast, not everyone wants to believe. Among modern commentators it is particularly Schnackenburg (2:45–48) who has highlighted this other, complementary, aspect of the text. In fact, he puts most of this section under the heading: "The Need for Faith."

The need to believe had already been mentioned in the center of the opening dialogue (v 29). Now, in what looks like a counter-balancing (chiastic?) structure, it is referred to first and last in the second section (vv 35–36, 40). A similar phenomenon was noticed in the structure of the first two sections of the discourse in chap. 5 (5:19–23 and 5:24–29). The idea which in the first section occurs in the center—that of the Son's giving life to humans (5:21)—in the second section occurs at the beginning and end (5:24–25,28–29). In any case, whatever the details of structure, the need to believe certainly is emphasized.

The text begins with an image of incipient believing. Those who speak to Jesus address him as *Kyrie* and ask for "this bread" (v 34). But *Kyrie* is ambiguous ("Sir" or divine "Lord") and, as in the case of the similar request by the Samaritan woman (4:15), they do not seem to have grasped what it is that Jesus is offering.

Believing is then compared to moving towards someone. Such is the implication of the parallel between "the one who comes to me" and "the one who
believes in me." The accompanying picture of Jesus satisfying hunger and thirst,
suggests "that the deepest, most elemental needs of humanity find their fulfillment
in Christ" (Kysar, 101).

Seeing does not lead to believing, at least not necessarily. At the beginning of
this section it is said that those who have seen Jesus do not believe (v 36). This
superficial seeing would seem to be akin to the superficial seeing of signs (v 26),
in other words akin to seeing them in a way that misses their significance. But the
conclusion of this section does, in fact, link believing with seeing, presumably
with a perceptive seeing (v 40, "everyone who sees the Son and believes in
him"). (At a later stage the gospel will speak of something which is still better—
believing without any form of seeing; for discussion, see Brown, 530–31).

What is important is that neither the feast, nor even the seeing of the feast, is
enough. There must be an engagement with it, a process of coming to it, a believing.

Once such a process of believing is present, however, a form of union begins
to develop. At this stage the idea of union is expressed through negatives—the
one who comes or believes shall not hunger or thirst, shall not be cast out, and,
finally, shall not perish (vv 35, 37, 39). Even if such negatives are dramatic
understatements—a form of litotes—they indicate a restraint of expression, and
they give to the picture of union a form that is tentative.

**[6:41–51] The discourse—Section 3: A more developed idea of union; a por-
trait of the essence of internal union with God.**   While section 1 emphasized
the removing of human obstacles, and section 2 the basic plan of God, it is in
section 3 that the human and divine really come together. This is a picture of
inner harmony.

One way to regard this text is to say that it is a reworking, in the Johannine
mold, of the prophetic idea of the new covenant, a covenant in which people
depend primarily not on each other, but on the internal dialogue that comes from
God (cf. esp. Jer 31:31–34). The actual text, which is quoted here, and which to
some extent dominates the section, is just a brief phrase—"And they shall all be
taught by God"—but it is taken from the climactic chapters of Second Isaiah (Isa
54:13), with all that that entails concerning emphasis on the transcendent word
which comes down to the heart of human reality. It has been seen by a number
of commentators as similar to Jeremiah's idea of a new covenant (cf. Brown, 277;
Schnackenburg, 2:51; Lindars, 264).

What is at stake is a phenomenon which is frequently spoken of, particularly
by psychologists, artists, and theologians, but which is very difficult to articulate:
the fact that the human spirit, if it is to mature fully, must have a quality of
independence, a positive solitude in which it becomes aware both of itself and of
a higher spirit, God. It is something of which St. Paul speaks (especially when
speaking on freedom in Galatians 1–4), and it is found in a unique way in Jesus.

In the present text the uniqueness of Jesus receives considerable emphasis. In
terms which recall the prologue and the discourse to Nicodemus, it is said that it

is he alone who has seen the Father, that he is the one who has come down from heaven (6:41,42,46,51; cf. 1:1–2,18; 3:13). The implication is of a unique intimacy with God.

But the emphasis is not on Jesus alone. The text speaks also of how others communicate with God. The previous section (vv 34–40) had spoken of God's will to save, to give life. Now comes the developed form of that process. Toward the center of communication which is Christ, the Father "draws" people (v 44). Lindars (263) interprets this drawing as "inner attraction" and writes: "There are several classic passages in the OT which express the attractive power of the love of God, notably Jer 31:3 (where the LXX uses John's word) and Hos 11:4." This incidentally would imply that both v 44 ("draws") and v 45 ("all . . . taught by God") are reminiscent of Jeremiah 31.

And while God is drawing, people are responding. Apart from referring to inner teaching, Jesus speaks also of people "hearing and learning" from the Father, and then of their coming to him (v 45b). The picture, therefore, is of people being drawn into communication with the one who has seen God. It is a picture of wholeness, and perhaps it is also related to mysticism (Lindars, 264).

Preceding this positive message is the contrasting picture of the Jews, who murmer against Jesus (vv 41–43). The sudden reference to "the Jews," in a place so far from Jerusalem, may seem surprising, but it suits the presentation of the message. Apart from the fact that their murmuring provides a foil for the image of increasing communication, what they say acts as a complement to what is being said by Jesus: he is, from one point of view, a very ordinary person; they know his father and mother. Jesus does not contradict them, nor does he insist, if his message is to hold true, that the Jews must agree with him. Inner maturity and communication with God is not gained through dependence on parents and authorities. It does not matter who his parents are or what the (Jewish) authorities say. His most basic identity, and the basic identity he gives to others, does not depend on being taught or approved by humans, but on being drawn and taught by God.

This communication with God is not something which leads to any form of frozen immobility. In the final verses of this section (vv 47–51) the emphasis is on life and living. Life and "to live" are used a total of five times, and it is with the word *life* that the Greek text concludes. This emphasis on life is introduced with a solemn "Amen, amen . . ." and then it is said not just that the believer should have eternal life (cf. v 40) but that the believer actually has it (v 47). Again, as earlier (v 35), Jesus says "I am the bread of life" (v 48), but the emphasis in this later instance appears to fall on the later part of the phrase— "the bread of life." The manna is recalled, but only to state that those who ate it died—and thus to highlight the contrast with the bread which Jesus gives (vv 49– 50).

Paradoxically, however, this repeated emphasis on life is accompanied by intimations concerning Jesus' death. Such is the implication of saying that his flesh is to be given for (*hyper*) the life of the world (v 51c; cf. Bultmann, 235). Thus it is through the surrendering of life that life comes. With this enigmatic thought the way is prepared for the final section of the discourse.

[6:52–59] The discourse—Section 4: Coming down from the mountain of spiritual union and living out the flesh-and-blood reality of human life. It is hardly an accident that, within the NT, pictures of intense spiritual union or strength are frequently followed by insistence on the practicalities and limitations of life. The climactic hymn on love and union which occurs at the end of Romans 8 gives way, after an interlude, to practical advice and plans (Romans 12–16). A similar transition occurs between the powerful prayer at the end of Ephesians 3 and the exhortation which follows (Ephesians 4–6). Paul's intense insistence in Galatians on a God-centered faith and freedom is followed by an equal insistence on practical service, on bearing one another's burdens (Gal 5:13–chap. 6, esp. 6:2). And in 2 Corinthians the account of a heavenly vision is followed immediately by the account of the stubborn thorn in the flesh (2 Cor 12:1–10). It would also seem to be of significance that in the canonical text of Isaiah and Jeremiah, the lyrical high points which extol God's love (Isaiah 40–55, esp. 54–55; Jeremiah 30–31) are followed by texts dealing to a considerable extent with practical living (Isaiah 56–66) and with the harsh realities of life and death (Jeremiah 32–45). To some extent, of course, these transitions may be explained through theoretical conventions and historical circumstances but, whatever the reasons, they are present, and they would seem to be of help in understanding the transition which occurs towards the end of the discourse.

It could be objected, of course, that such transitions have nothing to do with the bread-of-life discourse, yet in the first part of chap. 6 (6:1–21), in the account of the day which provides the immediate context of the discourse, there is such a transition: the picture of reclining and eating on the grassy mountain gives way abruptly to the harsh reality of rowing through darkness and being buffeted by the storm. And in chap. 2 the scene of the wedding wine gave way to the ominous scene of the cleansing of the temple. Besides, any major sapiential statement, if it is to be genuinely wise, must turn to the more difficult aspects of life and death.

It is to the down-to-earth reality of life and death that section 4 of the discourse is addressed. The text speaks above all of Jesus' flesh and blood. ''Flesh and blood is a Hebraic way of speaking of the whole person and describing the earthly character of human life'' (Kysar, 107; cf. also Brown, 282; Lindars, 268; John 1:13; Matt 16:17). In this particular context ''flesh and blood'' refers also to death. Jesus says that he will give his flesh for (*hyper*) the life of the world (v 51) —a phrase which, as noted earlier, alludes to his death (Bultmann, 235). And the fact that the flesh and blood are spoken of as those of the Son of humanity (v 53) —a title which refers to Jesus as going through death and glory (Brown, 84)—is a further indication that ''flesh and blood'' is a way of speaking of the fullness of Jesus' earthly experience, the incarnation and passion, and indeed of the fullness of earthly experience as such. It is this earthbound experience, with all its limitations, that people are being asked to embrace.

Jesus himself, of course, led the way in embracing this existence. The Word had become human flesh. He then lived among us. He washed people's feet—a gesture which is about as expressive as any could be of embracing earthbound existence.

In this final section of the discourse the idea that earthbound existence must be embraced or received is spoken of in the language of eating and drinking. Scarcely any image could be more expressive of acceptance, of total receptivity. To eat is to receive (cf 6:6, 23). And it is precisely because drinking also is so expressive of acceptance that Jesus ends his life by drinking (John 19:30).

There is, of course, at the heart of this text a considerable paradox: to live, one must accept death-oriented limitation. It is reminiscent of glorying in weakness (2 Cor 12:9–10), of losing one's life in order to save it (Mark 8:35, cf. John 12:25), and it is related to the fact that some people are so preoccupied with death, are so set against it, that they never really live. It also related to looking squarely at the deadly serpent (3:14–15), and at the idea, put forward by philosophers as different as Plato and Heidegger, that it is only through the forthright grasping of death that one really understands life and becomes fully human (cf. O'Donoghue, 1986, 369).

In stark contrast to the idea of life-giving receptivity is the picture with which it begins—that of Jews fighting each other (v 52). Once again, as in section 3, the Jews provide a dramatic foil.

At the end of the section, they—or at least their ancestors—provide a further foil: of people who "ate and died." Jesus, however, is offering a food that gives eternal life (v 58).

What is essential is that the primary meaning of eating and drinking the flesh and blood is that of embracing the fullness of God's down-to-earth, Jesus-shaped, death-related providence.

But the language of eating flesh and drinking blood has other dimensions. It may, perhaps, have an overtone suggesting intimate union. More obvious, however, is the fact that it is quite revolting. Yet this revolting character is altogether appropriate in view of the fact that God's providence includes death. For death is revolting. Even Jesus as he came close to it found it difficult to take, and he asked that he not have to drink it (cf. esp. Matt 26:42). He went ahead, of course, and it is not insignificant that the final drink which he deliberately "received" is described as being bitter (John 19:30).

Yet, paradox of paradoxes, the language of eating flesh and drinking blood is also eucharistic. While this eucharistic coloring does not appear to be primary— no eucharistic text in the NT uses quite such stark imagery as "eating flesh" and "drinking blood" (they are generally more discreet or distant [cf. Mark 14:22, Matt 26:26, Luke 22:19, 1 Cor 11:24])—yet the eucharistic coloring is strong and significant. Thus, the horror of death is absorbed into the eucharist, into thanksgiving. In other words, the literary complexity of the text—it uses language which simultaneously encompasses revulsion and thanksgiving—is a way of indicating that the horror of death is swallowed up in thanksgiving. Thus, though from one point of view death remains immensely bitter, from another it is something one can accept with equanimity and—when it is set in the context of the fullness of God's life-giving providence—even with thanksgiving. It is when one's thanksgiving includes death that the idea of surrender to the glory of existence takes on further meaning. Such an approach—of thanksgiving even in the face of death— seems, in fact, to have been the attitude of the early Christians (cf. O'Donoghue, 1986, 368–69).

The primary effect of a full acceptance of this message is peace: "The one who feeds . . . abides in me . . ." (v 56). This picture is one of mutual indwelling and is "the climax of the discourse" (Lindars, 57), a climax which was prepared for, through a similar emphasis, in chap. 5 (5:37–38). It is a peace which is deepseated, for by living through Jesus one is also living ultimately through God (v 58).

[6:60–65] The reactions—Section 1: The difficulty of the message and the need to put it in the context both of the ascending of the Son of humanity and of the Spirit; the providence surrounding belief and unbelief. The teaching about death being swallowed up in new life was regarded by many as offensively fantastic (literally, "hard"; cf. Brown, 296; Barrett, 320) and murmur-inducingly scandalous (vv 60–61)—roughly the same reactions as those evoked by Paul's doctrine of the wisdom of the cross (1 Cor 1:18–25, esp. 1:23). Within the fourth gospel itself these reactions are like an elaboration and intensification of the way Nicodemus once reacted to a related teaching—that of new life through rebirth (3:4, 9; compare 3:3 and 6:53, "Amen, amen . . . unless one is born . . . unless you eat . . ."; cf. Lindars, 264, 267; Bornkamm, 1956).

When Jesus responds to this incredulity he does not deny that what he is teaching is difficult. Rather he places the difficulty in a higher context, a context in which it can be resolved. This higher context consists of the world of the spirit and the supernatural—a world that is first evoked in this text by the reference to Jesus' supernatural knowledge: "Jesus, knowing in himself this his disciples murmured . . ." (v 61; cf. Brown, 296). The implication of the phrasing is not only that Jesus is on a higher level, but that the murmuring disciples are not.

When Jesus speaks of this higher world his phrases are unusually cryptic—a mysteriousness which can be frustrating for the hurried reader but which is appropriate to what he is talking about.

He refers first of all to the possibility that the disciples will "see the Son of humanity ascending to where he was before" (v 62). The basic idea here is that Jesus has come from God and, through death and glorification—such is the implication of the title "Son of humanity"—will ascend back to God. If they can perceive this reality, if they can see how this human Jeus ascends to God, then— so runs the implied argument—they will also see how death is absorbed into greater life.

Obviously such a process might seem quite impossible, and therefore, apparently to counter the "It's impossible" reaction, Jesus reminds them of the world of the Spirit. It is through the Spirit, not through ordinary physical growth, that one passes from death to new life: "It is the Spirit that gives life; the flesh accomplishes nothing" (v 63a). It is in the Spirit, therefore, that Jesus ascends to where he was before.

And the Spirit is not limited to Jesus; he is not the only one who enters this elevated realm. Rather, the Spirit is made available also to the disciples, and therefore it is, in fact, possible for the disciples to grasp the reality of how Jesus' death is transformed into life. The way in which Jesus expresses this presence of the Spirit is extraordinarily low-key and cryptic. All he says is, "The words that I have spoken to you are spirit and life'' (v 63b). The implication, however, is that his words are spirit-bearing. (The Greek *pneuma,* of course, does not distinguish spirit and Spirit.) Despite the difficulty, therefore, the Spirit is present, at least in some sense, and so the message can be grasped.

"But," adds Jesus, "there are some of you who do not believe."

This entire scene, as well as echoing much of the discussion with Nicodemus (3:1–21), contains also a proleptic synthesis of the account of the post-resurrection events—Jesus' ascension back to God, the granting of the Spirit, and the failure of some to believe (20:17–29).

There has been much discussion of whether the need for spirit (v 63) applies to Jesus or to the disciples (see esp. Schnackenburg, 2:71–73). This way of posing this question, in either-or terms, does not seem to do justice to the text and to its broad context. The reference to the need for spirit (to the inability of the flesh to produce spiritual life, v 63), occurs midway between the emphasis on Jesus (v 62) and the growing emphasis on the disciples (v 64–65). This ambiguous midway position suits the complexity of the reality: flesh as such, whether that of Jesus or his disciples, cannot generate a higher form of life. All such generation needs spirit. There is need therefore both for Jesus to be spiritualized and also for the spirit to be granted to the disciples.

When the text says that the flesh accomplishes nothing (v 63) this does not mean that Jesus' flesh, the flesh which is to be eaten in the eucharist, is useless. The whole phenomenon of Jesus, his life and death, his flesh and blood, is already in contact with another dimension, that of spirit. (This other dimension is visualized as a place to which one ascends, but the movement is spiritual rather than spatial.) What is useless is flesh on its own, flesh which has no reference to spirit. Since the body which is consumed in the eucharist is that of a Jesus who has entered the realm of the spiritual, the eucharistic body is spiritualized.

To say that the eucharistic body is spiritualized does not make it less real, does not detract from the idea of the real presence. Obviously it does not have many of the qualities of an unspiritual body—it does not for instance, weigh so many pounds—but it is nonetheless real. A warm-hearted disposition, for instance, cannot be weighed or measured, yet it is real. All the more so, the spiritualized eucharistic body which contains within itself, in a transformed way, the full reality of Jesus' humanity. Once one enters the world of the spirit, the word "real" begins to take on a different meaning.

The sense of touching on another world is reinforced in the final lines of this section when Jesus is referred to as knowing "from the beginning" the identity both of those who would not believe and also of the one who would hand him over; and then he reiterates, as a kind of fulfillment of his own words, the idea that believing depends on God's giving (vv 64–65). The effect of these lines is, first of all, to break the normal bonds of time—he knew from the beginning, and he spoke in advance of the facts. The further effect is to gather disbelief and evil into the mystery of the divine knowing and giving.

Thus, in this section as a whole (vv 60–65) both believing and disbelief are brought together under God's spirit-filled guidance. Believing in death-into-life is difficult—yet within the context of the spirit it can be done. And disbelief is highly negative—yet it has in some way been incorporated into God's supra-temporal process of giving.

[6:66–71] The reactions—Section 2: The emergence, at the end, of a believing group, life-filled but fragile; an evoking of the church. The narrative could have ended with the summarizing statement about the dynamics of believing and not believing and about the mystery which surrounds them (vv 60–65). It would have made a good general conclusion. But the text goes on to speak of something more specific and down to earth—the emergence of the twelve and of Peter.

Though in some ways the text maintains continuity with what precedes, it is also sharply different. There had indeed been reference to hesitation and discontent among Jesus' hearers (esp. vv 41, 52, 60), but never before had anything been said about disciples going away. On the contrary, they had always been visualized as coming or following. In fact, the language of the departure is such —"many of his disciples," "going away," "walked with him no more"—that it is exactly the opposite of the process of coming to discipleship (cf. 1:35–39), a picture of reversal which breaks new ground. This sense of newness is even more pronounced in what follows. The twelve had never before been mentioned in this gospel, but now they are referred to three times. Neither had there been any mention of the name of Judas. And though Peter had indeed been referred to, once, back in chap. 1 (1:40–42), he had never before spoken. That he should now appear as speaking for the twelve is, therefore, a major new development. The effect is heightened by his use of "Holy One of God"—a title never before mentioned in this gospel.

This latter title provides an initial clue to the nature and purpose of the whole scene. Occasionally in the OT, the phrase "Holy One of God" seems to be used somewhat casually (cf. Judg 13:7; Ps 106:16), but if one may speak of the essence of God, then, as the vision of Isaiah implied (Isa 6:3, "Holy, holy, holy is Yahweh Sabaoth"), that essence is holiness. In Schnackenburg's words (2:77): " 'Holy' expresses the closest possible intimacy with God, a participation in God's deepest and most essential being." To acknowledge Jesus as the Holy One of God is to say that the essence or heart of God is present in Jesus. In other words, the divine, after all, is not far away, is not distant from humans. Furthermore, to acknowledge it with such solemnity is to indicate that the holiness in question is not something which terminates in Jesus. It is something which, through Jesus, has entered the hearts and minds of the twelve ("... We have believed and have come to know"). Peter's "You are ..." (*su ei*) reponds to Jesus' statement of "I am ..." (*Egō eimi;* cf. Schnackenburg, 2:77; Bultmann, 448–49). It is a further, detailed acknowledgement of the presence of the divine.

What is important for understanding the nature of the scene is that this final acceptance, by Peter in the name of the twelve, has close links with the acceptance of the God-like Jesus by those in the boat. Among these links one may mention the following: both form dramatic conclusions of successive "days" (or divisions); both highlight the holiness of Jesus and also the acceptance of that holiness; and both use the words *thelō* and *hypagō,* "to will" and "to go" (vv 21, 67). In v 21 these latter words are used to introduce and conclude the climactic sentence which tells of the acceptance of Jesus. At the end, in v 67, they have been brought together, synthesislike ("Do you . . . will to go? . . .") to form the question which evokes that acceptance.

The essential point is that Peter's acceptance on behalf of the twelve clarifies and complements the acceptance of the disciples who were in the boat. As suggested earlier, while those in the boat may indeed have been going to Capernaum, their more essential destination was the God-like Jesus. Once they were willing to receive him, they had reached where they were going. And so have Peter and the others of the twelve. The unbelieving disciples may turn back, but not they. Nothing is said of their moving anywhere; in fact, they explicitly exclude it: "*Kyrie,* to whom shall we go?" Like the boat, they have reached their destination.

Given the images which are so conspicuous in these scenes—a boat and the Peter-led twelve—it seems reasonable to conclude that, whatever may have happened historically, the text as now constructed is concerned with the church. In other words, having done with the general questions—with the mystery-filled issues of death and life, spirit and belief, unbelief and God's plan (vv 60–65)—the evangelist then went on to give some idea of the practical working of God's plan in the church. This does not necessarily mean the concern with the church is primary. On the contrary, a reasonable case can be made that the text's primary concern is with the depth of the human heart and with the enigmatic process of discernment and decision-making. But, as with the eucharistic coloring of the multiplication account and the discourse, there is here a color which evokes the church.

The image of the church which thus emerges seems at once both strong and weak, life-filled and fragile. It is strong because Peter speaks with a dramatic clarity which indicates firmness. And it is life-filled because he has obviously absorbed Jesus' words—the "words of eternal life" (v 68), the "words which . . . are Spirit and life" (v 63b). The two life-related phrases are in careful continuity (Schnackenburg, 2:73), and they indicate to what extent Jesus' message has found a home in Peter and in those for whom he speaks. They are also in exact contrast to the last phrase in chapter 5: "How will you believe my words?" Thus the fading of Jewish belief (end of chap. 5) and the emergence of the church (end of chap. 6) are carefully correlated.

Yet around this luminous intimation of the church, as around the boat, lie various shadows. On the one hand, there are those in whom Jesus' words had indeed found a home, but not a firm one—those disciples who receded. On the other hand, there is Judas, chosen, one of the twelve, yet an instrument of the devil who will later hand Jesus over. And even Peter will not be immune.

Part 2 Conclusion

In the unfolding narrative of the gospel, chap. 6 is a dramatic high point. Here, more than before, the stage is broader, the crowds are bigger, the discourse is longer, and the reactions are more diverse and decisive. The only accounts to compete with it are 4:1–42 and especially chap. 5. But even chapter 5, with its initial multitude and its profound discourse, cannot quite match chapter 6.

The two chapters, 5 and 6, are closely related. They have essentially the same structure and are in many ways complementary. One emphasizes creation; the other providence. One breaks barriers of time; the other, those of space. One intimates the fading of the Jews; the other, the emergence of the church. And while the discourse in chap. 5 begins with an image of childhood, that in chap. 6 concludes with allusions to the acceptance of death. The list could go on. Even in details of structure there is complementarity. At the beginning of chap. 5, the three scenes become shorter by degrees. But in chap. 6, focused as it is towards the emergence of something new, the third scene, that of the boat, is longer than the one which precedes.

Both chapters take up the images and issues of the earlier episodes. The father–child imagery, for instance, which occurs a few times in chaps. 3–4, reappears in new form in chap. 5. And the imagery of food and drink, found especially in 4:1–42, is found again in chap. 6.

Similarly with the issues, above all the issue of human woundedness. In the case of the man at the poolside, the fact that he is handicapped is obvious. But in various ways, beginning with the introduction to the Nicodemus scene, it had been stressed that others too had problems. All are handicapped. All have to face various forms of dichotomy, especially the dichotomy which looks at reality in a very narrow way. What chaps. 5 and 6 are saying had already been suggested in chaps. 3 and 4: that the dichotomy does not have to rule, that in Jesus there is a harmonious union of the human with the fullness of God's reality, and that through him there is offered to all—if they will to receive it—a gift of integrity, of wholeness. Chap. 3 began by emphasizing the dichotomy. But at the end of chap. 6, though the dichotomy is recalled and reemphasized, there is also an image of mutual indwelling, and, in Peter's declaration, a suggestion of the attainment of divine intimacy.

Here, in this sixth chapter, "the revelatory words of Jesus reach their penultimate level" (Kysar, 114). Only in the farewell discourse will they be surpassed. A case could be made that they do not need to be surpassed, that in chaps. 1–6 the basic realities and problems have already been discussed. So they have. But to some extent the problems have only been touched. While evil and death have indeed been spoken of, their full reality has not yet engulfed the stage. Despite threats in Jerusalem, Jesus has gone through his ministry with relative ease. He has dialogued at night, and spoken to thousands by day. He has, so to speak, been to weddings and wells, over seas and over mountains. Such images are valid, and they are part of the wonder of life. But evil is not to be dealt with lightly. As Schnackenburg (2:78) notes about chap. 6: "the resounding finish, 'one of the twelve,' emphasizes the dark mystery." The shadows, in all their power, are on their way. And with them the shadow of death. Now comes the hard part.

Excursus 3: Repetition and Variation in the Bread of Life Discourse

Repetition, Variation, and Intensification in the Relationship between the Four Sections of the Discourse. Exploratory Comments.

The various forms of highlighting, as given in the accompanying table help to indicate elements of continuity. It would also be useful to mark this table in a way which highlights elements of newness.

It needs to be emphasized that the relationship of the four columns is not primarily one of parallelism. There is indeed continuity, and there are similarities, but the highlighting of similarities, especially verbal similarities, as done by the typographic style of certain words, tends to obscure the fact that each column represents a significant advance on what precedes. Once that caution is borne in mind, however, it is worth focusing on some of the more important similarities and continuities.

Each of the columns (vv 25–33, 34–40, 41–50, 51–59) may be broken roughly into four rows—a, b, c, d.

Row a acts as a foil. It provides a mounting negative picture of failure to perceive providence and achieve union. It refers to failure to see signs (vv 25–26), failure to believe (vv 34–36), growing superficiality and animosity (vv 41–42), and, finally, outright fighting (v 52). Thus it functions within the discourse somewhat as the dark image of Lot functions within the story of Abraham (Genesis 12–25).

Row b generally provides the basic positive thesis of the various columns—the initial idea of being given a special food and of working for it (vv 27–28); the further idea of a saving will, a will which does not want to let someone perish (vv 37–38); the more developed idea of drawing someone into positive, spiritual union (vv 43–46); and, finally, the climactic image of asking people to do something which is difficult and death-related but the acceptance of which brings life.

Row c tends to be an elaboration of row b: "This is the work . . . ." (vv 29–31), "Now this is the will . . . ." (v 39), "This is the bread . . . ." (vv 47–50), "For my flesh is . . . and my body is . . . ." (vv 55–57).

Row d also may provide elaboration of row b, but it tends particularly to draw the table to a pregnant close. Between these various closing sections there is considerable continuity (vv 32–33, 40, 51, 58).

With regard to further details, the relationship of the four columns is complex, subtle, and at times, intriguing. A few examples will suffice.

With regard to columns 1 and 2 (vv 25–33 and 34–40) there is at first a fairly obvious similarity: the speakers, who are not explicitly named, address Jesus directly (Rabbi, *Kyrie*) and they ask him (for) something. (Contrast the beginning of columns 3 and 4: the speakers are explicitly named as Jews, but Jesus, no longer addressed directly, is simply *houtos,* "this person.") But, as columns 1 and 2 develop, the relationship between the texts becomes very sophisticated: the *superficial seeking which lacks seeing* ("you seek me, not because you saw . . . .")

Repetition, Variation, and Intensification in the Relationship
between the Four Sections of the Discourse

SECTION 1	SECTION 2
Breaking through *to people and suggesting belief* *(Initial contact)*	*Inviting people to the feast* *of God's life-saving providence* *(A tentative idea of union)*

²⁵When they found him on the other side of the sea,

a. they said to him, "Rabbi, when have you come here?" ²⁶Jesus answered them and said, "Amen, amen, I say to you, you seek me, not because you saw signs, but because you ate of the loaves and were filled.

b. ²⁷*Do not* **work** for the food which perishes, but for the food which abides to eternal life, which the *Son of humanity* will give you; for on him has God the Father set his seal." ²⁸They therefore said to him, "What do we do that we may work the works of God?"

c. ²⁹Jesus answered and said to them, "This is the work of God, that you believe in him whom he has sent." ³⁰So they said to him, "Then what sign do you do that we may see, and believe you? What work do you do? *Our fathers ate the manna in the desert,* as it is written, 'He gave them **bread from heaven** to eat.' "

d. ³²Jesus therefore said to them, "Amen, amen, I say to you, *it was* NOT *Moses* who gave you bread from heaven, but my Father gives you the true bread from heaven. ³³For the bread of God is that *which comes down from heaven* and gives LIFE to the world."

---

³⁴They then said to him, "Kyrie, give us this bread always."
³⁵Jesus said to them, "I am the bread of life. The one who comes to me shall not hunger, and the one who believes in me shall never thirst.
³⁶But I said to you that you have seen me and yet you do not believe.

³⁷*All* that *the Father gives* me will *come to me*; and the one who comes to me I will not cast out; ³⁸because *I* **have come down from heaven,** not to do my own will, but the will of him who sent me.

³⁹Now this is the will of him who sent me: that I let perish nothing of all that he has given me, but should raise it up on the last day.

⁴⁰For this is the will of my Father, that all who see the Son and believe in him should HAVE ETERNAL LIFE, and I will raise them up on the last day."

SECTION 3	SECTION 4
The relationship that really counts and gives life—that with God (A more developed idea of union)	*The need to stomach the full dimensions of providence—including death (The consequence—full union)*

⁴¹ The Jews murmured at him, because he said, ''I am the **bread which came down from heaven,**''

⁵² The Jews then fought among themselves, saying,

⁴² and they said, ''Is this not Jesus, the son of Joseph, whose father and mother we know? How does he now say, 'I have come down from heaven'?''

''How can this person give us his FLESH TO EAT?''

---

⁴³ Jesus answered and said to them, ''*Do not murmur* among yourselves. ⁴⁴ No one can **come to me** unless **the Father** who sent me draws him; and I will raise him up on the last day. ⁴⁵ It is written in the prophets, 'And they shall all be taught by God.' All who have heard and learned from **the Father come to me.** ⁴⁶ Not that anyone has seen the Father, except the one who is from God; he has seen the Father.

⁵³ Jesus therefore said to them, ''Amen, amen, I say to you, unless you EAT THE FLESH of the *Son of humanity* and drink his blood, you do not have life in you. ⁵⁴ The one who feeds on my flesh and drinks my blood HAS ETERNAL LIFE, and I will raise him up on the last day.

---

⁴⁷ Amen, amen, I say to you, the one who believes HAS ETERNAL LIFE. ⁴⁸ I am the bread of life. ⁴⁹ *Your fathers ate the manna in the desert, and they died.* ⁵⁰ This is the **bread which comes down from heaven** that whoever EATS of it may not die.

⁵⁵ For my flesh is true food, and my blood is true drink. ⁵⁶ The one who feeds on my flesh and drinks my blood abides in me and I in him. ⁵⁷ As the living Father sent me, and I live throught the Father, so the one who feeds on me shall live through me.

---

⁵¹ I am the living bread **which came down from heaven**; whoever EATS of this bread will live forever, and the bread that I will give is MY FLESH for the LIFE of the world.''

⁵⁸ This is the **bread which came down from heaven,** NOT *such as the fathers ate and died*; the one who feeds on this bread will live forever.''

⁵⁹ He said this in a synagogue teaching in Capernaum.

gives way to a *superficial seeing which lacks believing* ("you have seen me, and yet you do not believe"). The essence of the two texts is a picture of failure: despite partaking of satiating bread the speakers could not see below the surface (v 26); and despite having seen the bread which removes all hunger they could not believe (vv 35–36). But this continuity of essence has been expressed in a way which plays with thoughts, phrases, and words, and which strains the mind and imagination. It involves, to some degree, a delving into the depths of language. (On the contrast between a certain modern tendency towards superficiality in examining language, and an earlier tendency, especially among ancient Jewish writers, towards appreciating the depth of language, see Steiner, 1975, 48–73, esp. 57–58; cf. 227–35.)

Column 3 (vv 41–51), as well as building on column 2, builds also on column 1. Thus in row b the image of coming to Jesus (vv 43–46) is an elaboration of the similar idea in column 2 (vv 37–38). But the form of its opening phrase, "Do not murmur, . . ." provides an echo of an opening phrase in column 1—"Do not work . . ." (v 27). More substantially, the themes of manna and life (column 3, rows c and d), build carefully on the corresponding subsections of column 1.

Column 4 (vv 52–58) intensifies and synthesizes the three preceding columns. In row a, for instance, the question (*"How* can this? . . .") brings together the basic elements of two questions in the preceding column ("Is this? . . ." and "*How* does he? . . ."). And the striking phrase "flesh to eat" and "eat the flesh" (rows a and b) similarly constitute more and more explicit combinings of elements which in the previous column had been separate (vv 50–51). In row c (vv 55–57) the ideas of abiding and living offer an implicit contrast to the image of the fathers who ate the manna and died (row c in columns 1 and 3). In the climactic row d, that implied contrast becomes explicit.

Part 3A □ The Third Year

In the Shadow of Death

For Jesus, the Approach of Death Essentially Means Not a Narrowing of Life but an Opening of New Horizons—a Move towards the World and towards the Fullness of Revelation

From its opening verse, this part of the gospel (chaps. 7–12) is shadowed by the threat of death. The Jews seek to kill Jesus, and so he stays away from Judea (7:1). Death had been referred to before, but it had never had such an immediate influence on Jesus' decisions.

In subsequent episodes the threat of death increases. During the feast of Tents (chaps. 7–8) Jesus alludes to his departure, and thus to his death (7:33–34; 8:21). At Dedication, when the Jews surround and almost stone him (10:22–39), the threat comes even closer. Then he loses a friend, Lazarus (chap. 11). And finally his own death is decided and, at Passover, it closes in (11:49–55; 12:7,16,23–27).

The entire section, in fact, is like a portrayal of human existence under the threat of death. As such, and in light of the way the gospel as a whole is organized (around three Passovers), it seems to adapt the story of Jesus so as to reflect the third and final stage of life, that of advancing maturity and old age.

In some ways the portrait is harsh. The growing hostility towards Jesus suggests an environment which is more and more alien. There are indications too that believing is becoming more difficult. In fact, the developing divisions among the Jews (7:43; 9:16; 10:19) show an intensifying pattern of downright refusal to believe. At one level this hostility and negativity reflects the story of Jesus and the Jews, including the Jews of the late first century. But at another level it reflects the difficulties of the later stages of life.

The sense of the harsh environment is heightened by the fact that the action in these chapters takes place in the darker time of the year—roughly from October (the feast of Tents) to March (Passover). The feast of Dedication, which stands at the center of this period, is set, very explicitly, in winter (10:22).

Yet amid this harshness the sense of life is greater than ever. The man born blind is surrounded by darkness, but through him Jesus works a sign which, more dramatically than any previous sign, indicates that the various stages of down-to-earth human existence are a revelation of God. The beloved Lazarus may die, yet from the subsequent sadness there emerges the death-conquering faith of Martha. Now, more than ever, there are encouraging signs.

The same positive tone pervades the discourses, even those which are darkest.

The discourse in chap. 8 is probably the most obscure in the gospel, yet its diverse parts are inaugurated by the ideas of light and freedom (8:12,31–32), and its final words are a sovereign "I am" (8:58). The discourses in chap. 10 bring death closer than before, yet this tenth chapter is not only placed between signs of light (chap. 9) and life (chap. 11); at its own center (10:21) there is an explicit reference to the idea of the opening of the eyes. Furthermore, chap. 10, far from associating the approach of death with isolation, portrays instead an image of solidarity—the flock, under the care of the good shepherd. The final "chapter" (11:54–chap. 12) begins, ominously, near the desert and portrays the week before death, yet it is colored by the sign of the raising of Lazarus (12:1,9,17); and the entry into the fateful Jerusalem has evocations of entering the Jerusalem of everlasting life.

Even the winter-centered setting (October to March) is not all darkness. On the contrary, in a move which turns things around, the dark part of the year is marked by feasts—Tents, Dedication, and Passover. In various ways these feasts light up life and reinterpret it, and, as indicated earlier (in summarizing the gospel's theology), they are bound up with the concept of sabbath and sabbath rest, and thus with the idea of abiding with God, of relaxing in God's presence.

Structure-Related Notes

The unity of chaps. 7–12 and their distinctness from chaps. 13–21 have been indicated, in broad terms, by Bultmann (111). This division (between 7–12 and 13–21) seems to be confirmed by the way in which these two major parts are mutually contrasting and complementary (see outline in Introduction, Chapter 5). Furthermore, there are a number of other factors which in various ways confirm and illuminate this division.

The Contrast of Beginnings

There is a similarity and contrast between the beginning of section A (chaps. 7–12) and the beginning of section B (chaps. 13–21). The texts are related insofar as they both occur in the context, quite unique, of an implied contrast between "Simon Peter," who shows exemplary faith in Jesus, and "Judas the son of Simon Iscariot," someone who reflects the devil and who, as Jesus knew, would betray him (cf. 6:64–71; 13:2–11). But while the beginning of chap. 13 will emphasize that the time has come, the time to depart (*meta-bainō*, literally, "to go over," "to change's one's residence") out of this world to the Father (13:1), the beginning of chap. 7 emphasizes the opposite: despite his brothers' exhortations to depart (*meta-bainō*) to Judea and to ascend, Jesus declares that the time has not yet come (7:1–9). Apart from one other instance (5:24), the word *meta-bainō* does not occur elsewhere in John. There are, in fact, several detailed correspondences between the texts (6:64–7:9; 13:1–11), but the main point is the contrast concerning time. By the feast of Passover (13:1) the time will have come, the hour. But at Tents (chap. 7) the time is not yet; it is not complete.

This contrast, between what is incomplete and complete, is an important clue to the relationship of chaps. 7–12 to chaps 13–21. The revelation which is given to the Jews, in the temple and around Jerusalem (esp. chaps. 7–8), is lacking something. It is accompanied not by the giving of the Spirit, but merely by its veiled promise (7:37–39). The revelation to the disciples, on the other hand, in chaps. 13–21, is much more complete: his revelation has taken on an added completing dimension—love (cf. esp. 13:1,34–35; 15:11–17; 17:24–26), and the Spirit is not only spoken of clearly but is also actually given (14:15–17; 16:7–15; 20:22).

The Thematic Unity of Chaps. 7–12

In discussing the unity of chaps. 7–12 it is necessary to distinguish between plot and theme. With regard to the plot, the basic sequence of actions, there is a break at the end of chap. 10. For four chapters (7–10) Jesus worked in Jerusalem, but when, in winter, the stone-bearing Jews issued a resounding rejection, he finally went away—away from the temple, away from Jerusalem, away to the other side of the Jordan to the place where John had first baptized. "And he remained there" (cf. 10:22–42, esp. 10:40). He will, of course, come back for the Lazarus scene, the scene which seals his fate, and for the solemn entry to Jerusalem. But, as some writers have noted (e.g. Brown, 414), the departure to the other side of the Jordan seems to indicate the end of the basic public ministry.

On the other hand, with regard to the theme, chaps. 7–12 seem to show a pervasive unity. There is a steady emphasis on the multifaceted process of life-giving revelation; and the incidents involving Lazarus and the entry to Jerusalem (chaps. 11–12), far from interfering with that process, help rather to bring it to a higher level.

These two facts—diversity at the level of plot, and unity at the level of theme —may seem at first sight to be at odds. Yet, as Alter (1986, esp. 38) has indicated, biblical narrative tends to work in just this way. In order to reflect the untidyness of history—an untidyness reflected in Toynbee's oft-cited definition of history as "one damn thing after another"—it tends to describe history as a series of episodes that seem to be related imperfectly, if at all. On the other hand, that same biblical narrative, to bring out the coherence of God's purpose even amid the complexity of life's episodes, shows "disparate materials that are purposefully linked by motif, theme, analogy, and, sometimes, by a character who serves as a bridge between two different narrative blocks otherwise separated" (Alter, 1986, 30).

The Unity of Chaps. 7–12 as Reflected in References to the Greeks, Galilee, and the Crowd

Despite the obvious emphasis which chaps. 7–12 lay on the Jews—on the way Jesus revealed himself to them and many of them rejected him—there is also a carefully constructed emphasis, first and last, on the Gentiles. Unlike earlier references, particularly the rather enigmatic references to "Galilee," to Philip, and "the crowd" (cf. 1:43; 2:1; 4:3,43,45,54; 6:1–2,22,24), the references in chaps. 7–12 are explicit: "Does he intend to go to . . . the Greeks and teach the Greeks?" (7:35), "Now . . . at the feast were . . . Greeks. So they came to Philip . . . and told him . . . 'We wish to see Jesus' " (12:20–21). John does not otherwise use the word *Greeks,* but he uses these three occurrences of the word in such a way as to constitute two balancing texts, one near the beginning of Part 3A, the other near the end. Furthermore, around the word *Greeks* he clusters references to "the crowd" and to Galilee.

This clustering of "the crowd" is particularly striking. Altogether John uses the word *crowd* (*ochlos*) twenty times. However, apart from five references near the end of Part 2 (5:13; 6:2,5,22,24), in other words near the end of that part which by and large indicates a movement from Jerusalem to Galilee, to the Gentiles, the word is found nowhere except at the beginning and end of Part 3A. And in these latter instances it is clustered around references to the Greeks. Thus while the Greeks are referred to in 7:35 and 12:20, the crowd is referred to in 7:12 (twice),20,31,32,40,43,49; and 11:42; 12:9,12,17,18,29,34. Hence despite the fact that "the crowd" would seem at first sight to refer to a crowd of Jews and is sometimes used, especially in chap. 7, as if it were synonymous with the Jews, there are indications that it is meant to evoke the Gentiles. John, in fact, never speaks of a "crowd of Jews." The nearest he comes to it is in a reference to the "*great* crowd *from* (*ek*) the Jews" (12:9). "The great crowd" (*ochlos polys*) is a broader term than "the crowd" and may perhaps be meant to evoke the coming together around Jesus of both Gentiles and Jews—a grouping which is quite distinct from "the Jews." In any case, as Brown (456) notes, the Jews who pertain to the great crowd in 12:9 "are clearly distinct from the Jewish authorities," in other words, as Brown sees it, clearly distinct from John's usual references to "the Jews."

It is better therefore that "the crowd" and "the Jews" not be taken synonymously. Rather, "the crowd," clustered as it is around the word *Greeks,* seems to derive much of its meaning from it.

Something similar may be noticed with the word "Galilee." John's use of it is somewhat more complex than his use of the word "crowd." Unlike "crowd" it is used towards the end of Parts 1 and 3B (cf. 1:44; 2:1,11; 21:2). But otherwise he uses it in a similar way—towards the later part of Part 2 (4:3,43,45,46,47,54; 6:1), and at the beginning and end of Part 3A, clustered or connected with the word *Greeks.* Thus while the word *Greeks* is used in 7:35 and 12:20, Galilee is referred to in 7:1,9,41,52 (twice) and 12:21.

This last detail, 12:21, is particularly instructive. The action in chap. 12 is located in and around Jerusalem, so one hardly expects a reference to Galilee. But when (in 12:20–21) the Greeks approach Philip, he is referred to as being "from Bethsaida in Galilee." As factual information this is redundant. The reader had already been told that Philip was from Bethsaida (1:44). Yet the detail, however trivial or redundant it may at first appear, is neither casual nor confused. It is John's way, even in this Jerusalem scene, of inserting a Galilee reference which gives artistic balance to his work and which exploits the tendency of the word

Galilee to evoke the Gentiles. It also serves as a clue that at least some of his geographic references have a symbolic aspect. Such an interpretation of 12:21 is not new. As Brown (466) notes at this point: "Some have thought that Galilee is mentioned here because of its association with the Gentiles (Matt 4:15, citing Isa 9:1)."

It is also noteworthy that when chap. 7 is laid out schematically, the reference to the Greeks (7:35) conterbalances a reference to Galilee (7:52).

The essential point, amid all these details, is that John's references to the Greeks, the crowd, and Galilee are not at all as confused or haphazard as they may at times appear. On the contrary, within Part 3A (chaps. 7–12) they have been carefully woven into its beginning and end, and they indicate both the importance of the Gentile theme and the unity of these chapters as a whole.

It follows therefore that however great the break at the end of chap. 10, when Jesus goes away across the Jordan, the text as we now have it is a well-wrought unity.

The Emphasis on the Greeks as an Indicator
of the Perspective of Chaps. 7–12

In Part 3 the evangelist has changed the perspective or angle from which the drama is being seen. In Part 1 his first and last geographic references were to Jerusalem (1:19, 2:13). In Part 2 there is a shift: he begins with Jerusalem and moves more and more toward Galilee and Capernaum (2:23; chap. 4; 6:1, 59). Part 3 begins and ends with Galilee (7:1; 21:1–2; so does 3A: cf. 12:21). In other words, even though Part 3 is largely set in Jerusalem, it is primarily the affair not of the Jews but of the whole world. Originally, of course, the Jews were first— and consequently Jerusalem was mentioned first and last. But no longer. The perspective now is somewhat like that of the later part of the epistle to the Romans: what Jesus has done is for all of humankind, and the Jews to some degree have been left behind, have lost their priority. It is noteworthy in chaps. 7–12 that it is "the crowd" which first believes, which first divides (7:31,43). Only later is it said that the Jews do so (8:30–31, 9:16, 10:19).

What emerges overall is that while the revelatory drama of chaps. 7–12 is set largely among the Jews and is in many ways preoccupied with the Jewish rejection of Jesus, it is also giving indications of the Gentile reaction and of the fact that ultimately it is among the Gentiles that Jesus' revelation is to meet the greatest acceptance. In chap. 7, when the crowd first begins to react to Jesus, the Pharisees take action by trying to have him arrested (7:33). But in chap. 12, as he enters Jerusalem and the Greeks approach, they realize that somehow they have brought themselves to a situation of being left behind. And they say to one another, "You see that you accomplish nothing. Behold, the world has gone after him" (12:19).

As already indicated, there is a certain sense in which John 7–12 is reminiscent of Romans 9–11. Like the epistle, it discusses the wrenching question of how the revelation, which was first directed to the Jews, was rejected by many of them and passed increasingly to the wider world. But while Romans 9–11 offers a prophetic resolution to the problem of the Jews' destiny (cf. esp. Romans 11), John does not, at least not in chaps. 7–12. By the end of chap. 12 they seem strangely isolated and blind, in a sense shrouded in darkness (cf. esp. 12:36b-43). Though Jesus' final words in chap. 12 are basically words of life (12:44–50, esp. v 50) there is little indication of how these words will ever reach the Jews.

The Discourses at the Feast of Tents

The Process of Advancing Revelation, Particularly of Revealing Jesus as Christ and Divine Son

The (Sinful, Death-Dominated) Rejection of Revelation Leads to Increasing Alienation and Final Separation

The text consists of 7:1–52 ("chap. 7") and 8:12–59 ("chap. 8"). As mentioned earlier, the story of the adulteress (7:53–8:11) is a late insertion which is best treated separately from the basic drama of chaps. 7 and 8 (see Excursus 4).

The basic sequence of events is relatively simple. Jesus is in Galilee, but following a disagreement with his unbelieving brothers, he goes with them to the temple, and during the feast of Tents he teaches and reveals as never before. Though some respond positively, the dominant reactions reflect the encounter with his brothers—disbelief, harsh disagreement, and separation.

The setting of this drama helps to make it remarkable. First there is the place —the temple. For Jews throughout the world this was the geographical focal point of their religion, to some degree the center of their universe. Here Jesus speaks: he enters in 7:14 and does not leave till 8:59.

There is also the timing—the feast of Tents. This feast, variously referred to as Tents, Tabernacles, or Huts (Hebrew, *sukkôt*; Greek, *skēnopēgia*) usually began around October 1 and was a magnificent week-long celebration—the most important and popular of all Jewish feasts. It was a joyful harvest festival with temple ceremonies involving both water and light. Its full significance is somewhat uncertain, but it was particularly associated with the idea of "the day of the Lord" and thus with the idea of the Lord's moment of revelation and the appearing of the Messiah (cf. Brown, 326–27, 344). When the brothers tell Jesus to show himself to the world (7:4) their words have an ironic sense: he should manifest himself as Messiah to Israel (Dodd, 1953, 351). Though Tents had some of the aspects of an *Oktoberfest* (cf. De Vaux, 1965, 495–502, esp. 496), Josephus referred to it as "the holiest and greatest of Hebrew feasts" (*Ant.* 8:4.1).

However promising the setting, the actual text is at times quite obscure, particularly in its sequence of thought, and so its unity is not obvious. Consequently, Bultmann, for instance, breaks it into fragments and scatters it. Schnackenburg (2:130–35) and Becker (247–59) remove part of chap. 7 (concerning the law, 7:15–24) and put it with chap. 5. And Brown (338,346,352), while leaving the text in its present order, views some of the material as rather haphazardly organized: he puts chap. 8 under the heading of miscellaneous discourses. Haenchen (II,3), following Wellhausen and others, concludes: "It is generally known that the several individual discourse scenes in chapters 7 and 8 do not form a real unity.''

But obscurity, including obscurity in the sequence of thought, need not mean disunity. It may be a deliberate literary technique, prosopopoeia—a way of suggesting, through the form of the text, what the text's content is about (cf. Kurz, 1980, 186). In the Prologue, for instance, the perplexing form reflects the content —the increasing change from soaring poetry to prose reflects the descent of the Word into flesh. Given that chaps. 7–8 are concerned not only with revelation but also with disbelief and the fading of the light (cf. 8:12,59), and given also that these two chapters are framed by balancing references to secrecy or hiddenness (7:4,10; 8:59), it is appropriate that the text should become more and more obscure. A modern variation on this technique is found for instance, in the deliberate obscurity which occurs in Joseph Conrad's *Heart of Darkness* (cf. Wilcox, 1960, esp. 2–3).

In any case, when chaps. 7–8 are taken as they are, they appear to have their own coherence. That coherence may be summarized as follows.

Within the gospel as a whole, and particularly within Part 3 (chaps. 7–21), the teaching at Tents (chaps. 7–8) serves in part as a preliminary last discourse. It is not, of course, a genuine last discourse nor does it follow the literary convention for such a situation. But in relation to the last discourse it acts both as a preparation and as a contrast. It is a preparation insofar as it introduces topics which are related to the last discourse, particularly that of the departure of Jesus (7:34,36; 8:14,21). And it is a contrast insofar as the revelation is being rejected and the final outcome is a picture not of union (as in chap. 17) but of alienation and separation (8:31–59). Thus it involves two interwoven dramas—one of advancing revelation and another of increasing rejection.

With regard to advancing revelation, this is first hinted at in the opening narrative (7:1–10)—in its suggestion of a new space and time. The new space is implied by the fact that, in a way that had not happened before, Jesus has chosen to be in Galilee rather than Judea (v 1). And he also emphasizes the need to wait for the right time (vv 6, 8). But it is in the main body of chap. 7 that the idea of development is seen clearly. During two related moments (the middle of the feast and on the feast's last day), Jesus speaks respectively of the law (7:14–24) and the Spirit (7:37–39). The result is a clear sense of progression: the law prevails during an intermediate time, but the final time is that of the Spirit. One gives way to the other. The implication is that through Jesus—through his life-giving interpretation of the law (7:23) and through his granting of the Spirit—God is giving increasing insight, increasing ability to lay aside superficial judgment and to recognize the truth of things (7:24). There is a deepening capacity to see spiritually.

From a human point of view, the result of this increasing insight is that people begin to recognize who Jesus is; they begin to see that this ordinary-looking person is God's anointed, the Christ (cf. 7:25–36, 40–52). This insight into Jesus is accompanied by two other perceptions—that he is born of God, and that he must die.

Born of God

The phrase "born of God" does not occur in these chapters, but there are discussions concerning Jesus' origins (7:27,41–42), and in chapter 8 there is a discussion which concerns the fatherhood or origin of Jesus and the Jews. The essence of these texts is that in speaking of parenthood, of what it is that has generated a person, it is necessary to make a distinction. On the one hand, there is an external process of generation, a process which can bring immense prestige or lack of prestige. (Jesus' origins are regarded as unimpressive, commonplace, inappropriate, 7:27,41–42; but the Jews, because of their descent from Abraham, feel complacent, and they tell Jesus that he is a Samaritan, 8:33,39,48.) On the other hand, there is a process which is more internal—the fact that one's deepest origin lies in God and that, if one is willing, God continues to be one's place of origin, to generate one's life. Thus no one knows where the Anointed comes from (7:27) because, even though at one level Jesus is an ordinary person, at another he is from God. And God is with him (8:18–19, 27–29). Those who reject him, however, while they may have a prestigious ancestor, in fact, depend for their continued generation on the devil (8:44). Natural prestige, therefore, is not enough. What is needed is birth of another kind, birth from above.

Hence, what is developed in chaps. 7–8 prepares the way for the story of chapter 9. The contrast between the two forms of generation finds dramatic expression in the story of the man born blind.

Bound to Die

Alongside the alluring idea of Jesus as the Anointed, there is a further, sobering, perception—he must die. His death is not mentioned explicitly, but as soon as people start to ask if he is the Christ, he begins to intimate that both his origin and destiny lie with God, and that in a "short time" he will depart to God (7:28–29, 33–34). Furthermore the increasing efforts to arrest him (7:30,32,44) foreshadow his passion. And the granting of the Spirit is associated with his death-involving glorification (7:39). In fact, one aspect of the balance between the beginning of chap. 7 and the beginning of chap. 13 concerns death's approach. In 13:1,3 it is put as positively as possible: Jesus is about "to depart from this world to the Father . . . [he is] going to God" (13:1–3). In 7:2 the same reality is viewed from a different angle: "the Jews sought to kill him." "Being killed" and "going to God" tend to evoke diverse feelings, diverse interpretations of reality. What John does is bring these things together. He shows how something as negative-looking as a killing may be part of a larger positive process. From now on, through a good deal of Part 3, he will be seeking to evoke and interpret the felt reality of death and of its approach.

In previous chapters there had of course been some references to "the dead" (5:21, 25) and even to Jesus rising from the dead (2:22). There had also been a reference to killing—the Jews sought to kill him (5:18)—and to the threat or actuality of dying (4:47,49; 6:49,50,58). But it is in chaps. 7 and 8 that these references multiply—both to killing (7:1,19,20,25; 8:22,37,40), and to dying

(8:21,24 [twice],52,53 [twice]). Thus even though the basic idea of death is recognized from the beginning of the story of Jesus, it is only as the story advances
that the reality of death begins to be felt.

One of the questions which arises in considering these chapters is whether
their emphasis on death and their evoking of the fragility of life have anything to
do with the image which to some degree overshadows the entire text—that of a
tent. The idea of pitching a tent evokes the whole world of the nomad, the pil-
grim, the person with no lasting city. In the OT the word "tent" occurs not only
in the context of God's dwelling place among the people (e.g., Exodus 26–40)
but also as a way of referring figuratively to life (e.g., Jer 10:20). The same
figurative sense is found in Wis 9:15 and is developed at some length by Paul (2
Cor 5:1–5). More decisive, however, than these rather distant references is the
fact that at the beginning of John's gospel the entire phenomenon of living in a
corruptible body, a body of flesh, is referred to as living in a tent: "the Word
became flesh and *eskēnōsen* among us," i.e. pitched his *skēnē*, "tent," among us
(1:14). This reference to a tent may, of course, also be seen as evoking God's
way of dwelling among humankind, but, particularly in John, one meaning need
not exclude another. In the text just mentioned (1:14), the emphasis on the flesh
evokes the fragile and temporary quality of the tent. In other words the tent suggests life in the flesh, transitory life.

Given John's practice of literary continuity, it is probable that this figurative
reference to a tent is meant as background for the later references to tents—at the
feast of *skēnopēgia*. Thus while it may be interesting from some points of view
to read the details concerning the feast of Tents, details about its history and
ceremonies, the primary clue to its meaning in John's gospel appears to be provided by the gospel itself, by the prologue. Human life is life in a tent. It is
appropriate, as the reality of death is perceived, that such an image be brought to
mind: "After this . . . the Jews sought to *kill* him. Now there was at hand the
Jews' feast of *Tents.*"

Yet death is not allowed to make the narrative morose. Jesus implies that death
is like going home—a return to the one who sent him (7:33). And the Spirit-
related text (7:37–39) implies that death is a glorification.

Thus the overall positive message from chap. 7 indicates that on God's part
there is an increasing revelation of the world of the Spirit, and that at the same
time there is an increasing emergence both of Jesus' dignity as Christ and of his
God-oriented death.

In chap. 8 this positive message is viewed from another angle. Unlike chap.
7, with its numerous references to places, movement, and time (general and specific), chap. 8 contains virtually no reference to time and space. (The puzzling
reference to Jesus as being "in the treasury," 8:20, will be seen as referring to a
supra-spatial union with God.) What chap. 8 does is spell out the deeper implications of chap. 7. To some degree chap. 8 is like an underwater view of a scene
which previously (in chap. 7) had been visible only from above the surface. The
emergence of the law-surpassing Spirit means a new world order, one in which
Jesus is the light of the world (8:12). And the emergence of Jesus as the Christ
means that he has a special relationship to the Father. The singular form of the

word "father" is not used in chap. 7, but in chap. 8 it occurs about nineteen times. Though the concept of "son" is indirect and scarce in chap. 8, it is present (three occurrences, vv 28, 35, 36), and when taken in conjunction with the repeated emphasis on fatherhood and the divine Father, it implies that Jesus is a divine Son. Thus while chap. 7 shows Jesus as the Christ, chap. 8 implies that he is the Son of God, one who emerges as divine, someone who is identified as the God-like "I am" (8:12,24,28,58).

Again, as in chap. 7, Jesus' status is linked to his death, to the fact that, having come from God, he will return to God (8:14,21). In fact, it is precisely when he has been "lifted up" as Son of humanity that he will be known as the God-like "I am" (8:28).

One of the main functions of chap. 8 is to picture things from the divine viewpoint. The events in chap. 7, tied as they are to time and space, are seen in a way that is largely human. In chap. 8, a higher world is brought more directly into focus, a world which, through the life and light of the ever-living God ("I am"), overcomes even death.

But while this entire drama of revelation is unfolding, the predominant reaction is one of rejection. Some people do accept it and do recognize clearly that Jesus is the Christ (7:40–41), but, like the brothers in the opening narrative (7:1–10), most listeners are tied to appearances. Unable to enter the emerging world of the Spirit, they do not recognize Jesus' dignity as Christ, nor do they see any possibility of overcoming death.

Their situation is somewhat like that of Nicodemus. When Nicodemus first came by night (2:23–3:21, at the beginning of Part 2), Jesus challenged him to accept the world of the Spirit and thus to rise above the dividedness of human nature (3:3–9). The challenge now (at the beginning of Part 3) is to rely even more on the Spirit and thus to rise not only above dividedness and sin, but also above death. Only through the Spirit can a person go to God; this is true in life, and it is true also in death. It is because they insist on living at the level of the superficial and refuse to accept a world that is deeper, more spiritual, that Jesus tells his hearers that where he is going they cannot come (7:34,36; 8:21–22).

Essentially the same challenge will be issued at the beginning of the last discourse: where Jesus is going Peter cannot follow (13:33–37). And the reason is that unaided human effort cannot overcome certain barriers. Only when the Spirit has been given will the way be open for Peter.

The final reaction in chap. 7 is a decisive rejection (7:45–52). And as the authorities spurn the idea of a prophet arising out of Galilee their final two words are *ouk egeiretai,* "does not arise." Though intended by them in one sense, these two words seem full of irony; they are a summary of their own inability to rise, of their insistence on the supremacy of death.

One of the purposes of chap. 8 is to get to the underlying cause of their rejection. Just as the initial section of chap. 8 (8:12–30) shows Jesus as being the Son who is rooted in God as Father, so its subsequent section (8:31–47) shows the superficial believers as being rooted in the fatherhood of the devil. The two texts (8:12–30 and 8:31–47) are complementary.

Finally, as a form of summary of the two divergent points of view, there is a concluding exchange which is like a variation on the idea of the two ways (8:48–59): Jesus speaks more and more about life, but the unbelievers are taken up with death, and thus at the end ''the light'' goes away.

In summary, chaps. 7–8 are like a two-act drama of revelation's progress and rejection. In Act 1 (chap. 7), as there is an increasing emphasis both on spiritual (supra-literal) interpretation of the law (7:14–24) and on the Spirit (7:37–39) and as Jesus is revealed more and more as the Christ, the reaction is one of increasing division and rejection. In Act 2 (chap. 8), the absence of specific references to time and space is an indication, not that the chapter is a collection of texts which are miscellaneous and largely unrelated, but that the entire phenomenon of revelation and rejection is being examined from a deeper point of view, one which leaves aside superficial details and which traces what is happening both to its original underlying roots (in God, 8:12–30; or the devil, 8:31–47) and to its ultimate implications (of life and of death, 8:48–59).

"The Brothers" and Jesus: Contrasting Sketches of Unbelief and of Waiting upon Revelation

Introduction: Unravelling the Structure of 7:1–13

As in chaps. 5 and 6, chap. 7 begins with a relatively brief episode or narrative section which suggests the essence of what is to come. But, as in the case of chap. 5, the extent of this initial narrative is not immediately obvious. Most commentators regard 7:1–13 as an introductory text which should be divided in two, but there is considerable disagreement over whether the thirteen verses should be divided into 1–9 and 10–13 or into 1–10 and 11–13—in other words, whether the division should be placed immediately before or after the account of Jesus going up to the feast (v 10). Many commentators place it before (Westcott, 117; Lagrange, 200; Bernard, 265; Hoskyns, 308; Lightfoot, 72; Morris, 393; Bruce, 169; Becker, 261; Kysar, 115; Maier, 320; Beasley-Murray, 101), but an impressive number of others place it after (Brown, 305; Schnackenburg, 2:138; Mateos and Barreto, 357; and, in modified ways, Marsh, 324, and Bultmann, 294). By and large, commentators do not articulate their reasons for choosing one option over the other.

It seems better that the division be placed after v 10; in other words, that the text be divided into (1) the account of how Jesus, after a time of witholding himself, went up to the feast (7:1–10); and (2) the scene at the feast itself, as "the Jews" and "the crowd" seek Jesus (7:11–13). Such a division gives, on the one hand, an episode which in varying ways is at some distance of time and space from the feast (cf. v 10, "*to* the feast"), and, on the other, a scene which takes place at the actual feast (cf. v 11, "*at* the feast"). It also gives distinction of characters: in the first text (vv 1–10), Jesus and his brothers; in the second (11–13), "the Jews" and "the crowd." And there appears to be a further distinction in the fact that while 7:1–10 is replete with references to various forms of moving or traveling, 7:11–13 has no such references; people are already in place. What is particularly significant is that 7:11–13 begins by repeating a phrase from the beginning of 7:1–10 ("the Jews sought . . ."), and within John's text such repetition is often a clue to a new division. Furthermore, 7:11–13, with its emphasis on seeking, and with its two references to both "the Jews" and "the crowd," emerges as a variation on the similarly brief introductions which preceded the long discourses in chaps. 5 and 6 (cf. 5:16–18; 6:22–24).

It seems reasonable therefore to conclude that the initial part of the text consists of 7:1–10.

It is doubtful, however, if 7:1–10 should be regarded as an unbroken whole. A number of scholars have suggested that the opening verse or verses (i.e. 7:1 or 7:1–2) be regarded as distinct (cf. Hoskyns, 281, 308; Marsh, 319; Mateos and Barreto, 357). Hendriksen (2:3) makes a further division—after v 5. And, as already noted, several scholars put a division immediately before v 10.

These suggestions seem to reflect significant data in the text, and when taken together they help to indicate that 7:1–10 should be divided into four subdivisions. First there is an introduction (7:1–2), and then there are three scenes: the brothers' disbelief (vv 3–5), Jesus' witholding of himself (vv 6–9), and, later, the going up to the feast (v 10).

The most questionable element in this proposal is the division after v 5—the division between the account of the brothers telling him to move and the account of Jesus' reply. Is it reasonable to assign a command and a reaction to distinct scenes? It would seem that it is, both because the command is followed by a faith-related comment which gives a certain sense of closure ("for even his brothers did not believe in him"; cf. closing faith-related statements in 2:11, 22; 4:42, 53; 8:30), and also because the basic division in the account of the cleansing of the temple is exactly of this nature; it is a pause between the account of telling some-one to get their things "out of here" (*enteuthen*, 2:16; cf. 7:3) and—following an authorial comment (2:17, cf. 7:5)—the account of someone's reaction (2:18, cf. 7:6).

This structure—an introduction and three scenes—is essentially the same as that found at the beginning of chaps. 5 and 6 (5:1–15; 6:1–21). And, as in 5:1–15 and 6:1–21, the third scene, v 10, is quite distinct, in time and space, from those that precede. It was not without reason that so many authors put a division between vv 9 and 10.

[7:1–2] Introduction: Walking in Galilee, under the shadow of death and Tents. The story begins by showing Jesus as more linked to Galilee than ever before. In previous references (1:44; 2:1,11; 4:3,43–54; 6:1) Galilee was either a destination or the object of an apparently brief visit. But now, instead of being a destination, it is a residence and starting point. The geographical focus has shifted. And while Galilee has become a place of "walking" (*peripateō*)—a word which may simply mean to go about, but one which has also an overtone of generating disciples (cf. 1:36–37; 6:66)—Judea has become a place in which "the Jews" threaten death. Thus the contrast is sharp—between a place suggesting disciple-ship (Galilee) and a place of death (Judea).

The reference to the feast of Tents heightens the threat of death. As mentioned in the introduction to chapters 7–8, and as 1:14 suggests, the image of tenting evokes human fragility and mortality. Though Jesus took due account of the dan-ger of being killed, he is not presented as being mastered by that danger. As the text says—following the more probable reading—he decided or willed (*thelo*) not to walk in Judea. The picture therefore is of someone who indeed acknowledges pressure but who also retains freedom.

[7:3–5] Scene 1: Jesus' brothers and the twisted logic of their unbelief. In John's only previous reference to Jesus' "brothers" (2:12), no details were given about their number or their exact relationship to Jesus—whether they were cous-ins, or half-brothers, or brothers-in-law, or brothers in the strict sense. What was faintly suggested, however, was that—in contrast to the disciples, though not at all in contrast to the Jews—they did not believe. Now, as the feast of Tents approaches, that suggestion will become an explicit statement.

As they re enter the drama, their message to Jesus is urgent: if he is to become known then he should move to Judea and reveal himself to the world.

At one level this sounds like the voice of sweet reason. Disciple-gathering requires publicity. At another level, however, their words form a web of half-truths and contradictions. They acknowledge he has unusual power—he performs "works" (miracles)—yet they speak to him almost as if he were a slave ("Depart from here . . ."). They suggest that he is working in secret while seeking to be known openly, yet the truth of such statements is not clear. They want him to be revealed to the world, yet they tell him to leave Galilee, the place which thus far in the gospel has been most associated with the wide world, and to go to the relatively small land of Judea. They seem to be concerned for his welfare, yet they want to send him to a place of death.

Whatever the full subtleties of the text, the basic point seems clear: under the guise of good advice, they are violating the truth and Jesus' freedom. In a way that is reminiscent of those who wanted to force Jesus to be king (6:14–15), they seek to turn his mission into a spectacle which may suit their own purposes. Brown (308) suggests that their words are Satan-like. And the text explains why —"they did not believe."

What the first scene gives, therefore, is an initial mini-portrait of unbelief: it seems so reasonable, yet ultimately it is confused and narrow.

[7:6–9] Scene 2: In the face of (the world's) unbelief, Jesus speaks of an impending time of revelation and witness. Jesus' response involves an elaboration of the picture of unbelief. He speaks of it as an unhealthy compliance with what is negative in the world. It involves no sense of a time other than one's own ("your time [*kairos*] is always ready"), and no tension with the world's evil deeds ("The world cannot hate you . . ."). In other words, in every way one simply goes with the flow of things.

Kairos refers to time not so much in its quantity as in its quality. It alludes to the fact that each moment has a special place before God and that at certain times God offers a unique *kairos,* a unique moment of revelation and meaning—a special challenge (Schnackenburg, 2:140). The picture, therefore, of unbelief, is of a life where the basic creative tensions are missing—the tension of following a positive challenge, and the tension of leaving behind what is evil. It is a life which may seem easy, but insofar as it tends to be engulfed meaninglessly by the dictates of the moment and by the power of what is evil, it is a life of "the deepest unfreedom" (Schnackenburg, 2:141).

In contrast to such enticing slavery, there is the example of Jesus, and it is on this contrasting figure that the scene's emphasis falls. Unlike his brothers, he waits for the appropriate moment of challenge, and he witnesses to what is evil. What he awaits, of course, is not easy. The coming "time" is related to the coming "hour." (One is the obverse or alternate of the other. *Kairos* regards time as a challenging opportunity, a gift. "Hour" sees that moment from the point of view of the giver, as something *from God,* divinely decreed; cf. Schnackenburg, 2:140; Brown, 306.) And the hour is the moment of death and glorification. Yet, though *kairos* has this unspoken difficult side, Jesus concentrates on what is positive.

When he adds "I am not ascending to the feast because my time is not yet fulfilled,'' he communicates not only freedom under pressure but also a sense of expectation. And so saying he remained where he was—''he abode in Galilee.''

The use of ''abide,'' with its overtones of abiding with God and with the disciples (e.g., cf. 1:33,38–39), links up with the similar overtones of ''he walked (*peripateō*) in Galilee'' (7:1, cf. 1:36). It is as though Galilee has become a place of creative quiet, a place of learning and abiding, of waiting till the time is right.

[7:10] Scene 3: Surprisingly, Jesus goes up to the feast. In responding to his brothers' pressure that he reveal himself, Jesus had said, ''I am not going up to this feast.'' But when his brothers had gone up, then so did he—in secret.

This seems to be a contradiction but, as commentators ancient and modern have indicated (Brown, 308; cf. Schnackenburg, 2:143) the word *anabainō*, ''go up/ascend'' is ambiguous and may refer not only to going to Jerusalem but also to ascending to God. In other words, when Jesus says that he will not ascend to (*or at*) this feast he is speaking at the higher level, he is saying that at this feast he will not ascend *to God*. But he may ascend in a more mundane sense. Some scholars reject this explanation (e.g. Schnackenburg, 2:142–43; Lindars, 284), yet it is supported by the context—both the immediate context which shows Jesus as on a higher level than his worldly, unbelieving brothers, and the broad context of several episodes where apparent contradictions or confusions are accounted for by the fact that Jesus is speaking on a higher level (cf. 2:19, 3:4, 4:11).

It is also true, however, as is emphasized by Barrett (313) and Schnackenburg (2:142), that Jesus is doing something more than speaking at this God-related level. In face of the pressure of unbelieving brothers, he is establishing his own freedom. These two elements—God-relatedness and freedom—are interconnected. He will not yield to their command to go up, and when he does go, he does so in his own appropriate way—in secret—a way which directly contradicts their demands.

Thus from the ''he willed'' in 7:1 to his going up in 7:10 there is an emphasis on his God-related freedom.

The overall effect of this brief episode (7:1–10) is to give a brief portrayal of what is negative (the desire to kill and unbelief) and, in contrast, to suggest the approach of a decisive time of revelation, the time (*kairos*) when Jesus, through his impending death (cf. 7:1–2), will be revealed to the world. It is something which has not yet come, but already, in secret, the process is underway. And through the confrontation between Jesus and his brothers it may be seen that, when it comes, this revelation will confront the world's unbelief, lies, and lack of freedom.

Jesus at the Death-Evoking Feast of Tents

A Drama Illustrating the Progress of Revelation and the Diversity of Responses

Introduction and Structure

In accordance with the idea of 7:1–10 that revelation must await the right time, the drama of 7:11–52 shows Jesus as imparting revelation progressively—first at the midpoint of the feast and then on its final day.

The structure of the text follows that progression. Once vv 11–13 have been isolated as forming an introduction—a matter already seen in discussing the structure of 7:1–10—most commentators are agreed in dividing 7:14–52 into two major sections: Jesus' teaching midway through the feast (7:14–36) and Jesus' revelation on the feast's last day (7:37–52). Furthermore, each of these major sections may be divided into three subsections or scenes. In simplified terms these scenes are as follows: first, Jesus teaches or reveals (vv 14–24 and 37–39); second, the listeners discuss his identity, particularly the question of whether he is the Christ (vv 25–30 and 40–44); and third, the authorities' demonstrate greater and greater rejection and hostility (vv 31–36 and 45–52).

[7:11–13] Introduction: At the feast, "the Jews" and "the crowd" look for Jesus; their receptivity and hostility. Like the brief introductions in 5:16–18 and 6:22–24, this introduction also prefaces Jesus' words by summarizing the audience and its mood. It is more complex, however, than those other introductions. As noted earlier, it refers twice both to "the Jews" (as in 5:16–18) and to "the crowd" (as in 6:22–24). Furthermore, it combines apparent hostility (as in 5:16–18) with apparent receptivity (as in 6:22–24). Thus, in its increasing complexity, it represents careful grading. The drama intensifies.

The expressions, "the Jews" and "the crowd," are used in a way that is so stereotyped, so mathematically exact (especially in relation to 5:16–18 and 6:22–24), that it seems likely that they are to be regarded as representative, as allusions to the diversity of the world—Jews and Gentiles ("the crowd").

Further intensification is found in the diverse perceptions of Jesus. On the one hand, there is something immensely positive—an instinctive recognition of Jesus' basic quality of goodness. On the other, there is the accusation that Jesus misleads the crowd—a very serious charge (Schnackenburg, 2:143) and one which is expressed more directly than the sabbath-related charges in 5:16–18.

Furthermore in the phrase "the fear of the Jews" there is yet another element of graded tension. So far the Jews' hostility had been directed only at Jesus. But now it reaches a new level—it aims at those who might be his followers.

The audience which emerges from this introduction is complex in composition and attitude. It is like a great swirling ("murmuring") sea, holding within itself much that is both positive and negative. Toward this vast potential Jesus now approaches.

313

[7:14–24] Midway through the feast: Jesus teaches the law, and he does so in a way that is God-based and life-giving (not letter-bound and deathly). The text begins with a scene-setting statement—that midway through the feast Jesus went up to the temple and taught (7:14). In fact, of the ten references which John makes to Jesus as involved in a process of teaching (*didaskō*), or as delivering a teaching (*didachē*), seven occur in these chapters (cf. 7:14,16,17,28,35; 8:20,28: the other three in 6:59; 18:19,20). In other words, more than ever before in the gospel, Jesus emerges as a teacher.

Jesus' teaching consists largely of a declaration on the law, and it falls into two statements of roughly equal length. The essence of these statements is that, in contrast to the literalist, death-oriented Jews, Jesus is interpreting the law in a way that is God-based (first statement, vv 16–19) and life-giving (second statement, vv 21–24). These two ideas (God-based and life-giving) are interconnected —like the connection between a tree and its fruit.

One of the problems associated with this text is that of its location within the gospel. It has many links with chap. 5, including a reference to the healing of the man on the sabbath (7:21–23, cf. 5:1–15), and for that reason is sometimes placed immediately after it, in other words before chap. 6 (cf. Bultmann, 247–78; Schnackenburg 2:90–136, esp. 130).

But it also has links with chap. 6. There are, first of all, several connecting details: the use of scene-setting statements (6:25,59; 7:14) and of introductory questions (6:25,28,30,42,52; 7:15,20); the use, at the beginning of the discourse or teaching process, of *two* balancing statements (6:26–27, 32–33; 7:16–19, 21–24; see comments on 6:25–33); and the use of specific phrases or words: "teach" (used for the first time in 6:59; 7:14); "How can/does this person? . . ." (6:52; 7:15); "the fathers" (6:31,49,58; 7:22); "Moses gave you bread/the law/circumcision" (6:32; 7:19,22). And there are other words and phrases, which, while they are indeed linked with chap. 5 (Schnackenburg, 2:130), are found also in chap. 6: the will and willing (6:11,21,38–40,67; 7:17) "of the one who sent me/him" (6:38–39; 7:16,18). Even the emphasis on "work" (7:21) may be found in varied form in chap. 6 (6:29).

Whatever the final, debatable, details, the basic point is clear: in a variety of ways, Jesus' declaration on the law takes up again the form and phrases not only of chap. 5 but also of chap. 6. Thus, just as the introduction (7:11–13), by its double use of both "the Jews" and "the crowd," fuses elements from the introductions in chaps. 5 and 6 (5:16–18, 6:22–24), so also the opening declaration on the law effects a similar fusion.

More important, however, than the progression of details is the progression of basic ideas. The law, however much it is founded on the creative word, is founded also on providence (chap. 6). In other words, it comes not only from the divine word, but also from divine care. Not just a bright idea, it is prepared as carefully as a parent provides food for a child. It is hardly an accident that, in the OT also, the giving of the law is set in the context of the giving of food (Exodus 16, 17, 19, 20). Nor is the gospel phrasing an accident: "[Moses] gave bread . . . gave the law . . . gave circumcision" (6:31–32; 7:19, 22). If the law is set in any

context other than that of life-giving providence then, as Jesus will imply (cf. esp.
7:19), it tends to kill.

Having set the text in its context—against the background of chap. 6—it is
now possible to look at it in greater detail.

The first statement (7:15–19) begins by emphasizing, in diverse ways, that
while Jesus does indeed know letters, and by implication knows the scriptures, he
is much more than a letter-bound scribe. The Jews put it negatively by saying that
his knowledge does not depend on human learning (v 15). Jesus puts it positively
by saying that his teaching comes not from himself but from the one who sent
him (v 16). He is pictured therefore as someone whose teaching is set in its true
ultimate context, as someone whose teaching does not depend exclusively on mere
intellect.

Nor does the response to his teaching and the recognition of its origin depend
on intellect alone; it depends rather on whether someone "wills to do [God's]
will" (v 17). The meaning of this verse has been much disputed (see esp. Bultmann, 274; and Haenchen, 2:13–14), but what it seems to be saying is that "predisposition determines one's response to Jesus" (Kysar, 120). A similar emphasis
on the will was seen in the preceding chapters (5:6,30,35,40; 6:11,21,38–40,67).

In contrast to this God-centered disposition is that of the one who seeks personal glory. Such is the attitude of the Jews. Though Moses gave them the law
none of them implements it. Rather they seek to kill Jesus (vv 18–19). The reference to killing may seem illogical, yet it has a terrible coherence. Set as it is in
the context of the Jewish betrayal of the law, it implies that in their hands the law
kills. (The connecting of apparently disparate elements by mere context or juxtaposition is a feature of biblical narrative; cf. Alter, 1981, 26.) A similar view of
the law—as something which kills—is found in Paul (cf. esp. Romans 7). The
contrast which finally emerges is between a God-centered teacher "who is true,
[in whom] there is no injustice" (*adikia*, v 18b), and a glory-hungry approach
which turns the law into a killer.

The second statement (7:20–24) gives an initial indication of how these diverse
approaches bear fruit. On the one hand, there are Jesus' interlocutors. They are
not in contact with reality, for, unlike those who are God-centered (v 17), they
do not recognize Jesus as being from God—they say he has a demon—nor do
they recognize the desire to kill in Jesus' opponents (they ask who seeks to kill
him; 7:20, cf. 7:1). In this context it is worth noting the comment of Duke (1985,
74): " 'The Jews' are strangely unaware of their real role in the death of Jesus."
Thus concerning good and evil in people, their most basic perceptions are flawed.
As for their implementation of the law, only one aspect is mentioned: their insistence, even when it is the sabbath, on circumcising, in other words, their involvement in a process which consists of inflicting a physical wound (literally, a cutting). This does not necessarily deny the dignity of circumcision in Jewish eyes
(cf. Hoskyns, 316), but it is a reminder of the fact that in the NT, circumcision
is not esteemed. It is sometimes treated as a matter of gashing or cutting (Gal
5:12, Phil 3:2), and at best it is regarded as something very limited. On the other
hand—in contrast to the literal interpreters—there is Jesus, someone who per-

formed a work which evoked wonder: on the sabbath day his action was not to cut but to make whole an entire person. Given the shallowness of their perceptions, it is not surprising that he concludes by warning against superficiality (v 24). Jesus teaches not as one who is attacking the law, but as one who has plumbed its depths, who knows its origin and essence, and who seeks to bring out its true meaning.

[7:25–30] Reinterpreting the law leads to a partial perception of the Christ; Jesus' origin in God.   In contrast to Jesus' interlocutors in the previous section, those in this text—a limited number ("some")—have a glimmering of who he is. In a questioning way they identify Jesus as the one whose life is threatened (v 15), and then, in a manner which is both questioning and indirect ("Can it be that the rulers have recognized? . . .") they wonder if he is the Anointed (v 26). But their perception of the Anointed, as well as being indirect, is also very weak: as soon as they see the possibility that Jesus might be the Anointed they withdraw from it; they argue that since Jesus' origin is known he cannot be the Anointed. The Anointed (according to some Jewish traditions) was supposed to be of unknown origin (v 27). Thus their insight falters.

In face of this faltering, Jesus "cried out." Yes, they know him and his origin, but only in a superficial way. He has another, unknown, origin, one who is an authentic ("true") source or sender (v 28). And this sender is not remote or cold. There is, rather, a personal relationship ("I know him"), and it is this personal relationship which underlies Jesus' mission (v 29).

Thus the scepticism surrounding Jesus' origin is countered, and there is a suggestion that he is indeed the Anointed.

The most important question in this text is why the emphasis on the law (7:14–24) should be followed by an emphasis on the emergence of the Anointed (7:25–29).

The essence of this law–Anointed relationship would seem to be that a true interpreting of the law (as found in 7:14–24) prepares the way for the initial emergence of the Anointed (as found in 7:25–29). In other words, the law prepares the way for the Anointed. And the nature of the link between the reinterpreted law and the Anointed has to do with breaking away from superficiality and developing an appreciation of persons and personal relationship—particularly relationship with God. True law has a sense of a person's dignity. And awareness of dignity tends to lead to the recognition that someone is special, anointed (*christos*), ultimately from God.

The final verse (30) reports a first attempt at arresting Jesus. It may seem superfluous and awkward, especially because of the later and more elaborate attempt to arrest him (v 32), but its tentative nature suits the narrative—it suits the account of the tentative recognition of the Anointed. And when it is combined with the closing words ("his hour had not yet come") it serves as a faint reminder that whatever one's God-based dignity, at some stage one will have to face an ominous hour. There is dignity, and there is death.

[7:31–36] A fuller perception of the Anointed—The prospect of Jesus' rejection and of his return to God. In this scene there is a significant advance. The Anointed is now perceived, not falteringly by "some" (as in vv 25–27), but more steadily, and by "many" (v 31). Their belief, insofar as it is sign-related, may not be the best, and like those in the previous scene they formulate their perception in a question, but now the implied answer is positive: "When the Anointed comes, will he do more signs? . . ." The time is at hand, therefore, for the revelation of the Anointed.

The evoking of a later time is corroborated by other factors. In contrast to the attempted arrest of the previous scene, one which was expressly connected with the absence of Jesus' hour (v 29), the attempt in this scene, with its involvement of "officials [sent by] the high priests and the Pharisees" is a harbinger of that hour, of the time when these forces will, in fact, arrest Jesus (18:3). Furthermore, as these forces are mentioned, Jesus begins to speak of his going (*hypagō*) to the one who sent him—an allusion to going to God in death (13:3). The Jews in their misunderstanding (v 35) add to the effect; they ask if he will go to the Gentile world ("the Dispersion of the Greeks")—something which is closely linked to the hour of Jesus' death (12:20–24).

What emerges, therefore, is a proleptic scene, one which summarizes basic aspects of the forthcoming passion, particularly the implied idea of Jesus' return to God. But the Jews cannot grasp it. All they can do is misunderstand (v 35) and parrot (v 36).

Note: Collective Terms in 7:14–36

In these three scenes the use of such phrases as "the Jews" and "the crowd" changes subtly. Initially they seem to be on an equal footing, though it is the Jews who are mentioned first (vv 15, 20). (Further balance between "the Jews" and "the crowd" may be noted *between* 5:16–18 and 6:22–24, and *within* 7:11–13.) Then, in another set of balanced phrases, "some from the Jerusalemites" is mentioned before "many from the crowd" (vv 25, 31). But though "the Jerusalemites" are referred to first, they are not as many, nor as believing as those from the crowd. Finally when "the Pharisees" hear "the crowd" murmuring there is a suggestion of antagonism between the two, an antagonism that threatens to be exacerbated by the Pharisees' alliance with the chief priests (v 32). In the end (vv 35–36) Jesus is referred to as being with "the Dispersion of the Greeks" and then simply with "the Greeks"—and "the Jews" are left behind. Thus there seems to be both a group of Jewish terms (Jews, Jerusalemites, Pharisees, high priests, and, perhaps, Dispersion) and a group of terms more suited to the Gentiles (crowd, Greeks). Initially the two are balanced, but though the Jews may be first, the overall movement is towards the Gentiles. This does not exclude all Jews; the words "Jerusalemite" and "Dispersion" are sufficiently ambiguous to suggest an openness of some Jews to Jesus and of Jesus to the Jews. And the whole setting, at a Jerusalem feast, implies some such openness. But there is a definite suggestion of an impending rift between, on the one hand, the Jewish leaders and the Jews, and on the other, some Jews and "the [Gentile] crowd."

Such usage of terms may be perplexing. It contributes to making the narrative seem confused—at least when it is read as straightforward reporting. Yet if it is seen as a form of art, as a way, within a brief specific episode, of suggesting a complex general movement (from the Jews to the Gentiles), then it is highly coherent and expressive.

[7:37–39] The last day of the feast: Jesus' declaration on the Spirit. On the last great day of the feast Jesus stands and cries out offering drink to the thirsty. It is an offer which echoes earlier offers, especially that made to the woman of Samaria (4:7–15, cf. 6:35), an offer which the text interprets as referring to the Spirit.

Among the controversies surrounding these verses two stand out: To what scripture does v 38 refer when it says that "Out of his heart shall flow rivers of living water?" And whose heart is involved—that of Jesus or of the believers? The punctuation is ambiguous. (For discussion see Brown, 320–23; Haenchen, 2:17–18; and esp. Schnackenburg, 2:151–57.)

With regard to identifying the scripture, there are a number of texts which show significant affinity with John's apparent quotation (e.g. Prov 18:4, Isa 43:20, 55:1; cf. Ps 78:15–16; 105:40–41; and esp. Zech 14:8 and Ezek 47:1–11). But none is adequate, and while it is indeed useful to indicate kindred texts, it seems better not to attempt to identify one specific text as being the precise one intended. In the context, no single reference could possibly be adequate. One of the most basic ideas of chap. 7 is that in Jesus something quite new is being revealed. The very word "cry" (*krazō*) suggests prophecy or revelation. The way is being prepared for a presence which is distinctive—the Spirit that has not yet been given (7:39). It is significant that, at the end of the preceding scene, "the Jews" are shown as unable to make sense of Jesus' "word"; all they can do is parrot it (cf. 7:34,36). Their incomprehension reflects the fact that Jesus is saying something that does not fit the old mold. As the would-be arresters report, he is speaking as no one has ever spoken before (7:46). Thus there is nothing in the past, not even in scripture, which articulates in a single statement what is now about to happen. What the evangelist has given strikes a delicate balance. On the one hand, Jesus' statement is indeed in accordance with the scriptures. As Brown (323) concludes, it is a kind of composite of various texts. On the other hand, it says something that had never been said before. Thus there is both continuity and innovation. Scripture is not destroyed, but fulfilled.

With regard to the other problem—the ambiguity concerning the source of the waters (Jesus or the believer?)—it seems better, as so often in John, to respect the ambiguity. On the one hand, it is appropriate to say that the source of the waters is Jesus: at several stages he offers something to drink (4:10–14; 6:35, 53–56; 7:37), and at his death there will be an outflow of blood and water (19:34). Furthermore, such an outpouring is associated in various ways with his giving of the Spirit (4:21–25; 19:30; 20:22). It makes sense then to see this text as referring to the fact that at Jesus' glorification there will flow from him the waters of the Spirit.

On the other hand, it also makes sense to see the Spirit as flowing from the believer. The woman of Samaria, as well as receiving from Jesus, became for others a source of believing (4:27–30, 39). And those who eventually receive the Spirit become for others a source of the forgiveness of sins (20:20–23). Within chap. 7 also there is, overall, a gradual shift of emphasis from focusing on Jesus and Jesus' words to focusing on the believer. In each succeeding scene he says less and less (cf. vv 14–24, 25–30, 31–36), and in the final two scenes he says nothing at all (cf vv 40–44, 45–52). What emerges instead is a series of voices of believers, first tentatively, but then more assertively—even in the face of division and authority (cf. vv 31, 40–41, 46, 51). Thus, according to chap. 7 the truth of revelation flows not only from Jesus but also from the believers, and the ambiguity in question (vv 37–39) falls right at the turning point in the shift of emphasis. In other words, the ambiguity is not a problem to be solved. Rather, set at the heart of chap. 7, and, to some degree, at the heart of the gospel, it is a rich microcosm of a much larger reality: life flows out from Jesus to the believer; and from the believer life flows out to others.

One of the curious details of the text is the opening phrase: *En . . . tē eschatē hēmera, . . .* "On the last day. . . ." This phrase, which is here used in the context of introducing the great day of the festival, appears to echo the earlier use of the same phrase in the context of giving life to the dead "on the last day" (6:39,40,44,54; 11:24; the reference in 12:48 is to judgement on the last day). The phrases in chaps. 6 and 7 are so connected—by their proximity to one another, and by the striking nature of the actual phrase—that some inherent relationship is quite possible. Though the contexts are different, a gospel which makes deliberate use of ambiguity could also accommodate such diversity of meaning. Furthermore, Jesus' cry "on the last day" (7:37–39) has many links with the scene of his death (see comment on 19:28–30). The avenue of research which seems most worth exploring is that the last day of the feast of Tents, the day on which Jesus stands up and alludes to the life-giving Spirit which is conferred at his glorification-through-death, that day is in some sense a proleptic portrait of what the Spirit, given through Jesus' glorification, will do for the dead on the last day.

[7:40–44] Revelation of the Spirit leads to recognition of the Anointed—and to division. Unlike "the Jews," who misunderstood Jesus' words or simply parroted them (vv 35–36), there are people in the crowd who, on hearing Jesus' words, reach new levels of understanding and recognition: "This is truly the prophet"; "This is the Anointed." The reference to the prophet recalls, word for word, the reaction of some to the multiplication account (6:14); in clear contrast to that earlier statement, however, it omits both the world-centered qualification ("who is to come into the world") and the power-centered effort to make Jesus king (6:15). In other words, unlike 6:14–15, they see Jesus as a prophet in the best sense—without qualification. It is an appropriate response in a chapter where

Jesus is portrayed as seeking not to put on a spectacular show for the world, but to bring revelation in its due time (cf. 7:3–9).

Then comes the further recognition—that he is the Anointed. This builds on the declaration that he is a prophet—it is like an intensification of the prophet idea—and it is a high point in the development of the entire chapter.

There are some who protest against seeing Jesus as the Anointed: they say the Anointed must come, not from Galilee, but as scripture says, from the descent of David and from Bethlehem. These objections, however, are not to be regarded as convincing. According to Matthew and Luke, Jesus met these criteria (Matt 1:20, 2:1; Luke 1:27, 2:4–6). More important, even if the reader were not aware of Matthew and Luke, John's own text circumvents the problem: in the earlier discussion of the Anointed (vv 25–30) it was implied that such criteria are not important, for if the origin of Christ is supposed to be secret (vv 28–29) then one cannot demand that the Anointed originate in a known lineage and place. Hence, as the narrative implies, those who saw Jesus as the Anointed simply discounted the objections and held to their insight.

Discounting such objections, however, was no easy thing. After all, they were based on scripture. Yet, in the context of a revelatory Spirit-related cry, which broke the limits of all known scripture (vv 37–38), it makes sense that people should take a stand against a reliance on scripture which is pedantic and "carnal." (The quotation in question invokes "the descent [lit. "seed," *sperma*] of David." Thus its very content confirms the idea of an unspiritual or letter-bound reading of scripture.)

Hence while the scene of the revelatory cry implied that Jesus was forging a new scripture, the present scene implies a complementary phenomenon: that those who recognize him are breaking the limits of the old scripture; they can see beyond the superficial proof-texting of the unbelievers. Given such tension, the next line is highly appropriate: "So there was a division (*schisma*) . . . because of him." It is the first time that such a word occurs in John, and it indicates that in a certain sense the decisive break with the old order is already under way. The following verse (44), which tells of a failed attempt to arrest Jesus, is similar to an earlier report from the midpoint of the feast (v 30), but, in sharp contrast to that previous account, nothing is said about his hour not having yet come. In other words, the contrast tends to confirm what the preceding scenes (vv 37–39, 40–44) imply: that in some sense the final hour is already looming on the horizon, that some of its dynamics are already in motion.

Just as it was necessary earlier to ask why the reinterpreting of the law (7:14–24) led to a partial recognition of the Anointed (7:25–36), so here too the question arises of why the scripture-breaking promise of the Spirit (7:37–39) leads to the fuller recognition of Jesus as both prophet and Anointed. The least one may conclude is that while the law imparts an obscure sense of the Anointed, the Spirit is associated with a sense of the Anointed which is clear or full.

A further implication of the text is that the Anointed is to be understood not in any crass way, but in a spiritual way which breaks established categories. Those who concentrate on physical externals—on a superficial sense of scripture and on questions of genealogy ("seed/descent")—cannot grasp the presence of the

Anointed, cannot see that an ordinary-looking person is special, anointed. But those who ''hear these [Spirit-related] words'' (v 40) are able to see beneath the surface; they recognize the Anointed.

Thus, without mentioning the virgin birth, John communicates the idea that the Christ is associated, not with physical descent, but with the Spirit.

[7:45–52] Recognition gives way to rejection. The emergence and recognition of the Anointed, so emphasized in the preceding scenes, receives in this text one crowning comment: an acknowledgement from the would-be arresters that Jesus was speaking in a way never known before. There is also some support from Nicodemus—a brief reference (7:50–51) which, when taken with the other Nicodemus texts (2:23–3:21, 19:39), draws a deft picture of a Jewish leader who is intent on seeking the light.

Most of the scene, however, is focused not on recognition of the Anointed, but on his rejection. Though the officials (*hypēretai*, ''officials/servants/officers/police'') speak positively about Jesus, their presence, when combined with that of the hostile Pharisees and high priests, creates something of the mood of the final rejection of Jesus at his Passion (18:3, 12–13, 22). So does the use of ''lead''— ''Why did you not lead him [here]?''—the word frequently used of Jesus during his final hours (18:13, 28; 19:13). There is furthermore the rejection by ''the rulers'' (7:48)—an expression which may indeed be connected with the Sanhedrin, but which, as it stands, has also a suggestion of rulers in general, the rulers of ''this world'' (18:36). It is a rejection which will be illustrated in Pilate, and one which was already alluded to broadly in saying that the world hates Jesus (7:7).

Apart from thus evoking final and widespread rejection, the text also gives some idea of the basic character of that rejection, its twisted nature—at least as seen in the Pharisees. It is a twistedness that was already suggested in the bizarre logic of Jesus' brothers (7:3–4). First they turn a breakthrough into an aberration: someone has spoken as never before, but despite the credibility of the witnesses, they do not pause to consider what these witnesses say; in contrast to Nicodemus they simply dismiss them as misguided (vv 46–47). Then they invoke the reaction of the authorities (v 48)—an unreliable procedure in a gospel where it is nameless disciples and servants rather than conspicuous leaders who tend to recognize things first. Next they declare an arrogant curse on the crowd, but while the curse is based on the crowd's alleged ignorance of the law, Nicodemus' question shows that they themselves, despite all their learning, are fundamentally ignorant of the law (vv 49–50). However, instead of cursing themselves, or even pausing in their rush to judgement, they simply ignore the central issue and seize on an isolated truth—the fact that the scriptures do not say, at least not explicitly, that a prophet (or, in some important mss., *the* prophet) is to rise from Galilee. And with their minds thus focused on this limited truth they begin to use it in a way that is bizarre and misleading—they suggest that Nicodemus is from Galilee. Such an idea dismisses Nicodemus, but since he is described as ''one of them,'' it also casts a doubt over themselves. Furthermore, in an ironic twist, their anti-Galilean reading of the scriptures (v 51) contains an echo of the pedantic exegesis of some of the crowd (vv 40–41)—the crowd they had dismissed as damnably ignorant of the law. Thus even as they cling to their isolated truth they heap doubt and damnation on themselves.

They do not actually use the word "scripture[s]." They simply say "search" —a technical word for scripture study. The implication, given the context of the scene as a whole, and given their fundamental misreading of the law, is that in the pursuit of their technique they have lost sight of the essence of the scriptures. A similar idea was put forward earlier (5:39–40). Thus while the scenes of the final day begin by showing Jesus as bringing the scriptures to a new Spirit-related level, they continue and conclude by showing that, as understood by Jesus' opponents, the scriptures are being increasingly parroted, misunderstood, and eclipsed.

At one level the process of rejection is clear and forceful: dismiss possible evidence, invoke authority, caricature other views (the crowd, Nicodemus), and seize an isolated truth or half-truth. But at another level it is confused and self-condemnatory, and it is an indication of the nature of some of the forces of darkness. It is the presence of such darkness which prepares the way for much of the conflict of chap. 8.

Behind the Drama of Rejected Revelation:
A Drama of Contrasting Roots and Relationships

As already mentioned, in the general introduction to chaps. 7–8, the text of 8:12–47 is more coherent than may at first appear. It is a diptych which, in the wake of the picture of Jesus' revelation being largely rejected, at least by the Jews (chap. 7), seeks to examine the deeper dimensions both of the revelation and of its rejection. Thus it leaves aside details of space and time and concentrates on the unseen relationships which give identity and character. At first, it looks to Jesus, the one who through his relationship with the Father is a guiding light for the world (8:12–30). Then it tells of "the Jews" and of the way in which, through their very different relationship to another father, they are enslaved in a pattern of lies and death (8:31–47).

What is at stake in this discussion of fatherhood is not one's genealogy, one's past, but rather one's present—the fatherhood or living force which now operates within. In other words, what is it that now generates one's life, which makes one act in a specific way?

Structure

Jesus' life-giving union with the Father (vv 12–30)
   Life-giving union is suggested (12–20)
   Life-giving union is stated more clearly (21–30)

Superficial believers' union with their father (vv 31–47)
   Deathly union is suggested (31–38)
   Deathly union is stated clearly (39–47)

As in the scenes with Nicodemus and the Samaritan woman, Jesus' statements tend to become longer and longer. At times, however, when one might expect a statement to be lengthy, it turns out, apparently for dramatic purposes, to be brief. A similar phenomenon occurs in chapter 9. Further discussion of the structure of 8:12–47 may be found in Excursus 5.

[8:12–20] Jesus, the guiding light, begins to reveal his self-identifying relationship to the Father. As in the Nicodemus episode, so in this three-part scene, Jesus begins with an arresting declaration and then proceeds to develop aspects of its meaning. The arresting declaration, "I am the light of the world, . . ." when taken along with the subsequent light–darkness contrast ("the one who follows me will not walk in darkness, but will have the light of life," v 12), may, to some degree, be understood against a complex background—the OT ideas of "the light of life" (Ps 56:13) and of God or God's glory as light (Ps 27:1, Bar 5:9), the Qumran contrast of light and darkness, and the way in which the light ceremonies of Tents recalled the guiding pillar of flame (Exod 13:21–22, 40:38; cf. Brown, 340, 343–344). What is equally important however, is the context provided by the gospel itself—the broad context provided by the prologue as it sets light between the life-giving divine Word and darkness (1:1–5), and, above all, the immediate context which uses the image of a guiding light to introduce the idea of Jesus' self-identifying relationship to God (8:12–30). In other words, when Jesus reveals himself as a guiding light, a light to be "followed" (v 12), he does so in the context of showing himself to be in union with the Father. The light, therefore, is not an isolated Jesus but a Jesus in relationship. The same is implied in the prologue: the light comes from a Word who is in relationship with God (1:1).

The Pharisees do not grasp the meaning of the light. All they see is an apparent legal infringement—an isolated individual testifying about himself—someone whose isolated witness is not true (v 13; cf. Num 35:30; Deut 17:6; 19:15; Mishnah, Ketub, 2:9).

And so in a second statement (vv 14–18), Jesus begins, indirectly, to introduce the idea of his relationship to the Father. The statement is quite long and, apart from some harmonizing manuscripts, the word "Father" does not appear until the very end. He starts by saying that he has a sense of direction—he knows where he comes from and where he is going (v 14). Later he says he is not alone —and he refers cryptically to one who sent him (v 16). Finally he identifies the sender as the Father (v 18).

The essence of this statement is positive, a preliminary portrait of someone in a profound relationship, but as it advances, it suggests that the Pharisees are in the opposite situation—they do not know his sense of direction, and they judge superficially ("according to the flesh," vv 14–15). The divergence between the two is heightened by the fact that Jesus refers to the law as "your law."

Light, insofar as it shows things for what they are, may be regarded as judging. But unlike the judgmental Pharisees, Jesus' immediate purpose is not to judge; and even to the extent that his (light-filled) presence must bring judgement, that judgement is not superficial (vv 15–16). There is an implication that his inner parental relationship sets a true standard for judging reality.

What emerges then is that the concept of light, instead of being seen as something glaring, as coming from an abstract force, is seen as relational, as coming from a parent.

In chap. 7 something similar had been done with the ideas of the law and the Anointed. They had been shown not as absolutes, but as relational. The law is to be interpreted in the context of caring providence (chap. 6), and it is for the sake of the whole person (7:14–24). The Anointed is to be understood in the context of personal knowledge, knowledge of the sender (7:26–29), and in the context of a Spirit which flows from the heart (7:37–41).

Thus in various ways the discourse at Tents seeks to remove a number of basic institutions or images from their possible positions as absolutes and to place them in the context of a living relationship.

In referring to the illegality of testifying to oneself, the Pharisees are right, and, in fact, at an earlier stage (in 5:31), Jesus himself had invoked the same principle. But that was a different context, one in which Jesus, in surveying and contrasting the old era and the new (5:31–40), had been speaking from within the viewpoint of the old. In doing so he acknowledged that the law, with its emphasis on eternal procedures, did have a value. But chap. 7 had indicated the need to reinterpret and surpass the law, to pass into the realm of the scripture-breaking Spirit, and to a significant degree it is within such a realm that chap. 8 operates. His reference to "*your* law" (8:17) appears to be a further indication that he has moved beyond the Pharisees' approach. The inner union makes a total of two persons—and, as far as the requirements of valid witness are concerned, that fulfills the law! (vv 14–18). In other words he is not a destroyer of the law; rather, he is following it, but at a higher level, a level which fulfills it. As in 7:14–24, but more so, he is interpreting the law in a holistic spiritual way which surpasses superficialities and which seeks the underlying God, the God within, the Father.

At this point they ask, "Where is your Father?", but Jesus' reply—his third statement—is the brief and negative "You do not know . . ." (v 19). It is a reminder that knowledge of the Father is not easy or superficial.

However, by adding "If you knew me you would know my Father also," Jesus begins to suggest an important message: that in some way he and the Father are identified. The Father, therefore, is not far away; in fact, God is within the human.

Yet because the third statement is surprisingly brief, the drama appears for the moment to withdraw from any further elaboration. Such a suggestion, of a temporary withdrawing or witholding, receives reinforcement from the final comment—that his hour had not yet come (v 20b). In other words, the unveiling of the Father, like the granting of the Spirit (7:37–39), is being held back. The Father is revealed, but the Father is also secret. And the failure to "sieze" him is sufficiently ambiguous to suggest a failure to grasp or understand.

It is this final idea, of a secret knowledge of the Father, which gives meaning to a puzzling detail—that Jesus spoke these things "in the treasury" (not "opposite" the treasury, as in Mark 12:41, but "in"). As Lindars (319) remarks, "it is hardly likely that Jesus taught in the temple strong-rooms." Brown (342) is even more decisive: "As far as we know, the treasury was a storage chamber, and hence Jesus would not be inside it." It is perhaps possible, as Brown suggests, that Greek prepositions were so fluid that "in" (*en*) means "opposite" (*katenanti*), but it seems much more plausible that, as with other puzzles of location, the evangelist is trying to say something. The word "treasure," as well as referring to something external, may also refer to what is internal, to what is spiritually most precious—union with the heavenly Father (cf. Matt 6:1–21, esp. 19–21). That the enigmatic location has to do with the Father is further suggested by the preceding context —by the fact that the Pharisees do not know the Father's location (19). Hence while the external meaning of treasure or treasury is puzzling, the theological meaning makes sense: within Jesus there is a hidden treasure, a secret not yet revealed, and when he speaks of the unknown Father, it is from within that treasury that he speaks.

The fact that, because Jesus' hour had not yet come, no one arrested him (v 20b), would seem, as Haenchen (2:27) suggests, to indicate the protective activity of the divine will. Hence while at one level Jesus stands vulnerably in the presence of the Pharisees, at another he stands in the treasury—in the rich and secret presence of a Father who brings him protectively to his appointed hour.

Thus, having depicted Jesus as challenging his hearers to rise above the level of the external meaning of things, the evangelist, in a final puzzling comment about the treasury, poses a similar challenge to the reader.

[8:21–30] Jesus reveals more fully his true identity, especially his self-identifying relationship with the Father. In some ways this scene is like that involving Nicodemus. It has the same kind of structure—three increasingly long statements, the third of which is twofold—and it builds up both towards a central declaration concerning Jesus' identity and mission, and, in particular, towards a declaration concerning the lifting up of the Son of humanity (8:28, cf. 3:14; the third such lifting up statement occurs in 12:32).

But while the Nicodemus scene is relatively relaxed—Jesus has plenty of time so to speak (he has just come from God), and Nicodemus, whatever his problems, is well-disposed—this later scene (8:21–30) is quite urgent. The atmosphere is one of considerable hostility, and time is running out. Jesus is presented not as someone who has just come from God (3:2), but as one who is soon to return ("I am going away, . . ." 8:21). And instead of declaring positively what must be done to reach the realm of God—a person must be reborn (3:3)—Jesus, in his first statement here, warns of the consequences of having failed to do anything: ". . . you will die in your sin. Where I am going you cannot come" (8:21). The sin in question is the refusal of all that Jesus embodies—the light of life, life itself. To reject this light is to invite death.

As Nicodemus had misunderstood, so do the Jews. When Jesus says that they cannot come where he is going, they ask whether he will kill himself. This is a reflection of their own sin-based orientation towards death, yet ironically it speaks a truth—it refers to Jesus' departure through death.

Then Jesus speaks again (vv 23–24), and, like his second statement to Nicodemus (3:5–8), his words emphasize a certain duality. But instead of being a duality of a general kind, a duality between flesh and spirit, it is a down-to-earth duality among people: "You are from below, I am from above. You are of this world, I am not of this world" (v 23). (The phrase "this world" refers to the world considered apart from God.) This difference too indicates that the scene in chap. 8 is more urgent: the fact that there are people on the wrong side of the divide means that something must be done. And so this statement of Jesus speaks also of the need to believe: "For if you do not believe that I am (*Egō eimi*) you will die in your sins" (v 24). "Sins," plural, refers to the many specific deviations which flow from the one basic "sin" which is the refusal of life (v 21). The "I am" (*Egō eimi*) is the divine name which calls people away from deathly sin and towards life. In effect, Jesus is speaking to them as if they were on a sinking ship, and he is saying, "If you want to find life, come to me."

"Who are you?", they ask.

This question is not unlike that posed by Moses at the burning bush (Exod 3:13). And it is exactly the question which had first been posed to John (1:19). When John answered he began with negatives, by saying who he was not, and only afterwards did he state positively and rather enigmatically who he was: "I am the voice of one crying . . ." (1:20–23). He might have said "I am John, from such and such a place." But instead, his answer was enigmatic, a voice from another dimension.

Jesus' answer is even more enigmatic: "Why from the beginning I speak to you." The details of the Greek are ambiguous and elusive (cf. Brown, 347–48; Schnackenburg, 2:200–201; Haenchen, 2:28). The phrase which is translated "from the beginning," *tēn archēn*, could, in strict grammar, be equally rendered "primarily" or "first of all"—in other words, "I am, primarily/first of all, what I say to you." Or the whole phrase could be turned around so that it seems to be a refusal to reply: "Why do I talk to you to begin with?" or, as the RSV alternative translation puts it "Why do I talk to you at all?"

For a translator or commentator the uncertainty is somewhat frustrating. Yet the elusiveness of the text—its ambiguity and suggestion of refusal—is altogether appropriate. What is at stake is the revelation of the divine name. In the context of speaking of his secret, his union with the Father, Jesus' reply cannot but be elusive, cannot but suggest that something is being refused, withheld. However, this does not at all mean (pace Schnackenburg, 2:200–201) that Jesus is refusing to talk. The whole context shows Jesus as revealing, and in this particular passage he goes on talking, and he wins people to belief. Far from being some kind of sulky refusal to reveal, Jesus' reply, with its evocations both of communication and of withholding, manages, in a minimum of words, to suggest something of both the proximity and the incommunicability of the divine.

It is true, of course, that when taken in isolation, the use of *archē* is indeed ambiguous and, arguably, insignificant. But account must also be taken of the context, a multifaceted context. First, the chapter as a whole (8:12–59) is considerably concerned with roots, with people's ultimate starting points and presuppositions. Its opening verse, which speaks of the world, light and darkness, evokes the beginning of the prologue (1:1–5). Furthermore, there is the immediate context, the fact that the discussion (8:12–30) is concerned first with what is most secret within Jesus, his relationship to the Father (8:12–20), and also with his closeness to the divine, to the I am. In fact the reference to the *archē* (v 25) occurs between two references to the I am (vv 24, 28). In addition, when the two main subdivisions of the chapter are laid out schematically, side by side (12–30 and 31–47), the ambiguous reference to *archē* is balanced in the later part of the chapter by a further use of *archē,* one which clearly refers to the primordial beginning ("The devil . . . was a murderer from the beginning," 8:44).

Given this context, this preoccupation with beginnings and this many-sided suggestion that Jesus is divine and out of time, and given also the incisive nature of the question ("Who are you?"), the fact that it tends to go to the root of things, there is no way that the word *archē* can fail to evoke the idea of a beginning, and obscurely, of some kind of primordial beginning. To concentrate on ambiguous grammatical technicalities to such an extent that any reference to a beginning is excluded is to imitate what Jesus even in this very passage is fighting—concentration on externals to the point where the deeper dimension of things is lost. What Jesus is saying, saying more enigmatically than John (the Baptist), is that he is a voice from out of time, a voice which even in the enigma of his name, calls people to see beyond the ordinary and external, to leave their path of sin and death.

The encounter with the divine, however, is not smooth sailing. Just as many of the prophets found that the divine call was a searching and searing affair, and just as the Nicodemus episode contained both a general emphasis on the difficulty of the ascent to God and also a specific moment of probing confrontation (3:10–12), so now Jesus indicates that he will use his speech, his revelatory words, to judge and confront the Jews and the world (v 26). And the basis of this confrontational speech is the one who sent him, the one whom Jesus hears and who is true.

This is all rather unnerving and perplexing—a warning of death (v 21), a suggestion of a sinking ship (vv 23–24), and the picture of a life-giver who is mysterious and challenging (vv 25–26). Consequently, rather as the Nicodemus scene relented from emphasizing difficulty and began, in the later part of the third response, to speak of God's love (3:16), so now, as the text moves into the second part of the third statement, there develops an emphasis on the guiding presence of the Father, a Father who teaches and who does not abandon one—not even in the moment of death (literally, of being lifted up) (vv 27–29). In fact, it is in death, in the death of the Son of humanity, that the reality of God, of the I am, is particularly revealed. Thus, the picture which finally emerges (esp. in vv 28b–29) is not of an alien God, but of a parent with whom one can be in perfect harmony.

Given the nature of Jesus' appeal—its solemnity, urgency, and attractiveness, and also the fact that what he says is a reflection of the voice of the Father—it is appropriate that the account concludes by telling that as he spoke "many" believed (v 30).

Thus while the preceding scene (vv 12–20) had suggested the secret presence of the Father and had concluded with a picture of failing to grasp Jesus, this later scene (vv 21–30) evokes a further period of revelation—a time when Jesus, in being lifted up, will reveal his union with the Father and thereby draw "many" to himself. It is in this role, as the alluring revelation of a Father who is present even in death, that he is truly the light of the world.

[8:31–38] Jesus, the giver of freedom, begins to reveal the enslavement of superficial believers.

Jesus now speaks to "the Jews who had believed in him" —a puzzling reference since "the Jews" is normally used to refer to those who do not believe, and since the believers in question seem, in fact, not to believe. In the Greek phrasing, the word "Jews" comes last, after "believed," and so the implication seems to be that these believers are "Jews," in other words, believers who do not really believe, or, more simply, superficial believers.

Thus in chap. 8, as in chap. 7, there are two groups. There are those who react positively to Jesus, who recognize him and believe in him genuinely (7:40–41a; 8:30), and those who cling to what is superficial and reject him (7:41b–42; 8:31,33). There is no need therefore to say that the puzzling phraseology is an editorial addition. Within the context of the diptych arrangement of 8:12–30 and 8:31–47, it helps to build a coherent contrast.

As for the identity of these superficial believers, Dodd (1957, 5–7; pace

Schnackenburg, 2:205) appears to be right in connecting them with Judaizing Christians, those who, while professing to believe in Jesus were still following the enslaved tradition of Judaism—a tradition which at one point is represented in variant form by the text concerning the son of Abraham's slave-girl (cf. Galatians, esp. 4:21–31). What Dodd is implying is that while 8:31–38 is set in the time of Jesus, it has a further level of reference—that of the period after Jesus. This makes sense. It receives support from the use of the term "disciples" in 8:31, a term which has not been used since 7:3, but which now, in its place at the beginning of the scene, functions like a headline announcing a new moment, the time of the disciples (a moment which echoes the new moment of the Spirit in 7:37–39). And this interpretation receives further corroboration from the fact that, as Martyn (1979, esp. 24–62) has demonstrated, the very next chapter (chap. 9) has a level of meaning which refers to the time when the disciples were in conflict with the Jews. It is noteworthy that in chap. 9 also there is a headline usage of the term "disciples" (9:2). It is not unreasonable, therefore, within chap. 8, to identify portraits of diverse aspects of the history of Jesus and the church. The first part (8:12–30) spoke of Jesus' emerging identity and mission. The second part (8:31–47) portrays an aspect of the time after Jesus—the persistent problem of the Judaizers.

However, while including a reference to the Judaizers, the picture of the superficial believers has a far wider scope. It refers to all those who abuse religion, and all who, in place of genuine believing, substitute some form of triviality, superstition, idol or lie. (Cf. Peck, 1983, esp. pp. 150–81.) It also illustrates the ancient proverb that the corruption of the best is the worst: it shows that the corruption of religion and of religion-like beliefs provides a place where evil may flourish.

There is a sense then in which John 8:31–47 functions somewhat like Conrad's *Heart of Darkness:* it "discovers the potential hell in the heart of every man." (Cf. Lillian Feeder, 1955, esp. 281–82).

Jesus begins (vv 31–32) by saying that his word leads to discipleship and truth, and by declaring "and the truth will set you free." The implication is that his word sets people free, and his declaration is one which in various ways complements his earlier statement that he was the light of the world, the light which leads to life (8:12). In fact, these two lapidary statements, concerning light and freedom, are like complementary pillars which introduce the two basic divisions of this chapter. The first, which is largely symbolic, begins with Jesus (as divine light) and then moves on to the implied idea of descipleship ("the one who follows," 8:12). The second, which is more ethical, begins with the idea of discipleship, and then moves on to the further notion of discipleship's consequences (truth and freedom, 8:31–32).

To say that truth gives freedom refers particularly to the fact that humans tend to become enslaved by a variety of idols or lies—unreal expectations, empty roles, hollow prestige games, nationalistic nonsense, dehumanizing practices and dependencies—and that it is only by recognizing these various things for what they really are, as enslaving lies, that one can achieve basic freedom. In the words of the modern slogan: "Addiction is slavery."

But the striking statement on freedom, instead of setting the tone for what follows, seems rather to provide a contrasting foil. The Jews interpret freedom in a very external or legal sense, and in accordance with this emphasis on what is external, they claim they have always been free. To some degree they are right—externally they are not slaves. But the claim to an ancient bloodline becomes, at least in their case, a confusing smoke screen, something which obscures the fullness of reality and causes them to focus on a mesmerizing sliver of the past. Bloodline or no bloodline, internally they are slaves.

Jesus on the other hand looks to what is inside. As he had earlier reinterpreted and internalized the idea of witness (8:12–20), so now (8:31–38) he reinterprets and internalizes the idea of freedom. And while he grants that in a purely carnal or physical sense they are indeed descended from Abraham, he implies that such a level of parentage is secondary to the issue of their internal or spiritual parentage.

Having spoken of freedom in his initial statement (8:31–32), Jesus then goes on to develop that theme (34–38, second statement). In contrast to the image of the slave—one who has no permanent place in the house and who ultimately must leave—Jesus speaks of the son, the one who abides forever (v 35). The slave-son contrast, which has considerable affinity with the imagery of Gal 4:21–31, may at first seem puzzling and awkward, but, as so often, it makes theological sense: like those who will die in their sin (cf. vv 21, 24), the sinful slave has no future in God's house; but the son, being God's child (cf. vv 27–29), abides forever in God's house (cf. 14:2, abiding in God's house). It is the son, therefore, who can really grant freedom (v 36). The son of course, is Jesus. But the Jewish believers, instead of accepting the freedom he offers, seek to kill him. What they want is to stifle the word which he speaks, a word which he has seen with the Father, and which, so it is implied, is in contrast to what they have heard from their father (vv 37–38).

The overall implied image (vv 34–38), reminiscent in some ways of the mother-haunted killer in Alfred Hitchcock's *Psycho,* is of a slave who, because he is haunted by a deviated father, seeks to kill the wisdom-bearing (or word-bearing) son—the very one who would free him and establish him in the house forever. It is an image which, among other things, expresses the way in which humans tend to avoid the truth and to kill the would-be free person in themselves and in others.

[8:39–47] The liars' rootedness in a death-dealing father. The scene opens with a Jewish assertion: "Our father is Abraham." It is a proud statement which is simple and clear. Jesus' reply, however—according to the best-attested reading —is a rather illogical sentence involving a mixture of moods and tenses: "If you are children of Abraham, you would do the works of Abraham." The illogicality does not mean that Jesus or the evangelist is confused. Rather it is a way of indicating, even through the literary shaping of the sentence—through the grammatical discrepancy between its two parts—what the sentence is all about: that in the Jews' relationship to Abraham there is a discrepancy; for they say they are his children, but do not do his works. Within them, as within the sentence, something is out of joint (v 39).

And then (v 40a) he explains the distortion: they seek to kill him, a person (*anthrōpos*) who speaks the truth which he had heard from God. There is an implication here that what really offends them is the truth and that their suppression of it leads to killing a person.

Having isolated their worst symptom—a death-bearing suppression of the truth—Jesus begins to uncover the underlying cause, and it is in doing this that he returns to the question of their father. He had indeed granted, in the previous scene (v 37), that they are physically descended from Abraham, but, given their conduct, Abraham may not be referred to as their father. Fatherhood, so it is implied, involves moral and spiritual continuity, and in this case there is none (v 40b, "That is not what Abraham did").

Though Jesus' words are low-key, even to the point of being obscure, their implications are ominous. It is being suggested to his hearers that their inspiration is evil, that there is something radically wrong with them.

It is enough to set alarm bells ringing: "We were not born of infidelity [*porneia*]. We have one father—God." In some ways this is a scream: "No, we do not have a serious problem. The only thing really inspiring us is God." But, like the claim to Abraham, the invoking of God is another smoke screen, and this too Jesus puts aside: "If God were your father, you would love [*agapaō*] me, for from God I came. . . ." Thus, in the final analysis they truly reflect neither Abraham nor God.

Incidentally, with regard to the contrast between *porneia*, "infidelity/fornication," and *agapē*, the best background seems, once again, to be that represented by Galatians. In that epistle the list of things that are opposed to the Spirit begins with *porneia*, and the list of things that are the fruits of the Spirit begins with *agapē* (Gal 5:19, 22). In other words, while it is generally agreed that there is dualism in this scene, and that in some ways it reflects the Qumran doctrine of the Two Spirits (cf. Lindars, 329; Brown, 365), part of that dualism is no further away than the tradition represented by Galatians. So it is hardly necessary, in explaining the word *porneia*, to appeal to such relatively distant documents as Origen's *Against Celsus* or the *Acts of Pilate* (Brown, 357; cf. Kysar, 144). Neither is it necessary to say that the "we" is emphatic ("We [*hēmeis*] were not born . . ."). A similar use of a pronoun, with no apparent emphasis, occurs in the previous sentence: "You [*hymeis*] do the works. . . ."

Having challenged the two empty claims (to Abraham and God), Jesus emphasizes what it is the Jews refuse to accept—"I have come forth from God and am here" (v 42b). This statement, which is not concerned with later trinitarian doctrine, is intended to present his mission with unusual solemnity (Brown, 357). It is as though he were giving a reminder: "If only you left aside these lies and saw the God-sent presence which is right in front of you, which in some sense is within you." But they do not, and the problem is why: "Why do you not understand what I say?" (v 43a). The question is fundamental.

The initial reply suggests that the problem is not really in the understanding at all: "It is because you cannot hear my word" (43b). In other words, the message never even reaches the understanding; it is blocked on the way in—at the hearing stage.

Then (v 44) Jesus goes to the core of the problem: ''You are of your father the devil and the desires of your father you will (*thelō*) do.'' And he then refers to the devil as the primordial (''from the beginning'') person-killing liar, someone whose lies come from his very own nature. His answer, therefore, is twofold. From the human point of view the core of the problem is in the will—in the choice or decision to hear or not to hear, to take or refuse a particular course of action. This is not something obvious or trivial. M. Scott Peck (1983, 178), for instance, indicates that it is basic, but that nonetheless it has been ''almost totally ignored'' even in so sophisticated a science as American psychiatry. The other factor is even more elusive: it is the primordial person-killing force which, from the beginning and on the basis of its own inherent perversity, plays upon the will. Given the fact that the role of the will has often been ignored, it is not surprising that even less attention has been paid to the second, diabolical, factor.

Having spoken of evil, Jesus then goes on (vv 45–47) to set it in context and to give a balancing emphasis. He refers to the truth and goodness (sinlessness) which is found in himself, and he indicates that the ultimate answer to the problem of evil is yet more elusive: ''You do not hear because you are not of God'' (47b). This is an ambiguous phrase which could refer either to the cause or the result of the refusal and which, therefore, places God in an uncertain position. What is clear is that however one approaches the problem, however much one invokes the will and the perverse force, the ultimate answer is in God. Thus the problem of evil is subsumed into the greater reality of God. Essentially the same approach had been adopted in the book of Job: the problem of evil was not solved, but false solutions were rejected. Evil was described, named (thus lessening its demonic force), and, above all, evil was set in the context where faith could deal with it —the context of God (cf Job 38:1–42:6).

Jesus' Vision of Life and the Jews' Vision of Death: The Parting of the Ways

This passage is closely bound to the rest of chapter 8, yet it is useful to treat it separately. Doing so highlights its distinctness—particularly the fact that while 8:12–30 and 8:31–47 together form a diptychlike study of contrasting origins and relationships, 8:48–59 is more focused towards contrasting destinies, towards contrasting visions of the future. Thus while 8:12–30 and 8:31–47 highlighted the contrast between Jesus' rootedness in the Father and the Jews' rootedness in the devil, 8:48–59 brings out the basic consequence of that contrast—the fact that Jesus is focused on life and the Jews are focused on death. It is a divergence which had already been suggested by earlier parts of the chapter (cf. Lindars, 316; Schnackenburg, 2:190–91) and which to some degree evokes Moses' culminating image of the two ways (Deut 30:15–20).

The root of the Jews' negativity has already been indicated—a willful sunkenness in deathly (diabolical) lies; it comes down to a lack of faith, to fear. Like craving, fear distorts; it prevents a person from seeing reality.

Structure

As Mateos and Barreto (414) indicate, the structure consists of a threefold pattern wherein "the Jews" speak and Jesus replies (vv 45–51, 52–56, 57–58). And at the end (v 59), when Jesus hides and leaves the temple, the ways separate.

As Jesus speaks, his statements seem at first to be becoming longer (cf. vv 49–51, 54–56), but the third statement, though it is climactic, is the shortest of all, and it ends in a striking two-word revelation: *Egō eimi,* the divine "I am" (v 58). Thus, here as elsewhere—see the discussion of the detailed structure of 8:12–47 (Excursus 5)—the pattern-breaking brevity achieves a dramatic effect.

As noted earlier, 8:48–59 balances 7:1–10. Details aside, the essence of this balance is that while 7:1–10 is concerned with belief's most basic aspects—belief is implicitly contrasted with the brothers' twisted logic and glory-oriented impatience—8:48–59 is more centered on belief's final outcome. Unbelief leads to death, and the truth leads to life. Thus, the entire drama (chaps. 7–8) opens and closes with a basic contrast involving belief and unbelief, life and death.

This rough balance between the drama's opening and closing sections (7:1–10 and 8:48–59) lends further likelihood to the idea that "the brothers" (in 7:1–10) are in some way representative of the unbelieving Jews.

[8:48–51] First reply: Jesus challenges death. "The Jews" open the scene with a confident statement ("Do we not speak well . . .") that Jesus is a Samaritan and has a demon. The meaning of this sweeping accusation is obscure, but one thing is clear—they are glaringly wrong. The woman of Samaria could tell immediately that Jesus was a Jew (4:9), but they, after extended conversation, can still not see it. And it is this "warped perception" (Kysar, 145) which acts as background for the remainder of the scene. Everything they say, about life or death, will be judged on the presupposition that they cannot see even the basics.

Jesus' reply begins (v 49) with an elementary clarification, first of what he is not (he does not have a demon), and then of what he is (someone who does the most fundamental of things—he honors his father). At the same time, by referring to the dishonoring practice of his hearers, he implies that between himself and them there is a division. And by alluding (v 50) to glory-seeking (a sensitive topic with the Jews, cf. 5:41–44) and judgement ("there is one who judges"), he heightens the sense of division, suggests his own union with God, and evokes an atmosphere of judgement.

Then he makes his declaration (v 51): "Amen, amen, I say to you, whoever keeps my word shall not see death for ever." It is faintly reminiscent of the initial declarations to Nicodemus and the Samaritan woman (3:3; 4:13–14)—the idea that Jesus is bringing a message or gift which opens the way to God and life eternal. And it echoes much of what is said in chaps. 5 and 6 about Jesus as the source of life, as having "the words of eternal life" (6:68). But, as so often happens in one of John's graded texts, it is expressed negatively. Rather than speaking of life, it refers to not seeing death. The conclusion, therefore, of this initial exchange is a declaration, solemn yet understated, that Jesus' word, which is based ultimately on the Father, is an effective challenge to death.

[8:52–56] Second reply: Jesus affirms joy. The Jewish reaction, echoing Nicodemus and the Samaritan woman, is a misunderstanding which sees things in a physical or external way: they think Jesus is offering the avoidance of physical death. This reaction, too, reflects the fact that they cannot perceive him correctly. Even in repeating his words they misquote—instead of "*see* death" they say "*taste* death." But Jesus did not exclude the taste of death. He had spoken earlier of *eating* and *drinking* a death-related providence (6:52–58), and not even about the beloved disciple did he say that he would not die (21:23).

Jesus' reply (vv 54–56), as well as being a self-defense, raises the focus of discussion to a new level—that of the glory that comes from the Father. But even as he speaks of knowing the Father who glorifies, Jesus tells also of the opposite phenomenon—of the Jews who, despite their invoking of God, do not, in fact, know God and so are lying. Thus while building to a positive culmination, the text is also building a more and more negative contrast.

Resuming the positive emphasis, Jesus speaks not only of knowing the Father who glorifies, but also of keeping his word. The word is like a life-bearing force, and in the first reply (v 51) the keeping of the word meant not seeing death. Now, as Jesus returns to the idea of the word, he expresses its life-bearing quality, not negatively as earlier (not seeing death), but positively—by speaking of Abraham, the one whom Jesus describes as rejoicing and as seeing beyond his limited time and into Jesus' own day (v 56). In other words, Jesus goes from challenging death (first statement) to affirming joy (second statement).

Abraham's Joy and Vision (8:56): A Note

Concerning the details of the reference to Abraham, it seems likely that when Jesus speaks of a double joy—Abraham "was overjoyed" and "rejoiced"—what is in question is the double joy which surrounded the birth of Isaac. First there was the overwhelming laughter which surrounded the announcement of Isaac's birth (Gen 17:17, cf. 18:12). And then there was the later joy, particularly on Sarah's part, which attended the birth itself (Gen 21:6). Even linguistically there is some connection:

Gen: laughed (17:17, 18:12), laughter, rejoice with (21:6)
e-gel-asen, gel-ōta, sug-char-eitai

John: was overjoyed, rejoiced
ē-gall-iasato, e-char-ē

Abraham's joy, therefore, was his joy at Isaac.

But as Gal 3:16 suggests, "the birth of Isaac is prophetic of the birth of Christ" (Lindars, 335), and so to have rejoiced over Isaac is to have rejoiced over Christ. The connection between Isaac and Christ is strengthened by the fact that Isaac was a symbol of victory over death—he was born to two people who were judged to be dead (in this regard cf. the triple use of dead/death in Rom 4:17–19; cf. also Heb 11:12). And his being saved from sacrifice meant that he was regarded as one whom God brought back from the dead (Hebr 11:17–19). As Spicq (1957, 83) notes concerning Hebr 11:19, the saving of Isaac from death prefigures the resurrection of all people, and in traditional exegesis, it prefigures the death and resurrection of Christ. Through Isaac therefore, Abraham had a distant vision of what Christ would bring. (See Hebr 11, esp. 11:9–10, 13, 19: "By faith Abraham [and others] . . . lived as an alien . . . in tents [*en skēnais*, v 9], . . . looking forward to the city . . . [of] God; . . . died . . . not having possessed what was promised, but *having seen it and greeted it from afar. . . .* He considered that God was able to raise . . . the dead.")

What aspect of Christ did Abraham see? What is the day ("my day") to which Jesus refers? It has long been disputed whether it refers to the incarnation (the birth of Jesus), the glorification, or the whole of Jesus' life. If one is to judge according to the broad context of prevailing Jewish ideas, then "the evangelist must mean the day of the Messiah's appearance" (Schnackenburg, 2:222), in other words, the day when Jesus is revealed as the Anointed. The more immediate context supports this: it tells of a day, the "great day" of the feast of Tents, when Jesus was perceived to be the Anointed (7:37–41). But as the declaration on the great day of Tents indicated, the revelation of Jesus is inextricably linked with his glorification (7:39), and therefore, while the Anointed may be partly revealed during life, the glorification also is essential. Thus it seems best to conclude that Jesus' day refers to the way in which, during his entire life, and especially in his death, he was revealed as the Anointed. It was this revelatory life and glorification which, through Isaac, Abraham saw.

Thus, while at one level Abraham may indeed have died, at another he reached across death and time to enter a vision of joy.

[8:57–58] Third reply: Jesus reveals timeless divinity. The Jewish failure to grasp the word now reaches a new level. They might have asked, given Jesus' preceding statement, how *Abraham saw Jesus*. Instead they ask how *Jesus*, not yet fifty years old, *has seen Abraham*. The surprising twist in the question has led some copyists to rewrite the text along more logical lines, but the puzzling phraseology has its purpose: it suggests a complete breakdown of coherent perception. Kysar (146) describes it as "still another ridiculous misunderstanding." It forms a very appropriate background for the story of blindness (chap. 9).

Yet ironically, in asking if Jesus has seen Abraham, they prepare the way for a crowning revelation: "Amen, amen, I say to you, before Abraham came to be (*ginomai*), I am (*Egō eimi*)." The distinction between *ginomai* and *eimi* is the same as that used in the prologue to distinguish the being of creatures from that of the Creator Word. As Brown (367) comments about the *Egō eimi:* "No clearer implication of divinity is found in the Gospel tradition."

Incidentally, it is generally agreed that the reference to fifty does not help in the reconstruction of history. If it has a symbolism, then perhaps it should be read as in some way connected with the earlier references to related numbers, to ten (1:39), five (4:18; 6:9), and five thousand (6:10). Is it, for instance, a variation on the perfection implied in ten, and so an ironically suitable introduction to the climactic revelation of divinity?

Whatever the possible meanings of such debatable details, the reference to fifty years highlights something important: that in this timebound human being there is a timeless presence, something divine. Thus the way is prepared for the later worshipping of the Son of humanity (9:35–38). More immediately, however, something else is being implied: let time and the ravages of time do what they will to an earthbound human, there is in that human something greater, something which time cannot destroy.

[8:59] Conclusion: rejection and separation.   Jesus' revelation—of divinity in humanity—evokes from the Jews not worship but hostility. Instead of seeing God they see blasphemy, and they react accordingly—with an attempt, as prescribed in Lev 24:16, to stone the blasphemer. Thus their fear, based on their faithlessness, takes its inevitable toll—it issues in violence. Faced with their intransigence he "hid himself and went out of the temple." The light (cf. 8:12) has gone, and it is time to speak of blindness.

Note: Chap. 8 as an Oblique Repetition of Aspects of 2:23–4:42

One of the subtle features of chap. 8 is the way in which it complements aspects of 2:23–4:42. First, the three-part upward spiral from darkness ("night") to the revelation of the Son of humanity (2:23–3:21) is found in a form that is complementary and more complex in 8:12–30. Then the two-part episode involving tension with the old Jewish order, along with its images of the bride and groom and the one from above (3:22–36), finds oblique echoes and counterimages in the two-part clash with the believing Jews—particularly in the references first to the son and slave and then to the devil (8:31–47). And finally, the three-part encounter with the Samaritan woman, an encounter in which Jesus reveals himself as source of life (4:1–42), is reflected in the final three-part exchange during which Jesus, accused of being a Samaritan, reveals himself as the one whose word is the source of life (8:48–59).

As an example of the subtle complexity of the relationship of the texts one may note 4:12 and 8:53:

"Kyrie . . .

Are you greater than our Father Jacob	"Are you greater than our Father Abraham
who gave us the *well,*	who *died?*
and *drank* from it himself	And the prophets *died.*
and his sons and his cattle?"	
	Who do you make yourself to be?"

The texts form a contrast. The woman, in interpreting the past, sees life and also the continuation and expansion of life (". . . the well . . . and drank . . ."). But what the Jews see, and see as continued, is death (". . . died . . . died"). In both texts there is an awareness that Jesus claims to be bringing a new form of life, but while the woman, despite her initial scepticism, is open to that possibility —the *Kyrie,* however mundane, is open to a higher meaning (cf. Duke, 1985, 102),—the Jews are closed; far from addressing Jesus as *Kyrie,* they see him as a pretender.

What is essential,however, is the larger relationship: while 2:23–4:42 moves towards an ever greater acceptance of Jesus, including his acceptance among the Gentiles, the Jews of chap. 8 move towards blind rejection.

Excursus 4: The Story of the Adulteress and the Accusers

It is generally agreed that this passage was not part of the original gospel. The oldest manuscripts do not contain it, and there are some manuscripts which, though they do reproduce it, suggest that it be located elsewhere—either after John 21:25, or after Luke 21:38. (For details, see esp. Schnackenburg, I, 181–82). The Council of Trent considered this text, but voted by two to one not to make a special declaration about it (Hoskyns, 563).

The origin of the passage is unknown. U. Becker (1963, 150–64) has argued that it came from Jewish-Christian circles in the second century, and that it was included with the gospels about the year 200.

Whatever may have been the text's original relationship to living people (to the person or group who first recorded it), it appears to be dependent in part on two sets of written sources—the synoptic gospels and the book of Daniel. The general picture of Jesus given here—moving from the mountain of Olives to confrontation in Jerusalem —accords broadly with the synoptic account of Jesus moving from Bethany to confrontation in Jerusalem (Mark 11:11,12,19,27; Matt 21:17; see synoptic references to the mountain of Olives [Mark 13:1–3; Luke 21:37,38; 22:39]). And the specific drama, concerning the hypocritical accusation of adultery, involves an adaptation of episodes from the life of Daniel (especially concerning Daniel and the accusation of Suzanna [Daniel 13, LXX; see Brodie, 1993, 157–59]). Like Daniel 13, John 7:53–8:11 lies close to the dividing line between what is canonical and what is not.

Whatever the origin and sources of 7:53–8:11, it is dramatic and meaningful. Jesus confronts the empty accusations of the authorities, yet the emphasis is not on confrontation but on mercy. Rather than tell the authorities their sins, he leaves them alone to face them. And in dealing with the woman, who is already quite aware of her sinfulness, he opens up for her a new place of forgiveness and peace. In the clash involving opposite elements of society—the power-hungry authorities and the vulnerable lone woman—Jesus does not hesitate about taking her side and about literally standing alone with her. Yet he does it with a kind of serenity.

In its present location, between chaps. 7 and 8, the story of the adulteress can be disruptive. It obscures the delicate unity and structure of these two chapters. Yet this location has some appropriateness. Jesus' treatment of the woman illustrates what chap. 7 had indicated—that in Jesus' hands the Law of Moses is a source of life rather than an instrument of death (7:14–24). And the contrast between Jesus and the Jewish authorities, which pervades chap. 8, finds vivid expression in the scene around the woman.

Excursus 5: The Structure of 8:12–47

8:12–30

It is generally agreed that this text, which is focused on Jesus' union with the Father, may be divided into two subsections or "scenes"—the initial indication of union (vv 12–20) and a more developed statement both about that union and about Jesus' identity (vv 21–30).

The distinction between these scenes is confirmed by some repetition involving their opening and closing sentences (cf. "Again, . . ." 8:12, 21; "These [things] . . . he spoke . . . teaching/[he] taught . . . speaking," 8:20, 28–30).

Within each scene Jesus makes three statements (within the first scene, cf. vv 12, 14–18, 19; within the second scene: cf. vv 21, 23–24, 25–29). But while the interlocutors' utterances become shorter, Jesus' three statements become longer, and the third is twofold. This follows a variation on the pattern seen earlier in Jesus' statements to Nicodemus and the Samaritan woman, yet it contains one striking variation: in the initial scene, Jesus' third statement, far from being prolonged or twofold, is disappointingly brief and negative: "You do not know, either me . . ." (v 19).

This rather startling variation on the pattern will be found again in chap. 9. In that chapter also there are two balancing scenes in which the healed man makes three statements of increasing lengths (initial scene: 9:9, 11, 12; later scene: 9:25, 27, 30–33), but in the initial scene, the third statement is disappointingly brief and negative: "I do not know" (v 12).

In both chapters this arrangement has the effect of making the initial scenes seem inadequate. Though they represent genuine progress they are but the preparation for the later and more developed scene. To some degree, this implied contrast, between what is preparatory and what is full, is to be seen in the light of one of the main ideas underlying the structure of chap. 7: a contrast between the time of the law and the time of the Spirit.

The distinction between these scenes (vv 12–20 and 21–30) does not mean that they belong to different redactional levels (cf. Neyrey, 1988, 37–58, esp. 37–43). The role of Jesus as judge, for instance, though initially denied (8:15), is present in both scenes—tentatively in the first (8:16) and clearly in the second (8:26). Similarly with Jesus' use of "I am," *Egō eimi:* in the first it is introduced (8:12, "I am the light . . .") and in the second it is used in a stronger form (8:24,28, ". . . believe . . . know that I am"). Such development is typical of John's graded text.

Nor does the continuity between 8:12–20 and chap. 7 (cf. Neyrey, 1988, 38–39) mean that 8:12–20 belongs more with chap. 7 than with the rest of chap. 8. Such continuity, insofar as it is accurately portrayed, is part of the larger continuity between chaps. 7 and 8.

As Neyrey indicates (1988, 37–51, esp. 37) the language of chap. 8 reflects that of a courtroom. Yet the courtroom language is not so dominant that it determines the very structure of the text. Rather, the process of giving judgement, while it is indeed significant, has been subjected to the requirements of the evangelist's own more basic plan. A similar phenomenon was noted in 6:25–59: the form of a midrashic homily, though important, was subjected to the evangelist's own structure.

8:31–47

The next major section of chap. 8 focuses not on Jesus but on the Jews, and especially on the questions of *their* identity and their relationship to their father (8:31–47). The distinctness of this section is not as well established as that of 8:12–30, yet there is significant support for the idea that v 47 forms some kind of conclusion (cf. Marsh, 364; Morris, 454; Brown, 361; Schnackenburg, 2:210; Mateos and Barreto, 413).

What is more difficult to judge is how this section (vv 31–47) should be subdivided. The various subdivisions proposed by the above-mentioned writers all involve a subdividing of one of Jesus' statements, and as such are highly questionable. (It is unusual in the account of a dialogue for a single statement which has no obvious interruption to begin in one subdivision or scene and to continue into another.) It seems best, therefore, with the UBSGNT and RSV, to make a subdivision at the end of v 38 (when Jesus refers suggestively to "your father"). This means that the following "scene" begins with "[They] answered and said to him . . ." (v 39)—a plausible beginning since that is also how the next division begins (vv 48–59, cf. v 48). Furthermore, it means that when the two proposed scenes are compared (vv 31–38 and 39–47), the conclusion of the first is echoed in various subtle ways in the conclusion of the second (cf. vv 37–38, 46–47, esp. the idea of not being from God ["you are the *sperma* of Abraham/not from God"] and of not hearing what Jesus says). Such balancing of conclusions—a balancing incidentally which involves some intensification in the later conclusion—fits the pattern noted in the two scenes of the preceding division (cf. vv 20, 28–30) and fits the tendency of the evangelist to use repetition in dividing texts.

Within each of these scenes (vv 31–38 and 39–47) the question of Jewish identity and sinfulness is examined, but while the first gives the question a treatment which is brief and preliminary, the second is prolonged and probing.

In both scenes Jesus speaks not three times, as in the preceding division, but twice (in the initial scene, cf. vv 31–32 and 34–38; in the later scene, cf. vv 39–41 and 42–47). This change, from a pattern that is threefold to one that is twofold, fits with the fact that the earlier threefold patterns, those involving Nicodemus and the Samaritan woman, both are followed by patterns that are twofold (cf. the basic "two-scene" structure of 3:22–36 and 4:43–54). It also fits with the fact that in chap. 9, the scenes where the man speaks three times (9:8–12, 24–34) are followed by scenes in which he speaks twice (9:13–17, 35–41; cf. vv 15 and 17; 36 and 38).

One detail is puzzling: the two sets of two statements (in vv 31–38 and 39–47) become progressively longer, but in chap. 9, they become much shorter; in fact, they become statements which, though striking, consist of only two Greek words (9:17, *profētes estin,* "He is a prophet"; and in 9:38, *Pisteuō kyrie,* "I believe, Lord''). Such brevity is surprising, particularly in a context where statements tend to become longer, yet precisely because it is rather surprising it appears to fulfill a purpose—it achieves a certain dramatic intensity.

What seems certain in any case is that, while the patterns sometimes contain variations of surprising brevity—whether those of the anticlimactic kind noted earlier (''You/I do not know, . . .'' 8:19 and 9:12), or those of the intense striking kind (9:17, 38)—the text as a whole shows careful coordination, and the general pattern is of texts and statements becoming longer and longer.

The Sight-Giving and the Shepherding

The Man Born Blind

This dramatic account tells of a man who not only received sight but who then went through various stages of advancing insight. After his eyes had been anointed (*chriō*, v 6), he came to see Jesus first as an *ordinary person* (v 11) and then as a *prophet* (v 17). Later, after his parents had shied away from confessing Jesus to be the Christ (*christos*, v 22), he went on to see Jesus as *from God* (v 33) and, finally, as *the Son of humanity* (v 37). The picture is one of steady progression.

His Jewish interrogators, on the other hand, become more and more blind. They go from a rather divided and critical acceptance of the healing (vv 13–16), to disbelieving that it ever happened (v 18), to vilifying the man's effort to bear witness to it (vv 24–34). They end in abiding sin (v 41).

Thus while chaps. 7–8 had spoken of an advancing process involving revelation and divergent responses, chap. 9 presents a drama in which that process is illustrated and developed.

The text is strongly ironical (Duke, 77–78, 117–26); several statements are quite out of line with the full reality of the situation. When, for instance, the Jews say, "Give glory to God. We know that this person is a sinner," there is multiple irony (Duke, 1985, 78, 121). They invoke God, but in fact deny God; they ask for the truth, yet they refuse the truth; and they say they know, but they do not. Thus truth and reality are elusive—a context which is very appropriate to a story of blindness and sight.

It is widely accepted that the text has more than one level. Though it tells of just one person from the time of Jesus' ministry, there is considerable agreement, particularly because of the work of J. L. Martyn (1979), that the man is a representative figure—that in him and in his expulsion by the Jews one may see reflected the fate of many Christian disciples of a later decade.

The present commentary seeks to indicate the presence of a further, complementary level: in the account of the healing and development of the man there is a persistent evoking of the complex process whereby a person is created, comes to birth, grows up, and matures.

Structure and Unity

It seems best, along with commentators such as Lindars (341–52) and Schnackenburg (2:239), to regard the text as composed of six scenes:

1.   1– 7   The creationlike receiving of sight;
2.   8–12   People wonder about the startling phenomenon;
3.   13–17 Pharisees' interrogation; the man gains insight;
4.   18–23 The parents talk and say little;
5.   24–34 Second interrogation; the man's greater insight;
6.   35–41 The climax of insight and blindness.

Brown (203, 376–77) would subdivide the introductory scene by regarding vv 6–7, the actual healing, as a distinct unit. And several authors (e.g., Martyn, 1979, 27; Resseguie, 1982, 295–301; Kysar, 1984, 49–51; Duke, 1985, 118; Holleran, 1990, 5–10) would subdivide the final scene—with one unit for the insightful man (vv 35–38/39), and the other for the blind Pharisees (vv 39/40–41). Noack (1954, 115) would subdivide both the first scene and the last—thus bringing the total number of scenes to eight.

These suggestions appear to reflect a genuine aspect of the text—namely the complexity of the introductory and concluding scenes—and, as Holleran (1990, 5–10) in particular emphasizes, there is little doubt but that the concluding scene, with its repetition of "Hearing, . . ." is in some way twofold or divided. But dividedness is something which in various forms is found in all the scenes—from the mild divergence of opinions in Scenes 1 and 2 (9:2–3, 8–9), to the "division" in Scene 3 (9:16, *schisma*), and to the development in Scenes 4 and 5, first of the threat and then of the reality of some kind of expulsion (9:22, 34). Therefore in itself dividedness is not a reliable indicator of the distinction of scenes.

What is necessary is to identify if possible the formal clue or criterion which sets the scenes apart. It is not accurate to say that each scene contains only two (groups of) speakers or actors. Several of the scenes are in some way three-cornered—containing three (groups of) speakers or actors. The criterion which distinguishes the scenes seems rather to consist of physical movement. In other words, as an indication that a scene is ending or beginning, someone either comes or goes or is called or is thrown out. Essentially the same criterion—some suggestion of movement—is used elsewhere in John, especially at Samaria (4:1–42) and in the trial before Pilate (18:28–19:16a). In chap. 9, such indications are found five times (in vv 7, 13, 18, 24, and 35), thus giving six scenes. But in the final verses, when Jesus speaks to the Pharisees, no such movement is indicated. On the contrary, it is explicitly ruled out: the Pharisees with whom he speaks are described as being *met autou*, "with him" or "near him" (9:40). It is the sort of detail which at first sight is puzzlingly unnecessary, but in the context of using movement as a stage direction, it has a purpose. And it means that the statement on the Pharisees' blindness belongs to the same scene as that which shows the man coming to full insight. Thus, in a way that is somewhat reminiscent of the climactic contrast between Peter and Judas (6:66–71), the final scene is one of stark divergence.

With regard to the unity of the chapter, it has been said that the verses which speak of the parents' fear of being cast out from the synagogue (9:22–23) "may well represent the hand of an editor . . . for they are somewhat intrusive in the narrative" (Brown, 380). But as Martyn (1979, 33) and Resseguie (1982, 299) have indicated, the reference to expulsion from the synagogue is integral to the dramatic presentation. In particular its image of the parents as fearful provides an appropriate foil for the subsequent picture of the man as courageous. Furthermore, the image of casting someone out of the synagogue forms part of a larger pattern of dividedness. And as the anaylsis of the drama shows, this dividedness is not something alien to the text. It is integral to every scene.

Overall therefore it seems best to regard the text as a unity, in six scenes.

Chapter 9 as a Diptych: Exploratory Observations

Without attempting to unravel the full complexity of the structure of chapter 9, it is worth noting that, like some earlier chapters (particularly 2:23–chap. 3, chaps. 7 and 8), it has some of the traits of a diptych. At least there is some extent to which features of Scenes 1–3 are balanced by features of Scenes 4–6. Most noticeable perhaps is the fact that in Scenes 1 and 4 the man does not speak at all, in Scenes 2 and 5 he speaks three times, and in Scenes 3 and 6, two times. In other words, as far as the frequency of the man's speaking is concerned, the scenes in both halves of the chapter show a pattern of 0, 3, 2. That the man should speak the same number of times (five) in each half is improbable. That the five utterances should follow the same pattern (0, 3, 2) is even less likely. There is also a certain balance with regard to the length of the man's utterances. In each half the five utterances first become progressively longer (utterances 1, 2, and 3) and then (utterances 4 and 5) progressively shorter. The only exception to this further element of balance is the brevity of the man's third reply—his *ouk oida,* "I do not know," when asked where Jesus was (9:12, Scene 2). This rather unexpected brevity and ignorance could be seen as discounting the idea of a planned pattern with regard to the length of the man's utterances, but it can also be seen as part of that pattern—as an appropriate foil for the man's third reply in the second half of the chapter, a reply which explicitly takes up the idea of knowing and not knowing, a reply in which the man amends overwhelmingly for his earlier ignorance (9:30–33, Scene 5).

Chapter 9 may, perhaps, have a chiastic structure, but the arguments thus far put forward are not clear and consistent (cf. Duke, 1985, 118–26; Holleran, 1990, 6–7). The problem is not only the claim to seven scenes but also the unreliability and/or vagueness of the criteria for maintaining that the scenes are balanced.

[9:1–7] Scene 1: Jesus, reflecting the Creator, performs a birthlike healing. As the curtain rises the main actor is a virtual nonentity. Blind from birth, he has never known light and so—given John's linking of light and life—there is a sense in which he is without life. Later it will be said that he begged, but in Scene 1 nothing so energetic even as begging is mentioned. The portrait instead is of one who is simply the object of others' conversation. He says nothing and does nothing—and so, in a sense, is nothing.

Around him hover two possible worlds—a vindictive world of sin and punishment and a world in which one may reveal the works of God. As Jesus passes by and sees him, it is the vindictive world that is on the minds of his disciples.

"Rabbi," they said, using a form of address which portrays them as beginners (e.g., cf. 1:38, 3:2), "who sinned . . . that he was born blind?" The fact that suffering is often caused by sin is clear, but how does one explain the suffering of a baby? Some biblical and rabbinical opinion seemed to attribute it to a sin on the part of the parents or to a sin which occurred during pregnancy and which therefore involved a certain participation by the unborn baby (cf. Exod 20:5; StrB, 2:528–29, 535–36). In this view such suffering appears to be a punishment, part of a process which seems implacable, even vindictive. What is at stake ultimately is the entire problem of evil, a problem which, insofar as it consists of sin, had just been attributed in chapter 8 first to the human will and then, even more fundamentally, to an underlying diabolical force (8:44). In that case Jesus had not denied the reality of sin and its diabolical roots, but he had gone on to set the evil in a positive context: he had moved from a negative emphasis to an emphasis on sinlessness and God (8:45–47), and so in a certain sense the image of evil was swallowed up in the image of a greater good.

To a significant degree, that is what Jesus does here also. The issue now, however—and here chap. 9 seems to complement chap. 8—is suffering rather than sin. He discounts the sin theory of the disciples, and he accepts the reality of the suffering in a positive context, a context wherein the virtually lifeless man is to reveal the works of God (9:3).

Then, turning from the individual case of the man, Jesus indicates that such in fact is the purpose of everybody's life—to reveal the works of God (9:4–5). And in these two verses, mixing pronouns so that everybody's fate is linked with his own ("Us . . . me . . ."), he gives a summary of life which is both chilling and alluring: it is like a period of light, which though faced with encroaching darkness, supplies a providential opportunity to share in something which surpasses oneself—the works of the Sender or Creator (*dei*, "it is necessary," suggests providence). The idea that life is lived amid encroaching darkness, amid encircling gloom, is central to John. The darkness refers to all that is evil, and it apparently includes a certain aspect of death. Judas' deathly betrayal is associated with night, darkness (13:30). The fact that Jesus is discussing the potential of human life in general, rather than simply the potential of one man, is borne out by his use of very general terms: "It is for *us* to work . . . night comes, when *no one* can work" (9:4). Then Jesus repeats what he had said at the beginning of chap. 8 ("I am the light of the world"), but he precedes it with a clause which, particularly in the context of encroaching night, can appear ominously limiting: "*As long as am in the world* I am. . . ." Thus human life, even when doing God's works and when in solidarity with Jesus, is faced by the prospect of deathly night. The bread of life discourse (esp. 6:52–58) had spoken in general terms of the need to absorb the reality of providential death, but now, in the shadow of the feast of Tents, the reality of that approaching night is beginning to impinge more fully: "As long as I am in the world. . . ."

Thus instead of focusing exclusively on why babies lack light or life, Jesus looks to the larger phenomenon—the darkness ("To be or not to be . . .") which surrounds all of human existence. And he sees it all, darkness notwithstanding, as coming from a providential Sender. Thus both the general limitedness of life and the specific limitedness of certain forms of suffering are put in the context of a greater providence. In other words, however painful it may be, there is a sense in which suffering can work for good. Human life, therefore, once set in the context of light—for that is his final emphasis (". . . I am the light of the world")—is worth living.

And with that, Jesus, light of the world, launches the virtual nonentity into being. As Irenaeus (*Adv. Haer.* v 15:2) noted, the process, with its use of clay, symbolizes or evokes the process of the original human creation (cf. Brown, 372). The act of spitting is perplexing but, when seen in the context of the actions of later chapters, including Jesus' weeping and bleeding (11:35; 19:34), would appear to be part of a pattern of texts which suggest a process of divine self-giving or self-emptying. If this is so—and judgement on its accuracy depends considerably on how one reads subsequent texts—then the action which recreates the blind man is one in which the Creator, far from being some kind of detached manufacturer, is personally involved.

Then, in a touch which highlights the dignity of this new birth, the eyes are described as being anointed (*chriō*). This is the verb which underlies "Christ" (*christos,* "anointed"). It is not to be translated casually for it is an intimation of the essence of the man's status and vocation. And given that in this case the eyes are everything, there is a suggestion of an anointing which extends to the entire person. (Early church tradition tells of a baptismal ritual which involved a complete anointing of the person; cf. Tertullian, *On Baptism* 7.)

Then, with a simple word of command, Jesus tells the man to "go, wash" in the nearby pool of Siloam, and when he did just that—"he went and he washed" —he came seeing. Again the process is evocative of both creation and birth— evocative of the commanding word which preceded creation and evocative also of the way in which water or washing is sometimes associated with birth or rebirth (cf. the Nicodemus scene, 3:1–5; the "rebirth" of Naaman, 2 Kgs 5:10, 14; and perhaps the physical process whereby, in coming to birth, a baby passes through a form of water). And the fact that Siloam means Sent (a rather free interpretation; cf. Brown, 373), reflects the idea that the man, in being made, is given a mission, is sent—as Jesus also had been sent (9:4). Humble though he seems, he reflects Jesus.

[9:8–12] Scene 2: The emerging figure is observed and questioned; he begins to speak. When the seeing man emerges among neighbors and acquaintances, some see him as the one who used to sit and beg, and others said, "No, but he is like him."

At this stage the person is still quite passive, still the object of other people's discussions. It is they who seem to determine his identity. The idea of passivity, of a kind of helplessness, is heightened by the information that at an earlier stage in his life the person used to beg, sit and beg. The two successive images, of begging, and of sitting and begging, while used primarily of a beggar, may also be used even of successive stages of childhood—of a tiny baby and of a sitting baby.

Then come his first words, *Egō eimi,* "I am" or "I am he," a minimal statement of existence and identity. It is often said that this very human *Egō eimi* has nothing to do with the God-related *Egō eimi*. But the context suggests otherwise. From the prologue onwards, the gospel as a whole is concerned with the fact that the human and divine are interwoven; and the next chapter will express that idea in a stark form: "I said you are gods" (10:34). Furthermore, the immediate literary context of the man's very human *Egō eimi* is the increasingly clear divine *Egō eimi* of Jesus in chap. 8 (8:24,28,58). In other words, from a literary point of view, the man's *Egō eimi* is an echo of the divine *Egō eimi*. Thus while Scene 1 indicated that human birth and life issue from the Creator, the man's first words reinforce that idea: they are like an echo or image of God.

Thus far, anything said in the man's presence consisted of either a command or a comment. Now for the first time he is addressed in a new way—as one capable of replying. From one point of view the question is fairly simple: "How were your eyes opened?" The man's answer, which is reasonably long ("The person called Jesus made clay, . . ." 9:11), consists, in fact, of an almost parrotlike repetition of the original account of the event (9:6–7). Thus within the present narrative it is an answer which in some ways is like that of childish imitation.

At this stage he seems incapable of anything more. When asked another question, one which demands more than simple repetition—they ask him, "Where is he?"—all he can do is say, *ouk oida*, "I do not know." His failure at this point is all the more striking because in earlier parts of John, in texts involving Nicodemus and the woman of Samaria, there were patterns of three statements or utterances, each one longer than the one before. The man seemed, perhaps, to be moving in that pattern. He had gone from a very short *Egō eimi* to a reasonably long account of the healing. But when the time came for his third utterance, he failed utterly—*ouk oida*.

The second scene, then, tells of the tentative emergence of the person, an emergence which is in some ways evocative of childhood and which is shadowed by diverse perceptions.

[9:13–17] Scene 3: The Pharisees' interrogation; the man gains insight.   As the scene opens "they lead him to the Pharisees." This action may seem relatively harmless, but it has ominous resonances of the fate of Jesus (cf. 7:46; 18:13,28), and the sudden reference to the sabbath (9:14) is such that it recalls the hostility which surrounded the earlier sabbath healing (5:9–18). Yet despite these dissonant notes, the text, employing a degree of repetition which may seem unnecessary (Lindars, 349, describes it as "almost wearisome") reiterates the wonder—the creationlike transition from being blind to seeing (9:13–14). Thus the scene begins with notes of both dissonance and creationlike harmony.

Once again the man is questioned about how the healing occurred, and this time his answer, while straightforward and factual, sounds much less like a verbatim imitation or repetition and more like a reasonably intelligent summary of what had happened: "He put clay on my eyes, and I washed, and I see."

At this stage, diversity of perception reenters the drama. "Some," by concentrating on the technical infringement of the sabbath, conclude that Jesus cannot be *from God.* But "others," echoing Nicodemus (3:2), said, "How can a man who is *a sinner* do such signs?" And "there was a division (*schisma*) among them." (The essence of this division, "from God" versus "a sinner," recalls the initial difference of perception between Jesus and the disciples: "Rabbi, who sinned? . . ." [9:1–3]. However, in this case the division is not about the one who was blind but about the one who gives sight.)

During the development of the debate and division among the Pharisees it is not said what the man was doing, but the implication is that he was present. And apparently he was not idle. As he listened to the two opinions—"from God," and "a sinner"—his own processes of perception were developing. When they asked him for his view he not only sided with the positive opinion—something he had done earlier in a very simple way by saying *Egō eimi*—but this time he expressed the positive viewpoint in a new way: "He is a prophet."

In Scene 3, then, the person enters the world of law and debate, and in that world he goes from a process of summarizing intelligently to expressing an opinion in a way that is slightly original.

[9:18–23] Scene 4: The parents' limited role—The man is of age, independent of his parents. The drama now enters a major new phase. The man begins to be seen not just as an emerging person but as one who is quite distinct from his parents.

The parents become involved when the Jews, who now refuse to believe that the man had originally been blind, decide to question them. In the ensuing process the person's relationship to others becomes clarified significantly: he is indeed his parents' child, but something has happened to him which sets him apart from them. He has been given a basic form of life—light—which is independent of his parents. And the parents realize the fact. With what seems to be considerable humility and poignancy they recognize the limits of what they gave their child: "We know that this is our son and that he was born blind." That much they understand, that much they know—basic externals. But the whole phenomenon of light, how it came to him and from whom, that is something which they say they do not know. And it is in the context of speaking of this enigmatic receiving of light, of sight, that the person is finally declared to be an adult: "Ask him; he is of age, he will speak for himself." The implication, from the juxtaposition of the texts, is that adulthood and light go together, in other words that his adulthood comes not from his parents but from his other source of light. It is that which makes him who he is, which enables him to speak for himself.

His parents, on the other hand, seem somewhat alien to the light. They themselves say that they know neither the underlying process *nor the underlying person* —". . . who opened his eyes, we do not know." They had not been directly asked this final question, so one might wonder why they seem eager to answer it or at least to get it out of the way. The text goes on to explain why: they were afraid that if they became involved with the question of identifying Jesus, and more specifically of confessing him to be the Christ, the Anointed, they would be put out of the synagogue. So they said, "He is of age; ask him."

Again the scene is basically positive. Despite all the parent–child ties it becomes clear that the emerging person is not some kind of clone. He is, so to speak, his own person. He has a gift of sight, of light, which sets him apart even from his parents, which gives him a fundamental independence.

[9:24-34] Scene 5: The second interrogation and the man's coming to maturity—intellectual, moral, and emotional.   This scene belongs to the man. He is now an adult, and more than ever he is fundamentally independent of other people. When he is called once more, the text explicitly notes that this is "the second time" (9:24), thus underlining the idea of a distinctively new phase.

The renewed encounter is high drama. The authorities, unaware of the full extent of what is developing within the man, apply immense pressure. *"Dos doxan tō theō,"* they begin. "Give glory to God" (or "Give praise to God"). The formula, brief though it is, should have been extremely intimidating. It was used to remind people of God and God's worship, and particularly to induce condemned criminals solemnly to honor God by confessing their guilt (cf. Jos 7:19, 1 Sam 6:5, 2 Chr 30:8, Jer 13:16; StrB, 1924, 2:535). It was a call to worship, but it was also a call to surrender. It will not have been weakened by the fact that, in their own way, the man's parents had already surrendered. And the authorities then followed this call to surrender with a solemn assertion which intensified the intimidation: "We know (*hēmeis oidamen*) that this man is a sinner (*hamartōlos*)." The *oidamen*, "we know," is solemn enough—an echo of the initial confident assertion of Nicodemus: ". . . We know that you are . . ." (3:2), and one of a triple series of confident assertions about Jesus (cf. 9:16, 26, 29). The *hēmeis* adds emphasis to the "we." And the subsequent statement, "that this man is a sinner" (*hoti . . . hamartōlos estin*), is not only a fundamental condemnation of Jesus, it is also, through its phrasing, a stark contradiction of what the seeing man had last said—"He is a prophet" (*hoti prophētes estin,* 9:17). Their words, therefore, form a ringing statement of confrontation, condemnation, and contradiction.

"Whether he is a sinner," replied the man, weighing the central charge, "I do not know"—again *ouk oida,* but this time the assertion of ignorance comes from a mind that is calm, clear, and firm. And then with strict adherence to what he is sure of, he begins slowly to build towards a positive statement of perception: "One thing I know, that though I was blind, now I see."

Through this brief statement the man avoids becoming entangled in their confused condemnatory world, and he manages instead to bring the debate back to the central facts.

The interrogators therefore say that they want to know the facts: "What did he do to you? How did he open your eyes?"

In an earlier scene the man would and did answer such questions. But he had now gone beyond the process of childish verbatim repetition, and he was not going to go back to it—not even in the face of threats. "I told you already," he said, "and you did not hear."

And with that simple answer, the forward march of the interrogators came, so to speak, to a halt. Their effort at intimidation had been an bluff, and now their demand for the facts was likewise shown to be empty, a masquerade.

But the man is not satisfied with bringing them to a halt. He begins, so to speak, to go after them.

"Why do you wish to hear it again?" he asks—a simple question, his first in the drama, but one which, almost imperceptibly, changes roles, which makes him the interrogator. Then, as he apparently begins to relish his new role, and as he allows some of his anger at this empty and pretentious process to come to the surface, he adds another question, this time spiced with sarcasm: "Do you also want to become his disciples?"

The sarcasm stings and his opponents fire back abuse: "They reviled him and said, 'You are his disciple.' " The "his" (genitive case, cf. *ekeinos,* "that [man]") seems to have a pejorative meaning—"that fellow." As Brown (370) puts it: "You are the one who is that fellow's disciple." In their eyes such discipleship is contemptible. The discipleship of Moses, on the other hand, is seen differently: ". . . But *we* are disciples of Moses. We know (*oidamen*) that God has spoken to Moses. . . ."

And they are right. Amid all their empty pretentiousness there is a profound truth—God did speak to Moses. And they know it. In their debate with the man they momentarily recapture the high ground. They may indeed have retreated from both their call to surrender and from their pretended attempt to know the facts, but in their claim to an ancient and revered tradition they have found a refuge and a new source of strength: "We know that God has spoken to Moses. . . ." Their position, in a sense, is unassailable.

And from that position they begin, on a low key, to resume their abuse: ". . . but as for him, we do not know (*ouk oidamen*) where he is from."

Their position is doubly strong. Insofar as they are making positive statements, they are based on an ancient tradition, and so they must be right. And with regard to this new phenonmenon, this person, they are not saying anything positive ("we do not know"), and therefore they cannot be wrong. The logic seems impeccable. They stand righteous and vindicated.

At an earlier stage, in Scene 2, when it fell to the emerging man to speak for a third time, to go beyond simple repetition, he had faltered, pitifully almost, into an *ouk oida,* "I do not know." Now as the possibility arises once more of speaking for a third time, he is faced with the task not only of going beyond simple repetition, but of replying to a formidable combination of intimidation, authority, tradition, and apparent logic. To falter here would hardly be surprising.

"Why, this is a marvel!" he said, "You do not know where he is from, and yet he opened my eyes." He does not attack Moses, the tradition which they claim to know. Instead he focuses on what they exclude—the possibility that behind this new person there may be something immensely positive, another manifestation of the divine. For the moment, of course, he does not say that explicitly. However, his initial exclamation, "Why, this is a marvel!" has an overtone pointing in that direction. In the OT, the word "marvel" or "wonder," a noun derived from the adjective *thaumastos,* "wonderful," "marvelous," is almost always used to refer to God or to a manifestation of God (e.g., cf. Exod 11:15, 34:10; Deut 28:58, 59; Jos 3:5; Judg 13:18, 19). And in other NT usages of *thaumastos* it is always so (cf. Matt 21:42; Mark 12:11; 1 Pet 2:9; Rev 15:1, 3). Since the context of John 9 is dealing with precisely this problem—whether there is present a manifestation of the divine—the word "marvel" or "wonder" cannot but connote something of its usual meaning. So when the man exclaims, "Why this is a marvel!" there is a certain sense in which he is saying cryptically what he will finally say openly, "Why, this is an overwhelming wonder, something unutterably magnificent, something divine."

And he, the once blind wordless man, proceeds to hold forth on being sensitive to the divine. "God does not hear sinners," he says, thereby expressing, in a way that is familiarly biblical but also rather negative, the fact that sinfulness can block off communication with God, including all sensitivity to God (e.g., cf. Isa 1:15, Ps 66:18). And then he goes on, "But if anyone is a God-worshipper (*theo-sebēs*) and does his will, [*theo-sebēs* evokes the piety of the Hellenistic world, and "doing his will" that of the Hebrews (Brown, 375)], God listens to that person." In other words, thorough acceptance of God induces God's communication, God's manifestation. And the opening of the eyes which had been born blind was a manifestation that was unparalleled: "Never since the world began" had such a thing been heard. Given such a manifestation there is no way that the person who induced it could be a sinner. He had to be related to the very source of life. "If this person were not from God," he concluded, "he could do nothing."

He had spoken of sensitivity to God, yet what he was also speaking of was sensitivity to a human person and to what was being manifested in that person. While not attacking their tradition, he was asking them to see the reality in front of them, the reality of God in "this fellow." It was not to some peripheral reality that he called them, some theological nicety or trivial curiosity, it was to a manifestation and perception of God such as had never before been known—not "since the world began." It did not negate Moses, but it introduced something which Moses had never known, something which in that sense surpassed him. And it meant that in relating to God, fidelity to Moses was not enough. God was doing something and they were refusing to see it. At the heart of all their assertions of fidelity to God there was, in fact, a basic denial of the actual reality of God, of what God was doing for them, here and now—in this man. This person was doing something special. If he were not from God, "he could do nothing."

But their minds were focused on sin. Relying on a claim to tradition, they had decided, regardless of what new way God might act, that Jesus was sinful. And now they applied the same blind mind to the man who was speaking to them. "You were born wholly in sin," they said, "and would you teach us?" Then, "they threw him out."

Once again the scene contains division, no longer merely the general word ("division") or a particular idea (to put out of the synagogue) but the reality, an actual physical division—"they threw him out."

Yet the basic picture provided by the scene is positive. Despite the fear shown by his parents and the forces ranged against him, he had remained true to what God was doing within him. He had not become unfaithful—not even under the threat of being cast out.

[9:35–41] Scene 6: The climax of insight—the humble acceptance of (God in) one's humanity. The text gives no comment on the man's mood following his expulsion. There is, in a sense, no time for such details. He had said, at the high point of his discourse, that if someone were faithful, *God would hear.* He had been faithful, even to expulsion, by saying Jesus was from God, and so the opening line of the next scene is almost predictable: *"Jesus heard. . . ."*

What Jesus asks for at this final stage is belief in the *hyios. . .anthrōpou*, the "Son of humanity" or "human child." This refers first of all to Jesus himself, to the fact that "Jesus, the Son of man is . . . the revelation of the nearness of the glory of God" (Schnackenburg, 2:254). But the glory of God is not immediately obvious in Jesus, and when the man inquires about this person in whom he is to believe, in other words, this bearer of glory, Jesus in effect says, "You are looking at him." And the man, faced with sheer humanity, perceives the divine: "I believe, Lord," and he bowed down before him. The phrase used here, *prosekynēsen autō*, "he bowed in worship before him," is first used in the NT about someone who seems equally unlikely as an object of worship—the baby before whom the Magi bowed down (cf. Matt 2:2, 8, 11). For the healed man this humble worship is the final insight, the final stage of development.

As well as accepting Jesus, this worship implies also a self-acceptance. This link is suggested by the fact that, in the course of the drama, the man, who remains nameless, is described in a way which persistently relates him with Jesus. Jesus is an *anthrōpos* and the *hyios. . .anthrōpou* ("person/man" and "Son of humanity," 9:11, 16, 24, 35). The man is an *anthrōpos* 9:1, 24, 30) and a *hyios,* "son" (9:19, 20). Jesus is *Christos,* "Anointed" (9:22), and the man also is anointed (*chriō,* 9:6). In the structure of the narrative he emerges in the context of Jesus' action: Jesus sees him at the beginning (9:1) and at the end. In the final act of worship, he flows back to Jesus, as it were, and is heard of no more (9:38). (In the kindred account in 5:1–15, the healed man who to some degree personifies the Jews blends back into them [5:15].) In the fifth scene, when the man confronts the interrogators (9:24–34), his fate, as an emerging disciple, is clearly linked to that of Jesus. When, therefore, he finally and fully accepts the humanity of Jesus, there is also a basic self-acceptance.

This climactic acceptance of humanity builds on the climactic section of the bread-of-life discourse—the emphasis on the complete acceptance (eating and drinking) of all that is truly human (flesh and blood) (6:52–58). A connection with chap. 6—namely the need to come to terms with the impending reality of death—had already been indicated in analyzing Scene 1 (9:1–7). Now, in Scene 6, that connection is found again, and it is a reminder that the full acceptance of the Son of humanity involves not only humble self-acceptance, but acceptance of a self who faces death.

Self-acceptance has often been emphasized in later centuries, particularly in the closing paragraphs of Georges Bernanos's *The Diary of a Country Priest,* but it was something for which the Jews, in clinging to a distorted tradition, were not ready. The scene ends, therefore, by speaking of their embeddedness in blindness and guilt.

Despite the concluding darkness, the drama as a whole is positive. Its six scenes are like portrayals of the six ages of a maturing person: birth, infancy, adolescence, independence of parents, mature perception and interactions with others, and finally a humble spirituality.

Continuity with Chaps. 7–8

As already partly indicated, chap. 9, despite its difference of style, builds carefully on the drama of chaps. 7–8. Both the idea of the gradual progress of revelation (chap. 7) and the appearing and hiding of the light (chap. 8, esp. 8:12, 59) find practical expression in the gradually increasing sight and blindness of the man and of the Pharisees. There is continuity also, for instance, with regard to the idea of recognizing Jesus as (the) prophet and as (the) Christ (cf. 7:26–27,40–42; 9:17,22). And the element of dividedness, which is first mentioned explicitly after Jesus' climactic cry (7:43) pervades the drama of chap. 9. There is further continuity in relation to the idea of sin. In chaps. 1–12 John refers seventeen times to the words "sinner" and "sin." (The remaining chapters have seven such references.) Of these seventeen occurrences, all but two (1:29, 5:14) appear in chaps. 8 and 9 (six times in chap. 8, nine in chap. 9). In a variety of ways then, chap. 9 continues and develops the themes of chaps. 7 and 8.

Continuity with Chaps. 3 and 5

In its picture of someone emerging gropingly from darkness, trying to discern the significance of signs and to struggle against a narrow Jewish background, chap. 9 recalls various features and details of the Nicodemus story—the background of night (3:1; 9:1–4); the Jewish claim to know ("we know") and the countering of that claim by others (by Jesus, 3:2,9–10; by the man, 9:24,29–31); the discerning of signs and of the fact that Jesus is from God (3:2; 9:16,33); and the role of Jesus as light, bringing judgment into the world (3:19–21; 9:5,39). That this continuity is really present has been indicated in varying degrees by several writers (see, for instance, Brown, 376; Haenchen, 2:41).

It has also been indicated, especially by Culpepper (1983, 139–40), that the story of the blind man is in remarkable continuity with the story of the man by the pool (chap. 5). Thus in both texts one notices:

- There was a man, inept or passive, who had been sick a long time (thirty-eight years—5:5, 7; from birth—9:1);

- Jesus sees the man and takes the initiative to heal him (5:6; 9:1,6). In both texts Jesus is seen as working in accordance with the Father (5:17) or the one who sent him (9:4).

- In diverse ways the setting and story involve a pool which, in some way, is associated with healing (5:2, Bethzatha; 9:7, Siloam). The first man does not enter the pool. The other does.

- In diverse ways the sickness is related to sin. It is seen as associated with it (5:14) and, curiously, as not being associated with it (9:2–3).

- At a rather late stage the narrative mentions that the healing occurred on the sabbath and that this led to objections—by the Jews (5:9–10) and by the Pharisees and Jews (9:14,16,18).

- The man is asked about Jesus and does not know—does not know who he is (5:12–13); does not know where he is (9:12).

- In diverse ways the man is associated with the Jews—he seems to blend back into them (5:15–16); and he is cast out by them (9:34).

- Jesus finds the man and issues diverse invitations—not to sin further and become worse (5:14); to believe, in contrast to the sinful Pharisees (9:35,41).

What emerges from a comparison of the three stories (Nicodemus, the poolside man, and the blind man) is a sustained mixture of continuity and diversity. The Nicodemus story, set in Jerusalem, shows a Jew emerging from darkness and being faced with a basic decision—whether to remain where he is or to accept rebirth in water and the Spirit. Little or no indication is given of which way he is leaning. Then, in chap. 5, during Jesus' second visit to Jerusalem, there emerges a man who, despite receiving healing, does not enter the water and does not come to know Jesus or believe in him, but who seems instead to fade back into identity with the resisting Jews. The man in chap. 9, on the other hand, *does* enter the water, does come to know Jesus and believe in him. And, far from fading back into his Jewish identity, he is cast out by the Jews. Thus while Nicodemus emerges as a Jew who is faced with an option but is undecided, chaps. 5 and 9 seem to show diverse reactions to that option—rejection (chap. 5) and acceptance (chap. 9). In other words, the men of chaps. 5 and 9, despite all their dissimilarities, are like diverse faces of Judaism.

While this seems reasonably plausible as a general conclusion, its details are not immediately clear. What, for instance, is to be made of the three references to water—to being born of water (3:5), to not entering the water because "another" goes down first (5:7), to washing and seeing (9:7)? Is there a deliberate continuity between these three references? From a literary viewpoint, in other words the viewpoint of the completed canonical text, it would seem that there is. The references are linked by similarities of both context and detail.

The Question of Baptism

Literary continuity is important when trying to assess whether the washing of chap. 9 involves an allusion to baptism. There is ample evidence from early Christianity—the art of the catacombs, the use of chap. 9 in preparing candidates for baptism, and the comments of early church writers—that the story of the blind man was interpreted as referring in some way to baptism. (For details, see Hoskyns, 351; Brown, 380; Schnackenburg, 2:257–58, 499–500.) Nonetheless, Schnackenburg (2:258) rejects this interpretation as something imposed on the story, something which has no basis in the text itself. If, however, the washing of chap. 9 is in literary continuity with the baptism-related reference to being reborn of water and the Spirit (3:1–8, cf. 3:22–23) then a reference to baptism is integral to the text.

What is more difficult to discern is whether in chap. 5 also, in the fact that the man does not go down into the water, there is yet another allusion to baptism, a negative one. In other words, does the failure of the man to descend into the water—the man is in some ways representative of the Jews—have something to do with the failure of many Jews to descend into the waters of baptism? And does the "other" (*allos*) who goes down before him (*pro emou,* "before me") have something to do with the fact that others, the Gentiles, accepted baptism more readily? Paul, in Romans 11, proposes a similar idea—that, in the order of the salvation brought by Christ, the Gentiles now precede a section of the Jews (Rom 11:25–26). Is it better, perhaps, in the present state of research, to leave the matter open.

John and Images of Children

One of the striking features of John is that, unlike the other gospels, it gives almost no direct role to children. Even Mark, while not having an infancy narrative, tells of Jesus embracing and blessing the little children (Mark 10:13–16). Still, within chaps. 4–9, John gives a number of references which relate in some way to children or infancy. There is the background appearance of the official's son, a child apparently (*paidion,* a diminutive of *pais,* "child," 4:49). There is a reference to a son, seemingly a small child, imitating a parent (5:19). Then, when the crowd is hungry and weak, there is the intervention of what appears to be a small boy (*paidarion,* a double diminutive of *pais,* 6:9). And in subsequent passages there are increasing references, not so much to Jesus' infancy, as to his origin—to Joseph and his mother (6:42); and to the place of his origin, particularly to questions involving the coming of the Christ, Bethlehem, and Galilee (7:27–28,41–42). Finally, in chap. 8, Jesus speaks with increasing clarity of his own roots—not of his infancy in this world, but of his roots in God, of his existence in the distant past: "Before Abraham was, I am" (8:58). In other words, while chaps. 4–8 do not speak much of children or infancy they do evoke aspects of both and aspects also of Jesus' origin.

Should the various references to children and origins which are found in chaps. 4–8 be seen as an introduction to chap. 9? The link is not immediately clear, but given John's general practice of building careful continuity, some connection is likely. What he seems to have done is speak first of the origins of Jesus, of the fact that his identity and abilities come primarily, not from his parents and village, but from God (chaps. 4–8, esp. chaps. 5–8); and then, having established Jesus' primordial roots in God, he uses the story of the blind man to speak of a similar phenomenon in Jesus' disciples. The man did, of course, seem to have natural parents, just as Jesus seemed to come from Joseph and his mother. Yet, quite apart from those parents, he went through a total process of growth, from creation to full maturity. There is a sense then in which it could be said of him, as it was of Jesus, that in one way people knew where he was from, yet in another sense they did not (cf. 7:27–28). Thus without ever speaking explicitly of the virgin birth, John manages to convey the theological essence of that idea—the fact that Jesus' birth was primarily not from human parents but from God. And having said that of Jesus, he then indicates that something similar is true of Jesus' disciples— whatever their natural origin, their primary identity and origin lie with God.

Chapter 9: The Central Message

It seems likely that part of John's message is apologetic: to show to what extent the Jews reject evidence and Jesus' disciples accept it. In other words, in a trial between the Jews and Jesus' disciples, the evidence is on the side of the disciples.

The central message, however, concerns the basic optimism which pervades John's gospel and which comes to a new expression in chap. 9. Here more than ever one may see that this optimism is not naive, for the entire chapter is shadowed by sin. The disciples take it for granted that either the blind man or his parents sinned (9:2). Jesus rejects this idea (and its implication of a spiteful tyrannical God; 9:3), but the notion reappears with full force in the pronouncement of the Jewish authorities: "You were born wholly in sin" (9:34). Thus the man's affliction tends to be misinterpreted as indicating a more basic disorder.

Paradoxically, the healing of that affliction is also regarded as indicating disorder, sinfulness. Apart from regarding the healed man as sinful, the Jewish authorities also regard Jesus as sinful and, despite the man's objections to such an interpretation of the healing, they refuse to abandon it (9:16–17, 24–34). Thus the authorities live in a world in which sin is overpowering. They imply that God is spiteful and lifeless, and they see people accordingly as cowed creatures living pettily under sin.

The irony is that it is precisely this interpretation of God and people, and the refusal to leave this interpretation, which is sinful. John 9 sees sin, not where the Pharisees see it, in those who suffer affliction and who, like Jesus, relieve it, but in the authorities' refusal to move from their cramped view of reality (9:41).

A Parable of Divine Providence (Jesus as Good Shepherd, 10:1–21), and a Down-to-Earth Picture of Consequent Human Dignity and Destiny (Jesus, at Dedication, as Messiah and Son, 10:22–42)

Introduction and Structure

As far as the gospel's story line is concerned, chap. 10 makes an important contribution. In narrating Jesus' final fateful year, it moves the action from some time after the autumnal feast of Tents to the winter feast of Dedication (10:22). And then, following the ominous trial-like confrontation with the Jews (10:22–39), it tells of Jesus finally leaving Jerusalem and going away, across the Jordan, to the place where John had first baptized (10:40–42). As Brown emphasizes (414), the effect of this departure and of going to the transjordanian place where the ministry began (1:28–29), is to suggest that something has now come to an end, that in a certain sense Jesus' public ministry is over.

At another level, that of theme rather than story development, this chapter, which itself deals with the idea of the giving of life, forms a bridge between two kindred chapters, both concerned with essentially the same idea—chap. 9, with its suggestion of the original giving of life, at creation and birth; and chap. 11, with its message of a later giving of life, after death. A symptom of the unity of chaps. 9–11 is found, for instance in the fact that the healing of chap. 9 is recalled in both chaps. 10 and 11 (10:21; 11:37).

These two levels (of story and theme) are not at odds with each other. As will be seen in dealing with the story of Lazarus (11:1–53), the suggestion of a break in the story, at the end of chap. 10, far from interfering with the development of the theme, helps it.

The realization that there are two levels help to make sense of the text. At first sight the narrative may sometimes seem rather jagged or confused—like life itself. But when seen from a higher, theological level, it is coherent and meaningful.

The beginning of the chapter ("Amen, amen, I say to you . . .") has occasionally been regarded as strangely abrupt, bereft of appropriate introduction, and for that and other similar reasons, it has sometimes been suggested, notably by Bernard (xxiv–xxv, 341–71) and Bultmann (357–94), that the text be rearranged in various ways (for discussion, see Schnackenburg, 2:276–78). Nonetheless, a considerable number of authors, including Schnackenburg (2:278), see no benefit in such a process. Hoskyns (382–83), in particular, emphasizes that the chapter as a whole is coherent and that it is built carefully on what precedes. And Brown (390) concludes: "We agree with Dodd, Feuillet, Schneider, and others in accepting the present order in John as a purposeful arrangement and not as a product of accident or confusion."

The impression of most scholars, in fact, is that the various rearrangement theories are arbitrary and unhelpful. Yet these theories have the advantage of highlighting certain significant features of the text, and it is necessary, especially in discussing structure, to take account of such features.

As is generally agreed, the chapter consists of two major sections of equal length (10:1–21 and 10:22–42). And it is possible, using simplified terms, to summarize these sections as follows:

A timeless parabolic discourse—the life-giving shepherd (1–21);

A down-to-earth trial-like confrontation—Jesus, at Dedication, is Messiah and consecrated Son (22–42).

The relationship between the two sections of the chapter is akin to that between chaps. 7 and 8. Like chap. 8, the parabolic discourse gives virtually no indications of time or space. And the divine, timeless, "I am," which opens and closes chapter 8 (8:12,58), is echoed repeatedly in 10:1–21: "I am . . . I am . . . I am . . . the door/the good shepherd" (vv 7, 9, 11, 14). It is because the passage as a whole is so deliberately bereft of indications of time and space that it is appropriate that it begin abruptly, that it have no "normal" introduction. The trial-like confrontation, on the other hand, has the concreteness of chap. 7: it is linked very deliberately to time (the feast of Dedication, winter) and place ("in Jerusalem . . . in the temple . . . in the portico of Solomon," 10:22–23; cf. 7:1–2,14,37). Chap. 7 is echoed even in some details: a feast; "Jesus walked about in . . ."; the impatient demand of the unbelieving brothers/Jews for *parrēsia*, "openness" (7:1–5; 10:22–25); the increasing disagreement with the brothers/Jews, which leads to his abiding in another place (Galilee, 7:6–9; beyond the Jordan, 10:40). Thus in various ways the concreteness of chap. 7 and the timelessness of chap. 8 are balanced by the timelessness and concreteness of 10:1–21 and 10:22–42 respectively. And this balance helps to forge all of chaps. 7–10 into a unity.

What is essential from the point of view of chapter 10 is that its two sections, different though they are, complement each other. One emphasizes a Jesus who, initially at least, speaks an enigmatic language and who echoes the divine. The other shows a Jesus who, despite his unity with the divine, is enmeshed in the tangled reality of history. The first may be said, to some extent, to show God's plan from the inside; the second shows it more from the outside, from the way it is received in human experience.

As some presentations of the text imply (see esp. the RSV and UBSGNT), each section consists of three subsections. These subsections may be summarized as follows:

1–6   The enigmatic parable of the sheepfold

7–18   Interpretation: "the good (*kalos*) shepherd"

19–21   Reaction: division, and a sketch of developing belief

22–30   The enigmatic Messiah who gives life to the sheep

31–39   The consecrated Son who shows the Father's good (*kalos*) works

40–42   Reaction (as Jesus goes away): developed belief

As will be seen, two of these subsections may be further subdivided—vv 7–18 into three parts, vv 31–39 into two—but such further subdivisions should not

confuse the fact that the basic division of the chapter as a whole is sixfold.
Schnackenburg (2:288–303) does include some of these further subdivisions, and,
partly for that reason, divides the chapter into seven parts.

The relationship between the six subsections is complex and subtle. Number
1, for instance, the parable (vv 1–6), is developed by number 2 (vv 7–18), the
interpretation. But it is also mirrored obliquely by its opposite number in the other
half of the chapter—the Messiah text (22–30). And so on: 1, 2, and 3 are variously mirrored or balanced by 4, 5, and 6. To a very limited degree, the same
phenomenon was noted in the six scenes of chap. 9. To some degree, therefore,
chapter 10 is like a diptych.

Overview of Content

It is useful at the beginning—even if it means going ahead of the detailed evidence—to give an overview of the chapter as a whole, particularly of the balance
between 1–21 and 22–42.

The essence of the relationship between the two halves of the chapter is not
only that the first is more divine and the second more human. There is a sense
also in which, in a unique way, these texts give working definitions of what is
meant by the divine and the human. The divine, at least insofar as the divine is
known, is defined as the good shepherd. And the human is defined as one who is
an anointed (Messiah), and better still, a consecrated child of God, a child whom
God sends into the world. In Jesus both elements, divine and human, are held
together.

The centrality of these definitions is such that it gives chap. 10 a unique status.
Though less known as a unity than some other chapters, it is in fact a focal point
in the gospel. The designation ''interpretative interlude,'' which Culpepper (1983,
93) uses of 9:1–10:21, may be applied to all of 9:1–10:42, and especially to chap.
10. Coming at the end of Jesus' public ministry, it has the role of a clarifying
culmination.

The fact that the two sections are defining the divine and the human, helps
explain the relationship between them. Since from one point of view the divine
and human are so diverse, it is appropriate that the two sections look different and
in many ways be different. But since the human and divine are also so interwoven
—one cannot in practice understand one without the other—it is also appropriate
that the two sections be closely related.

As indicated, the first major idea—in the opening subsections (vv 1–6, 22–
30)—is that of something secret; there is the implied secret of the parable and the
implied secret of Messiahship or anointedness. Diverse though these things are,
they are also closely related. The secrecy of the parable, its enigmatic nature, has
to do with the secrecy of God's activity (in Jesus), and as such is far beyond
the human. Yet it is precisely that secret activity which engenders in the human
heart a further secret, that of the special dignity of the human—a dignity expressed by the idea of being anointed. In the turmoil of life, however, it is not

easy to hear these secrets, and so in both texts there are various references to the difficult process of hearing and understanding.

The second major idea—in the central subsections (vv 7–18, 31–39)—is that of something good, even beautiful (*kalos*). Again, the good things in question are very diverse. There is the inherent goodness, primordial, of the divine, a goodness that is seen in the good shepherd, in other words, in God's Jesus-centered providence. And there is the other goodness, quite distant, of all God's works, the "good works" from the Father which are shown by Jesus—a reference apparently not just to the specific miracles recounted in the gospel, but through these miracles, to all that is good and wonderful. Again, however, despite the diversity, the two things are closely related: it is the goodness of the divine shepherd which brings into human life so much that is wonderfully good, and these good things help a person to come to the realization, not just of having the dignity of one who is anointed, but of being something more—a child of God, a consecrated child.

Despite their profound sense of all that is good, these various texts are not naive. The emphasis on the positive is set against a background that is chilling. The threat of brutality and death is pervasive—from the first verse of the parable, with its suggestion of a night stalker (10:1), to the final Jewish effort at lynching (10:31–33,39). Yet it is precisely amid such darkness that one may grasp the secret and its wonder.

The problem, of course, is that such a secret is not easy to grasp. Even when shouted it is elusive. It is for that reason that the final subsections (vv 19–21, 40–42) deal largely with the question of people's reactions. Some of what these subsections portray is negative, but the main emphasis is positive: they contain carefully graded portraits of the process of coming to believe. This needs to be examined in greater detail.

The Reaction Accounts

The position and authenticity of the reaction accounts (19–21, 40–42) have often been questioned (e.g., cf. Becker, 323). The first (vv 19–21) tells of the coming into being of a division "among the Jews," the second (vv 40–42) goes further by showing the working out of that division: Jesus is rejected in Jerusalem, yet, when he leaves Jerusalem, the followers of John come to him.

One of the features of these reaction texts, and of other references in chap. 10 to reactions (cf. 10:6,31–39), is that they repeat, often in intensified form, the reactions first recorded in preceding chapters, especially in chapters 7 and 8:

- Failure to understand: 8:27; 10:6

- Division: among the crowd, 7:43; among the Pharisees, 9:16; and, finally, among "the Jews," 10:19

- Accusation of demonic possession: 7:20; 8:48,52; 10:20

- Attempted stoning: 8:59; 10:31–33

- Jesus' escape from their hands: 7:30,44; 10:39
- Many believe: 8:30; 10:41–42

The process of intensification may be noted, for instance, in the fact that in chap. 10 the accusation of demonic possession is accompanied by that of madness, the attempted stoning uses the word "stone" with greater frequency, and the escape from their hands implies—in contrast to 7:30,44—that to some degree he had actually been in their hands. In the context of such a process of intensification, the final intensified statement of belief (10:41–42) is altogether appropriate.

Quantity Analysis: Exploratory Observations

A curious aspect of the text is the variation in the quantity of its subsections, specifically the fact that, in comparison with 10:1–6, 10:7–18 is quite extensive. A similar phenomenon may be seen in Part 1 (1:1–2:22): though the quantity of text allotted to the successive days is graded evenly, the quantity of the subsections varies sharply, particularly between the call of Philip (2 verses) and that of Nathanael (7). The minuscule quantity given to the call of Philip appears to reflect the undeveloped nature of its subject matter, the call of the Gentiles, and it seems likely that within chap. 10 there is a similar purposefulness in the variations of quantity. This likelihood is strengthened by the fact that it is in the context of chapter 10 that Brown (415) notes the decrease in the quantity of the references to John the baptizer (cf. 10:40–41). In other words, in chapter 10, as in earlier passages, the quantity is not haphazard.

Why exactly the first text (1–6) should be so much shorter than the second (7–18) probably has to do with the basic content of these texts. One is a parable, and as such is like something that is closed. The second, being an explanation, is more open, and so, unlike the first, it tends to unfold—and thus to be more expansive. Hence, the increasing quantity would appear, primarily, to reflect the idea of increasing clarification. A further reason may be the fact that vv 7–18 bring up the idea, more clearly than previously, of a new and more complex gathering—one which would, in fact, be twofold (Jewish and Gentile, cf. 10:16)—and it is appropriate that the text which envisages that twofold expansion should itself be significantly expansive.

Jesus as the Good Shepherd (10:1–21):
A Parable of Divine Providence

[10:1–6] The parable of the sheepfold.   The positive picture which is presented here is essentially quite simple: as the door of a sheepfold (*aulē*, yard/fold) is opened by the doorkeeper, a shepherd comes in, calls those who are his own sheep, and leads them out.

Along with the positive picture, however, there is one which is negative—

that of another figure, described as a violent thief (literally "a thief and a robber"), who, by some way other than the door, climbs into the fold.

As Wikenhauser (194) implies, the contrast between the thief and the shepherd is literally like that between darkness and dawn: the thief breaks in at night; the shepherd, following local custom, comes in the early morning and leads the sheep out to pasture.

While the contrast between the night thief and the dawn shepherd provides a vivid background, most of the dramatic action centers on the interaction between the shepherd and his sheep—the various things he does to call them out (comes, calls his own by name, leads out, puts out, goes before), and the various aspects of their response (they hear his voice; they follow him and know his voice).

The drama is heightened by the fact that, even as they follow the shepherd, whose voice they now know, it is emphasized that they will not follow a stranger, but will, in fact, flee from anyone with an unknown voice.

A Single Parable

There has been much scholarly discussion about whether the text should be seen as a parable (sometimes regarded as a story or illustration with a single point) or, rather, as an allegory (a story or illustration in which every detail has a figurative meaning). But, as Brown (390) emphasizes, this Greek-based distinction between a one-point parable and an all-points allegory may not be rigorously applied to the world of biblical literature, a world governed by the fact that the single Hebrew word *mashal* had been used with great ambiguity; it referred to all kinds of figurative stories and illustrations (parables, allegories, riddles, proverbs, similes, etc.). The word used by the text itself, *paroimia* (10:6), does not, of course, mean either parable or allegory, at least not in any restricted sense. Rather, as Schnackenburg (2:283) indicates, it reflects the broad range of the word *mashal,* and, given that background, it would seem at first sight that it should be translated by the wide-ranging word "figure." However, the word "parable," despite its narrowness as a Greek literary term, may also be taken in a wide-ranging sense—a sense which, to some degree, is suggested by its manifold use in the synoptic gospels—and it is in this wide-ranging sense, not distinguished from allegory (pace Wikenhauser, 194), that the word "parable" is used here.

It is disputed whether the text consists of one parable or two. Brown (392–93) and Kysar (159–60), for instance, largely by emphasizing the difference between the negative background in the opening verses (vv 1–3a) and the more positive emphasis in the final verses (vv 3b–5), conclude that the number of parables is two.

But contrasting background is an integral part of good art, and one can no more separate the polemical background from the positive message than one can separate the increasingly blind Pharisees from the story of the increasingly insightful man (chap. 9).

Nor does a variation in the designation of the negative figure (*thieves and robbers* in v 1, but *strangers* in v 5) indicate disunity—any more than the variation in chap. 9 from "Pharisees" to "Jews" indicates disunity (9:13,18). The designation of the thief as a "stranger" makes sense in the context. For the first time in the parable the shepherd has just been described as one whose voice is *known* (v 4). Inevitably, anyone who is contrasted with that known figure must now be regarded as in some way unknown—as a stranger.

Besides, however one translates *paroimia* (figure, parable, allegory), one thing is certain: in 10:6 it is used in the singular (*"this* parable").

A Parable of Providential Shepherding

While the action in the parable is relatively easy to follow, its ultimate meaning is not immediately clear. To some degree it is like the story which Nathan told to David about the two men and the lamb (2 Sam 12:1–15): the story was very easy to follow, but David had no idea what it was referring to. In the present text none of the figures is identified. Not even the speaker is named. (Only in v 6 is Jesus mentioned.) It seems strange too that a shepherd should know each of his sheep by name, and stranger still that, despite being so well-known, and despite knowing the shepherd's voice, the sheep have to be "put out" (literally, thrown out, *ek-ballō,* v 4). Thus in many ways the text is a puzzle, or, as Schnackenburg (2:285) says, it is "a real riddle."

It seems better not to attempt straightaway to explain the riddle fully. The purpose of the passage which follows (vv 7–18) is largely to provide such an explanation. It is necessary, however, even if only in preparing for the explanation, to highlight some basic elements.

The opening formula ("Amen, amen . . .") suggests a revelatory declaration. The riddle, therefore, is not trivial; it has to do with the action of God.

The repeated references to sheep and a shepherd cannot but evoke something of the well-known OT background in which the people were referred to as a flock, and "shepherd" was used of such central characters as Moses (Exod 2:16–3:1), Joshua (Num 27:6–7), David (1 Sam 16:11; 2 Sam 5:2, 7:8), and above all of God's own self (Ezekiel 34). In other words, what is evoked obscurely is the entire world of God's shepherding of the flock. In such a context it makes sense that the shepherd should know each sheep by name.

"The thief and the robber" refers first of all to a single negative attacker, but at the end of the parable, when the plural is used ("strangers"), it is clear that it refers also to a multiplicity of enemies, to a variety of thieves and robbers. As a single attacker it is like the fundamental force of evil or darkness which opposes the divine shepherding. And as representative of various thieves and robbers it refers to all those who play a part in opposing that divine work. Given the role played by the Pharisees in chap. 9—they seemed opposed to the whole process of the divine giving of life and light—they cannot but be included among the thieves and robbers. It is possible too, given the gospel's earlier linking of Pharisees with priests (1:19,24; 7:32,45), that the mention of thieves and robbers alludes also to the priests. Such an allusion would be an appropriate preparation both for the mention of Dedication (10:22)—a feast associated with rapacious post-Maccabean priests (cf. Brown, 392–93)—and for the later confrontation in the yard (*aulē*) of the high priest (18:12–27).

What the parable, therefore, suggests is a fundamental conflict of forces. On the one hand, there is the broad world of divine shepherding. On the other, there is a complex destructive power, one which may indeed be identified with the Pharisees (and priests), but which in its very vagueness tends to evoke a larger world of negativity. And, in the middle, there is an actual shepherd, one who amid this potentially destructive setting, manages to go to the sheep, call them by name, and lead them out.

Yet, in a strange way, what is negative and positive work together. The Pharisees and Jews had "thrown out" the formerly blind man (*ek-ballō*, 9:34–35), and the shepherd "throws out" the sheep (*ek-ballō*, 10:4). In other words, by stretching the language—Culpepper (1983, cf. 199) would probably say by deforming it—the evangelist manages to use the same word both of the expulsion of the disciple from the circle of the Jews and of the shepherd's calling of his sheep. The overall effect is not only to evoke the providential shepherding of the people, but to link that providence with the complex negative process of the Jewish expulsion of the disciples.

It is against the background of this complexity, this elusive *paroimia* of God's providence, that Jesus then proceeds to clarify.

[10:7–18] The interpretation of the parable: Jesus as door, as good shepherd, and as dying in the Father's love. The interpretation begins in classic form. Nathan had said, "You are the man" (2 Sam 2:7). Jesus says, "I am the gate. . . ." But as Jesus goes on talking, and, as he changes to "I am the good shepherd," it becomes clear that the NT case is not nearly so simple.

As presented in the canonical text, the interpretation consists of an unbroken address by Jesus, and it is clearly distinguished both from the parable which precedes (10:1–6) and from the reaction which follows (10:19–21). It would seem, therefore, to form some kind of unity.

Yet the text changes a good deal, and what is particularly perplexing is that at certain points, especially in the final verses (17–18), the sheep-related imagery seems to be quite absent. Hence the nature of its unity is not clear, and it is partly true that the final two verses "seem to lie somewhat outside the picture of the parable and its explanation" (Brown, 399). Schnackenburg (2:298–303), in fact, in a rather unusual move, breaks off the final *three* verses (16–18) and places them in the same subunit as the account of the reaction (vv 19–21).

An initial clue to the structure of the text is provided by commentators such as Brown (393–99) and Kysar (160–63), who, while not defining the nature of the unity of the text, suggest that in practice it should be divided into three parts:

7–10 Jesus as the gate
11–16 Jesus the good shepherd
17–18 Jesus' death in the loving plan of the Father

This division seems to be reliable. The beginning of the good shepherd text (v 11a) recalls the beginning of the gate text (v 7), yet it leaves aside its solemn opening ("Amen, amen . . .") and is clearly distinct from it. And the beginning of the third text (v 17, Jesus' death in God's loving plan) repeats the first idea of the good shepherd text, that of laying down one's life, yet, with more down-to-earthness than ever, it leaves aside even the limited solemnity ("I am . . .") of the opening of the good shepherd text, and it embarks on a more direct mode of discourse. The overall effect is of a threefold division which advances from parabolic obscurity to increasing clarity.

A further clue is provided by those who emphasize that even within each of these divisions there are significant variations. Thus within the gate text (vv 7–10), Bultmann (375) and Brown (393) note that at first (in v 8) the interpretation stays very close to the imagery of the parable. But, as the interpretation develops, that imagery fades, and in its final sentence (v 10b) "there is straight theological language, and not one word is drawn from the allegory" (Lindars, 360). In other words, within the gate text there is an initial stage which is quite close to the parabolic imagery (vv 7–8), an intermediate stage which is less so (v 9), and a final stage in which it eventually disappears (v 10).

A similar phenomenon occurs within the good shepherd text (vv 11–16). Kysar (162–63) and Haenchen (2:48), for instance, subdivide it into three stages (11–13, 14–15, 16), and—even though the good shepherd text as a whole is considerably further from the language of the parable than the gate text—within those three stages, the first has much more sheep-related imagery than the second. The third (v 16) has a good deal of such imagery, but by speaking of "other sheep," it breaks away even more. (Thus, while Schnackenburg's grouping of v 16 with what follows [2:298–303] may not be accurate, it does help to underline that v 16 is quite distinct.)

Whether the dying-in-God's-love text (vv 17–18) should also be divided in three is not immediately clear. What is reasonably evident, however, is that, while it has none of the language of the parable, such shepherd-related language as it does have—"I lay down my life"—gradually fades.

What finally emerges, therefore, is not just a threefold division, but a threefold spiral. Within each division (7–10, 11–16, 17–18) there is a progressive relinquishing of parabolic language. This is seen most easily in the opening phrases. Verses 7–10 pass from "I am the door of the sheep" to "I am the door" and finally to the simple "I came. . . ." And vv 11–16 moves from a double use of the phrase "good shepherd" (11), to a single use of it (14), to the simple phrase "I have . . ." (16). In the final part (17–18), parabolic language has been left behind completely, and the only symptom of the descending spiral would appear to be the ever more brief and varied expressions of the idea of laying down one's life—an idea first found as a virtual definition of the role of the good shepherd (11).

In this context it is worth noting that in the Greek text the use of *egō* ("I") and *echō* ("I have") form an interesting pattern. (*egō* is used in conjunction with three verbs, *eimi*, *ēlthon*, and *tithēmi*, respectively, "I am," "I came" and "I lay down.")

7–10   Amen, amen, *egō eimi* the gate of the sheep
        egō eimi the gate
        egō ēlthon

11–16   *egō eimi* the good shepherd. The good shepherd lays down . . .
        egō eimi the good shepherd
        echō [other sheep]

17–18   *egō tithēmi* my life
        egō tithēmi it
        echō [power] . . . *echō* [power]

The basic pattern is one of fading or narrowing, and part of that fading is that *egō* gives way to *echō*. But at the very end the pattern is reversed: the *echō* occurs twice. This reversal in the form reflects a reversal in the content: having spoken repeatedly of laying down his life, Jesus at this point, in the final *echō*, speaks of having power to take it up again.

Apart from relinquishing language which is parabolic, the text also leaves aside language which is divine. The opening "Amen, amen, . . ." with all its suggestion of supreme authority, is never repeated. And the use of "I am" gradually fades away. The only thing left at the end is the authority to die and take life up again. And even that finally gives way to a reality that is yet more humble —the receiving of a command from the Father (18c).

There is a suggestion, therefore, of a self-emptying, and the overall effect is like that of the prologue—a descent from the divine to the human, a descent described in language that, with complete appropriateness, is less and less high-flown (less poetic in the prologue, less parabolic in 10:7–18).

There are, of course, major differences between this descent and that of the prologue. In particular, this one is told from the inside. And it is closer in position and emphasis to the point at which the descent becomes really difficult—at the threat of death. Yet, as will be seen from a closer examination, it manages, like the prologue, to encompass a wide view.

[10:7–10] In the face of the destroyer, Jesus as the door to life. Jesus begins with a solemn revelatory statement—"I am the door of the sheep"—a statement which to a significant degree echoes the solemn opening of chapter 8: "I am the light of the world" (8:12). Even in the surrounding details there are echoes:

8:12	10:7–8
Again, therefore, Jesus spoke to them, saying,	Jesus, therefore, again said, "Amen, amen, I say to you,
"I am the light of the world.	I am the door of the sheep.
The one *who follows me* will *not walk in darkness,*	All *who came before me* are *thieves and robbers,*
but will have the light of life."	but the sheep did not hear them."
	[10:10, "The thief comes . . . to kill.
	I came that they may have life. . . ."]

Without dwelling on the details, it is useful to mention that the continuity is all the greater because both the light and the door are regarded as sources of *life* (". . . will have the light of life," 8:12; ". . . that they may have life," 10:10), and also because the opposing force(s) may be visualized in terms of *darkness* (8:12 speaks explicitly of darkness; and the murderous thief of 10:10 is so described as to be "a general representative of darkness" [Brown, 395]).

What is essential is that Jesus' proclamation of himself as the door or gate is not some secondary statement. In its solemnity and content it has echoes of chapter 8 and of the prologue (1:1–5). And its intermediate verse (10:9, "I am the door. Whoever enters through me will be saved") will itself be echoed later in Jesus' memorable declaration, "I am the way and the truth and the life . . ." (14:6). (For details, see Schnackenburg, 2:292; the German original, 2:368, is more complete.)

The overall effect is of a divine voice which solemnly declares its unique role as the origin of life. And it is in this context of the divine that one should probably understand the difficult and controverted statement, "All who came before me are thieves and robbers, but the sheep did not hear them" (v 8). Those who come before Jesus are those who come before God, in other words, all those who in any way are false gods. The "before," therefore, refers to coming first not in time, but in preference. Whatever comes before God is like a thief and a robber —it is destructive of life. Even love destroys, unless God comes before it. It is a matter so basic that it is addressed in the very first commandment: "You shall have no other gods before me" (Deut 5:7, LXX, literally "before my face," *pro prosōpou mou*).

The fact that Jesus uses the past tense ("all who *came* . . .") *appears* to be explained by the context of the parable and its explanation. The explanation, by its very nature, is looking to the past—not to the course of history, but to *the things that happened in the parable.*

It is not necessary, therefore, to take "those who came before me" as referring primarily to false messiahs, and still less to the figures of the OT. This does not, however, rule out all reference to historical figures. The gospel text often moves on diverse levels, and Brown (393–94) is probably correct when, on the basis of the literary continuity between the explanation and the parable, he sees the "thieves and robbers" (v 8) as containing an allusion to the Pharisees (and priests). But while granting this historical allusion or dimension, it would seem that the primary emphasis is on the basic idea of the conflict between all that is from God and all that tries to put itself before God.

This sense of the exclusiveness of God is, of course, reflected in and through the figure of Jesus, the incarnate Word of God. Hence, the picture given here of Jesus is one of a life-giver who has a unique claim. As Bultmann (377) concludes: "All pretended revealers of all ages are swept away by the 'coming' of Jesus which is experienced in faith."

The Image of the Gate/Door

What is not immediately clear is why the central image is that of a door (*thyra*, door/gate). For many people, the idea of a door does not grip the imagination.

But for someone seeking a way out of slavery or imprisonment, or for someone seeking entry to a place of well-being, there is nothing of greater interest. The door is the key, the beginning of greater life.

The image of the door was used by the Gnostics, especially to refer to the heavenly door through which the soul enters after death, and Schnackenburg, who summarizes the Gnostic references, may be right in concluding that "one cannot rule out a certain influence from the world of Gnostic imagery" (2:290). But the image of the door or gate is found as early as the OT (see Ps 118:20, "This is the gate of the Lord; the just may enter through it"), and the synoptic gospels have several references to similar or associated images—the door, the doorkeeper, the keys, the way. And Acts 14:27, in the context of admitting the pagans— an idea which is very close to the thought of chapter 10 (cf. 10:16)—speaks of God as opening a door. Thus the background to the use of the image of the door may have been quite complex.

What is important is that as it now stands the image of the door has several aspects. It has a certain aloofness or emotional distance. At a later stage in the descending spiral of vv 7–18, the figure of the good shepherd almost invariably strikes a responsive chord. But the idea of the door—not completely unlike that of the Word—may leave one wondering. However, in the context of the text's emphasis on the solemnity of the divine, this sense of distance is appropriate.

The Gateway to Life

For all its distance, this door or gate is the source of life. It is both the path *to* the sheep—it is through Jesus that "humans gain affiliation with the sheep of God, the elect community" (Kysar, 161)—and it is the way through which the sheep are nourished. In v 9, as the text begins to unfold, this nourishing role of Jesus is spelled out. Through him a person *is saved* (is thus brought from what is harmful to what is good), and *goes in and out* (a process which suggests ease and freedom), and *finds pasture* (a symbol of fundamental well-being and fulfillment). Brown (394) refers to this pasture as the pasture of life and compares it to the gospel's earlier references to living water and the bread of life.

Then, in v 10, the crowning statement about this role: in contrast to the murderous thief, Jesus has come to bring life, life to the full. Life to the full refers to everything from the kind of natural exuberance that is suggested by the wine at the Cana wedding to the suggestions in chaps. 5 and 6 of giving life to the dead. It refers above all to a quality of interior life, life in the spirit.

The passage as a whole, therefore, refers first of all to the divine process, mediated through Jesus, of giving life abundantly and of doing so even in the teeth of murderous attacks.

But because of its immediate context (its relationship to the parable and, through that parable, to chap. 9), the passage refers also, in an obscure way, to a more limited, historical phenomenon—the process by which, even in the teeth of death-minded Jewish leaders ("thieves and robbers") who threw out those who were coming to the light, God was leading other Jews to a place of greater life.

[10:11–16] Jesus as the good shepherd—the one who turns death into love, knowledge, and union.   The reference to the good shepherd introduces into the discourse a distinctive change of mood. In comparison with the image of the door, that of the shepherd is much more human. And this sense of humanity is accentuated by the fact that the shepherd is immediately spoken of as dying—an idea which "appears rather abruptly" (Brown, 395).

As indicated earlier, this abrupt shift, from a divine and rather distant level to one which is more human, is not unlike that which occurs in the prologue when John is introduced (1:6). But the change which occurs here, insofar as it speaks not just of what is human but also of death, goes considerably further.

The text (vv 11–16) consists of three interwoven steps: Jesus' total generosity towards the sheep, even to the giving of his life (11–13); his knowledge of his sheep and theirs of him (14–15); and his bringing of other sheep so as to form a unity (16). Thus it goes from the idea of (implied) love to that of (mutual) knowledge to that of a yet greater scope for his love and knowledge. Beginning with total self-giving, it is an expanding process.

The initial theme, that of implied love (vv 11–13), has a startling quality, for the idea of dying is not only rather abrupt, it is also complemented by the sudden appearance of a further image—that of the mercenary shepherd who allows the wolf to sieze and scatter. The main problem with this money-minded worker is his implied lack of love, an implication that is developed at some length: "he sees . . . and leaves . . . and flees" (a vivid three-verb description), and he allows the wolf to achieve the opposite of (unitive) love—to seize and scatter. He does this because he is not bonded with the sheep (they are "not his own," v 12), and, to put it more crudely, as the text finally does, "he does not care" (v 13).

The overall effect of these contrasting images—total giving and not caring—is to establish, with a sense of surprise, the foundational role of an implied love.

The next theme, that of knowledge (vv 14–15), is also rather surprising, because even though it had been referred to in the parable (v 4, they follow him and know his voice), it is spoken of here in a way which indicates a rather extraordinary knowledge which is personal and mutual, a knowledge which is like nothing less than that between Jesus and the Father. This may be called mystical if the word is used in a positive sense—as referring to "a thoroughly *personal* relationship in which the integrity of the persons is preserved" (Kysar, 163). Yet, as if to guard against the danger that this knowledge be regarded as some exotic cerebral game, there is a further reminder (15b) of the reality underlying this knowledge—Jesus' loving even unto death.

Then, in the third step (v 16ab), the text opens up yet a further horizon, that of the "other sheep" whom it is necessary (*dei*—providential necessity) for Jesus to bring—a reference, above all, to the providential coming of the Gentiles. A similar sense of providential necessity, in other words, of providential guidance, governed Jesus' first encounter with non-Jews—the Samaritans (cf. 4:4).

And finally (v 16c)—following what seems to be the slightly more difficult reading (Brown, 387)—"*they* shall become one flock, one shepherd." In other words, both groups, the responsive sheep who were in the original *aulē* (fold/ yard), together with the "other sheep," will form a new unity, a unity which is centered in Jesus himself, and which, in fact, consists of Jesus or at least is contained within him: "they shall become . . . one shepherd." However puzzling this phrasing may seem, it makes theological sense: it suggests that, as Ephesians, for instance, emphasizes (cf. esp. Eph 2:11–18), the union of Jews and Gentiles is accomplished in the person of Christ, in his body and through his self-giving in death (his "blood"). In his crucified-and-risen body they are brought into one. The fourth gospel's later references to unity also occur in this context—the context of Jesus' impending death (cf. 11:52–53; 17:19–26).

It is because of this connection—between Jewish–Gentile unity and Jesus' death—that, *pace* Bultmann (383), the theme of the providential coming of the Gentiles is so appropriate to the passage on the good shepherd. For the good shepherd is presented first of all as giving himself in death, and it makes sense that the picture of such self-giving should include one of its most basic accomplishments—the bringing together into unity of Jews and Gentiles.

Thus the passage as a whole (vv 11–16) goes from the idea of self-giving in death, to mutual knowledge, to unity. The three factors are closely connected. It is the total self-giving which, by saving the sheep and warding off the disruptive wolf, opens the way for mutual knowledge. And "the purpose of this knowledge is to bring these followers into union" (Brown, 396).

The Power of the Shepherd Image

The extraordinary power of the good shepherd passage depends considerably on its ability to hold together two very distinct areas of experience. On the one hand, it manages to suggest, particularly by its repetition of the quietly majestic "I am, . . ." and especially through the evocative power of the image of the good shepherd (an image which, among other things, recalls a rich OT background, especially Psalm 23 and Ezekiel 34), it manages to suggest the all-encompassing majestic providence of God. On the other hand, by speaking of shepherds and sheep—an image which is heightened by that of the mercenary and the destructive wolf—it manages also to touch a whole world of human feeling. As is shown by modern greeting cards, national symbols, and children's books, and as was implied by the earlier references to a lamb and a dove (1:29–34), animals have considerable power as evocative symbols. Nor is this a modern phenomenon. A major area of Greco-Roman literature was pastoral. And as Brown notes in the context of the good shepherd (397), "even when agriculture became dominant in Israel, there remained a nostalgia for the pastoral." Thus, in a manner which echoes the prologue's bridging of the pre-existing Word with the Word-made-flesh, the good shepherd text links the all-encompassing providential God with the world of personal feeling.

What is at stake ultimately is the idea that supporting each human life, there is a foundational love, a love which gives even to death. The relationship of such a love to human existence, particularly to the existence of those who are most wounded, is reflected indirectly in a comment once made about a group of emotionally disturbed children in New England: "What those kids need is someone who will go to the wall for them." The message of the good shepherd text is that such a love exists, but initially it is shrouded in parable, and its revelation comes but slowly.

What is also in question is the fact that this love-unto-death does not remain private. More and more it both brings knowledge and breaks barriers—so that eventually all may become one.

Why death should be associated with unity is a complex question. Death, of course, is the great leveler, the point at which scepter and spade are equal, and likewise Jew and Gentile. What is important is that this ultimate human experience, common to all, has become an expression or revelation of divine love; as is shown in Jesus, love has taken over death. Death has become a place where the loving unity of Father and Son, already present in Jesus' lifetime, becomes fully transparent; a dark chasm has been bridged. To some extent the bridging of this chasm of death may be visualized, even in John, as a sacrifice of expiation (Schnackenburg, 1:157). But the primary picture is not of Jesus sacrificing to God, but of a single God, who is both Father and Son, working to show that even in death, in fact, most of all in death, love is present and creative. In other words, death is a high point for God's creative love. Hence, the death of Jesus, the divine good shepherd, is like a beacon which lights the human scene. And for all who accept it and who realize how deeply it speaks to their own experience and to their own ultimate fate, it becomes a profound bond of unity. Thus the awareness of the death-related shepherd gathers people into one.

[10:17–18] Jesus' death as love-based, life-oriented, and free.

The connection between death and love, which in the preceding section was merely implied, now comes clearly to the fore.

Death is often seen as making a mockery of life, love, and freedom, but when Jesus speaks of his own death he sees it otherwise. Having said earlier that the Father's love for the Son is expressed in showing him how to create and give life (5:19–21), he now states that this Father's love is particularly expressed in Jesus' dying: "Because of this the Father loves me, that I lay down my life, in order that I may take it up again." As Lindars (364) emphasizes, it is not that the Father's love is dependent on Jesus' death. Rather, that love is presupposed; but in Jesus' dying the Father's love is expressed in a special way and is grounded yet more firmly. Furthermore, this death is inextricably bound to life. The "in order that I may take it up again" reflects the fact that in NT thought in general and in Johannine thought in particular, Jesus' death, resurrection, and ascension constitute one action, the "indissoluble salvific action of return to the Father" (Brown, 399). Thus, contrary to appearances, death is seen as grounded in love and oriented towards life.

Death may also seem to express one's final failure, one's utter powerlessness. But here too Jesus takes a different approach: his life is not taken from him; rather, he has power both in laying it down and in taking it again.

Yet, having claimed this extraordinary sense of being in command of his own destiny, he states that it is based on something distinct from himself—on the *entolē* ("command/charge") received from the Father. Thus as he speaks of death he has a sense both of power and of surrender.

[10:19–21] Reaction: division among the Jews, and a sketch of developing belief. As noted in introducing chap. 10, this reaction is part of the chapter's larger pattern of reactions, and it is an intensification of various reactions in chaps. 7–9, especially of the accusations that Jesus was possessed (7:20; 8:48,52).

When Jesus first told the parable (vv 1–5) he was met by a lack of understanding. Now that he has clarified it, there comes division. Ultimately this division is a variation of that between those who did and did not receive the light (1:11–12), between those who do and do not come to the light (3:20–21).

The accusation of possession or madness seems to express a fundamental rejection of the message concerning life and light. It was used in 7:20, in the context of Jesus' interpreting of the law as life-giving, by those who had turned the law into an instrument of death. And its use in 8:48,52 occurred in the context of affirming death and denying Jesus' message of life. Now, as Jesus comes closer to the reality of his own death, and as he affirms, more than before, the reality of love and life, the rejection based on alleged possession or madness is stronger than ever. It is like some kind of revulsion with regard to life or the idea of further life.

Those who accept Jesus at the end of this explanation (10:21) do so partly because to them his words do not sound demonic, but especially because his granting of sight to the blind man had disposed them to interpret his words in a positive way. Thus, at this stage, the decisive factor is Jesus' work rather than his word. It is not an ideal form of response, but it is positive, and it prepares the way for the later, more developed, reaction (10:40–42).

With light strokes chap. 10 is providing an outline of the process of coming to believe. First, in parabolic language, there is the reaction of the sheep in recognizing the voice of the shepherd (v 3), a reaction which suggests an instinctive affinity for what is good and true. Complementing that instinct there is a lack of knowledge, a lack of response, concerning what is destructive (vv 4, 5, 8). Then, in the reaction accounts (vv 19–21, 40–42), when parabolic language has been left aside, chapter 10 gives two portraits of believing, one partial, the other more complete. Thus, through these texts and through some other features, this chapter speaks not only of revelation but also of response.

Jesus at Dedication as Messiah and Son (10:22–42): A Down-to-Earth Picture of Consequent Human Dignity and Destiny

[10:22–30] The trial-like confrontation at the Feast of Dedication: amid death-evoking winter Jesus has a hidden (messianic) dignity which comes from union with the Father; his care for "his sheep". As was emphasized in the introduction to chap. 10, the later part of the chapter, in contrast to 10:1–21, is set in a definite time and place.

The events at Dedication fall essentially into two scenes. In the first, the Jews surround Jesus, yet, as the Messiah, the Anointed, he affirms that he and the Father are one (vv 22–30). In the second, they increase their hostility—they take up stones to stone him—but now, more than ever, as Son, Jesus asserts his union with the Father (vv 31–39). The overall effect is that of an intensification of death and darkness, and the countering of these negative forces by an intensified statement about the presence of light and life.

Initially, when the text first refers to the feast of Dedication, the presence of darkness is not obvious. Dedication (*egkainia,* literally "renewal"; in Hebrew, *hannukah*) was an annual celebration of the reconsecration, following the Maccabean war (167–164 B.C.), of the altar and temple. Despite its origin in the Maccabean period, however, it had wider overtones. It was "somewhat evocative of the consecration of all the houses of God in Israel's history" (Brown, 402). And it was a feast associated with light.

At this stage in John's gospel, however, light and consecration belong not to the temple and its altar, but to Jesus. He is the light of the world and has left the temple (8:12,59). And it is he, rather than the temple and its altar, who will be spoken of as consecrated (10:36).

And so, having mentioned Dedication, the text adds, "It was winter." The phrase, however matter-of-fact it may seem, is unnecessary—like saying (in the Northern Hemisphere), "It was during Christmas, and it was winter." But the phrasing has its purpose: in many human contexts "winter" is a loaded term, a word which, as is shown for instance by its use in book titles and poetry, is evocative of much of the bleakness and darkness which assail the human heart (cf. *The View in Winter* [old age], *The Winter of Our Discontent, A Lion in Winter*). Hence, just as "It was night" (13:30) is generally regarded as being both matter-of-fact and symbolic, so, as Schnackenburg (2:305) suggests, "it was winter" seems also to be symbolic, evocative of darkness. A similar evoking of darkness was found in the figure of the death-bearing thief (10:10; Brown, 395).

Against this ominous background, the evangelist tells that Jesus walked in the portico of Solomon. This detail also may be read at two levels: historically the portico provided shelter from winter's cold; dramatically, the image of being in Solomon's portico suggests that, even in winter, in the valley of darkness, the vulnerable Jesus, who had just spoken of the good shepherd, is not without protection. And in fact, he needs protection, for immediately it is said that the Jews surrounded him. (A somewhat similar sequence of ideas and images occurs in 18:1–3: the ominous "winterflowing" Kedron; the reassuring "garden," and the approach of the hostile forces.)

The scene in the portico is vivid, as vivid as the earlier portico scene in chap. 5 (5:1–6), but it is much more hostile—an intensification not only of the sometimes latent hostility of chap. 5 but also of the further hostility of chap. 7 (esp. 7:1–5).

When the Jews begin to question Jesus the atmosphere of hostility is in no way lessened. As many commentators have noted, the tense questions and answers, about whether Jesus is the Anointed and the Son of God (10:24–25, 33, 36), are significantly similar to those found in the synoptics' account of Jesus' trial on the night before his death (cf. esp. Mark 14:61–64, Luke 22:67–71). In this winter scene, therefore, the atmosphere is evocative of that fateful night. The difference is that in John's gospel Jesus does not have to wait until death is at hand to have a sense of being surrounded by encroaching darkness. It is felt even in midgospel, in midlife.

Against this background the reply of Jesus constitutes an expanding spiral of light. Even in the Jews' question, when they demand that he say openly whether he is the Christ, there is an indication that their hostile power is not what it seems. Though they surround Jesus, they express themselves in a way which suggests ironically that it is Jesus who is in command: "How long do you hold our lives in suspense?" (literally, "How long do you take away our lives?" 10:24). It is he who holds life. Furthermore, as Hoskyns (386) indicates, the idea of taking away someone's life had already been used at the end of the sheep-and-shepherd text to refer precisely to the fact that even in death, when Jesus seems most helpless, no one takes away his life; it is he, under the Father, who is in command (10:18). (Bultmann, 361, is highly skeptical about this continuity between 10:18 and 10:24, but given Bultmann's lack of appreciation for the continuity of the text as a whole, this skepticism is not convincing.) Thus both at the end of the shepherd text and also as the image of the sheep is about to be reintroduced by Jesus (cf. 10:26), there are indications that, contrary to appearances, the forces of darkness do not have the power to destroy life.

But it is at the level of appearances that "the Jews" operate. Like the unbelieving brothers who wanted Jesus to reveal himself openly to the world (7:4), they want Jesus to state openly if he is the Anointed (24). What they do not understand is that, while there may have been some expectation of a Messiah who would be spectacular and openly powerful, the Messiahship revealed by Jesus is shown not to the outer eyes but to the inner. Messiahship, the fact that Jesus and his disciples are anointed—that people are discovered to be special, special and worthy even as those who traditionally were anointed—such Messiahship is not seen by those who concentrate on externals. The first to appreciate Jesus' Messiahship were the two disciples who followed him in anonymity and abode with him (1:37–41). The next to do so was the nameless Samaritan woman who, despite her initial skepticism, stayed in conversation with Jesus, and in doing so grappled increasingly not only with the identity of Jesus, but also with her own troubled identity (4:7–30). A further character who wrestled with the issue was the formerly blind man, equally nameless. As a disciple who, to a significant degree, had to operate in Jesus' absence, he sought honestly, amid the conflicts of life, to realize not just who Jesus was but who he himself was and what had happened to him. He had been anointed in his very coming to light (9:6), but it is only in the final scenes that his dignity comes fully into evidence. (The reference to acknowledging the Anointed in 9:22 is just about ambiguous enough to allow a momentary suspicion that what is in question is the Messiahship not of Jesus, but of the man.) And the blind man does justice to his true anointed self, not by being spectacular, but by his integrity, by being rejected and by his full acceptance of (the Son of) humanity.

As Lindars (369) indicates, Jesus' reply to the Jews—"I told you and you do not believe" (10:25)—finds its nearest parallel in the earlier reply of the blind man: "I told you already and you did not hear" (9:27). Such continuity suggests that their difficulty in understanding Jesus' Messiahship is of a piece with their difficulty in accepting what had happened to the man—and that means difficulty in accepting the God-given process, wonderful yet ordinary, of human life.

As Jesus continues to speak (vv 25–30), he confirms what was suggested by those earlier Christ-related texts (1:37–41, 4:7–30, chap. 9): the perception of anointedness is achieved not by external spectacle but by believing in Jesus' word and by accepting the witness of the works which he does in the name of his Father (v 25). In other words, if they are willing to receive it, there is enough assurance and evidence.

But they will not, and, in accounting for their unbelief, all Jesus will say at this point is that they are not of his sheep (v 26). This does not deny their guilt, but it suggests that their refusal be seen in the context of a kind of predestination —and, therefore, ultimately within the positive plan of God.

Having said that, Jesus goes on (vv 27–30), in this most unlikely of settings, to give a further summary of God's positive work and especially of his own role within it. He is, in fact, involved in the entire process of salvation. Those who hear are his sheep, and he knows them, and they follow him, and he gives them eternal life, and no one shall seize them from his hand (vv 27–28). Then, after making that final statement about himself ("no one shall seize . . .") he says it of the Father also (v 29b). And finally, with an arresting flourish, he concludes (30): "I and the Father are one." For someone whose Messiahship may have seemed unimpressive, he is very self-assured.

Between the two almost identical statements about no one seizing from his hand or that of his Father, there is the phrase which has been translated here as, "My Father, what he has given me, is greater than all" (v 29a). The Greek text is unsure and, to a significant degree, is ambiguous (for discussion, see Schnackenburg, 2:307–8). In the context, however, this ambiguity seems appropriate: it suggests that while the Father is indeed greater than all, what has been given to Jesus is also greater than all. Thus the way is prepared for saying that from neither of them (the Father; Jesus) can anything be seized; that the two, in fact, are one.

In later centuries such statements about unity with the Father would be used as a basis for articulating the doctrine of the Trinity and for asserting unity of essence or nature. However, most modern commentators hold that the more basic purpose of the text is to speak of functional unity, unity of power and operation (Kysar, 167; Brown, 407).

The reality of Messiahship, therefore, is found, not in externals, but in something that is profoundly hidden—union with a parentlike God. On the outside the world may be bleak—wintery and hostile—but at the center there is union.

[10:31–39] Amid intensified hostility Jesus reaffirms the Father's works and word, and his own consequent identity as God's child; his mission to "the world". As the Jews take up stones (v 31), the hostility which had been suggested by the surrounding of Jesus (v 24) becomes more explicit and hostile, and the drama moves into a further stage or scene.

Brief though it is, this scene is climactic. Apart from the subsequent reaction (vv 40–42), it is the final scene of what might be regarded as Jesus' public min-

istry. And because it is climactic, it is also quite dense; it gathers up certain basic
strands and knots them together to form a new striking synthesis. Finally, after it
has delved the essence of evidence (works), tradition (Word), and logic, it builds
resoundingly to a statement which is of limpid simplicity: *Hyios theou eimi,* "I
am God's Son," or alternatively, "I am a child of God."

The scene is framed by the Jewish threat of stoning (v 31) and by Jesus'
escape from their hands (v 39). The basic structure is twofold—a fact that is first
suggested by the unusual repetition of the term "the Jews" (vv 31, 33), and by
the exact repetition of the phrase "Jesus answered them" (vv 32, 34).

The first part (vv 31–33) deals with Jesus' works. At this stage Jesus does not
refer just to one or two works. Rather, as is fitting in a final confrontation, he
reviews the broad sweep of what God has shown through him, and he refers to
the works as "many" and "good" (*kalos*), and as being "from the Father." The
word *kalos* (beautiful, good) which is here repeated (v 33), was also used in
repeated form of the shepherd (vv 11, 14), and—since the evangelist generally
uses no such adjective about Jesus' works—its use here links these works with
all that is suggested by the figure of the shepherd, i.e., life-giving love and an all-
encompassing providence. It is also used of the abundant fine wine at Cana, the
beginning of Jesus' works (2:10–11).

As well as being good or beautiful, the works are also many. At one level
Jesus is referring to the particular works of his brief ministry. At another, however, there is an evoking of all that has been created through the Word. The
description of the "work" done at Cana as a "beginning" (*archē,* 2:11) links it
with the Word through whom *all* things were made (1:1–3). And the healing of
the blind man is such that, in another way, it too evokes the process of creation
(cf. esp. 9:6). Thus from first to last the works to which Jesus refers suggest all
that has been made, all that is good and beautiful.

And these works are "from the Father." In other words, they have in them
something of a God who is a Father, a caring parent.

If God is a parent, then there is an implication that the one who receives these
works is a child, a child of God. Thus parent and child, God and human, are
profoundly bonded. Or as Jesus had just said, at the conclusion of the previous
scene (v 30), he and the Father are one.

But "the Jews" cannot grasp the connection. They say they have no objection
to the good works, and to some degree that is probably true. But they cannot see
what the works imply about Jesus—that even though he is human he is bonded
with the divine. And so, in a new development, they accuse him of blasphemy.
Previously (8:59) the charge of blasphemy had simply been implied. Now, however, it is climactically explicit. From what is known of their own laws they seem
unduly eager with this accusation: the Mishnah (Sanh 7:5) limits blasphemy to the
saying of God's sacred name (YHWH)—something Jesus had not done. The essential thing, however, is not the questionable legality of their action but their
blindness: where they might have seen a parentlike God, all they see is an offense
against their self-made God.

The irony, of course, is that instead of realizing that they are making God into their own narrow image, they accuse Jesus of a related distortion: "you, being a human (*anthrōpos*), make yourself God." Having narrowed God, they demand a corresponding narrowing of humanity.

This is the last thing they say in chap. 10, the last thing, in fact, which they say in Jesus' public ministry, and it is a final expression both of their failure to understand and also, ironically, of the truth. Even with the evidence of all the works in the world, they cannot understand that humans, limited though they are by flesh and blood, have another higher dimension, one that is ultimately divine. And in their own way—this is the irony—they also pronounce one of the basic truths of the gospel: that Jesus is God.

The second part (vv 34–36) deals with the role of the word(s), with the fact that the divine dimension of humanity is attested to by the word of God—both by the form of the word which is found in the old order (the OT), and by that found in the new. The OT quotation, "I said, 'You are gods,' " is taken from the Psalms (82:3) and is restricted in its original meaning, but, in a manner which seems akin to his spirit-filled exegesis at Tents (7:38–39), Jesus interprets it freely as being representative of the whole old law (". . . written *in your law*"). (For extensive discussion, see Brown, 409–11.)

As well as alluding to the law, the text manages to evoke something even broader. Through a fourfold use of the word *theos* (god/God, vv 34–36), as well as a reference to the action of the word of God (v 35, *logos . . . theou egeneto*), there is a linguistic reminder of the *logos* through whom all things were made (1:1–3). The idea that Jesus is referring to a wide panorama seems to find support in the reference to being sent "into the world"; thus, rather as 10:1–21 eventually opened out to refer to the Gentiles (10:16), so 10:22–42, which initially refers to "my sheep" (10:27), seems to open out increasingly, especially in the later part of vv 31–36, to a broader world.

Then, with an implication that the word of God (*logos tou theou*) which was found in the old order is present in even greater form in the new, he indicates that he has a better claim to a divine dimension: he is the one whom the Father has consecrated and sent into the world.

To consecrate (*hagiazō*) means, above all else, to make *hagios*, "holy"—and that means to make something or someone *other*, different, very special. In the OT, consecration was used, for instance, of Moses (Sir 14:4), Jeremiah (Jer 1:5), the priests (2 Chr 26:18), and especially the Tabernacle, the "dwelling place" of God (Num 7:1). Hence while anointing indicated that someone was special, consecration heightened the process. And as one who was "sent," Jesus' status is further assured; in Jewish thought the one who was sent—the *saliah* or deputy— was one who, from the point of view of law, enjoyed the Sender's authority and identity (Brown, 411; Bühner, 1977, 191–235). And this consecration and sending are from "the Father."

It all adds up to a statement which, far from being blasphemous, expresses a central truth: "I am God's Son/child." As well as being true of Jesus, it recalls also the blind man—the one who was anointed and sent (9:6–7)—and thus it is true of all who are created and who, sent into the world, seek the light.

Having made his most basic declaration, Jesus adds a kind of epilogue (vv

37–38), a statement that his ministry, and, in fact, all that the Word has done, faces people with a choice. It is phrased in two balancing sentences, a further variation (following 3:20–21, 36) on the idea of the two ways: "If I do not do the works . . . [then] do not believe. . . . But if I do . . . [then] believe. . . ." Thus it is, in effect, an appeal to believe. The first alternative is unreal; it envisages a situation in which Jesus does not do any of the works of the Father, and— since the creation of everything depends on Jesus, the Word (1:3)—that means a situation in which there is nothing. So, in effect, he is saying: If there is nothing, do not believe.

But if there is, then, even if they do not believe him, let them "believe the works." At first sight this may seem startling. The ideal which the gospel often proposes is to believe on the basis of the Word (cf. esp. 2:22, 6:68–69, 20:29). But it acknowledges also that works or signs help the process, that they dispose a person to trust. And since "works" and "signs" refer to everything that has been made, Jesus, in effect, is concluding with an appeal not only to accept his ministry, but to look around, to see the reality of creation with all it suggests of a parentlike providence, and on that basis to begin to trust. The ideal of further belief is not abandoned, however. Once the initial trust has developed, the rest can follow: "believe the works, that you may know and understand that the Father is in me and I in the Father." This is not only an image of personal union, a union which surpasses the earlier image of functional union (at the end of the preceding scene, v 30: "I and the Father are one"); it is also an invitation to others to enter increasingly ("know and understand") into that world of union, into mutual indwelling.

This invitation is all the more striking because of the circumstances in which it is made. His earthly body seems in danger of being crushed brutally—stoning, particularly by an encircling crowd, is horrible—yet, even amid the threat of such horror, he can know the reality of dwelling in intimacy and can invite others to share it. And it is with that invitation that the words of the ministry conclude.

The overall effect of these verses (34–38), particularly because of the extraordinary complexity of vv 35–36, is of a solemnly ascending spiral. There are affinities with the prologue but also with other ascentlike texts, especially with 3:20–21, and, above all, with chapter 17. Thus in chap. 10, as a whole, there is not only a descent (vv 7–18) but also some of the elements of an ascent. Whether 10:22–33 should be included in this pendulum effect seems difficult to say and is best left to further research.

At the end of the scene (v 39) they seek to seize him, but even though he had been surrounded, "he went out of their hands." This ability to get away, literally "out of their hand," provides a contrast and a complement to the conclusion of the preceding scene where it was said that no one could seize the sheep "out of the hand" of Jesus or of the Father (vv 29–30). Thus, the protecting hand is sure, but the attacking hand, whatever its evil, cannot hold.

[10:40–42] Jesus goes back across the Jordan, and many believe in him there; a sketch of mature believers. Jesus' return to the point where John first baptized serves in many ways to bring his public ministry to an end (Brown, 414).

Within the structure of the narrative he had come from God and from beyond the Jordan (1:1,28–29). Now, under the shadow of death, he returns there. It is not, of course, said that he is returning to God—such an idea does not become explicit until 13:3—but the only word used of his activity beyond the Jordan is "abide" (*menō*), and that word, particularly as first used by John (1:33), has overtones of abiding *in union*, especially union with the divine. Thus, while at one level of the text Jesus is very much on *terra firma*, at another there is a suggestion or intimation of his returning to God. As Schnackenburg (2:314) says of this passage in general: "The geographical data . . . have a theological significance."

The suggestion of union with God maintains continuity with the preceding scene—with the idea of being one with the Father (vv 30, 38). But there is yet more continuity, and of a clearer kind: as Jesus abides beyond the Jordan, he encounters exactly what, in the confrontation at Dedication, he had asked for and failed to encounter—people who believe on the basis of word and sign (work). The "many" who come to him do so first of all because of the word—because "all John said" of Jesus was found in him to be true—but also, so it is implied, because of the signs ("John did no sign, but . . ."). Since John represents the old order, the OT, there is in this brief scene, as in the previous one in which Jesus quotes the OT (34–35), a sense that the word which issues from the old order is fulfilled in the new, and that it should be an adequate basis for believing. Though a role is also assigned to works or signs, it appears in both scenes to be subsidiary. Yet, between these successive scenes, there is a crucial difference: the Jews in the temple do not believe, but the faithful followers of John do.

With this brief account, the chapter completes its portrayal of the process of coming to believe. The introductory parabolic section, by emphasizing recognition of the voice (vv 3–5, 8), had suggested the basic idea of responding to the word. The initial reaction (v 21) and the Dedication scene (vv 25–27, 31–38) had indicated aspects of the interplay of word and work. Now, at the end, the role of works is accepted, but the final emphasis is on the word.

Who are these believers? There is nothing in the text to suggest that they have anything to do with sectarians of any kind. On the contrary, placed as they are at the conclusion of Jesus' ministry, they represent the mainstream of the positive response which that ministry evoked. Given that John the baptizer is the high point and representative of the old order, they are the ones who were able to see that the old order is fulfilled in Jesus. In other words, in contrast to those Jews who rejected Jesus, they are the true Jews, the true Israel, those who saw that in Jesus the words of the OT voices were fulfilled and surpassed. Within the context of chap. 10, they are the sheep who, when the shepherd came, recognized his voice, and, as he left the darkened temple, followed him out of the restrictive Jewish fold.

Their arrival at Jesus' dwelling place, far from being intrusive, fits perfectly into the narrative. The initial reaction in chap. 10 had indicated "a division among the Jews" (10:19). And chap. 11 will presuppose a division between "many" sympathetic Jews (11:19,31,45) and others who are death-bent (11:8,46–53). It is appropriate, therefore, while the Dedication scene itself showed those Jews who were hostile (10:22–39), that the complementary episode, beyond the Jordan, should tell of those who were receptive. They are sectarian only in so far as Christianity as a whole in its origin was sectarian—a breakaway from Judaism. Their positive reaction—of believing because of the signs, but especially because of the word —is of a piece with the earlier climactic responses of the initial disciples (2:22, cf. 2:11) and of Peter (6:68–69). They constitute, therefore, a thumbnail sketch of the early believers.

The temple, abandoned by the light in chap. 8, may indeed now be shrouded in winter darkness, but there is in Jesus—as earlier episodes suggested (2:18–22, cf. 4:20–24)—a new consecrated presence, a new temple. The old order breaks apart, but in him, sundered and restored, there will be a new abiding place.

At the end of this sketch there is a curious detail. With what looks like unnecessary repetition the text uses the term "many" not once, but twice: "And many came. . . . And many believed. . . ." It has been seen again and again, however, that what at first seems puzzling or unnecessary in the gospel text is, in fact, quite purposeful; and the same may, perhaps, be true here. The following is one possible explanation: even though the entire text (vv 40–42) is speaking primarily of responsive Jews, at another level the repetition of "many" leaves a teasing hint not of one "many" but of two, the Jews and the Gentiles. That the text contains such an idea makes sense. It accounts for what seems unnecessary in the text itself; it recalls one of the important elements of the whole chapter (Jew and Gentile in one flock); and, placed at the end of the chapter, it prepares the way, by faint intimation, for the more explicit Jew–Gentile statement at the end of the upcoming story of Lazarus (11:52).

Conclusion to Chapters 9 and 10

However diverse at first sight, chaps. 9 and 10 are closely related. This is suggested first of all by some externals. They are of similar length and have essentially the same structure—six parts, but with a certain diptych effect (parts 1, 2, and 3 are echoed respectively in 4, 5, and 6), and with subdivisions which are threefold and twofold.

More important, however, is the fundamental complementarity of underlying theme: chap. 9 deals with creation—the creation and development of human life; chap. 10 deals with providence. A similar complementarity was noted between chaps. 5 and 6.

The essential difference between 5 and 6, on the one hand, and 9 and 10, on the other, is that while 5 and 6 are rather general, 9 and 10 are more specific, and, in particular, they deal more with the felt reality of human life. Thus in contrast to chap. 5, chap. 9 portrays the diverse stages of the development of a life. And while chap. 6, especially in the final section of the bread of life discourse, speaks of the general need to face death, chap. 10, especially in the scene at Dedication, shows Jesus as actually doing it—as speaking boldly even when surrounded by those who seek to kill him.

In both 9 and 10 there is a progression of diverse reactions. While the blind man gains sight, the Pharisees become blind. And while some of the Jews of chap. 10 become more hostile, others grow in belief. Chap. 9 ends by emphasizing the negative reaction (''your sin abides''), chap. 10, the positive (''and many believed in him there'').

Among the many other elements of complementarity, a few are particularly important. Chapter 9 emphasizes the individual; chap. 10, the larger body (the flock). The role of anointing, scarcely perceptible in chap. 9 (9:6, 22)—a low-key beginning which is appropriate to the secrecy or elusiveness of human mes-siahship—becomes much more pronounced in the conspicuous references to Jesus as Messiah and as consecrated (10:24, 36). The build-up in chapter 9 to the full appreciation of the human dimension (''Son of humanity,'' 9:35) is balanced by the build-up in chap. 10 to appreciating the divine dimension (''God's son,'' 10:36). And the Jews' expulsion of the disciple (9:34) prepares the way both for the leading out of those sheep who hear the shepherd's voice and for the formation of a new flock comprising both Jews and Gentiles.

The Raising of Lazarus and Its Consequences

| The Story of Lazarus | 11:1–53 |

The Lord Descends into Death and Invites
People to See beyond Death to Life

The crisis of Lazarus's sickness is all the more dramatic because Jesus' response to it seems so measured. First he waits for two days, and afterwards he talks to the disciples. Later there are the two meetings—first with Martha, and next with Mary and the Jews. Only then does he call forth Lazarus. Yet the event is far from being anticlimactic. In fact, it is so striking that it leads the Sanhedrin to the most pivotal decision in the gospel—that Jesus must die.

It is probably in this story, rather than in any other single NT episode, that one receives a sense of the day-to-day human reality of coping with sickness and death. Here there is no immediate intervention, no painless solution. The deceased is buried. Feelings vary. The days begin to pass.

But the story does not confine itself to that human experience. On the contrary, as Schneiders (1987) particularly has shown, it weaves human experience with theology, and thus it provides a framework in which the experience of death can be integrated with faith.

As already indicated—in discussing the gospel's design (Chapters 4 and 5) and in introducing chap. 10—there is a sense in which chap. 10 concludes Jesus' public ministry, and, for that reason, chaps. 11 and 12 stand somewhat apart. Furthermore, though the story of Lazarus is dramatic and decisive, it is not even mentioned in the other gospels.

But this does not mean that in the composition of the fourth gospel the raising of Lazarus is in any way an afterthought. On the contrary, it is central to the development of the gospel as a whole. It is in this story that the various signs reach a high point. Previously Jesus had healed, first the official's son, someone who had been sick for a limited period, then a man who had been sick for thirty-eight years, and finally a man who had been blind even from birth. But now, at last, and very appropriately, he deals with the ultimate crisis—someone who is dead. It is in this story too that the recurring motif of the death-threat finally coalesces into a form that is decisive. In the context of the gospel as a whole, particularly in the context of his own death and resurrection, the story constitutes a "penultimate climax" (Kysar, 54). It brings together several elements of the preceding chapters and at the same time it helps to set the scene for the gospel's final drama. In particular, it dramatizes powerfully the idea of life, an idea which, from the beginning, is integral to the gospel. In other words, nothing could be more appropriate to the gospel's thought. As Schnackenburg (2:316) puts it: "Together with the healing of the man born blind, the raising of Lazarus expresses the central Christological idea of the fourth gospel, that Jesus is the light and life of the world (cf. 1:4)."

Structure

It has sometimes been said that the structure of the Lazarus story is "clear" (cf. esp. Schneider, 210; Schnackenburg, 2:317). A glance through a variety of studies, however, shows considerable disagreement—including disagreement among those who say it is clear. Nor is there agreement about where the story ends; in particular, there is uncertainty about as to whether it includes the Sanhedrin's decision to kill Jesus (vv 45–53).

In discussing how the text has been composed, perhaps the best starting point is the fact that the crisis which the story presents is twofold: it tells not only that Lazarus is sick but also that Jesus is in danger of being killed (vv 1, 8). If the crisis is twofold then the resolution is also likely to be twofold, and therefore one may reasonably expect the narrative to deal not only with the fate of Lazarus but also with the threat to Jesus. This suggests inclusion of the decision that Jesus be killed (vv 45–53).

Working on the hypothesis that the story consists of 11:1–53, one seeks then to discern its basic divisions or scenes. As so often in John, particularly in the case of chap. 9, an important criterion is provided by the idea of movement. This does not mean that every reference to movement introduces a new scene, but there is no new scene without reference to movement. Thus in v 7, for instance, Jesus says "Let us go. . . ." In fact, he appears for the moment to stay where he is, but the "Let us go" is enough to indicate a new scene. Further new scenes begin with the coming of Jesus (v 17), Martha's going to call Mary (v 28), the coming of Jesus to the tomb (v 38), and the account of how some who had come went away and told the Pharisees (v 45). The result is six scenes:

1–6   Lazarus and his sisters—a scene of sickness and love
7–16   The disciples; Lazarus dies; Jesus in danger
17–27   Martha comes to meet Jesus
28–37   Mary and the Jews come to Jesus; Jesus cries
38–44   The calling forth of Lazarus
45–53   The decision to kill Jesus

To some degree the meaning of these six scenes may be found in the fact that they constitute a reasonably coherent story, one which is placed in the life of Jesus. Yet as a straightforward story the coherence is not complete. In Scene 2, for instance, "the disciples . . . appear . . . and [then] play no further part at all" (Schnackenburg, 2:319). Various parts are repetitive or may seem unnecessary. One could make a plausible Lazarus story with little more than Scenes 1, 3, and 5—or even with just six or seven verses (see Becker, 345).

To find the key to the coherence of the present text—to what it is that holds these scenes together—it is necessary to go beyond the level of straightforward story and to enter the level of theological portrayal.

The Involvement of God: 11:1–53 as a Three-part Spiralling Descent

One of the notable features of the Lazarus story is that when Jesus is most wanted he is absent. Furthermore he does not hurry to return. Thus, at one level, the story conveys something of the impression that when death strikes, the Lord is both absent and indifferent.

But at another level the text suggests otherwise. First of all, it is remarkable that instead of being in Bethany with Lazarus, the absent Lord is in the place where John had first baptized, in other words across the Jordan, *in Bethany*—the Bethany that is unknown to geographers (10:40; 1:28). Thus in the familiar Bethany Jesus is absent, but in the more elusive Bethany he is present, across the Jordan. Somehow as far as ''Bethany'' is concerned he is both absent and present.

Furthermore, far from being indifferent, Jesus is immensely involved. When the text is divided into three fairly even parts—Jesus hears and sets out (vv 1–16), he comes and speaks in the presence of Martha and Mary (vv 17–37), he raises Lazarus and is condemned to death (vv 38–53)—the result is a spiralling picture of divine descent.

Within vv 1–16 Jesus seems at first (vv 1–6) to be like the distant God. He dwells apart, he views death as something which gives glory to God, and his words do not involve him in a real conversation. Yet his love is increasingly revealed (vv 3,5), and in the second scene (vv 7–16) he begins to set out, and he enters into a conversation which is not only real but which becomes more and more open, less parabolic. Furthermore death now begins to be seen in terms which are increasingly painful—as connected with the threat of stoning and as being not just a sleep but as involving real death. Thus the text as a whole suggests a transition from a God-like Jesus who is distant to one who sets out to become involved, involved even in death.

Within vv 17–37 Jesus does not begin at the same distant point, yet here too there is a marked transition. At first (vv 17–27), when Martha meets him, death is looked at from a very elevated point of view: Lazarus will rise; Jesus is the resurrection and the life (''I am . . .''). But when Mary comes, there is a sense of something which goes from being secret to being open—Mary at first receives the message about Jesus in secret (v 28)—and there is a further sense of Jesus as being involved with humble human reality and especially with death: by the end of the scene he is crying, and some people see him simply as ''this [fellow].''

Finally in vv 38–53 there is a further transition. Beginning from yet a lower point than in the preceding texts—here there is no distant God and no ''I am . . .'' (vv 4, 25)—Jesus, nonetheless, through prayer, once again asserts his authority over death and raises Lazarus (vv 38–44). But again, and now more than ever, there is a transition in which he enters the painful reality of death: he is referred to simply as ''this person'' and, instead of crying for a friend, he is himself condemned to die (vv 45–53). Here too there is a suggestion of something secret or mysterious being revealed: the murderous plan of Caiaphas contains an unsuspected prophetical dimension concerning the role of Jesus' death.

Thus in each of the three major sections of chap. 11 there is first a sense of Jesus' power over death, then, in ways that are increasingly easier to understand, there is a sense that a hidden dimension is being revealed, and finally an increasing sense of Jesus' involvement in the full painful reality of death. At the end (vv 16, 37, 53) the texts dovetail: "that we may die with him"; "that . . . [he] might not die"; "that they might kill him."

The text as a whole is like an elaborate development of the good shepherd text (10:7–18): more and more, the language of divinity and parable is left behind and in its place there is an increasing sense of openness and of Jesus' involvement in death.

Human Response, Representative Roles

As well as portraying the role of God, God's self-revealing in Jesus, chap. 11 is also concerned with human response, and that response is portrayed largely through the figures of Martha and Mary.

Mary is mentioned first and, through the reference to the anointing, her prominence is underlined (vv 1–2), but already by the end of the opening scene Martha's name has taken priority, and Mary's name has faded (v 5).

In subsequent scenes Martha and Mary show diverse reactions. With identical words both express some bitterness ("Lord if you had been here. . . . Lord if you had been here, . . ." vv 21, 32), but while Martha rises above her sense of loss, Mary does not.

In the final two scenes they are both mentioned, but in very different ways. Martha's faith helped to bring Lazarus to life (v 40), but some of those who had been with Mary triggered the meeting which decided to kill Jesus (vv 46–47).

The role of Mary is such—her moving from first place and her association with a form of disbelief and with the Jews—that, though she is loved, she in some way represents the unbelieving Jews. Martha, on the other hand, who is more associated with "the crowd" (vv 39, 42), is like a representative (vv 39–42) of those who believe. The fact that these roles are representative helps in turn to explain the appearance of "the disciples" (Scene 2, vv 7–16): the disciples are not intrusive; rather, like the disciples in 4:1–42, their role is interwoven with that of the representative woman—in this case with the believing Martha.

However, the primary level of the text deals not with representative roles but with individuals: Martha and Mary show the two basic possibilities open to everyone who is faced with bitter loss—to rise above the bitterness or to sink into unrestrained mourning.

The Puzzle of the Role of Lazarus

Lazarus is associated not only with his two sisters, but also with John the baptizer and with the beloved disciple. With John he shares the distinctive fact that within a relatively short text (two scenes, 10:40–42 and 11:1–6) both their names are mentioned three times. And like the beloved disciple he is referred to as being loved by Jesus (11:3, 5; 13:23). Furthermore, as indicated by Johannes Beutler (in conversation, May 6, 1988), these three characters seem, as it were, to take over from one another: it is after the last reference to John (10:40–42) that Lazarus appears (11:1), and it is shortly after the last reference to Lazarus (12:17) that the beloved disciple is introduced (13:23). Thus between them there is continuity.

But the problem is more complex. The fate of Lazarus is interwoven with that of his sisters, and the role of the beloved is also interwoven with others—particularly with the women who stood by the cross (19:25–27) and with Peter. Thus while it appears to be true that Lazarus is in some way representative of all those whom Jesus loves, and thus of all Christians (Brown, 431), it is also true that that role needs to be placed in the context of the roles of the other characters.

[11:1–6] The sickness of Lazarus: Human fragility portrayed in the context of Jesus' death and love.

The basic story line seems simple. When a man called Lazarus is sick, his two sisters send word to his friend Jesus. When Jesus hears of the sickness he says it is for the glory of God, and he stays where he is for two days.

Yet on closer inspection the account is quite puzzling. How can Jesus love someone and yet delay in responding? And there are other problems. The introduction (vv 1–2) seems "awkward and ill-formulated" (Hoskyns, 399). In fact, many commentators regard the reference to Mary's anointing of Jesus' feet (v 2) as an editorial insertion. Furthermore, the second reference to Jesus' loving someone (v 5), insofar as it is repetitious, is also often regarded as a gloss. Thus the narrative may seem both difficult and bungled.

The narrative indeed is difficult, yet that is appropriate, for so is the topic—the relationship of God's love to human suffering and weakness. (*Astheneō*, the verb used of Lazarus' sickness, v 1, evokes much of human fragility; it is also used in 4:46, 5:3, and 6:2.)

The problem of knowing how to view sickness, where to locate it in one's understanding of things, is first suggested by a geographical puzzle—where to locate Lazarus. He is said to be from Bethany (11:1), but as noted earlier, "Bethany" in v 1 is ambiguous—it could refer to Bethany beyond the Jordan (cf. 1:28, 10:40)—and clarification is not given until v 17.

The basic effect of the introduction (vv 1–2), particularly the reference to Mary's anointing of Jesus (v 2), is not only to present the fatal sickness of Lazarus, but also to set it in its appropriate context—that of the death of Jesus. For the anointing is related to Jesus' death (12:7), and the placing of this reference at the beginning of the story provides an initial intimation that the story as a whole, with its triple descent, is focused towards Jesus' death, particularly towards the concluding plan to kill him (v 53). The reader who was wondering where to locate the sick Lazarus is led away from the confusion about Bethany and into a new landscape, a world of enigmatic beauty—"anointed the Lord"; "with perfume." The idea of a deliberate change of landscape is confirmed by the fact that the second verse begins exactly as did the first (*en de* . . . "Now there was . . ."/ "Now Mary was . . ."). There is beauty not only in the image of a woman anointing the Lord, and with perfume, but also in the suggestion of an extraordinary blending of the divine with the human. It is enigmatic, of course, particularly because of the association with death (12:3–7). But for the moment death is not mentioned explicitly, and the implication rather is of something very alive. The sense of vitality is underlined by what follows: "and wiped his feet with her hair." And with these final words—"her hair"—the focus comes back again to Mary and to the fact that her "brother was sick."

The introduction, therefore, which at first looks so confused, turns out to be a challenge to the reader to rise above the level of the superficial and to set the sickness in the appropriate higher context, that of the vitality surrounding Jesus' death. In 9:6 the rebirth of the blind man was accompanied with anointing. Now, in 11:2, the fatal illness of Lazarus is set in a similarly elevated context.

The events which follow reinforce the build-up of a positive context. When the sisters send to Jesus he is addressed as Lord, and next to the verb "to be sick" there is placed the verb "to love," *phileō* (v 3). Thus the sickness, literally the weakening, is surrounded by power ("Lord") and love. And when Jesus speaks of this sickness, he sees it as leading not to death but to glory—to the glory of God and thus to the glory of God's Son (v 4). In other words, the sickness does not make a mockery of life and of God. On the contrary, the end result will be the glorifying of God's human representative—and thereby a glorifying of all that is truly human, a manifestation of the wonder which God works in humans.

And with that, in a manner which is faintly evocative of the classic, "For God so loved (*agapaō*) the world . . . ." (3:16), the text opens out to speak of a love which extends beyond Lazarus: "Now Jesus loved (*agapaō*) Martha and her sister and Lazarus" (v 5). In the introduction (vv 1–2), Martha had been mentioned last and had been outside of the action. Then, in the appeal to the *Kyrios,* she gained an equality (vv 3–4, "The sisters . . . sent . . ."). And now, at the end, she is first: "Jesus loved Martha. . . ." The subtle literary changes suggest a love which reaches out to what has been excluded, to those who are essentially unknown.

The overall effect of the narrative is to provide for something as negative as the ebbing of life a context which is immensely positive—that of a love which, through the death of Jesus, reaches out and leads to glory.

Note. 11:1–6 as Maintaining Continuity and also as Breaking New Ground

As many commentators indicate, some aspects of the narrative are very much of a piece with all that has preceded. The introduction to Lazarus' sickness (vv 1–2) recalls 4:46:

- "So he came again to Cana . . . where he had made the water wine, and *there was a certain . . . whose son was sick . . .*"
- "Now *there was a certain . . . whose brother Lazarus was sick.*"

Cana is further recalled by the calm factual requests:

- The mother (2:3): "They have no wine."
- The sisters (v 3): "Lord, the one whom you love is sick."

At Cana, Jesus' hour had not come; in the Lazarus story, Jesus himself has not come. And the fact that the sickness has a positive purpose, the glory of God and of God's Son (v 4), is a variation on the idea that the blindness (9:3) had a similarly positive purpose—the revelation of God's works in the blind man. Such echoes, both of the first signs (at Cana) and of the sign which was most recent (chap. 9), provide initial indications that the Lazarus story maintains continuity with earlier episodes.

But, in a rather startling way, it also breaks new ground. Having gone through episode after episode without mentioning a new name, the narrative suddenly tells of "Lazarus"—a shortened, Greek form of the Semitic name *El-azar*, "God helps." Also new are the names "Mary" and "Martha." And the name "Bethany" (*Beth-anya*, "House of Affliction") will eventually be seen clearly to refer to a new location. The next scene will produce yet another new name—Thomas (v 16), and later there are references to the Romans and Caiaphas (vv 48–49). The overall effect is to suggest that, while at one level the story of Jesus may be progressing methodically, at another a whole new drama has developed.

This effect is heightened by the fact that the end of chap. 10 had suggested that Jesus' ministry was over, and there had been an intimation of his return to God. Now in chap. 11 that idea is maintained and developed. Lindars (386) notes that 11:2 "seems to imply that the anointing has already taken place." Thus, though set in the time of Jesus, this drama of new names seems to be outside of Jesus' ministry and seems even to be looking back at it. It would appear, therefore, that just as chap. 9, with its different levels, manages to speak both of Jesus' lifetime and also of the subsequent experience of the disciples, so chap. 11 seems to contain a level which has to do with a later phase.

In this context Jesus' delay in returning may be seen as incorporating something of the early church's discussion about the time of the Lord's coming—both about its delay and about the need to be ready to go to meet him. In fact, the Lazarus story makes several references to time—two days (v 6), twelve hours (v 9), four days (v 39), that year (vv 49, 51), that day (v 53)—and together they reinforce the idea of God's plan having its due time and of the need for being ready to meet him.

[11:7–16] The disciples and death: The parable of the journey and the light. As the story is told in John, the two days during which Jesus abode where he was seem to last a long time. The author brings them to an end with a repetitive phrase, *epeita meta touto*, literally, "then, after this" (11:7a). Barrett (391) regards the repetitiveness as "a pleonasm, but perpetrated with full consciousness, and for emphasis," and he translates: "Then, after the delay just mentioned." Brown (421) translates, "Then, at last. . . ."

What follows is a conversation with the disciples. In its first part (vv 7–10), it deals largely with *Jesus* and the danger of his projected journey to Judea. In the later part (vv 11–16), the journey of Jesus is still important but the focus shifts increasingly to what had previously been less emphasized—the beneficiaries of that journey, namely *Lazarus* and *the disciples*. (Lazarus is closely related to the disciples. Jesus refers to him as "our friend," v 11.) Thus two poles are envisaged in this conversation—on the one hand, Jesus, and on the other, the disciples and Lazarus. Increasingly, however, and particularly in the last verse—when Thomas says "Let us also go, that we may die with him" (v 16)—the two poles come together, and the emphasis on Jesus' death leads to an increasing emphasis on the role of the disciples.

The most basic image in this conversation is that of journeying. Three times there is an occurrence of "Let us go . . ." (vv 7, 15, 16). And Jesus at one point says about Lazarus, "But I go (*poreuomai*) to awake him" (v 11). Furthermore, the brief illustration or parable (vv 9–10) deals with images of walking or travelling. Against the immobility of the previous scene it presents quite a contrast.

One of the most important features of this conversation is not its content but simply its occurrence. After the enigmatic and tight-lipped reaction of the previous scene, a scene in which there was no direct exchange, Jesus is finally talking. Furthermore, his speech becomes clearer and clearer—he goes from the dense parable concerning walking in the light and dark (vv 9–10), to the simpler idea of death as sleep (vv 11–13), and finally to the declaration, made openly, that Lazarus is dead (vv 14–15).

Thus in contrast to the opening scene—one in which the power of healing love remained within a sphere of silence and immobility—this scene of journeying towards the beloved is one of increasing communication.

The two ideas—of speaking and journeying—are closely interwoven. The journey is towards Judea and towards Lazarus. The speaking is with the disciples. But, as already noted, the disciples are interrelated with their friend Lazarus, and Jesus is as interested in putting new life in the disciples as in Lazarus ("Lazarus is dead and I rejoice . . . so that you may believe," vv 14–15). In fact, there is a certain sense in which, while talking of journeying to Judea and Lazarus, the ones he is really journeying towards are the disciples, trying to reach them, trying to impart to them the light which will enable them to face the dark. Lazarus is like the lens through which that reality is communicated.

vv 7–10: Faced with death, a disciple needs (spiritual) light

Looking at the text in more detail, the first part (vv 7–10) focuses on the death of Jesus and on the disciples' response to it. Their reaction, when he pronounces a very deliberate "Let us go, . . ." is to shy away, to dissuade him. For they know that Judea, the place to which he is going, is one which threatens imminent death—stoning.

In one sense their reaction is admirable; unlike the unbelieving brothers (7:3), they seem really concerned about him. But the "Rabbi" with which they address him shows they do not understand him, and mixed with their concern is fear. After all, Jesus did not say "*I* am going," but "Let us go. . . ." The danger is there for all.

In face of this fear Jesus gives a brief example or parable. Using the ancient system of counting time he refers to the daylight as consisting of twelve hours, and then he draws the lesson—the need for the one who travels or walks to do so in the light. The parable is framed in two ways, first by saying that the one who walks in the day does not stumble (because that person sees "the light of this world"), then by saying that the one who walks at night does stumble (because within that person "the light" is not present).

That a traveller needs light is clear, but what does that have to do with Jesus' proposed journey to Judea and with the disciples' fear? Of the various interpretations that have been proposed, the most accurate seems to be that of Schnackenburg (2:325–26). The first part of the parable (about the traveller who uses the daylight) takes light in its ordinary sense, and it refers to Jesus. In fulfilling his mission, his father's work, he is like a traveller who watches the hours and keeps on schedule. As he had said earlier (9:4), night is coming when no one can work. And so he presses on, not stumbling. The later part (about the traveller who in the night stumbles) takes light in a deeper sense, and it refers to the disciples— to those who, when challenged to travel towards death, cannot meet the challenge; they stumble. What they lack is not daylight ("the light of this world"—the phrase used in the initial part of the parable) but "the light" (the term used in the later part of the parable), in other words, the inner light which is given by Jesus who is himself the light. (This parable involves intricate continuity with 7:3–6; 8:12; 9:4–5; 10:7–10.) It is precisely their failure to grasp this light which causes them to address him as "Rabbi." Thus within the parable there is a shift from Jesus to the disciples.

The reliability of this interpretation is corroborated by the fact that, as Kysar (174) indicates, the discussion between Jesus and his disciples, one which in many ways is an interlude, contains variations on an earlier discussion in 4:31–38— also an interlude and also containing a little parable—in which the focus shifts from the unstinting but exhausting work of Jesus to the challenge and opportunity which is being placed before the disciples.

But just as the disciples in chapter 4 were rather slow in grasping the challenge to work, so in the initial part of this interlude they are slow. Death is like night, and they do not have the light to face it.

vv 11–16: Faced with death, intimations of the need for love
The second part (vv 11–16) occurs "after that" and portrays the disciples as being in solidarity not only with Jesus but also with Lazarus, and it is around the death of Lazarus that the discussion moves. Rather as the parable (vv 9–10) contained two meanings of "light," one mundane and the other more profound, so the discussion here contains two meanings of "sleep"—sleep as ordinary sleep, and sleep as death. Again the disciples have problems with the more profound dimension of things, and eventually Jesus has to tell them "openly" that Lazarus is dead.

Overall, however, despite their initial fear, the disciples make some progress. They now see Jesus as *Kyrios,* "Lord". Even in their superficial understanding of "sleep" they utter an ironic truth—that Lazarus will recover, literally "will be saved." And when Jesus leads them beyond their superficial understanding and brings them at last to the reality of death and to the fact that the awaking of Lazarus is to enable them to believe, then they seem ready to face death. When Jesus first had said "Let us go, ..." they withdrew (7–8). Now, when, in a

modified way, he repeats the challenge, they take it up: "Let us also go," said
Thomas, but then he adds "that we may die with him," a phrase which leaves a
question about whether he has really understood the message.

One of the features of this text (vv 11–16), subtle but important, is the idea
of solidarity, of love. Lazarus is not just an object lesson, nor even just a friend
of Jesus, he is "our friend." The journey in the later part of the scene is no
longer simply "to Judea" (as in v 7) but "to him" (v 15). And among Jesus and
the disciples there is a far greater sense of communication: they call him *Kyrios;*
he speaks to them plainly; he rejoices at the prospect of their believing. Thomas
is ready even to "die with him." And it is within this context that "Thomas" is
interpreted as meaning *twin* and that he is portrayed as speaking to his *co-disciples*
(*sym-mathētai*)—the only time such a word occurs in the NT.

Whatever the final details, there are indications that the idea of death is being
increasingly confronted by that of love, and there is an implication that it is by
some form of love that death is to be overcome. Already in chap. 10 death had
been placed in the context of love, the context of a union which would not allow
a person to be destroyed (cf. esp. 10:17–18, 28–29, 39). Now that a death has
actually occurred it is in that same context that it is being placed. And the love in
question comes not only from Jesus but also from those to whom he increasingly
reveals himself—his disciples.

**[11:17–27] Martha comes to meet Jesus; in the face of death, Jesus offers life
and Martha proclaims belief.** Rather as 4:1–42, following the interlude with
the disciples (4:31–38), returned to the story of the woman of Samaria, so now
this story returns to Mary and Martha. What the interlude has done is to suggest
that among the disciples there is to be a developing process of revealing and
believing, and in this next scene the working out of that process is portrayed in
the lives of Mary and Martha.

For Mary the process of revealing and believing is absent. When Jesus comes
Lazarus seems irretrievably dead—in the ancient world three days meant decom-
position and the final departure of the soul (Lindars, 392–93)—and Mary, accompanied by many sympathizing Jews from Jerusalem, "sat in the house." Sitting
was a posture appropriate to mourning (cf. Job 2:8,13; Ezek 8:14), and Mary's
embeddedness in this inert state is underlined by fact that in the Greek text the
word "sat" falls emphatically at the end: "but Mary in the house sat." Concerning her role in this scene that is the last word.

In clear contrast is Martha. When the scene opens with the coming of Jesus
she seems to be in the same state as Mary; both are being consoled. But in a
manner that is left quite unexplained, one hears and the other does not. And so,
while Mary sat in mourning, Martha came to meet Jesus. As the closing verses of
the first scene suggested (vv 5–6, "Jesus loved Martha . . ."), Martha has moved
into a position of priority.

"Lord," she said, "if you had been here my brother would not have died."
Despite Schnackenburg's statement to the contrary (2:329), there is an ambiguity
in these words, for they can be read as expressing either faith or bitterness. How-

ever, as she continues to speak it is faith which gains the upper hand: "And even now, I know that whatever you ask of God, God will give you."

The drama at this point is delicately poised. In the background is the inert figure of Mary. In the foreground, trying to hear clearly, is Martha. Somewhere within her there is a shadow of bitterness, but it is receding, and her mind is beginning to focus on what is still possible. And she realizes that in a sense everything is possible: "whatever you ask, God will give." This is not something that she sees clearly. The "whatever" is left unspecified, her vision is obscure. But she "knows." How she came to know is not spelled out—any more than how she first came to hear. The parable of the sheepfold, initially at least, leaves a similar mystery concerning the way the sheep hear and know (10:3–4). The only things told about her are her trust in Jesus, the fact that Jesus loved her, and her willingness to come to meet him (vv 3, 5, 20). Somewhere in that mixture of trust and love and willingness there awoke an awareness that, even in grief, with God everything is possible.

"Your brother will rise again," said Jesus.

The idea of a general resurrection of the dead on the last day was fairly common among the Jews (cf. esp. Dan 12:2, Acts 23:8), and that is the sense understood by Martha: "I know that he will rise again, in the resurrection on the last day."

But as so often, Jesus' words have further meaning. The idea of rising again, of resurrection, while it may indeed be used of the distant future and of a decayed body, may also be used of the present and of a dead heart. "The physical life which returns to a rotting body is only a feeble reflection of that true life that Jesus calls forth in believers" (Schnackenburg, 2:330). And once Martha has grasped the basic idea of resurrection, it is this further dimension which Jesus emphasizes: "I am the resurrection and the life. The one who believes in me, even if that person die, shall live. . . ." The "I am . . ." recalls the divine, not a divine that is distant but one that transcends time and that is everpresent to give resurrection, and thus new life, to the believer. As Brown indicates (434; following Dodd, 1953, 365) this power of resurrection applies not only to internal spiritual renewal; it also refers to the fact that even if such a person dies physically, that person shall come to eternal life—and so Jesus concludes, "and all who live and believe in me shall never die."

Then he adds, "Do you believe this?"

The question may seem unusually stark, yet this starkness has a purpose: it highlights the fact that all the resurrectional life in the world is useless unless a person reaches out for it and receives it; it is like water which a parched soul refuses to touch. Jesus is resurrection and life only to those who enter into communion with him—in other words, who believe in him.

The moment is climactic. Never before in the gospel has the idea of resurrection been spelled out so clearly. It comes, therefore, at the end of a long process. And for Martha, too, it is the end of a long process. At the beginning of Scene 1 (11:2) she seemed on the periphery. Now she has been brought in, but she has also been brought through grief, and she has had to struggle to rise above bitterness. Finally, having come through all of that, she is asked if she can receive this giving of life. Thus, even before she has seen the sign, the actual raising, she is asked if she can believe the word.

Her answer is strong and memorable, a variation on the climactic declaration of Peter (6:69) and on the purpose of writing the gospel (20:31): "Yes, Lord, I believe that you are the Anointed, the Son of God, the one who is coming into the world." It may seem curious that she does not say, "Yes, Lord, I do believe that you are the resurrection and the life." It is not that she avoids such an answer —in fact, the "Yes, Lord" includes the acceptance of that idea—but that she goes beyond it. The titles which she uses of Jesus are titles which, following the later part of chap. 10, reflect his role not so much as the divine giver but as the human receiver. In chap. 10 Jesus was presented as the Anointed and as God's Son sent into the world (10:24, 36). Now he is addressed as the Anointed, the Son of God who is coming into the world. The emphasis falls on the final phrase "coming into the world"—a phrase which indicates that Jesus is "the bringer of salvation sent by God" (Schnackenburg, 2:332), or as Bultmann (404) puts it, Jesus involves "the breaking of the beyond into this life." It is that which Martha grasps—not just the statement about what is divine and what is "out there," but its impact on a human life, on the life first of all of Jesus, and thus on the life of all who believe. In saying he is the Anointed, the Son who is coming into the world, she is also affirming her own dignity as an anointed child who has received God's salvation.

[11:28–37] Mary and the Jews come to Jesus and lament; Jesus' anger and tears. In contrast to Martha's ascending faith is the sorrowful state of Mary and the Jewish sympathizers. The preceding scene had already suggested such a contrast, but now it becomes much more developed. At first it may not seem so; when she comes to Jesus, her initial words are those of Martha: "Lord, if you had been here my brother would not have died." But she does not add, "And now I know. . . ." Thus unlike her sister, she never moves beyond what might have been.

In many ways she provides an advance sketch of the later Mary, Mary Magdalene, who, while others advance in believing, will likewise be left behind crying (20:1–18). Though she rises quickly, and having fallen at Jesus' feet, addresses him as *Kyrios* (vv 29, 32), the title seems to mean no more to her than it will to Mary Magdalene—as a way of referring to someone whose power she does not understand and whom she does not recognize (20:13–15). And though Jesus is calling her and she is anxious to come to him, it is never said clearly that Jesus spoke to her directly, nor is it said, as it was of Martha, that she heard or knew or believed. It is as though, despite her eagerness, there is some kind of veil over her perception. The last activity ascribed to her is that of crying (33).

Almost identified with her are the Jews. They are introduced in this scene as being "with her in the house" and, like her, their minds are focused on death— they presume she is going to the tomb to cry.

Instead they all go to Jesus—and cry. The verb here, *klaiō*, refers to unrestrained wailing. It is used three times, once of what the Jews thought Mary was going to do (v 31), then, twice, of what Mary and the Jews actually did (v 33).

The result is a crescendo of lamentation—a direct contrast to Martha's crescendo of believing. They are in the presence of "the resurrection and the life," but there is no belief, and their perceptions are those of people at a tomb.

Then come Jesus' reactions: he bursts into anger, asks where they have placed Lazarus, and breaks into tears (vv 33–35). Some manuscripts and many translations soften the notion of anger and suggest instead a rather general emotional disturbance. But as has been recognized from the time of the Greek Fathers, the basic meaning of the verb in question, *embrimaomai*, is to sniff or snort with anger, and it indicates, in fact, "an outburst of anger" (Schnackenburg, 2:335). The anger happens *tō pneumati*, "in spirit," meaning that Jesus' breath or spirit goes out in anger. In other words, he breathed angrily. And then he was "disturbed" (literally, "and he troubled himself," or "disturbed himself"). These two terms, of anger and disturbance, are very closely related (Brown, 426), and it is probably best—as Schnackenburg (2:331) says of two other closely related terms ("resurrection" and "life," 25)—to see the second not as introducing new meaning but as elucidating the first, as something which "unlocks the inside of the first term." The basic idea, therefore, is of unfolding anger: he breathed angrily and was shaken. This then is the moment when, in face of the ravages of death, Jesus protests angrily.

And then, after asking where they had laid Lazarus, Jesus cries. The word used of Jesus' weeping is *dakryō,* "to shed tears." The particular grammatical form used here—the aorist—means "broke into tears" (Hoskyns, 403). Thus there are two outbursts—first of anger, and later of tears.

Two questions arise. Against what is Jesus reacting? And what do his reactions mean? In the history of interpretation these problems have been much discussed (see esp. Hoskyns, 403–5).

As the context (v 33) strongly indicates, the immediate reason for this anger is the unbelief of Mary and the Jews. (For detailed discussion, see Hoskyns, 405; Schnackenburg, 2:336.) In Schnackenburg's words, the lamenting Jews are "representatives of unbelief." And as such they represent the essence of sin.

But bound up with sin is death. "In Christian thought death and sin are inseparable" (Hoskyns, 404), and, in fact, the problem with the Jews, at various stages (e.g., 8:48–59), and particularly here, is that in several ways they are death-oriented, overwhelmed, in fact, by death. Hence while maintaining that the anger is focused first of all on unbelief, it seems necessary also, particularly because at a later stage the idea of being troubled or disturbed is linked to death (12:27; 14:1, 27; cf. Brown, 435), to conclude that Jesus' unfolding anger is directed at sin-and-death. Insofar as sin and death come ultimately from the devil (8:44; cf. 13:2,21–30), Jesus' anger may be seen as directed against the realm of Satan (Brown, 435).

The same would seem to be true of the tears. They are a reaction to the complex phenomenon of sin-and-death, especially death. It is at the moment that his focus shifts from unbelief to death—from "seeing" the wailing to being invited to "see" the dead Lazarus (vv 33–34)—that Jesus cries.

There remains the further problem—concerning the meaning of this double outburst and of the intervening question about where they had laid Lazarus. The purpose apparently of these outbursts and of the question is to suggest something of the idea of self-emptying and death. The death of Jesus will be accompanied both by the handing over of the spirit and by the outflow of blood and water (19:30, 34). There is a literal emptying. Given that the Lazarus story, from start to finish (11:2, 53), is so closely connected to the death of Jesus, it is appropriate that in this story also, this "rehearsal" of Jesus' passion-and-glorification, there should be an initial process of self-emptying. The burst of spirit-disturbing anger and the flow of tears suggest such a process. The fact that these outbursts have something to do with death is confirmed by the fact that they are preceded by the image of Mary being at the feet of Jesus (v 32)—thus recalling the death-related introductory reference to Mary wiping Jesus' feet (v 2). It is also confirmed by the death-related question, "Where have you placed him?"

Furthermore, the question itself represents a form of self-emptying. When the Lazarus story began Jesus was first referred to rather surprisingly as "Lord" (v 2). And he dwelt apart in love, knowing the mystery of Lazarus's death even before it happened (vv 1–6). Then in Scene 2 (vv 7–16) there was a suggestion of a descent in his mode of discourse. In Scenes 3 and 4, beginning at a lower level, there is a partial repetition of the same process: in Scene 3 Jesus is very much in command and there is a suggestion, at the beginning of the scene, that he knows all about Lazarus and the tomb (v 17). But in Scene 4 Jesus is a very pale figure; his only utterance is a question, "Where have you placed him?" This is not the Jesus who dwelt afar, knowing mysteries. The question, in fact, is somewhat akin to that of the weeping distracted Mary Magdalene who knew not where they had placed the one she sought (20:13). And there is an immense irony in the fact that he is invited to "come and see" (v 34). There was a time when it was he, in a sovereign way, who told others to "come and see" (1:39). The irony is heightened by the *Kyrie* (*"Kyrie,* come and see") and by its ambiguity (v 34). He has, therefore, been emptied of his sovereign status and knowledge. And it is at that point that the self-emptying takes a further and more conclusive form—he bursts into tears.

The fact that the tears represent a profound self-emptying does not mean that they were not an indication that Jesus loved Lazarus. They were—and the Jews, in seeing them, were right in detecting that love (v 36). But it was no superficial love, no mood of the moment. It was a love of complete self-giving.

[11:38–44] The Creatorlike Jesus calls forth Lazarus. The initial sight at the tomb is forbidding: "It was a cave, and a stone lay upon it." The simple-sounding image is unclear (cf. Schnackenburg, 2:337–38, 517; Brown, 426; Lindars, 399), but, as so often in this gospel, the puzzling lack of clarity at a superficial level helps to focus attention on a further level—in this case on the fact that "cave" and "stone," whatever their architectural implications, have heavily negative overtones. "Cave" suggests a place of darkness, and "stone" in this gospel, including this chapter, has always been used in contexts where the forces of darkness seek to bring about Jesus' death (8:59; 10:31–33; 11:8). In other words, once certain elements of puzzle and wordplay are taken into consideration, the cave and the stone suggest darkness and death.

Within this cave there will be a stench, and at the root of the stench a dead man who from feet to head is wrapped and bound. The overall effect is of something dark and rotten and knotted.

When Jesus comes to the tomb he is described once again as being angry. Yet his state is not as weak as at the end of the previous scene. Here there are no tears, and he asks no humble questions. Even the anger is different; it is confined within himself. And he no longer shakes. Instead his conduct at the tomb evokes the Creator.

An evoking of Jesus' creative power had already been given at the end of the preceding scene—in the remark about his having opened the eyes of the blind (v 37). But the remark had been skeptical and had suggested not so much the presence of creationlike power as the absence or loss of it. Now, however, that power is very much in evidence. The calling forth of Lazarus is like a fulfillment of the Creator-like power, emphasized in chap. 5, of calling the dead from their tombs (5:24–29). As Brown concludes (437), "in many details ch. xi acts out the promise of ch. v."

The continuity with chapter 5 is strengthened by the fact that, like the healing of the sick man (5:8, "Rise, take up . . . walk") the raising of Lazarus involves a form of triple command:

"Take away the stone" (*Arate* . . .);

"Lazarus, come out" (*Lazare, deuro* . . .);

"Loose him and let him go" (*Lusate* . . . *aphete* . . .).

A further variation on this pattern may be found in 9:7—"Go, wash . . . Sent."

However, unlike the cases in chaps. 5 and 9, where the life-giving commands follow each other immediately, the unfolding of the commands at the tomb must wait upon the development of faith. Thus between the first command and its fulfillment there is a faith-related interlude—waiting for Martha to trust in the command (the taking away of the stone, vv 39–40). And between the fulfilling of that command and the pronouncement of the next decisive one, there is a further interlude—Jesus prays so that those who see the sign may believe (41–42). The implication of this structure is that, while the initial giving of life comes from God, its further and final giving, though equally from God, depends upon believing.

That Martha should have a problem of faith may seem surprising; as already noted, her earlier declaration (27) had been nothing less than a variation on the climactic declaration of Peter (6:69). But just as closeness to the reality of death causes Peter to lose faith (13:36–38; 18:12–27), so, to some degree, Martha too falters. It is to indicate this idea of her closeness to death that she is introduced into the scene in a way that at first sight may seem unnecessary—as "the sister of the dead [man]" (v 39). Then, in a phrase which, by its reference to the glory of God, recalls the opening scene (11:4), Jesus speaks to her, and with an implication that her faith is thus renewed, the command goes into effect—they lifted (*ēran*) the stone.

With that, Jesus lifted (*ēren*) his eyes and began to pray. The literary continuity ("lifted . . . lifted") has theological meaning: it underlines the continuity of the process, underlines the connection between Martha's faith, obedience to the command, and the prayer which leads into the calling of Lazarus. A similar phenomenon is seen in the first sign, at Cana: the process of turning the water into wine depends both on believing Jesus' word (something communicated by the mother to the servants) and on the strenuous carrying out of that word (by filling the stone water jars and so on, 2:5–8).

The prayer (vv 41–42) is the first of three such prayers in John's gospel (cf. 12:27–28; chap. 17). All three are said in the face of death, but all presuppose that death will be overcome, and so their basic mood is one of thanks or praise.

In this prayer Jesus speaks as a son who is in constant union with the father, as one whose prayers are, therefore, heard and who, at this moment, gives thanks. He does so for the sake of those standing around—that they may believe. Earlier he had said to his disciples, "Lazarus is dead and I rejoice (*chairō*) . . . that you may believe" (v 15). Now for essentially the same reason he gives thanks: "I thank (*eucharistō*) you . . . that they many believe that you sent me" (vv 41–42).

What is essential is that however much Jesus is presented as Creator-like, the bringing of life depends also on human activity and interaction. Through such activity death is transformed—through believing, through cooperation, through thanksgiving.

[11:45–53] The Sanhedrin's providential plan to kill Jesus.   The change from one scene to the next involves a major transition: the Jesus who had been the master of life is now revealed as being subject to death. Yet the two scenes form a unit; as noted earlier (in analyzing the three-part descent of 11:1–53), together they form part of a larger pattern, and together they help to portray the divine participation in human life, even in death.

The human drama which is here portrayed is highly negative. Those who report the Lazarus incident are as skeptical as they had been beforehand (cf. vv 46, 37, "But some . . ."), and thus they show that their fundamental human perceptions are blocked. The Sanhedrin freely admits that Jesus is working signs, but with a perversity which seems more calculated than that of the skeptics who brought the report, they deliberately reject the whole phenomenon of signs and believing in order that, whatever else happens, they may retain the structure which gives them power, prestige, and security ("our place [the temple] and nation"; cf. 5:41–44; 12:43). And finally, with a clear-mindedness which surpasses even that of the calculating Sanhedrin, the bullying ("you know nothing") high priest explains that it is expedient that Jesus should die. Thus with a terrible logic, there is a progression from the initial blocking of perceptions and signs to the final decision to kill.

Yet it is precisely in the midst of this scene of moral and physical death that the divine is somehow present. Such a presence is shown most obviously in the irony of the statement of Caiaphas. When he speaks of the fact that the nation must not be destroyed, he is also referring, without intending it, to the process by which Jesus' death both saves the nation and gathers all of God's children into one. His very death-plan contains a prophecy, an element of the divine word. Thus even in the most dreaded councils of the wicked the plan of God goes forward. This does not in any way lessen the reality of evil, but it places that evil within a larger framework which is ultimately positive, the framework of divine providence.

The idea of providence contributes towards understanding the puzzling phrase that Caiaphas was high priest "(of) that year." It is puzzling both because he was high priest for nineteen years (A.D. 18–37) and because it is repeated three times (11:49,51; 18:13). Bultmann (410) sees it as evidence that the evangelist is mistaken with regard to history. But such a mistake is unlikely; if someone has been in what is virtually a people's highest office for nineteen years in the beginning of a century, it is relatively easy, even at the end of the century, to know that the period of office was not just one year. Besides, why say it three times? Rather than being a mistake, the puzzling detail would seem, as so often, to be suggesting something else, something beyond the level of reporting historical details.

A clue is provided by those authors, beginning with Origen, who believe that the purpose is to highlight the year in question: Caiaphas was high priest during that significant or fateful year (cf. Brown, 440; Schnackenburg, 2:348–49).

A further clue is provided by the fact that all three references to "that year" are accompanied by references to Jesus dying for the people (11:49–52, 18:13–14). "The people," as 11:51–52 explains, refers to the coming together of Jews and Gentiles, and in some early Christian traditions—for instance, in that represented by Ephesians—the fact that Jesus' death would bring Jews and Gentiles together was inextricably bound up with the idea of an age-old providential plan (*boulē*) which would go into operation at a specific time (Ephesians 1–3, esp. 1:11; 2:11–18; 3:1–10).

Thus John's highlighting of the year emerges as a way of highlighting the time —the time of God's hidden providence. Far from being a mistake in history, it represents a theological insight. Furthermore, by evoking providence it complements the preceding evocation of creation (in Jesus' Creator-like commands at the tomb, 38–44).

The idea that the Sanhedrin scene is concerned with unity and providence is confirmed by the fact that, as Brown (439, 443) indicates, it has echoes of 6:1–13—a text which, through the sharing of bread, suggests unity and providence. Both texts contain certain broad outlines:

• the seeing of signs which he did (6:2; 11:45–47)

• the sense of being in a quandary (how to provide bread; how to prevent belief) and of wondering what to do (6:5–9; 11:47: Jesus knows; the Sanhedrin knows nothing)

• the solution: breaking the bread and gathering the pieces (6:10–13); killing Jesus and gathering the dispersed into one (11:50–52).

Further connecting details could be found, but it is the main point that is significant: even the meeting of the Sanhedrin contains aspects of the providence which gives bread to the hungry.

The Sanhedrin scene may also be usefully connected both with the cleansing of the temple (2:12–22) and with the Pauline idea of the body of Christ (Brown, 443). It is in his body, destroyed and renewed, that a new temple is prepared. And it is in his body that all are gathered into one—a new people. Again, the thought is not unrelated to that of Eph 1–3.

The scene closes on what looks like an ominous note: "from that day they planned [lit. took counsel, *ebouleusanto*] to kill him" (v 53). But within this murderous design the emphasis on the exact time ("that day") constitutes an echo and a focusing of the earlier emphasis on the exact time of the providential plan ("that year"). And within *ebouleusanto* ("took counsel") there is essentially contained the word *boulē* ("plan")—the term which, as already noted, is elsewhere used to describe the plan of God.

What is essential is that even though Jesus is no longer present in this scene as he had been in the preceding, neither is he entirely absent. Rather the divine power, which previously allowed Jesus to act like the Creator, has now humbled itself so that it works through human realities, including the plot to kill Jesus.

Jesus Comes to Jerusalem

The Ascent to Death and Glory Offers Life to All

The account of Jesus coming to Bethany to give life to Lazarus (11:1–53) is followed by the story of Jesus coming to Jerusalem and effectively offering life to all (11:54–12:50). The Lazarus story evoked a process of descent, but the coming to Jerusalem is more evocative of ascent. Thus the two "chapters" complement one another. Even in length they are virtually the same (53 verses and 54).

The text has two major sections.

Jesus' day-to-day path to death in Jerusalem (11:54–12:19)

* An introductory episode: from the desert to the feast (vv 54–57)

1. The Bethany anointing—evoking burial (12:1–11)

2. The entry to Jerusalem—evoking resurrection glory (12:12–19)

Jesus, as if beyond death, is the timeless center of all (12:20–50)

3. The approach of all people ("the Greeks")—evoking glorification (20–36a)

4. The departure into hiding—reflecting unbelievers' blindness (36b–43)

* An epilogue: the divine word and the two ways (44–50)

The distinction between the two main sections (between the coming to Jerusalem, 11:54–12:19 and the subsequent episodes, 12:20–50) is somewhat like the distinction between chaps. 7 and 8: the first is set clearly in time and space, but the second has a timeless quality and, with regard to space, leaves aside fixed confines.

Furthermore, between the first section and the second, there is a considerable change in the *dramatis personae:* the first part (11:54–12:19) refers to Lazarus and his sisters (cf. 12:1–3, 17), but the second (12:20–50) makes no mention of them, and it speaks instead of Philip, Andrew, and the Greeks (12:20–22). Part of the reason for this transition is that, to some degree, these characters are representative. Lazarus, with his Semitic name, represents something of the Jews; but Philip, Andrew, and the Greeks represent a new, wider, group; and the transition from one to the other, though perplexing at one level, is an indication that the ascent of Jesus inaugurates a new, wider, order.

Continuity with the Lazarus Story

There is a sense in which the story of Lazarus and his sisters (11:1–53) continues into the account of the coming to Jerusalem (11:54–12:19). In fact, the idea of Jesus coming to Bethany, though mentioned in 11:17–18, is not explicitly spelled out until 12:1. And it is within 11:1–12:19, and nowhere else, that the gospel speaks of people coming to "meet" Jesus (11:20,30; 12:13,18).

But the unity between the Lazarus story and this chapter goes beyond 12:19 and includes all of chap. 12. Thus there is continuity, for instance, between the

prayer of 11:41–43 and that of 12:27–28: Jesus' reliance on his Father to raise
the buried Lazarus (11:41–43) is partly echoed in his reliance on the Father when
faced with the prospect of his own death and burial (cf. 12:7,23–28).

A Picture of Ascent

The idea of an ascent emerges slowly. At first Jesus seems to be going nowhere;
he is, in fact, in the desert (11:54). But people are going up to Jerusalem, and
there is a sense of expectation that he also will come to the feast (11:55–57).
Then, in two stages, he does so—first to Bethany (12:1–11) and, on the following
day, to Jerusalem (12:12–19). (In the synoptics the Bethany and Jerusalem incidents are in reverse order and well separated; cf. Mark 11:1–11; 14:3–9.) At one
level, the Johannine progression is simply that of an earthly journey, but the events
at Bethany and Jerusalem suggest Jesus' burial and glorification (12:7,16), and so
there is an evoking of Jesus' coming to the heavenly Jerusalem.

In the second major section (12:20–50) certain aspects of an earthly succession
of events are retained (the Greeks come; Jesus confronts death; later, Jesus goes
away), but increasingly the dominant perspective is that of a Jesus who, at one
level, has already conquered death and entered heaven. As already mentioned, in
this later section (vv 20–50) there are virtually no references to time and space—
a strong contrast with 11:54–12:19. Jesus speaks as one who, when lifted from
the earth, will draw all people to himself (12:32).

Four Main Texts

The bulk of 11:54–12:50 consists of four main texts: vv 1–11, 12–19, 20–36a,
and 36b–43. These passages play off one another in various ways. (See, for instance, the use of scripture in vv 12–19 and 36b–43.) Of these four texts, the
emphasis falls on the third—the coming of the Greeks and the appeal to discipleship (vv 20–36a.) This is the moment when the glorified Jesus is placed before
the world as it were, and when the people of the world, both Greek and Jewish,
come to Jesus and are challenged by him.

In the opening verse(s) of each of these four texts there is an emphasis on
physical movement by Jesus and/or towards him (cf. 1, 12–13, 20–22, 36b). In
a manner similar to what was noted in analyzing the initial call to discipleship
(1:35–42), these movements seem to suggest something of the dynamic of discipleship. Jesus, in coming to Bethany, makes the first move (v 1). Then, as he
comes to Jerusalem, those who hear respond, and there is a much greater sense
of movement and reaction (vv 12–13). Finally, as the Greeks approach, there is
a threefold pattern of movement towards Jesus (vv 20–22). The result, in the text
as a whole, is an increasing sense of action and counteraction, in other words of
revelation and response. In the fourth text (vv 36b-43), however, that increasing
pattern is broken. Jesus, instead of coming forward, goes away and hides (v 36b).

At the end of each of each of these texts there is a final subsection dealing
largely with reactions (vv 9–11, 17–19, 29–36a, 42–43). At first these reaction
texts are roughly of equal length (9–11, 17–19), but in the climactic Jesus-before-

humanity scene the reaction text is much longer (29–36a), and in the final scene of unbelief it is significantly shorter (42–43). Thus the reaction texts seem proportioned to the (potential) presence of belief.

With regard to the main body of these four sections (vv 1–8, 12–16, 20–28, 36b–41) the structure varies slightly. In the first two scenes, at Bethany and (near) Jerusalem, the texts are best seen as divided in two. At Bethany, the second part begins with the intervention of Judas ("But Judas, . . ." 4), and at the coming to Jerusalem, with the reaction of Jesus ("But Jesus, . . ." 14). In the third scene, however, the text is much more complex, and, as will be indicated later, is organized on a basis that is threefold. The final scene (vv 36b–41) does have something of the twofold arrangement found in the opening scenes—particularly because of its twofold use of scripture (38–40, cf. 13–15)—yet the division of the scene in two is not so clear. Thus, while the centrality of the climactic scene is heightened by a structure which is threefold, the negativity of the final scene of unbelief seems to be reflected in a brief text which is scarcely twofold. The final scene, therefore, not only speaks of people who are incapacitated, its very structure limps.

Note. Of the many details of structure, there is one which seems to need particular emphasis: the reference to Jesus going away and hiding (v 36b), though frequently regarded as the conclusion of the scene concerning Jesus' appeal to humanity (20–36a), should be seen rather as the beginning of the following scene on unbelief (so Bernard, 2:449; Lindars, 437; UBSGNT; RSV). Such a division is supported by a number of factors. With regard to essential content, the idea of Jesus as hidden seems connected to what follows, to the idea of unbelief, rather than to what precedes. Furthermore, with regard to the pattern of movements, since the other scenes have movement, above all, at their beginning (1, 12–13, 20–22), the account of Jesus going away would seem also to be a beginning. None of the other scenes have movement by Jesus at their conclusion. Finally, with regard to phrases and linguistic details, there are elements of 36b which seem to connect with what follows: both with 37 and, in a relationship of balance, with 41 (36b, "Thus [*tauta*] spoke . . . and . . . from them [*autōn*]"; 37, 41, "So many [*tosauta*] . . . before them [*autōn*] . . . thus . . . spoke . . ."). Such linguistic details may seem to constitute fragile evidence, yet in the context of the way the fourth gospel frequently uses elements of repetition to indicate divisions, they seem to have some significance. In any case, given the other factors—the essential content and the pattern of movements—the weight of evidence favors regarding 36b as a beginning. This conclusion will be corroborated by the fact that within chaps. 13–17 the wording of 36b (*tauta elalēsen* . . .) suggests the beginning of a final text, not its ending (cf. esp. 13:21; 14:25; 15:11; 16:1, 25).

Structure: Affinity with Other Texts

The structure of 11:54–chap. 12 is related both to chaps. 7–8 and to 19:38–chap. 21. With regard to chaps. 7–8, the opening verses (11:54–55) contain a brief but close echo of 7:1–10, and there is further affinity between 11:56–57 and 7:11–13.

Each text goes on to speak of two incidents related to each other by time (7:14, 37: midway through the feast, and on the last great day of the feast; 12:1, 12: six days before Passover, and on the next day). Then the texts change gears, and move into a sphere that is outside specific time and space (8:12–47; 12:20–43). At first these "timeless" texts focus on the positive (8:12–30; Jesus' roots in God; 12:20–36a, Jesus' appeal to humanity), then on the negative (8:31–47, the roots of Jewish unbelief; 12:36b–43, the providence of Jewish unbelief). Finally, both texts give a concluding contrast—between life-oriented Jesus and death-oriented Jews (8:48–59), and between belief and unbelief (12:44–50). Thus, in a form that is compressed and adapted, the structure of chaps. 7–8 is echoed in 11:54–chap. 12.

But 11:54–chap. 12 has a deep affinity also with 19:38–chap. 21, particularly with 19:38–chap. 20. The basic pattern of ascent which dominates 11:54–12:43, also dominates 19:38–chap. 20, though in varied form. In each case there is an introduction (11:54–57; 19:38–42), and then four main texts (12:1–11, 12–19, 20–36a, 36b–43; 20:1–10, 11–18, 19–23, 24–31). In each case there is a major shift after the second main scene (i.e., after 12:19 and 20:18). Finally at the end of both texts there is a further passage, an epilogue—a text which at one level stands apart (12:44–50, chap. 21).

The details of these affinities are extremely complex, and it seems best to leave them to further research.

Bethany, Jerusalem: The Evoking of Jesus' Death (11:54–12:19)

[11:54–57] Preliminary episode. From the desert to the feast. The "chapter" begins with two balancing journeys: Jesus went away from Judea "into [*eis*] the country" (v 54), and many ascended to Jerusalem "from [*ek*] the country" (v 55). The connectedness of the two journeys is emphasized by the double use of the unusual word "country." (Apart from 4:35, "country," *chōra*, does not occur elsewhere in John.)

At first sight this journey-centered account seems very matter-of-fact, but, like the opening episodes in chaps. 5, 6, and 7, it has a special role: it provides a preliminary glimpse into the rest of the chapter. And it contains echoes of other preliminary events, particularly of the balancing journeys which preceded the cleansing of the temple (2:12–13, Jesus descended to Capernaum, and he ascended to Jerusalem). Furthermore, in a number of ways, especially in its portrayal of Jesus as going away to spend some time with the disciples, it also echoes the introductory text concerning Jesus' initial withdrawal to the Judean countryside (3:22–24).

The first indication that the text is more than matter-of-fact comes from the reference to Jesus' destination: he went away "to the country near the desert, to a city called Ephraim" (11:54). Like "Aenon near Salim" (3:23), Ephraim is not known to geographers (cf. Brown, 151, 441; Schnackenburg, 1:412, 2:351; but cf. Schwank in De Jonge, 1977, 377–84). As in many of the evangelist's geographic puzzles, the purpose apparently is to challenge the reader to go beyond the level of externals. The clue in this case would seem to lie in the fact that, as Lindars (409) notes, the name "Ephraim" means "fruitful." Thus, at one level of reading, one gets the effect, especially in the Greek wording, of Jesus going "to . . . the desert to fruitfulness." This picture, of a transition from wilderness to fruitfulness, provides a very appropriate background for all that is going to happen to Jesus, and particularly for the way in which he will summarize his fate: as that of a grain of wheat which undergoes a similar transition—from dying to fruitfulness (12:24).

The fruitfulness in question is not just that of personal growth; it involves also a relationship with others. Jesus in the desert is sojourning (*diatribō*) "with the disciples," and the subsequent scenes show how, in going towards death and glorification, he attracted many followers. At an earlier stage, while John was in Aenon near Salim, Jesus was similarly sojourning with his disciples (3:22–23), and as already mentioned, the two pictures (3:22–23; 11:54) have some affinity. But now the process of developing disciples has reached a more advanced stage, one which—as the desert intimates—will involve his death.

The sense of the involvement of other people is strengthened by what follows —by the fact that Jesus' journey "into the country" is balanced by the ascent of "many from the country." There is a suggestion, faint but real, that in some invisible way the two events are connected: when Jesus goes into the country, "many" come out of it. Later the idea will become clearer and clearer: when the seed dies it bears fruit (12:24), and when Jesus is lifted up he will draw all people to himself (12:32).

For the moment, however, that fruitfulness is scarcely perceptible. The two references to the country, however balanced, are far enough apart that the reader may miss the connection. Besides, the attitude of those who go up to Jerusalem is not clear. At first sight they seem preoccupied with Jewish ritual (with the purification that was sometimes needed before celebrating Passover; cf. Schnackenburg, 2:364; Num 9:1–14; 2 Chr 30:15–19; Acts 21:24,26), and it is only in the later part of the scene (vv 56–57) that it becomes clear that they are looking for Jesus.

But the encounter with Jesus is not going to be easy. The authorities have given a command (*entolē*, cf. 12:49–50) that anyone who knows Jesus' whereabouts should inform, so that they might arrest him. Thus within the minds of those who talk about Jesus there is a profound tension: they seek someone new yet they are under pressure, as soon as they find out about him, to betray him.

The suggestion given by this preliminary scene is of a quiet fruitfulness in which many are ready to take part, but which some others wish to reject.

The double journey which preceded the cleansing of the temple evoked faintly all of Jesus' life—his few days on earth, encompassed by a descent and an ascent (2:12–13). The double journey here evokes just the final point of that life—when Jesus descends into a death which will raise up many others.

[12:1–11] The supper with the extravagant anointing: a symbol of Jesus' burial; the coming of the great crowd.   As presented in the fourth gospel, the supper at Bethany occurs six days before the (Friday) Passover, in other words, on the preceding Saturday evening. Despite all the threats which surround it, the scene suggests an atmosphere of profound celebration. Jesus is with people he loves (Lazarus, Martha, Mary; cf. 11:3,5), and so the sense of togetherness, which was first implied by the brief verse on Ephraim (11:54, ". . . with the disciples") is maintained and developed.

The sense of celebration is heightened by the fact that this supper scene has affinities with the wedding scene at Cana (2:1–11). The details, of course, are very different, yet, apart from some resemblances with chap. 13, it is with the Cana feast, rather than with any other episode, that the Bethany supper shares the elements of celebration—togetherness, a meal, Jesus, the disciples/Lazarus and others, the woman/women, the intervention of the mother/Mary, the profusion of something wonderful (fine wine/expensive perfume). Furthermore, both events are linked to specific weeks—the Cana wedding to the gospel's opening week (especially to what seems to be its sixth day) and the Bethany supper to what seems to be the gospel's closing week (cf. 12:1,12; "Six days before Passover. . . . The next day . . .").

In any case, the atmosphere at Bethany can hardly have lacked a mood of celebration. As far as the narrative is concerned, one could expect such an event. After prolonged sadness and tension, Jesus had called forth Lazarus—but nothing was said about the positive reactions of all those involved. Now, at last, as if to make up for that lack, a supper is given.

It is not immediately clear for whom the supper is intended—whether for Jesus or for Lazarus. In the circumstances it could be for either. The text refers primarily to Jesus, and eventually does so clearly, yet it has enough ambiguity to suggest, at least for a moment, that it could also be Lazarus. And in various ways, in this text as in 11:1–53, the fates of Jesus and Lazarus are interwoven. The opening sentence (v 1), which is sometimes regarded as (poorly) edited because of its repetition of the name "Jesus," may also be seen as a balanced construction which, with deliberate artistry, begins and ends with "Jesus" and which places "Lazarus" in the middle (see esp. the phrasing in Greek). The following sentence (v 2) refers to Lazarus as being "with him." And at the end of the scene, when the great crowd comes, the interweaving of the names and roles of Jesus and Lazarus is particularly clear (vv 9–11). Furthermore, both here (vv 9–11) and later (vv 17–19) the text describes Lazarus in words and phrases which repeat and echo what had earlier been said about Jesus—particularly about the plot to kill him and about the different attitudes of the "many . . . Jews," on the one hand, and of the high priests and Pharisees, on the other (cf. 11:47, 49 ["You know nothing . . ."],53,55,57; 12:10–11,18–19 [" . . . you accomplish nothing . . ."]).

The basic effect of this interweaving of the roles of Jesus and Lazarus is to suggest that, even though the spotlight during this final week is on Jesus, his fate is not his alone but is shared by Lazarus and by all those whom the beloved

Lazarus represents or evokes. What was done in Jesus is in some way continued in and through Lazarus. And, as already noted (in dealing with 11:1–53), the role of Lazarus is in continuity with both John the baptizer and the beloved disciple. It is hardly an accident that the phraseology used to describe the reclining Lazarus (v 2) finds its nearest equivalent in the reference to the reclining beloved disciple (13:23). Thus at Bethany—as at Cana, to some extent—there is an unspoken suggestion of love, of interwoven fates, and of a celebration which is not for Jesus alone but for many others. The involvement of others is made more explicit by the references to the believing Jews and the crowd (vv 9, 11, 17, 18).

This celebration, however, is not escapist; it does not run away from the reality of life, least of all from death. A hint of death had already been present at Cana—in the reference to Jesus' hour (2:4)—but here it is much stronger. This is seen, first of all, with regard to Jesus. The supper is set in the context of Passover, a feast which has always been linked with Jesus' death (2:13,22; 6:4,71; cf. 19:14). The fact that Lazarus is described unnecessarily as having been raised from the dead (v 1) does not mean that the reference is an editorial gloss; rather it is a further way of putting the supper in the context of death—the death not only of Jesus but also of Lazarus. The actual phrase "raise/rise *from the dead*" is never used in the Lazarus story proper, 11:1–53. It is primarily associated with Jesus (cf. 2:22; 20:9; 21:14) and is used of Lazarus only in relation to Jesus, and within the context of the Jesus-oriented Passover (12:1, 9, 17). Again therefore, on the question of death, the fates of Jesus and Lazarus are interwoven.

It is not with Lazarus alone that Jesus' fate is interwoven. It is bound up also with Martha and Mary. The self-giving and self-emptying, which in chaps. 10 and 11 were seen in Jesus (in his role as good shepherd, 10:7–18, and in his involvement with death, 11:1–53) are now seen in the sisters—in Martha's serving (*diakoneō*, v 2) and in Mary's outpouring (the perfume, her hair). Thus here, even more than at Cana, it is not Jesus alone who makes the occasion; a decisive role is played by the woman/women and the servants/service (cf. 2:5–9).

The perfume was from real nard—a plant found in the mountains of northern India—and the word used for "real" is *pistikos*, literally "faithful" (cf. Brown, 448). The anointing and wiping of the feet (rather than the head), is to be seen in the context both of the previous time Mary was at Jesus' feet (11:32–36), when Jesus poured out anger and tears, and of Jesus' subsequent washing and wiping of the disciples' feet (13:5; cf. Lindars, 416). In other words, her self-giving is in continuity with his. And Lazarus also will have to give and give totally: at the end of the episode he will receive from the high priests exactly what Jesus received—condemnation to death (12:10, cf. 11:53).

Perhaps the emphasis on the feet should also be related to the theological idea that everything, including death, is to be put under Jesus' feet (Eph 1:22, 1 Cor 15:24–26). Thus the fact that through the fragrance of the perfume the house was filled (*pleroō*) would evoke not only the filling of the church or world by means of the word or message (cf. Bernard, 2:418; Bultmann, 415; Brown, 453), but also the related idea of the fullness (*plerōma*) which fills creation (Eph 1:23).

The overall effect, therefore, of the first part of the scene (vv 1–3) is to suggest a supper which, far from being escapist, integrates the realities of service and death, but which manages, precisely because it integrates these realities, to be genuinely celebrative—a house filled with the atmosphere of high class perfume.

But Judas, though physically present, lives in another world (vv 4–6). With feigned concern for the poor, he protests against the waste of a perfume which, on his calculation, could have been sold for three hundred denarii (the equivalent of three hundred days' wages). This is surprising. At first sight he does indeed seem to be in the same world as everyone else at the supper; the apparently unnecessary description of him as ''one of his disciples'' (v 4) not only underlines his discipleship; it also echoes the preceding description of Lazarus as ''one of those reclining with him'' (v 2). But while Lazarus, Martha, and Mary are in solidarity with Jesus and seek to emulate the self-emptying which goes back in a special way to his role as good shepherd, Judas is a traitor, and he is described in a way that reflects the sheep-destroying characters of chapter 10: he is a thief (12:6; 10:1,8,10), he is mercenary (he thinks money, 12:5; 10:12), and he ''does not care for the poor/sheep'' (12:6; 10:13). Nor does he lay down anything, least of all his life (10:11, 15, 17–18); rather, he lifts or carries something—money (12:6).

Whatever the final details, the basic picture is clear: in comparison with the self-giving of Jesus and those around him, the figure of Judas provides a thorough contrast.

Then (vv 7–8) Jesus intervenes: ''Let her be—that she may keep it for the day of my burial. For the poor. . . .'' Anointing was part of the burial rite, and Jesus' words suggest that ''the occasion is symbolically equivalent to the day of burial'' (Lindars, 419). This reinforces the idea that the supper integrates death, and it seems to challenge the readers, even in the face of complex social and economic problems ('' . . . the poor . . .''), to look beneath the surface of things and to see the dignity and value that is found in one person who is soon to die. It does not mean indifference towards people; in fact, Jesus is soon to give his life for everybody. But it implies that concern, including concern for the poor, should go beyond the level of the superficial.

Mary apparently was not fully aware of the significance of the anointing; unknowingly she has performed an action that is symbolic or prophetic (Brown, 449, 454), and it is Jesus who interprets it. Thus, as in the case of the high priest who unknowingly prophesied (11:50–52), there is an implication of the activity of a deeper (divine) dimension.

Reactions (vv 9–11). In reacting to the supper (vv 9–11) the leading priests plot to kill Lazarus. Thus while Judas, during the supper, had been negative, a thief, the priests are even more so.

But most people react positively: the seeing of Lazarus leads them to believing in Jesus. Incidentally, they are described curiously—not as ''*a* great crowd *of* Jews'' but as ''*the* great crowd *from* the Jews.'' The effect of this phrasing is to evoke the fact that from the Jews there developed a widespread Christian community (''the great crowd'') comprising both Jews and Gentiles.

The allusion to this widespread community is in continuity with the image of the fragrance which filled the house. Hence the dynamics which in one form are present in the supper scene (the filling fragrance and Judas) are reflected in more down-to-earth form in the reaction (the great crowd and the authorities' plot).

[12:12–19] The festive coming to Jerusalem, and the symbolism of resurrection and of another realm; the crowds bear witness and hear. "On the next day" the great crowd hears that Jesus "is coming . . . to Jerusalem." Though he had been to Jerusalem before (2:12–22; 5:1; 7:10), this is different: for the first time in the gospel, Jesus' approach to Jerusalem is described not as a going up (or ascending), but as a *coming;* and, again for the first time, the reception is immensely festive—the great crowd comes to meet him with cries of "Hosanna . . ." and with branches of palm. On the other occasions on which Jesus ascended to Jerusalem, there was a sense of his arriving in a limited city at an unfulfilled time. On this occasion, however, the city includes the presence of the Gentiles, and Jesus declares that now at last there has arrived the hour of his glorification. Thus, in comparison with the previous visits, this depicts a different Jerusalem.

And so on two successive days, apparently a Saturday evening and a Sunday, Jesus is surrounded by a festive atmosphere. In the synoptics the coming to Jerusalem is accompanied not by branches of palm but by ordinary branches or greenery (Matt 21:8, Mark 11:8). It is John, and John alone, who provides the two elements, "palm" and "Sunday." The successive festive days, one with perfume and the other with palm, together constitute an intensifying picture of celebration.

The first part of the scene (vv 12–13) is open to misunderstanding. Branches of palm were often used to suggest immortality—in much ancient art, the palm was the tree of life (Trever, 1962; cf. Rev 7:9; note use of palm at Tents, Lev 23:40; Neh 8:15)—but they were also used in connection with the nationalistic capture of Jerusalem by the Maccabees (1 Macc 13:51). And the cry of "Hosanna, . . ." a word which means "Save" but which had taken on the meaning of an exclamation of praise ("Salvation!"), was also not clear. Though the crowd follows the words of the Psalms (118:26–27) and connects salvation with "the name of the Lord," they also hail Jesus as king, and, like the people who after the miracle of the bread wanted to inaugurate a kingship based on force (6:14–15), it is not evident that they have understood the nature of Jesus' kingship. The coming to Jerusalem, therefore, threatens to become superficial—to turn into a nationalistic triumphal march.

It is in the context of superficiality that it seems appropriate to consider one of the puzzles of this scene. As far as is known, palm was not available in first-century Jerusalem (Brown, 456–57). Yet with emphatic repetitiveness the Greek text uses two palm-designating words (*baion, phoinix*). The question which arises is whether this puzzle is to be regarded as so many other of the evangelist's puzzles—as challenges to the reader to see beyond the superficial, in this case to see that, apart from the level of the historical earthbound Jerusalem, there is an allusion to the Jerusalem which is above, the heavenly Jerusalem which Jesus is soon to enter.

In any case, Jesus then (vv 14–16) challenges the apparently nationalistic enthusiasm. While a nationalist or political movement would expect its king to enter on a horse or war chariot, Jesus takes a different approach: "finding . . . a little donkey [*onarion*] he sat on it." On other occasions, Jesus' "finding" is associated with aspects of his supreme authority (2:14; 5:14; 9:35; 11:17), and the apparent ease with which he finds the animal—the narrative gives no hint of effort or search—accords with that suggestion of intervening authority. His action, therefore, indicates a breaking of the mold. Even more indicative of such a break is the animal. *Onarion* is the diminutive of *onos,* "donkey." This is the only time the NT uses the word, and, as is implied by Wikenhauser (228) and Schneider (226), it suggests an animal that is not only young but small. The diminutive takes on further significance when seen against the background of the diminutive figure (*paidarion,* small boy) who was instrumental in the multiplication of the bread (6:9). The combined action of finding such an animal and sitting on it suggests a form of authority, of kingship, which is not of this world. In fact, through the picture of the little donkey, it seems gently to mock worldly authority. And the actual phrase, "he sat [*kathizō*] on it" has no counterpart in John except in the account of how—according to one level of the text—Jesus "sat" (*kathizō*) on the judgment seat (19:13). Thus in various ways the account is already suggesting what Jesus will later say clearly to Pilot—that his kingdom, his realm, is not of this world (18:36, cf. Kysar, 193).

The picture of this other kind of realm or kingdom is developed by a quotation from scripture. The quotation is based on Zech 9:9, but instead of beginning with "Rejoice greatly . . ." as does Zechariah, the evangelist substitutes an equivalent biblical phrase: "Do not fear. . . ." Wherever he quarried this phrase (perhaps from the festive text of Zeph 3:14–17, a text which could also have supplied the reference in 12:13 to the "king of Israel") its effect in the narrative is to heighten the contrast with Pilate—the Caesar-related ruler who "was afraid" (19:8). (In John 10–21 these are the only two uses of the verb "to fear".) In the kingdom of Caesar there is fear but not in the realm of the one who sits on a little donkey.

The nature of this other realm is not easy to grasp, and so, as the text notes (v 16), it was only after Jesus was glorified that the disciples, in remembering, understood the scripture and the corresponding events (cf. 2:22). The implication, therefore, is that the realm has to do with Jesus' glory, and that, if the disciples could only have grasped it, it was in some sense already present in the picture of Jesus seated on the donkey.

The Continuity of the Scenes

Kysar (193) regards Jesus' action (sitting on the donkey) as symbolic. Brown (463) sees it as prophetic. Thus in three successive texts there are prophetic words or actions:

- Caiaphas's prophecy about the need for Jesus to die (11:50)
- Mary's anointing of Jesus for his burial (12:3–8)
- Jesus' action signaling his own glorification and the inauguration of a glory-based realm (12:14–16)

Mary's action focuses attention on Jesus' burial and body and, for that reason, is important in the threefold pattern. For if all are to be gathered into one (as in 11:52), and if a new realm is to emerge (as in 12:14–16), it is through Jesus' body, through his death and the reconciling of all in his death, that it will be done.

There is a special continuity between the anointing and the entry to Jerusalem. While the anointing is symbolic of Jesus' burial, the coming to Jerusalem refers more to his resurrection. In other words, both of them are celebrational and prophetic, and they follow each other as do Jesus' burial and glorification. One fills the house, and the other evokes a further form of completeness or fullness—the coming of God's kingdom in Jesus and the seeking of Jesus by the world. Both together inaugurate a new realm, a realm built on the glorification of his body. (In 2:21–22, verses so akin to 12:16, the theme of the body is more explicit.)

One of the features of the successive prophetic interventions (by Caiaphas, 11:50–52; Mary, 12:3–8; and Jesus, 12:14–16) is that they show an increasing consciousness concerning the divine dimension or presence. Caiaphas is quite unaware of it. Mary's situation is ambiguous, but the fact that it is Jesus who interprets her action, and that he does so then and there, means that awareness is close at hand. And when Jesus acts, the impression is that he knows fully the meaning of what he is doing. The overall impression is of a process of revelation which, even in dealing with death, is becoming clear.

Reactions (vv 17–19). Just as the anointing scene is followed by a picture of response—the believing of many in the great crowd (vv 9–11)—so the coming to Jerusalem is followed by a complementary scene of belief (vv 17–19). But the later scene goes further. It tells not so much of people coming to believe, but of believers who "bear witness" and of others who "hear." It is a process which has affinity both with the Samaritan woman's witnessing to the people (4:29–30,39–42) and with the disciples' reporting to Thomas (20:24–29). The implication, with regard to those who hear the witness, is that they progress from hearing about a sign to an actual meeting with Jesus (v 18). A similar progression may be found with the people of Samaria and Thomas (4:42; 20:27–28).

In these verses (vv 18–19) the evangelist tells not of "the great crowd" but of two "crowds"—one which bears witness and one which hears. The implication, however, is that both meet Jesus, and that together they form "the great crowd" (12:12–13, 17–18). Thus, while depicting the ageless process of witness and hearing, the evangelist keeps the basic idea of everybody, Jews and Gentiles, gathering around Jesus as he goes, symbolically, through burial and resurrection. The Pharisees have lost. In a phrase which echoes the uselessness of relying on flesh, on externals (6:63), they tell one another that they accomplish nothing (v 19). And in a faint but ironic echo of the receptive Samaritans (4:42), they complain that the world has gone after (the soon-to-be-gloried) Jesus.

[12:20–28] The coming of the Greeks signals Jesus' glorification in death. Jesus' fruitful acceptance of death reveals the essence of discipleship. The story of Jesus, apart from his death, might have ended with the account of his anointing and of his coming to Jerusalem. These events are climactically festive. They include a certain symbolizing of his burial and resurrection, and they indicate what an impact he made on the world.

But they are described in a way that is tightly compressed and, as if to unpack their density, the narrative goes on to articulate their implications. In the account of the coming of the Greeks (vv 20–36a) a closer look is provided both at Jesus' fate and at its implications for those who would accept it. And then (vv 36b–43) there is a brief account of those who would reject it. To some degree both these texts are timeless: they look beyond Jesus' ministry, and they summarize the permanent essence of acceptance (discipleship) and rejection.

The text on discipleship, on Jesus' challenge to humanity (vv 20–36a), consists of two parts. The first (20–28), though it begins with the coming of the Greeks, focuses on the fate of Jesus, on his pain and glory; and only secondarily, at its center, does it speak of discipleship in general. The second part (29–36a), by focusing on the crowd and by addressing it directly (''you''), indicates more clearly what Jesus' actions mean for others. In the accounts of the anointing and the coming to Jerusalem there was a similar shift of focus from Jesus (12:1–8, 12–16) to the crowd (12:9–11, 17–19).

The first part (vv 20–28), in its focus on Jesus, is typically Johannine in structure: three times three. First, the coming of the Greeks is recounted through three repetitive movements (vv 20–22, esp. 21–22). Then, when Jesus replies (vv 23–26), he uses three sayings, each containing a parallelism. And finally, when he speaks of himself, of his distress, and of his relationship to his father (vv 27–28), he inaugurates a threefold pattern of Father–Son statements (two statements by him to the Father, and one in reply, from heaven). In outline, and literally:

The coming of the Greeks (20–22)

"[The] Greeks . . . came . . . telling . . . Philip."

"Philip comes and tells Andrew."

"Andrew comes and Philip and they tell Jesus."

Jesus' reply concerning the glorification of the Son of humanity (23–26)

"Unless [*ean mē*] the grain . . . dies. . . .
. . . but if [*ean de*] it dies. . . .''

"Those who love their life . . .
. . . and whoever hates their life. . . .''

"If anyone serves me, let that person follow. . . .
. . . If anyone serves me, the Father will honor that person."

In distress, Jesus speaks to the Father (27–28)

"Father, save me from this hour?"

"Father, glorify your name."

"I have glorified it, and I will glorify it again."

Within each set of three, the third involves a variation in the pattern. It is not Andrew alone who comes to Jesus (as the pattern and the singular "comes" might suggest), but both Andrew and Philip. And when Jesus replies, his third saying, instead of being antithetical, either-or, is more both-and, a form of synonymous parallelism. Finally, when Jesus speaks to the Father, the third saying is not a prayer but a reply ("I have . . . and I will . . ."). Each of these variations has a certain both-and effect.

The overall impression is one of steady intensification. In the Greek phrasing, the first set of three culminates in the word "Jesus," the second begins with Jesus and culminates in "the Father," and the third refers twice to the Father and culminates in the voice from heaven saying, "I will glorify." Altogether the text uses the words "Jesus" and "Father" three times.

The Coming of the Greeks (vv 20–22)

The initial picture, that of the Greeks (vv 20–22), makes explicit a theme that had often been intimated—the inclusion of the Gentiles. They are not to be understood as Jews, yet the fact that they have come to worship at the feast shows that they are open to all that is good in the Jewish heritage. And in accordance with that openness they come to Philip and say, "*Kyrie,* we wish (*thelō,* will/wish) to see Jesus." The basic impression is of people who in their search for true worship, for God, made their way first towards Judaism, and then, within and through Judaism, towards what they saw as its true expression—Jesus.

Furthermore, the reference to Philip as being "from Bethsaida of Galilee," a reference which, strictly speaking, is both unnecessary and inaccurate—Philip's origin in Bethsaida was given earlier (1:44), and Bethsaida was not in Galilee but in Gaulinitis—this reference has the effect of evoking Philip's call (1:43–44), a call which referred to Galilee and Bethsaida and Andrew. One of the basic elements of that call was the intimating of the coming together of Jew and Gentile. And in varied form the same idea reappears in the present text. Bethsaida may not be in Galilee, but while "Bethsaida" is thoroughly Semitic, "Galilee" is more associated with the Gentiles (cf. Matt 4:15), and the joining of the two, though geographically questionable, makes theological sense: it evokes the union of Jews and Gentiles.

Thus the text speaks not only of how the Greeks approach Jesus, but also of the intermediary role of Judaism and of the fact that the approach of the Greeks takes place within a larger Jewish-Greek union.

Jesus' Parabolic Principle: Death Leads to Life (vv 23–26)

When Jesus replies (vv 23–26) he does not refer to Jews or Gentiles. Rather, in accordance with the larger union implied by the previous verses, he uses of himself an inclusive title, Son of humanity, and he refers to the process through which that Jew–Gentile union is to be accomplished—through glorification: "The hour has come for the Son of humanity to be glorified."

At this point the text refers first of all to Jesus, to the fact that, like the dawning of one's last day, his decisive hour has finally struck. Three times in earlier chapters the gospel had stated solemnly that it had not yet come (2:4, 7:30, 8:20). But now it is here, and beginning with this text (12:23), the narrative will go on to state three times and with equal solemnity that it has in fact come (cf. also 13:1, 17:1).

It is a crucial moment, one in which the focus closes in on Jesus to catch his reaction. But the reaction is momentarily postponed, and in the meantime, just when the reader is likely to be most attentive, Jesus pronounces three central sayings:

- (v 24) In the world of nature, the fate of the wheat grain shows that the path to fruitfulness, to life, is through death.

- (v 25) The same principle applies to human life: it is by letting go of one form of life, life "in this world," in other words by letting go of all that ties one to what is of earth and flesh, particularly to what is dark or empty, that one achieves a higher form of life, life which endures forever. Thus, to really live a person must first die to the world.

- (v 26) This process of dying and of coming to greater life is accomplished by serving (*diakoneō*) Jesus—by following him, by being there with him, and by receiving honor from the Father. Thus, the serving of Jesus involves a letting go, a dying.

But in this relationship Jesus is not a killjoy. The words and ideas with which that relationship is described—serving, following, being there—all reflect aspects of the celebratory dinner and of the coming to Jerusalem (12:1–19; Martha *served* him *there,* v 2; and it is implied that people followed him, v 19). Even in the shadow of burial there was festive life.

Above all, serving Jesus means being honored by the Father (v 26)—a reversal of the idea of honoring one's mother and father, and a startling indication, therefore, of one's dignity, of the extent to which one's value is esteemed. Thus the process of letting go of relationship with the world leads to the development of a relationship which is supreme.

As with the statements about Jesus as the good shepherd (10:7–18) and Jesus' danger-filled journey to save Lazarus (11:7–15), the language in these sayings goes from being divinely solemn and parabolic (v 24) to being more and more personal and plain. And, like those other texts, these three sayings (vv 24–26) refer not only to Jesus, to his fruitful self-giving in death, but also, with increasing clarity, to would-be disciples (cf. v 26; 11:11–15).

Insofar as these sayings deal with one of the most basic truths of the gospel, it is not surprising that they may be connected fairly easily with a wide variety of parables and sayings—in the OT, the synoptic gospels, the epistles, the rabbinic literature, and perhaps the mystery religions (Bultmann, 424–26; Brown, 471–75; Schnackenburg, 2:383–86). As an illustration of this widespread affinity, reference may be made, for instance, to Galatians. In that epistle Paul manages, often in what may seem at first sight to be an erratic manner, to establish his freedom from every earthly tie—from his mother, from his friend Barnabas, from the law, from church authorities, in fact, from every human being (Gal 1:10,15–24; 2:13–14). And he asserts his firm union, through the cross of Jesus, with God (Gal 1:2, 2:20–21). Thus he has died to all that is of this world and bases his life on union with God. But this death leads to greater life. In the later part of the epistle he shows that on the basis of detachment, of inner freedom and sureness of one's identity, one comes to a greater degree of care for others, thus to a greater degree of life (Gal 5:13–14,22; 6:1–2). The fourth gospel speaks more emphatically of life which is eternal, but eternal life is expressed here and now, in service and presence; and so in broad terms, both Galatians and John are speaking of the same dynamic of death leading to life.

The complementary principle is also true: clinging to life ("loving one's life," v 25) leads to destruction, to death. This refers especially to the refusal to move beyond a limited image of life, beyond a private reality, whatever form that limited reality may take, whether particular possessions or relationships (including structures), or particular ways of living, thinking, or imaging. Within that narrow world—anything from addictive pleasure to a superstitious theology—there is a certain security, and so a certain sense of life and vitality, but like the seed that will not die, such a soul remains alone, immobile, and it never comes to know all it might have been and what honor it might have received even from God. In Bultmann's words (425): "Life is of so peculiar a character, so completely eludes any desire to have it at our own disposal, that it is lost precisely when we desire to hold it fast, and it is won when we give it up."

Jesus Applies the Parabolic Principle to Himself (vv 27–28)

Then, in vv 27–28, Jesus goes from simply stating the principle to turning it into action. He is in profound distress ("Now is my soul troubled") and there is a temptation to turn back ("What shall I say, 'Father save me from this hour'?"— the question is rhetorical, yet it may also be read as a prayer to be spared). But he steadies himself and prays his way towards embracing his fate: "Father, glorify your name." And in response—to some degree as an illustration of what it means to be honored by the Father—there comes the voice from heaven.

The prayer that God's name be glorified is essentially a prayer that the fullness of God be revealed—God's "essence . . . holiness . . . inviolable will . . . mercy and love" (Schnackenburg, 2:387). It is a revelation which is to take place through Jesus' death and resurrection. In other words, it is his death-leading-to-resurrection which will show forth the nature and wonder of God.

But the showing forth of God is not limited to Jesus' death and resurrection. When the voice from heaven says, "I have glorified it and will glorify it again," the reference is very wide—back to the past and into the future. The past includes not only Jesus' entire ministry (cf. Brown, 476; Schnackenburg, 2:388) but also the fact that, as the expression of God's creative Word, Christ was in some way present in the old dispensation. As 12:41 expresses it, his glory was seen by Isaiah.

Thus, as Jesus embraces his fate, the Father whose voice we hear both looks back on all that he has already accomplished and forward to all that will be. It is like God's answering embrace, a resounding voice of encouragement as Jesus faces the final challenge.

Yet he did falter, at least momentarily. It is not as conspicuous as in the synoptic scene of the agony in the garden; on that occasion he asked unambiguously that he be spared (Mark 14:36 and parr.). But, as on no other occasion, except when close to the death of the beloved Lazarus (11:33), he was rattled (v 27).

When he recovers, as he does immediately, the basic effect is that the shadow of death is overtaken by the reasserted presence of glory. Thus the crisis passes, and he is once more ready to speak to others.

[12:29–36a] Reactions among people: The victory of Jesus provides salvation for all; It challenges people to decide and to accept the light.   Having shown Jesus' overcoming of the forces of fear, the text next focuses on "the crowd," on what Jesus' achievement means for them. Though they do not immediately understand him, there is nothing to indicate that they are hostile. Rather, like the perplexed Nicodemus and the woman of Samaria, they are struggling to figure out what is being said and what it means.

Their identity is not stated explicitly. When they are first mentioned (v 29) it would seem, given the context of the coming of the Greeks, that they are to be understood as representing Gentiles. And the fact that they interpret the heavenly voice as thunder or an angel—both interpretations seem inadequate—does nothing to discount that view. But when there is a further reference to "the crowd" (v 34), it is clear, given their reliance on the law, that they are Jewish. Thus "the crowd" is mentioned twice, first as apparently Gentile, then as apparently Jewish. The texts which follow both references are virtually equal in length and, as will be seen, are complementary in content. Thus, the twofold use of "the crowd" is a stylized way of referring to all those people, Jews and Gentiles, who hear of Jesus and wonder. Variations on this stylized presentation are found in the earlier references to "the great crowd" (12:9), and the twofold "crowd" (12:17–18). A further variation on this technique was noted in analyzing the beginning of the bread of life discourse (6:25–30): at first Jesus spoke as if to Gentiles (6:26–27), then as if to Jews (6:31–33). And, as already noted, the beginning of this later episode (12:20–22), when the Greeks approach Jesus, shows a profound intermingling of what is Gentile and Jewish. The crowd, therefore, is everybody. The fact that they are not explicitly named, and that the scene as a whole has almost no details of space and time, tends to make their role even more representative. They are the people of every time and place.

vv 29–33: Through Jesus' conquering of death and its fear,
the way is now open for all others
Jesus' first reply may be described as good news. The crowd did not understand what came from heaven; yet, as he says, it was not for him, but for them. In other words, what has just happened to him—his passage from fear to an awareness of the Father—is to happen to others.

And then he takes up the "now" which he had just applied to himself ("Now is my soul troubled'') and shows that it affects the world of the crowd: ''Now is the judgment of this world, now shall the ruler of this world be driven out; and I, when I am lifted up. . . .'' Like the ''now'' that brought trouble to his own soul, the other ''nows'' allude also to turbulence—the turbulence involved in showing up or judging those who refuse the message; and the turbulence of contending with the underlying cause of all evil, ''the ruler of this world''—Satanic darkness. In other words, when Jesus confronted darkness, when he was shaken by fear and death but managed nonetheless to keep a clear focus on God, in that moment the nature of evil was seen clearly (''judged''), and its supremacy was defeated.

More positively, Jesus speaks of an implied invitation: if lifted up from the earth he will draw all people to himself. The lifting up refers both to dying (on the cross, cf. v 33) and to ascending to God. Thus the seed which fell to the earth and died will be lifted up from the earth and will indeed bear much fruit. As in the bread of life discourse (6:44), ''drawing'' refers to a profound inner action upon the human heart. And ''all people'' has a sweeping universalism.

Thus to people everywhere who may be cowed by fear and death Jesus offers a strengthening vision: one need not be immobilized by the forces of darkness; rather one may be drawn, along with others, towards one who is above the earth.

Insofar as this text refers both to evil and then to universalism there is a further indication here of an idea that has already appeared elsewhere (cf. 8:44–47, 11:49–53): that ultimately the forces of evil are in some way turned to good account. Consequently, while there is indeed in the text a certain dichotomy or dualism, one which has overtones of Qumran and its doctrine of the two Spirits (see esp. Schnackenburg, 2:391; Lindars, 433), there is also a suggestion that ultimately the dualism is to be resolved and that, in principle, for those who will accept the fact, it is already resolved.

Yet the solution, though available, is not facile. At the end of Jesus' positive statement there is a telling note: that being lifted up referred to the way he would die (v 33). After the many intimations of death, beginning in 2:19–22, the spectre of what will actually happen now begins to appear. That I will die is one thing; that this is it is another. The allusion to crucifixion brings to center stage the pain of death, and its acts as a final reminder that it is through death that the vision is to be grasped.

vv 34–36a: Time is short. Instead of dreaming, people need to face
reality, accept the light, and thus become children of light
The crowd objects to accepting death. In contrast to what is said by Jesus, they propose the idea, based in the law or OT, of a Messiah who will abide ''forever.'' In a sense, ironically, they are right: Jesus will·eventually abide forever. But what they want is a splendid undying Messiah, someone of the kind suggested in the famous oracle of Isa 9:1–6, of whom it was said that his reign would last ''from now and forever'' (Isa 9:6). In other words, they want to circumvent death. And they question Jesus about what he means when he says it is necessary (*dei*—indicating providential necessity) that the Son of humanity be lifted up. Thus they bring to the fore the contrast between the idea of a spectacular unending

existence and that of a very human existence which is destined to die. To some degree they are still caught in an old unreal idea. Yet, insofar as they have pieced together various elements of what Jesus has said and have formed them into a leading question, they are making appropriate use of their capacities and are on the brink of a major insight and decision. With advancing understanding they then come to the question which was previously stated in chap. 9 (9:35–36): "Who is this Son of humanity?" It is a way of saying, "Who are you?" And it is also a way of asking, "What is a human being?"

To these people, hovering between an unreal dream and a courageous confrontation of reality, Jesus offers a challenge (vv 35–36): the light, far from lasting "forever," is with them but "a short time," and they must walk in that light, must make the most of it. If they do not, they are in danger of being overcome by darkness—the primordial danger referred to in 1:5—and so are in danger of not knowing where they are going. But while the light is there they can commit themselves to it ("believe in" it) and so finally become children of light. The short time refers first of all to the shortness of his own stay. It is therefore a challenge to seize the opportunity, to believe in him while he is there.

But this passage, which involves something of a synthesis of several leading texts (1:4–5; 8:12; 9:4–5; 11:9–10), would seem also to refer to a more general truth: for a short lifetime human beings are offered the light; and they may refuse it and thus end not knowing where they are going; or they may walk in it, and so enter a realm of trust in which they become children of light. The idea of walking in the light is not just intellectual; it is also moral (cf. Brown, 479), and so the challenge offered by Jesus asks not only that they use their wits but also that they commit the depths of their hearts. It is precisely because this involvement is so thorough that it provides an identity—that of being a particular kind of child. The phrase "sons of light" is used both in Qumran and by Paul (1 Thess 5:5, Eph 5:8), but what is more crucial to its meaning in chap. 12 is that the larger phrase "become children/sons of light" is a variation on the phrase which is at the heart of the prologue, that of "becoming children of God" (1:12). It is a phrase which, whatever its background, suggests a thorough serenity, and its connection with the prologue heightens it further.

The challenge is not exclusively individualistic; it includes an involvement with other people. In this passage as a whole (12:20–36a) there are no fewer than three references to Jesus as the Son of humanity (vv 23, 34)—a title which underlines his solidarity with every human being. This emphasis on solidarity is reinforced by the statement that his exaltation will draw all people (v 32).

The implication is that while Lazarus has disappeared, and the Greeks say no more, what they represent—the emergence of a new complex community—has been absorbed into the humanity-related figure of the Son of humanity.

What is being offered, therefore, is an invitation not only to enter into the mystery of Jesus' life-bearing death, and thus into the mystery of divine life itself, but also to find in that life a force which, like a light, draws people together.

Attractive as this may be, it is not easy. The leading verse (11:54) had suggested a quiet withdrawal to the desert, and Jesus' later statements (12:24, 27,

32–33) emphasize the need to face the full reality of death. Thus, in various ways, there is a demand both for letting go and for accepting.

The story does not say how the crowd reacted, whether they rose to the challenge. All that is known is that in similar circumstances, the formerly blind man had reacted positively (9:38). Now, in the absence of such a response, the challenge falls to the reader.

[12:36b–43] The providence of willful unbelief. As noted earlier, all of the three preceding scenes had begun with suggestions of people coming together, of people responding to Jesus or coming to him (vv 1–3, 12–13, 20–22).

But in this text (vv 36b-43) there is no movement or meeting, except of a negative kind—Jesus goes away and hides (v 36b). Part of the idea in this image is that, when shut out by disbelief, God seems to go away (cf. Rom 1:24,26,28). And the text as a whole is concerned not with any meeting of minds but with the refusal to meet—with unbelief, above all with the agonizing question of the unbelief of the Jews.

The primary concern of the passage is not with the human side of unbelief, with why it is that people reject God's call in Jesus. Such an analysis, including a picture of Jesus going into hiding, has already been given (cf. esp. 5:36–47; 8:31–47,59), and it left no doubt about the full involvement of the human will (5:40; 8:44). That aspect is now taken for granted, and it is reinforced by the reference to the fact that even though Jesus' signs were so many, people still did not believe (v 37).

The concern here is with the relationship of unbelief to God's providence. The main idea would seem to be that "unbelief is a part of the divine economy of salvation and does not surprise or frustrate God's redemptive efforts" (Kysar, 202). This does not mean that God wills unbelief—as already noted, unbelief comes from the human will—but that God works around it, so to speak, and maintains providence.

Part of the problem is that while the human will is responsible for unbelief, the human will alone is not capable of belief. In Kysar's words (202), "faith is more than human will." Thus while human willing is decisive, there is a further element, divine, which is also decisive. The discussion at this point touches central theological dimensions concerning the interaction of God and free will. Rather than enter into these questions—they seem insoluble—it seems best simply to say that at this point the evangelist's main concern is with the divine element.

To indicate how the divine element operates in this case, how providence encompasses human unbelief, the evangelist draws on Isaiah. The actual name "Isaiah" is mentioned three times, and the triple reference forms a crescendo effect.

In passing, a subtle question of structure may be mentioned. It was noted earlier that this scene scarcely contains the twofold structure of the earlier scenes at Bethany and Jerusalem (vv 1–19)—a limpness of form that may perhaps be connected to limpness of content, in other words to the scene's emphasis on human failure. Yet its reference to Isaiah is threefold—an element of structure which connects it with the strong and climactic scene of Jesus relating powerfully to humanity (vv 20–28). This curious blending of diverse aspects of structure, one weak and the other strong, may, perhaps, be a reflection of a blending of diverse elements of content—the weak element of human unbelief and the strong element of God's encompassing providence.

The first idea in the crescendo (vv 37–38), one which is illustrated by the fact that a text concerning unbelief (Isa 51:1, "Lord, who has believed? . . .") had to be fulfilled, is that unbelief was foreseen. It might even be said to have been prophetically decreed; in Brown's words (483), "The prophecy brought about the unbelief."

The second idea (vv 39–40), illustrated by "[God] has blinded their eyes . . ." (Isa 6:10), is that God has allowed the unbelief, and in a certain sense has caused it. To say that God caused it is a simplification, however, for it does not take account of human willfulness; and God caused human ill-will only insofar as God did not somehow prevent it. As Hoskyns (429) comments, though the passage looks like a crude statement of predestination, it is not so. Instead of being read in the light of later theological controversies, it should be read in the context of the basic ideas of John: the Jews could have accepted Jesus, however, in view of the OT, the fact that they did not is not surprising. The evangelist has expressed teaching concerning divine foresight in a way which indicates "the inevitability of that which is foreseen." The fact that the Jews could have believed is highlighted by the statement, which follows closely, that many of them, in fact, did do so (v 42).

The third idea (v 41) is that the phenomenon of unbelief is ultimately part of the process of manifesting God's glory—for it was in the context of seeing the glory of God in Jesus that Isaiah spoke of unbelief.

Reactions (vv 42–43).   Having spoken of the initiative of God or Jesus, the text then goes on, as it does in the three preceding episodes, to recount a human action or reaction (vv 42–43; cf. 9–11, 17–19, 29–36a). It tells of the fact that, contrary to appearances, from among the rulers "many believed"; but because of the Pharisees, lest they be put out of the synagogue, they did not confess it. And the same reason is operative as in their original refusal—love of human glory rather than of the glory of God (v 43, cf. 5:41–44).

Much as this text (vv 36b–43) contrasts with all three preceding scenes (in vv 1–36a), it contrasts in a particular way with the coming to Jerusalem (vv 12–19). The contrast involves many details, but the most central factor is that while the entry to Jerusalem was a moment of meeting and revelation, the hiding is a moment of departure and darkness.

[12:44–50] Epilogue: the implications of belief and unbelief in Jesus' Godoriented mission   (a reformulation of the prologue and of the Nicodemus scene into a statement of the two ways). Just as, at the beginning of chaps 1–12, the prologue stands somewhat apart and summarizes much of what is to come, so at the end there is a proclamation, an epilogue, which, in another manner, stands apart and summarizes the message. It is an epilogue which reflects the fact that in a certain sense the basic account of Jesus' life is over; he has already spoken as if from beyond death, from glory (12:20–36a), and what follows (chaps. 13–21) is largely focused on the central mystery of the Passover.

While the prologue is so formulated that it leads the reader into the story (''In the beginning . . .'') these final verses are shaped in such a way that they press the reader to come to a decision. More elaborately than the prologue, they highlight the contrast between ''the one who believes in me'' (v 44) and ''the one who rejects me'' (v 48). The one who believes in Jesus sees the Father and does not abide in darkness (vv 45–46; cf. vv 49–50); but the one who rejects Jesus is condemned (v 48). It is appropriate therefore to regard this text as including a variation on the idea of the two ways.

This idea of two ways appears explicitly or implicitly as the conclusion of several texts—the discourses of Moses (Deut 11:26–28; 30:15–20; re Deut 18:18–19 and John 12:48–50, see Boismard, 1988, 12–14); the Sermon on the Mount (Matt 7:24–27); the missionary discourse to the seventy (Luke 10:16); and some earlier discourses in John (3:20–21,36; see the introductory comment on 8:48–59). It is not surprising then that a variation on the two ways idea should be incorporated into the conclusion of chaps. 1–12.

That the final proclamation stands apart is agreed upon by all commentators. As Wikenhauser (240) notes, it is given no specific time or place or audience. But despite many suggestions to the contrary, it is not alien. As is shown particularly by Schnackenburg's discussion with Boismard (Schnackenburg, 2:420–21), there is no strong evidence for invoking the intervention of a later editor. On the contrary, once its role is understood, it may be seen to be an integral part of the text. It is like the earlier revelatory ''cries'' of John in the prologue (1:15) and of Jesus at Tents (7:28,37), and its apartness heightens its ability to speak to all ages.

When it is first examined it is found, above all, to echo the discourses of chap. 3, especially that to Nicodemus (3:16–21, cf. 3:34–36; cf. Boismard, 1961, 507–14; Schneider, 238; Brown, 147, 490). The challenge which is put before Nicodemus, to choose between light and darkness, between salvation and judgment, is reformulated to become a challenge to the reader. Actually, even in chap. 3 the challenge has a certain timelessness—in 3:16–21 Nicodemus has faded into the background and the words of Jesus are becoming addressed to everybody—but at the end of chap. 12 the open challenge is more obvious. The reader might have shrugged off the implications of the Nicodemus scene, but not so here.

As well as issuing a Nicodemus-related challenge, the concluding proclamation also ''takes up the message of the prologue'' (Schnackenburg, 2:425). It speaks of the light coming into the world to free people from darkness (v 46; 1:4–5, 8–9), of faith-based communication with God (v 44; 1:12–13), and finally of Jesus as expressing faithfully the word (*logos*) which is spoken by the Father (vv 48–50; 1:1,14,18). Thus ''chaps. 1–12 end . . . much as they started—with the claim that Jesus is the Word of God, and he has been the Word of God by constantly obeying the Father's will'' (Kysar, 204).

As seen earlier, in examining 2:23–3:21, the prologue and the Nicodemus scene are inherently connected. The first depicts God's descent to humanity and the second the challenging possibility of humanity's ascent to God. What one finds in the closing proclamation is a blending of aspects of both. There is a challenge which is set in the context of Jesus being the down-to-earth expression of the *logos* of God.

It is because this final cry is a challenge, a decision-provoking statement of two possible ways, that it speaks of judgment. Jesus did not come to judge, but in bringing God's gift of salvation he inevitably provoked a distinction, a judgment, between those who accepted it and those who did not (47–48; 3:17–18). Refusal has a condemnatory effect—it deprives one of salvation both immediately (realized eschatology) and in the long term ("on the last day"—final eschatalogy, v 48). The two eschatologies are intertwined (Brown, 491).

The more basic emphasis of this final cry, however, is not on judgment but on salvation. Like someone who from a great distance shouts aloud that he has found the way, Jesus cries out that he can provide the way to God—to healing and life. For it is about God ultimately that he is talking and not about himself: "whoever believes in me believes not in me but in the one who sent me" (v 44). It is thus that he begins in this passage, and it is with a similar emphasis that he ends: what he says comes not from himself but from the one who sent him, the Father (v 49–50). Believing is seeing, and what is seen above all is not Jesus but God (v 45). In the words of Hoskyns (430):

> Christian faith is not a cult of Jesus; it is faith in God (13:20; Matt 10:40; Luke 9:48; 1 Thess 1:9). Faith therefore does not rest in Jesus, but in the Father who sent Him and commissioned Him. There cannot, moreover, be two objects of faith or of sight.

THE COMMENTARY: BOOK TWO
PART 3B: THE CENTRAL MYSTERY
PASSOVER

John's gospel falls into two main parts, two "books" (chaps. 1–12 and 13–21) and, as indicated in the introduction (chapter 5), these may be designated "The Flow of Years (The Life of Jesus)" and "The Central Mystery (Passover)." Book One tells the life of Jesus, and it does so in such a way that, at one level, it includes the essential elements of his death and resurrection (see esp. commentary on 11:54–chap. 12). Thus it has a certain completeness; it narrates his entire life.

Book Two has a distinct interest. By concentrating on Jesus' final Passover (something already mentioned in 11:55 and 12:1; cf. 12:20) it stands back as it were from the flow of time and focusses on the central mystery—the Passover mystery which contains the essence of biblical revelation.

The text consists of three parts:

- Chaps.13–17, the last discourse, reveals the central message.
- 18:1–19:16a, the arrest and trial, reveals even amid evil.
- 19:16b-chap. 21, the glorification, reveals the working out of the message.

The Last Discourse

A Unified Portrayal of Three Stages of Spiritual
Development Based on God's Loving Action as Expressed
in Jesus' Death and Resurrection

Introduction and the Debate Concerning Unity

These five chapters have a unique appeal. Here the deeds and words of Jesus reach a new level of calm intensity, and this shared quality lends to the entire text a certain unity.

This general unity of quality is reinforced by a unity of setting: within John's gospel these five chapters are placed in the context of Jesus' final supper and as such they stand out clearly from all that precedes and follows.

Furthermore, there is general agreement among researchers that in writing this account the evangelist made use of a specific literary convention, "the well-established literary pattern of attributing to famous men farewell speeches delivered before death'' (Brown, 598; see Cortès, 1976). Examples or partial examples of this convention may be found not only in Greco-Roman literature (cf. Stauffer, 1950, 29–30) but also in the OT, particularly in the stories of Jacob (Genesis 48–49) and Joshua (Joshua 23–24), and, above all, in the story of Moses (Deuteronomy 31–33; see Lacomara, 1974). There is some evidence of it also in other areas of the NT, for instance, in Paul's farewell to the Ephesian elders (Acts 20:17–38) and in the suggestions of final farewells which are found in 2 Timothy 3–4 (esp. 4:1–8) and in 2 Peter (esp. 1:12–15). The writing of such speeches was particularly noticeable in the intertestamental period (see esp. *Testaments of the Twelve Patriarchs* and *Jubilees*), and, in some of the accounts, one of the features of the farewell is a meal (*Jub* 35:27, 36:17; *Testament of Naphtali* 1:2). This latter element, together with the well-established elements of words of farewell and a final blessing or prayer, provides a precedent for the basic contents of John 13–17: a meal, words of farewell, and the concluding prayer (chap. 17).

The fact that a writer followed this literary convention does not in itself decide the question of historicity. That depends on the quality of the sources and the way they were used. Even if the person in question made no such speech before dying, the attributed discourse could reflect accurately the person's character or earlier speeches. What the convention sought was a dramatic synthesis—to distill the essence of the person's thought and, by setting it at the memorable time of death, to impart it strikingly to later generations. Such discourses, therefore, had a dramatic unity, and the fact that John 13–17, with the meal, farewell, and prayer, follows that convention, provides additional evidence of these chapters' unity.

There is further general agreement that within chaps. 13–17 there are two fundamental points of division: at the end of chap. 14, when Jesus (having said "Arise . . .") begins what seems almost like a new discourse (chaps. 15–16); and at the beginning of chap. 17 when Jesus lifts up his eyes and begins a further new form of discourse, the prayer.

But there the agreement ends, and there has been a major debate about whether, despite some overall interrelatedness, chaps. 13–17 can really be regarded as a unity. The problem is not one of sources (though it is sometimes confused with it); like a well-written article, a text may be based on dozens of different sources and still be a well-wrought unity. The issue rather has to do with the finished product: is the present text a coherent whole or is it rather a composite, a text in which parts have been placed together by editorial efforts, which, whatever their fidelities and intentions, were never fully coordinated? The problem of editorial insertions refers not only to particular verses but to three whole chapters—chaps. 15–17. As Bultmann (459) sees it, "chs. 15–17 are left in mid-air. . . . The conclusion is unavoidable that [these] chs. are either a secondary insertion, or they are not in their right place."

Many other researchers have taken a similar position (cf. esp. Brown, 582–86; Schnackenburg, 3:4, 123–24). And, largely on the basis of a comparison of John 13–17 with 1 John, it has been proposed by Becker (1970) and Segovia (1982, 96–131) that it is an editor who has inserted 13:34–35 and 15:1–16:15. (For a review of opinions on the structure of chaps. 13–17, see Simoens, 1981, 1–51.)

The main reasons for holding that the text is composite are as follows:

1. At the end of the chapter 14, the words of Jesus, especially "Arise, let us go from here" (14:31), seem to give the impression that the discourse has ended, but then he goes on talking for three more chapters, and it is only in 18:1, which could blend smoothly with 14:31, that he actually departs. The three chapters therefore seem to be an awkward secondary intrusion.

2. Much of what is said in 16:4b–33 repeats what had been said earlier in 13:31–14:31 (for details, see Brown, 589–91), and such repetition may be seen as reflecting the presence of two distinct discourses, the second of which is an editorial addition.

3. Between chaps. 13–14 and 15–17 there are apparent contradictions. In particular, Peter asks, "Lord, where are you going?" (13:36), but in 16:5 Jesus says "None of you asks me, 'Where are you going?'"

4. Some of the material in chaps. 15–17 seems to have no necessary connection with the theme of the last supper—that of Jesus' departure. This is particularly true of the image of the vine (15:1). It speaks not of departure, but of union.

5. There is apparent variety of theological outlook, something seen most clearly in the varied expectations about the mode of Jesus' return and presence. It would also seem to be seen in the fact that, with regard to the world, the Paraclete is first seen as inactive (14:17) but later as active (16:8–11).

Despite the weight of these objections, other writers see in chaps. 13–17 a text which, whatever its tensions, is carefully coordinated. Yves Simoens (1981,

52–80), for instance, has argued that these chapters constitute a single chiastic structure, centered on the idea of love as found in 15:12–17. Even though Simoens's complex structure has been criticised as being too rigid (see esp. Lamouille, 1982), the essence of his thesis seems insightful (Lamouille, 1982; Cahill, 1983). It is with a double use of the word "love" that chaps. 13–17 begin and conclude (cf. 13:1 and 17:26), and within that striking framework it makes sense that the text as a whole should be centered, even in terms of its structure, on love.

It is necessary, however, as Lamouille (1982, 629) and Cahill (1983, 710) indicate, to move beyond such chiastic or concentric studies and to seek other aspects of the text, particularly its linear progression. It is also necessary to engage directly the arguments against unity. To do all this however, it is first necessary to make a positive proposal.

Chapters 13–17 As Reflecting Three Stages of Discipleship

The proposal made here is that the three fundamental divisions within chapters 13–17 (13–14, 15–16, 17) reflect three advancing stages of discipleship, of spiritual development. Thus, while one of the basic ideas of the gospel as a whole is to evoke the advancing stages of maturity, from youth to death, chaps. 13–17 focus on the fact that, whatever one's age, there is an ideal of advancing through different stages of spiritual development. And these stages capture the essence of the biblical revelation, the essence of the encounter between God and humanity.

The fact that the discourse deals with advancing discipleship does not mean that it is unconcerned with Jesus' departure, with his death-and-resurrection. It is thus concerned; in fact, it provides an analysis of the enigmatic Passover event ("the Passover mystery"). But it so depicts Jesus' departure as to highlight the implications for the believer. And it uses the language of departure-and-return to indicate a process of internal loss and gain. This is particularly true in chaps. 14 and 16. The sense of disturbance and sadness which accompanies the loss of the familiar physical Jesus is used as a way of referring to painful aspects of spiritual experience—to the way in which the advancing disciple must let go of much that is easy and familiar, in a sense let go of life itself. And the return of Jesus to the disciples, his coming so that they see him, likewise has a reference to a spiritual experience. As mentioned earlier, "seeing Jesus [in 16:16–23a] has been reinterpreted to mean the continued experience of his presence in the Christian" (Brown, 730); "To 'see Jesus' is essentially to experience him as indwelling" (Schneiders, 1975, 635).

Thus the text has two levels: a historical or historylike level which tells of Jesus' actions and words; and a theological level which explores the stages of discipleship. Furthermore, it is the theological level which determines the structure of the text. In other words, what Schnackenburg (3:6) says of 13:1–30 is true of the entire discourse: "The whole presentation is subject to . . . theological thought."

The theological truth in question is that the death and resurrection of Jesus open up for the believer a profound realm of the spirit, a place where, if the believer is faithful, there is advancing intimacy with God. In other words, while Paul speaks of Jesus' death-and-resurrection as taking place, in a sense, within the believer, and as thus opening a realm of spirit and of union with God (e.g. Romans 5–8, esp. 6:1–11; chap. 8; Col 3:1–4), so John brings the death-and-resurrection down to earth, into the believer's experience, and he explores, in a concrete way, the nature of that spiritual realm.

The proposal that chaps. 13–17 are concerned with discipleship as something which advances does not exclude the possibility that these chapters are also concerned with other aspects of discipleship. Discipleship may be seen, for instance, as having both an outside aspect (as being oriented towards perceiving the outside world and learning from it) and an inside aspect (as listening to what is within a person, especially to the inner spirit). And this distinction may perhaps be a factor in the distinction between chaps. 13–14 and chaps. 15–16. At least the outside/inside distinction has a role in later chapters (see introduction to 18:1–19:16a, under the heading "Two dramas of revelation and rejection," and the more tentative comments which introduce 19:16b–chap. 21).

The Divine Initiative

However much the text emphasizes the believer, there is no suggestion that it is on the believer that spiritual advancement ultimately depends. The believer's co-operation is indeed essential, but the initiative comes from God; and it is the loving action of God, manifested in Jesus' death-and-resurrection, which guides the movement of the text.

This divine action is of three basic kinds—cleansing (chap. 13), purifying (chap. 15), and sanctifying (chap. 17). The initial process, God's loving cleansing of the believer, is illustrated dramatically in Jesus' washing of the feet (13:1–20). The next stage, one which involves a radical departure from past habits, is that in which the believer, now joined to Jesus as a branch to its vine, is pruned or purified by a loving parentlike God ("the Father," 15:1–10). The final stage—in which the emphasis is not so much on a break with the past as on a coming to union with God, to a certain vision of God—is that in which the Father, the holy one ("Holy Father . . .") makes the believer also to be holy (sanctified/consecrated, 17:6–19).

That the ideas of cleansing and purifying have a leading role is reasonably clear. The texts from which they come, the foot-washing and the parable of the true vine, are set strikingly at the beginning of their respective chapters.

The situation in chap. 17 is different. The idea of consecrating or making holy does indeed seem to be the key process which is described in the text—so much so that Westcott (236), Hoskyns (494), and Beasley-Murray (291) all refer to the entire chapter simply as "The Consecration Prayer" or "The Prayer of Consecration." But, unlike chaps. 13 and 15, this key process is emphasized not at the beginning of the chapter but towards its conclusion, particularly at the conclusion of the major central section (cf. 17:17–19). This reversal, this move of the pivotal action to the end of the chapter, is surprising. But it makes sense. It reflects the fact that in chap. 17 the sense of closeness to the transcendent God, the God who consecrates, is primarily at the end of the chapter rather than at its beginning. (In chaps. 13 and 15, both of which imply a process of descent, the sense of the transcendent God is primarily at the beginning.) Thus the three actions—of washing, purifying, and making holy—all come from the transcendent God. But while chaps. 13 and 15 evoke this God at the beginning of their respective texts, chap. 17 does so at the end.

That the ideas of cleansing, purifying, and making holy stand in literary and theological continuity is corroborated by various affinities between the texts. For instance, while the foot-washing uses the phrase "you are clean" (*katharos*, 13:10–11), the parable of the vine, in the context of speaking of the way in which a vine is pruned or cleansed (*kathairō*, 15:2) repeats the phrase. It also develops the central idea: it attributes the cleansing to the word: "You are already clean (*katharos*) because of the *word* which I have spoken to you" (15:3).

The final process, that of making holy (chap. 17), does not repeat any of the vocabulary of cleansing—such concepts belong to the preliminary stages—but it retains and further develops the emphasis on the word: "Make them holy in truth; your *word* is truth" (17:17). Thus, in subtly changing ways, the "word" is associated with all three—cleansing, purifying, and sanctifying. Other aspects of the continuity between these texts may be found, for instance, in Swank (1965, 46, esp. on 13:10 and 15:3) and in Forestell (1974, 155–57, on all three).

The essential point is that through chapters 13, 15, and 17 the discourse portrays, on the part of God and God's incarnate word, a threefold initiative, and it is this initiative which carries the believer into the realm of the spirit.

The Communitarian Aspect

The foregoing triple process does not cause the believer to retreat into a private spiritual world; it does not isolate the individual. Though a certain element of retreat into the spirit remains necessary, the basic impulse of the threefold divine initiative is to bring the individual farther and farther into community, into some form of love and unity with other people. The shape of that community is not specified, and in following the divine impulse it may be necessary to leave one form of community to develop another, but the orientation towards other people, ultimately towards all people, is basic to the text.

It begins in chap. 13 when, following the discussion with Peter, Jesus tells the disciples that, as he has washed their feet, so they are to wash one another's feet (13:14). His action implies "a radically new order of human relationships" (Schneiders, 1981, 87), and it is in the wake of this implication that he goes on to impart the new commandment of love (13:34–35).

Likewise, chap. 15. When Jesus speaks of purifying (15:2–3), he does so in the context of the vine, a symbol closely related to the idea of a whole people, community, or church (Brown, 670; Schnackenburg, 3:108). And he then repeats the commandment of love—but in a heightened form, that of love unto death (15:12–13).

Finally, in chapter 17, the process of making holy, far from leading to isolation, is closely linked to unity. In fact, the very first mention of the word "holy" leads to the idea of unity (17:11, *"Holy* father, keep them in your name . . . that they may be *one"*). The later explicit emphasis on holiness introduces a similar emphasis on unity—a unity which implies some ideal of community (Brown, 778), and which is so described, in Jesus' prayer, that it speaks to the whole world and involves a further variation on the commandment of love (Schnackenburg, 3:190–91). It is with love, in fact, and with intensifying images of eternal togetherness, that the whole discourse both begins and ends (13:1, 3; and, with more people, 17:24–26).

Thus the three-stage divine initiative leads the believer more and more deeply into the realm of the spirit and into (comm)unity.

This blending of the individual with the community may help to explain why, as the discourse develops, individual disciples become less intrusive. In chaps. 13–14 several disciples speak, and some are named. In chaps, 15–16, they rarely speak, and they are never named. And in chap. 17 there are neither names nor intrusions. In 19:16b–chap. 21 a further, complementary, phenomenon may be observed: against the background of the formed community, there is an increasing emphasis on individuals. Thus, the later text (19:16b–chap. 21) provides a counterpoint to chaps. 13–17.

The Human Point of View: The Believer's Experience and Response

The emphasis in chaps. 13, 15, and 17 on the triple divine initiative is balanced, in chaps. 14, 16, and 17 by an emphasis on how the process is experienced from the human point of view. Thus while chap. 13 describes a divine washing, the first effect of which is to impart to a person a form of God-given radiance or cleanliness ("clean all over," 13:10), chap. 14 shows people, in the context of Jesus' departure and return, as trying to discern, first in Jesus (14:1–11), and then in themselves (14:12–24), how the divine is present and how, with the Spirit's help, to cooperate actively to make the divine more present.

And while chap. 15 (cf. 15:1–10, the parable of the true vine) describes a more intense form of divine activity and a more developed form of divine union, chap. 16 (cf. 16:4b–24) shows people, again in the context of Jesus' departure and return, as cooperating, with ever greater help from the Spirit, in arriving at a new stage of insight (16:4b–15) and then, through a painful birthlike process, as reaching a breakthrough in seeing Jesus, in other words, a breakthrough in awareness of the divine (16:16–24).

Finally, in chap. 17 there is a combined picture of divine initiative and human response. The spiralling text which builds towards the divine process of sanctification (17:1–19) contains within it, at the beginning of its second part (17:6–10), a dense picture of human cooperation: "they have kept . . . they know . . . they have received . . . they have believed." In fact, 17:6–10 "contains, in a compressed form, the whole Johannine theology of revelation and the community of salvation" (Schnackenburg, 3:174–75), and part of that compressed picture is the emphasis on human cooperation. The activity which had been mentioned in chap. 16 is surpassed. Thus the process of coming, Spirit-led, to the truth (16:12–15, "The Spirit of truth . . . will announce . . . all whatsoever") appears in 17:6–

10 to be further advanced ("Now they know that all whatsoever you have given me is from you . . .").

The combining of the two sets of actions, divine and human, into a single culminating prayer, would seem to be a way of expressing, through the literary shaping of the text, what the discourse is all about—the increasing union of the divine and the human, to the point where the two blend prayerfully into one.

Thus, in simplified terms, the discourse consists of two diptychs and a single synthesizing prayer.

Relationship to the World

As a result of the fact that the believer's relationship with God changes, there is also a change in the believer's relationship with the world, particularly with the world in its negative sense as something which harbors evil. Such a result is inevitable; one cannot come closer to God without changing one's relationship both to everything that is evil and to everything in the world which tends to set itself in God's place. And the discourse has several references to everything and everyone who in various ways contend against God's love—in particular, the devil (13:2), Satan (13:27), Judas (13:2,26), "the ruler of this world" (14:30) and, with great frequency, "the world" (see esp. 15:18–27). To some degree all these factors blend into one another and constitute a single challenge to God.

In accordance with the three stages, the believer relates to the world in three distinct ways. At first (13:1–20) the believer and the world's evil are intermingled, and the task is to drive out the root of the evil. The foot-washing scene, however much it reflects God's far-reaching love, is shadowed by several references to the presence of the devil and the betrayer (13:2,10,18). Unlike Judas, Peter manages to take the foot-washing to heart, but he has problems in doing so, and his hesitation and confusion are indications of the extent to which his thoughts had been those of the world, almost those of the devil.

In the second stage (15:1–16:4a), when the root of the evil has been driven out and God is purifying the believer, there is a certain withdrawal from the world, a painful struggle to be free from all that chains the heart, and this withdrawal or confrontation is indicated dramatically by a bold literary procedure: within 15:1–16:4a there is not just one major flow of action (as with the cleansing in 13:1–20 and the making holy in chap. 17); rather there are two—the purifying action of God (15:1–17) and the hating action of the world (15:18–16:4a). In other words, a key function of the picture of the world's hatred is to highlight the idea that in following Christ, in drawing close to God, one must go through a stage of letting go of the world, a stage of separation, and one must place one's roots where they truly belong—in God. The world, feeling challenged or spurned, tends to feel resentment, and from this comes an antipathy, a hatred.

In the third stage (chap. 17), when one's identity in God has been firmly established, there is a return to the world—not as something to be either exploited or idolized, but as something in which, despite its evil, one works for faith and understanding (chap. 17, esp. 17:11,15,21,23).

Practical Effects: the Conclusions

At the conclusion of each major passage, each portrayal of action, there is a picture of practical effects, of what the action implies for real life. In each case this down-to-earth picture is introduced by the word *tauta*, "these things" (cf. 13:21–38; 14:25–31; 15:11–17; 16:1–4a; 16:25–33; chap. 17, as usual, is exceptional).

It would also seem that in each case the text may be divided in two. The striking account of the foot-washing, with all the divine love which it suggests, is followed by two complementary scenes, each of which introduces an arresting picture of what God's love (in Jesus) implies: the appearance, for the first time in the gospel, of the figure of the beloved disciple (cf. 13:21–30); and the imparting of the new commandment of mutual love (cf. 13:31–38). In other words, the result of God's human-shaped love is first that people realize they are beloved (vv 21–30) and then that they love one another (vv 31–38). There are, of course, many other things going on in these two texts, particularly in the threatening pictures of Satan-related betrayal and denial. But the mainstream of chap. 13, the central momentum which holds it together and which sets all of chaps. 13–17 in motion, that mainstream is the flow of divine love which issues in the beloved and in mutual love.

In chap. 14, which is essentially a portrayal of the human being trying to respond to all this, trying to see and admit the divine presence, there is a related twofold conclusion: first, there is a picture of spirit-based peace (14:25–27b), and then there is a picture of all that threatens that peace (14:27c–31). Thus just as the picture of God's love in chap. 13 is threatened to the very end by Satan-related betrayal and denial, so in chap. 14 the believer's loving response and the resulting spirit-based peace are under threat. The overall picture, therefore, in chaps. 14–15—and it is a picture which advances slightly from one chapter to the next—is of the development of a love, or of a love-related peace, which is present but threatened.

In 15:1–16:4a the same two components, love and threat (hostility), are again present in the concluding texts, but since 15:1–16:4a is composed of distinct parts (15:1–10 and 15:18–27), so, correspondingly, the concluding components are distinct and apart (love in 15:11–17 and threat or hostility in 16:1–4a).

Within 15:1–17, therefore, with its picture of God's care-filled but deeply probing action (the purifying of the vine) the conclusion consists of the picture of deepened love (15:11–17). Thus, just as God's action in purifying (15:1–10) goes deeper than did the initial action of washing (13:1–10), so also the resulting love (15:11–17) is deeper than that which followed the washing (13:21–38). Where 13:31–38 had referred to mutual love, 15:11–14 speaks of a mutual love which goes even as far as death. And while 13:21–30 had spoken of a beloved who asks the Lord a question, 15:15–17 suggests a friendship which in some ways is deeper and more explicit: the disciples are friends who have already been told everything.

Within 15:18–16:4a, with its picture of the world's hatred, the rather general picture of hatred and persecution (15:18–27) is followed in the conclusion by a picture of dire practical results—expulsion and death (16:1–4a). Again there appears to be a certain intensification of chap. 13, this time of its negative side: the earlier formation of a devil-inspired intention to betray (13:2,11,18) has been replaced now by what seems to be a more intense personal hatred (15:18–20), and the conclusion which shows Judas as expelling himself, so to speak, with a view to deathly betrayal (cf. 13:21–30), has given way to a conclusion which speaks of inflicting expulsion on others and of personally killing them (16:1–3).

In 16:4b–33, where it is presupposed that the believer is experiencing both intensified divine care and intense antagonism in relation to the world, and where the believer's response consists first of the Spirit-led discernment of the truth (16:4b–15) and then of a painful new birth (16:16–24), there is a further conclusion, which again is in two parts and which again contains a variation on the elements of love and threat. In the love-related text (16:25–28) the essential picture is of a breakthrough to union with a loving, parentlike God, "the Father." In the threat-like text (16:29–33) there is the image of being scattered and of being left quite alone. These final texts have several affinities with the texts at the end of chap. 14, but again they appear more developed, more intense. In particular, instead of experiencing what the Father sends (the spirit-based peace, 14:25–27b), the believer now receives the Father's love directly (16:26–27). What has been achieved, therefore, is a new proximity to God's very self. Even amid the picture of being left alone amid the distress of the world (16:29–33) there is a reminder that in the last analysis what is negative does not win; one is not alone and beaten. On the contrary, as Jesus' words suggest, the distress of the world, though very real, has been overcome, and in the presence of the Father there is a deep peace. Hence the final phrase: "I have defeated the world."

In chap. 17 the fundamental love–threat conflict has been largely resolved and partly for this reason apparently, there is no such double-edged conclusion. The general emphasis is on sanctifying what has already been united to God, and the conclusion, such as it is, consists of a picture of ultimate unity and love (17:20–26).

What emerges from a study of the various conclusions of chaps. 13–17 is a gradual disentangling of the forces of good and evil. At first (13:21–30) when all recline together and when the betrayer could be almost anybody (13:21–30), good and evil seem very interwoven. It is difficult, just from a literary point of view, to find the division in the text. But in the very next scene (13:31–38) a division is reasonably clear: the commandment to mutual love is quite distinct from the foretelling of Peter's denial.

By the time one reaches 15:1–16:4a, the two are not only distinct, they are well separated—the good in 15:11–17, the evil in 16:1–4a.

Finally, in chap. 17, there is a sense in which evil has been left aside. One might even say, on the basis of the last phrase of chap. 16 ("I have conquered/defeated the world") that, from one point of view, evil has been defeated. One lives in the midst of the world, yet at another level one's life is in God.

Thus it is in the conclusions particularly that one perceives a reflection of what the discourse as a whole is about—Jesus' God-oriented battle against evil and the believer's consequent journey to God.

Eschatology

The journey to God is ultimately a journey into the future, a journey which concludes in the eternal abodes of God's house. It is to this end that Jesus is going (13:1–3), and it is to this end also, in order to be fully with Jesus, that the believers are traveling (14:1–3; 17:24–26). In other words, these three references, placed strategically at the beginnings of the opening diptych and at the end of the final prayer, provide for the journey a broad framework of future eschatology.

But in the last analysis the nature of the final union with God is unknown, and what the evangelist wants to explore is the process by which one comes to union with God here and now. Thus, while maintaining a future-oriented framework, the essential emphasis is on "realized" eschatology, on the journey which takes place in the present.

A Spirit-oriented Last Discourse

What the evangelist has done is adapt the literary convention of a last discourse towards a spiritual goal. Instead of emphasizing the meal—one of the conventional elements of a last discourse—he has taken what might be a detail in the meal account, the preparatory washing of feet, and, placing it *during* the meal, has given it a major role. "It forms [the meal's] focal point" (Schnackenburg, 3:46). This role is spiritual; for though the pouring of the water may be seen as a simple factual process, the context is such—both the context of the gospel as a whole and the context of chapters 13–17 (including the purifying, 15:1–10; the sanctifying, 17:11–19; and the conversation with Peter, 13:6–11)—that the water has overtones of a significance which is clearly spiritual. What the water evokes is the pouring forth of Jesus' love, ultimately of the saving love of God. And having given the discourse that orientation, the evangelist completes the convention with the spirit-oriented farewell and the prayer.

The result is something akin to the account of the woman at the well (4:1–42). In that case the standardized betrothal account was introduced with a strong emphasis on Jesus' giving of spirit-related water, and then the account as a whole was turned into a form of spiritual betrothal. The woman, struggling to rise, went in rapid time through a spiritual progression or journey. In chaps. 13–17, with equal literary originality and theological insight, a further kind of journey is spelled out in greater detail.

The idea that faithful believers go through a threefold progression would seem to be borne out by subsequent experience. The French spiritual analyst, Joseph de Guilbert (1877–1942), for instance, speaks of three stages—*quiet, union,* and *transforming union*—stages which to some degree correspond to the gospel's threefold progression (de Guilbert, 1954; for discussion, see W. Johnston, 1974, 68–79). "Quiet" refers to a state of recollection, a state which is dependent on a rather surprising wave of the divine presence (cf. John 13–14). "Union" is a state in which the person is intensely united to God and in which "one is asleep as regards the world" (W. Johnston, 1974, 70; cf. John 15–16). In "transforming union," the stage which Teresa of Avila refers to as "spiritual marriage" (1961),

212–18) the intense union becomes a calm plateau. There is now "a great freedom to act and to work and to love. This in some ways resembles the Zen 'return to the marketplace,' a stage in which the enlightened person comes back to ordinary life to redeem all sentient beings" (W. Johnston, 1974, 72; cf. the consecrated return to the world in John 17).

A Reconsideration of the Objections to Unity

1. In discussing the perplexing "Arise, let us go . . . ." (14:31) the first thing that needs to be said is that the editorial hypothesis is not satisfactory. Not that the editing idea is inherently unattractive; there is, in fact, an immense credibility to the general idea of an editor who, given difficult material, makes the best of it. But this general idea does not fit the case; the material (in 14:31) is not difficult. In fact, one could scarcely imagine an easier editorial task than moving "Arise, let us go . . . ." to the end of chap. 17. Not that any editor would want to play fast and loose with the text; one may presuppose that there was care, even reverence. But any editor who felt free to insert three chapters is unlikely to have had qualms about moving half a verse. In fact, it would not even have been necessary to move "Arise, let us go. . . ." If, as is sometimes said, it immediately preceded the account of Jesus going out (18:1), then, particularly since there were no chapter divisions at that time, all the editor had to do was choose the right place for the insertion—in other words, *before* "Arise, let us go. . . ." The logic of the editorial hypothesis leads to the idea that in some strange way the editor was both careful and bungling, free and scrupulous. Thus, it is a hypothesis which lacks internal coherence.

More decisive, however, than this internal weakness or incoherence is the fact that the editing hypothesis is simply unnecessary. Within the context of a portrayal of a three-stage spiritual progression, the phrase "Arise, let us go from here" makes eminent sense. First, because "the formula of rising and going . . . is one of the prevalent biblical conventions for marking the end of a narrative segment" (Alter, 1981, 65). Furthermore, it is a way of inviting the believer to leave a previous situation and to rise to a new level; within chaps. 13–17 it is complemented by the later lifting of the eyes to heaven (17:1), a movement which, physically speaking, is minimal, but which as an indication of spiritual progression is of major significance: it shows an advance to a further stage, one in which the believer is focused on God and, in a certain sense, now clean at heart, sees God. Thus the two rare references to anyone moving during the actual meal, the only two in chaps. 14–17, combine to suggest an upward spiritual movement. And with immense appropriateness, while the first lays the emphasis on a form of departure, on a leaving of the past (". . . from here"), the second places the focus on a form of arrival, on coming fully to God (". . . to heaven"). Thus there is an overall sense of a departure and arrival, in other words, of a journey. And it is precisely because the first looks to the past to some extent and the other looks forward that the first is attached to the passing of stage one (to the *end* of chap. 14) and the other to the inauguration of stage three (to the *beginning* of chap. 17).

The idea that indications of physical movement are used as a way of dividing the text is corroborated by other passages. In chap. 9, for instance, physical movement is the basic clue to its division, but apart from the journey to and from the pool (9:7) these movements are extremely vague. They do not tell the reader that anyone is going anywhere; they are simply literary indicators of a new scene, a new stage in the man's coming to sight. Similarly with the woman of Samaria. After the woman has become interested, Jesus says to her "Go call your husband and come here" (literally, "hither," 4:16). Jesus might have used any of a hundred ways to bring up the decisive subject of her husband(s). But the one used is physical movement: "Go . . . and come hither." The woman, of course, does not move, but the suggestion of movement, though somewhat perplexing, accomplishes its purpose: it makes a division in the text and opens the way to a scene in which Jesus' revelation to the woman is more developed.

As to why movement should be used as a divider between scenes or stages, the reason would seem to lie in the fact that movement, by its very nature, suggests some kind of development or progression, whether that progression be physical or spiritual. Immobility, on the other hand, can suggest that one is dispirited; refusal to move or change often reflects spiritual paralysis. The suitability of movement as an indicator of spiritual progression is particularly appropriate in the broad context of the fact that discipleship is often described as a process of *following* Jesus (*akoloutheō*, cf. 1:36–38,40,43; 6:2; 8:12; 10:4,5,27; 12:26; 13:36–37; 18:15; 20:6; 21:19–22) and especially in the context of a chapter which highlights Jesus as the *way* (14:6). Thus when Dodd (1953, 409) concludes that "Arise . . . ." has a meaning that is theological, that it indicates "a movement of the spirit," the details of his explanation may be questionable but his basic conclusion is not farfetched. On the contrary, it is in accord with basic ideas both of the gospel and of chap. 14.

Note.   Also in accord with the gospel plan as a whole is the discourse's diptych-like use of two balancing texts (chaps. 13–14 are balanced by chaps. 15–16). By and large it is through twofold complementary texts that the gospel is built up. To some degree the phenomenon may be noticed even as early as chaps. 1 and 2. There is a significant degree of complementarity between the initiatory trial (1:19–28) and the initiatory vision (1:29–34), between the variety of calls (1:35–42) and the variety of people(s) (1:43–51), and between the vitality of life at Cana (2:1–11) and the intimation of death in Jerusalem (2:12–22). But it is in the subsequent episodes that this phenomenon of balancing sections or chapters becomes more evident: Nicodemus and John; the woman of Samaria and the official from Capernaum; chaps. 5 and 6; chaps. 7 and 8; chaps. 9 and 10; 11:1–53, and 11:54–chap. 12.

Among the various examples of complementarity found elsewhere in the gospel, the case of chaps. 7 and 8 is particularly instructive. As indicated in discussing the overall plan of the gospel, chaps. 7–8 provide a kind of foil for chaps. 13–17. Furthermore, like chap. 7 with its emphasis on specific times and places and on the need to wait for the appropriate time (cf. esp. 7:1–10,39), the first discourse (chaps. 13–14) has a certain concreteness, particularly with regard to time and the fact that the time has come (cf. esp. 13:1,31).

The second discourse, on the other hand, is like chap. 8: without any references to time or place, it begins abruptly with a divinelike pronouncement of Jesus.

7:52–8:12	14:31–15:1
". . . does not arise" (*egeiretai*).	"Arise (*egeiresthe*), let us go from here."
". . . I am the light of the world."	"I am the true vine. . . ."

A somewhat similar transition occurs between chaps. 9 and 10 (9:41–10:1): the idea of movement (or failure to move—"Your sin abides") is followed by an authoritative pronouncement: "Amen, amen, I say to you. . . ."

All three transitions (between 7 and 8, between 9 and 10, and between 14 and 15) revolve around some idea of movement. But in the first two cases (at the end of chaps. 7 and 9) the people in question are the Pharisees and the notion of movement is negative. In other words, their spiritual negativity shows up in various forms of nonmovement—that of a prophet who does not arise (7:52) and that of a sin which remains (9:41). In the last discourse, on the other hand, Jesus is leading the disciples forward spiritually, and so the sense of movement is emphasized (14:31).

In addition, the phenomenon of repetition, quite strong in the relationship between chaps. 13–14 and 15–16, finds a significant precedent in the relationship between chaps. 7 and 8 (cf. Brown, 343, 349).

2. The presence of repetition, in chaps. 14 and 16, need not be seen as an unlikely phenomenon to be explained by uncoordinated editing. It was indicated earlier (Excursus 1) that, as a general principle, repetition is an integral part of much art and poetry. In this particular case, the fairly clear similarities between chapters 14 and 16 are but one part of a much larger phenomenon—the complex pattern of continuity which pervades all of chaps. 13–17. As already noted, there is a delicate blend of repetition and variation between the discourse's three leading actions, the cleansing, purifying, and sanctifying in chaps. 13, 15, and 17. In addition, as Kysar's outline (235) shows, many of the elements found in chaps. 14 and 16 are found also in chap. 15. And the relationship between parts of chaps. 13 and 17 is so close that Bultmann (486–90) placed the two together. What emerges, therefore, is not one major ill-fitting instance of repetition (chaps. 14 and 16), but a subtly moving text in which, amid progress, there is both continuity and variation. For most readers and hearers the effect of this pattern of repetition is not to confuse what has already been said, but rather to deepen it.

3. The contradiction between "Where are you going?" (13:36) and "None of you asks me 'Where are you going?' " (16:5) is to be seen within the context of the changing stages and moods of spiritual development. At an early stage of discipleship the idea of the journey towards God can inspire a form of facile enthusiasm, and at this point, perhaps relying unduly on one's own resources, there is an eagerness to go, to follow Jesus—hence Peter's "Where are you going?"

But as the journey goes on, and as the cost of discipleship becomes clear, there often comes a faltering and a subsequent sadness. It is to this crisis that Jesus refers (16:5–6): "None of you asks me. . . . Instead, because I have said these things to you, sorrow has filled your hearts." God's process of purification (15:1–10), a purification which the disciple experiences as some form of death (16:4b–24), has become too much, and there is no longer a desire to follow—to know where Jesus is going. The situation has some broad affinity with mood changes of the kind recorded in Deuteronomy 1 (cf. esp. Deut 1:19–33, 41–66), but a closer analogy is found in the account of the rich man who knelt before the journeying Jesus (Mark 10:17–22). He had accomplished one stage of development, having kept everything from his youth, and his eagerness is reflected in the fact that as he approaches Jesus, he runs. One would have thought he was ready to follow. But the price of the next stage was too great: "His face fell, and he went away, sorrowful." The apparent contradiction in John is one more challenge to the reader to rise above the physical level, where the contradiction is real, and to hear the text at a level that is spiritual or theological.

4. The idea of union (in the parable of the vine), far from being alien to the discourse, is central to it. From the foot-washing and the picture of the beloved (in chap. 13) to the final prayer for unity, it is precisely union which is the guiding purpose of chaps. 13–17. But union with God demands dying to this world, and so along with the theme of union there is the complementary theme of loss or death, and it is this latter theme which is reflected in the references to Jesus' departure. In other words, the evangelist has indeed used a literary convention which is concerned with death and departure, but in accordance with the theological idea that dying is a pathway to life and to union with God, he has rewritten the convention so that the process of departure is set within the larger process of the movement towards union. Again, of course, to find the coherence of the text it is necessary to read it at a level that is theological, spiritual.

5. It is true that there are varied views within the discourse, but by and large these may be seen fairly easily as fitting into the context of the various stages of spiritual development and of the varied points of view within particular stages. In stage one, for instance, chap. 13 tends to emphasize the divine; chap. 14, the human. That there should be variety concerning the mode of Jesus' return and presence is to be expected, for it is precisely with the varied stages and views of the divine presence that the whole discourse is most concerned. What is necessary is to rise above some of the contradictory superficialities of the story line and to see that, theologically, the viewpoints converge into a process that is developing but coherent; similarly with regard to the changing picture of the Spirit—first as relatively inactive with regard to the world (14:17) and later as active (16:8–11). What has changed is the believer—from being spiritually underdeveloped and only partly in touch with the Spirit to being fully Spirit-led and much more aware of the need to resist all that is worldly.

CHAPTER 13

The Foot-Washing and the Response

God's Descent through Jesus into the Human—A Portrait of Shadowed Love and Mixed Reactions

Introductions: The Basic Structure

At one level chap. 13 consists of narrative which is fairly straightforward. Its dominating image is that of Jesus washing the feet of the disciples (1–20), and there is considerable agreement that the account falls into three parts: 1–5, 6–11, 12–20. These three parts may be put under the following headings:

- The complex introduction and the action itself, 1–5.

- The foot-washing as evocative of Jesus' saving death; Peter's misunderstanding, 6–11.

- The foot-washing as an ethical example; the disciples apparently understand, 12–20.

It would appear, furthermore, that each of these three parts has three subsections: the action itself (13:1–5), which begins with an indication of time (*"Before the feast . . ."*), is divided by two further time indications (*"And during supper. . . . Then* he put . . ."). The exchange with Peter (6–11) consists of a triple pattern of question/statement and response. And the subsequent explanation (12–20) contains two uses of "Amen, amen, . . ." a phrase which often acts as a divider, and which apparently does so in this case also, thereby dividing the final text in three.

The remainder of the chapter (21–38) is generally divided into two main scenes:

- The beloved-related foretelling of betrayal, 21–30;
- The glory-related love and the foretelling of denial, 31–38.

The Structure of the Final Scenes (vv 21–30 and 31–38)

As already noted, in discussing the various conclusions in chaps. 13–17, each of the final scenes may be divided in two. In the scene of the betrayal (vv 21–30) there is an apparent division between the prediction (vv 21–27a) and the action (vv 27b–30). And in the final scene (vv 31–38) there is a widely accepted division between the initial emphasis on glory and love (vv 31–35) and the later foretelling of Peter's denial (vv 36–38).

The idea that there is a division within vv 21–30 is indicated, as so often in John, by elements of movement and repetition. The movement is found in the arrival of Satan ("Satan entered him"), and it is reflected in the departure of Judas ("he went out. . . . It was night"). The repetition is found especially in the two references to the morsel of food—first at the end of 21–27a, and then, somewhat suprisingly, at the end of 27b–30.

The resulting subdivision is as follows:

The emergence of a betrayer (and of a beloved) (21–27a);

The action of the betrayer (with allusions to love) (27b–30);

The glory-related commandment of love (31–35);

The spectre of Peter's denial (36–38).

What is important in this subdivision (21–30, 31–38) is that it gives an idea of the extent to which the positive and negative are interwoven. In the first scene (21–30) this is particularly the case; each subsection (21–27a and 27b-30) has both positive and negative. In the final scene (31–38), however, the two are beginning to be distinct; the first part (31–35), with its glory-related commandment of love, is largely positive, and the final part (36–38), telling of Peter's denial, is largely negative. It is this increasing distinction which makes it relatively easy to detect the division in the final scene.

Structure: The Relation to 12:20–36a

The chapter therefore consists both of a major section built on the basis of three threes, and of two smaller two-part units. Thus from the point of view of structure, it is an elaboration of the picture which dominates chap. 12, that of the coming of the Greeks and Jews (12:20–36a).

With regard to content also, chap. 13 stands in close coordination with chap. 12, especially with the anointing of the feet (12:1–11) and with the ideas of death and glory in the Greeks-related scene (12:20–36a).

Objections to Unity

Despite the general impression of straightforward narrative, the text is sometimes seen as lacking unity and as containing editorial insertions (see esp. Schnackenburg, 3:7–15, 53; Brown, 559–62). The reasons for this perception are manifold:

- Within vv 1–5 there is striking variation in style: 1–3 is very complicated, "linguistically overladen" (Schnackenburg, 3:7); but 5, which describes the actual washing, is of "extreme simplicity" (Kysar, 208).

- Within vv 6–20 there is considerable variation in content: 6–11 sees the washing as Christological, as a symbol of Jesus' death (Brown, 565–66); but 12–20 regards it as ethical, as an example to be imitated (Schnackenburg, 3:4; Brown, 558–69, esp. 566). The two interpretations, one symbolic, the other ethical, are sometimes regarded as independent in origin. Richter (1967, 308–13, esp. 312), for instance, claims that the person who added chaps. 15–17 also added the second interpretation. Thyen (1971, esp. 344–45, 350) would say that most of it (vv 12–17, 20) was inserted by the church-concerned writer of 1 John. Furthermore, while the first interpretation (6–11) sees Jesus' action as something that will not be known (or understood) until later (7), the second presumes that one can know right now.

- The final section (vv 31–38), beginning as it does with the sudden intro-duction of the idea of glorification ("Now is the Son of humanity glori-fied . . ."), is often seen as introducing a major new division, one which is quite distinct from the account of the foot-washing.
- Within that final section (vv 31–38), with its apparent emphasis on im-pending departure and denial, the new commandment of mutual love may appear out of place, inserted.

The Unity of the Text

In proposing the editorial hypothesis it is sometimes said that the text obviously reflects a variety of sources. This observation appears to be right, but that is not the issue. What is in question is whether a single author worked these many sources into a coherent unity.

A basic clue to the nature and unity of the text is provided (though never fully developed) by Schnackenburg (3:6): "The whole presentation is subservient to . . . theological thought."

The thought which dominates chap. 13, and indeed all of chaps. 13–17, is indicated by the opening sentence: ". . . having loved his own who were in the world, he loved them to the end" (13:1). It is a sentence which both echoes and develops the climactic "For God so loved the world . . ." (3:16), and as such it indicates that God's love is expressed in Jesus, in his final self-giving in death and in his immediate self-giving in the foot-washing. It is this self-giving love, flowing from God through Jesus' life, and from Jesus into the lives of the disci-ples, which holds the chapter together.

To summarize: Jesus' loving "descent" into the washing of feet (13:1–20) is like an encapsulated form of the incarnation: he leaves his original place, becomes like a servant, and then takes up his place again (cf. Beasley-Murray, 239). In vv 1–5 there is, so to speak, the picture of the descent. Then, as he speaks to Peter (vv 6–11) it becomes clear that the foot-washing symbolizes in a particular way Jesus' saving death (the foot-washing is the key to gaining eternal life and eternal reward—literally it is the source of heritage or share [*meros*] with Jesus, 13:8—and as such it has a role which is as pivotal as Jesus' death). Finally, after he has resumed his place, a process of self-giving continues, but not so much in Jesus as in others: in the "ethical" section, the divine love is something which goes from one person to another, so much so that in receiving another person one may re-ceive Jesus, and thus receive God (vv 12–20, esp. 20).

The overall picture (vv 1–20) is of an unbounded love which flows out from God in self-giving and death, and which ultimately comes back to God.

But all is not sweetness and light; there is a shadow side. The reference to Jesus as loving is followed immediately by a reference to the devil as infecting the heart with murderous treachery (13:2). Furthermore, elements of darkness are found not only in Judas and in the repeated references to betrayal (13:2, 10b-11, 18–19) but also in the confusedness and reluctance of Peter, someone who, to a certain degree, represents the disciples. God's love may indeed eventually conquer, but only after it has contended with deadly opposition.

Following this capsule picture of the incarnation (vv 1–20), there are two scenes which summarize its practical effects (vv 21–30 and 31–38), and inevitably, given the preceding combustion of love and darkness, these scenes are a dense mixture. The first begins with the negative: Jesus looks into God's plan and, seeing that it allows a place for a treacherous death, his spirit is shaken (v 21). But as the scene advances he manages to swallow the bitter pill—he even tells Judas to do it quickly—and, having done that, he is able at the beginning of the second scene to see the positive, able to realize that however painful the death-related plan, it is not one which will annihilate him in God-denying absurdity; on the contrary, through that death he will blossom into new life, and in the God-given blossoming, God also will be affirmed, manifested—glorified (vv 31–32). This is what the talk of glorification is about; it is not a departure from the foot-washing-centered chapter. Rather, it is the flowering which completes that chapter. Thus the picture of the death-focused incarnation and of its consequences ends not in meaninglessness but in an outburst of life—the very phrasing of vv 31–32 is exuberant—an outburst which shows forth the true character of both humanity and God.

The concluding two scenes, despite the contrast in the way they begin, are not monolithically diverse, one negative and the other positive. As already indicated, both contain a mixture, and given this deliberate mixture, the theme of love fits well with the idea of denial (vv 31–38). The foretelling and carrying out of the betrayal (vv 21–30) is relieved by the picture of the beloved, and also by the presumption, ironic in the circumstances, that Jesus' disciples are involved in helping the poor. On the other hand, the scene, which waxes poetic about the glorification of Jesus and God, and about the resulting outflow of a covenant of mutual love (vv 31–38), is shadowed nonetheless by the spectre of Jesus' departure and Peter's denial.

It is a further sign of the unity of chap. 13 that the negativity found in these final scenes (21–30, 31–38) is in continuity with that found in the foot-washing. The taking over of Judas by the devil, a process which was begun in v 2, is completed in v 27. In comparison with the first stage (''the *devil* had put it into *the heart that Judas,* . . .'' 2), the second is more personal and indicates a more complete possession (*''Satan entered him,''* 27).

Peter also goes from bad to worse. The elements which are found in the foot-washing scene —*Peter does not know,* then *swears against being washed* by Jesus, and then in *impetuous misunderstanding* offers feet, hands, and head for washing (6–9)—all of these factors turn up in varied and often aggravated form in the subsequent picture: he *does not know . . .* but will follow later (22–24, 36); in *impetuous misunderstanding* he offers to lay down his very life (37); and in place of his emphatic swearing that Jesus will never wash him, Jesus tells him, with *yet greater solemnity,* that before cockcrow he will distance himself even more radically—he will deny him three times (38, cf. 8). There would also seem to be a continuity between the initial bewilderment of Peter (6) and the later and more general confusedness of those for whom Peter appears as the spokesperson —the disciples (22, 28–29). In any case, when the focus turns to the disciples, the weaknesses which first appear in the washing of Peter's feet, all reappear in aggravated form.

The two characters—Judas and Peter—are in some way related. Judas ("a devil") was first presented in the shadow of Peter's climactic recognition of Jesus (6:68–71). Now it is Judas (with the devil) who is mentioned initially, and Peter, not at all as clear-sighted as earlier, is partly in his shadow (vv 2–9). (They even share a name—Simon. Curiously, in a text with many triads, Peter is referred to as Simon on only two occasions, 6, 9. To find a third "Simon" one has to include "Judas, son of Simon," 2.) In this context it makes sense that, in the subsequent portrait of the disciples, the foretelling of Peter's denial should be set in the shadow of the foretelling of Judas' Satan-based betrayal.

What emerges then in chap. 13, is a picture where love is at its strongest, but where the devil also is exerting full force and where the consequent negativity and darkness are spilling over into the fate of Jesus and into the confusedness of the disciples.

Yet there is a sense in which the negative is never out of control. Jesus himself foretells his own betrayal, and even commands it. He also foretells his departure and Peter's denial. Thus the negative is somehow encompassed by his word. The "somehow" may plague the reader, but the evangelist's message is clear: what-ever the burden of death and denial there is a greater weight of love and glory.

Unity: A Reconsideration of the Objections

The striking change of style, from complexity to simplicity (13:1–5), may now be looked at afresh. It is, in fact, appropriate to the theological content—to the mind-bending idea that, in a sense, God is washing feet. In other words, the extraordinary complexity ("linguistically overladen"), instead of reflecting edito-rial confusion, may also be seen as a sophisticated literary device to suggest so-lemnity, and this solemnity is appropriate to introducing the high point of God's plan in Jesus. But because this plan involved Jesus' self-emptying, the solemnity gives way to a style which is expressive of that self-emptying—to simplicity.

This transition in style is a variation on previous Johannine transitions, partic-ularly those found in the prologue and good shepherd text. (In fact, Grossouw, 1966, 127, refers to 13:1–3 as "a minor prologue".) In each case the transition is considerable: from poetry to prose (1:1–18), from parable to openess (10:7–18), from solemnity to simplicity (13:1–5).

With regard to the two interpretations of the footwashing, one Christological (6–11) and the other ethical (12–20), these are not mutually exclusive. On the contrary, taken together they express the fact that it is God's self-giving in Jesus' saving death which provides the context for Christian ethics. Kysar (210), for instance, emphasizes their compatibility, and elsewhere (in discussing 13:34 and 14:9–11) articulates the pertinent theological principle: "The model and source of love is Jesus' death" (217); "ethics is founded on Christology" (239). Alcoholics

Anonymous, for instance, cannot establish abstinence without rooting it in some form of acceptance of God. As will be seen later, Peter's blunder (13:36–38) is to confide in a detached ethic—one which is not built on Jesus' death. Furthermore, there are other texts, such as the conversations with Nicodemus and the Samaritan woman, in which an initial emphasis on the symbolic eventually turns to morality (cf. 3:19–21, 4:16–29). The love which is poured forth in Jesus, and which brings those who are washed to eternal life, does not operate in a vacuum. It is to be expressed in a similar outpouring in their own lives.

Concerning the alleged contradiction between not knowing until "after these things" (v 7) and knowing now (v 12), there is indeed a tension, but given the fundamental unity and complementarity between the larger sections of the text— between the symbolic (vv 6–11) and the ethical (vv 12–20)—it is more appropriate, rather than invoking confused editing, to seek to locate that tension within the larger context of the enigmatic question of knowing (including Jesus' knowing, vv 1, 3). Paul, for instance, speaks of both knowing and not knowing: "Now I know in part, but then . . ." (1 Cor 13:12). And even during this life there are levels both of knowing and unknowing.

What has already been indicated with regard to the idea of glorification (vv 30–31)—that it is an appropriate culmination of the foot-washing text—may also be said of the commandment of mutual love (vv 34–35). Far from being alien, it is the practical outcome of the whole dynamism of the incarnation, particularly as the incarnation is expressed in the foot-washing.

[13:1–5] The foot-washing: a further stage in God's descent into the human.   Jesus' washing of the disciples' feet is surprising yet terribly appropriate. Their feet, bearing in a special way the dirt and fatigue of the day, are representative of all their needs, including the needs that are humblest. Even physiologically the body is so organized that a massage of the feet has the effect of renewing the body as a whole. And, as Jesus will say to Peter, there is no need to wash the hands and head; the washing of the feet cleans everything (13:9–10). In the feet, therefore, and in their lowliness, human need is focused.

When Jesus begins to wash he does so not only as a human being but as someone in whom there is present all the majesty and love of God. The puzzling change of style, from mind-bending complexity and solemnity (vv 1–3, esp. 1) to increasing simplicity (vv 4–5, esp. 5), is a literary way of expressing the theological truth that the awesome God has taken this humble feet-washing form. The love that was previously attributed to God (3:16 ". . . so loved the world"), is now expressed in a specific form in Jesus (13:1 "having loved . . . in the world, he loved . . . to the end"). The connection with God's love is reinforced by the ambiguity of the "having loved": while it may indeed refer to a specific time and action, it may also refer to a love which is beyond time, a love like that of God (Brown, 549).

This ambiguity—of something which is simultaneously greater than time, yet within it—is reflected in the way the text is structured: even though initially, at least, it is almost mind-transcending, it is contained within a three-part framework which is very down-to-earth, which is, in fact, time-based: "Before. . . . And during supper. . . . Then . . ." (13:1, 2, 5).

Within this framework the text is quite repetitive and, when combined with the "descending" form of the style (its decreasing complexity), the effect of this repetition is to suggest a descending spiral. And so the overall picture is something like that given in the prologue: the transcendent God enters into time, into human history.

But the foot-washing scene goes further than the prologue. The emphasis at this stage is not on "the beginning" of God's involvement, but on its conclusion: having loved, the question now is of loving "to the end." In the parable of the good shepherd the evangelist had already provided a variation on the prologue and in doing so had begun to change the emphasis towards Jesus' death. Now, however, that change of emphasis goes further. All three parts of 13:1–5 evoke Jesus' death. First, ever so faintly, in the initial reference to the "end" (*telos*, v 1). Then in the vocabulary of "laying down" and "taking up" (*tithēmi . . . lambanō*, v 4)—an echo of the death of the good shepherd (10:17–18; Brown, 551; Kysar, 208; the use of "his own," 13:1, may also be seen as reflecting the good shepherd text, 10:3–4,12–15,27—cf. Schnackenburg, 3:16). And finally, the pouring of the water on the feet stands in continuity both with the burial-related anointing and wiping of the feet (12:1–8; cf. Lindars, 416) and also with the water which, following the "end," and the repeated use of end-related words, flows from Jesus' side (19:28,30,34).

The overall impression, therefore, is of a God who, in the face of human need, gives, and gives totally. In a certain sense what Jesus pours out is himself. Käsemann (1968, 4–26) and Schnackenburg (2:410) contend that the Johannine Jesus is never lowly, that there is no self-emptying. But the evidence of individual texts is uncontestable: he shudders, he cries, he bleeds. He rises from the settledness of supper and lays aside the protectiveness (and perhaps attractiveness) of clothing. And he washes feet.

Given this extraordinary responsiveness on God's part one might imagine that human problems would be solved immediately. But the situation is not so simple. Just as the drama is developing there is a major complication: the solemn announcement of God's outpouring of love in Jesus is followed by the news that the devil has infected the heart with murderous treachery (v 2). The text does not say that "the devil had put it into *the heart of Judas,* son of Simon . . ." but (following the more difficult reading) "when the devil had put it into *the heart that Judas,* son of Simon . . ." (13:2; cf. Beasley-Murray, 229). In other words, by straining the phraseology it lays the emphasis not on Judas and his specific heart, but on the heart as such. Satan, therefore, is seeking entrance to every heart, including that of Simon Peter.

This complication, this deadly infection of the heart, is not something peripheral. The literary construction is such that the actions of the devil and of Jesus (vv 2, 4–5) form an acute antithesis:

"During supper, when the devil had already put (*ballō*) it into the heart.
. . ."

"He rose from the supper. . . . Then he put (*ballō*) water . . . and began
to wash the feet. . . ."

There is an implication that the disciples are experiencing two opposing forces
—one infecting the heart and the other washing the feet to cleanse away all that
is wrong. The balance between the images is hardly coincidence. The repeated
reference to the supper is unnecessary, but it makes sense as a way of recalling
and balancing the initial reference. Furthermore, it seems strange that the relatively rare word *ballō* should be used twice—unless the two usages are connected. The word does not otherwise occur in chaps. 13–17, except for a further
double usage in the account of the purifying of the vine 15:6 ("anyone who does
not abide will be *put* out . . . and they will *put* it in the fire"—*ballō, ballō*).
The effect of this further double usage (in 15:6) is not to lessen the significance
of that which occurs in 13:2, 5 but to strengthen it: it means that at the beginning
of both major diptychs, God's purifying action is described, in part, by the double
use of a single verb. It is, of course, used differently; in 13:2, 5 the repeated *ballō*
describes the initial battle, whereas in 15:6 it is used of a process which, very
appropriately, is more advanced. The effect is to provide a double linguistic link
which both solidifies the connection between the washing of the feet and the purifying of the vine, and which also places the action of the devil, frightening
though it may be, within a verbal pattern which is governed ultimately by God.

A similar sense of the devil being governed ultimately by God is found within
the account of the foot-washing itself. Jesus' action is indeed a response to that
of the devil, yet the account of the devil's action is placed in a subordinate clause
(v 2), and the introduction to what Jesus does (v 3) has a majesty which echoes
the solemn opening concerning the further manifestation of God's eternal love (v
1). Thus the devil's action is encompassed by a greater love, a love manifested in
the down-to-earth action of meeting people where they hurt most.

A similar optimism had been suggested by the setting, by the way in which
the text began with a climactic emphasis on the Passover (13:1, "Before the . . .
Passover"). Variations on that phrase had already been used twice (11:55, 12:1:
"the Passover . . . before the Passover"). But the third occurrence, as well as
being climactic, is more solemn and festive: "Before the *feast* of Passover." It is
an initial indication that whatever the sadness of death, the ultimate background
is that of a God-given festival, a festival of human freedom and salvation.

What the foot-washing does above all is provide a reminder that even though
salvation is not easy, even though the devil and death do, in fact, wreak havoc,
God is present in the trenches. The second and final sections of the text end with
intensifying images of Jesus as girded or tied ("he girded himself . . . he was
girded," vv 4, 5). This is the imagery of service, of slavery (Beasley-Murray,
233). Whatever the sin or pain, whatever the need, God comes in Jesus, not to
lord it over people but to join them where they are and to go with them through
a new Passover.

**[13:6–11] The washing (symbol of Jesus' death) brings eternal inheritance;
Peter's problems with the process.** When Jesus comes to Peter and talks to
him, what had been suggested in 13:1–5 becomes clearer: the washing of the feet,

so prosaic at one level—the epitome of a menial life—has a far higher significance: it is something that will not be understood until "after these things" (v 7); it is the key to obtaining an eternal reward with Jesus (literally, an inheritance, *meros,* v 8b; cf. Brown, 565); and, despite its apparent limitedness, it means that one has been completely bathed (v 10; cf. Lindars, 451, "It is an act which is done once for all"). In other words, the washing of the feet opens the way to salvation, here and hereafter. As such it has a role similar to that of Jesus' saving death. It is, in fact, a central expression of the self-emptying which finished in death.

But it will not be understood until "after these things," an expression which, in the context, is ambiguous: it suggests, first of all, an understanding associated with the eternal reward (the final kind of understanding or knowing referred to in 1 Cor 13:12); and it also leaves open the possibility of an understanding which comes in the near future following Jesus' death (cf. 2:12; 12:16). What is certain is that while Jesus is offering complete salvation, he is not immediately offering complete understanding.

Peter is dissatisfied. His conversation with Jesus consists of a triple exchange, and it has echoes of earlier conversations, particularly of the opening triple exchange with the woman of Samaria (4:7–15). Very briefly, both the woman and Peter first express shock at Jesus' approach (something to the effect of "You and me—like this!" 4:9; 13:6); then they rule out Jesus' proposal (the woman implies that it cannot be done, 4:11–12; Peter swears it will not be done, ever, 13:8); and finally, in an abrupt turnabout, both ask Jesus to go ahead (to give the living water, 4:15; to wash, 13:9).

There are, of course, great differences between the conversations. But sometimes, even in the differences, there are connections. The woman cannot believe that Jesus can reach so high ("Are you greater? . . ."). Peter cannot accept that Jesus should reach so low. The essential stumbling block for both of them is the difficulty of grasping the union of extremes, the union of what is above and what is below, of divinity and humanity.

In the course of the exchange the portrait of Peter is quite sympathetic; all his mistakes, so it seems, can be explained on the basis of his high regard for Jesus. But Peter has a serious problem: he is not able to receive the washing and all that it symbolizes—God's love poured out in Jesus and in Jesus' death. Despite his high-flown acknowledgment of Jesus as the Holy One of God (6:69), he cannot accept the actual shape which God takes. God may be in the words of eternal life (6:68), but not in feet and in death. At first he holds the washing at a distance, and, in fact, swears that it will never happen (v 8). Then he is ready to accept it, but he wants more (v 9). In both reactions he shows that he cannot see the appropriateness of God's unique Jesus-centered gift to his own life; he cannot see his own place in relation to what God has actually done in Jesus. The implication, as yet unclear, is of an incompatibility between God and himself. And therein lies a further implication: rejection of self and rejection of God.

The problem is not limited to Peter. As the switch to the plural indicates ("and you [plural] are clean"), Peter is the representative of the other disciples (Schnackenburg, 3:22).

Furthermore, the literary unit which describes the conversation with Peter contains also an allusion to Judas and to his outright failure to be cleansed. Thus, though Judas is distinguished from the others, he is also associated with them. And this situation is aggravated by the fact that, as mentioned earlier, he is associated with Peter in other ways. Peter's hesitations, therefore, could be ominous. The difficulty is serious because the washing, love-filled yet death-related, reflects the entire divine plan. What is curious and perhaps highly significant is that Peter's problem is not so much with the death as with the love. For, in the simple process of having his feet washed, the emphasis is on love, and it is that particularly which Peter finds difficult to accept.

But despite the hesitations and misunderstandings, the overall emphasis is on the positive. Each of Peter's problems is answered by Jesus, and even the undercurrent of treachery is encompassed by Jesus' knowledge and words. This mystery-filled action is not to be turned away by problems and threats.

[13:12–20] Given the divine presence in the human, an exhortation to corresponding recognition and action.   Jesus' return to his former place is described in more detail than may seem necessary. The text, instead of using something brief (such as "Afterwards, he said to them . . ."), employs a triad of verbs: "So when he had washed . . . he took [*lambanō*] . . . and he reclined. . . ." At the level of straightforward narrative, this adds a touch of drama and solemnity. At the level of theological overtones it evokes what the introduction to the foot-washing had already referred to—Jesus' return to God (13:1,3). Such a return is further evoked by the use of *lambanō*, the word used about the good shepherd's resumption of his life (10:18; cf. Brown, 551, Kysar, 208), and especially by Jesus' increasingly solemn language (including, twice, "Amen, amen, I say . . ."), particularly his increasingly solemn references to himself: as teacher, as Lord, and, above all, as "I am" ("that you may believe that I am," v 19). This is the language of divinity, and, given that the laying down (*tithēmi*, also used of the good shepherd, 10:18) of the clothes and the washing of the feet symbolize Jesus' death, symbolize the emptying, as it were, of his divinity, the taking up (*lambanō*) of his clothes and the use of the solemn "I am" indicate a return to divinity, to his former position with God. So when, with that touch of drama, he resumes his place, his identity has an air of ambiguity: his work placed him among slaves, yet he now evokes the divine.

The subsequent address, uninterrupted apart from the two instances of "Amen, amen, . . ." is quite perplexing. In fact, given its sequence of obscurely related sayings, the reader may have to struggle to put the pieces together, and the lack of clear unity may lead to the impression that this indeed is the result of unpolished editing.

But this puzzling form—this obscurity and lack of obvious connection—is appropriate to the content. What Jesus is talking about is recognition and the consequences of recognition, in other words, the difficult and often obscure process of piecing together the human and divine, of seeing—as he expresses it in summary form at the end (v 20)—of seeing that in receiving Jesus' messenger one receives Jesus and that in receiving Jesus one receives God. This is the challenge, to meet an ordinary person and to recognize the presence of the divine. Of course, Jesus is also talking about ethical conduct and community, about a situation in which "the exercise of power and . . . the superiorities and inferiorities of nature and grace are . . . transcended by friendship" (Schneiders, 1981, 87–88); such is the implication of the conversation with Peter and of the subsequent command to wash one another's feet. But service and community are not the foundational elements; they are simply some of the consequences of the central factor of recognition.

The text begins (vv 12–15) by mentioning the question of knowledge, of perception ("Do you know what I have done? . . ."), and then it uses the disciples' insightful recognition of Jesus (as Teacher and Lord) and the example of what he has done as a basis for exhorting them to wash one another's feet, in other words, as a basis for expressing, in a very practical way, that not only in Jesus, but also in one another, there is someone special to be recognized. Thus the first consequence of recognition is profound respect and care.

Then (vv 16–19), having said that if he can do it so can they (such, apparently, is part of the meaning of "The servant is not greater than the Lord . . ."), Jesus speaks of the other consequence of recognition—blessedness: "blessed (*makarios*) are you if you do . . . these things." Blessedness is no mean state; the word *makarios* is not otherwise used in John except in the climactic post-resurrection statement to Thomas, "Blessed are those who have not seen and yet believe" (20:29). In other words, the whole heritage of believing, all that it bestows, may be summed up as blessedness. And it is that same heritage which is gained by appropriate recognition and action.

But Jesus is aware that not all will do this. In a further allusion to the impending treachery, he cites the scripture about the table companion who "raised up his heel" (Ps 41:9)—an action which in any Middle Eastern context would express contempt, but which in a situation of washing feet has an added edge of rejection. Yet, in some sense, even this rejection is encompassed by the divine knowledge and words: it accords ultimately with Jesus' choice and with scripture and with Jesus' prediction, so much so that when it happens it should lead not to discouragement but to believing: "that you may believe that I am." This is the ultimate recognition, to see even amid hatred and its results an aspect of the divine presence.

Recognition, therefore, as well as leading to a course of action, leads also to a faith-filled blessedness which not even hatred can destroy.

The final synthesizing part (v 20) not only highlights the central idea that in being receptive towards something Jesus-like in people one is ultimately being receptive towards the divine, but it also makes repeated use of *lambanō*, "to take/receive," the verb used to indicate Jesus' resumption of life and status (as good shepherd, 10:18; and as foot-washer, 13:12). This connection may at first seem flimsy; *lambanō* is a rather common word, and in the synoptics there are phrases which are similar to 13:30 (cf. Brown, 572). Yet in the entire NT there is not another verse where *lambanō* is used with such frequency—four times, culminating in a double (back-to-back) usage: *lambanōn . . . lambanei . . . lambanōn lambanei.* And given the apparent deliberateness with which *lambanō* was used at the beginning of this passage (v 12), it is hardly coincidence that it now recurs so forcibly at the end. What is being indicated apparently is that the process of re-suming life, begun in v 12 and reaching a high point with the divine ''I am'' (v 19), now overflows from Jesus to the disciples: they also receive or take up, even to the point of receiving the divine.

Hence, if the beginning of the foot-washing (13:1–5), with its puzzling change from complexity to simplicity, expresses the emptying of the divine into the very human, the conclusion goes further: it challenges the mind to recognize that in the human the divine is to be encountered. Thus is the pendulum movement complete, out from God and back to God.

The Foot-washing and Baptism

The primary message of the foot-washing is that, through Jesus' incarnation and death, God's love is poured out in a cleansing which awakens the believer to a new awareness, especially to a new recognition of the divine in the human. But in a significant part of Christian practice and experience, such an acceptance of Jesus' saving death, such an awakening cleansing, is associated with baptism (see especially Rom 6:1–4, and the baptizing of the eunuch, Acts 8:26–40). It is ap-propriate, therefore, that the description of the washing should have some sugges-tion or overtone of the associated sacrament. And that apparently is the case: the word ''to bathe'' (*louō*, 13:10) belongs to the ''standard NT vocabulary for bap-tism'' (Brown, 566). The foot-washing, therefore, does refer to baptism, second-arily.

Insofar as baptismal bathing is associated (in Eph 5:25–27) with Christ's spouselike love, the foot-washing may be seen as expressing such a love.

[13:21–30] The prediction of betrayal: even in the shadow of death, various shades of love. This scene and the following (vv 31–38) show the practical effects or outward manifestation of what was suggested in a general way in the foot-washing—that despite God's outpouring of saving love, there is also at work a strong but subordinate process of deathly treachery and of human reluctance.

The initial emphasis is on the treachery. Within the scene, both subdivisions begin with Jesus speaking about the treachery, first to predict it (v 21), then to precipitate or even command it (v 27b). And at the end of these subdivisions the essence of that treachery is compressed into two words which, in the Greek, fall like dead weights at the end of their respective sentences: ''. . . Satan''; ''. . . night.''

Yet amid this ominous setting there is repeated emphasis on love. In the initial subdivision, for instance, the emphasis on treachery may seem to be over-whelming: as noted earlier, the account of Satan entering Judas is the second of two subtly differentiated grades of possession (cf. vv 2, 27). But before that crude second stage is mentioned, one encounters—for the first time in the gospel—the figure of the beloved. Not only is he in conversation with Jesus, but in the course of that conversation, even while he is engaged with the problem of the evil one, he moves closer: from having been ''reclining [*anakeimenos*] next to Jesus' bosom [*kolpos*],'' a phrase which may be understood as simply indicating that he was close to Jesus, he is next described as "leaning back (or falling back, *anapesōn*) on Jesus' breast (or chest, *stēthos*)," an expression which refers to greater closeness.

Underlying these images of the beloved as being on the bosom of Jesus is that of Jesus as being in the bosom of the Father (1:18). In other words, between the advancing stages of diabolical possession there is a glimpse of advancing stages of divine intimacy. The contrast is heightened by Culpepper's conclusion (1983, 123–24) that the beloved disciple embodies the Paraclete and that Judas "represents the humanization of the cosmic forces of evil." In other words, one embodies all that is supportive and uplifting; the other all that is alien and injurious. And while Judas is indeed possessed, the picture of the beloved disciple, as he leans back on Jesus, is one of complete ease and freedom.

Likewise in the second subdivision (vv 27b–30) there is a contrast. Judas sets about his work, but the minds of the others are set on things that are positive— celebrating a feast (nothing too extravagant, simply what is needed) and giving to the poor. Thus the scene as a whole is a tense blend of good and evil.

Pivotal in this scene is Peter. However one reconstructs the arrangement of the disciples at the last supper—and such reconstructions tend to be "highly speculative" (Brown, 574)—one thing is certain: in the canonical text, in its literary construction, Peter is in the middle; the single slender verse in which he appears (v 24) is placed right at the center of the subdivision which makes repeated references to the beloved and to the betrayer. In previous texts he appeared in some form of proximity to Judas (6:68–71; 13:2, 6). At this point, in v 24, he beckons to the beloved—and he asks about the betrayer. He is not himself the beloved or the betrayer, yet in his own way he will be involved both in betraying and in loving. Now, at the supper, the two ways lie open.

And what is true of Peter is true of all the disciples; he is, after all, in some sense their representative. When Jesus announces the impending treachery, the phrasing is such that it could, in a sense, refer to any of the disciples: "'one of you. . . .' The disciples looked . . ." (vv 21–22). And then, in the next verse, when the beloved is introduced, it could again be any of them: he is simply "one of the disciples" (v 23). The phrasing, as well as being open-ended, is also overlapping (from betrayer to beloved), and it all indicates a single idea: any of them could be the betrayer, and any of them could be the beloved. Brown (577) remarks, "the evangelist . . . is . . . showing the good and bad extremes in the spectrum of discipleship." And, as disciples, that spectrum lies open to all. It is therefore unrealistic for the reader to think, "I could never be so evil," or, on the other hand, "I could never be the beloved." Everyone is capable of both.

This emphasis on freedom has added importance when considering the role of Judas. It is true, as Becker (432) has noted, that Judas can seem like a puppet in the plan of salvation: the morsel of bread which Jesus offers him has the effect of precipitating the entry of Satan. But, however much the resulting evil was encompassed in the plan of salvation, the morsel did not destroy Judas' freedom, did not push him into the grip of Satan. On the contrary, since it was about as gentle and affectionate a gesture as one could imagine—like something a parent would do for a child or one lover for another—it was an effort by Jesus to recall Judas from his developing entanglement with Satan. But, just as the washing failed to cleanse him, so also did the food fail, and he turned it instead, as one can turn almost anything good, into an occasion of evil. In some way the mystery of the interaction between his freedom and the plan of salvation is as complex ultimately as the similar mystery surrounding the fate of Judaism as a whole (cf. Romans 9–11).

When he went out "it was night"—a reference not only to chronology, but also to the presence of the power of darkness and to the end of Jesus' day (cf. 9:4; 11:9–10).

[13:31–38] Glory, departure, and love: the glory of the God-human union opens the way, through Jesus' departure, for a new identity and for love. But presumptuous Peter will deny it. The complexity of the preceding heading reflects one of the basic features of the text—that, rather like the final part of the foot-washing (vv 12–20), it is composed of elements which are difficult to place under a single title, difficult to piece together. In fact, when this text (vv 31–38) is read in the liturgy, part of it is sometimes omitted. But, regardless of the diversity of its sources, the difficulty of putting its pieces together need not mean that it lacks unity. On the contrary, as in the case of vv 12–20, the difficulty of putting the pieces together may be seen as a way of suggesting, through the very form of the text, what the content is all about, namely the difficulty of piecing together glory, departure (into death), and love, ultimately of piecing together the complex interaction and union of the divine and the human. It is a difficulty which is so great that when, later on, Peter is faced with the human reality—with what actually happens to Jesus—he will in effect deny that any such union exists.

The text begins with the idea of glorification. Thus far chap. 13 had made no mention of glory or glorification, but, as was indicated in the general introduction to the chapter, far from being alien to it, it is like a blossoming which, though surprising in character, has been well prepared for.

The essential idea in the first part of the scene (vv 31–35) is that when Jesus looks at his death and beyond it, he sees that his human life, far from being a meaningless God-denying absurdity, something which chills the heart into fear-filled immobility or devouring self-indulgence, is instead a place of unprecedented divine generosity and regeneration, a place in which God shines forth and in which God's shining reveals Jesus' own true glorious self. And he sees that this mystery-filled generosity—like gentle sunshine which invites children to come out and play—this generosity invites people to discover another rejuvenated self and to throw themselves into its spirit of love. In other words, God's glorious presence so lights up life that it invites people to love.

But love is not easy. One cannot love as Jesus has loved, one cannot give oneself as Peter proposes to do, without outside help. There are barricades which make love inaccessible, and so, before speaking of it, before issuing the invitation, Jesus refers to his own going away (v 33), to what is, in fact, a mission to clear the barricades. Through his departure in death he will release, a stream of spiritual life which, while sweeping away all obstacles, will impart a new life, a new power of loving.

This is what Peter does not understand (vv 36–38). He thinks that he already has all he needs. In fact, he is so capable of loving that he is going to lay down his life for Jesus. As for this other, divine, dimension—the dimension which is already in Jesus (hence the talk of glorification) and which Jesus will make available to others—all that is not clear to him. The only thing he can grasp is the purely human, and when, in the case of Jesus, the purely human seems to be collapsing, he will lose faith in that other dimension.

A detailed exposition (vv 31–38)

Jesus' statement on glorification, given after the exit of Judas, is somewhat similar to his earlier statement on glorification, given after the coming of the Greeks (12:20–23,28). In fact, the two processes, the Greeks' coming and Judas's going, seem to complement one another—as though both were necessary for the full revealing of God's glory in the Son of humanity. In both texts there is a repetition of the word "glorify"—in 12:23, 28, four times; and in 13:31–32, five (following the longer reading—cf. Schnackenburg, 3:50).

This fivefold poetic repetition has a powerfully climactic effect. Its basic message is that in the Son of humanity, in other words, in Jesus as "the true self of the human race" (Dodd, 1953, 249) and especially in Jesus' death, the wonder of God is shown forth. And in the wonder of God, the wonder of the Son of humanity is seen. Thus in the human the divine is revealed, and in the divine, the human. The understanding of one leads to the understanding of the other (for discussion see esp. Schnackenburg, 3:50–52). A practical implication of this is that unless one is receptive towards people one is not receptive towards God, and unless one is receptive towards God, one's receptivity towards people is limited. A humanity seen apart from God is a humanity which is out of context and which consequently is misunderstood and mistreated.

The blending of humanity and divinity is reflected in the text's enigmatic allusions to time. On the one hand, the glory in question is beyond time, is something external; it "is past, present, and future since the whole process is viewed from an eternal viewpoint" (Brown, 610). Hence one finds here (13:31–32), as in the voice from heaven (12:28), a mixing of past and future: glorification has happened and will happen. It includes all that God has ever revealed through the Word in humanity. On the other hand, from the moment that Judas's departure is imminent, there appears a succession of time-related words (13:27–33): "After . . . then . . . quickly . . . the feast . . . immediately . . . night . . . when . . . now . . . immediately . . . yet a short while . . . now." The details are debatable, but the general emphasis seems clear (cf. Schnackenburg, 3:49–53), and the basic impression which emerges is that however much God may always have been at work revealing God's own self in humans and humans in God, and however much the divine is beyond time, there is at hand now a moment which is distinctive, new.

It is at this climactic moment, in this context of a breakthrough in revelation, that Jesus uses two significant words or phrases which he had never used before in this gospel—"little children," and "new commandment" (33–34). The implication is that the breakthrough brings for the disciples a new identity and a new role or morality.

Even though *teknion,* ''little child,'' is a diminutive (of *teknon,* ''child''), it always refers, in its eight other NT occurrences, not to small children, but to disciples (Gal 4:19; 1 John 2:1,2,28; 3:7,18; 4:4; 5:21). It is best seen, therefore, in the context of the central NT idea that with the coming of Christ and of the realm of God, those who are receptive are reborn in the Spirit and are revealed as God's children (see, for instance, Gal 4:1–7; Rom 8:14–17; Mark 10:13–16 and parr.; 1 John 2:1–4:6, esp. 3:1). It is used here because the context is that of Jesus' glorification and, since glorification implies the granting of the Spirit (7:37–39; cf. 19:30,34), it is appropriate to evoke the new Spirit-given identity—''little children.''

And with this new identity (and its implied presence of the Spirit) comes the new commandment—to love one another, as Jesus loved. As is indicated by several commentators, and, indirectly by 1 John 2:5b-8, the commandment of love, from one point of view, is not new (cf. esp. Lev 19:18, 34). But it is set in a new context, and context gives meaning. The context in this case is the unprecedented revelation of God's love, a revelation which is seen in Jesus (3:16) and especially in Jesus' washing of the feet (13:1–20, esp. 13:1). As Schnackenburg (3:53) indicates, even the striking phrasing of the commandment (''that as I . . . [so] you also,'' 34) is best compared to that of the foot-washing (15). Once so much love is revealed—one might say, once a new covenant is formed (Brown, 614)—the whole idea of love takes on new meaning. In Schnackenburg's words (3:54):

> The love that has been given to us in anticipation by God opens up for us a new living space in which we can and should love . . . in an entirely new way. . . . In the light of . . . 1 Jn [2:8; 3:14–16; 4:9] . . . this ''new commandment'' is not presented simply as a moral demand. It is rather expressed above all as a new possibility which calls . . . for realization.

Jesus' Departure and Return

Jesus, the Human Way, Reflects the Divine and Leads People to Union

It is sometimes said that chapter 14 is concerned with Jesus' departure and return (see esp. Becker, 1970, 222–23; Segovia, 1985, 477–78; Schnackenburg, 3:58). To some degree this is true; Jesus does, in fact, speak both of going and coming (see esp. vv 2–5, 18, 28). And in so doing he evokes both the resurrection and the final coming, or Parousia. But the conversation with Philip (vv 7b–11), for instance, "should not be brought under the rubric of the 'departure' of Jesus; the passage sets forth the relation of Jesus to the Father" (Beasley-Murray, 244). For Mateos and Barreto (627–35) it is this relationship with the Father, this ideal of union, which dominates the chapter. In fact, Haenchen (2:124) regards the chapter as so dominated by the evangelist's "experience of the Spirit" that the traditional language of the return seems to him to be unintegrated.

Yet the images of departure and return have their place. They help to achieve purposes which cohere with the gospel as a whole and particularly with the discourse: they lend to the central ideas (of union and spiritual experience) an added dimension of personalism and power; they imply, as is appropriate in speaking of achieving personal union with the Father, a process of loss and gain; and they maintain a limited suggestion of some form of eschatology or eschatological union in the future.

The essence of the chapter, therefore, is about union with God—to some degree union hereafter (vv 1–3), but above all union now—and with the process of achieving that union. Chapter 13 had spoken primarily of God as giving, of entering through Jesus' washing of the feet into the full reality of human experience. Now, in chap. 14, the emphasis is on the other side of the process, on the disciple as receiving. The relationship between the chapters, therefore, is something like that of a seal to wax. One evokes God's descent into what is very human (the feet). The other shows the human as accepting and possessing God, as being God's abode.

There is also in chap. 14, as in chap. 13, a persistent negative note. The dissonance which is found in the references to the devil, Judas, Peter, and the confused disciples (13:2,6–11,18,21–30,36–38) is echoed in various ways in 14:1–11. Thus while the two main sections of chapter 13 (13:1–20 and 13:21–38) virtually begin with references to the devil's influence on the heart and to the consequent human shuddering or shaking (13:2,21; cf. 13:27; Brown, 435), chapter 14 begins by speaking of the shaking heart (14:1). Furthermore, as will be seen later, the kind of confusion which is found in Peter (13:6–11,36–37) is found also, in variant form, in the questions of Thomas and Philip (14:5,8). In simplified terms, Peter does not want a revelation that is so human, so lowly; Thomas and Philip want something higher. And while the first part of chap. 14 (14:1–11) thus adapts and synthesizes the negativity of chap. 13, the remainder of the chapter (14:12–31) goes on to introduce negativity under a further image: "the world" (14:17,19,22,27,30,31). "World" at this point refers especially to those people who do not accept God's abiding. Thus both the giving and receiving of God's abiding are shadowed by evil, confusion, and refusal.

But the focus, clearly, is on the positive. In fact, just as chap. 13 contained a distinctively new and explicit emphasis on God's love being poured out even in death, so the subsequent picture of loving union, of abiding together (chapter 14), breaks new ground.

Structure: Main Divisions

The dividing of chap. 14 is unusually difficult. The easiest decision, though it has sometimes been contested, is that there is a conclusion which is marked off by the words "These things I have spoken to you . . ." (vv 25–31; Bernard, 2:552; Hoskyns, 461; Bultmann, 625; Behler, 1960, 72; Lindars, 483; Brown, 652; Schnackenburg, 3:82).

Then comes the basic question—finding the major division within vv 1–24. It is sometimes placed at 15, the chapter's first explicit reference to love, but even some of those who follow this division acknowledge that there is a problem: the verses which surround 15 (vv 12–17) are closely interwoven in various ways, particularly because of their emphasis on asking (Brown, 623, 644), and so it is better that they not be broken up. The unity of vv 12–17 is also indicated in varying degrees by, for instance, Schnackenburg (3:70–76, esp. 73) and Woll (1981, 69–96, esp. 81). Details of this unity will be seen later.

Once the section from verse 12 through verse 17 is regarded as essentially forming a unity, then the major dividing line has to fall either at its beginning, at v 12, or immediately after it, at v 18. If the text were primarily structured around the two ideas of departure and return then it would be plausible to make the division at v 18, for at v 18 there is a particularly strong reference to some form of coming or return, and that reference could appear as the dividing line between the two ideas (so Becker, 1970, 223–28; and Schnackenburg, 3:58; cf. critique of Becker by Woll, 1981, 17–21, esp. 19).

But, as indicated earlier, the ideas of departure and return, though they do occur, are not dominant. The determining idea is that of an abode, of achieving an abiding union with God. And as far as that notion is concerned the central division occurs at v 12. In simplified form:

vv   1–11   The shaken heart finds God in (the human) Jesus, in him who
            is the way to union.
vv 12–24   Finding God's abode in oneself, Spirit-led.

Further analysis of chap. 14 (as found especially in Excursus 6) indicates that its detailed structure is as follows.

Finding God in Jesus, the way (vv 1–11)

   Introduction: the ultimate finding of God—in a future abode (1–3);

   Finding God now, in the human Jesus, the way (4–7a);

Finding God in Jesus (an elaboration of 4–7a) (7b–11).

Finding God in oneself, Spirit-led (vv 12–24)

    Indwelling, stage 1: believing, leading to Spirit-led loving (12–17);

    Indwelling, stage 2: increased sense of union with Jesus (18–21b);

    Indwelling, stage 3: the Father-Jesus presence, a new creation (21c–24).

Conclusion: Spirit-based peace (vv 25–31)

    The peace . . . (25–27b)

    . . . Even in face of loss and death (27c–31)

Commentary

[14:1–3] Evoking the ultimate destination: In the face of fear, Jesus goes to prepare the final abode. Before looking at 14:1–3 in detail it is necessary to place it within the context of chap. 13 and of 14:1–11.

Chapter 13 had alluded to the coming death not only of Jesus, but also of Peter, the representative of the disciples (13:36, "You will follow later"). In 14:1–11, therefore, Jesus is speaking to people who are threatened by the limitedness of life—threatened primarily by his own imminent departure, but also to some degree by the fact that sooner or later they will all have to follow. It is a situation in which life's uncertainty may cause the heart to falter.

"Let not you heart be shaken" he begins, echoing earlier references to how he himself had been shaken by the increasing proximity of death (cf. 11:33; 12:27; 13:21). And then he gives a basic twofold message: appreciate what lies far ahead of you, an (eternal) abode with God (11:1–3); and, above all, appreciate what you have here and now, access to God through a way which is very down-to-earth, through the human Jesus and all he represents (14:4–11). Thus, there is a twofold focus, on the future and on the present.

The unity of future and present is underlined by some of the literary qualities of the text. First, the entire passage (vv 1–11) is bound together, first and last, by repeated calls to believe (vv 1, 10–11). The interwovenness of these references to believing is quite intricate. The initial use of the word "believe" may be read either as an indicative ("you believe") or an imperative ("believe"), but in the subsequent references there is no such ambiguity; they are all imperatives: "believe . . . believe . . . believe." Thus, the text goes from an imperative which is negative ("Let not your heart . . .") to one which is ambiguous, to ones which are clearly positive. The overall effect of this subtle literary grading is to bind the text into a unit and to highlight its role as a call to believe.

A further literary indication of the unity of the future and present is that the transition from one to the other, from future to present, occurs almost without a ripple; one glides from v 3 into v 4, and the scholarly difficulty in discerning a dividing line (cf. Excursus 6) is a reflection of the underlying unity.

This blending of future and present provides a corrective to the either/or approach which is sometimes applied to the question of John's eschatology. The prospect which the gospel holds out is not narrow. It emphasizes the present, but places that emphasis in the context of the future. Thus it is both comprehensive and challenging.

At the center of 14:1–3 is the alluring image of a *monē,* an "abode"—a word which takes the gospel's pivotal idea of active abiding (the verb, *menō*) and converts it into a form which suggests something final, stable. The old translation "mansion" ("In my Father's house there are many mansions . . .") had its limitations, but it also had the advantage of evoking something distant and wonderful.

But the image, however alluring, is not clear; in fact, the text is quite obscure.

vv 1–3 as "extraordinarily difficult." When one looks more closely at vv 1–3 one meets a perplexing situation. Jesus suggests the image of a house which has rooms for everybody and he indicates that after he has gone ahead to this house "to prepare a place" for the disciples, he will "come again" and take them to himself. In one sense the image seems simple; as Lindars (470) remarks, it is like the idea of going ahead to book people into a hotel and then coming back for them when all is ready.

Yet it has qualities which raise it far above the commonplace. It has a haunting suggestion of a restful place of well-being and final togetherness. And, in the details of its description, this brief passage is mind-bending.

The mind-bending quality is found in the fact that Jesus' words (vv 2–3) contain a striking number of ambiguities and obscurities. As Brown (625) remarks, the text is "extraordinarily difficult."

The difficulties may be summarized as follows. It is not clear whether the reference to Jesus "telling" the disciples forms a statement ("if not, I would have told you") or a question ("if not, would I have told you?"). Nor is it clear whether the telling refers to what precedes (the existence of the house with many abodes) or what follows (Jesus' going away to prepare a place). And the relationship of the telling to what follows is made even more uncertain by the ambiguity of the connecting *hoti,* "for" or, more simply, "that." (The omission of *hoti* in some manuscripts would appear to reflect an effort to limit the ambiguity.) Furthermore, if the telling refers to preparing a place, when did it occur? There is no previous reference to Jesus telling such a thing. Thus the notion of telling, and particularly telling about preparing a place, is set in obscurity and ambiguity.

In v 3 there is further uncertainty. Jesus says, "I will come again and take you to myself," but it is not clear to what he refers—whether to the post-resurrectional appearances or to taking people to himself at their death or to the final coming in the Parousia.

Without attempting a complete analysis of these difficulties, it may be said that in many ways they strain and baffle the mind, particularly with regard to place and time. The fact that the telling ("I have told you") can refer to distinct aspects of place—either to the (preceding) "house" or the (following) "place" —means that the mind cannot get a clear focus on the location. In other words, the announcement of the place has a certain fluidity. And the fact that the "coming again" can refer to diverse times provides a level of meaning wherein diverse times are collapsed into one. Thus, in various ways, there is a suggestion of the breaking of the normal boundaries of space and time.

What is essential is that what at first may look like confusion would seem rather to consist of sophisticated literary art with a definite purpose. In the face of death Jesus evokes another form of existence, an abiding with God which is beyond time and space, an existence which is grasped only through a mystery-filled (i.e., revelatory) telling and through the response of believing.

In discussing the extraordinary complexity of 14:1–3 it is appropriate to remember the extraordinary complexity of 13:1–3. Both texts allude to God and God's plan in Jesus. The first (13:1–3) is largely concerned with the origin of that plan, with its beginning, yet it alludes also to its end. The second (14:1–3) refers more directly to the end. Essential to both texts, despite their great differences, is that they are trying to describe the indescribable or, at least, to evoke the unutterable. Given that context, their mind-bending language is very appropriate. Like certain forms of art, they appeal not so much to the superficial intellect as to a deeper level of understanding.

[14:4–11] Appreciating the present revelation: the role of Jesus as the way. Having evoked the ultimate destination, the final abiding with God, Jesus focuses attention on the more immediate task of discerning how to get there and of recognizing that it is possible even now to see the Father.

The opening sentence has a certain disjuncture and consequently has sometimes been seen as ''not good grammar'' (Lindars, 671): ''And where I am going, you know the way'' (4a). He does not say ''where I am going you know *and* the way *you know,*'' even though, as is reflected in some manuscripts and translations, some such variation would have brought a welcome simplicity. Instead, in the middle of the short sentence there is a very slight jolt, as with a train changing tracks, and the theme shifts to the way. ''The way is made the theme even by the linguistic form of this verse, in which the emphasis falls at the end of the sentence'' (Schnackenburg, 3:63–64). The effect of this disjuncture, within so compact a sentence, is to underline both the unity and distinctness of the themes, of the future abode, and of the present way.

But Thomas and Philip are not satisfied. Thomas complains that they do not, in fact, know where Jesus is going; and thus he implies that they need a better view of the destination. Philip is more positive and forthright: ''Lord,'' he said, ''show us the Father; and that will be enough for us.'' What he is asking for, effectively, is a vision.

Their dissatisfaction echoes that of Peter during the foot-washing (13:6–11). Peter was unable to appreciate a divine presence which was so lowly, so human. Thomas and Philip want something higher, something visionlike.

It is at this point that Jesus alerts them to appreciating what they already have: ''I am the way. . . . Whoever has seen me has seen the Father . . .'' (14:6, 9). The phrase ''the way'' may also be found in other contexts. In Hellenistic religions it refers to ''the process by which the initiate became divine'' (Kysar, 223; cf. Bultmann, 603–4). In the OT it indicates the path laid down by the law (Ps 119:30, 34). And in Qumran and Acts it designates a community and its life (1QS ix 17–18,21; Acts 9:2, etc.) But Jesus uses it of himself, and he thus indicates that, above all, it is by focusing on the human person that one discovers the reality of God. When he adds ". . . and the truth and the life," these are not new ideas; they simply spell out what is already suggested in the term "the way." Focusing on the human person is a way to the truth, and even though aspects of the truth may be frightening, the acceptance of it finally leads to greater freedom and vitality, in other words, to life.

The image of Jesus as *the way of truth and life* synthesizes and develops the earlier image of Jesus as *the gate to salvation and life* (10:1–10, esp. vv 7–10; see Schnackenburg, 2:292, and for more detail, the German original, 2:368). One of the distinctive aspects of the more developed form (in chap. 14) is the more explicit emphasis on knowing and on Jesus as the way to knowing.

Precisely because this way is rather frightening the reader may want to find another one. And so, as if in answer, Jesus adds, "No one comes to the Father except through me." The contrast here is not with other religions, but with any approach which bypasses what Jesus represents, namely an emphasis on the human. While Thomas and Philip want something more ethereal, the way is this Jesus who is soon to die.

The exchange with Thomas ends on a negative note, on what seems to be a touch of rebuke or regret at the fact that the disciples have missed an opportunity: "If you had known me you would have known my Father also" (v 7a).

But Jesus does not linger on the past. He immediately moves on and thus uses the missed opportunity as added motivation for the present: "And now. . . ." Then comes the exchange with Philip (vv 7b–11), more positive, more prolonged, more explicit: "Whoever has seen me has seen the Father" (v 9).

The two exchanges complement each other. In relation to the first and its statement on Jesus as the way, the second may be described as commentary (Brown, 631) or clarification and intensification (Schnackenburg, 3:68).

One of the features of this intensification is that the discourse moves more and more inward. The reply to Philip is repetitious and personal. Philip is one of the few people, along with Lazarus, Mary, and Simon Peter (11:43; 20:16; 21:15–17) whom Jesus addresses by name. And Jesus emphasizes that he and Philip have been together: "So long a time I am with you. . . ." The basic effect of this discussion is to suggest an interaction which is immensely human, and to indicate that it is precisely through such an interaction that one sees the Father. Not that the seeing is inevitable or easy; it requires an act of believing: "Do you not believe that I am in the Father and the Father in me?" And the emphasis on believing goes on to become more and more explicit and intensive (vv 10–11).

At this point (10–11) there recurs the familiar idea (see esp. 10:37–38—which also gives a triple use of "believe") of believing first of all in Jesus' words, or failing that, in the works. Ultimately both the words and works come from the Father. But while chapter 10, especially 10:22–39, had highlighted Jesus' unique God-based dignity, his union with God, the present text (14:1–11) is going a step further by emphasizing, more than before, that, through Jesus, this presence of God is perceptible to others—provided they believe—and that this presence is perceived above all in human life and interaction.

The most central idea in vv 4–11 is that the perfect human being reflects God, is God's mirror. And Jesus was such a being. "He was the true self of the human race, standing in . . . perfect union with God'' (Dodd, 1953, 249). This true self is set within space and time, yet in another sense it is outside these factors; it is in the world of the divine ''I am.'' In the words of William Johnston (1981, 46):

> It is principally in the fourth gospel . . . that we find a Jesus who is acutely aware of his identity. . . . This is the Jesus on whose lips the evangelist puts those words of Exodus: ''I am.'' . . . The deep self of Jesus is outside space and time, since he is the eternal word of the Father. And Jesus can finally say: ''He who has seen me has seen the Father'' (John 14:9). For he is the perfect image of the Father, the mirror in which the Father is reflected. Here we are at the very heart of Johannine theology.

[14:12–24] Spirit-led union: how ordinary people begin to discover God in themselves. Jesus' closeness to God, as described in 14:1–11, is not some exotic showpiece, to be preserved so to speak in a museum; it is above all a way, in other words, a way for other people. Consequently, Jesus now goes on (vv 12–24) to indicate how others arrive at, or are brought to, a similar closeness.

The fact that this process of discovery is open to all does not mean that it is easy. Though the gospel's positive-sounding opening passages (1:1–2:22) suggested that the heart is naturally oriented towards making this discovery, a human being has serious weaknesses or wounds, and there are many patterns of action and thought which in various ways clog the workings of the heart and prevent it from seeing. Hence moral conduct is important; ''there is no spiritual union which is not also a moral union'' (Hoskyns, 460).

This process of spiritual discovery may be described as a journey, one which follows the way constituted by Jesus. In him humanity was combined with divinity, and those who follow that way find that not only within Jesus but also within themselves there is a presence which is extraordinary. Something of the feeling of that voyage is captured by Johnston (1981, 47):

> What a journey! As we pass through the outer layers of turbulent darkness . . . of . . . consciousness . . . and approach the core of our being what will we find? If we have the courage to answer the call to look into the mirror of our own souls, we will see our own beauty and the beauty of God. And that will be a great enlightenment.

One is not alone on this journey. As the washing of the feet suggested, and as the death and resurrection will make clear, God has entered the world, has essentially overcome weakness and woundedness, and has made available, through the companionlike Spirit, a reservoir of healing and strength. Hence, however much may be demanded of the individual, however difficult or frightening the journey, this gentle Spirit is present, humanlike yet much more, to lead the way, to renew the heart, and, even in this life, to bring the person home to God.

The text consists of three main sections, and these emphasize, respectively, the Spirit (vv 12–17), Jesus (vv 18–20), and the Father (vv 21–24). Together they speak of God and, in the final analysis, it is on God's initiative that progress depends. So true is this that, even though the text as a whole is largely governed by the implied image of the believer following a way, undertaking a journey, within each section of the text it is to the Spirit, Jesus, and the Father that movement is attributed: the Spirit will be given (vv 12–17); Jesus will come (vv 18–20); and, finally, with a climactic sense of energy and movement, "we will come . . . and we will make our abode" (vv 21–24).

vv 12–17. The first section (vv 12–17) presupposes that the person who is journeying is a believer, in other words, that there is a basic conviction that the journey is worthwhile, that Jesus really does reflect ultimate goodness. And with believing (v 12) there is hoping (vv 13–14) and loving (vv 15–17). The word "hope," of course, is not used—in fact, apart from a single negative reference ("Moses in whom you hope," 5:45) the word never occurs in the entire gospel— but in the repeated idea of asking (vv 13–14), hope is implied. And so, in simplified terms, this first section begins with the presence of faith, hope, and love. And with these, inextricably interwoven with them both in the literary structure of the text and in reality, is the Spirit.

These four elements (faith, hope, love, the Spirit) are not presented as realities which are either inert or separate. Faith, hope, and love are all described as various verbs, thus implying movement. And the Spirit also is connected with movement—both with the believer's loving and the divine giving. Furthermore, all these verbs are interwoven; one leads to the next. What is implied, therefore, is a single complex dynamism through which the traveler reaches out to God and God to the traveler.

The sense of dynamism is heightened by a closer look at the structure. Each of the subsections—those dealing respectively with faith, hope, and love—has two steps:

Faith	leads both to works such as Jesus does
	and also to greater works,
	"because I am going to the Father" (v 12);
Asking	involves asking in union with Jesus (lit., in his name)
	and, still in union, asking Jesus himself,
	"that the Father may be glorified in the Son" (v 13);
Love	implies keeping Jesus' commandments
	and Jesus will ask the Father
	"and he will give you another paraklētos to be with you . . ." (v 15).

In each case the second step involves a certain advancement or intensification of the first, and the final intensification, flowing from love, is inseparable from the *paraklētos* ("counsellor" or "companion"). (The reference to the *paraklētos*, therefore, is integral to the text.) Furthermore, interwoven with believing, asking, and loving, there is a kind of summary of what Jesus' work accomplishes—his going to the Father, the Father's glorification, and the giving of the Companion. Thus, there is a sense in which the death-and-resurrection, with all that it implies about overcoming weakness and woundedness, takes place in the heart of the hopeful traveler.

This implies a profound transformation, and so it is not surprising to find that the entire passage (vv 12–24) has suggestions of a new creation. This is first hinted at by the reference to the believer doing "greater works" (v 12). The traditional (and apparently correct) interpretation of this is that the basic work of Jesus, his mission to the world, finds its "greater" expression in the period after his own ministry, the period in which, through the believers, his word is really brought to the ends of the earth. What is being spoken of, therefore, is not just the performing of miracles, though these are included, but the larger work of which the miracles were merely signs—the renewal of the world and, indeed, of creation.

The idea that Jesus is envisaging some form of new or renewed creation is confirmed by a number of factors. His own works had had various echoes of creation (cf. esp. 2:11; 5:1–18, esp. 5:6–9, 17; 9:1–7). Furthermore, in this text itself there is another creation-related echo: the passage has several points of affinity with the creation-related discourse of 5:19–47, particularly with 5:19–24 (see esp. 14:12 and 5:19–20; note the roles of the life-giver, 5:21; 14:19; of the believer, 5:24; 14:12; of right conduct, 5:29; 14:15,21,23; of the word, 5:24; 14:23–24. Some of the points of contact are noted by Lindars, 475–76). And the text also makes striking use of *poieō*, "do/make," the verb which is used repeatedly to describe the making or creating of everything (Gen 1:1,7,11,16,21,25,26,27 [3 times],31; 2:2 [2 times], 3,4,18). In 14:12–24, it is first said, twice, that the believer will "do/make" the "works", *poiēsei . . . erga* (12). Then Jesus says twice that *he* will "do/make" whatever is asked, *poiēsō* (13, 14). The connection with the process of creation is heightened by the fact that creation was described as "works" (*erga*, Gen 2:3).

At each stage of this process, as the believer comes closer, Jesus is active, is doing what the believer asks. There is no impeding of this process. Provided what the believer asks is in union with Jesus ("in my name"), Jesus does it.

There comes a point, however, when Jesus grants something extra—the Companion, the Spirit of truth. The gospel does not say that the believer asks for it. It is as though the Spirit were in some way beyond the believer's initial knowledge. But because the believer has been seeking and has been faithful, *Jesus* asks for the Paraclete, and the Father gives it.

The word *paraklētos* is found once in 1 John (where Jesus is described as "our paraclete" or heavenly intercessor with the Father, 1 John 2:1), and four times in the last discourse (14:16,26; 15:27; 16:7). It does not otherwise occur in the NT or in the entire OT. The word itself, formed from *para-kaleō*, "call to one's side/appeal to/exert/comfort/encourage," is variously translated as "advocate," "counselor," "intercessor," "protector," "comforter," or "helper." The suitability of "companion" as a translation is indicated by the context—by the emphasis on *being with* the disciples (vv 9, 16), and by the discourse's central emphasis on friendship (15:11–17).

As used in the canonical text of the last discourse, *paraklētos* refers to the Holy Spirit (cf. 14:16, and esp. 14:26), and despite its difficulty as a term—it is difficult both in background and meaning—it has a very definite effect: it brings the idea of the (Holy) Spirit down to earth in an arresting way. In fact, the very difficulty and richness of the term constitute much of its strength. Like yet another thought-provoking puzzle, it engages the mind and implicity challenges it to expand, to rise to a new level. As Jesus is about to go away, the Companion emerges as another rich personal presence. It is a presence which, precisely because of its character as mind-bending, mind-surpassing, cannot be accepted or seen or known by a glib material world. But for those who have believed and searched and truly loved, it becomes a presence which is permanent (''with you forever'') and which is right at the person's center (''it abides with you and is in you'').

vv 18–20. The second section (vv 18–20) shifts the emphasis from the Spirit-related activity of the traveler (believing, asking, loving) to the corroborating activity of Jesus, above all to the idea of his coming.

The picture is quite vivid. Following a form of spiral structure, the text looks afresh and sees the traveler as an orphan, as alone. But it immediately goes on, in three intensifying stages, to speak of the presence of Jesus:

''I will come to you'' (v 18);

''Yet a short while . . . you will see me, and because I live, you also will live'' (v 19);

''On that day you will know that I am in the Father, and you in me and I in you'' (v 20).

When Jesus speaks of his own coming (18–20, ''I will not leave you orphans; I will come to you . . .'') it is quite possible at first sight to understand that coming as referring to a specific time—either to his final coming in the Parousia or to his return after the resurrection. The reference to ''a short while'' (19) may appear to suggest a coming that is post-resurrectional, but it can also be stretched to refer to the Parousia (cf. 1 Cor 7:29, ''The time is short''; Brown, 645, 607). In fact, the phrase ''On that day'' has an eschatological ring which may be taken as confirming the idea of an allusion to the Parousia.

Yet, though Jesus' words do indeed evoke both the post-resurrectional appearances and the Parousia, they go beyond these specific times, and they suggest something more permanent—the abiding presence of Jesus, in other words, the union of Jesus, as life-giver, with those who believe in him. This idea is confirmed by the fact that, as described in the text, Jesus' presence is closely linked to that of the abiding Companion. Like the Companion, Jesus may not be seen by the world, but he is seen by the believers and is ''in them.'' In fact, it is essentially with the phrase ''in you'' that both texts conclude (17, 20). Furthermore, the phase, ''I will not leave you orphans,'' is placed so close to the description of the coming of the Spirit that, on first reading the text, one may receive a momentary impression that it is the Spirit rather than Jesus who saves the disciples from orphanhood.

The role of the *returning* Jesus, as *saving from orphanhood,* complements the earlier connection between the image of *small children* and the *departure* of Jesus (13:33). Thus it is Jesus and not the Spirit who is explicitly linked with the images of small children and orphans. But in both texts, both in the reference to the small children and the orphans, the idea of the Spirit is not far away. In 13:33 it was the implied need to send the "child-forming" Spirit of love which made sense of the fact that Jesus used the term "small children" and said he had to go away. And now, in 14:17–18, the reference to not being orphans is placed immediately after the mention of the abiding Spirit.

What is essential is that the role of Jesus as the one who saves from orphan-hood—the one who gives fundamental identity and strength—is closely linked to that of the Spirit.

The journey, therefore, is like a spiralling process in which the disciple, having first reached an awareness of a love-related Spirit, then discovers a reinforcing presence, the personal life-giving presence of the risen Jesus.

vv 21–24.   The third section (vv 21–24) swings back to an initial emphasis on the believer, but instead of going through the triple activity of believing, asking, and loving, it starts with loving (v 21a) and then goes on, with increasing intensity, to present that love as being returned by God.

Again the text would appear to contain three steps, and again the climactic third is more elaborate than the others. Separating these steps is difficult, and the following division is tentative (the apparent division which begins at v 21c is somewhat similar to that which begins at v 4).

The first step extends to the idea, passively stated, of being loved by the Father (v 21ab). Then comes the idea, actively stated, that to such a person Jesus gives not only love but also revelation; and the sense of something new is heightened by the introduction into the discourse of a new character, "Judas, not the Iscariot," someone previously not mentioned in the entire gospel (vv 21c–22). Finally (vv 23–24), there is the active statement of the Father's love, and with it the resounding promise: "And we shall come . . . and we shall make our abode. . . ."

The suggestion of a new creation, a suggestion which had been faintly evoked through the "greater works" of vv 12–17, and through the eschatological-sounding "in that day" of vv 18–20, finds here significant backing. There is, in effect, a new Judas, one who, in contrast to the Judas who was last mentioned as being inhabited by Satan and enveloped by night (13:27,30), opens the way, through his question, to the revealing of Jesus and to the idea of being indwelt by God. Furthermore, the climactic "and we shall come . . . and shall make [*poiēso-metha*] our abode" has, within vv 12–26, much of the same climactic meaning and function as does "Let us make [*poiēsomen*] humankind" within the first creation story (Gen 1:26). The Genesis story indicates that the human is essentially an image of God. The text of John is a promise that that image, however fallen and battered, is to be restored and strengthened.

The key to this restoration is love. This does not mean that for the reader the word "love" always suggests something positive. On the contrary it may evoke deep pain, the experience of being "a frayed . . . survivor in a fallen world" (Farley, 1986, 24, adapting Annie Dillard). Yet it is through love, through a deeper love, that the heart is to be renewed. So far the gospel has used the verb *agapaō* sparingly, but now, with climactic intensity, it is used four times in a single verse (21). And at one point in the middle of that verse it occurs three times with little interruption:

> . . . *ho agapōn me*; *ho de agapōn me agapēthēsetai* . . .
>
> ". . . who loves me; the one who loves me will be loved . . ."

The love which is given by the one who keeps the commandments is a love for Jesus, but the love which is returned comes not only from Jesus, but also— and this is mentioned first—from the Father. Thus through loving Jesus (and all that Jesus represents) there is finally a kind of breakthrough to the Father. Ultimately, of course, it was the Father, in loving the world and giving the Son (3:16), who first set the cycle of love in motion. But now that that original expression of love has been fully accepted—now that Jesus has been loved through keeping his commandments—there is given by the Father a crowning love, one which involves mutuality, the mutuality of Father and Son, and the mutuality of both with the Spirit-helped believer. In earlier texts Jesus had spoken of his own union with the Father (cf. 5:16–18; 10:30, 38; 14:9–10). But now, following the reference to the Companion, the believer is also brought into this divine union, first into union with Jesus (20) and now, finally, into union with both the Father and Jesus (21, 23).

The final image (v 24) is of hearing the "word" (*logos*). It is not an isolated reference; within vv 12–26 there is a pattern of texts which speak of "keeping" the "commandments" and/or "words" and that pattern is focused into the final image of hearing the word. What is evoked therefore in v 24 is the accepting and retaining of "the whole of Jesus' activity in the sphere of revelation" (Schnackenburg, 3:74), in other words, the whole of God's self-communication. The implication is of having God in one's heart.

[14:25–31] Conclusion: Spirit-based peace, even in the face of (Jesus') departure and death.   These verses form a kind of interlude or pause. They allow the Spirit-based process to take hold so to speak. It is like stepping back from a carefully planted garden to see whether or how it will begin to come to fruition. Just as the thought of the foot-washing (and of other texts) is reflected and developed in the final scenes of chap. 13 (13:21–38), so here also the thought of preceding texts, especially the idea of an abode, an abiding union which is established through Jesus' departure and death (14:1–24), is summarized and developed.

It is extremely difficult to find the division(s) in the text. Some writers see the reference to peace (v 27ab) as indicating a new subsection (e.g., Lagrange, 392– 93; Blank, 4/2:130; Becker, 475; Beasley-Murray, 245). And Bultmann (627) regards the reference to peace as forming a unit with the following reference to not being disturbed (27c). But one of the divisions made by Brown (654) is between the peace (v 27ab) and the disturbance (or threat, v 27c), and, on balance, this would appear to be the most significant division in the passage. It yields a text which is divided between an initial picture of Spirit-based peace (vv 25–27b) and a later more negative picture in which Jesus reassures the disciple who has to fight off certain disturbing threats, especially the disturbance caused by the threat of loss (Jesus' departure) and by the implied hostility of the world (vv 27c–31).

Support for this division is provided by some details. The word which the first part uses repeatedly to conclude its phrases, *hymin,* "(to) you" (vv 26–27b), had already been used in the preceding text precisely to form conclusions (vv 17, 20). And the major word with which the second part begins *tarassō,* "disturb/trouble/ shake" (27c), had similarly been used in the preceding text as a beginning (v 1, cf. 13:21). Thus within the chapter as a whole there are precedents for the role of these words as dividing the text.

vv 25–27b, Jesus' Spirit-based peace.   Having alluded to the sad fact that something is coming to an end, that the former togetherness ("abiding") is over (v 25), Jesus goes on to refer to another form of togetherness, that which is achieved through both the Holy Spirit's action of bringing to mind what Jesus had said (v 26) and also through the giving of peace (v 27ab). The two elements, the Holy Spirit and peace, are not explicitly linked to one another, yet—as if associated by juxtapositioning or mere contact (Alter, 1981, 26)—they do seem to be inherently connected. Thus, the possibly disruptive effect of losing something is offset by the prospect of a greater, spiritual, gift.

Furthermore, at this point the spiritual gift itself begins to emerge more clearly: in comparison with the initial reference to the Companion (vv 16–17), the Spirit is now seen with increasing clarity, activity, and personality. Apart from just two other references (1:33; 20:22) this is the only time the gospel refers to the Spirit as holy. And this sense of definiteness is increased by the reference to the Holy Spirit as the one "whom the Father will send in my name" and as *ekeinos* "that one" (masculine). The primary effect of using a gender which is either masculine or feminine (rather than neuter, as in 17) is to give an increased sense of personality to the Spirit. As Brown notes (650), the Spirit is thus "more then a tendency or influence."

And then, following the reference to the Spirit, comes the reference to peace (27). It is a peace which is granted by Jesus rather than the Spirit, but given the Spirit's union with Jesus (the Spirit is given in Jesus' name, 26), it is a peace which is Spirit-related. (Later, in 20:19–23, Jesus' peace introduces the Spirit.) The context, plus the fact that this peace is distinguished from that of "the world," indicates its essence—the Spirit-based divine indwelling which is repeatedly depicted as set apart from "the world" (17, 19, 22). Thus for the believer, peace is not based on the world and not on externals or on the absence of external conflict, but on a vigorous harmony with the deepest personal elements of the divine.

vv 27c–31, reassurance against loss and hostility.   The Spirit-based harmony need not be destroyed—neither by departures, nor the devil, nor death. In the remaining verses (27c–31), as he speaks of his impending death, Jesus alludes to many of the tumults and fears that invade the heart, and the essence of his message is that no circumstance or threat should cause the disciples to lose faith in him or cause them to break the abiding union.

There is, in fact, a certain universality to his message. In speaking of his own words to them, he refers to the past, present, and future:

"You have heard me say to you . . ." (28);

"And now I have told you . . ." (29);

"I will no longer talk much with you . . ." (30).

Part of the meaning of this pattern is that all his words (past, present, and future) form a kind of global unity which counters what he had just warned against (27c) —insecurity and fear.

Then he begins to spell out the matters that may cause a break in the sense of union. First of all, disturbance may be caused by his departure. Yet if they really loved him they would be glad for him . . . "for the Father is greater than I" (28). This latter phrase was used by the Arians to argue against the divinity of Christ. But in the context, especially the context of the foot-washing, what is meant is that within the complex process of salvation there was a particular time when the divine Son and messenger played a role which was, in some way, subservient to the Father (and even to later believers, cf. 13:16; 14:12; see esp. Westcott, 213–16). The basic idea is well illustrated in the hymn on self-emptying (Phil 2:5–11) where Christ, though divine, abandons equality with God in order to enter the human condition. As in Philippians, the return to God is something immensely positive. His departure, therefore, is something which should bring joy.

Furthermore (29) since what will happen to Jesus has been told by him prophetlike in advance, there is an implication that his fate falls within a known plan, a plan which is ultimately divine. And so, he tells them that when it happens, their reaction, far from being one of despair, should be one of believing.

Finally (30–31), not even the approach of "the ruler of this world"—a reference to the devil (working through Judas) as the leader of all that is worldly, all that is not of God—not even that death-bearing agent should destroy the sense of union with God. For that ruler has no power over Jesus, no place in him, no abode (literally, "in me he has not anything"—a phrase which in isolation refers to having no legal claim, but which in the context forms a contrast with the idea of an abode). It is the Father who has an abode in Jesus, not the devil. And if Jesus goes to his death it is ultimately not because of the devil, but because it is communicated ("commanded") by the Father, and because it is something which Jesus does with love.

Thus once again, as so often in preceding passages (e.g. 8:44–47; 11:49–53) the gospel locates what seems most negative (devil-related death) within a larger positive framework (God-related love).

Despite this positive attitude there is a suggestion that Jesus has now reached a low point. Not only is he lesser than the Father (v 28), he is also obedient unto death (v 31). The self-emptying is being increasingly evoked. But precisely by reaching such a low point, by dying, the seed comes to new life. And so when Jesus says, "Arise, let us go from here," he is not saying that they must leave the room. He is talking, as he did, for instance, to Nicodemus and the woman of

Samaria, on a higher challenging level, the level of spiritual birth and development. He is evoking the whole process of resurrection and of journeying to God. It is a process of growth which is found first of all in himself, but it includes also those in whom his divine Spirit has been planted (cf. vv 12–24) and in whom it has begun to take root (cf. vv 25–27). Together he and they are now ready to rise. Thus the way is prepared for a surprising new development—the growth of the vine and its branches.

Excursus 6: The Structure of John 14

In introducing chap. 14 the following structure was proposed:

- The shaken heart finds God in Jesus, the way (vv 1–11)
- Finding God's abode in oneself, Spirit-led (vv 12–24)
- Conclusion: Spirit-led peace (vv 25–31)

This proposal, however, needs to be tested and developed. For instance, on either side of the main proposed dividing line (at v 12) there are references to works-related faith (cf. vv 10–12), and this may seem to call the division into question. However, in these verses the idea of faith is used in diverse ways. In vv 1–11 (including vv 10–11), faith is something that Jesus encourages, something to be striven for. In v 12, on the other hand, it is presupposed.

The plausibility of v 12 as the dividing line is heightened by the fact that vv 1–11 are bound together like an *inclusio*—bound by the opening and closing emphasis on the need to believe (vv 1, 10–11). Furthermore, v 12 itself begins with "Amen, amen, I say to you," a phrase which frequently acts as a divider, and which is doubly likely to do so in a chapter where more conspicuous dividing signs are missing, and in which the conclusion is marked off by the analogous, "These things I have spoken to you" (v 25).

The confusion which surrounds the dividing of chap. 14 has some affinity with the confusion which surrounds the dividing of chap. 17. In both cases the essence of the chapter is concerned with union, and it is that idea which provides the clue to detecting how the chapter is structured. But in both cases there are other factors which, though important, are not fundamental, not governing—the idea of departure and return in chap. 14 and the making of petitions in chap. 17.

Subdivisions

In subdividing vv 1–11, the first task is to mark off the introductory section. It is disputed whether this consists of vv 1–3 (Boismard, 1961, 519) or whether it also involves v 4 (Bultmann, 598; for other opinions, see Brown, 623–24).

The problem is clarified significantly by comparing 14:1–3 with the end of Jesus' prayer, 17:24–26. Unlike much of the discourse, focused as it is on this life, both these brief texts are focused on the hereafter, on the final abiding with Jesus and God. Set as they are at the extremities of the texts, at the beginning of 14 and the conclusion of 17, they provide, along with 13:1–3, a certain ultimate framework. Thus they have balancing roles; one opens and the other closes. Within this context of balance, a further element of balance is to be noticed, between 14:3 and 17:24:

14:3   "that where I am you also may be."
17:24   "that where I am they also may be with me."

Given that 17:24 acts as a divider (it opens 17:24–26), the same would seem to be true, in a balancing way, of 14:3 (it closes 14:1–3). The argument has a certain mathematical quality, but that is not inappropriate, and it tips the balance of the debate in favor of closing with v 3.

Once vv 1–3 are in place as introductory, the remainder of vv 4–11 divides fairly easily into two exchanges, one involving Thomas (vv 4–7a) and the other Philip (vv 7b–11). The beginnings of these exchanges contain elements of repetition and complementarity:

"And where . . .	"And now already
you know . . ."	you know . . ."
Thomas said to him,	Philip said to him,
"Lord . . ."	"Lord . . ."
Jesus said to him,	Jesus said to him,
"I am . . ."	"So long a time I am . . ."

This balance helps to confirm the subdividing of vv 1–11 into 1–3, 4–7a and 7b–11.

In subdividing vv 12–24 there is considerable agreement that the text falls into three segments (cf. Brown, 642–48, esp. 642, 644, 647), but while there is little problem in locating the first point of subdivision (18, "I will not leave you orphans, I will come to you . . ."), it is not clear whether the other occurs at 21 ("Whoever has my commandments . . .") or at 23 ("Jesus answered [Judas] and said . . ."). A symptom of the difficulty is the fact that, in reviewing the discussion, Brown (642–43, 647) shows considerable sympathy with making the division at 23, but then goes on to suggest tentatively that it begins at v 21. Thus the subunits would consist of vv 12–17, 18–20, and 21–24.

This, in fact, seems to be the better division. It takes account of 22, which otherwise tends to become stranded between sections—an indication that something is probably wrong—and at the points of division it manifests elements of repetition: "The one who believes/keeps . . ." (12, 21); "(is) in you" (end of 17, 20).

The resulting text is one which, from one point of view at least, lays emphasis first on the Spirit (12–17), then on Jesus (18–20), and finally on the Father (21–24). And it suggests a spiritual process of increasingly receiving God. First the advancing efforts of the believer are aided by the *paraklētos*, the Spirit of truth (12–17). Then there is the reinforcing and vivifying of that process through the (Father-related) presence of Jesus (18–20). And finally there is the full flowering, in the abode of the heart, of God's (Father-based) multifaceted love (21–24).

As will be seen later, it would seem also that within each section there are three subsections. These begin at 12, 13, 15, 18, 19, 20, 21, 21c(?), 23. Most of the subsections appear to have two parts, but the final climactic subsections, numbers 3, 6, and 9, seem to be more elaborate.

Be that as it may, a central problem remains unsolved: What is the basis of the fundamental division into three sections (into 12–17, 18–20, and 21–24)?

The relative brevity of the Jesus section (18–20) may be a reflection of the fact that at this point his status is reduced. The Father is greater (28b); Jesus is obedient unto death (31).

The two longer texts (12–17 and 21–24) may be referred to, in simplified terms, as pictures of increasing indwelling. Apart from the scene-setting "Amen, amen, . . ." both begin with the third person (12, "The one who believes in me . . ."; 21, "The one who has my commandments . . ."), and they have several elements of affinity and duplication: an initial sense of the disciple's link with Jesus and thus, somehow, with the Father (12, 21); loving Jesus brings something from the Father (15–16, 23); and a reference to what is negative (17, the world; 24, the one who does not love). One of the main differences between 12–17 and 21–24 is that in the later subunit the connection with the Father is more immediate, and thus there is a greater sense of full communication with the Godhead. The later one (21–24), therefore, may be seen as an intensification of the first (12–17).

The brief intervening text (18–20) begins, not with the third person, but with "I will not . . ." (in Greek the "not" is first). It repeats elements of 12–17 (the idea of not seeing, and especially the concluding ". . . in you," 17, 19–20), but its main characteristic, apart from referring to indwelling, is to highlight the coming of Jesus. This it does in a way that is not done in the other texts.

Thus while the first and third subunits (12–17 and 21–24) reflect advancing communication, and do so in a way which lays considerable emphasis on the role of the believer, the central subunit (18–20), with its brief picture of the coming of Jesus, provides a reminder of the extent to which the entire process of communication depends on God's action in Jesus. It is union which governs chap. 14 as a whole, and it is also union which governs the subdividing of vv 12–24.

The Parable of the True Vine

A Picture of Advancing Purification and of Deepening Love

As already indicated in the general introduction to chapters 13–17, 15:1–16:4a is essentially a single unit which deals first with what is positive (God's purifying of Jesus, the true vine; 15:1–17) and then with what is negative (the world's hatred, 15:18–16:4a). In chaps. 13 and 17, of course, positive and negative are variously interwoven, and 15:1–16:4a could have done likewise, but since one of the essentials of its content is the theme of a purifying or separating, it is appropriate that the form reflect that theme. Thus the fact that the advancing disciple has to go through a certain process of separation—of breaking free from the world with all its enslaving habits, values, and relationships—that separation is reflected in the very form of the text, in the dividing of it into two units which are distinct (15:1–17 and 15:18–16:4a).

The essential purpose of the parable (15:1–17) is to portray how God works to bring people more fully into divine union, into their full potential of fruition and joy.

While there is considerable agreement that 15:1–17 is a single text, its interpretation is obscured by uncertainty concerning its structure. Some writers do not attempt to find a major point of division, and among those who do, a sampling of opinion shows widespread disagreement:

1–6, 7–17	Brown (665), Mateos and Barreto (652)
1–8, 9–17	Lagrange (405), Hoskyns (472), Bultmann (539), Becker (484), Segovia (1982, 99)
1–10, 11–17	Westcott (216 [1–10, 11–16]), Borig (1967, 19), Beasley-Murray (269), UBSGNT
1–11, 12–17	Schnackenburg (3:96), RSV

Before attempting to solve the problem it is necessary to set the passage in context, particularly in the context of the gospel.

Broad Context

The ultimate background for the image of the vine would appear to be found in the OT, in those texts where the focal area of God's activity, Israel, is described as a vineyard or vine (cf. esp. Isa 5:1–7; Ezek 17; and particularly Jer 2:21, LXX, "I planted you as a vine, fruit bearing . . . true," (*egō . . . ampelon karpophorōn . . . alēthinēn*). This does not exclude an incorporation of Gnostic elements, particularly those related to the Mandean picture of the vine as the tree of life (for discussion, see esp. Borig, 1967, 79–194; Schnackenburg, 3:104–6; Brown, 669–72). Furthermore, in the synoptics several parables indicate that "the vineyard, or persons connected with it, represent[s] Israel, or a section of Israel" (Barrett, 471; cf. Matt 20:1–16, 21:28–32, 21:33–41, and parr.; Luke 13:6–9).

Within John's gospel certain elements of context are provided by earlier references to wine and bread and fruit-bearing. The surprise production of abundant glory-filled wedding wine, achieved through listening to Jesus' words of command (2:1–11), helps both to prepare the way for the idea that Jesus' words and commands bring the vine to rich fruition (cf. 15:3,7,10,12,17) and also to invest wine-related images with extra meaning. The bread of life text also, insofar as some of its words and phrases are echoed in the vine passage (cf. 6:33,35,41,48,56; for some further details see Brown, 673), helps to invest the later passage with some of its own meaning, particularly that of increasing union with the divine. And the gospel's only previous image of fruit-bearing, insofar as it is clearly based on death (12:24), suggests that for the vine also and for its branches the cost of bearing fruit will be high.

Further context is provided by the preceding chapter and by its emphasis on the idea of an abode (cf. 14:2,23); this prepares the way for the repeated emphasis which 15:1–17 places on the idea of abiding. The essence of the abode/abide language is the concept of union; chap. 14 establishes it, and 15:1–17 develops it. Associated with abiding union is the following of "the word": the repetitive pattern of 14:12–24 ("my commandments . . . my commandments . . . my word . . . my words . . . the word," 14:15,21,23–24) prepares for what follows ("the word . . . my words . . . my commandments . . . my Father's commandments . . . I command you . . . I command you," (15:3,7,10,14,17). In chap. 14, which views increasing union from the human point of view, the sense of movement is from the human to the divine—from keeping the commandments towards the (divine) center, "the word." But in chap. 15, written from the divine point of view, the movement is outwards—from "the word" to the (human) keeping of the commandments.

The Context Provided by 1:1–18, 10:7–18, and Chapter 13

The most fundamental context for 15:1–17 is that provided by three other leading texts—the prologue (1:1–18), the parable of the good shepherd (10:7–18), and the foot-washing (chap. 13). They are leading insofar as they provide advancing portrayals of the foundational divine initiative—the initial incarnation (1:1–18), the willingness to go further, even to death (10:7–18), and the symbolizing and partial enactment of that death (chap. 13). The parable of the true vine is in that same leading category; it too is a portrayal of divine action. And it goes further still: it suggests not only a certain self-giving or descent on the part of Jesus, but also a form of death for those who are in union with him: the branches, in order to be fruitful, must undergo a radical cleansing.

Some further details of this continuity with earlier texts may be noted. The emphasis which 15:1–17 places on the "word" and on its several aspects, while it does indeed mirror 14:12–24, is ultimately a variation and development of the emphasis on the Word which is found in the prologue. Both texts suggest an increasing descent of the divine word into the day-to-day reality of human life. The prologue, of course, starts at the very beginning, then alludes first to the prophetic word, as found in John's witness, and finally speaks of the Word becoming flesh (1:1,6,14). The parable, which presupposes that the word has already entered life, first ascribes to it a basic function, the God-like function of pruning or purifying those who are with Jesus, in other words, the fundamental role of bringing God's vine to greater life ("Now you are clean by reason of the word, . . ." 3). And then it refers to the word in ways which by and large are increasingly related to practice: "my words" (7), "my commandments . . . my Father's commandments" (10), "I command you" (14), "These things I command you . . ." (17). Thus, as in the prologue, but more so, the word becomes flesh.

Yet, significant as is the link between 15:1–17 and the prologue, the links with 10:7–18 and chap. 13 are greater. As a parable—using "parable" in the broad sense of the Hebrew *mashal* and the synoptics' *parabolē*—it has a unique affinity with the parable of the good shepherd. Together the two texts constitute "the grand allegories of this gospel" (Kysar, 236). And with chap. 13 it shares both the central image of a cleansing and a leading role within the last discourse.

With this context in mind it is now possible to return to the problem of the structure.

Structure

The most immediate context, that of chap. 13 and the last discourse, provides the first clue: it uses the word *tauta*, "these things" (or some longer form such as "these things I have spoken to you"), to divide the text, particularly to signal some form or sense of conclusion (cf. 13:21; 14:25; 16:1,4a; 16:4b,6; 16:25; 17:1), and by so doing it suggests that within 15:1–17 also the word *tauta*, which occurs in 15:11, should play a similar role. In other words, it suggests that 15:1–17 be divided into 15:1–10 (the main body of the text) and 15:11–17 (the section which concludes, which portrays practical results).

As a matter of incidental detail, this does not mean that the concluding use of *tauta* in chaps. 13–17 follows a uniform pattern; there are variations. In chaps. 13 and 14, the use is very simple—to introduce the concluding subsections (cf. 13:21, 14:25). Then, within chaps. 15 and 16 it is used in a way which is slightly more complex—not only to introduce the concluding sections but also to round them off (cf. 15:11,17; 16:1,4a; 16:25–33). Thus there is a form of double use or inclusion. Finally—and this involves some overlapping—in the concluding "chapters" (16:4b–33 and chap. 17) it is used in an introductory role (16:4b,6— a double use; and 17:1). In other words, its use changes from introducing chapters' conclusions to introducing concluding chapters. What is essential is that through all the variations it retains its role as signaling conclusions, and, as such, it signals also that the concluding section of 15:1–17 begins at 15:11.

Schnackenburg (3:92–93) remarks that the *tauta* phrase is an important "structural element," but he does not press his investigation into whether it belongs to what precedes or what follows. And so he includes v 11 with vv 1–10—even though he indicates later that, with its theme of joy, v 11 belongs to the category of results (3:104: "the joy resulting from community with Christ"). Westcott (216, 219) also had regarded joy as a result and, for that reason, had separated it from the initial picture of union (vv 1–10). Beasley-Murray (266, 269) endorses

Schnackenburg's basic insight about the concluding role of *tauta*, but in organizing the text makes the necessary adjustment: 1–10, 11–17.

Next comes the problem of subdividing 15:1–10. Like Schnackenburg, Brown (665–68) underlines a fundamental insight: the structure of the good shepherd parable could act as a guiding model in unraveling the structure of 15:1–17. But again, it is an insight which is difficult to apply. The parable of the good shepherd is preceded by the obscure figure of the sheepfold (10:1–6), and if this figure is included in the guiding model, it will tend to lead to the conclusion that, like chap. 10, 15:1–17 also should be divided after v 6—thus giving 1–6, 7–17. However, as Schnackenburg (3:97) indicates, such a cryptic discourse, pronounced in the presence of unbelief, has no role here; the situation here is one of openness, one of direct revelation to the disciples. Therefore the model to be used is not all of 10:1–18 but simply 10:7–18 (the central parable about the gate and the good shepherd).

When the two parables are placed side by side (10:7–18 and 15:1–10) the divisions within one do, in fact, cast light on how to divide the other. First, the division which begins with "I am the good shepherd" (10:11) finds a counterpart in "I am the vine" (15:5). There is a sense in both cases of "a new start" (Lindars, 489). Second, the division which begins "Because of this the Father loves me . . ." (10:17) finds a counterpart in "In this is my Father glorified . . ." (15:18). In more detail:

10:17	15:8
Because of this the Father *loves* me—	In this is my Father *glorified*—
that I *lay down my life*. . . .	that you *bear much fruit* . . . As the Father has
	loved me. . . .

Within the gospel's thought pattern, the italicized words are inherently connected: love leads to glory, and death to fruit-bearing. And within their respective chapters these are the first occurrences of the words "love" and "glorify."

Without attempting to unravel either the other affinities between 10:17–18 and 15:8–10 or the full subtlety of the way in which 10:7–18 as a whole is reflected and developed in 15:1–10, a tentative conclusion may be drawn: the main body of the parable of the true vine consists of vv 1–10, and it is to be subdivided into 1–4, 5–7, and 8–10.

A case may also be made for further subdividing 15:1–10, into nine units. In this division vv 1–2 would constitute the first unit, and the remaining eight verses would each constitute one unit. However, as in the case of 10:7–18, it may be better, particularly at this stage of research, not to press this subdivision.

In 15:1–10, as in 10:7–18, parabolic language gives way to language that is direct, open. In the synoptics, of course, something of this transition may also be found: the parables of the sower and the weeds are followed almost immediately by explanations that are quite direct and open (Matt 13:1–43). But John's technique is quite different; here the two forms of language are interwoven, and the transition from one to the other, accomplished through spiralling repetition, is gradual. One of the effects of this is to suggest a gradual process of revelation.

As for the picture of the results or practical effects, vv 11–17, it will be seen later to constitute an entity that is divided in two: 11–14 and 15–17.

What emerges, therefore, is a structure which, insofar as its main body is threefold and its conclusion is twofold, follows the essential lines of chapter 13, but which, precisely because of the nature of its main threefold division, retains an affinity both with the prologue and especially with the parable of the good shepherd.

[15:1–10] Union with Jesus, the true vine: from abiding to fruit-bearing in love. Chapter 15 takes up where chap. 14 left off—with the idea of abiding union (cf. 14:23), the union of believers with Jesus. In vv 1–10 the word "abide" is used ten times, a frequency not matched elsewhere in the NT. The image in question, the vine and its branches, is particularly effective in suggesting unity, for unlike other trees where one may distinguish clearly between trunk and branches, such a distinction is not clear. The vine consists of its branches; all flow together into one. Furthermore, it is an image that "is remarkably similar to the figure of Christ as the Body that includes the Church (1 Cor 12:12–27; Col 1:18, 2:19; Eph 1:22–23)" (Beasley-Murray, 272); as well as being individual, it is ecclesial (Borig, 1967, 250–52).

But unions can be inert, and if there is one thing which this parable and its structure communicates it is a sense of vitality. In a gospel where believing is always a verb, abiding union is something which moves, which develops. "Bearing fruit" suggests that one's whole makeup is in ferment.

The sense of vitality is implied in the very opening phrase: "I am the true vine. . . ." To some degree the word "true" has a negative connotation; it suggests that other possible claimants to being a vine (ancient Israel or the Hellenistic religions) were not altogether true. But its primary meaning is positive: "true" suggests "above the earthly/ordinary," the real thing so to speak, ultimately something that is divine. Such also is the connotation of the "I am." The sense of vitality is heightened by the fact that vines by their nature are full of a slightly unpredictable energy—as Noah to his cost found out (Gen 9:20–21). But this vine, precisely because it is true, is particularly thriving. The energy in question is above that of natural life.

The sense of vitality is further increased by the fact that the vine is surrounded by intense care, for the vinedresser is a God who works like a caring father, and nothing is overlooked: "every branch" is seen to. Those that are unfruitful he takes away (*airei*), and those that give fruit he prunes or cleanses (*kath-airei*), that they may bear more fruit. The overlapping of the verbs suggests an activity which is coordinated, flowing. This vinedresser knows what to do.

In the central part of the parable (vv 5–7) there is a further overlapping of verbs: what does not bear fruit is put out (*ballō exō*, "put/throw out," aorist tense) and "they" put (*ballō,* present tense) it in the fire (v 6). Evidently the same vibrant vinedresser is still at work, yet that vinedresser is hidden behind words which are passive ("is thrown out") or impersonal ("they"), and behind changes of tense. The seeming implication is of a phase in which God's working is obscured.

But in the final stage (vv 8–10), when much fruit is borne, the situation changes: "The Father is glorified"—God's obscurity is ended.

Thus, as the vine comes to fruition, the parable suggests a certain flow of history or time, and this idea of development seems applicable to the individual or the community. In other words, God works to develop the individual, and this development takes place in the context of a community and of a larger history. Ultimately, this history is an advanced variation on the history implied in the prologue.

Important in this process is the role of Jesus. The picture of him that is given here follows one that by now is rather familiar in the gospel. At first (v 1) he is "the true vine"; then (v 5) he is simply "the vine"; and finally (v 8) he has momentarily disappeared from view and is replaced by the fruitful emergence of the disciples. The descent, while related to that found in the prologue and foot-washing, is particularly close to that found in 10:7–18: starting with the same "I am" formula, Jesus (in chap. 10) had gone from being the gate (10:7), to being the good shepherd (10:11), to a titleless laying down of his life (10:17). In neither text does this imply that Jesus is reduced to meaninglessness. In 10:17–18 his dying had been surrounded by his Father's love and command, and it had been used to underline his authority. And in 15:8–10 his fruit-bearing is likewise surrounded by the Father's love and commands, and his own love becomes a center for others. But the descent does involve a diminution, and it means that if the branches are beginning to flourish, if people are developing and emerging, it is because in Jesus there has been poured out a divine love which makes people realize they have a home, a place in which to abide.

As for the people who are the focus of all this divine attention, the three-part text implies a progression—from initial mutual indwelling or abiding (v 4a), to an increasing union of wills (v 7, "you shall ask whatever you will and it shall be done to you"), to a final blossoming, a bearing of "much fruit," which is characterized by a profound development of love (vv 8–10).

Fruit-bearing is not just a manifesting of virtue or good works. It involves, first of all, a deep union with the vine, ultimately with God. And it is from the basis of this union that action flows.

As suggested earlier, in comparing this parable with the prologue, one of the basic features of the text is that the imagery of the vine gives way increasingly to the idea of "the word" (*logos*, v 3), and to variations on "the word" that are more and more down to earth—"my words" (*rhēmata*, v 7), "my commandments . . . my Father's commandments" (v 10; cf. vv 12, 17, "this is my commandment. . . . these things I command you . . ."). The first reference to "the word" (v 3) is somewhat surprising or intrusive—so much so that it has often been regarded as an editorial insertion. But this puzzling reference, like the puzzling texts in 13:1–3 and 14:1–3, appears to be a way of challenging the reader, in this case challenging the one who already believes, who has already received the word, to be surprised by the word once again, and to advance to a further stage of discipleship.

The emphasis on "the word" serves also to interpret the parable, for the practical way in which one grows in God's vine is by letting the word of God, God's communication, sink in ever more deeply. The shift in persons, from third person to second ("Now *you* are clean, ..." v 3) increases the sense of God reaching people in dialogue, and so also does the transition from parabolic language to language which is more direct. Thus 15:3, with its surprise and its linguistic "descent" (from parabolic to plain) is another variation on the theme of the descent of divine revelation into human life.

How exactly this word is communicated in one's life is secondary—whether, for instance, through quiet meditation or through experience, ordinary or unusual, or through a religious service. What counts is that it should reach a receptive heart.

The absorbing of the word is deeply purifying, and it is this purifying process which is described through the strong image of cutting and clearing the branches and of burning what is fruitless. As well as referring to the individual, this purifying would seem also to refer to the community—to the removal of apostates or of members whose presence is destructive (cf. Brown, 676; Schnackenburg, 3:98; Kysar, 236).

The process of purifying leads to life. In the second part (vv 5–7), when Jesus decreases ("the true vine" becomes "the vine"), the believers increase. For the first time they are spoken of explicitly as the branches, and instead of simply bearing "more" fruit (as in v 2), they now bear "much" fruit (v 5). Then, against the contrasting background of being expelled and burned—an image which refers above all to the soul's total alientation from God (v 6)—there is the picture of profound union, of the blending of wills (v 7).

Finally (vv 8–10) comes the sudden blossoming. The believers "become . . . disciples," a phrase which in this context refers to a form of breakthrough, to an entering into the sphere of divine love. Thus far in the parable the word "love" had not been used, but at this stage, when the vine-related language has almost disappeared, it suddenly occurs five times, and it is when that happens that God is manifested, that "the Father is glorified." In other words, through the presence of love, God is revealed, glorified.

This climactic reference to the link between discipleship and love complements Jesus' earlier statement that his disciples would be recognized by their mutual love (13:35). In both cases (13:35, 15:8–10) the basic message is clear: the essence of discipleship is love; love reflects God. The primary emphasis now, however, is not on loving, but on receiving love.

As already suggested, in comparing the structure of 15:1–10 to that of the prologue, this breakthrough into divine love and into the implied idea of community is ultimately a variation on the breakthrough which was first effected in the incarnation itself (1:14). As Kysar (238) comments about 15:8: "The incarnation of God's presence moves from Jesus of Nazareth (1:14) to the community of faith." The Word which became flesh went on, as it were, to become love. And the glory which was seen then, when the Word dwelt "amongst us" (1:14), was seen further when loving discipleship led to the Father being glorified (15:8).

The union which is thus achieved is not cheap. In speaking of the purifying of the vine, the parable evokes the dying of Jesus, and in doing so inevitably implies the dying of those who abide in Jesus. The two deaths, of Jesus and of the disciple, are inseparable. Thus the final blossoming, the breakthrough into the realm of divine love, is preceded by a form of death. Teresa of Ávila, in describing what seems to be such a breakthrough, refers to the way in which the silkworm changes into "a beautiful butterfly" (1961, 104). But she emphasizes too that the silkworm, as such, has to die. A variation on that same message is found is the life experience of Dietrich Bonhoeffer.

In practical life this means that union with God is unlikely to be achieved when one is unduly warm and fed and flattered. In Galatians 1–4, esp. 1–2, Paul receives the good news of God in profound solitude. For many people, in fact, the reality of God comes home amid both solitude and shock, often in middle age and rejection (W. Johnston, 1978, 147–48).

But "the pain of rejection is the herald of unutterable joy" (W. Johnston, 1978, 149). And what is true of the rejection which shocks one into an awareness of God is also true of the thorough purifying which accompanies God's increasing union: despite the process of dying, in fact *through* the process of dying, the way is cleared for God's love to take hold and to bring forth joy.

The True Vine and the Eucharist

The primary significance of the parable of the true vine is that God works to bring the advancing disciple into abiding divine union. The ways in which such a union is accomplished may vary greatly from one person to another, but for most Christians union with the divine presence is particularly associated with the eucharistic ceremony of bread and wine. The eucharist, when well celebrated, expresses and nurtures that union. It is very appropriate, therefore, when speaking of union, to use an image which is associated with the eucharist, which reflects it and evokes it. And that is what the vine does. It has an inherent affinity with the eucharistic symbol of the wine, and elsewhere in the NT, when the eucharist is referred to as the fruit of the vine (Matt 26:29, Mark, 14:25), that connection is made explicit. The true vine therefore refers primarily to union and secondarily to the eucharist.

[15:11–17] The practical effects of union.　When a person accepts the realm of divine love, the result is joy, love for others, and divine friendship. Joy is like an initial gift, and with it come the down-to-earth love and the divine friendship. The text is so written that the themes of love and friendship are interwoven, yet it seems to contain a distinction. There is an initial part (vv 11–14) which lays the primary emphasis on love for others and the secondary emphasis on divine friendship. And the second part (vv 15–17) reverses the priorities—first friendship and then mutual love.

This division is confirmed by elements of repetition (cf. the initial idea of "telling/calling" you: vv 11, 15; and the concluding "I command you": vv 14, 17) and it is somewhat akin to the subdivision in 13:21–38, especially in 13:31–38 (cf. the use of *legō* "I say," in 13:27b, 36; 15:15).

Joy had already been hinted at following the initial picture of God coming to abide (14:28), but it is only when the abiding deepens that the joy really blossoms.

In the gospel as a whole, joy is generally a reaction to Christ, to some aspect of all that he mediates—to the marriagelike union which he inaugurates (3:29); to the work, begun by him, of gathering fruit into eternal life (4:36); to his "day" (8:56); to his overcoming of death (in Lazarus, 11:15; in himself, 14:28); to his risen appearance as *kyrios* (20:20); and especially to his post-resurrection coming to the disciples (16:16–24). The overall impression is that God has a wide-reaching providence of life and love, centered on Jesus and his resurrection, and that when one really sees this providence, when it enters one's heart, one reacts with joy. This sense of God does not enter the heart easily. First, there must be a thorough process of cleansing, of letting go. But when the joy does enter, it becomes a sign, in the person's disposition, that God is indeed present.

The opening picture of joy (15:11) functions somewhat as does the opening picture of glorification in 13:31: it expresses a blossoming which flows from God's realm. The glorification is more in the outer sphere, and the joy in the inner. The result of both is to bring a person to mutual love. In 13:34–35 this love theme is strong, but in 15:12–13 it is stronger still: as well as speaking of loving as Jesus had loved, it makes explicit the idea of loving unto death, of laying down one's life for one's friends. When Jesus first refers to friends he is speaking about friends in general (v 13), and the connection with himself and his own love may not be clear. But then he removes the doubt: "You are my friends . . ." (v 14). The conclusion at this stage is that the disciples are indeed being challenged to the greatest love possible.

Then (vv 15–17) the focus shifts. The notion of friendship which had been simply a subtheme, something used to explain the idea of love, now becomes the central focus. Friendship was an important value both in the OT and in Greco-Roman culture (cf. esp. Schnackenburg, 3:109–12). And it was emphasized in the story of David and Jonathan (1 Sam 18:1–4; 20:1–42; 23:15–18) and in the wisdom literature (esp. Eccles 6:5–17). But perhaps even more significant is the fact that the most basic figure in the OT, Moses, precisely in the process of receiving God's communication and law, is described as a friend: God would speak with him as a person would speak to a friend (Exod 33:11). It is for this reason that Moses has been portrayed as a mystic (W.Johnston, 1984, 24–35). Thus at the heart of the OT, understanding of the law is connected with a relationship of friendship.

Within John this relationship is to be seen in the context both of the preceding references to love and the earlier picture of the beloved disciple (13:23–26). In fact, to a significant degree what 15:15–17 does is to spell out what was implied in 13:23–26: that the one who is loved, who has become a friend, has a special knowledge of the incarnate God. This is not the slave's knowledge of a master. In a statement that removes from the words "command" and "commandments" any such ring of authoritarianism, Jesus now excludes that slave–master relationship (v 15a). For a time it had its place, but not anymore. The knowledge in question includes a genuine mutuality such as one finds among friends who know one another's hopes and plans (v 15). And, as he goes on to speak of what may be called the divine plan (". . . I chose you and appointed you so that . . ."), there is an implication that from now on the disciples have a sense of this plan, in other words, that as Jesus' friends they have a certain knowledge of all that God has planned in Jesus.

Friendship, therefore, gives a kind of inside knowledge. But this knowledge is not any kind of arrogant private domain. It is related first and last to love; in the text it is literally encased in references to love for others (12–13, 17). Thus the essence of the friendship is not in a dominating knowledge but in a self-giving love. And in speaking to his friends, Jesus does not address them as an exclusive club. Rather they are to go and bear fruit, a reference apparently to moving out and bringing their friendship with Jesus to others. The impression is of an expanding process, and it is heightened by the fact that whatever they ask will be granted (v 16). In referring earlier to a form of prayer (v 7) it was not clear whether the prayer was exclusively for the sake of the one praying or whether it was also directed outwards. The present context, insofar as it is that of an outward mission, indicates that the prayer does indeed have a further vision.

The World's Hatred

In Contrast to the True Vine, the Portrait of a Realm of Hostility and of Its Limits

Having given a portrait of how God brings disciples into the realm of divine love (15:1–17), Jesus goes on to give the other side of the picture, the realm which is constituted by the world's hatred for God and for all who are associated with God.

In itself, of course, the world is good. It was made good by God (Genesis 1), and God thoroughly loves it and wishes to save it (3:16). But there is a part of it, found especially in the human will, which can resist God's process of salvation, and as John's gospel advances that resistance is placed increasingly under the heading of "the world." The gospel never refers to this opposition, this sphere, as a kingdom, but on three occasions there are references to "the ruler of this world" (12:31, 14:30, 16:11), and so there is a suggestion that, in contrast to the realm of God, there is another realm, that of Satan and darkness.

This may suggest two equal realms, or at least that the negative realm, "this world," is quite independent and out of control. But even when evil is at its worst, the gospel does not see things in that way. However chilling the imposing title ("the ruler of this world"), it is a title which always indicates someone who has lost power or is under judgment. And "this world," whatever its negativity or ferocity, is always placed within the sphere of God's encompassing plan or providence.

The contrast, which is presented in 15:1–16:4a, is not new. Already in Part 2 (2:23–chap. 6), particularly in speaking to Nicodemus and in concluding the bread-of-life discourse (see esp. 3:5–8, 6:63), Jesus had indicated that people are caught in a tension between two worlds—an earthbound world of petty prestige or pleasure, and a higher or heavenly world which calls to the chained heart to break free and to set up its abode in the realm of God's uplifting presence. This change of abode does not exclude human loves and interests (in fact, it enhances them), but it does mean that the heart has to make a fundamental decision about where its ultimate values lie—whether in the narrow petty world or in the world of (God's) love.

When the tension which faces individual people is reflected in groups, then the sense of two worlds becomes all the greater. One group, by and large, has opted for one world, and the other for the alternative. At the beginning of chapter 7 the unbelieving brothers are all associated with "the world," and Jesus is in the opposite position; he is hated by the world (7:5–7). Thus the tension mounts in the drama, until by chap. 15 the tension between the two worlds is reflected in a picture which is divided starkly in two: on the one hand, there is the true or heavenly realm, that of all who abide in union with God; on the other, there is "the world," those who follow the path of resistance to (God's) love, and who bitterly resent the challenge to their limited vision.

485

Structure and the Central Issue

Amid considerable divergence of opinion a good case has been made (especially by Brown, 693–95) that the text extends as far as 16:4a and consists of four main parts—the three leading statements (vv 18–21, 22–25, 26–27) and the conclusion (16:1–4a). Bultmann's analysis (556–57) suggests one further point: the concluding section has two balancing clauses or subsections, one negative (16:1–3) and the other positive (16:4a). Thus the main text is three-part, and the conclusion twofold—a structure which is essentially the same as that of 15:1–17, and, like 15:1–17, a variation on the structure of the foot-washing and its consequences (chap. 13).

The connection with the foot-washing scene is underlined by the fact that Jesus explicitly refers back to it: "Remember the word which I said to you, 'A servant is not greater . . . ' " (15:20, cf. 13:16).

This connection, with the parable of the vine and with the foot-washing, helps to locate the account of the world's hatred within John's gospel. Far from being some form of afterthought, it belongs with the mainstream texts, especially those which provide much of the context for the foot-washing and the vine, namely the prologue and the parable of the good shepherd (10:7–18). Those earlier passages (1:1–18; 10:7–18; chap. 13) presented pictures in which good and evil were intertwined. In 15:1–16:4a they are largely distinct—first good (15:1–17) and now evil (15:18–16:4a)—but, despite the distinctness, this text retains some of the basic features of those other passages.

One of those features is that its three main parts form a threefold progression, three stages:

18–21   The way the world has "first" hated Jesus
22–25   Following Jesus' coming, the world's guilt (sin)
26–27   Following the Spirit's coming, the giving of witness [to the world]

Although Jesus is describing future evil, he manages at another level to evoke the way in which, from the "first," from the beginning, the entire phenomenon of evil has been engaged and combatted by the history of salvation, in particular by his own coming and by the coming of the Spirit.

The presence of this wider dimension or level is indicated not only by the broad relationship with some of the gospel's mainstream texts but also by specific details. The word *archē*, "beginning" (v 27), for instance, may seem initially to refer simply to the time when Jesus called the disciples. But there is a further meaning. In Schnackenburg's words (3:120): "This 'beginning' does not establish a departure in time. . . . This principle of the 'beginning' is evident at various levels and especially at those of the personal Logos, existing from the beginning." In other words, in a gospel where "beginning" is associated with something which is beyond time—with God and the whole realm of the divine (1:1–2; 2:11; 6:64; 8:25,44)—there is a suggestion of having been with the world before time began, in other words, of having been predestined. A similar idea had been suggested by the earlier emphasis on Jesus' free choosing (15:16,19; cf. Kysar, 241; Eph 1:4).

Within this context it would seem that the word "first" (v 18)—even though it refers primarily to the fact that the rejection of Jesus precedes that of the disciples—manages also to evoke the "first" period, that which was before Jesus' coming. In other words, the initial rejecting of Jesus (v 18) refers also to the way in which Jesus had already been partly present even in the pre-incarnation period ("Christ in the OT") and had already been rejected. Such an allusion is a further echo of the prologue—a text which was itself concerned with the place of Christ in the OT.

As well as evoking something of the first period of salvation history, the text then goes on to refer to the two other major periods, those inaugurated by the coming, respectively, of Jesus and the Spirit. Granted that at first sight the two uses of the common verb "to come" may seem casual ("If I had not come," v 22; "when the Companion comes," v 26), yet, in a chapter where this verb does not otherwise occur, these two references stand out. Furthermore, by their positions they are inherently connected: each is placed at the bridgehead of one of text's major divisions. If they occur in different tenses ("had come," "comes") it is because Jesus stands in the middle and, in that context, must look both to the past and the future.

The essential point is that Jesus' discourse on the world's hatred is not any narrow preaching or prophecy; it refers to the entire struggle between evil and good, between "the world" and the agents of God.

The general picture which emerges may seem very negative, particularly in the initial stage (vv 18–21). But as the text advances, emphasis falls increasingly on the positive. This is true both within the basic three-part picture (15:18–27) and also within the concluding text, which depicts the practical working out of the struggle (16:1–4a).

[15:18–27] The hatred of the resenting world. The first section (vv 18–21) consists of a grim sketch of tension and hatred. The implied picture is that of a world which is set in its ways (which "loves its own") and which, when Jesus calls people to another awareness, hates both him and all who respond to him. "Hates" may be something of a Semitic hyperbole, yet it is difficult to overstate the crusading anger of those who find their narrow world being threatened. In fact, something of this fierce resistance exists within everybody. And even if the resistance consists of indifference, the indifference may be more deep-seated than a disease. Thus in its suggestion of something which reaches far into the soul, the concept of hatred expresses a basic truth.

But however grim this picture, it does not have to be overpowering. The weight of the world's negativity need not cause despair. Starting on a low key, Jesus indicates that such negativity can be resisted. And the primary way of resisting it is by Jesus' word, in other words by grasping in the heart and mind all that Jesus represents, the entire providence which is centered in him. A corresponding emphasis was found in the picture of the true vine: it is through the word(s)/commandment(s) that the realm of love is built. And now it is through the word that the realm of hatred is countered.

The specific form of the word, as cited here by Jesus, is that taken from the foot-washing—"A servant is not greater than his lord"—and it reminds the disciples to be ready for hostility. But it does much more. By referring to the relative positions of "servant" and "lord" it evokes the entire process, already reflected in the foot-washing, of the divine self-emptying in which Jesus eventually went from being servant to Lord (13:1–20, esp. 13:4–5, 13–16; cf. Phil 2:7, 11). And by doing this it sets hatred and hostility in the context of God's greater gift of love. Jesus is reminding them, when they feel like abused servants, that, even within a state of servanthood, they need not forfeit, anymore than he did, a deep and uplifting union with (the Lord) God. Such a notion may be misused—for instance, to perpetuate slavery or harsh conditions. But it also contains a fundamental truth: that people who are in many ways disadvantaged or impoverished often manage, amid their poverty, to discover in God a rich joy. They do not feel the need to go on a safari because in God they find their adventure. "Blessed are the poor. . . ."

In the preceding text (15:15) Jesus had presented himself as friend. When he now refers to the disciple as a servant and to himself as Lord, it is not to contradict that idea but to complement it. The disciple is both friend and servant: friend as being the abode of the indwelling God; servant as one who, following the divine example, goes through a process of suffering and self-emptying.

Furthermore, as well as using the word to set hostility in context, Jesus then goes on (v 20c) to evoke the possibility that the world may respond to the word: "If they have kept my word, they will keep yours also." Given the preceding bleak picture of the world's hostility "this positive possibility surprises the reader" (Kysar, 243). It brings a faint note of hope that the word will speak not only to the disciples but also to the world. At the very least it indicates that the world should not simply be left to its own devices; it should be faced with the word.

And having thus faintly evoked the presence and action of the word, Jesus explicitly emphasizes its absence, the fact that "they do not know the one who sent me" (v 21b). Thus, for all its energy, the world is in fundamental ignorance; it is unaware that there is a sender, that there is someone out there, and unaware of all that that means.

The second section (vv 22–25) highlights a further dimension of the world's hatred, its sin, or its guilty ignorance, and in doing so it deepens the idea of negativity. But it also speaks increasingly of Jesus, of his coming, and of what he said and did. And it concludes by seeing the fundamental phenomenon of hatred as fulfilling the word (v 25). Thus in the final analysis, the world's hatred is subject to the word, serves even to fulfill it.

The picture of sin implies that people have turned away from the evidence which speaks of God. They have even looked God's presence in the face and resented it. For God is not some distant alien. As Jesus speaks, he refers to the fact that in him God has come to people. And he summarizes the two basic ways in which he has sought to communicate with people—through words and works. The words were such that they should have convinced the thoughtful heart and mind. Those who rejected these words are thus left without any reason, without any excuse (22), and in resenting those words they resent God (23). The works also, all the wonders emanating from the down-to-earth Word, all the goodness and beauty, these at least, because they are so striking to the eye, should have provoked reflection. But people looked at them and hated both them and all they represented: "Now they have both seen and hated both me and the Father."

The primary achievement of these verses is to give a theological sketch of unbelief. Insofar as they may also be seen as giving a negative portrait of specific unbelievers, particularly of those Jews who rejected Jesus and his work, they may also be seen as apologetic (cf. Schnackenburg, 3:116).

Yet, even unbelief is somehow within the sphere of God's providence. The word of God, as well as being a support against the world's hatred (as in the first section, esp. v 20), is also something encompassing; it contains a reference to such hatred. With a rather elaborate introduction which helps to emphasize that it really was written and foretold ("this is to fulfill the word [*logos*] which is written in their law"), Jesus quotes (freely) from the OT: "They hated me without cause" (cf. Ps 35:19, and esp. 69:4). Thus, in the final analysis, hatred is subject to the word.

The third section (vv 26–27) does not refer explicitly to a conflict or meeting between the world and the word, but, in modified form, that idea is present—in the picture of the Companion, "the Spirit of truth," bearing witness. Witness-bearing suggests stating the truth in a difficult situation, and the phrase "Spirit of Truth" was used at Qumran in the context of a dualistic conflict against the forces of evil who are led by the Spirit of Falsehood (cf. Brown, 1138; Lindars, 496). In John the dualism is not as stark—ultimately everything is under God—yet the context suggests that there is indeed a need to confront a deep-seated falsehood or lie, the lie which blocks out God. Thus, once again, there is a picture of tension between the world and the word.

It has often been suggested that this third section (26–27) is a late insertion, that it does not fit smoothly with what precedes. To some degree, this is true. These verses are different, even "strange" (Becker, 2:492). And the opening phrase, "When the Companion comes, . . ." sets this section somewhat apart. But in the gospel's three-part constructions, the third part is often set apart some-what (e.g. 5:14–15; 6:16–21; note 10:17–18; 13:12–20, and 15:8–10). Besides, as Schackenburg (3:114, 117) in particular, has indicated, the idea of bearing witness, of bringing the word to the world, is a coherent development of the preceding ideas (of relying on the word, 20; and of Jesus, the incarnate Word, coming to the world, 22–24). Furthermore, as already mentioned, the "coming" of the Companion (26) is in continuity with the "coming" of Jesus (22). The most coherent explanation of this text's newness is not that it is a late insertion, but that it is saying something new, something which may seem strange or star-tling. It is replacing the sense of acute conflict with a more positive process of witnessing. A certain degree of conflict is indeed still present, but there is an implication that the Spirit will speak positively to the world, and the reader is left wondering what the outcome may be.

The sense of the Spirit's involvement is heightened by the fact that, in contrast to the two earlier references to the Companion (14:16, 26), the picture of the Companion which is suggested here is quite active. These earlier references (esp. 14:16) had spoken of the Companion in a way that was rather passive, as one who was given and sent. But now (15:26) the Companion is described not only as being sent but also as "coming," and then, in a parallel phrase which puts intensified emphasis on the idea of an active role, the Companion is described simply as "proceeding" ("the Spirit of Truth who proceeds from the Father"). The emphasis of the text then is not so much on the inner dynamics of God as on the increasing role of the Companion in the outer world, a role which consists of witnessing about Jesus.

Yet, however active the Companion, the role of bearing witness is carried out through people. Hence the addition (27): "And you also bear witness. . . ." The implication is that bearing witness does not consist of two processes, one by the Companion and the other by people, but rather that there is a single process in which both play their roles.

The final picture then is of the Spirit-led disciples bearing witness to the world. Such a process could be visualized as lonely, as a picture of voices wasting their breath. But the depiction of the Spirit had been strong, and concerning the disciples, Jesus adds a final strengthening note: "Because from the beginning (*archē*) you are with me." As already mentioned, within the context of John's other uses of "beginning," uses which, in various ways, suggest the realm of the divine (1:1–2; 2:11; 6:64; 8:25,44), such a phrase suggests not only the time-bound meeting of Jesus with his disciples but also the larger divine plan which first chose those disciples and brought them to Jesus. And the evoking of that plan lends to the process of witness-bearing a sense of purpose and peace.

[16:1–4a] The practical results of the world's hatred.   Rather as the picture of God's vine concluded with a picture of the fruits or results of that vine (15:11–17), so the picture of the opposing world concludes with a summary of concrete results (16:1–4a).

As noted earlier, the text has two sections, one quite negative, a picture largely of expulsion and murder (16:1–3), and the other more positive, a picture of recalling what Jesus has said, or, to state it otherwise, a picture of recalling Jesus' words(s) (16:4a; cf. Bultmann, 556–57). Thus the tension, which is fundamental to the main text (15:18–27), the tension between evil and the word, is reflected also in the picture of the results.

In many details also the results reflect the main text—the intensifying hostility (16:1–2; cf. 15:18,20), the accompanying ignorance of both the Father and Jesus (16:3; cf. 15:21,24), a two-phase process of development or "coming" (16:2,4, "an hour is coming . . . when their hour comes"; cf. 15:22,26), and the fact that the word is to be both recalled and fulfilled (such is the implication of 16:4a; cf. 15:20, 25).

The essential point is that the underlying conflict (15:18–27) is closely reflected in the resulting reality of life.

In the first section (16:1–3) two major expressions of hostility are mentioned: being expelled from the synagogue and being put to death by those who think that in killing they offer service (*latreia*) to God (2). The irony is that in both cases the hostility appears to be based ultimately on religion, yet as the context suggests, and as the next verse emphasizes (3), it is precisely the lack of genuine religion, the lack of openness to a parentlike God, which underlies the hostility ("because they have not known either the Father or me"). What Jesus is talking about, therefore, is not only the blocking out of the true God, but the consequence or result of that process—the fabrication of a false god or false religion, a fabrication which becomes the basis for exclusion and murder.

At this point the text appears to be referring to two levels. To some degree, particularly because of the mention of expulsion from the synagogue, it is speaking of evils which are quite specific—the hostile activities of the Jews. In fact, some commentators hold that the evils are quite local, that what is in question is the attitude of the Jewish synagogue in John's own city or village. But within John's gospel, specific people or groups (including the Jews) often have roles which are representative, and for that reason the text seems to have a further level, one which speaks of evil in general. Furthermore, even though the Jews historically did expel Christians (beginning around AD 90), and even though it is easy to imagine the (Jewish) Zealots as indulging in self-righteous killing, yet—despite the statements of some Christian apologists, especially Justin—it is simply not clear to what extent Jews sought to kill Christian "apostates" (cf. Brown, 691–92). What is certain, however, and what the gospel seems intent on underlining, is that idolatrous unbelief, including idolatrous religion and politics, leads to treating others with rejection and death. In the course of history it is an aberration from which many, including the Jews, have suffered much.

Given the reality of thoroughgoing campaigns of rejection and murder, it is understandable that Jesus should have begun this section by appealing to the disciples not to be scandalized (16:1), in other words, not to allow the weight of the world's woes to make them abandon believing and yield to despair.

The final section (16:4a), however, the final result, is not one of faith being shattered. On the contrary, it speaks of Jesus' words being borne in mind and fulfilled, and thus it implies a picture of vision being retrieved, of faith being sustained and strengthened.

It also refers—following the more difficult reading—to the coming of "their hour." This is ominous, for it suggests the time when the forces of rejection and murder come to power. But it is highly ambiguous, for the coming of one's hour can also refer, as it often does in John, to the coming of a time of death and transformation. Furthermore, the phrase which heralds the coming of their hour, *hotan elthē,* very literally "when comes," is exactly the phrase that was used to herald the coming of the Spirit (15:26). Thus even what is most menacing is surrounded, somehow, by the divine action, and, as in the case of the basic text (15:18–27), the final picture suggests that the world, even at its worst, is being engaged by the divine word. To the disciple falls the task of cooperating in that action, the task of recalling that word, and—so runs the implication—of bringing it to the world.

Jesus' Departure and Return—a More Intense Portrayal

At Another Level, the Disciples' Painful Spirit-Led Way of Experiencing More Fully the Indwelling Jesus and of Attaining More Direct Access to the Father

Introduction and Structure

It is becoming more fully recognized by researchers that, as far as chap. 16 is concerned, the traditional chapter division needs an adjustment. The unity which one expects from a chapter is to be found not in 16:1–33 but in 16:4b–33 (see esp. Behler, 1960, 177; Brown, 587; Schnackenburg, 3:123; Kysar, 246; Beasley-Murray, 270–71).

Within this unity the following structure may be observed:

4b–15   The work of the Spirit (confronting and guiding);
16–24   The birthlike seeing of Jesus;
25–33   Conclusion: "These things . . . I have said. . . ."

Several scholars concur in placing the chapter's major division after v 15 (among them, Lagrange, 424; Hoskyns, 487; Barrett, 491; Van den Bussche, 1959, 127; Behler, 1960, 196; Brown, 703; Schnackenburg, 3:125; Becker, 493).

There is also strong scholarly support for the distinctness of vv 25–33; as so often in the last discourse, this final section begins with a variation on the conclusion-related phrase "These things (I have said to you)" (Lagrange, 428; Bernard, 552; Bultmann, 586; Strathmann, 219; Schnackenburg, 3:160; Beasley-Murray, 267). The fact that this conclusion (vv 25–33) repeats ideas from the preceding verses sometimes leads to confusion—to the idea that it should not be separated from what precedes. However, as Strathmann (220), for instance, indicates, Jesus at this point is looking back, and so it is appropriate to repeat aspects of what precedes. The same phenomenon was found in chap. 14: as Brown (652) noted, its conclusion (14:25–31) repeated several elements of the preceding text.

The Substructure of 16:4b–15

Following fairly closely on the suggestions of Brown (709) and Schnackenburg (3:125), this text may be divided into a brief introduction (4b–6, a picture of paralyzing sadness) and two complementary passages, both dealing with the Spirit (7–11 and 12–15).

The accuracy of this division is supported by some details of repetition. Both Spirit passages begin with variations on I-am-speaking-to-you (v 7, *egō . . . legō hymin*; v 12, *echō hymin legein*). And later, with an emphasis on the personal pronoun *ekeinos* "that [person]," both refer to the Spirit's coming (vv 8, 13).

At first sight these two Spirit passages may seem somewhat unrelated. In the first (7–11) it is to "the world" that the Spirit (as Companion) speaks. In the second (12–15) it is to Jesus' hearers. But "the world," in other words, the world's unbelief, can be present in Jesus' hearers. As Brown (712) remarks about the confrontation with the world: "The courtroom is not in some apocalyptic Valley of Jehoshaphat (Joel 3:2,12) but in the mind and understanding of the disciples." Hence the first task of the Spirit is to confront, as Companion, all that is worldly in the disciple. The second task, described in the second Spirit passage, is to go on from there and lead the disciple(s) into the fullness of the truth.

This fullness of truth does not mean any truth beyond that given by Jesus. As God's Word, Jesus embodies all truth, but the worldly disciple has a long way to go before entering the fullness of that truth. In other words, what is in question is not the development of the church's truth or dogma, but the spiritual development of the Spirit-led disciple(s). Obviously insofar as dogma is the expression of the disciples' advancing understanding, the progression may have some relation to the development of dogma. But the primary emphasis is on the journey of the heart to God.

Though the initial confronting of the world takes place within the disciples, it is not limited to them. For they are witnesses, co-witnesses with the Spirit (15:26–27), and so there is an implication that, having themselves experienced the purifying action of the Spirit, they will then carry that action further—they will become instruments for confronting the outside world.

The challenging of what is worldly involves three steps—confrontation concerning sin, justice, and judgement (9–11). And the subsequent process of leading into all truth also involves three steps—a progression which is indicated by the threefold repetition of "will announce to you" (13b–15). Thus in each Spirit passage there is a leading statement and then a three-step elaboration of that statement.

The overall picture is a summary of the way in which those who are embedded in the world are led to God. Earlier in the gospel such a process was carried out by Jesus—see, for instance, 4:1–42—but in the future it will be done by Jesus' Spirit or by those in whom Jesus' Spirit dwells.

The structure of 16:4b–15 seems to be essentially the same as that of the first part of chapter 14 (14:1–11). In both cases there is a brief opening statement which provides a backdrop or perspective (the union hereafter, 14:1–3; the separation now, 16:4b–6). And then there is a two-part summary of what it is that guides the disciples in the interim—Jesus as the *way* and as the reflection of the Father (14:4–11), the Spirit as the one who challenges and who *shows the way* to truth (16:7–11). The complementarity of the texts is complex. One of the most basic developments from one to the other is an obvious one: that the guiding role of Jesus is being taken over in large part by the Spirit.

Incidentally, there appears to be some detailed linguistic complementarity in the sentences which introduce the subsections of the texts (14:4–6, 8–9; 16:7, 12). In various ways these introductory sentences give echoes of such introductory phrases as "I am" (*egō eimi*) and "I say to you" (*egō legō hymin*):

14:4–6 [*egō*] . . . *legei autō* . . . *legei autō* . . . *egō eimi*
14:8–9 *legei autō* . . . *legei autō* . . . *eimi*

16:7   *egō . . . legō hymin*
16:12   *echō hymin legein*

The Central Problem of the Seeing of Jesus

The focus of this entire "chapter" (16:4b–33) is the dramatic account of seeing Jesus (vv 16–24), yet its meaning is not easy to discern. Brown (729), in fact, refers to "the great difficulty of determining what is meant . . . by the return [or seeing] of Jesus." The importance of this seeing is highlighted by the fact that it is compared with the wonder of birth, with all of birth's sorrow and joy.

The obscurity which surrounds the meaning of seeing Jesus is reflected, for instance, in Beasley-Murray's suggestion (270–71) that the statements concerning the Spirit (vv 7–15) have been inserted. This opinion highlights the fact that it is not clear what the Spirit has to do with the return or seeing of Jesus.

A further aspect of the puzzle is the relationship of 16:4b–16 to the preceding chapters. Brown (588–91) notes many of the similarities with chap. 14. Schnackenburg (3:124–25) goes further: 16:4b–33 is "to some extent modeled on chapter 14, [but] . . . from a different point of view. . . . The evangelist . . . also knew chapter 15 and linked his discourse particularly to the second part (with its theme of 'separation from the world')." Yet the nature of the relationship remains elusive, and that elusiveness again reflects the obscurity surrounding the idea of seeing Jesus.

The proposal put forward here is that the seeing of Jesus, while at one level referring both to the return after the resurrection and to the final return, refers above all to the indwelling, to Jesus coming to abide within the disciples. This idea is not new. As mentioned earlier, it is found in Brown (730), and yet more explicitly in Schneiders (1975, 635): "To 'see Jesus' is essentially to experience him as indwelling." Thus what is in question once again is the idea of abiding union, but instead of using the language of mutual indwelling ("abide in me and I in you," 15:4; cf. 15:5–10), Jesus now uses the language of mutual seeing ("you will see me . . . I will see you," 16:16,22; cf. 16:17–19). In this way mutuality is not only maintained, it also becomes more developed, more personal. The seeing brings a further dimension of communication.

Once the seeing of Jesus is understood as an intensified form of mutual abiding, the other elements of the puzzle begin to fall into place. The work of the Spirit (vv 7–15), far from being secondary, is a necessary preparation for the seeing. Left to oneself one cannot see Jesus, one cannot have an inner sense of the human face of God, a sense of personally seeing and being seen. Such a process requires that, in various ways, the Companion or Spirit first confront and guide the disciple.

Relation to Chapters 14 and 15

The role of the Spirit, as preparatory to indwelling, helps, in turn, to clarify important aspects of the relationship of 16:4b–33 to chap. 14. For in chap. 14

essentially the same Spirit-indwelling phenomenon is found: within the focal section (14:12–24) the build-up towards mutual indwelling requires the initial involvement of the Companion or Spirit. First there is the love-related sending of the Spirit (14:15–17), then the coming or seeing of Jesus (14:18–20), and finally the climactic picture of the establishing of the divine abode within the disciple (14:23). What chap. 16 has done is to take these focal verses and unpack them so to speak. The role of the Companion/Spirit, so brief in chap. 14 (vv 16–17) is now deepened and expanded (16:7–15). And the description of the coming or seeing of Jesus (14:18–20, "I will not leave you orphans . . .") likewise gives way to something much more developed and dramatic—the birthlike seeing (16:16–24). Thus the two major sections of chap. 16 (vv 7–15 and 16–24) are essentially a deepening of two brief texts in chap. 14 (vv 16–17 and 18–20).

This is not, of course, the full story on the interrelationship of these chapters. Many other elements of chap. 14 are reflected in chap. 16. The extensive opening image of Jesus as the way (*hodos,* 14:4–11) has been absorbed in brief form into the description of the Spirit—into the role of the Spirit as guiding or leading the way (*hodēgeō,* 16:13). And the final climactic picture of creating a divine abode within someone (14:21–24) has been absorbed into the more dramatic picture of the birth of a new person (16:21). Thus in simple quantitative language, the kernel or center of chap. 14 (vv 16–20) has been expanded and highlighted, and its two ends (vv 4–11 and 21–24) have been synthesized and absorbed.

More important than the details and the quantity is the basic difference: the picture of Spirit-led union, so brief in chap. 14, is replaced in chap. 16 by something which is more developed. The union now is deeper. Now the Spirit is fully active, and the result is like a whole new birth. There is great pain and sorrow, pain even like death, but there is also great joy.

Relationship to chap. 15 (15:1–16:4a). The deeper union depicted in chap. 16 may already be noticed in chap. 15. It is in 15:1–10 that the idea of abiding first reaches explicit repetitive intensity. And it is in 15:18–27 that the sense of Spirit-related confrontation with the world (cf. 16:7–11) likewise becomes uniquely explicit. Both aspects are important for union—confronting what is detrimental and abiding in what is divine. In chap. 15, when the unifying action is presented from the divine point of view, the initial emphasis is on the divine action, on the Father as union-building vinedresser; and later comes the idea of both the Word and the Spirit confronting the world. But in chap. 16, since the point of view is more that of the human, of someone who is already involved with the world, it is the need to confront the world which is first emphasized (16:7–15, esp. vv 7–11), and only later does the text speak of mutual seeing, of deep union (16:16–24).

Thus the first stage of union, initiated in chap. 13 and viewed from a more human viewpoint in chap. 14, gives way to a second, deeper stage, which again is pictured from diverse viewpoints, divine (chap. 15) and human (chap. 16). From one stage to the next (from chaps. 13–14 to chaps. 15–16) there is a major advance, but even within each stage, in moving from one point of view or chapter to the next, the picture of union grows ever deeper. With the account of the birthlike seeing of Jesus that union reaches a new level.

[16:4b–6] The barrier of backward-looking sadness. At this point Jesus looks backward for a moment (v 4b), and then he refers to the sadness which surrounds his impending departure and death (v 6). The result is to suggest that the disciples are in the grip of a paralyzing backward-looking sadness. At the same time he says that none of them asks, "Where are you going" (v 5)—an extremely puzzling statement since at an earlier stage they had, in fact, asked exactly that question (13:36; cf. 14:4). Thus once again (as in 13:1–3; 14:1–3, and 15:1–3) the text begins with a challenge to the reader.

A partial solution is provided by the observation (Lagrange, 417–18; Barrett, 405) that the text does not exclude the possibility that the disciples had, in fact, asked earlier; the emphasis after all is on the idea that they do not ask now (present tense). However, as so often—and as with Nicodemus and the Samaritan woman—the more essential solution is that the apparent contradiction be set in the context of a spiritual reality. As mentioned earlier, it is a way of saying that the advancing disciple goes through different phases—at first eager, perhaps even overeager, to know the way, but then, as the necessity emerges for some form of dying, the eagerness is lost, and the disciple, turning sadly backwards, no longer wants to follow nor even to ask the way.

Now that critical phase has been reached—a fact which is reflected apparently in the double use of the conclusion-related *tauta,* "These things . . . I (have) said to you" (vv 4b, 6). Now is the conclusive hour. Just as the seeing of Jesus (or Jesus' return) refers above all to a spiritual seeing, so the departure and death of Jesus contains a reference to a spiritual process, to a letting-go which is a form of dying. But now that that hour of spiritual death is at hand, the sense of loss is overpowering, and the heart is filled with sadness.

It is at this point that it would appear that the disciple cannot make it. And it is at this point also that Jesus begins, more than ever, to speak of the Companion, the Spirit.

[16:7–11] Amid paralyzing sadness, the Paraclete provides an awareness of underlying problems and of positive possibilities. As Jesus addresses the saddened hearers, his manner of speaking suggests a moment of revelation: "But I tell you the truth. . . ."

And then he speaks of the benefit of undergoing a loss: "It is expedient/good/beneficial (*sympherei*) for you that I go . . ."—a reference, as elsewhere when *sympherei* is used (11:50; 18:14), to his death. So deathlike loss is beneficial! ". . . For if I do not go the Companion will not come." Again the very strangeness of the word *parakletos* has the effect of challenging the saddened disciple to look beyond the loss to a new horizon.

Jesus then goes on to speak of the Companion as confronting the world. However, as noted when introducing 16:4b–33, this confrontation occurs, first of all, within the disciples; they must deal with the unbelieving world which is in themselves.

The confrontation is under three headings—*sin, justice* and *judgement.* As the gospel often implies, and here states more clearly, *sin* consists essentially of failing to believe, of giving up (v 9). An awareness of sin does not always come easily, particularly for one who has made some limited progress in discipleship. The disciple may, for instance, retain considerable anger or self-pity. It is not easy to see and accept that included in one's reaction there is a stubborn refusal of the good.

As well as indicating what is wrong, the Companion also gives an awareness of something immensely positive—*justice,* in this case a justice which comes from God and which is manifested in the fate of Jesus. Such is the implication of Jesus' going to the Father (v 10); it is a way of saying that, however harsh Jesus' fate, his exaltation to God shows that there is justice, the justice of God. To one who is sunk in bitterness such an awareness is challenging and uplifting. The fact that Jesus' presence is not physically visible ("and you will see me no longer") is meant to emphasize that the disciple is being challenged by the realm of the invisible, the realm of Jesus' presence through the Companion. Thus the paralyzed disciple is being drawn into a realm which is wholly other. The full extent of this realm is underlined by the fact that "justice," as well as applying to legal justice, has a wider field of reference; the "justice of God" involves also God's holiness and majesty (Brown, 706). Thus from a paralysis that by its nature tends to be inward-looking, the disciple is being drawn outward to see something holy— something alluring.

Also uplifting is the awareness of where final *judgement* lies (v 11). The world, and all that is worldly or disbelieving in a disciple, may tend to think, especially because Jesus is out of sight ("and you see me no longer," 10), that whatever justice God may have shown in Jesus, the final outcome or judgement lies with the powers of darkness and negativity. But here too evil has lost. "The ruler of this world," far from having the last word, has already (perfect tense) been judged, already been condemned.

The three elements, sin, justice, and judgement, form a graded unity. The awareness of sin helps the person to realize the need to turn from what is evil and, by implication, to seek the good. (This, to some degree, may be called the I've-got-a-problem stage.) The awareness of God's justice in Jesus provides an alluring good. And, though Jesus is out of sight, the awareness of the nature of the final judgement indicates the scope, the lasting nature of that good. In other words, when the disciple is plunged in darkness, the Companion confronts it and draws it from its sin to an increasing awareness of the world of goodness and truth.

[16:12–15] The further work of the Spirit.   Having described the foundational stages of the work of the Spirit—how it raises the discouraged soul to an awareness of God's saving justice and judgement—Jesus goes on to refer to the Spirit's further work, to the way in which it leads the disciple into a full understanding of Jesus and God. This further work involves another stage of spiritual development.

But advanced spirituality, whether of an individual or church, is not something that comes easily. As Jesus speaks to those who not long previously had been so overpowered by sadness, he tells them that for the moment they are not able to bear many other aspects of his message (12). The situation is somewhat akin to that later found in Corinth, where Paul's readers were so weighed down by worldly considerations (literally, the flesh) that for the moment they were not able to receive mature spiritual teaching (1 Corinthians 2–3, esp. 3:1–4).

But later the Spirit of truth will come, and "will show you the way [*hodegeō*] into all the truth" (13a). Since this builds on the earlier statement that the way (*hodos*) is Jesus (14:4–6), there is an initial indication of what it is that the Spirit will communicate, namely the truth which is embodied in the life of Jesus.

The Spirit's process of communicating all truth is described in three sentences with repetitive endings: the Spirit ". . . will announce to you. . . . will announce to you. . . . will announce to you." The result is to suggest an advancing process of revelation.

The first picture of this process (13b) gives only a limited idea of what the Spirit will reveal. Negatively the text states that the Spirit will not speak on its own authority, and then there is a note which is positive but very low-key, cryptic almost: the Spirit receives what it will say from someone else, someone from whom it hears ("whatsoever he will hear he will speak"). However, while the Spirit's source remains obscure, there is real communication: "and the things which are to come he will announce to you." As Bultmann (575) emphasizes the background for this sentence seems to come from "the common Christian idea of the spirit of prophecy," yet as it is used here it refers not to a foretelling of the distant (apocalyptic) future, but to the fact that "the future . . . will be illuminated again and again by the word" (Bultmann, 575). Schnackenburg (3:135) gives essentially the same interpretation but makes greater allowance for some idea of having a sense of the future: the Spirit "will guide . . . into the future and make clear . . . what is coming." Against the background of paralyzing preoccupation this refers above all to recovering and maintaining a sense of direction.

The second picture (14) refers to communicating an awareness or recognition of Jesus, and, since recognizing someone involves a certain glorifying of that person, this process is referred to as the Spirit's glorifying of Jesus. What is essential is that the sense of direction, which had been given earlier, develops now into something more rich and personal: an awareness of what is implied in the person and mission of Jesus ("he will take what is mine and announce it to you").

Finally (15), in a third picture of what the Spirit communicates, there is an articulating of what is implied in Jesus: "all whatsoever the Father has." In other words, a person who is guided to a recognition of Jesus will then be guided to the highest source of all, the one who is present in Jesus, namely God the Father and the Father's encompassing care.

As with the graded progression between awareness of sin, justice, and judgement, so there is a graded progression between gaining a sense of direction (a sense of a way forward), coming to a developed sense of Jesus and coming to an awareness of the Father.

The entire process, from sin to the Father, has overtones of the story of the woman of Samaria (especially of its second stage), the story which Brown (178) described as "the drama of a soul struggling to rise from the things of this world to belief in Jesus.'' The overtones are not simply of the broad thematic kind; there are also some linguistic links (4:25; 16:13–15):

"When he [the *Christos*] comes he will announce to us all things."

hotan elthē ekeinos, anaggelei hēmin hapanta.

"But when he comes, the Spirit . . . he will announce to you . . . all."

hotan de elthē ekeinos, to pneuma . . . anaggelei hymin . . . panta.

With one exception (5:15), the word "announce," *anaggelō*, does not otherwise occur in John's gospel. There is, furthermore, a complementarity between Jesus revealing "all whatsoever" the woman has done (*panta hosa . . . panta hosa,* 4:29,39) and the Spirit revealing all whatsoever it receives from Jesus (*hosa . . . panta hosa;* 16:13,15).

Whatever the details, the impression which emerges is that just as Jesus helped the woman of Samaria to reach a new level, so will the Spirit help those who are "struggling to rise from the things of this world."

[16:16–24] The divinely led breakthrough to union with God.   The description of the work of the Spirit (16:7–15) had indicated the build-up of a certain momentum: through the Spirit the disciple is led from worldliness to an increasing awareness of Jesus and of all that the Father has given to Jesus. Now that momentum reaches a new level: in vv 16–24, when the text speaks of seeing Jesus, there is a kind of breakthrough, a significantly new degree of union.

In chap. 15 also there had been a sense of breakthrough, but in that chapter the breakthrough was spoken of primarily from God's point of view: the Father as vinedresser brought the disciple into the realm of divine love (15:8–10). Now the emphasis is on the experience of the disciple, an experience which in some ways is like that of coming through a painful birth.

The text falls into three parts, each set off from the next by "Amen, amen . . .":

16–19   The preliminary confusion
20–23a   Breakthrough: the birthlike seeing of Jesus in joy
23b–24   The new level of intimacy with the Father

In the history of interpreting the meaning of seeing Jesus the primary emphasis has been on the resurrection, on the moment when his reappearance to the disciples would bring them joy (20:20; cf. Brown, 729). And for Lindars (506), for instance, that view still holds: "It is clear that John means the resurrection."

But the question is not so simple, for unlike the brief joy of seeing the resurrected Jesus, the joy which is spoken of here is "a joy that no one can take from you." Hence Brown (729) speaks of "a more permanent union with Jesus," and Lindars (709) qualifies his emphasis on the resurrection by speaking of the establishing of "a permanent relationship." The permanence is given an added ring of finality by the use of "On that day . . ." (v 23), a phrase which, particularly because it evokes the final "Day of the Lord," has eschatological overtones. Hence Schnackenburg (3:159), though excluding a reference to the Parousia, speaks of a joy which "anticipates the eschaton."

What emerges then is a joyful union which sees the risen Jesus not in any transient way but with a vision which is more permanent. The vision, therefore, has to be within, in the realm of the Spirit, " 'Seeing' Jesus has been reinterpreted to mean the continued experience of his presence in the Christian, and this can only mean the presence of the Paraclete/Spirit" (Brown, 730). It is an awareness —no matter how ordinary life may be—that deep within oneself there is the living face of the eternal God.

This awareness is not easy or superficial. The image which is used to illustrate it, that of childbirth, emphasizes pain and has overtones even of death ("weep and lament" was previously used concerning the death of Lazarus, 11:31–33). But the image of childbirth is also very positive. In various ways it was used to express the most decisive processes and moments in salvation history—the coming of the saving Messiah in Isaiah 1–12 (see esp. Isa 7:14; 9:5–6), the divine intervention which includes raising the dead (Isaiah 26, esp. 26:16–19), the apocalyptic renewal which brings joy to Jerusalem (Isa 66:5–16), the great recovery and consolation of the people (Jeremiah 30–31, esp. 30:6–7), and the groaning even of the whole of creation as it moves from decadence to renewal (Rom 8:22–23). Without attempting to be comprehensive, it may be seen that in essence it is an image which is capable of expressing the entire divine process of giving forth life. And that is what it means for the disciple; it signals a God-given transition from a narrow form of preoccupation with the world to an involved awareness of a whole other dimension of reality, a dimension which brings great joy.

Verses 16–19, with their picture of preliminary confusion, have the effect of highlighting the fact that this new awareness is God-given, not the result of human effort or knowing. When Jesus says that the disciples will see him in a little while, they do "not know" what to make of what he says. Fastening on the phrase "a short while," they become preoccupied with time and departure (his going away), and the account of their conversation suggests a process which is repetitious and unproductive. They seem unable even to ask—so much so that, with God-like knowledge, Jesus eventually tells them exactly the question which is on their minds. He even reproduces for them a tiny variation which they had introduced into his own words—*ou* ("not") in place of *ouketi* ("not yet"; vv 16, 17, 19). In other words, in the journey from sad inability to joyful recognition of the Jesus within, one needs the help not only of the Spirit, but of a God who knows one's confused thoughts and questions and who leads one through them to a new birth. Not that Jesus softens reality. On the contrary, he tells them of impending sorrow and of a form of death. But beyond the death is birth. The overall effect is something like that of God's reply at the burning bush (Exod 3:13–15). The anxious Moses wanted clear-cut answers—God's name. All God would give was an assurance of saving presence. And when (vv 23b–24) the new birth has already occurred, when the stormy transition has already inaugurated a new calm (v 23a, "you will not question me any more"), then there is a sense of reaching a new level of intimacy with the Father.

One aspect of this move to a new level is the change from the verb *erotaō*, which can mean either "question" or "petition" (23a) to *aiteō*, which means "petition," and which refers more properly to prayer. In these few lines (23b–24), *aiteō* is used three times, and it helps to build the picture of what Hoskyns (487–89) calls "the new economy of prayer."

The most distinctive aspect of this new prayer situation is that the disciple has direct access to the Father (23b, following the more difficult reading). This does not mean that Jesus has no role. On the contrary, the Father who responds and gives, does so in union with Jesus (literally, "in my name"), and (because of the post-resurrectional granting of the Spirit) the disciple also is in union with Jesus (24a). And it is on the basis of that double union—of Jesus with both the Father and the disciples—that the way is open for the further unifying move, that of the (Spirit-led) disciple directly with the personal seeing God.

The practical outcome of this complex-sounding picture of union and, indeed, of the whole divine action of leading and knowing (16:7–24) is that at this stage prayer is not so much an address to God as an attentive allowing of God to pray within one. The person who prays is not excluded from this praying process or made to feel unimportant; on the contrary, one is never more involved and more at peace about one's own worth. But by various means, whether with tangible words or in silence, it is God who is leading the way.

And it is within such prayer that the union of wills—something already spoken of in 15:7 (cf. 14:13–14)—reaches a new level. One receives what one asks (v 23b) because one's very asking is directed by God. However severe one's problems and cares, when they are brought through prayer into the depth of God's inner dialogue they are experienced otherwise, and, therefore, one's way of asking about them changes. That does not mean developing an indifference to problems; on the contrary, one often brings from prayer a greater sensitivity and a certain power of healing. But within the prayer there is a mode of asking which is so dependent on God that it is itself God's gift and is itself an answer—not perhaps the answer one had originally been looking for, but one which reflects the goodness of God and which brings a deep joy.

[16:25–33] Practical results: a clear sense of the Father's love, even amid the loneliness of the world.   The breakthrough to seeing the inner face of God has effects on one's life in the world, and it is these effects which are summarized in the concluding verses. The text would seem to fall into two parts—first (vv 25–28), a positive picture of having a clear sense of God's love; then (vv 29–33), even amid the spectre of falling away, of loneliness and of distress, a renewal of the sense of God's presence and victory.

This division (into vv 25–28 and 29–33) seems to be confirmed by some details. The conclusions of the two parts contain repetition ("world . . . world"; in vv 28, 33). And the beginning of the second part uses a form of *legō*, "I say" —the same verb which occurs at or near the beginning of all the other subdivisions in this chapter (cf. vv 7, 12, 20, 23b).

One of the basic features of the text as a whole is that it broadens the horizon of the discussion. In the first part (vv 25–28), Jesus seems to look back on all that is past. (His initial mention of having spoken in parables, v 25, refers apparently to his entire life and teachings; cf. Kysar, 252; Brown, 735; Lindars, 511; Schnackenburg, 3:162. And later, v 28, he reviews his entire existence, his going forth from God into the world, and then his going from the world back to God.) In the second part (vv 29–33), the essential focus is on the future, particularly on the future of the disciples in the world.

One of the results of this wider view is to confirm what was implied in the opening verses of this "chapter" (in 16:4b–7), namely that the discourse as a whole is coming to an end, that it is time to step back and see things in context, in the flow of time. It is within this expanding context that he now speaks of the implications of the breakthrough into the divine realm.

In vv 25–28 he announces that the coming hour—the reference is to his glorification, but there is a suggestion also of the "hour" of childbirth, the hour when the glorification takes regenerating effect on the disciples (16:21–22)—this hour will bring a transition from parabolic language to the language of openness: Jesus will tell them plainly of the Father; he will announce it to them (v 25). Then (vv 26–27) he explains what he is referring to: a form of prayer in which, in union with him ("in my name"), they are in direct communication with the deepest personal dimension of God, with "the Father" who loves them. And this love is a two-way process, for the Father's love, even though it is mentioned first and *is* first, is also a reciprocation of their loving faith in the one who came forth from God and who returns to God. Thus in prayer they are led to a participation in the dialogue of divine love. It is appropriate, therefore, that these verses begin with the eschatological-sounding phrase "On that day . . ." (v 26). In this depth of prayer they are in living contact with the ultimate.

The quality of this contact is that of friendship. As Schnackenburg notes (3:163) the use of *phileō*, "to love" (27, twice), "was certainly chosen with great deliberation." It builds on the word *philos,* "friend" or "beloved," which was used in describing Jesus' friendship with the disciples, a friendship based on communicating all he had heard from the Father (15:14–15), and it extends the notion of friendship to include the friendship of God.

In vv 29–33 the process of communicating with God is set in the context of harsh reality, the context of the failure of faith, of aloneness, and of distress. This negative side surfaces in the statement of the disciples, a statement which at first sounds like a resoundingly positive declaration. It begins with a rather solemn "Behold," and consists of three ascending steps:

> "*Behold, now* you are speaking plainly and not in any parable.
>
> *Now we know* that you know all things and that you do not need that anyone question you.
>
> Through this *we believe* that you came forth from God."

There is a progression here in the way of perceiving. They go from the dawning realization of "Behold, now . . ." to the more confident "we know" and "we believe." There is also a progression in the content—from Jesus' clear speaking, to a realization that he knows all things, and then to the further explicit realization that he is "from God." (The fact that he does not need to be questioned is a variation on the idea that he knows all things; as was illustrated in the discussion about the "short while" [v 19], he knew exactly what they wanted to ask, and so it was not necessary that they actually pose the question.) The first two statements have a carefully crafted balance between positive and negative ("you are speaking . . . and not . . ."; "you know . . . and you do not . . ."), and the third has a simplicity which gives it a clinching ring: ". . . you came forth from God."

Yet for all its artistry and confidence this profession of faith is surrounded by ambiguity. It may justly be seen as quite negative, as a superficial confession which, whatever its enthusiasm, is, in fact, an ironic expression of misunderstanding (see esp. Duke, 1985, 56–59). The misunderstanding is seen particularly in the fact that while Jesus had just indicated that his parabolic speech would be made plain only through his glorification, they, in their overconfidence, say that it is already plain, that already they understand and believe.

The ambiguity is heightened by the fact that the exchange as a whole (vv 29–33) echoes Peter both at what seems to be his best (6:69; Dodd, 1953, 392) and also at his most brash and overconfident (13:36–38). Thus the way is prepared both for the showing up of Peter's superficiality (18:1–27) and also for his later, humbled, reinstatement (21:15–17).

When Jesus replies, therefore, his words are deflating. After an initial "You now believe (?)," a phrase which may be read either as a declaration or a question, he gives an answering "Behold," one which counters that of the disciples, and then he tells of them being utterly scattered—"each to his own and will leave me alone."

It may seem strange that the discourse at this stage should suggest such a fiasco. The essential picture after all had been one of advancing discipleship—not of discipleship collapsing. But the image of a collapse would seem to have a positive purpose—to underline the fact that it is only through the coming "hour," the hour of glorification and of the giving of the Spirit, that solid discipleship can be built. Thus implicitly it reestablishes the "hour" as pivotal to believing.

Besides, the image of the disciples as scattered each to his "own," while applicable to some degree to the fact that Jesus was largely left alone, would seem even more applicable—especially in a gospel which puzzlingly does not actually say the disciples were scattered, and in which one of them, in fact, stood right by the cross—to their subsequent scattering in the world. In other words, at another level it is "a prediction of the suffering to be endured by the Christians scattered in the hostile world" (Brown, 737). Thus is it an indication of the future condition of the believer.

This evoking of the hostile world opens up a new horizon, and the final verses (31–33) develop it: they refer to Jesus as being "alone," and to the disciples as experiencing the world's "distress." Both ideas—"alone" and "distress"—sound negative, yet both are overcome: even when Jesus is alone, the Father is present; and even amid the world's distress the disciples can have peace and take courage —Jesus has conquered the world. In fact, the word "distress," *thlipsis,* had just been used of the positive pain of childbirth (16:21). The implication is that the distress of the world, far from causing faith to die, should be a place where it is reborn.

Needless to say, this is not easy. Among the documents on display in modern Dachau are two which refer to a Munich locksmith who had opposed the Nazis. The first records his imprisonment, and the second, written five years later, records his release. In the space for recording the person's religion, the first reads "Catholic," the second "without confession." The challenge, even amid one's personal Dachau, is to retain faith, and somehow, through the *thlipsis,* to renew it.

Thus while these concluding verses (25–33) allow for a temporary collapse of faith, their basic effect is to bring down to earth the message of 16:4b–24: you have reached the realm of God's love, and not even the loneliness and distress of the world can take that from you. On the contrary, such conditions can be the occasion for growth.

The Prayer of Holiness (Wholeness/Sanctification) and Unity

A Prayerful Ascentlike Review, with Petitions, of the Process of
Glory-Based Sanctification and of the Consequent Emergence
into the World of a God-Reflecting Community

Meaning and Structure: The Prayer as an Ascent
Which Signals Holiness and Unity

Almost from the beginning, and particularly since Part 2 (2:23–chap. 6), the gospel has been dealing, directly or indirectly, with the ravages of sin and division. This does not mean that these negative forces have been seen as uppermost or out of hand; rather, they have always been placed within the context of a greater, more positive, development, a development which is based ultimately on God's love and which is focused towards holiness and unity.

Nowhere is the movement towards holiness and unity clearer than in the last discourse, especially in chap. 17. The depicting of this process by which God makes people holy begins with the washing (chap. 13) and the purifying (15:1–17), but it is in chap. 17, with the explicit emphasis on "holy" and "to make holy" (*hagios,* 17:10; and *hagiazō,* 17:17–19), that it reaches its full development (cf. Forestell, 1974, 155–57). Likewise with the related idea of unity: in various ways it was the implied focus of chaps. 13–16, but in chap. 17 it becomes explicit (17:11,20–23).

The centrality of *hagiazō* to chapter 17 was particularly emphasized by Westcott (236) and Hoskyns (494). It is variously translated "sanctify," "consecrate," or simply "make holy," and, in general, refers to the process by which something ordinary, for instance a person or place, is brought into the sphere of the holy, the sphere of God. In the case of a person, this coming to God involves a coming to one's true self, to wholeness.

But holiness (or wholeness) is not something isolated. The God who is holy and who makes holy is a God of communication and creation, a God in whom Father and Son are one; "unity is the mark of divine being" (Schnackenburg, 3:192). And so holiness is inextricably related to other people, to community. Thus within chap. 17 the emphasis on holiness gives way to an increasing emphasis on unity, to an implied image of the unity of the church and to a sense of the relation of this unity to the whole world (vv 11, 20–23). In fact, the text is so written that to some degree the voice in the prayer is the voice of the church (Rosenblatt, 1988).

But the voice is also the voice of Jesus, and it is through him that holiness and unity come. His role is not immediately clear. Is he on earth, at the supper, or is he in some sense already in heaven? In the history of interpretation the fact that he is heaven-related and petitioning has sometimes led to seeing him as the heavenly petitioner, the high priest, who is described in Hebrews (Hebr 7:25, 9:16; cf. 1 John 2:1, Rom 8:34). And so chap. 17 has been called "the high priestly prayer." But is this accurate?

To clarify the role of Jesus it is useful first to clarify the literary role of the chapter. At one level, chapter 17 breaks the literary mold. Unlike chaps. 13–16, in which chapters are paired together in diptychs (13 with 14; 15:1–16:4a with 16:4b–33), 17 stands alone. Nor does it have any of the dialogue which marked some of the previous chapters; instead, it is a long unbroken prayer, virtually unique in the gospel. Even its structure is different from that of chaps. 13–16.

At another level, chap. 17 belongs to the last discourse. Single chapter though it is, it combines, almost as much as the paired chapters do (13–14, 15–16), an emphasis on both the divine and the human, on divine giving and on human keeping, receiving, and believing (cf. esp. vv 6–8). Its absence of dialogue had been prepared for in the discourse of 15:1–16:4a, and preparation had also been made for its prayer—not only through earlier prayers (at the tomb of Lazarus, 11:41–42; and at the Greeks-related onset of death, 12:27–28), but also through the fact that the literary convention of a last discourse allowed for a conclusion that was different (a prayer, song, or blessing). Such a phenomenon may be found as early as Deuteronomy 32 and 33. As for the difference of structure, chap. 17 does not ignore the arrangement found in the discourse's leading chapters (13 and 15). Rather it reaches behind these chapters, so to speak, to the texts on which they themselves are modeled, the good shepherd (10:7–18; cf. Schnackenburg, 3:171, 178, 181) and the prologue, and it produces a structure which is a new synthesis of all these mainstream texts. In fact, 13:1 is so closely related to chap. 17 that Bultmann (486) regarded one as the introduction to the other.

What is essential is that in relation to the unity of the last discourse, chap. 17 is both within and outside.

This literary ambiguity provides the setting for a theological ambiguity: in relation to the last supper, the Jesus who prays is both present and absent; he is still in the world, but he is also coming to the Father. This is not simply the usual tension which springs from the fact that Jesus is both human and divine. The text suggests an active process of coming towards the Father.

This heavenward movement is suggested initially by the fact that the first part of the text (vv 1–5) begins with the heavenward raising of the eyes (17:1). Then, in the main body of the text (vv 6–19), there is an increasing sense of coming to the Father (cf. vv 6, 11, 13: "I have revealed your name. . . . I am no longer in the world. . . . And now I am coming to you"). Finally, in the concluding section (vv 20–26, esp. v 24), Jesus speaks to the Father with sovereign power, as one who is already in heaven ("Father . . . I desire/will," *thelō*). The overall effect is of a heavenward movement which is threefold and spiralling.

The sense of a heavenward movement is particularly noticeable in vv 6–19. As Jesus speaks of coming closer to God ("I have revealed. . . . I am no longer in the world. . . . And now I am coming to you"), he becomes stronger as the intercessor or advocate. Thus, in the opening stage (vv 6–10) he simply makes a request, and he does so in a way which is modified, qualified ("I pray for them, I do not pray for the world, . . ." v 9). Then (vv 11–12), while granting implicitly that the supreme quality of holiness belongs to the Father, he asks with greater directness, using the imperative, for something approaching holiness: "Holy Father, keep them in your name" (v 11). And finally (v 13–19), with an imperative which is even more direct—in the context it has a certain abruptness—he asks that holiness itself be shared: "Make them holy . . ." v (17).

Within the concluding section also there is a grading in the assertiveness of the petitions. First comes the simple "I ask" (v 20), a request which recalls but surpasses the "I ask" of v 9 (unlike the modifier in v 9, asking for fewer people —"I ask . . . I do not ask for . . ."—the modifier in v 20 asks for more: "I do not ask for those only but for . . ."). And finally comes the majestic "I will . . ." (v 24).

What is being portrayed, therefore, is a Jesus who is not exclusively either on earth or in heaven, but who in some sense is moving from one to the other, who is ascending and is coming closer to the Father.

This implies that the designation of chapter 17 as "the high priestly prayer" needs to be qualified. The Jesus who prays is indeed in heaven to some degree, but he is also on earth, and the "high priestly" designation neglects that factor.

This ascending pattern also casts light on Käsemann's study (1968). Käsemann's interpretation restored a needed emphasis on glory. But it went too far; it neglected the more mundane human dimension of Jesus. Thus the final majestic "I desire/will" (*thelō,* v 24), for instance, is indeed significant, but it does not "dominate the whole chapter" (Käsemann, 1968, 5). It is rather the heavenly, climactic stage of a humbler process of petition which works its way gradually through the whole text. By focusing unduly on what might be called the most heavenly aspect of the most heavenly chapter, Käsemann (1968, 4–26) inevitably reached a position which is unbalanced.

On the other hand, the picture of Jesus as ascending vindicates the view of Dodd (1953, 419): "The prayer in some sort *is* the ascent of the Son to the Father." In saying this Dodd is not referring to a bodily ascension or to the physical act of dying; rather, "Christ's 'journeying' to the Father . . . is that spiritual ascent to God which is the inward reality of all true prayer" (1953, 419).

This ascent is not carried out in isolation. As true prayer it involves intercession, and so others are included in the ascent. "In thus praying," concludes Dodd (1953, 419), "Christ both accomplishes the self-oblation of which His death is the historical expression, and 'draws' all . . . [people] after Him into the sphere of eternal life which is union with God."

So when chap. 17 speaks of holiness and unity it does not suggest that their connection to Jesus' prayer is loose or secondary; prayer is not a slot-machine for producing holiness and unity. Holiness and unity may be gifts, but their connection with prayer is inherent. They require prayer, first the pioneering prayer of Christ, and then the prayer of the church, in other words, the prayer of those for whom he interceded and whose voice is reflected in the prayer.

If the Spirit is not mentioned in chap. 17 it would seem to be because, following the Spirit-led union of chaps. 15–16, especially the "seeing" or experiencing of the indwelling Jesus (16:4b–24, esp. vv 16–24), there is a sense in which the presence of the Spirit is now taken for granted. In other words, the Spirit is present—but in the people, in those who have believed, those who, as their voice echoes that of Jesus, carry his Spirit to one another and to the world.

For they do not retreat from the world. One of the striking features of chap. 17 is that, even though it implies an increasing ascent to God, it also suggests an increasing sense of mission to the world.

A Note on the Structure of Chapter 17

The preceding analysis implies that the structure consists of a threefold spiralling movement (1–5, 6–19, 20–26), and that the movement is accompanied by petitions. Many researchers agree with this threefold division, and some add a subdivision at 24. (See, for instance, Westcott, 237; Lagrange, 436; Strathmann, 231–35; Behler, 1960, 219; Barrett, 499 [subdivision at 25]; Lindars, 515; Schnackenburg, 3:168; Mateos and Barreto, 707; Beasley-Murray, 295; UBSGNT; RSV. For a review of opinions, see Becker, 1969, esp. 57–60; note also Schnackenburg, 1973.)

But the process of dividing the text is sometimes influenced decisively by the idea that Jesus is making petitions—particularly petitions for himself (vv 1–5), for the disciples (6–19), and for future believers (20–26). To some degree this is true; Jesus does, in fact, make such petitions. And it is particularly because of the emphasis on petitions that some other researchers would change the foregoing proposal. With considerable justification, they say that the petition for the disciples does not begin until v 9, and so they divide: 1–8, 9–19, 20–26.

But as commentators sometimes note, petitions are not the foundation of the text. The dominating factor is the movement towards unity: "this is more a prayer of union or communion . . . than it is a prayer of petition" (Brown, 748). In other words, it does not make sense first to say that the text is not primarily petition, and then to divide it as though it were.

The same caution applies when subdividing the main body of the text, vv 6–19. Schnackenburg (3:169), for instance, sees vv 6–19 as dominated by the two petitions or intercessions which begin in v 11b and v 17 ("Holy Father, keep them. . . . Make them holy . . ."), and so he divides accordingly: 6–11a, 11b–16, 17–19. These petitions are indeed high points, and Schnackenburg's analysis helps to clarify their interlocking roles. But they are merely part of the larger three-part pattern of petitions (9, 11b, 17), and besides, they are not the foundation, not the basis of the structure. The foundation consists of the three-part spiralling movement towards the Father, and within vv 6–19 that foundation is found in the graded pictures of Jesus being in the world and then coming to God (cf. vv 6, 11, 13).

As for the concluding segment (vv 20–26) it seems right, as most writers suggest, to subdivide it into two parts: 20–23, on the unity of believers; and 24–26, on final union with God.

Chapter 17 as a Variation on the Prologue

To a significant degree chap. 17 is a review of the process or history of sanctification. As such it is a variation on the prologue, a text which consists of "a description of the history of salvation" (Brown, 23–24). The prologue is meditative, chap. 17 is prayerful. Käsemann (1968, 3, 6) notes that "this chapter [17] is a summary of the Johannine discourses and in this respect is a counterpart to the prologue. . . . Its scope encompasses the total earthly history." Brown (745) also emphasizes the connection: "The prayer . . . and the Prologue have interesting similarities in their poetic quality, careful structure . . . and theme."

Of course there are also major differences. In comparison to the prologue's general idea of salvation, the prayer's emphasis on sanctification is more specific and developed. It represents a high point in the process of salvation. And while the prologue views things from the outside and at the beginning, the prayer sees things from within (from the viewpoint of Jesus and the church) and from near the end. Thus, it is like viewing a single object in distinct ways at distinct times. A great valley, for instance, which a small girl sees from the eastern end, playing amid the rich grass on a sunlit spring morning, is very different from the valley she perceives more than two generations later when she looks out from her western-end mountain home on an autumn evening.

But it is the same valley. And ultimately the prologue and prayer represent complementary views of the same complex process. In terms that are greatly simplified:

The history of salvation (1:1–18)	*The history of the sanctification of the church (17:1–26)*
A meditation	A prayer
1–5 *The beginning*	1–5 *The* glory-based *incarnation* ("glory . . . before the world was"), that "they" (the church) may know God.
6–13 *The coming* The intermediate period (OT): the light was coming into the world.	6–19 *The going away.* The intermediate process (the ascent): as Jesus comes closer to the Father, the disciples, who are in the world, advance towards holiness.
14–18 *The incarnation* of the Word, and "we" (the church) have seen his glory.	20–26 *The church,* built on the Word and glory, incarnates God's unity, that the world may believe and know. Final unity.

The essential view of history which underlies both schemas is that, apart from the divine dimension, which is outside of time and which is strongly present in both 1:1–5 and 17:1–5, there are three basic periods: the OT, the ministry of Jesus, and the time of the church. The prologue, precisely because it is a prologue, lays the emphasis on the explicit idea of the beginning and on the first two periods of history. The concluding prayer, however, precisely because it is concluding, regards the beginning only indirectly, as something to be looked back on ("glory . . . before the world was"), and the emphasis falls on the later periods of history. The idea of glory, which in the prologue lay in the distance, in the prayer is immediately visible.

Despite these great differences, there are subtle continuities. For instance, the first major change in the prologue has thematic and linguistic affinities with the first major change in the prayer:

- "There was a person sent . . . whose name . . . that all might believe" (1:6–7).

- "I have revealed your name to the persons . . . and they have believed that you sent me" (17:6–8).

Both texts speak of decisive moments in God's sending of revealers and also of the reactions to those believers. The second text, however, is much more developed. The revealer is greater, the process of believing has already begun, and the word *name,* for instance, has gone from a mundane meaning to a meaning which involves the divine. Thus there is a mixture of logical continuity and supralogical wordplay.

Likewise with the second major point of division:

- "And the Word . . . tented among (*en*) us . . . and we have seen his glory, glory as of the only Son from the Father" (1:14).

- ". . . I ask . . . for those who believe through their word . . . that they . . . may be one . . . Father . . . in [*en*] us . . . and the glory which you have given to me I have given to them" (17:20–22).

Again, there is a basic continuity: both texts refer to a basic step forward in revelation, a fundamental advance in the coming together of God and humanity. But more than ever there is a radical difference of perspectives. Instead of the implied picture of *people* telling how the *divine* Word came down into them, the *divine* persons are speaking of how *people* who have accepted the Word will be "brought up," into the divine. In other words, while one refers to God going forth and being received by people, the other is more concerned with the beginning of the return, with people being received into the unity of God. And the glory, which was first seen in 1:14, has now been handed on. In Kysar's words (262), "the glory perceived in the incarnate Word (1:14) is now perceptible in the church."

Leaving aside further details, a fundamental conclusion may be drawn: in content and structure chap. 17 has a central affinity with the prologue.

This affinity confirms the opinion of those who divide chap. 17 into 1–5, 6–19, 20–26. Furthermore, since the center of the prologue is dominated by a three-part picture of the coming of the light into the world ("There was a person . . . [who] came to bear witness to the light. . . . The light . . . was . . . coming. . . . He came to his own"), it provides added support for the idea that the center of the prayer is dominated by the complementary three-part picture of Jesus returning to God, in other words for the division: 6–10, 11–12, 13–19.

The relationship to the prologue also helps explain some of the prayer's density. The prologue is generally regarded as a form of synthesis. The prayer also is a synthesis, though in a manner which concludes rather than introduces. In

Dodd's words (1953, 417, 420), "The prayer gathers up much of what has been said. . . . This is the climax . . . of the thought of the whole gospel."

[17:1–5] Praying for glorification, Jesus reviews the incarnation and its purpose of imparting life-giving knowing. When Jesus begins by declaring, ". . . the hour has come," his words have considerable ambiguity. On the one hand, they suggest the striking of the dreaded hour of death. On the other, they surround the possible sense of dread with counterbalancing factors—the raising of the eyes to heaven, the invoking of the Father, and the request for glorification. Thus, even in face of death, he "enters the familiar . . . transcendent . . . space of God" (Schnackenburg, 3:170). Death is being absorbed into glory.

Jesus' purpose in seeking glorification is to glorify God, "to make God known" (Kysar, 255). For humans, of course, God is elusive, sometimes painfully so, and particularly so at death.

Jesus will reverse that. His death, despite all its brutality, will be surrounded not by absurdity, but by life, by a sense of divine presence—by glory. Thus will God be made known. Such, in fact, had been the purpose of the incarnation—to reveal the divine which is latent in the human—and so now, in a kind of flashback, Jesus reviews what he has done. He refers to the broad creation-related power which enabled him to impart the life which consists of knowing God (vv 2–3), and to the specific way in which he had made God known, namely by glorifying God on earth and particularly by "completing" God's work (v 4). "Complete" (*teleioō*) is used of Jesus' death (19:28), and so in describing God's work he alludes, once again, to his own dying.

Thus (v 5) he returns to the request with which he had started: "And now, you glorify me, Father, in your presence. . . ." And he intensifies the request by recalling the glory which he had had "before the world was."

The result is a text which, both in its pendulum movement (from one "glorify" to another; vv 1, 5) and in its content, summarizes the entire incarnation. It has echoes of earlier passages, particularly of the prologue, of the picture of the Son as Creator (5:19–29; esp. vv 21, 27) and of the pendulum movement in the foot-washing (13:1–20).

Yet it is quite distinctive. More perhaps than any other text, it emphasizes that the Incarnation is based on God's glory and thus on God's love (for it is love that gives rise to glory). Furthermore, it states more clearly than before that the purpose of the incarnation, the meaning of eternal life, is that people should know this God of glory (and love): "And this is eternal life—that they may know you the only [*monos*] true God and Jesus Christ whom you have sent." The sentence is central, as central, it has sometimes been said, as Islam's proclamation, "There is only one God and Mohammed is His prophet." The uniqueness of the statement is underlined by the fact that nowhere else does the gospel use the phrase "the only true God."

The authenticity of this central verse (v 3) has often been questioned. The fact that Jesus refers to himself, strangely, with the rather distant title of "Jesus Christ" has been seen as evidence that the verse does not really belong to his prayer, but has, rather, been inserted. However, the puzzle, which seems to be one of a series (cf. 13:1–3; 14:1–3; 15:3; 16:5), has its purpose: its churchlike language alerts the reader to the fact that Jesus is fading from the scene and that, in this chapter, attention will be turning more to the disciples and to future believers. Essentially the same phenomenon was found in the discussions involving Nicodemus and John the baptizer: to suggest the fading of John and of Jesus, their language became distant and began to sound like that of the evangelist or the church (3:16–21, 31–36). The gospel's only other use of the phrase "Jesus Christ," in the prologue, is likewise set in a church-related context, in proximity to the "we" who received the grace of the incarnation (1:17). In the prologue, of course, such distinctly churchlike language is kept, appropriately, until near the end. But in the final prayer, since the role of the disciples and the church is much closer, the churchlike title is used near the beginning.

The integrity of v 3 is confirmed by the fact that it forms part of a linguistic pattern (*hina . . . kathōs . . . hina . . . hina,* "that . . . as . . . that . . . that," vv 1–3) which recurs in variant forms in vv 21–23 (cf. Brown, 769).

As well as being regarded as inauthentic, v 3 has also been regarded as in some way gnostic. It may indeed reflect or absorb something of the Hellenistic idea that knowledge, *gnōsis,* was a way to salvation. But, despite Käsemann's implication (1968, 6) to the contrary, it does not use the noun *gnōsis* (in fact, the word never appears in the gospel); it uses the verb, "to know [*ginōskō*] . . . God", a word which is to be interpreted, first, through the immediate context— the idea in chaps. 13–17 of advancing discipleship and union—and, second, through the literature which stands directly in the background, the OT, wherein " 'knowing God' has the . . . meaning of 'having communion with God' " (Schnackenburg, 3:172).

The idea of knowing is, in fact, quite important to the evangelist, and his use of it here is not new. As Kysar (256) notes, "John uses "know" and "believe" in nearly synonymous ways (cf. 8:31; 10:38; 17:8, and 6:69)." But it is now that it becomes central, and this centrality is connected with the fact that the chapter as a whole is significantly concerned with holiness, with making holy. And holiness involves knowing; it is not just good ceremonial and moral excellence—even though generous morality is integral to it and some ceremonial almost inevitable. It is because the advanced stages of communion with God involve knowing that the idea of knowing is so emphasized, for instance, in the climactic "new covenant" of Jeremiah (31:33–34). Or as William of St. Thierry says in his *Song of Songs,* "Love of God . . . is knowledge" (1970, 64). And it is because knowing is connected to truth, that within chapter 17, "true" and "truth" are conspicuous (vv 3, 17, 19). The truth in question, however, is not an abstract truth, something detached, nor is it an arrogant or exclusive "knowledge." It has to do rather with the fundamental reality of God's saving involvement in human existence. It is the profound form of life which comes from knowing experientially, even in face of death, that the most basic reality is the presence of a loving God.

As well as suggesting that holiness involves knowing, these first verses (1–5) return to the beginning and discuss the roots of holiness—the process within God of a (Father-Son) knowing which is personal and mutual. And from this inner knowing of God there comes, in a reflected form, the knowing which characterizes holiness. Thus the human reflects the activity of the divine. For, like the washing (chap. 13) and purifying (chap. 15), but more so, sanctifying is an active process in which God is attending to the person, a process which is of a highly personal nature. To use a metaphor which builds on the image of seeing (cf. 16:16–24) and on Jesus' raising of his eyes (17:1), sanctifying is the loving gaze of God which, more even than the admiring eyes of friend or lover, raises the person to a new level of dignity, peace, and joy. Whether in life or in death, the person lives in the divine gaze and returns it. When Jesus raises his eyes and asks to be glorified he is, in effect, asking that something which is hidden in himself be brought out, that the divine gaze light up what is divine within him—so that, as he begins to rejoin the eternity of God, begins to ascend to God, something may be revealed of God's own eternal self.

[17:6–19] The Jesus-led ascent of the believers to holiness—even while they are amid the world and evil. As already described, the text is threefold (vv 6–10, 11–12, 13–19) and implies the ascent of Jesus to God. But at this point Jesus is also beginning to intercede for others, and the effect of his prayer as he comes closer to God is to open for others a divine space into which they also may enter. This is not a location above the clouds, but an inner spiritual place in which the one who believes gains increasing knowledge of God and comes finally to God's holiness. Already, in vv 1–5, Jesus had implied the existence of a form of divine state or place, a place of glory, and had also implied that people could come to know the divine. Now, in vv 6–19, he suggests how they come to this knowledge. In other words, this text unpacks the preceding passage, particularly its central verse (v 3).

The first step is the dense picture of the revealing of the divine name (vv 6–10), a process which, like the revealing of the divine name to Moses (Exod 2:23–chap. 4), involves entering a form of divine space and receiving the divine word ("they have kept your word"). As the many active verbs show ("kept . . . know . . . received . . . know . . . believed"), this implies deep human involvement, yet the whole process is something given. In fact, the verb "give" (*didōmi*)—already used four times in vv 1–5—is now used six times, and it leads up to the idea of Jesus being glorified (v 10): God "gives" the believers to Jesus and because of that he is "glorified." Even linguistically there is a curious continuity between the repeated references to those "you gave/have given to me" (*edōkas moi . . . dedōkas moi . . . edōkas moi . . . dedōkas moi*) and the final statement that in them "I am glorified" (*dedoxasmai*). Giving leads to glory. In other words, as gifts say something about the one who gives them, God's giving in Jesus says something about both God and Jesus; in the giving they are revealed, their glory is manifested. And it is within such a gloriously generous process that the divine name is given to people and is received by them. The believers are seen as set within the mystery of a divine exchange—a variation on the perception of Gerald Manley Hopkins: "I think that we are bound/by mercy round and round."

In the next stage (vv 11–12), as Jesus comes closer to the Father, there is an increased sense of the believers being within God's care ("Holy Father, keep them . . .") and also within the shepherdlike care of Jesus ("I kept . . . I guarded," cf. Schnackenburg, 3:181–82). It is in this context that there occurs the first prayer for unity: ". . . keep them in your name . . . that they may be one as we are." The unity, therefore, is primarily spiritual, something rooted in God, a togetherness within God.

Togetherness often brings joy, and so the closing section (vv 13–19) speaks of having joy in the world. And then, in the closing verses, Jesus prays about making the believers holy and making himself holy for their sake (vv 17–19). This combination, joy-holiness, which is somewhat akin to the joy-friendship combination in 15:11–17, is part of the larger flow which began with the reference to revealing the divine name (v 6). The mention of the name already implied holiness. In Semitic thought the name meant the person, and to reveal God's name was like revealing the essence of God, God's holiness. In the course of the passage (vv 6–19) that holiness becomes more explicit, especially its implications of unity and joy, and now at the end the explicitness is made complete: holiness involves joy and unity. And at this stage, far from abandoning the world, they are sent into it—as Jesus was: "As you have sent me . . . so I have sent them." Then, as if to enable those who are sent into the world to face the challenge, Jesus adds: "And for their sake I make myself holy." In 10:34–36 making holy was associated with receiving God's word, and here also it is the receiving of God's word which seems to be the meaning. This does not exclude the notion of sacrifice. Rather, the idea of sacrifice has been adapted to bring out its deepest meaning—the wholehearted acceptance of God's word. Thus "he refers primarily to his mission of revealing God . . . by fidelity to his Father's word" (Forestell, 1974, 78–82, esp. 81). Such fidelity, of course, involves his "laying down" of his life (10:17–18; 15:13–14) and so, in order that they may be "made holy in truth," he implies a reference to his death.

What emerges, therefore, at the end (vv 17–19) is a picture of Jesus' complete receiving of God's word, God's (saving) truth, and of Jesus thereby making that word accessible to others. Thus they may enter fully and freely into a space of holiness. This space is divine (holy); and it is also eminently human (it makes people whole). The revelation of the Father's holy name has led to the formation within people of a world of divine presence and meaning.

All of this, however, takes place amid the world's evil. Just as there is an increasing sense of the action of Jesus, so within the text's three stages there are progressively clear pictures of the world's antipathy. The first ominous sign is the fact that Jesus does not pray for the world (v 9). Then there is the sad reminder of the loss and destructiveness of "the son of perdition" (v 12)—a reference to Judas which reflects the fact that in the gospel he was "the tool of Satan" (Brown, 760). And finally (vv 14–15), with yet greater explicitness, there is a reference to the world's hatred and to (the) evil (one)—an ambiguity which encompasses both Satan ("the Evil One") and the entire phenomenon of evil.

This situation does not mean that the world is regarded with hostility. Schnackenburg (3:178) comments: "The unbelieving world has, in fact, excluded itself from the divine sphere and to pray for it, asking God to keep it in his name (v 11) and sanctify it in his truth (v 17) would, therefore, be meaningless."

What is also important when discussing hostility towards the world is the context of the ascent. It is Jesus' ascent, his bringing of the full dimensions of his human existence to God, which opens the way for a full exchange between humanity and God. "At the ascension Jesus carried humanity into God" (Spong, 1988). The ascent must come first. When Jesus says he does not pray for the world, he is merely beginning his ascent (17:9). But as the chapter develops, and particularly in the verses before and after his allusion to the decisive moment of death ("I make myself holy," v 19), the references to dealing with the world become much more positive: "I have sent them into the world . . . that the world may believe . . . [and] know . . ." (vv 18, 21, 22). The contrast with these later verses is underlined by the details of linguistic continuity and contrast which are found between vv 9 and 20. The implication seems to be that, at one level at least, the text is saying that there was a time, prior to Jesus' ascent to God, prior to the completion of the incarnation and return, when the world was, in some sense, outside of the scope of the divine revelation. But now that is changed. (In Eph 2:11–18 a similar idea is used about the former situation of the Gentiles.)

The fact that the later attitude toward the world is more positive does not, of course, mean that the world's values are approved or that the world will respond. Hatred and ignorance continue (cf. vv 14, 25). But the world's evil need not prevent progress towards holiness. Evil is presented as in some sense confined, confined by the fact that even the actions of a destroyer fall within the realm of scripture and even fulfill it (v 12), and also, by the textual arrangement, found in the third stage (vv 13–19), which effectively separates the dense picture of the world's negativity (vv 14–15) from the final climactic picture of making believers holy (vv 17–19). The believers are indeed in the world (vv 11, 15), but they are not "of" (*ek*) it (v 16); they do not draw their ultimate identity and strength from it.

The overall impression (vv 6–19) is that, while human efforts are important, it is Jesus' approach to the Father, and particularly his intensifying intercession, which both puts the world's evil in perspective and which brings people into the holiness of knowing God's word of truth. Jesus' revealing and return to God represent a dynamic which is indeed a transcendent mystery, but one which is also personal and which has a human aspect or face, including care to save from evil.

One of the effects of this section (vv 6–19) is to capture something of the Eastern saying, "After enlightenment, the laundry." Jesus may be opening the way to heaven, but he is simultaneously bringing heaven into the world, into daily life. The loftiness of the prayer does not take people away from their mundane tasks. Rather, it sends people to these tasks with greater calm and attentiveness.

[17:20–26] As if in heaven, Jesus looks to the future and petitions complete union—the world-challenging unity of believers and the final unity with God. Quite suddenly, as if the preceding allusion to death ("for their sake I make myself holy") marked a crucial transition, Jesus looks beyond his own lifetime and towards the future. Here especially he prays as if his earthly life were over and as if he were already in heaven. He no longer begins by reviewing his work or his approach to the Father. Instead, as a strong advocate, he makes his

wishes known immediately, first by petitioning ("I ask," v 20), and then, climactically, by an authoritative declaration ("I will/wish/desire," *thelō*, v 24).

This transition marks the final stage in the process of incarnation-and-return,
and it is from this new position of union with the Father that Jesus prays for the
unity of believers. The implication, which is made explicit by the phrase "as we
are," is that the unity among believers reflects the unity which is within God.
And, as mentioned earlier, the phrasing ("that they may be one . . . as we . . .")
builds on the commandment of mutual love ("that you may love . . . as I,"
13:34; 15:12; cf. Schnackenburg, 3:191). Thus the unity is both vertical and hor-
izontal. It is within God, yet it is reflected in a down-to-earth way in God's
commandment of love.

Amid the many interpretations of the practical meaning of this unity (for opinions, see Brown, 775), it may be said that it is more than moral, more simply
than mutual love. Love, though it is the crucial element, is not the only one. The
fact that the unity is "as we are" involves doctrine, and the fact that it must
challenge the world often requires organization. However, this does not mean that
it provides a pretext for uniformity and legalism—thus tending towards a totalitarianism which is the antithesis of mutual love. On balance, what seems to be
implied is a union with God which implies also "an ideal of community" (Brown,
778).

This ideal, of a community based on God and mutual care, is the high point
and synthesis of the discourse and of the chapter—indeed of the whole gospel.
As the incarnation is the finale of the prologue, so is the idea of unity the finale
of chap. 17; it is the down-to-earth realization of God—but more so. It is the
incarnation of the incarnation. The Word, which became flesh, is to become community. As 1:14 spoke of the Word and the Word's glory, Jesus sees the community as founded on the disciples' "word" (v 20) and as having been given
Jesus' glory (v 22).

The two realities, the *logos* and the glory, are complementary. The *logos* is
God revealed; the glory is the accompanying wonder, an added dimension—it is
"the fullness of divine life" (Schnackenburg, 3:192). The results which follow
from the *logos* (20–21), follow also, but more intensely, from the glory (22–23;
cf. Brown, 769).

This intensification shows up in the fact that, in comparison with 20–21 (and
with 11a, "that they may be one as we are"), 22–23 is more developed:

- It omits "all" (v 22, cf. 21) and thus achieves a greater focus on "one."

- Basic Father-Son unity is presupposed, and a further, third dimension is
  added, "I in them," thus making the unity three-way, complete.

- The unity (in vv 22–23) has the climactic elements of completion and
  love.

Thus the word of God brings unity (vv 20–21), and glory brings unity which
is complete (vv 22–23). Not that this glory means triumphalism. Kysar (262),
having noted that the glory perceived in the incarnate Word (1:14) is now percep-

tible in the church, goes on to say that "[this] glory . . . like [that of] Christ, [is] found in the midst of the suffering in mission."

In vv 24–26 attention switches from the implied ideal of a community and its realized eschatology to a yet further union of Father, Son, and people. Here there is a form of final eschalology which, along with 13:1–3 and 14:1–3, encases the whole discourse.

With a unique ring of authority (*thelō*, "I will") Jesus speaks to the Father of a togetherness in which the believers see a new degree of glory, glory as it reflects the Father's eternal love. The implication is of the believers entering fully into the divine exchange of love, entering the eternity of God.

Yet, even at this high point of envisaging eternal glory, there is a shadow (v 25): Jesus refers briefly to the fact that along with those who have known the Father, there is a second group who have not done so ("Just Father, the world has not known you, but I have . . . and these have . . ."). In other words, beside the suggestion of an eternal positive love and plan, there is an allusion to refusal and judgement. And it is in that context —a context which alludes to evil —that the Father is referred to, appropriately, as "just" (*dikaios*), in other words, as merciful and loving. Thus the presence of refusal, of evil, is not allowed to suggest that God has been unfair. Furthermore, the shadow side is placed in a form of subordinate clause, and so, as is often the case in this gospel, the final emphasis falls on the positive encompassing plan.

The Arrest and Trial

*Amid the Proceedings, Portraits Both of
Revelation and of Sinful Confusion*

Introduction and Structure

The text describes two dramas—first the arrest and Jewish interrogation (18:1–27), then the trial before Pilate (18:28–19:16a). One occurs at night and lasts until cockcrow. The other begins in the early morning and lasts until noon ("the sixth hour"). The division between night and morning acts as an initial indication of the division and complementarity of the two dramas.

John's account is quite different from that of the other gospels. He does not tell of a full meeting of the Jewish Sanhedrin (though such a meeting is reported as part of the Lazarus story, 11:45–53), and his picture of the trial before Pilate is much more elaborate.

That the trial before Pilate constitutes a single drama is generally recognized. Less obvious is the unity of the arrest-and-interrogation (18:1–27); the very fact that it has two distinct parts—"arrest" (vv 1–11) and "interrogation" (12–27) —suggests division. But the reality of this division does not take away from the overall unity, which is indicated by other factors, among them the encompassing presence of the night and the continuity which is found in the repeated references to a number of elements—to the cohort, to Peter, and to the servant of the high priest (18:3,10,12,26). Furthermore, the trial before Pilate, however unified, is divided by the scourging (19:1–3). Thus the overall pattern is of two dramas, each of which has two major sections.

This structure is somewhat akin, though in reverse order, to the overall structure of chaps. 9 and 10. In these earlier texts a drama which is unified (chap. 9) but which can also be divided in two (9:1–17 and 9:18–41), is complemented by a unified text (chap. 10) in which the twofold division is obvious (10:1–21 and 10:22–42). Thus in each case (chaps. 9–10 and 18:1–19:16a) there are two two-part texts, one in which the two parts form a tightly knit drama (the man born blind, the trial before Pilate), and another in which, despite their real unity, the two parts remain more obviously distinct (the shepherd and "trial" texts of 10:1–21, 22–42; the arrest and trial scenes of 18:1–27 and 18:28–19:16a).

This kinship of structure is not accidental. Within the larger body of the gospel these texts have complementary roles. Within chaps. 7–12—a division which places considerable emphasis on a struggle against dark disbelief—chaps. 9–10 provide a contrast: they place their primary emphasis on coming to the light and to unity. And within chaps 13–21—a division where the primary emphasis is on coming to seeing and to unity—18:1–19:16a likewise provides a contrast: it places the primary emphasis on the darkening degeneration not only of Judas and the Judeans but also of Peter and Pilate.

Subdivisions

The structure which is given here (see The Gospel in English, this volume) accepts all the subdivisions proposed by Schnackenburg (3:220), and it adds two more: following Giblin (1984, 218) and De la Potterie (1986, 50), it makes a break after the initial collapse of the hostile forces which came to arrest Jesus ("they fell to the ground," 6); and, as is implied by Kysar (275), it regards the bringing of Jesus to the praetorium (18:28) as a distinct introductory subdivision.

In making these subdivisions one of the criteria is that of repetition. This is particularly so with regard to the repeated question, "Whom do you seek?" (18:4,7). Significant repetition is also found concerning the idea of hearing (19:8,13) and the name of Caesar (19:12,15).

The most controverted area, with regard to subdivision, is the trial before Pilate (18:28–19:16a). Brown (857–59) endorses a sevenfold chiastic structure, but Giblin (1986) has given a more detailed analysis of the text and thus has helped to indicate that, while a sevenfold division may seem plausible at first, the trial, precisely as a trial, consists essentially of six scenes. Furthermore, there are two passages which act as introductions or interludes: the initial leading of Jesus from Caiaphas to the praetorium (18:28) and the scourging which, in a bizarre miscarriage of justice, occurs halfway through the trial (19:1–3). Bizarre though it is, the interlude has its purpose within the drama of the trial. Since the scourging is accompanied by the dressing of Jesus as a king, it acts as an introduction to the king motif in the subsequent scenes (19:5,14).

The four introductory texts (18:1–3,12–14,28; 19:1–3) have some affinities with the four introductory texts of chaps. 2–4 (2:23–25; 3:22–24; 4:1–6; 4:43–45). But the affinities are quite general, and they consist not so much of similarities as of contrasts. Thus the third introduction, far from being twice as long as the others (which is the case with 4:1–6), instead is twice as short (18:28). And instead of showing Jesus as being more and more on the move, going all the way from Jerusalem to Galilee, they depict a Jesus who is increasingly led and immobile.

Thus, at first (18:1–3) Jesus is indeed able to move; he goes out and he comes in (v 1). But this picture of freedom is overshadowed by the longer description of Judas and the approaching forces (vv 2–3). Then, in the second introduction (the interlude, 18:12–14), he is "taken" and "led" to Annas. Next (18:28) he is "led" to the praetorium. And finally, he is "taken" and beaten (19:1–3). The only movement in this last text is by those who come to him in order to insult him.

Two Dramas of Revelation and Rejection

One of the conspicuous features of the trial before Pilate, and one which helps to divide the trial into scenes, is the series of references to going in and going out:

the Jews are outside the praetorium, but Jesus is inside, and as the trial progresses Pilate goes in and out from one to the other.

It is possible to regard these exits and entrances as superficial details, but the systematic way in which they are emphasized suggests that they are important, and this suspicion is heightened when something of the same pattern is found in the drama of the arrest and interrogation: Jesus *goes out* with his disciples and *goes in* to the garden; then he *goes out* to meet the arresting force (18:1, 4); another disciple *goes in* with Jesus to the court of the high priest and then *goes out* and leads in Peter (18:15–16). As Giblin (1984, 218) remarks, it seems unlikely, given the emphasis on "in" and "out" in the trial scene, that the earlier references (in 18:1–27) are of no consequence. It seems even less unlikely in view of the fact that in Mark, for instance, the distinction between inside and outside is connected with the important idea of revelation: while those with Jesus receive the revelation of the realm of God, those "outside" remain in obscurity (cf. Kermode, 1979, 1–49, esp. 2–3, 32–33). In fact, in the opinion of Dauer (1972, 104), it is precisely the idea of revelation which gives added meaning to the inside/outside contrast of the trial drama: inside (the praetorium) Jesus gives the revelation (he speaks of the true meaning of the reign); but the Jews are outside —outside the praetorium and outside the revelation.

In the initial drama also (18:1–27) the idea of revelation is of central importance. Even as he is being arrested, Jesus makes a triple statement of the primordial "I am" revelation (*Egō eimi*, 18:5,6,8). And in the presence of the high priest, Jesus' primary assertion is about his revelation (18:20–21). But—and this is where the matter is initially perplexing—unlike the trial scene, there is no suggestion in 18:1–27 that the revelation is in any way secret, that it is restricted to those inside. On the contrary, it has been given openly to all (see esp. De la Potterie, 1986, 75–76).

Thus the two dramas give two quite distinct notions of revelation—one which is fully public (18:1–27) and another which is, in some way, restricted, secret (18:28–19:16).

There is a further puzzle. During the drama in which Jesus is speaking openly to everybody (18:1–27) there is conflict with various kinds of secret knowledge (the special insider knowledge which enables Judas to betray him, 18:2–3; and the further insider knowledge which leads Peter to the place of his downfall, the place in which he denies the "I am," 18:15–17). On the other hand, during the trial before Pilate (18:28–19:16a), when Jesus is speaking inside, giving, in effect, a kind of secret knowledge, there is conflict because his opponents do not share that knowledge (the Jews reject anything to do with Jesus' reign, 18:39, 19:15; and Pilate asks "What is truth?" 18:38). Thus his opponents have an inside knowledge which is destructive (18:1–27), but when it comes to the inside knowledge which is true, they know nothing (18:28–19:16a).

The overall situation is somewhat like that described in 1 Corinthians: Paul's message is plain and open—in contrast to the bankrupt knowledgeable wisdom of the world (1 Cor 1:17–2:5). Yet in another sense Paul *does* have a wisdom, a kind of secret knowledge of God's mysteries—and of this the world is quite ignorant (2:6–9). Perhaps there is also some connection with the two traditional types of mysticism—one in which the person looks outward, thus seeing God in nature, and the other in which the focus is inward, seeking God in stillness (see Murray, 1991b, 78–83).

The opening verse (18:1) seems to allude to the paradox of Jesus' message: the double movement of going out and coming in is in accord with the fact that, in general, his message is twofold—it is external, for all; but it also has an inner, secret, dimension.

Then in 18:4 Jesus "goes out," thus setting the scene for the open revelation which pervades 18:1–27. But Peter, and another disciple who misled him, "go in" (18:15–16), thus evoking the destructive inside knowledge which will issue in Peter's denial of Jesus.

Later, in the trial before Pilate, the situation is reversed: Jesus is inside, and those who reject him are outside.

The overall picture is one in which Jesus does indeed reveal, first publicly (18:1–27) and then privately (18:28–19:16a). But the process of revelation is overshadowed by an intensifying drama of people who abuse inside knowledge (18:1–27) and of people who choose to be left outside (18:28–19:16a). Given this overshadowing, this tragedy of knowledge and exclusion, it is an account which, in its broad theme at least, has heavy echoes of the Fall (Gen 3:1–4:16).

Two Dramas of Sin

Just as Genesis provides two complementary dramas of the Fall, first the sin of the couple (Genesis 3) and then that of the brothers (Gen 4:1–16; cf. Westermann, 1984, 285–86), so in its own very different way the fourth gospel provides two central portrayals of sin, first that of Peter (18:1–27) and then that of Pilate (18:28–19:16a). Obviously others are involved, particularly Judas and the Jews, but to some degree their role is to push Peter and Pilate to their downfall.

The sin of Peter begins when he cuts off the ear of the servant. Then, as pressure increases and Jesus appears more and more helpless, he simply ceases to believe.

In the case of Pilate, one of the first clear indications of oncoming tragedy is his failure to hear Jesus' message of truth. For a moment, when he asks "What is truth?" he seems to be on the brink of hearing. But then he goes away, out, and after that he listens increasingly to the voice of violence and death.

The two dramas, of disbelief and death, complement one another. Peter's initial violence prepares the way for his disbelieving, and the absence of believing provides an appropriate background for the further escalation of violence and death.

18:1–19:16a as a Reversal of the Last Discourse

Insofar as 18:1–19:16a is a portrayal of sin it constitutes a reversal of the positive vision which was offered in chaps. 13–17. Obviously the relationship (of 18:1–19:16a to chaps. 13–17) is not one of reversal only; there is also continuity. The Jesus who washed the feet and revealed now continues to offer himself and to reveal further. But the reactions now are primarily negative and, to a significant degree, the resulting picture is a contrast. This picture may be described as follows, without any attempt to be exhaustive.

The descent and self-offering implied in the foot-washing (chap. 13) are continued in the arrest (18:1–11), but the roles of Judas and Peter are more decisively negative, and the positive pictures, especially of the beloved disciple and of mutual love, are missing. Instead of the washing and wiping of feet, there is the striking and cutting of the servant.

Instead of the process of recognizing Jesus and believing (chap. 14), the initial trial (18:12–27) brings denial of Jesus and implicit disbelief. The result is not mutual abiding (as in chap. 14), but rather alienation.

In 15:1–16:4a the image of the vine and its implications of a deep union of love (15:1–17) precede and overshadow the picture of the world's hatred (15:18–16:4a). But in the initial stages of the trial before Pilate (18:28–40), the related picture of the kingdom of truth is swamped in a sea of confusion, deafness, and antagonism.

The seeing of Jesus, so central in 16:4b–33, is important also in 19:1–16a, first when Jesus is presented as a human being ("Behold, a human being!") and later when he is presented as king ("Behold your king!"), but instead of a birth-like joy, the later seeing arouses shouts of death.

With regard to chap. 17, one of its central elements, that of (sanctifying) truth, has been absorbed into the picture of the kingdom of truth (18:36–37). But the chapter as a whole is focused towards community and for that the later text has no equivalent. In other words, while the positive vision leads to community, sin leads to the absence of community, to nothing.

The Arrest and Interrogation

[18:1–3] Introduction: Peace and the approach of violent security forces. There are few things people remember so vividly as being arrested. This is particularly so if the charge is serious, if the forces involved are intimidating, and if the arrest occurs in the middle of the night.

The introduction (vv 1–3) is like a scene which precedes a tempest—darkening silence overshadowed by an ominous rumble. As Jesus goes out with his disciples and crosses the "winterflowing" Kedron, the picture of the vulnerable group is overshadowed by that of the treacherous Judas taking against them a massive force.

The word "winterflowing" (*cheimarros*), as well as reflecting the fact that it is only in winter that the Kedron valley flows with water, serves also to evoke the gospel's persistent motif of (death-related) darkness. Something of the same effect is achieved by other matter-of-fact references ("it was winter . . . it was night . . . it was cold," 10:22, 13:30, 18:17). As Brown (806) notes, in 1 Kgs 2:37 the crossing of the "winterflowing Kedron" is associated with dying.

The sense of impending death is heightened by the nature and size of the approaching force. It is cunningly treacherous, as is seen in Judas the former disciple who was last referred to as representing Satan (13:27) and who now uses his inside knowledge so destructively. And it appears overwhelming—a whole cohort (six hundred Roman soldiers). Even if cohort is taken in its occasionally reduced sense, as referring not to a cohort but to a maniple, one is still faced with a force of two hundred men. The later reference to "the commander" (18:12; literally, the commander of a thousand, *chili-archos*) does not encourage such a reduction. In any case, there is a massive representation of the greatest military force in the known world. And with them are officers from the high priests and Pharisees.

The overall effect is to suggest that while Judas may be seen as merely a guide, he may also be regarded as a leading figure, as embodying "the ruler of the world" (14:30). The two verbs used to describe his action confirm this idea of a commanding role: He "takes" the cohort, and he "comes" (*erchetai*)—exactly the word and grammatical form which (in 14:30) was used about the ruler of the world.

The darkness of the scene is intensified by the concluding words: "with lanterns and torches and weapons." In the context of the gospel's imagery of light and darkness, the reliance on lanterns and torches suggests an absence of the true light, suggests, in other words, that these are the forces of darkness, of sin (Brown, 809, 817). And the final detail translates the general notion of sinful darkness into a form that is all too clear and down to earth: "weapons." It was not necessary to say that a cohort had weapons. But the word has its purpose. In contrast to all that Jesus stands for, in contrast particularly to the gentleness of the foot-washing, it shows darkness as issuing in injury.

In such a situation there is little doubt about the nature of the tempest which awaits Jesus. Within twenty-four hours he will be dead.

Yet the picture is not one of unrelieved gloom. The "going out" across the winter-evoking Kedron gives way to the picture of a garden and of "going in." The image of a garden is highly ambiguous. It may be regarded, following some of the earliest commentators, as evocative of the primordial garden (Genesis 2–3; for general references see Schnackenburg, 3:442 n6), and as such it provides a very suitable background for the subsequent drama of sin. But it may also be interpreted, particularly in the context of the allusion to winter, as suggesting something surprisingly positive. The term "garden" is repeated in varied ways in the following episodes (cf. 18:26, 19:41, 20:15 ["gardener"]) and it "apparently functions as a motif, suggesting a place apart and close association" (Giblin, 1984, 218). In particular, as a place of food, flowers, and trees, it suggests life and salvation.

The sense of a contrast between "winter" and "garden" is heightened by the contrast, to be developed in the subsequent scenes (especially 18:28–19:16a), between "going out" and "going in." It is as though, in this first verse of the passion narrative (18:1), as in the first verses of the final discourse (13:1,3), the evangelist wanted to give a summary of aspects of the process of going forth from God and going back to God—of "going out" to the wintery reality of death, and of "going in" to life-giving union with the Father. Thus, despite the impending doom, there is a faint reminder that Jesus' life will not end in winter.

Nor will that of his disciples. With deliberate repetitiveness the text recounts that in both going out and going in he is accompanied by his disciples. They also will eventually cross over to salvation. Thus the sense of solidarity which was expressed at the beginning of the long discourse (13:1) finds an echo here.

Yet, as the beginning of the discourse had clearly indicated (in its reference to the devil and Judas, 13:2), the solidarity can be broken. All that Judas retains from his former union with the disciples is a knowledge which is empty and destructive. His triumph seems assured; but the image of the garden evokes a reality which is deeper.

[18:4–6] Jesus as divine.   At earlier stages Jesus had withdrawn or hidden. But not now. "Knowing all that was coming," he "went out" and questioned them: "Whom do you seek?" Thus despite the size of the deadly opposition, it is he who retains the initiative.

He retains, furthermore, his divine identity. An indication of this divinity is already contained in the "knowing all" (v 4, cf. 13:3), but it is seen still more clearly when, in answer to the demand for Jesus of Nazareth, Jesus replies "I am (he)," *Egō eimi*. This simple self-identification, while capable of meaning nothing more than "I am (he)," in fact contains also the higher meaning of the divine "I am." Thus at the moment of arrest—the very moment when, under normal circumstances, God may seem to be devastatingly absent—the emphasis falls on God being present.

The power of that presence is underlined by what follows: the ominous armed forces "went back and fell to the ground." If someone boldly identifies themselves it may indeed evoke surprise, even shock, but it does not cause a military force to fall to the ground. Thus as unadorned history the account does not make sense. But as a theological portrait it is clear. The clash is not just between Jesus of Nazareth and some soldiers; it is between the divine and the representatives of the primordial forces of darkness. The reality of that darkness is highlighted by the emphasis—unnecessary in a purely historical account—on the presence of Judas (v 5); it is his Satanic role which brings out the nature of those who are with him.

The phrase "they went backwards" had been used only once before in the gospel—to express rejection of belief (6:66). Now a similar negativity reappears in varied form. At that earlier stage, when so many others went backwards, Judas did not (cf. 6:66–71). But now he is the leader of those who do.

Unlike 6:66, however, where the backward movement comes from human refusal, the movement in 18:6 seems to come from the divine. It is as though the divine drives them away. This does not mean that God is destructively vengeful but probably has something to do with the idea that after one has rejected God, anything to do with God tends to cause one to recoil. The further occurrence, "they fell to the ground," indicates that the ultimate fate of God's enemies is collapse.

The first stage of the arrest, therefore, however ominous at one level, at another is a theophany, a manifestation of the *mysterium tremendum* (Schnackenburg, 3:224): it is a summary picture of God "going out" into the world and overpowering the forces of darkness.

[18:7–9] Jesus as divine and self-giving.   Once again Jesus asks "Whom do you seek?" and once again he identifies himself by saying "I am (he)," *Egō eimi.* Yet despite this repetition, the drama is not static, for by adding, "If you seek me, let these go away," Jesus moves closer to being apprehended. In other words, the arrest, precisely as an arrest, takes a step forward.

At one level this is a step closer to doom. But, as Schnackenburg (3:226) partly indicates, the text has a further theological level. Jesus' offering of himself so that the disciples may be saved contains also a variation on a central idea— that of the divine self-giving which achieves salvation.

The emphasis on the divine, even at this dark moment, is heightened by the fact that the text speaks of Jesus' words (concerning not losing people) as being fulfilled (v 9; cf. 6:39; 10:11, 28; 17:12), and thus it implicitly puts his words on a par with (divine) scripture. And the fact that Jesus' words are summarized as meaning that none of those given will be lost emphasizes again that through Jesus the divine is working to save.

Thus the picture of Jesus being arrested contains a portrayal of God's action: first, the divine action of going out to the world and overpowering the forces of darkness (stage one, vv 4–6), then the divine self-giving which enters life's brutality in order to accomplish salvation (stage two, vv 7–9).

[18:10–11] Peter resorts to weaponry; Jesus' further self-giving.   The account of the arrest might have ended quite coherently with Jesus' offering of himself to the armed men and with the implied departure of the disciples. But it suddenly emerges that Peter also is armed, and his cutting off of the ear of Malchus, servant of the high priest, adds a further twist to the story. It is a development which at the level of straightforward narrative may appear to disturb the flow of the story (Schnackenburg, 3:226), but, once again, at the level of theology, and in the context of the larger narrative, it fits well.

The description of Peter's action, with its wealth of verbs and detail, is like the final down-to-earth part of the descending spiral, the spiral which began with the lofty description of Jesus as knowing all things and as pronouncing the divine "I am" (vv 4–5). Something of the same effect was seen at the beginning of the last discourse: the lofty spiralling language, including a variation on the idea of "knowing all" (13:1–3), gave way rapidly to a succession of down-to-earth verbs and details concerning the washing and wiping of the feet (13:4–5).

But, unlike the washing and wiping, Peter's action consists of striking and cutting, and it is an aberration. Within the context of the arrest scene as a whole, his "sword" stands in literary continuity not with Jesus but with the final focal detail in the description of the assembled forces of darkness—their "weapons" (v 3). In other words, their weapons-focused darkness finds expression in his use of the sword. In retrospect then, it is not surprising that Peter did not understand the washing and wiping (13:6) and that, within chap. 13 as a whole, his darkness of mind is cast in the context of the Satanic darkness of Judas (13:2,21–38). Here too he shows shades of Judas.

The details of the incident—"servant of the high priest . . . right ear . . . name(d) Malchus [meaning king]"—seem to constitute a puzzle. Even if they were quite historical, it is questionable if the gospel would include them unless they had significance. But the significance is elusive. It is, however, remarkable that despite the massive Roman presence, Peter managed to strike the most sensitive Jewish target—"the servant" of "the high priest." (The proximity to the high priest is highlighted by the Greek word order: not "he struck the servant of the high priest" but "he struck *the* of the high priest *servant*," as though the servant to some degree "contained" or represented the high priest.) In any case it is a bad omen for those high priests who put their trust in weapons and Caesar (cf. 19:15, "We have no king but Caesar").

With regard to the ear, it was the right ear, which was considered the more valuable (cf. Brown, 812), and therefore the loss of it would suggest a major loss of hearing—an idea which seems appropriate to the general theme of rejecting God's word of revelation.

And the fact that the servant's name means "king" has the effect of strengthening the king motif, which becomes central in the trial before Pilate. It is as though in different ways, whether by failing to hear the word or by relying on the sword, both Peter and the Jewish high priests are straying from the realm of God and are clashing with one another on the level of rival realms of the world. In other words, the result of their common straying is not solidarity but fighting. Holiness brought unity (chaps. 13–17, esp. chap. 17), but rejection of God brings division. Similarly in chapter 6: refusal of the word led to fighting (6:52).

Whatever the details of Peter's aberration, Jesus does not allow it to continue. With a reference to drinking the cup, meaning the cup of death, he returns, in intensified form, to the motif of self-giving. No longer is there a reference to the "I am" of divinity. As in the parable of the good shepherd (10:7–10), such language has gradually faded. In the present text the movement has been from a double ''I am'' (stage one, vv 4–6), to a single ''I am'' (stage two, vv 7–9), to an implicit acceptance of death (stage three, vv 10–11). Thus once more, but in a form that is more advanced than ever, there is a portrayal of the process of divine self-emptying.

The result is an apparent absence of divinity, and in that absence Peter will find a daunting trial.

[18:12–14] Interlude: Jesus bound—and the trial prejudged. A new phase begins, and with it a reversal of roles. Jesus no longer leads the action as he did in most of the arrest scene. Grammatically, his name now generally occurs not in the leading (nominative) case, but in the more passive cases (accusative/dative). Even when it is nominative (vv 20, 23) there is a certain passivity: he is responding to the questions or actions of others.

The leading roles (the conspicuous nominative cases) are taken over by those who, in various ways, oppose or reject Jesus—particularly the arresting force (12), Peter (15, 25), and the high priest (19).

This does not mean that the situation is out of control. Rather, Jesus has voluntarily entered a phase where others are able in various ways to lead him and abuse him.

The opening line (''Then the cohort and the commander and the officers of the Jews . . .'') is surprising not only because the leading role has now passed to the arresting force but also because, in a further change of roles, the leadership within that force has now passed to ''the commander.'' Judas, the original initiator of hostility, has slipped into the background.

Jesus is taken and bound and led. This is captivity indeed. And when he is brought before Annas, a former high priest (AD 6–15), the reader is immediately given a piece of information which effectively puts to rest any hope of a fair trial: Annas was the father-in-law of Caiaphas—the presiding high priest who had already persuaded the Jewish authorities that Jesus must die (vv 13–14; 11:50–53). That the two, Annas and Caiaphas, were in communication about dealing with Jesus is indicated by the fact that Judas had received officers from the ''high priests'' (18:3; the plural, ''high priests'' was an accepted way of referring to a powerful group, a group which comprised ''the incumbent high priest [Caiaphas], . . . former high priests who had been deposed but were still alive, e.g. Annas, . . . and members of the privileged families from whom the high priests were chosen''—Brown, 808). The connection between Annas and Caiaphas is further confirmed by the fact that Jesus is led not to the presiding Caiaphas, the one who had made the decisive intervention in the Sanhedrin, but, for some unexplained reason, to the father-in-law. The implication is of a web of intrigue in which the father-in-law is a kind of godfather and in which Caiaphas is little more than a puppet.

The idea that Caiaphas is a puppet helps to explain the curious way he is represented in this trial. At the beginning, when he is quoted (v 14), the words give an almost exact (puppetlike) repetition of what he had said earlier (11:50), and in that earlier statement he had definitely been a puppet, though of a different kind—the puppet of prophecy (cf. 11:51, "he did not say this of himself"). Furthermore, even though Caiaphas is nominally "the high priest of that year" (v 13), the actual exercise of the role, the active questioning of Jesus, is taken over by Annas (18:18, 24). And finally when the role is returned to Caiaphas (18:24, Annas sent Jesus "bound to Caiaphas the high priest"), Caiaphas, left on his own, is not reported as doing anything. In other words, as far as the narrative is concerned, he has no role. Such glaring overlapping of roles, followed by Caiaphas's nonrole, indicates that the official high priest, the one who had swung the debate and accused the others of knowing nothing, was himself, in fact, a non-person, a controlled object.

When, therefore, Jesus is described as bound and led he may seem at first sight to be a hapless captive. But he has chosen freely to be where he is and, on closer inspection, it is the high priests who lack freedom.

[18:15–18] Peter's fall: his denial of the revelation. Peter's following of Jesus may seem impressive at first sight. But he is trying to do what Jesus had explicitly told him that, at this time, he could not do (13:37–38). Thus the process of following, coming as it does after the swordplay, is a further act of impetuosity (cf. Mateos and Barreto, 753) and ultimately a further expression of sinfulness.

With him is "another disciple"—possibly *"the* other disciple" (20:2,3,4,8) whom Jesus loved (20:2; 13:23; 21:7, 20), but there are objections to this idea, especially the discrepancy between "another" and "the other" (Schnackenburg, 3:235). It seems more likely that the reference is to Judas. Like the beloved, he is often grouped with Peter (6:68–71; 13:1–11, 21–30). In fact, in 13:21–30 there is a certain interchangeability between the beloved and the traitor: either could be any one of the disciples. It is more understandable also, given Judas's previous contact with the high priests (18:3), that he was "known" to the high priest. This being-known, therefore, like the knowing of 18:2, is not a positive thing; it is used abusively—in this case to enter the *aulē* ("fold/courtyard") and especially to lead in Peter, a step which brings him towards his fall.

At this point there are overtones of the original fall (Gen 3): the Satanic figure (the serpent, Judas) with the superior knowledge speaks to the woman, and when the woman speaks to the (representative) man ("Adam," Peter), he gives in and grasps for creature comfort (food, for Adam; warmth, for Peter). The essence of both texts is a denial of one's true relationship to God (Peter's "I am not," *ouk eimi,* is a direct contradiction of Jesus' divine "I am," *egō eimi,* 18:5,8).

Peter's fall, though Genesis-like, has been thoroughly adapted to John's own narrative. The woman's role, for instance, is less open to misrepresentation. The account has been so shaped that it is in delicate continuity with preceding passages, especially with the image of the sheepfold (chap. 10). There are various details, some of them quite rare, which connect the two texts—*aulē* ("court/yard"), follow, know, enter, exit, door, doorkeeper—but the essence of the relationship is a form of reversal: while genuine knowledge of the sheep can be used positively (10:1–18,26–29), the denial scene shows that there is also an inside knowledge which can be used destructively. The knowledge is not that of a serpent but of a disciple. And the creature comfort to which the fallen Peter turns is not food but—following John's motif of light—fire, artificial light, in place of genuine light.

The failure to name the disciple with the destructive knowledge would seem, as at the last discourse (13:21–30), to be a further way both of forcing the reader to ask, "Who is it?" and of suggesting that, in a sense, it could be anybody.

[18:19–26] The high priest questions Jesus; Jesus' revelation is rejected. Historically, Annas's interrogation of Jesus is perplexing. It is not mentioned by the other gospels, and no basis is given for Annas's right to hold a hearing of that kind. In Schnackenburg's words (3:236), such an interrogation "could not have been in any way official."

But dramatically and theologically the scene makes sense. In the midst of a drama which rejects revelation, Jesus' reply to the high priest affirms revelation resoundingly, and it emphasizes its openess and availability to all. He has spoken "openly to the world" . . . "always" . . . where "all" are gathered . . . and with "nothing . . . in secret." And his teaching has, in fact, been learned by others: "Why do you ask me? Ask those who have heard. . . . Behold, they know what I said." Thus what is given, even in the midst of this portrayal of increasing darkness, is a contrasting summary of Jesus' open revelation to the world (see esp. De la Potterie, 1986, 73–76).

The subsequent slap in the face by the policeman (or official, v 22) highlights the contrast. Hitting the revealing Jesus is a symbol of the rejection of revelation, a rejection which is being worked out in the denials of Peter (De la Potterie, 1986, 77–80).

The continuity between Peter's denying of Jesus and the official's slapping of Jesus is underlined by the fact that Peter, in warming himself, stands "with" the high priest's slaves and officials. All are part of the same negative network. It is further underlind by the fact that Jesus' reply to the official ("If I have spoken wrongly [*kakos*] . . . but if well [*kalos*] . . .") effectively accuses him of arrogating to himself the knowledge of good and evil, in other words, the power of an alternative god, and such a fundamental deviation is in continuity with the Genesis-like character of Peter's sin. Thus, in diverse ways both Peter and the police official reflect Genesis.

Furthermore, behind the deviations of both men there is a certain dependence on the high priest. It is knowledge of the high priest which guides Peter towards his sin. And it is mindless subservience to the high priest which leads the official to slap Jesus. Thus the high priest is one of the keys to the network of rejection.

Given this key role it is remarkable that the figure of the high priest is so vague. He is never quoted directly. As the interrogation begins it is not clear even who the high priest is—whether Annas or Caiaphas. The vagueness is accentuated by the directness and clarity of the response of Jesus. And though being known to him is significant, he, on the other hand, seems not to know the one thing that is important—the basic revelation which had been spoken openly to the world and to "all the Jews." Thus despite his power and knowledge, the impression which emerges is of a shadowy figure, someone who fits well into a drama of advancing darkness, and who in the end has nothing to say.

[18:25–27] Peter's continuing descent into darkness. Even though Peter's effort to follow Jesus had indeed come undone, there remained, theoretically, the possibility that, as Jesus moved on to the next stage of his fateful journey, Peter would recover sufficiently to follow him further. But after Jesus has been sent bound from Annas to Caiaphas the reader who expects action is going to be disappointed: the continuing description of Peter (v 25) is so repetitous of what had been said earlier (vv 17–18) that it suggests an almost complete paralysis. The account is of a further denial, and the only major addition, in comparison to the first one, is that the verb "deny" becomes explicit. Thus the denial intensifies.

Then, in a third encounter (vv 26–27), it intensifies further. The verb "deny" is repeated, and it is accentuated by "again." Furthermore, this time there is no direct speech, no "I am not." Instead the emphasis on the "I" is found in the words of the questioner: "Did not I . . ." (*ouk egō*; Schnackenburg, 3:240). Thus between the scenes of the arrest (1–11) and interrogation (12–27) there is a balance:

18:4, 6, 8	18:17, 25, 26
egō eimi, I am [he]	*ouk eimi,* I am not
egō eimi, I am [he]	*ouk eimi,* I am not
egō eimi, I am [he]	*ouk egō,* . . . not I

The fact that the series is completed not by Peter but by one of those who arrested Jesus is a reflection of Peter's confusion and alienation. His language has become the language of the enemy. And as if the presence of confusion and enmity was not clear enough, it is highlighted by the fact that the questioner in this third instance is a relative of Malchus—"whose ear Peter had cut off." Peter had struck Malchus; now his own faltering language is echoed by Malchus's relative. Such a person may perhaps be regarded as dangerously hostile, and, in the aftermath of Jesus' being hit, such hostility is particularly fearful. Peter, far from being impressively impetuous seems to shrink, to diminish. His repeated "I am not" and his ultimate failure to say anything, indicate a complete loss of identity. Yet at one stage he had been with the divine "I am" and, as if to highlight his alienation, the confronting relative reminds him of his former sense of belonging: "Did I not see you *in the garden with him?*"

The cockcrow is like an alarm which indicates that, as far as Peter is concerned, the worst has happened. But it is also an indication that the worst was foreseen (13:38) and that somewhere ahead lies the dawn.

The Trial Before Pilate

[18:28] Introduction: The arrival at the praetorium and the law-bound failure to enter. The scene seems simple enough: at dawn they lead Jesus from Caiaphas (or Caiaphas's house) to the praetorium, the temporary residence of the Roman governor, but they do not enter lest they break the laws governing ritual purity and thus be barred from eating the Passover meal.

Despite the simplicity of the scene, a number of things are unclear: the identity of those leading Jesus (the context suggests that they are Jews), the route which they took (the location of Caiaphas' house is unknown and that of the governor's residence is uncertain; cf. Brown 845), and the law in question (there is no known law which in the circumstances would have thus prevented them from eating the Passover meal; cf. Brown, 846).

Yet all is not obscurity. The auspicious nature of Jesus' entry to the praetorium is heightened by the fact that after the word "praetorium" there comes the significant detail: "It was dawn." The reference first of all is to the early hour, but in the context of John's emphasis on light and darkness, particularly in the context of "It was night" (13:30; note also 18:38, "it was cold"), a number of commentators have suggested a further, theological meaning: "the day of the victory of Jesus over the world is dawning" (Bultmann, 651; cf. Brown, 866). His entering of the Roman praetorium is evocative of a new relationship to the world. But the Jews will not join in. Jesus on his way of salvation may indeed enter a decisive new space and open up a new dawn for the world, but they are so preoccupied with obscure ritualistic law that they remain outside.

[18:29–32] Outside: Pilate and the Jews. The Jews see evil, and with minds on Jesus' death, follow the law. As the Roman governor enters the stage, his first act is to surrender to pressure from the Jews: instead of holding the entire trial within the praetorium he accepts their refusal to enter and goes out "to them." Though it is but a detail, it is indicative of what is to come (Mateos and Barreto, 765; cf. Sternberg on proleptic portraits, 1985, 321–41). Thus, whatever Pilate's character in history (for discussion and references, cf. Brown, 847), the reader already has a clue that Roman power is limited and that it is the Jews rather than the governor who will decide the outcome.

As if to reassert his authority and establish that this trial will follow proper procedure, Pilate begins with a formal inquiry: "What accusation do you bring against this person (*anthrōpos*)?" Thus it may seem that Pilate comes to the trial with an open mind, ready to learn about Jesus for the first time. But the involvement of a Roman cohort and commander in Jesus' arrest leaves a clear implication that the Roman authorities, particularly the governor, had already given considerable thought to dealing with Jesus and had already discovered a specific danger. The cohort has now disappeared behind the scenes, and the reader is left unsure both about the soldiers' whereabouts and about Pilate's intentions. Thus to a significant degree the formal question is a pretense, and beneath it lurks a sea of intrigue and suspicion.

When the Jews reply, their accusation confirms the impression of lurking violence: "If he were not an evildoer we would not have handed him over to you." Their words involve both a refusal to engage in reasonable discussion and the replacement of such discussion by added pressure. Furthermore, in saying that they have "handed over" Jesus, they use the verb which otherwise was not used except to describe the treacherous "handing over" by Judas—(6:64,71; 12:4; 13:2,11,21; 18:2,5), an action which stemmed ultimately from the devil (6:70–71; 13:2,27). In effect, from their position of power, the accusers have taken to themselves the defining of what is good and evil (Mateos and Barreto, 766).

Their bewildering logic seems to leave Pilate nonplussed; but, rather than confront them, he again gives in to them and seems interested only in extricating himself: "Take him you and judge him according to your own law." The Jews, however, are not cooperative; they reply that it is not lawful for them to kill anyone.

Historically speaking, the reference to the law is perplexing: it is not known just how much judicial authority was held under the Romans by the Jewish Sanhedrin. (Apparently they really did not have power to inflict the death penalty; for discussion, see Brown, 848–50.)

But theologically the message is clear: according to the law one should not kill; the law is not an instrument of death (see esp. the Decalogue, Exod 20:13; Deut 5:17). Yet the Jews show that they want death. Thus a tension is established: the law which forbids death is in the hands of those who want death. And the way is prepared for the later scene of using the law to kill (19:4–7).

But not even this compounding of moral disorder destroys the word of Jesus; on the contrary by returning the judgment to Pilate and thus directing the course of events towards Roman-style crucifixion, it serves to fulfill what Jesus had said about the way he would die—by being lifted up (v 32; cf. 3:14; 8:28; 12:32–33). The fact that Jesus' word is thus "fulfilled" means that, as in 18:9, his words have a scriptural, divine quality, and thus that even when the plotters are being most perverse their designs are encompassed by the divine word.

[18:33–38a] Within: Pilate asks about kingship—Jesus announces an otherworldly realm of truth. Following the emphasis on law and death, Pilate enters the praetorium and, having called Jesus, asks him: "Are you the king of the Jews?" Historically this question is plausible; it touches problems which would have concerned Pilate (and it is found also in the other gospels). What remains unexplained is its relationship to the preceding episode; the discussion of the charge against Jesus had said nothing about his being a king. It may seem, as Kysar (277) notes, that "this is a charge for which John has not prepared us."

The answer appears to lie in the fact the preceding episode had a powerful undertone of violence—the psychological violence of refusing to offer a straightforward charge and of bringing instead a form of crude pressure (v 30); and the more open violence of implicitly wanting to kill (v 31)—and, for the evangelist (and for Pilate too), *violence is a mark of kingship;* kings reflect violence and generate it. In an era of gentle constitutional monarchs such an association may seem strange, but that is because constitutions have effectively disarmed the monarchs, and the power lies elsewhere—hopefully in channels less open to capriciousness and corruption. However, from Israel's first experiments with monarchy, as reflected in Jotham's fable about the useless devouring king (Judg 9:7–15), until the Herods and emperors of the beginning of Christianity, the experience of kingship was often devastating. The effort by the satiated crowd to make Jesus king (6:15) had had a marked tone of violence, and it is allegiance to Caesar, both by Pilate and the Jews, which will ultimately kill Jesus (19:12–16a).

This does not exclude the possibility of a kingship that is positive. In fact, Jesus had already been referred to favorably as "king of Israel" (1:49; 12:13, 15), king that is, not of the Judeans or of the Jewish race, but of Israel's religious heritage. And in the subsequent discussion with Pilate, Jesus does allow a certain usage of the term "kingdom" (or "realm," *basileia*). But he does not accept the unqualified title of king. "King" is a word used by the political-minded Pilate.

The suggestion of violence is maintained as Jesus and Pilate exchange questions (vv 33–34). When Jesus asks Pilate whether his inquiry concerning kingship comes from himself or from others, he is, in fact, asking whether Pilate is his own man or whether he is governed by pressure. Pilate in replying ("Am I a Jew? Your own nation . . . handed you over to me") acknowledges the pressure, and in doing so admits, ironically, that he does not know who he is.

It is against this background of confusion and confinement that Jesus begins to speak of his realm ("kingdom"). First he says what it is not—it is not from this world, it is not established by fighting, and it does not originate here (v 36). Then, with a clear self-identity which contrasts with that of Pilate, Jesus speaks of himself as originating not only through a natural birth ("for this I was born") but also through an origin which is outside the limited visible world ("and for this I have come into the world"). And on the basis of this other origin he announces that he witnesses to the truth and that those who are of the truth hear his voice. In other words, within the area of Jesus' witnessing voice, people are gathered into a place or realm of truth.

Brief though it is, the text (including Pilate's response) involves a triple use of the word "truth," and thus it directs attention to the part of the gospel in which truth is most mentioned—the last discourse, particularly the later chapters (cf. 14:6,17; 15:26; 16:7,13[twice]) and especially 17:17–19 where there is another triple use of "truth." Jesus, therefore, is referring to the realm or kingdom which he had announced in the last discourse, especially in chaps. 15–17. The idea that chaps. 15–17 imply a divine realm or kingdom makes sense; Brown (670), for instance, sees the parable of the vine as reflecting part of the evangelist's transformed understanding of the synoptic term "kingdom of God." Furthermore, just as the last discourse, particularly 15:1–17, reflected the parable of the good shepherd (10:7–18), so also Jesus' brief presentation of his realm recalls the shepherd text (cf. "hears my voice," 18:37, 10:16). And just as the parable of the vine (15:1–17) stands in contrast to the hatred of the world (15:18–16:4a) so Jesus' realm stands out in contrast to the world and to the violence of his accusers (vv 31, 36, 40). The parable implied an inner space from which one could be excluded ("thrown out," 15:6)—an exclusion which is reflected in the fact that, while Jesus speaks of his kingdom, he is within, and the violent accusers are outside.

What is essential is that Jesus' brief speech (to Pilate) concerning his realm is an encapsulation of the realm which was implied in chaps. 13–17—the realm which, having been prepared for by his coming to wash feet, then developed into the union portrayed by the vine, and finally culminated in the truth that sanctifies.

While John does allow this divine sphere to be thought of as a kingdom, he keeps the suspect terminology of king and kingdoms to a minimum, and he prefers, in chaps. 15–17, to employ other images. If he now engages images of kingship, it is not so much to rely on them as to draw a contrast with them.

The highlighting of truth at this point makes the contrast all the stronger. Truth for John does not refer to scientific exactitude, whether historical or philosophical. It is a way of speaking of the deepest level of things, the level at which, despite sin and death, God works to bring salvation. In practice this means that it is the revelation of the mystery of salvation in Jesus, the Son of the Father; it is the possibility of becoming Spirit-led children of God (De la Potterie, 1986, 100–101; 1977, 471). Amid so many shadows of lies and death this announcement of saving truth constitutes a deep challenge.

Yet it scarcely affects Pilate. His question ''What is truth?'' shows that physically he caught Jesus' words, but his immediate exit indicates that he has not really heard.

[18:38b–40] Outside. Jesus the innocent king is offered to the Jews—They choose Barabbas the thief.   Having half heard the message of God's reign, Pilate goes out and, without being fully aware of what he is doing, offers the message to the Jews, offers them Jesus.

What he actually does is declare formally that Jesus is innocent (''I find no case against him''), and he asks whether, in accordance with their custom of receiving someone's release at Passover, they wish to receive ''the king of the Jews.'' Since they are expressly referred to as ''the Jews'' (38b) what Pilate is doing is offering them a king. The offer for the moment is merely implicit, but it is there.

Associated with this king are innocence and freedom, the innocence detected by Pilate and the freedom suggested by the reference to Passover. The historical details of the Passover custom of releasing someone are quite obscure (Brown, 854–55), but the theological implications of the canonical text are reasonably clear: the king is being offered in the context of innocence and Passover, and therefore there is an implication of a sinless reign which brings people out of their slavery. Thus, to the Jews, preoccupied as they are with law and death, something profoundly healing is being offered.

Instead of accepting it, however, they shout (again?) that they want Barabbas, a ''thief'' (*lēstēs*). Thus when faced with two diametrically opposed characters, the witness of saving truth and the thief (cf. 10:1–2,10–11), their choice is for the one who is destructive.

[19:1–3] Interlude: The scourging and mocking of the king—an introduction to final rejection.   Thus far the opposition to Jesus has been muted. In fact, despite the ominous Jewish adherence to the law and to the idea of death, it is Jesus' exposition of the reign which dominates the opening episodes.

However, from now on, from the scourging until the final episode, "the tone . . . change[s]" (Brown, 885). It is not so much that the charge moves from being political to being more religious, as that from now on the emphasis falls less on Jesus' reign and more on the rejecting of that reign. Thus, just as the trial before the high priest (18:12–27) was dominated by images of rejection, so here also rejection dominates, particularly in the reactions to seeing Jesus (19:5–6, 14–15).

But the rejected Jesus does not fade away. His death remains purposeful, and his human wretchedness gives him the role of an unpretentious but effective judge.

At one level, the scourging comes as a shock. Though it had been partly prepared for by the implicit violence of choosing the destructive Barabbas, its brutality brings a new dimension to the gospel story. In itself it is physically devastating, and thorns on the head add searing pain. Whatever strength is left is abused psychologically by the mocking and slapping.

The violence originates in Jewish pressure, yet there is no suggestion that Pilate is without guilt. Unlike a commander-in-chief who after a military operation shrugs off responsibility by saying "I never fired a shot," Pilate's role is highlighted. Though it is clear (in v 2) that it was the soldiers who did the actual beating, it is on him that the initial emphasis falls: "Then Pilate took Jesus and scourged (singular) him." However distant, he did it.

The emphasis then moves to the soldiers. There is no suggestion here that, because of due obedience, they are not responsible. The picture rather is of people who are fully involved and who, therefore, are guilty.

The guilt of the Gentiles (the Romans) is aggravated by the fact that, not just morally, but even legally, what they are doing is confused and questionable. Jesus has not refused to answer questions nor has he been found guilty of anything. Legally a scourging could be the initial stage of an execution, but not in this case, for thus far no sentence has been pronounced. Consequently, though the trial has some semblances of proper procedure, the effect of these elements is not to prevent injustice but to cover it with a veneer of legality.

The mocking of Jesus as king of the Jews suggests the end of Jewish hopes for a messianic kingship. Such an idea is something that the Gentiles laugh at (Mateos and Barreto, 783). Yet at another level the Gentiles' mocking homage of Jesus serves as an ironic intimation that at some stage in the future the Gentiles will indeed pay Jesus homage.

[19:4–7] Outside: "Behold a human being" . . . "a son of God." This episode, brief though it is, contains two distinct stages—first, Pilate's presentation of the scourged Jesus as a human ("Behold the *anthrōpos*," vv 4–5) and then, the statement of the crucifixion-seeking Jews that Jesus had made himself a Son of God (vv 6–7). The two ways of referring to Jesus, as human and as Son of God, suggest a complementarity between the two stages, and this idea of complementarity is corroborated by the fact that each stage contains a formal declaration of Jesus' innocence (vv 4, 6) and by the further fact—bizarre in light of Jesus' innocence—that the two stages refer implicitly or explicitly to the two major steps of his execution (the scourging reflected in stage one and the crucifixion heralded in stage two).

In chap. 1 of the gospel, it would seem that there is a similar complementarity between two of the titles of Jesus—between "Son of God" and "Son of humanity" (1:51; cf. 1:34). (Even if the word "son" is uncertain in 1:34, it is doubly implied in 1:14,18, and it recurs clearly in 1:49.) But while chap. 1 uses its titles favorably, the titles of the trial episode reflect a mixture of mockery (by Pilate) and condemnation (by the Jews). Pilate has used his particular power in a way that has already half-killed Jesus, and the Jews, by misinterpreting their law, want to finish the process.

At one level, of course, Pilate is anxious to be just; hence his repeated declarations of Jesus' innocence. And there is also a level at which the Jews want to follow the law, hence their insistence on referring to it. But these sentiments are superficial, and on both sides there is a failing which leads to death.

At the center is Jesus. From one point of view he is pitiable; he bears the marks of the world's confusion and reflects the reality of human misery and desolation. But "despite his pitiable appearance, he has a dignity which, shortly afterwards, is referred to by the chief priests in, 'Son of God'" (Schnackenburg, 3:257). In fact, it has been argued that Pilate's use of "the human" or "a human being" is a variation on "the Son of humanity" (for references to this discussion, see Schnackenburg, 3:256, 451). And the dramatic appearance of Jesus ("Behold . . . that you may know. . . . Behold. . . . When they beheld, . . ." vv 4–6) is like a down-to-earth version of the dramatic appearance which is frequently associated with the Son of humanity (cf. Mark 9:1, Acts 7:49–60). In any case, beneath the misery there is a divine element, and, despite all their adherence to the law, it is precisely this divine dimension which, with a resounding appeal to the law, the Jews reject.

[19:8–12] Within: amid Pilate's fear and the Jews' political pressure, Jesus appears ever more mysterious and divinely directed. The deviations of both Pilate and the Jews now take a new turn. Pilate, the godless politician, becomes superstitious. The reference to Jesus as a Son of God inspires in him a fear which, while evoking a fear that is genuinely reverential (cf. Schnackenburg, 3:260) turns out to lack such a quality. And the law-enforcing Jews become calculating politicians. They tell Pilate that if he lets Jesus go his career is in danger—he is no friend of Caesar. The fact that "friend of Caesar" may have been a specific honorific title (Brown, 879) highlights their manipulative expertise and aggravates the situation of Pilate. Trapped between conflicting fears, he still has to go through the motions of being in charge and of pretending to administer justice.

At the same time, even as Pilate and the Jews are straying ever farther from their proclaimed ideals, Jesus advances in stature and authority. The qualities of the previous episode—dignified human and Son of God—now take on a further dimension.

When Pilate asks him "Where are you from?" Jesus' silence acts as an indicator of mystery, of the fact that ultimately his origin goes back to God. And when Pilate in frustration makes a pretentious claim, filled with irony, of knowing more than Jesus and of having the power of liberty and death ("Do you not know that I have the authority? . . ."), Jesus asserts that his fate rests rather with an authority which is "from above" (*anōthen*), in other words, from God (cf. 3:3,27,31).

Incidentally, this is not the same as the idea, found in Rom 13:1, that civil leaders receive their authority from God (cf. Brown, 892; Schnackenburg, 3:261). Rather than solidifying Pilate's authority, Jesus is setting it in perspective and is saying something about himself—that he is in the hands of an authority which ultimately is greater than that of Pilate and that Pilate does what he does only because in some sense he is allowed to (cf. 10:18).

Like the "human" and "Son of God" of the previous episode, the "Where . . . from?" (*pothen*) and "from above" (*anōthen*) complement one another, and together they deepen the portrait of Jesus and increase his authority. This sense of authority becomes yet clearer when Jesus continues: "He who handed me over to you has the greater sin." These are the words, not of a criminal, but of a judge.

For the moment Pilate escapes the full weight of condemnation. Not to him but to the Jews goes the blame for "handing over"—the process that ultimately goes back to Judas and the devil (6:71, 13:2). Thus Pilate still has a chance to reverse the process and escape the judgment. But now, at the decisive moment, loud questions are raised about another issue—his patriotism.

[19:13–16a] Outside: The final betrayal of Jesus by both the Jews and Pilate —Jesus as judge and king, at Passover.   This final scene portrays the full weight of sin. Pilate turns away from any hearing—superstitious or genuine—of the idea that Jesus is from God and, having listened instead to the words of political danger (contrast vv 8 and 13, "When Pilate heard. . . . When Pilate heard"), finally "hands over" Jesus to be crucified (v 16a). Thus he concludes the Satan-inspired handing-over which began in Judas. The Jews meanwhile reject any reign except that of Caesar, and thereby they both break the covenant and join Pilate in his enslavement to Caesar, to the world.

Given this deathly betrayal and enslavement, there is a terrible appropriateness to the setting, to the fact that the place is called Stone-pavement (in Greek, one word, *litho-strōtos*). It is not known where in the city this place was located, and it is doubtful if it should be identified with the pavement which has been excavated at the Antonia fortress (apparently the Antonia pavement was not laid until a century after Jesus' death—Brown, 882). But given the fact that thus far in the gospel the word "stone" has always been associated with sin and death—with the disbelief of the stone-throwing Judeans (8:59, 10:31–33, 11:8) and with Lazarus' tomb (11:38–41)—it is fitting, in this climactic scene of death-bearing sin, that there be a massive presence of stone.

It is also fitting, given that the accusers and judge are the sinners, that there be an uncertainty about who is occupying the *bēma* or seat of judgement. The Greek text is ambiguous: "Pilate led out Jesus and he sat down (*kathizō*) on the judgement seat." Who sat down? In Greek the verb *kathizō* may indicate intransitive or transitive, to sit or make sit. What emerges then is that the Jesus who, even in the preceding episode, was already assuming the role of judge, now is presented—in one level of the text—as sitting in judgement over the sin of the world.

He is also presented as king, and the wording, "Behold, your king!" is in continuity with the earlier presentation of Jesus as a human (vv 4–5, "Behold. . . . Behold a human being!"). Thus, however mockingly Pilate may have spoken in making these presentations, his statements form part of a steady pattern which shows Jesus first as human and Son of God (vv 4–7), then as a mysterious person who reflects an authority from above and who judges (vv 8–12), and now finally as sitting in judgement and as king (vv 13–16a). Hence, as sin deepens, Jesus the human appears increasingly as judge and king. This supports the view that "a human being" is a variation on "the Son of humanity," but the Jesus who here appears in judgement is not a condemnatory spectator. Rather he is someone who takes to himself the full weight of sin and who endures the cries of those who shout "Take him away, take him away! Crucify him." It was, says the text matter-of-factly, the day before Passover, "about the sixth hour."

Yet in this dread scene of stone and "Take him away" there are enigmatic hints of a further reality. The place of stone, whatever its heavy negative connotations, is known in Hebrew as *Gabbatha*—meaning a place which is elevated or raised. The hour is the hour of the killing of the Passover lambs and thus suggests that Jesus' killing be viewed as that of the (Passover) lamb who takes away the sin of the world (1:29). And the repeated "Take him away" uses, as it happens, the same verb (*airō*) that is used both of the lamb's taking away of sin and of the taking away of the stone on Lazarus' tomb (11:39–40). Nothing is clear, but the hostile cries have haunting echoes, and the reader is left pondering.

The Glorification of Jesus

John does indeed tell fully of Jesus' death and resurrection, yet rather than speaking of two distinct processes—dying and rising—he tends, to a significant extent, to portray a single unified process, that of Jesus' glorification. The conclusion of the trial before Pilate had spoken of the sixth hour (19:14), and, given the association of "the hour" with glorification (cf. esp. 12:23), the implication is that from now on the glorification is under way. The horror of crucifixion may seem to deny this, but insofar as the crucifixion involves a lifting up of Jesus, there is also a sense in which, as 12:23–33 suggests, the crucifixion inaugurates the glorification. Thus, precisely in the face of the most numbing brutality, the evangelist implies the presence of a larger positive process.

The encompassing of death and resurrection under a single positive viewpoint is further seen in the fact that the entire text (19:16b–chap. 21) forms a literary unity. The details of its structure will be dealt with at later stages, but the main point may be stated here: the entire account consists of five interwoven panels: crucifixion (19:16b–27), death (19:28–37), the tomb-related accounts (19:38–20:18), the appearances to the disciples (20:19–31), and the revelation at the sea (chap. 21).

The relationships between these five panels is roughly analogous to the relationships between the five panels of the last discourse: the first two form a pair, and so do the next two, but the fifth panel (chap. 21, like chap. 17) stands somewhat apart.

As in the case of the last discourse, there is a complex continuity between panels one, three, and five. Thus between one (19:16b–27, the crucifixion) and three (19:38–20:18, the tomb accounts) there are several links, particularly the motif of Jesus' clothing (19:23–24; 20:6–7) and the picture of the woman/women who stood by the cross/tomb (19:25–27; 20:11–18). The clothing motif appears also in chap. 21, but it is adapted from Jesus to Peter (21:7).

The similarity with the last discourse is not simply one of structure; there is also significant similarity of content. The going forth from God—mentioned at the beginning of chap. 13 (cf. 13:3)—is echoed and continued in the going forth to be crucified (19:17). Even the motif of the clothing is a continuation of the clothing motif involved in the foot-washing (13:4,12).

The details of these complex continuities—both within the five panels of 19:16b–chap. 21, and between 19:16b–chap. 21 and the last discourse—would need a special study to themselves. At this point it seems better simply to make the following tentative observations.

Unlike the last discourse, where the initial emphasis is on the role of the divine (chap. 13; 15:1–17, chap. 17), 19:16b–chap. 21 tends to lay the initial emphasis on the role of humans. This is particularly clear in the resurrection account. In the opening resurrection panel (19:38–20:18) the narratives begin with ordinary people—Joseph, Nicodemus, Mary, the beloved disciple, Peter. In the account of the crucifixion and death (19:16b–37) there is an emphasis on the fulfillment of scripture such as is not found in the subsequent texts. Scripture fulfillment is seen first in the sharing of the clothing (19:23–24), then in the deathly thirst (19:28), and finally, following the piercing of Jesus' side, there is a climactic double fulfillment (19:36–37). Thus it is precisely when God's word might most seem to be mocked that the evangelist presents it as being fulfilled. In 19:38–chap. 21, however, the old scriptures seem to be left behind. It is as though they have been surpassed.

Unlike chaps. 13–17, where, as the text advances, the individuality of the disciples progressively fades, in 19:16b–chap. 21, their individuality becomes more and more pronounced.

As in the account of Jesus' arrest and trials where—particularly with regard to the location of Jesus himself—the essential drama seemed to move from outside (18:1–27) to inside (18:28–19:16a), so in the account of Jesus' death and resurrection the action moves significantly from outside (crucifixion and death, 19:16b–37) to inside (inside the tomb and behind closed doors, 19:38–20:31). As explained in introducing 18:1–19:16a (under the heading "Two dramas of Revelation and Rejection"), the categories of outside and inside appear to reflect aspects of the evangelist's understanding of revelation.

Finally, the account of Jesus' death and resurrection (19:16b–chap. 20) seems to have some broad connections with the twofold account of creation (Genesis 1–2). To some degree this idea has an initial plausibility: the breathing which accompanies the granting of the Spirit (20:22) "harks back to . . . Gen 2:7" (Beasley-Murray, 380), and one could scarcely find a more fitting way of expressing the new life wrought by the resurrection than by evoking the first giving of life at creation. But—perhaps to emphasize the newness—the evangelist, to some degree, has made a reversal: the *first* gospel text with its space-related picture of the cross in the middle surrounded by four soldiers (19:16b–27) sometimes has more affinity with the *second,* space-structured, creation text (Gen 2:4b–25); and the *second* gospel text, with its time-related account of events occupying about a week (19:38–chap. 20) sometimes has more affinity with the *first,* time-structured, creation passage (Gen 1:1–2:4a).

The Descent into Death

Introduction and Structure

Following the noise of the trial, the account of the crucifixion and death seems relatively quiet and uncluttered. Many of the synoptics' negative details are missing. "There are no taunts by the bystanders, no mention of the darkness at noon, no cry of dereliction. There is a pervading calm, like an Italian primitive painting" (Lindars, 573).

It is not immediately clear, however, how the text is structured. Some would see the next major division as occurring after the death (v 30: e.g., Tillmann, 321; Schulz, 234; Lindars, 573; Dauer, 1972, 165); others place it after the burial (v 42: e.g., Zahn, 651; Bultmann, 666; Brown, 911; Schnackenburg, 3:269; Haenchen, 2:191; Kysar, 286).

At first sight these suggestions seem plausible. In much human experience death and burial have a numbing finality, and so it is natural that in the text also they be seen as final, as points of division.

Lagrange (488), however, implies that the next major division occurs not after the death or burial but after the reaction to the flow of blood and water (vv 35–37). In this case the final mood is not one of numbing emptiness, but rather of faith and fullness: the one who has seen bears witness "that you also may believe" (v 35); and the effect of this deathly outflow is not to make a mockery of God's word but to bring it to fulfillment (vv 36–37). Thus the final say would go not to death and burial but to faith and God's (written) word.

Such a division involves a startling reversal of natural expectations but, in a gospel which frequently reverses expectations, it is not to be ruled out.

Suspicion increases when it is noted that both the death and the burial are introduced by "After" ("After this . . ."; "After these things . . ."), a word which is generally used, not at the end of a major section, but at some kind of beginning (cf. 2:12; 3:22; 4:43; 5:1; 6:1; 7:1). There is a suggestion, therefore, that death and burial are not conclusions but rather beginnings.

It may seem strange that either a death or a burial could act as a beginning. And indeed it would be if the evangelist's primary interest were in a biography as such, a biography for its own sake. But that is not what is being presented. As indicated in the introduction, the portrait of Jesus has been adapted to bring out its practical meaning, its impact on the life of the believer. And as far as the believer is concerned the death of Jesus is not an end; it is a beginning. As Brown (913) indicates at one point: "The death of Jesus is the beginning of Christian life."

Once the account of Jesus' death (vv 28–30) is seen as some form of a beginning, the overall structure becomes clearer. The whole text consists, as so often in John, of two panels: the first tells of the crucifixion (vv 16b–27) and the second of the death (vv 28–37). (The burial, as will be seen later, belongs to the resurrection account.) Both panels begin with decisive events: in the first, Jesus is *crucified* (vv 16b–18), and in the second, Jesus *gives over the spirit* (vv 28–30). Then—in both panels—come the actions, largely negative, of the Jews and soldiers (*after the crucifixion,* the Jews dispute Pilate's inscription, and the soldiers divide the garments, vv 19–24; and *after the death,* the Jews ask Pilate to have the soldiers finish off the bodies, vv 31–34). Finally, in a suprising turnabout, both panels conclude with pictures of *reactions which are positive:* the mother who stood by the cross is received by the beloved disciple (vv 25–27), and the one who saw the deathly outflow gives faith-inviting witness (vv 35–37).

The internal structure of these panels is not identical. Somewhat like the two complementary panels involving Nicodemus (2:23–3:21) and John the baptizer (3:22–36), the structure of the first (apart from its introduction) is essentially threefold, and the structure of the second (apart from its conclusion) is essentially twofold.

The presence within the second panel of a "conclusion" rather than an "introduction" is linked to the fact that the gospel as a whole is drawing to a close, and, as will be seen later, this conclusion, with its reference to the faith-inviting witness (vv 35–37), is part of that closing process.

The Crucifixion (19:16b–27)

[19:16b–18] Introduction: the going forth and the crucifixion. Jesus in this introduction may seem like an object, subhuman. "They took" him, like something passive; and "they crucified him." There is no indication here that he felt anything, or that anyone felt anything for him. His executioners may indeed be reasonably connected, from a literary point of view, both with the Jews who had called for his death and with the soldiers who carried it out, but at the moment of bringing him to crucifixion their faces are not to be seen; they are hidden behind the anonymity of the "they." And the name given to the place to which they took him is equally vague, topographically speaking (Brown, 899–900). Yet, at another level the place has a terrible clarity: *Golgotha,* "the Place of a Skull"—a grim evocation of the fact that, from one point of view, human life often leads to nothing more than becoming a nameless skull.

Yet there is another level in the text which suggests that, despite appearances, Jesus is not a doomed object. It is emphasized that he carried his own cross, a detail which, as well as being in contrast to the other gospels, takes up the theme of the good shepherd—"that he went to his death as sole master of his own destiny . . . that [he] would lay down his own life and that no one would take it from him (v 18)" (Brown, 917). And the expression "he went out," however prosaic at one level, at another cannot but evoke the studied, central usage of "he went out" in 18:1–19:16, a usage connected with the process of revelation and with the idea that Jesus, the good shepherd, "went out" in self-giving, from God (cf. esp. 13:3; 18:1,4).

The purpose of this going out is reflected in the scene. The fact that two others are with him, one on either side with Jesus in the middle, is best read not in the light of the other gospels and the information that they were thieves, one bad and one good (Luke 23:33, 39–43), but in light of John's own account—an account which told that Jesus, when lifted up, would draw all to himself (12:32; Mateos and Barreto, 805) and, in particular, which indicated that the good shepherd, in laying down his life, would bring to salvation two groups (10:16–18).

Even the cold picture of the skull is not without its glimmer of light. *Golgotha,* while indeed reflecting the Semitic words for skull (*Gulgolta,* Aramaic; *Gulgolet,* Hebrew), echoes also the word *Gabbatha* (19:13), meaning elevated or raised. The continuity between *Gabbatha* and *Golgotha* is found in their proximity (four verses apart), their similarity of function (place names, introducing two successive units), the unique similarity in the phrasing which introduces them (". . . Jesus . . . out . . . to . . . a place . . . called . . . in Hebrew"), and in the form of spelling (*-tha*). Thus, as the death-related image of stone was relieved by *Gabbatha* with its suggestion of being raised, so *Golgotha* extends that connotation to the image of the skull. Ultimately both of these faint subtleties reflect something central and clear—the idea that crucifixion itself, with all its degrading horror, was a lifting up (cf. 12:32–33, 18:32).

This introduction, therefore, is a picture of Jesus being brought low, but it has a further level of meaning—one in which he is raised up and in which, from his central position ("in the middle"), he is drawing people to himself. Again the text is not clear, but again the reader is led to ponder.

[19:19–22] Through Pilate's writing the realm is proclaimed; some Jews reject it, but the proclamation stands. The impression that the text has a deeper meaning is reinforced by what follows. Pilate, in an apparent adaptation of the occasional Roman custom of writing out publicly a culprit's crime (Brown, 901), indicates that this down-to-earth Jesus ("Jesus of Nazareth") is "King of the Jews," and he places the written statement on the cross. The result is that the crucifixion, instead of being a place of empty silence, becomes a scene of proclamation.

The Jewish reaction to this proclamation is described through a text which has a curious twofold structure (vv 20–21). First it is said that it *"was written,"* and that many Jews read it (v 20). Then it is said that it *"was written* in Hebrew, Latin, and Greek" and that the Jewish chief priests rejected it (v 21). As Brown's translation implies (897), it would make for a clearer text, logically, if the two "was written" clauses were combined into one.

Yet the present twofold structure, though initially puzzling, appears to have a purpose: it evokes two aspects of the Jewish reaction to revelation and scripture: first, many of them read it, but then, when faced with its universality ("in Hebrew, Latin, and Greek"), the chief priests rejected it. In other words, it reflects division among the Jews.

In describing the first stage it is said that the place where Jesus was crucified was "near" and that it was this nearness which allowed the Jews to read the proclamation (v 20). The idea of being "near" appears to have two levels of meaning—the meaning which is most immediately suggested by the word itself, that of being physically close at hand, and the more spiritual meaning, suggested by the context and found also, for instance, in Ephesians (2:13, 17), of being close to God's revelation, particularly as that revelation is seen in Jesus' crucifixion. In other words, the two pictures, of nearness and rejection, correspond to the two main aspects of the Jewish reaction to God's revelation—first they were near the revelation, then, when it became universal, they rejected it. This makes theological sense and explains the otherwise perplexing structure.

But at this stage, unlike that of the trial, the Jewish-inspired rejection does not win. By insisting that what he has written has been written irreversibly, Pilate becomes the instrument for communicating that a new order is being established. This need not mean that Pilate is being virtuous or insightful. His action rather is best seen as a (Roman) power play against the high priests. Like Caiaphas, the high priest who used a power play against the other high priests in order to keep the Romans at bay, and who thus became an unwitting prophet, Pilate is the unwitting source of scripture/writing (cf. Bultmann, 669). For this new order goes beyond that of the covenant-breaking Jews (cf. 19:15) and has its own writing or scripture (cf. Mateos and Barreto, 806: "*nueva Escritura*"). The idea of a new scripture had already been implied by the fact that Jesus' words were put on a par with scripture (18:9, 32). Now the implication of a new scripture appears again, and this time it is suggesting a kingship which is universal.

[19:23–24] The taking of the clothes: the soldiers' actions evoke universality, unity, and scriptural fulfillment.

Following the tense matter-of-principle exchange among the self-willed leaders (Pilate and the chief priests), the text goes on to tell of a more prosaic drama—the soldiers' dividing of the meager loot.

At first sight, the two episodes may seem unrelated and the later one rather meaningless (cf. Bultmann, 670–71). Yet they have their own coherence. Precisely because from one point of view they are so different, the two incidents provide a striking dramatic contrast, a form of upstairs-downstairs effect.

And, despite the contrast, there is continuity. This is seen first of all in the text's form:

> 21: So they said . . . ,
>
>   "Do not write . . . but . . .";
>
> 24: So they said,
>
>   "Do not let us . . . but. . . ."

A more fundamental aspect of continuity is that the upstairs-downstairs effect helps to form a basis for the evoking of Jesus' self-giving descent. In the rather high-flown discussion about the inscription, Jesus was proclaimed to be a king. But now there is a reminder that he was crucified, and it is added that they took his very clothes. A similar process was found at the (death-related) foot-washing: Jesus' removal of his clothes contributed significantly to the idea of the divine self-giving (13:1–5). Thus while the introductory picture of Jesus as "going out" freely with his cross (vv 17–18) evoked the general idea of the free self-giving of the good shepherd, the subsequent episodes develop and dramatize that self-giving idea, and they do so by implying a descent from kingship to nakedness.

Within this pattern of drama and descent there are further elements of continuity.

The universalism which had been suggested by the three languages is continued in the fact that the dividing of the clothes into four likewise suggests universalism (the four corners of the earth).

Attached to the sentence concerning the division into four is a reference to the (undivided) tunic. Admittedly the reference ("and also the tunic") seems to be "tagged on . . . somewhat clums[il]y" (Schnackenburg, 3:273), but the apparent clumsiness may also be seen as an indication to the reader that something is being signalled, namely that universalism is to be accompanied by undividedness—in other words, by unity (see esp. Cyprian, *The Unity of the Universal Church* 7; Brown, 921; Hoskyns, 529; pace Schnackenburg, 3:274).

Thus while the inscription episode was largely concerned with the attitude of the Jews—"many" read it "closely," but the high priests rejected it—the episode involving the clothes and the Roman soldiers is more indicative of the attitude of the Gentiles, and therefore it opens up more explicitly the question of the universal reaction to Jesus and thus the idea of the universal church.

At first sight the soldiers' attitude seems crass and rapacious; they simply take everything available. Yet in receiving each a "share" (*meros,* 23), they evoke the divine share or heritage which was promised to Peter at the foot-washing (13:8, *meros*), and thereby also they evoke the richness that the divine self-giving will bestow on all humankind. It is appropriate, therefore, that their number suggest universalism and that the tunic, woven "from above" (*ek tōn anōthen,* 23; cf. 3:3), suggest unity.

Thus the suggestion of a division among the Jews (vv 19–22) is complemented by a suggestion of the participation of the Gentiles and of the joining of both in one universal church (vv 23–24).

Furthermore, this new development is not contrary to what was written, to scripture. Here lies another element of continuity between 19–22 and 23–24. Pilate had replied that the inscription, in fact, was like scripture. And the soldiers, in sharing the clothing, fulfilled scripture. The final superfluous-looking detail, "and that is what the soldiers did," has essentially the same effect as Pilate's "what I have written, I have written": it solidifies the rightness of what was written. If Pilate unwittingly wrote a form of scripture, then something similar is true of the soldiers—they "unwittingly did exactly as prophesied" (Brown, 904).

The overall effect of these two episodes is to indicate that even as someone lies dying amid petty rivalry and rapaciousness, there is at work, through that very dying and pettiness, a divine self-giving which, in accordance with what was written, seeks to gather all people into one.

[19:25–27] The context and quality of the community—love, motherhood, sisterhood, and universalism. At one level this episode—of the women standing at the cross and of Jesus' addressing his mother and the beloved disciple— this episode is a scene of understandable human concern, the women's concern for the dying Jesus, and Jesus' concern for those being left behind. Such is the core of the text—a picture of profound care, even in very difficult circumstances.

This care, though portrayed in specific people, is not something which is either self-made or isolated. On the contrary, it has two self-surpassing dimensions: it comes down from God, and it constitutes the church.

The dependence on God, though subtle, is relatively easy to discuss. The preceding episodes, however barbarous, have portrayed at one level the advanced stages of the divine self-giving. Jesus, bearing his own cross, went forth to be despoiled. And it is at the conclusion of that picture of divine generosity, when his very clothes have been taken away, that the gospel introduces the scene of human concern. The implication is that human care flows from the divine. A similar dynamic is found in chapter 13: the care which Jesus showed in the foot-washing is to be reflected in care for one another.

The portrayal of the church is a much more complex problem. While there is considerable agreement that at least some of the characters in the scene are representative and that the text is therefore saying something about the community or church, it is not clear who represents what, and what exactly is going on.

Two aspects of this texts are immediately puzzling. How many women are in question—two, three, or four? And why does the picture of those standing by the cross seem to change? The change occurs between two successive verses (vv 25–26). At first (v 25) the text mentions the women (plural)—without any reference to the beloved disciple. But when Jesus begins to speak (v 26) what he sees are his mother and the beloved disciple. What became of the other woman/women? And why was the beloved not mentioned at the beginning? It would have been easy and more logical: "Now there stood . . . his mother . . . and the disciple. . . ."

This perplexing shift should probably be seen in the context of the shift which occurs in describing those who reacted to the inscription (vv 20–21). In both cases a seeming illogicality of phrasing is, in fact, a way of depicting diverse views of a single changing reality.

The initial view, the picture of the women (v 25), is like a picture of all those people, particularly Jews, who in one way or another were present at the cross. (Thus, to some degree, it is analogous to the "many" Jews who read the inscription.) Nothing much is said of their degree of involvement; they simply stood there.

The second view, which begins pointedly with the initiative of Jesus and continues with the active response of his mother and the beloved disciple (v 26), is like a picture of the first steps towards the emergence of the church. (Thus while the inscription scene first suggested open-minded observation and then the emergence of rejecting Jews, this later scene moves from an apparently open-minded presence to a picture of the emergence of the church.)

Within both these views, "the mother . . . represents Jewish Christianity that overcame the offence of the cross" (Bultmann, 673); she "represents the section of the [Jewish] population which was open to the 'King of Israel' " (Schnackenburg, 3:278). The beloved disciple, on the other hand, seems to represent Christianity—not so much Gentile Christianity, as Bultmann (673) suggests, but Christianity as a whole, the new reality which contained the Jewish-Gentile church, the reality into which faithful Israel was absorbed (he "took her to his own"). "He is the mediator and interpreter of Jesus' . . . revelation of salvation for [all] mankind" (Schnackenburg, 3:279).

Left behind in this process is at least one person, Mary Magdalene. She was at the cross, but she just stood there and was not involved in the emergence of the new grouping. She forms a contrast with the mother—as do the Jewish leaders who rejected Jesus' inscription (Schnackenburg, 3:278)—and the implication is that, in this gospel at least, she in some way represents those Jews who did not believe.

Thus the scene at the cross, while preplexing in its way of changing the *dramatis personae,* dropping at least one character and adding another, makes sense when seen as summing up positively what the previous scenes had suggested— that following a division in Judaism there would emerge through Jesus' death a new universal church, one in which believing Jews and other believers would behold one another with cross-inspired regard and in which Jews would be fully accepted.

As regards the perplexing question of whether the number of women at the cross is two, three, or four, this also would seem connected to the episodes which precede. If they are regarded as two (the mother, [called] Mary of Klopas, and her sister, Mary Magdalene), the two may be seen as representing the two Judaisms, one going forward in belief, the other fading into the background, holding back in negative sorrow, in disbelief. If, as in the RSV, they are regarded as three (his mother, her sister, [known as] Mary of Klopas, and Mary Magdalene), Mary Magdalene may still be seen as negative-oriented Judaism, and the two sisters become the church's two components—Jewish (the mother) and Gentile (Mary of Klopas). This level of reading is concerned not with the fact that faithful Israel is absorbed into a new and greater reality, but simply with the idea that, within the church, different ethnic groups are related to one another like sisters.

Finally, at yet another level, if the number of women is regarded as four, the four may be seen as providing a counterpart to the four soldiers (Hoskyns, 530; Lightfoot, 316) and as again evoking the emerging universalism.

What is important is not just that all three readings are possible, but that all three may be connected with what precedes. As often in John, therefore, it may be a mistake to choose one at the expense of the others. Besides, it simply cannot be done, at least not satisfactorily; Kysar (288) characterizes the process of trying to make an exclusive choice as "hopelessly problematic."

It may be more productive, and more true to the nature of the text, to see it insofar as it evokes a response from the reader. The reader looks at it and, initially perhaps, gets the impression that there are two women. But as one thinks about that some objections may arise, and so, on further reflection, are there not three? Or is it four? Thus within the reader there is a process of shifting from one combination to another, a process which in some ways is unsettling but one which corresponds to what is in question—the changing shape of God's people, the unsettling but fruitful process of moving towards a people that is one and universal.

The Mother

At Cana also, the mother of Jesus may be seen as responsive Judaism. She is the former people, the former church, the one who, before the decisive hour has come, takes the initiative and prepares the way for the intervention of Jesus. But in the later part of the Cana episode (2:6–11), when her preparatory role is over, she disappears from view.

Now, at the decisive and painful hour, she is seen again. Her reappearance, however, recalls not only Cana but also the woman who had sorrow because the hour had come when she would give birth (16:21; Lightfoot, 317). This is the time for a birth, the time for the emergence of something new—a reborn Jesus and a re-formed church.

The mother, far from being banished, is incorporated into the new spiritual order. Thus her presence is a reminder that in this new order too there is a mothering church.

The Beloved Disciple and Peter

There is also, however, a larger phenomenon—the world of discipleship which is more than the church, the world personified by the beloved disciple. It is a world which is closely bound to the church and which is also related with the sometimes questionable figure of Peter.

This is the one time in the gospel in which the beloved disciple appears without Peter. Yet the relationship to Peter is not forgotten. This episode, at the end of the crucifixion scene, occupies a role which is similar, both in dramatic effect and in structure, to that of the Peter episode at the end of the scene of the arrest (18:10–11). Peter brought a sudden note of violent resistance to death and was commanded by Jesus to put his sword away. The mother and beloved disciple bring a solidarity which is more positive, and they are commanded by Jesus to see one another. For Peter, Jesus' death was a source of alienation; for the mother and the beloved disciple it is a source of mutual acceptance.

This mutual acceptance ("Behold. . . . Behold"), as well as being in contrast to the violence of Peter, is also in contrast to the violence of the Jews who, on being told twice by Pilate to behold Jesus (19:5, 14), shouted back their death-filled rejection.

Thus, in comparison with Peter's failure, the Jews' rejection, and the soldiers' barbarity, this seminal picture of the church offers a strong contrast.

Jesus Hands Over (19:28–37)

[19:28–30] The bitter end, with glimmerings of a spiritual beginning. The death of Jesus is described largely through the imagery of thirsting and drinking. At earlier stages of his life it was he who offered drink to others—at Cana (2:1–11), at the well (4:7–26), and on the last day of the feast of Tents—to all who thirst (7:37–39). But now, crucified, his own next-to-last word is *"Dipsō,"* "I thirst." And having received a drink, he said "It is finished" and, bowing his head, handed over the spirit.

The brief account is dominated linguistically by the triple use of two sets of words—words suggesting an end, *telos*, (*teleioō*, "to complete/finish," 28b; *te-*

leō, "to bring to an end/finish," 28a, 30) and the word *oxos,* the name which was given to a common vinegary wine and which in itself indicated something which was sharp, bitter. The depth of the distastefulness is heightened by a triple repetition: "full of bitter(ness) . . . full of the bitter(ness) . . . Jesus received the bitter(ness)." The result, as Jesus pronounces, "It is complete," and drops his head, is to evoke not only death's physical depletion, the physical emptiness and thirst, but also all of death's bitterness and finality.

But, as always in this gospel, there are suggestions of a further reality. The opening phrase, "After this" generally indicates not an end but a beginning. The name, "Jesus," instead of being in the accusative case (like an object—as in 18:12,28; 19:1,16b) now appears in the nominative case, as a subject. His "knowing . . . all" evokes deity (cf. 13:1,3; 18:4). The verbs which suggest an end also indicate a positive completion. The scriptures, at this dread scene, are not made absurd; instead—particularly because the thirst reflects them (cf. esp. Ps 69:22)—they are fulfilled. The placing of the rather heavy drink on a weak hyssop plant (inexplicable as simple history) evokes what hyssop was used for—to sprinkle the saving blood of the paschal lamb (Exod 12:22); in fact, the light hyssop which bears the heavy weight of bitterness is like a variation on the picture of the (light) lamb who takes away the (weight of the) world's sin (1:29). Thus, the bitterness ultimately does not dominate; instead of fighting it, Jesus receives it, accepts it—and thus robs it of its oppressiveness. And finally, in stark contrast to the bitter drink, there is the suggestion of drink of another kind, that of the spirit, exactly the drink which Jesus had offered implicitly at the well (4:22–24) and at Tents (7:39), the supreme drink which was intimated in the fine wine of Cana.

A somewhat similar transition, from accepting the distasteful to receiving the life-giving, was offered in chapter 6: those who ate and drank the flesh and blood would have life and would be raised up on the last day (6:52–58). The great difference is that in his death Jesus is not receiving the life-giving spirit but instead is imparting it. He has accepted the distasteful in order that others may live. He is opening the way so that they may follow.

For the moment, of course, the spirit which is handed over is not referred to as life-giving. In fact, at one level, the imparting of the spirit simply means death. But, as just noted, the immediate context has suggestions of life, and these suggestions are strengthened by earlier passages. The climactic cry at the feast of Tents (7:37–39) is particularly close to the death scene: it speaks of thirst, of drinking, and of Jesus' glorification; it even contains a somewhat similar ambiguity in its opening lines (7:38, "the one who believes" can be attached either to what precedes or to what follows; and, in 19:28, the phrase "that the scripture might be completed" can likewise be attached either to what precedes or to what follows); and when 7:37–39 speaks of the spirit it does so as something intensely life-giving.

One of the curious features of the cry at Tents is that it occurs "on the last day" (7:37). This may be seen as a straightforward chronological detail, but the context of the gospel gives it further meaning. Because it is related implicitly to Jesus' death, it takes up the death-related "on the last day" which recurs in chapter 6 (6:39,40,44,54). Thus it acts as a kind of bridge between the repeated theme of raising people on the last day and the account of the death of Jesus.

The dropping of the head is a further reflection of the text's ambiguity. In itself it suggests the sinking of life. And it evokes the grim fact that in the final months or weeks of life, as death closes in, people are sometimes unable to hold up their heads. But in the context of a passage which began with a reminder of divinity ("knowing . . . all") and in the context of so many other passages which began with divinity and then descended into humanity, it is a sign of the divine outpouring, of the descent which partakes in the full frailty of the flesh, even in its final collapse.

[19:31–34] The reactions of the Jews and soldiers; the flow of blood and water. The grimness of death, already portrayed in the picture of thirst, bitterness, and finality, finds further emphasis in the aftermath—in this crude scene of dealing with the bodies. As in the scenes following the crucifixion—concerning the inscription and the clothes (19:19–24)—the action is largely dominated first by the Jews and then by the soldiers. And in diverse ways both groups are still being true to character. For the Jews, there was a law that bodies should not hang overnight (Deut 21:22–23), and presumably this would apply in a special way at the time of a feast such as the Passover (Brown, 934). Consequently, in their anxiety to keep the Passover legalities, they ask about breaking and removing the bodies (including the body of Jesus, the true unbroken Passover lamb).

They give no idea—the Jews and soldiers—that Jesus' death has made any impression on them. The handing over of the spirit has passed them by. In fact, the Jews apparently have not even noticed that he is dead. It is the soldiers in the midst of their brutal work who first realize what has happened. That simplifies the work; it is easier to prod a spear.

The two subsequent images, blood and water, complement each other. Blood, or at least the spilling of blood, lays the emphasis on death. It signals loss. In the bread-of-life discourse the drinking of the blood indicated an acceptance of death (6:52–58). In contrast, the flowing of water signals life and spirit (3:5; 4:7–24; 7:38–39; 9:7). Together they indicate loss and gain, death and life.

Again therefore, as in the proceding account of the death, the emphasis on the negative—whether on bitterness or brutality—is relieved by a suggestion of something positive. Even the detailed arrangement of the text seems positive: the use of "water" as the last word of this episode dovetails with the use of "spirit" at the very end of the death account.

The flow of blood and water furthers the continuity already found in the death episode, between the death of Jesus and the climactic cry at Tents (7:37–39). Both events occur on "the great day" (cf. 3:37; 19:31), and what was promised at Tents, that water would flow out of Jesus, now actually happens.

The blood and water is also in continuity with the repeated theme of the divine self-emptying. This theme had already been taken up in the death scene—in the implied idea of a descent (the divine "knowing . . . all" gave way to the bowing of the head). Now as the blood and water "come out" (*ex-erchomai*, "come/go out") of Jesus, he is literally emptied; and the "going out" from God, a process which, ever since the prologue had often been implied (see esp. 13:3; cf. 18:4, 19:17), is here brought to its final conclusion.

Insofar as blood and water are connected with the imagery of the sacraments —blood with the eucharist and water with baptism—the outflow has sometimes been seen as the source of the sacraments and even of the church (for patristic opinions, see esp. Westcott, 284–86). The reference to the sacraments is, at most, secondary (cf. esp. Beasley-Murray, 357–58), but the general idea of seeing the sacraments and church as coming from the side of Christ has a certain validity: it was through the incarnation, and especially through the completion of the incarnation in Jesus'crucifixion and death, that the church was born. Thus in all three texts—the prologue (1:1–18), the crucifixion account (19:16b–27), and the account of the death (19:28–37)—the emphasis on Christ gives way to an emphasis on the emergence of believers: the "we" who have seen his glory (1:14), the figures by the cross (19:25–27), and, following the outflow, the witness-bearing which leads to believing (19:35).

[19:35–37] Witness and writing—the two faith-inspiring records; the witnessing and its purpose. The flow of blood and water is followed by two double texts, one about a witness (v 35) and the other about scripture, writing (*graphē*, vv 36–37). The double text concerning the witness affirms solemnly that what has been narrated is true. And the scripture-related text affirms that what has been narrated fulfills written records, scripture. The combined effect of these two texts is to indicate that the flow of blood and water is in accord with both witness and writing, and that, as such, it is eminently faith-inspiring.

The repetitive solemnity of the passage may seem surprising, yet it is appropriate. The flow of blood and water from the unbroken Jesus is highly significant, both in itself, as an indication that even amid blood and emptiness there is life, and also as the final stage of the gospel's central story of the divine self-emptying. To look at a dead bloodied body and to be aware, even in doing so, of a world of divine compassion and life—such a recognition demands to be expressed, to be solemnly witnessed; and that is what this passage does.

vv 35–37: a note on authenticity and structure. Partly because of its arresting solemnity and conclusiveness, and partly because of its similarity to the supposedly added 21:24, the statement concerning the witness (v 35) has sometimes been regarded, with varying degrees of conviction, as an editorial addition. Bultmann (678) and Brown (945), for instance, regard the addition theory as certain, but Lindars (589) and Schnackenburg (3:287, 291) seem less sure.

This addition theory, however, is not necessary. Given the importance of what is being witnessed to, the solemnity is appropriate. And it will be argued later that 21:24, like all of chap 21, is not an addition.

Besides, the connection is not simply between 19:35 and 21:24. Rather, both 19:35 and 21:24 are part of a larger delicately woven pattern of three graded conclusions—19:35–37; 20:30–31, and 21:24–25. All three deal with variations on witness and writing, and all three either seek to inspire faith or imply that faith is already present.

The authenticity of all of 19:35-37, and especially of the picture of the positive witness (19:35), is confirmed by the way it fits into the passion account: it balances the picture of those who stood by the cross (19:25-27), and it counterbalances the final picture of Peter's denials (18:25-27). Thus while the two concluding pictures of Peter—at the arrest (18:10-11) and in the courtyard (18:25-27)—constitute a slide from deviation to denial, the two concluding pictures at the crucifixion and death portray a counterbalancing advance: from a positive church-building presence (19:25-27) to a solemn faith-building witness (19:35-37).

vv 35-37: solemn witness and saving scripture.   The question of the identity of the witness does not seem difficult; he would appear to be the beloved disciple (Bultmann, 679; Brown, 952). Apart from the women, he was the only sympathetic person present (19:25-27), and such an identification is suggested by 21:24.

Yet the picture is not so simple. Having spoken of the witness who has seen, the text adds "and he [*ekeinos*, lit. "that one"] knows that he speaks the truth. . . ." In other words, as well as a seeing there is a knowing. The fact that the knowing is different from the seeing is highlighted by the use of *ekeinos:* it would seem from one point of view to be the same person who saw, but the wording has a rather jolting ambiguity which suggests that someone else was involved, particularly someone divine (for discussion, see Bultmann, 678; Brown, 936-37; Schnackenburg, 3:290). This suggestion is heightened by the fact that, at the end of the prologue, the revealing Jesus is referred to as *ekeinos* (1:18). Brown (952) provides the key to the ambiguity when he emphasizes that the testifying disciple is not alone but is aided by the Spirit (cf. 15:26-27). The implication, therefore, is that while one may see with one's own eyes, there is a distinct process, that of knowing, which is accomplished through a fusion of persons, a divine indwelling. The perceiving of the truth, then, is not done by the eyes alone. They have their valid role, but it is the Spirit who knows.

The fact that the witness is "true" does not mean that it reflects scientific accuracy. "True" is used in the sense of something that is saving, in other words as reflecting the greatest truth; namely, that in and through the full reality of life, including death, God is actively involved to bring humans salvation.

And the process of seeing and knowing is directed to others: "that you . . . may believe." Thus the self-giving and outpouring which began with Jesus is continued in the disciple who, in union with the divine and the divine self-giving, looks out towards others. The self-giving goes on.

Then (vv 36-37) come two scripture quotations, one about unbrokenness and the other about piercing and seeing (or looking). These quotations refer back not only to what happened to Jesus—his being unbroken yet wounded—but also, through the idea of looking (or seeing) to the subsequent reaction, the seeing (v 35, "And he who saw . . ."). In Greek it is the same verb which is used for both seeing and looking (*horaō;* vv 35, 37).

The unbrokeness quotation (v 36) is a rather free composition, not corresponding exactly to any known OT text. It is close, however, to two texts which suggest salvation—the reference to God's providential care of the just (Ps 34:20), and especially to the description of the saving paschal lamb (Exod 12:46). Likewise the subsequent quotation (v 37) about looking at the one who was pierced (cf. Zech 12:10): though it obviously indicates a certain woundedness, both its OT context (Zechariah 12–14, esp. 12:9–13:1) and several related NT texts indicate that it too heralds salvation (see esp., Schnackenburg, 3: 292–94).

It is not only through their content, however, that these quotations suggest salvation; it is also through their origin, their role as scripture which has been fulfilled. The fact that an event fulfilled scripture meant that it accorded with God's word. And God's word was saving. As Bultmann (677) summarizes: "The double fulfillment plainly shows that God's plan of salvation is fulfilled in this event, that the crucified Jesus is the promised bringer of salvation."

The text of 19:35–37 has a double role. It refers, first of all, to the immediate fate of Jesus' body (to its being pierced, not broken). And, placed, as it is, exactly at the conclusion of the last of several graded portrayals of the central drama of the divine self-giving, it refers also to that drama as a whole. To have witnessed and understood the final act, as 19:35 implies, meant becoming a witness to the entire story. And the scripture texts (19:36–37), insofar as they suggest that Jesus is the paschal lamb, go back to the way in which Jesus was first sighted—the lamb who takes away the sin of the world (1:29).

The Open Tomb and the Appearances

In John's gospel there is no description of Jesus' resurrection, no account, for instance, which tells that at a particular moment the dead body stirred to life and then broke forth from the tomb. John's approach, however, is not exceptional: "the resurrection is never described in the NT . . . [and] in Hebr 9 [there is], seemingly, a direct progression from crucifixion to ascension, without an intervening act of resurrection" (Brown, 966). The victory over death in John is something which, after the fact, is discovered and revealed in various ways.

The absence of a specific description makes it difficult to know when that fact occurred and, consequently, where the resurrection account begins. Obviously Mary's coming to the tomb on the first day of the week (20:1) represents a major act of discovery, and thus a new division in the text, but the event itself, the event which will dominate all of chap. 20, has already taken place. The question therefore arises whether, before chap. 20 tells of the various discoveries and revelations, the text gives any inkling of what has happened.

The proposal made here is that, while there is no description of a resurrection, the account of the burial (19:38–42) provides enigmatic suggestions of a process of transformation, and thus, *pace* Bultmann (680), provides the opening section of the resurrection text.

At first sight it may seem incongruous that a resurrection account should begin with a burial. Burials at times seem final, dark, and bitter—far from any sense of a beginning or a resurrection. As the clay covers the coffin, or as the body is consigned in whatever way to the earth, the earth may seem alien and devouring, the final implacable enemy that will eventually reduce the last remains to nothing.

Yet in depicting the working of God it was above all to the earth, "the good earth," that Jesus appealed. When the seed fell on it, the earth became a source of transformation and new life (Mark 4:1–9,26–32, and parr). And when speaking of his own fate, it was a similar process which Jesus evoked: the grain of wheat falls to the earth and dies, but from it comes much fruit (12:24). It is not inappropriate, therefore, that the development of new life should be associated with consignment to the earth, in other words, with burial.

That the burial has an inaugural role is confirmed by several other factors.

- As a conclusion it can seem out of place. Brown (911), for instance, sees it as the final part of a chiasm which began with the crucifixion, but there is not enough at the other end of the chiasm (in 19:16b–18) to balance it, and so Schnackenburg (3:455) concludes: "the [chiastic] arrangement seems artificial, the 'correspondence' of the episodes is not convincing."

- The text which immediately precedes it, concerning faith-inviting witness and fulfillment (vv 35–37), is closely connected with texts which are conclusions (20:29–31; 21:24–25), and itself appears to be a conclusion. Thus the way is open for the following text, the burial account, to be a beginning.

- The burial passage begins with *meta . . . tauta,* "after these things," a

556

phrase which in John's text generally indicates a new section (cf. 3:22; 5:1,14; 6:1; 7:1; 21:1). Furthermore, when placed at the beginning of the first panel of resurrection texts, it forms part of a pattern of beginnings which are all time-related:

"After this . . ." (19:28);

"After these things . . ." (19:38);

"On the evening of that day . . ." (20:19);

"After these things . . ." (21:1).

The effect is somewhat akin to that found in the broken pattern of time-related beginnings in chapters 1–2 (1:29,35,43; 2:1,12; cf. 1:39). Other aspects of this broken-pattern effect appear to be reflected in the two references which first tell on which specific day certain things occurred (20:1,26). What is essential, however, is that the burial fits a general pattern of beginnings.

• It is the burial account which provides some of the most basic elements for the episodes in 20:1–18—particularly the tomb, the clothes, and the garden(er) (cf. Schnackenburg 3:295–96). In other words, as far as the narrative of 20:1–18 is concerned, the burial account acts as an introduction.

Once the burial account is seen as a beginning, the remainder of the structure falls into place fairly easily.

As so often, and as partly indicated by Brown (965), the text consists of two complementary panels: one is set largely in or near the tomb (19:38–20:18), the other behind closed doors (20:19–31). As in the case of the account of the crucifixion and death, the first panel consists of a brief introduction (Joseph's taking away of the body, v 38) and three episodes, and the second panel consists of two episodes and a conclusion.

The entire account (19:38–20:31) is not simply about diverse discoveries and appearances. Rather, as the detailed commentary will indicate, it describes and implies a single coherent process of development, one which, through stages, moves all the way from the first surprising mention of a garden to the climactic "My Lord and my God."

The fact that the text has two panels does not mean that the account is uncoordinated. Rather, the two are complementary. As noted earlier, the first emphasizes human initiative (19:38–20:18), the second, divine (20:19–28). Together they bring out that the process of resurrection is both divine and human.

Ascension and Unity (Beginnings) (19:38–20:18)

[19:38] Introduction: The respectful taking away of the body. It is just when Jesus seems finished that the text springs a surprise: it introduces the previously unmentioned figure of Joseph of Arimathea, "a disciple of Jesus." In the other gospels also he is referred to at this point (and this point only), but that does not nullify the surprise; in the aftermath of the callous attitude of the Jews and soldiers his sympathetic presence is a significant change.

Yet this presence brings a problem, at least for the reader: Joseph proceeds to do what the Jews had already done—to get permission from Pilate for taking away the body (vv 31,38). The result is an apparent contradiction, an "obvious duplication . . . [for which] no simple solution is possible" (Brown, 956–57).

The solution indeed is not simple, for it would seem, as so often in John, to lie in the realm of theology and symbolism. The Jews regard "the bodies" crudely. They are interested only in breaking their legs and having them removed. They do not distinguish the body of Jesus. But Joseph does, and he is explicitly set apart from the Jews (he had been afraid of them). There is, in fact, a studied contrast between the crudeness of the Jews' request for the taking away of "the bodies" (even the syntax is twisted, 19:31) and the repetitive solemnity and decorum surrounding Joseph's discerning request for "the body of Jesus." It is a contrast which corresponds broadly to the Pauline distinction between those who do, and do not, discern the body of the Lord (1 Cor 11:27–29). In other words, the two pictures of a request to Pilate are not the result of confused history or poor editing, but come rather from a deliberate effort to depict two contrasting attitudes and two contrasting groups.

The basic effect of the appearance of Joseph is to suggest that where some perceive death and destruction, others, because they are disciples, perceive something positive—a body which, far from deserving to be battered crudely, is to be treated with reverence.

To some degree, the role of the Joseph reference is related to that of other brief introductions—particularly 3:22–24; 6:22–24, and 11:54–55. Like Aenon (3:23) and Ephraim (11:54), the location of Arimathea is unknown (cf. Brown, 938), and—whatever one makes of the similarity of sounds (Eph-ra-im, Jos-eph of Ar-im-athea)—the texts have rather similar purposes: they present the mind with a puzzle, and thereby they challenge it, before reading what follows, to rise to a higher level of perception. In 3:22–24 the presence of the disciples helped to indicate a higher, spiritual, level of communication. In 6:22–24 the enigmatic interaction of the disciples and the boats demanded that reality be seen in a way that is not materialistic. And in 11:54 (the text which paves the way for the idea of the dying seed which becomes fruitful, 12:24) the phrasing "desert, to Ephraim [fruitful]" evokes a process of life which is above the ordinary, which surprises. Thus through these earlier texts the way is prepared for Joseph of Arimathea and for challenging the mind both to look beyond what is dead and to enter a new level of perception and life.

[19:39–42] The burial.   Quite distinct from the action of taking away a body, is that of burying it. So it is here. It is only after the account of taking away the body has been closed—"So he came and took away his body"—that the text goes on to speak of the burial.

The distinctness of the burial is further underlined by the introduction of another character—Nicodemus. Unlike Joseph, Nicodemus is someone whom the reader has met before (3:1, 7:50), but since the previous references left unanswered the central question of how this leading Jew was going to decide, it is altogether appropriate, before the gospel closes, that he appear again. Joseph also assists at the burial, but his name is not given again, and it is Nicodemus who brings the burial-related mixture of myrrh and aloes, and who accordingly assumes a leading role in this episode. Nicodemus has made a choice. At a difficult moment he steps out of the shadows and receives the body. It is a gesture which suggests an acceptance of Jesus. His acceptance appears to be conditioned by the fact that he is still following Jewish custom yet, in some form at least, he has moved towards Jesus.

The burial is described in two stages, first the wrapping of the body in linen cloths with aromatic oils (vv 39–40), and then the placing of it in a tomb (vv 41–42). The first stage, even though it is lavish (100 pounds = 75 modern pounds), and thereby fit for a king (Brown, 960; Kysar, 294), is nonetheless carried out according to standardized Jewish custom. But the second stage suggests, literally, a breaking of new ground and a certain tension with the Jews.

The idea of new ground is indicated by the surprising information that, in a place previously characterized by a skull, a symbol of decay, "there was a garden," a place of growth. It is also indicated by the fact that within the garden there was something new—"a new tomb." The sense of newness is underlined by the emphasis on the fact that in this tomb "no one" had "ever" been laid. The combined effect of these images—the garden and the brand new tomb—is to suggest a place which, instead of being a dead end, is in some way a beginning.

But with this new beginning comes tension with the Jews. This is hinted at by the fact that the mention of the garden and tomb is followed by a reference to "the Preparation [Day] of the Jews." At first sight this reference seems vague and superfluous (cf. Brown, 943; Schnackenburg, 3:299). Yet it has its purpose. The emphasis on "the Jews" follows John's typical usage of that term (cf. Schnackenburg, ibid), and as such it suggests tension or hostility. This implication of tension is reinforced by the fact that in the preceding reference to the Preparation Day, following Jesus' death (19:31), "the Jews" were pictured as asking that the legs be broken—in other words, they were seen as harmful and hostile. Thus, in the first part of the burial—in embalming the body (vv 39–40)—Nicodemus is following standard Jewish procedure. But when it comes to the actual burial (vv 41–42), there are indications that, in a way which will cause problems with the Jews, something quite new is in the process of developing.

There is a connection between the scenes of inscription (19:19–22) and burial (19:39–42): both texts suggest that Jesus is king or has a kingdom/realm (Brown, 960). In the inscription scene the kingship of Jesus is explicit. In the burial scene it appears to be implied—in the lavishness of the spices, fit for a king, and perhaps in the fact that like some OT kings (cf. 2 Kgs 21:18,26; Neh 3:16, LXX), Jesus was buried in a garden.

Apart from this thematic link, the scenes of inscription and burial are linked also by structure. Both texts are subtly twofold: in one there is the move from apparent Jewish acceptance (19:19–20a) to Jewish rejection (19:20b–22); in the other there is a development from following a standardized Jewish custom (19:39–40) to breaking new ground even in the shadow of Jewish tension (19:41–42).

And there are links which are verbal.

19:41–42   "Pilate . . . placed . . . of the Jews, because the place was near . . . where Jesus was crucified."

19:41–42   "There was in the place where he was crucified . . . of the Jews, because the tomb was near, they placed Jesus."

If the word "near" has a theological overtone in the inscription account (see comment on 19:19–22) then it is also likely to have this overtone in the burial text—a suggestion, even when speaking of placing a body in a tomb, of being close to God. The essential point is that while Pilate's description had proclaimed openly to the world that Jesus was king (and thus that he was inaugurating the realm of God), the burial account, by subtle hints, indicates that in the body of Jesus the realm of God is very near.

[20:1–10] Running to the tomb and seeing the face veil which signifies ascension and unity.   In a narrative where the disciples had either disappeared or come to a standstill, the picture of Peter and of the beloved disciple as running represents a major development. Not that there was no preparation for this; the burial scene had shown some movement and had given intimations of growth and newness. And the Lazarus story, after a slow start (11:6), had shown increasing indications of hurrying (of coming "quickly," 11:29,31). But this is the first time in the gospel that anyone runs, and the repetitive account builds a striking picture of movement and energy.

The narrative is not simple. Complexity is caused, for instance, by its dramatic repetitiveness and by the fact that to some degree the characters are representative. Thus Mary Magdalene speaks in the plural (". . . and we do not know . . .") (cf. Bultmann, 681–82; Brown, 995).

This complexity need not mean that the passage is an ill-fitting mixture of disparate material. However multiple its sources, the present text has its own coherence.

The drama advances in three stages: first, Mary Magdalene's discovery and pessimism (vv 1–2); then, the run to the tomb and the inconclusive seeing of the wrappings (vv 3–5); and finally, the entry into the tomb and, following the seeing of the face veil, the believing (vv 6–10).

Each stage begins with the idea of coming:

"Mary *came*" (v 1);

"Peter *went out* [first] and . . . they *were coming*" (v 3);

"Peter *came* . . . following . . . and *went in*" (v 6).

The latter two sentences, concerning Peter, balance one another finely.

The first stage (vv 1–2), concerning Mary Magdalene, may seem initially to be very hopeful. She comes in darkness, she sees that the stone has been taken away, and when she runs—and she is the first person in the gospel to do so—she comes, surprisingly, to both Peter and the beloved disciple. It is a surprise because, when last seen, these two seemed far apart, one denying that he knew Jesus, the other standing by Jesus' cross. Now, following her running—in a certain sense even because of that running—they are in some way together. The text does not say that they were together at first; Mary comes *"to* Simon Peter *and to* the other . . ."—as though they had been apart. It is through her, apparently, that some of that apartness is resolved.

But when she speaks, all she can see is loss: "They have taken away the Lord . . . and we do not know where they have placed him." The fact that she uses the plural ("we do not know") adds a further dimension to her negativity—as though she represented others. The discussion with Nicodemus, for instance, involved the use of "we know" (3:2, 11), and it did so because it reflected a larger discussion with Judaism. In the case of Mary Magdalene also it will have to be asked later (in discussing vv 11–20) whether or in what way she is representative. What is certain for the moment is that, despite her pessimistic conclusion, she has set something greater than herself in motion.

The run to the tomb (vv 3–5) has linguistic echoes of the preceding coming and running of Mary, but it is more intense. Peter apparently starts first, then they are together, and then the other disciple pulls ahead, running "faster." The whole scene, the "faster," suggests immense vitality. There seems to be nothing quite like it elsewhere in the Bible—except perhaps the dread running of the two men who brought to David the news of the beloved Absalom (2 Sam 18:19–32). Such a background, however, serves, if anything, as a distant foil.

The fact that the beloved runs faster does not indicate that he is younger; it simply means that he is, literally, in better running order. But in a gospel where discipleship is connected with images of "following" (1:37–38), of physical movement, being in better running condition is of considerable significance; it indicates that what is ultimately in better condition is the essence of his discipleship.

At one level, of course, Peter is first. In all three stages it is he, rather than the beloved, who is first mentioned. Yet at the significant level of running, of coming to the tomb, the beloved is "first" (v 4), and Peter is "following him" (v 6). The distance between the two is reflected even in the separateness of their names (vv 2, 3).

When the beloved arrives at the tomb and, bending down, looks in, what he sees are the pieces of cloth in which Jesus had been wrapped: "he saw the linen cloths lying there." The sight seems inconclusive. His seeing (*blepei*) appears to reflect the earlier limited seeing of Mary (*blepei,* v 1). And the significance of the wrappings is unclear. In any case, all he has is a partial view. "Yet he did not go in."

Then, in stage three (vv 6–10), it is clear that Peter is simultaneously follower and leader. He "follows" the beloved, yet he leads the way into the tomb. Again, within the tomb, he becomes the follower: it is he who first sees that, apart from the wrappings, there is the face veil; but it is the other disciple who first believes. And at this point, recalling the running, the "first" is explicit.

Thus in all three stages Peter's name is given first, yet on three occasions, and increasingly as the text progresses, it is the beloved who is spoken of as first— once in stage two (v 4, "first") and twice in stage three (vv 6, 8; "following him," "first").

When Peter first entered the tomb it was not only his body which was churning. His mind also was racing. As Brown (985) notes, the evangelist supposes that by now there was enough daylight to see within the burial chamber. But tombs suggest death, and unlike the beloved who stood by the cross, death was something with which Peter had had problems. He had either approached it glibly ("I will lay down, . . ." 13:37) or had run from it (in violence and denials; 18:10–11,15–27). Now, as never before, he enters death's place; he faces it.

What is he to make of it? As well as the wrappings, there is the face veil (*soudarion,* literally a cloth for wiping *sudor,* perspiration). It is not a trivial detail; in being distinguished from the general wrappings (*ta othonia;* cf. Brown, 941–42) it receives a whole verse of description: it had been "on his head"; and now it was not just lying there; rather it was "apart, wrapped up into one place." What has happened? Mary had implied that the body had been stolen. Do thieves tidy up? Peter apparently is trying to understand, but aspects of darkness and death still block his vision, and all he sees are pieces of cloth.

When the beloved then enters and, on seeing, believes, it is not because the tomb is otherwise, but because he is otherwise disposed (Schneiders, 1983). His closeness to Jesus, both at the supper and on the cross (13:23–25, 18:26–27), has given him a better sense of reality, particularly concerning love and death. Thus the clothes, especially the face veil, function like a Johannine sign; in themselves they are ambiguous, but for one who had a developed disposition they open the way to faith (cf. Schneiders, 1983, 95–96).

The significance of the cloths seems to be twofold. First, they show that Jesus has left behind the limitations of this world and has gone to God; he has *ascended.* In Schnackenburg's words (3:311), "He has left behind those wrappings used for the body, because he has risen and lives, because he has obtained a new, unearthly-heavenly existence." More specifically, the face veil appears to reflect the veil which Moses wore over his face but which he laid aside when he spoke to God (Exod 34:33–35). "Like Moses, who put aside the veil when he ascended to meet God in glory, Jesus, the new Moses has put aside the veil of his flesh as he ascends into the presence of God" (Schneiders, 1983, 96).

The further significance of the cloths, apart from ascension, is that they suggest *unity.* The idea of unity is found not only in the text—in the association of the veil with the "head" (symbol of unity in Eph 1:22, 4:15–16, 5:23) and in its being rolled "into one place"—but also in the context, in the similarity between *the "wrappings" and veil* as found in this scene, and *the clothes and undivided tunic* as found in the crucifixion scene (19:23–24). One is a variation on the other.

In particular, the face veil which is rolled into one place is a variation on the theme of the undivided tunic.

These two meanings—ascension and unity—are not placed together arbitrarily. Rather, they are connected inherently. As indicated elsewhere (chap. 17, Eph 4:1–16) it is Jesus' ascension, and the ascension's consequent raising of all humans, which brings humans into unity. The process is illustrated in prayer: the heartfelt repetition, for instance, of the simple words "Our Father" has the effect not only of raising the heart and mind to God, but also of dispelling divisive resentment—the effect, in other words, of bringing the praying person(s) to unity. The ascent is not physical; it is in the realm of the spirit and it is within that realm that it brings unity.

In the scene at the tomb the ascension is not presented as fully accomplished; it is merely intimated, like something which is underway. Yet already it has an effect: the very next sentence—which deals with not knowing the scripture and which "is intended to emphasize the faith of the other disciple" (Schnackenburg, 3:312–13)—is stated, not in the singular, but in the plural, as though it included Peter. In other words, the breakthrough in faith, the breakthrough into the reality of ascension and union, though achieved in the beloved disciple, is immediately reflected in Peter. The faith of one has become that of the other. Unity is already taking hold. In the preceding text there had been between Peter and the beloved disciple a tense mixture of distance and interdependence. At one point as they were running they had been described as being "together" (v 4). But only now does unity really begin to emerge.

Finally (v 10) the disciples "went back again to their home" (literally, "to themselves," *pros antous*). The phrase is a variation on 19:27:

19:27 ". . . the disciple took her to his own [home]";
20:10 ". . . the disciples went back again to their [homes]."

Somewhat as 19:27 indicates a coming together of distinct people or aspects, so does 20:10. As they go away they are no longer "Simon Peter" and "the other disciple." Rather, for the first time in the passage, they are both described simply as "the disciples." And in the Greek text it is that unifying description which is the last word.

The Two Disciples as Representative

The suggestion that Peter and the other disciple are in some way symbolic (cf. esp. Loisy, 500; Bultmann, 685) has sometimes been strongly rejected (cf. esp. Lindars, 602; Brown, 1006). This rejection is understandable insofar as the suggested symbolism often appears questionable—the idea, for instance, that "Peter and the beloved disciple are the representatives [respectively] of Jewish and Gentile Christianity" (Bultmann, 685). The figures of Peter and the beloved simply do not correspond accurately to Jewish and Gentile Christianity. In various ways Peter is related to the whole church, and so is the beloved disciple.

Yet, that the two figures are in some way representative seems plausible. The scene as a whole has considerable affinity to the crucifixion scenes which involve the clothing (19:23–24) and the figures by the cross (19:23–27), and these scenes are in various ways symbolic, representative. The problem is, what is the symbolism?

The relationship between the two may, perhaps, be connected to the earlier picture of the relationship between Peter and the two earliest disciples (1:35–42). At that stage it was indicated that the two brief portraits, first of the anonymous disciples (1:35–39) and then of the conspicuously named Peter (1:40–42), represented two faces of the church, the contemplative and the official. Despite the distinction, however, they formed a unity. In the race to the tomb something similar seems to be present—except that now the tension between the two is more evident. Yet, in the end, the result is the same: tension notwithstanding, it is possible—through shared faith in the ascending Christ—to be in unity.

[20:11–18] At the tomb: Mary's belated recognition of Jesus. Thus far Mary Magdalene has appeared in two scenes in the gospel—standing by the cross (19:25) and running from the tomb (20:1–2)—but on both occasions, as the action developed, she was left behind. Now, however, she remains on center stage throughout.

This passage is sometimes seen as reflecting editorial confusion—particularly because it is not clear how Mary came back to the tomb, and also because she seems to turn twice to Jesus (e.g., cf. Lindars, 603; Brown, 995).

But it is not necessary to explain how Mary came to be at the tomb—anymore than it was necessary to explain how the women came to be standing by the cross (19:25–27). In fact, these two scenes—of those who "stood by the cross" and of Mary who "stood at the tomb"—are in careful coordination with one another.

And the fact that Mary turns twice, though initially perplexing, falls into the pattern of her spiritual progression.

The scene may be described as one of recognition, and as such it has some affinity with the Greco-Roman recognition scenes which tell of gods being recognized as they move among humans (cf. Brown, 1009). But it has a far greater affinity with the scene of slow recognition on the way to Emmaus (Luke 24:13–35; cf. Bultmann, 686; Brown, 1009).

The action has three stages—the sighting of the two angels (11–13), the sighting of Jesus (14–15), and the recognition of Jesus (16–18). The stages are divided from one another by the variations in the process of seeing and also by several details of repetition (cf. esp. ". . . stood . . . turned . . . turning"; "where they have laid him . . . where you have laid him").

In stage one (vv 11–13), when Mary bends down into the tomb and sees two angels who make no impression on her, it may seem surprising and even blatantly inconsistent that she does not see what the beloved disciple had first seen—the linen cloths lying there.

An important part of the answer to this puzzle seems to lie in the fact that the resurrection is being pictured not as a single explosive event, but as a gradual progression in which each stage is soon replaced by a stage which is more developed. "The Lord's return to the Father, although . . . it occurred at the moment . . . of His death, is nonetheless also a process, even after His resurrection; nor is His union with His followers at once complete" (Lightfoot, 331). What is being described, therefore, is not just life, but life in process. An initial intimation of life was provided by the surprising reference to the garden. Then came the news of the removal of the stone, followed by the progressive references to the clothing, clothing which indicates that Jesus is ascending. And from this suggestion of a new heavenly existence, the progression moves to the picture of the two angels in white. These positions, sitting one at the *head* and the other at the *feet,* involve a variation on the twofold description of the clothing (the *cloths lying,* the *head cloth* apart) and they are explicitly linked with the body of Jesus: "sitting . . . where the body of Jesus had lain." Thus the idea of a new existence, previously suggested by the clothing, is now seen more clearly in the angels. As angels they reflect heaven, and white means victory, especially victory over death (Rev 7:9–10).

However, unlike the effect of the clothing on the beloved disciple, the angels make no impression on Mary. She is not seeing correctly. This will be evident in the next stage when she looks at Jesus and thinks he is the gardener, but even now her mind is not clear. Unlike the beloved disciple, whose state of mind is indicated by the fact that he had just been running and, apparently, running hopefully, she, when the time came for looking in, was far from running; instead she is described as *standing, outside, crying.* Each word is significant. Faced with the tomb her heart and mind have come to a halt. The result is that she is "outside," a word which within the context of the goings-in and goings-out of chaps. 18–20 indicates being outside the revelation, outside the sense of divine life. And the final consequence is that she is crying.

This does not mean grief is bad. Jesus cried. But, like the gradual process of transition from death to resurrection, the grief has a capacity to develop, to progress. Mary, however, seems embedded in her tears. Even at the moment of bending down she is described as crying. "Woman," say the angels in white, as they sit where Jesus had lain, "why are you crying?" But this extraordinary sight makes no impression on her, nor does she perceive the compassion which speaks to her. "They have taken away my Lord, and I do not know. . . ." The world has become a void, and its people have been divided into an impersonal hostile "they" and a lonely-sounding "I do not know. . . ."

And with that "she turned backwards . . ." (stage two, vv 14–15). The expression "backwards" (*eis ta opisō*) as used previously in John indicates a form of flight from the divine and from faith; it was used of those who rejected the bread-of-life discourse (6:66) and of the hostile arresting force which shrank before the divine "I am" (18:6). Both of these divine pronouncements, in chaps. 6 and 18, involved a readiness to accept death. Mary, however, cannot do it; far from making progress, she regresses.

When she turns she sees Jesus, the first person to do so since his burial. He is "standing" (*estōta*)—a description which, apart from possibly suggesting progress on his own part (he had previously been referred to as *lying,* and the angels as *sitting;* v 12)—places him in a certain solidarity with Mary as she had stood at the tomb (v 11).

His inquiry about why she is crying repeats exactly the words of the angels; but, with much irony, it adds a development: "Whom do you seek?"

She does not even hear it. Rather, like the man at the poolside (5:5–6), she cannot give a straight answer about what or whom she wants. With further irony she regards Jesus as the gardener, to be addressed as "Sir" (*kyrie*), and her reply, instead of being more developed, is less. She no longer says that she is looking for "my Lord" (*kyrion*); now she simply refers, rather confusedly to "him . . . him . . . him". And she sees the "him" as passive and dead: "If you have carried [*bastazō*] him [away]. . . ." But there is yet more irony here: *bastazō* was the verb used to describe Jesus as "carrying his own cross" and as thus expressing, even in face of death, his sovereign freedom.

Stage three (vv 16–18) brings a reversal. "Jesus said to her 'Mary' . . .", and she "turned." But this time there is no "backwards," and her address of recognition, "Rabbouni" ("Teacher") shows that she is emerging from her grief.

However, as the repetition of "Jesus said to her" helps to indicate (v 17), she has a further step to take. Jesus' words to her ("Touch me no more, for I have not yet ascended . . .") are an invitation to an intimacy which is not physical, but spiritual, an invitation which relates to Jesus as ascended, as united with God. And for the moment that process of ascension is still underway (Hoskyns, 543; Lightfoot, 331).

Then he continues, "But go to my brothers and say to them, 'I am ascending to my Father and to your Father . . . ' " This again is the language of union and intimacy. Jesus is already ascending to union, and he comes to the Father not in isolation, but as one of many brothers.

Thus the themes of the preceding scene (20:1–10)—the combined ideas of ascension and unity—now emerge once more. But at this point they are more explicit, and, furthermore, they are accompanied by a clearer sense of mission.

The final verse (v 18) is a picture of Mary fulfilling her mission. She has now reached a new level, one in which she sees Jesus not as Teacher, but as Lord, and, as at the end of the preceding scene, the final emphasis is on the simple shared term "disciples"—people who have learned of God. Thus the sense of sharing the faith, implied in the earlier scene (vv 8–10), here becomes more explicit.

The closing phrase is somewhat surprising—literally, "I have seen the Lord and *these things he said to her.*" There is a double transition here, first from the specific "I have seen the Lord" to the very general and far-reaching idea of "these things," and second, from direct speech to indirect. This need not mean that the final phrase is an editorial addition. Part of the explanation for these transitions seems to lie in the fact that they reflect a fading-out technique—as when the camera at the end of a scene on film sometimes pulls back and allows a significant figure to fade into a larger, more distant, setting. Besides, the use of "these things" (*tauta*) is not an isolated phenomenon. It coincides with the larger pattern, found in all three of the gospel's concluding texts (cf. 19:36, 20:31,

21:24), of using "these things" in a concluding role. Thus this picture, of Mary announcing, fits into the broader picture of the announcing activity of the gospel. In fact, when Mary's final emphasis on witness ("I have seen," *heōraka*) is taken in conjunction with the preceding scene's final emphasis on scripture (v 9, "as yet they did not know the scripture"), one finds a variation on the witness-plus-scripture combination which is found in the gospel's more formal conclusions (19:35–37; 20:29–31; 21:24–25). This not only confirms that the announcing activity of Mary is integral to that of the gospel, it also shows that the believing process of Peter and the beloved, which was first set in motion by Mary, also finds its completion in her.

Mary as Representative

At one level this scene at the tomb is a portrayal of one person's grief and of the way in which, despite a regression, an increasing awareness of the Lord enabled her to find new life.

But Mary appears also to be a representative figure. Left behind at crucial moments in the building of the faith of the community (at the cross, 19:25–27; in running to the tomb and entering it, 20:1–10), she corresponds significantly to unbelieving Israel. Other factors strengthen this impression. The picture of her as unable to recognize Jesus, apart from being suited to a recognition scene, corresponds also to the picture of Israel as temporarily blind (cf. Rom 11:25), as veiled in mind (2 Cor 3:12–18). When Mary is called by her name and then turns to Jesus, she resembles considerably the picture of blinded Israel who is still loved and who eventually receives mercy (Rom 11:28–31). When she turns, she speaks first in Hebrew. Those to whom she is sent are called "brothers"—the term Paul uses of the Jews (Rom 9:3). And the person whom in her grief she most resembles, Mary the sister of Lazarus, was also particularly associated with the Jews (11:31,33).

Whatever the details, it seems a reasonable conclusion that Mary represents one aspect of the unbelieving Jews and that her mission to the brothers represents a mission to the Jews. Until she speaks to the brothers, the faith process which began in Peter and the beloved will not be complete. The fact that the term "brothers" gives way to "disciples" (20:17–18) evokes the idea that her mission is to be successful, that the brothers will become disciples.

Ascension and Unity (Final Stages) (20:19–31)

[20:19–23] The disciples' fear—The coming of Jesus and the granting of the Spirit. In contrast to the initial episodes, from Joseph of Arimathea to Mary Magdalene (19:38–20:18), the episodes concerning the disciples and Thomas lay the emphasis not on human initiative, but on divine. In these passages it is Jesus, and Jesus alone, who is described as coming (vv 19, 26).

It is appropriate, therefore, that the initial coming of Jesus take place "on that day'' (v 19)—a phrase which, partly because it echoes earlier phrases in John (7:37; 16:23,26), has an eschatological ring (cf. Brown, 1019).

This eschatological note reflects a major change in the development of the narrative. Within the preceding episodes (19:38–20:18) Jesus went through a progression—from simply being a body, to passing apparently through the open entrance to the tomb, to being about to ascend. And within these later episodes (20:19–29) there is a further progression—from *perhaps* being able to come through closed doors (v 19—the text is ambiguous) to clearly being able to do so (v 26; cf. Brown, 1020). Thus there are many changes, but the change which is major, and which is accompanied by the introduction of this eschatological note, occurs between the meeting with Mary and the coming to the disciples. With Mary, Jesus is still on the way to the Father, but with the disciples he has already been to the Father—has already ascended—and now he returns as Lord. Mary had indeed seen him as Lord, but only at the very end (v 18). For the disciples, however, the perception of Jesus as Lord is the starting point (vv 19–20).

Thus in 19:38–20:28 as a whole there is both a single progression (in the status of Jesus) and two panels, one of human initiative, one of divine.

The scene with the disciples falls into two sections or stages. First Jesus comes and reveals (''shows'') himself to them as the crucified Lord (vv 19–20). And then he commissions them, granting them (''breathed on them'') the salvation-bearing Holy Spirit (vv 21–23). The distinction between the two stages is marked by several elements of repetition or duplication (cf. Brown, 1029).

In stage one (vv 19–20) the disciples go through a fundamental transition. At first they seem to be overcome by the evil and darkness of the world and of death. Such is the implication of the ''evening'' and of the fact that they are behind closed doors for fear of ''the Jews.'' But then, at a time which both suggests an eschatological event ''on that day'' and which recalls the resurrection (''the first of the week''), Jesus comes, stands in their midst, wishes them ''Peace,'' and shows them his hands and side. This is like a capsule-form incarnation story. In their place of darkness he has come to bring light. ''Peace'' means wholeness, the bringing into harmony of what is scattered and broken. And in Jesus that harmony is seen: when he shows them his hands and side there is an implication that they see in him both divine life and human wounds. The wounds have their cruel side; they reflect the weight of sin, particularly as experienced in the corruption of the system of justice and the de facto brutality of the world's leading defense force. Yet they place suffering in a greater context, that of a glorified body, that of a larger God-centered unity. Wounds remain, but within this greater light they are absorbed and transformed. The disciples, seeing this in him, rejoiced.

In stage two (vv 21–23) the sense of peace and of unity with the divine is the starting point, and Jesus goes on to speak of something further—active participation in the divine mission: ''As the Father has sent me, so I send you.'' The process of incarnation is to continue. The primary reference here is not to church activity or office, but to human existence. In other words, as is suggested by the use of ''send'' with regard to the blind man (9:7), the primary mission is that of entering the world as a human being and living an integrated life. In the course of such a life, the degree of involvement in specifically church-related activities will vary greatly from individual to individual.

However, whether one's work consists of driving a bus or preaching, an integrated life requires the Spirit. And so, just as Jesus' initial greeting of peace had been accompanied ("and saying this") by a revelation (wounds within glory) which made the peace possible (v 20), so now this mission is accompanied ("and saying this") by a gift which makes it too possible: he breathed on them and said "Receive the Holy Spirit." The breathing, reminiscent of the creation scene in which God breathed life into humanity (Gen 2:7), represents the giving to them of all that is alive within him. (Nothing is more basic to life and love than breath.) And what is alive within him now is not simply a physical breath, but the breath, the life, of one who has ascended to union with the Father. They no longer have to depend on their first creation, on the limited life and gifts that they were given through natural birth and upbringing. He is opening to them a further sphere, a divine Spirit which offers them a new sense of life, what might be called a new birth or a new creation.

A central factor in this new life is the forgiveness of sins (v 23). Like the removal of blindness, as narrated in chapter 9, the removal of sin opens the way to salvation. The fact that Jesus passes through closed doors dramatizes his role as opening the way, as breaking through sinful barriers. It is this sin-removing salvation which Jesus brought into the world and which the disciples are to carry further. And they are to do it with confidence, sure of their union through Jesus with God: "Whose sins you forgive, they are forgiven them." In view of the fact that so many people are weighed down with guilt, this gives to Jesus' disciples an extraordinarily positive task. This does not mean that the disciples are always accommodating. As long as there are Stalins and Hitlers in the world, of whatever color or creed, public or private, it is the task of the disciples, precisely because the holiness of the Spirit gives them a sensitivity to evil, to say and to insist that sin is sin, evil is evil: ". . . whose sins you retain, they are retained."

The social nature of forgiveness is to be seen not only in the context of related sayings in the other gospels (cf. esp. Jesus' words to Peter, Matt 16:19), but first of all in the context of the rest of John 20. In the opening episodes—the run to the tomb and the appearance to Mary—faith is something which is shared. The faith of the beloved is shared in some way by Peter (20:8–10), and the faith of Mary is shared with the brothers (20:17–18). In other words, to a significant degree one receives faith through others.

Likewise forgiveness. This is seen not only in "whose sins you forgive . . ." (20:23), but also in the subsequent Thomas episode. Thomas will find forgiveness (for his sinful disbelief) not in the presence of an isolated Jesus, but in a situation which emphasizes both the role of the other disciples and particularly the role of the body (20:26–28). At one level the body refers to the risen body which includes the community.

Overall, therefore, the journey to integration—particularly through faith and forgiveness—is not achieved alone; it involves community.

[20:24–29] Thomas's doubt: The coming of Jesus and Thomas's climactic confession of faith. This passage imitates the disciples episode (vv 19–23) not only by being twofold, but also in many of its phrases and images, particularly those concerning Jesus' body and the manner of his coming (compare vv 25–26 with vv 19–20; cf. Lindars, 613; Brown, 1033; Schnackenburg, 3:328).

Such obvious similarities, however, need not mean that the text is an afterthought. On the contrary, the passage is not only an integral part of the resurrection narrative, it is, in many ways, its culmination, its high point both of Christology and faith. Here, for the first time, it is clear that Jesus' ascension to the divine state is complete: he comes through doors which are unambiguously closed; he knows thoughts; and he is called "God."

As for the obvious similarities with the preceding disciples episode, they achieve a basic purpose: they establish that the two texts are in clear continuity. This is important. The disciples episode, insofar as it implied a new creation, the setting up of a new covenant, was foundational. The Thomas episode, on the other hand, insofar as it deals with someone who "was not with them," someone who encountered the Lord later, on the following Sunday ("after eight days"), represents something of the emergence and experience of the future church (Schnackenburg, 3:331–32; cf. Beasley-Murray, 385). It was important that the two scenes not be drastically diverse, that one follow from the other. The essential continuity is summarized by Schneiders (1975, 640): "In the disciples episode [Jesus] . . . fulfills the prophetic description of the New Covenant by communicating the Spirit. In the Thomas episode [he] . . . incorporates into the New Covenant all those who were not present at its inauguration."

The actual story of Thomas reflects one of the central dangers facing the new church. As in the case of Mary Magdalene, it is a story which is at once individual and collective. Like Mary, Thomas stands out. "Despite the brevity of the pericopes which treat them, each emerges as a strong, integrated, and unique religious personality. Their respective femininity and masculinity color their pericopes as do their respective temperaments" (Schneiders, 1975, 643). Mary gave way to sadness, Thomas to doubt. Essentially both lost faith. But then Mary "turned" (v 16), and Thomas also, in his own way, underwent a "turnabout" (Schnackenburg, 3:332).

In earlier references (in connection with the death of Lazarus, 11:14–16, and the impending departure of Jesus, 14:5), Thomas expressed a mixture of fidelity and doubt, particularly doubt about death—doubt about Jesus' ability to overcome it (he presumes they will all simply die), and doubt about where Jesus himself, after his death, will go.

Now he wants proof. His demand is reminiscent of the attitude of the royal official (4:48, "Unless you see signs and wonders . . ."). More ominously, he is introduced as "one of the twelve," a phrase previously used for only one purpose—to introduce the treachery of Judas (6:71). This association with Judas is heightened by the fact that at the conclusion of chapter 6 there are two negative pictures—those who went "backwards" (6:66) and Judas "one of the twelve" (6:71). Given that Mary had already turned "backwards" (20:14), the mention of "one of the twelve" heightens the suggestion that Thomas may yet imitate Judas.

His demand is set out in a repetitive triple progression: "Unless I see . . . and put [literally, 'throw,' *ballō*] my finger . . . and put my hand. . . ." Jesus, when he comes into the midst, gives a further triple progression, one which absorbs that of Thomas and surpasses it: "Bring your finger here and see . . . and bring your hand and put . . . and do not be unbelieving but. . . ." The effect (somewhat like that of the repetitive discussion in 16:16–19 about "the short while") is to show both that Jesus knows all the pedantic details of Thomas's arguments and that he is calling him to a reality which surpasses them. Combined with the fact that Jesus entered while the doors were closed, it presents Thomas with a realm which is beyond normal human limitations, a realm which is divine.

When Thomas says "My Lord and my God" his words have the effect of reflecting both some of the OT references to God (cf. esp. Ps 35:23, "My God and my Lord") and also apparently some of the pretentious imperial titles (Brown, 1047; Kysar, 307). In Barrett's words (573), "as frequently, John's language is . . . both biblical and Hellenistic." Thus the allegiance that might have been falsely claimed by an emperor is given to Jesus as the true incarnate God.

However, while granting this relationship to the OT and also apparently to imperial titles, the primary context for Thomas's profession is the gospel itself. In the words of Schnackenburg (3:333), this confession "takes its place in a whole series of confessions in John's gospel (1:49, 4:42, 6:69, 9:37f, 11:27, 16:30, 20:16) and forms their conclusion and climax."

There has been considerable discussion of whether Thomas actually touched Jesus, actually put his hand into his side (cf. Schnackenburg, 3:332). Both sides of the argument highlight an important truth: on the one hand, close contact is indeed prepared for, elaborately; on the other hand, it is not reported, at all. The text never says that Thomas actually put his hand into Jesus' side. Instead there is a declaration of faith. What the text apparently has done is set something up and then transform it: the notion of close physical contact is not forgotten; rather, it is transformed into a contact which is spiritual, the contact of faith. A somewhat similar transformation was found in the 4:1–42: as a betrothal scene it prepared the way for physical union, but what it delivered was a union which was spiritual. And in Mary Magdalene's case also, the momentum towards physical union gave way to the spiritual. By believing as he does, Thomas rises above the physical and joins himself spiritually to the body of Christ.

As well as being a vivid story of an individual, the Thomas episode is a reflection of the dangers facing the emerging church. Placed as it is in tandem with the story of Mary and with Mary's evoking of the lapse of the Jews, it indicates that the same fate could befall Christians.

Jesus' reply to Thomas (v 29) is a solemn pronouncement of blessing on "those who have not seen and yet believe." As such it has a special relevance for later Christians and also for readers of the gospel. Consequently, it leads naturally to what follows—the statement on why the gospel was written.

[20:30–31] The writing and its purpose. Like Jesus' pronouncement to Thomas (v 29), the statement on why the gospel was written is an invitation to faith. In fact, of the two invitations, the purpose-statement, despite some textual uncertainty, is much clearer (vv 30–31, ". . . that you may believe . . ."). The uncertainty concerns the tense (aorist or present?) of the word "believe," but whatever the original, there is growing agreement among researchers that the purpose is to deepen the faith of those who in some way already believe (cf. Schnackenburg, 3:338; Beasley-Murray, 387). Thus in their own way the two calls to believing (in v 29 and in 31) form a graded unity. As Minear (1983, 87) concludes, "These verses [30–31] are . . . very closely linked to verse 29."

The purpose of writing is not only "that you may believe" but that the believing should be rich in content ("that Jesus is the Anointed, the Son of God") and that through this richness of believing "you may have life in his name." The implication is of opening oneself to the dignity and divinity which was first found in Jesus. Thus while Jesus' words to Thomas pronounced those who believe to be blessed or fortunate (*makarios,* "blessed/happy"), the statement on the purpose of writing spells out some of the meaning of that blessedness.

The Role of vv 30–31 in Concluding the Gospel

The statement on the purpose of writing is frequently seen as constituting the gospel's conclusion. It does, in fact, help to conclude it, but that does not make it *the* conclusion. Such an idea is based largely on the perception that 20:30–31 stands apart from 20:1–29 (see esp. Brown, 1053; Kysar, 309), and on the impression that, placed in that detached vantage point, it has a better claim than any other text to being the gospel's true conclusion.

But 20:30–31 does not stand apart from all that precedes; it is linked to 20:29 and, in a special way, particularly because of its emphasis on signs, to all of chapter 20 (cf. Minear, 1983, 87–89).

Furthermore, when 20:30–31 is taken in conjunction with v 29, it forms part of a larger pattern consisting of 19:35–37, 20:30–31, and 21:24–25. Each of these texts has a double role—to conclude the passage which immediately precedes and to conclude the gospel as a whole. Each of the three speaks in some way of both witnessing (or seeing) and writing, but they vary in emphasis. For the first (19:35–37), the emphasis is on witness; for the second (20:30–31), it is on writing; and in the third (21:24–25), there is a culminating double emphasis— first on witnessing and then on writing.

One of the reasons why 20:30–31 has tended to monopolize the role of conclusion is precisely the fact that it is here rather than elsewhere that one finds an exclusive emphasis on the process of writing the gospel, and, when one is dealing with a book, the summarizing of the process of writing seems to summarize the book, to conclude it.

But the evangelist wants to emphasize that the book, however worthy in itself, rests on more than writing. Underlying it is witness (19:35), and—regardless of what one decides about whether, historically speaking, the beloved disciple had already died—there is a further process of witnessing which goes on (21:24). For the witness is not that of the beloved disciple alone; it is also that of the accompanying Spirit (cf. comment on 19:35; Culpepper, 1983, 123). In other words, the gospel is not just a literary production; it is founded ultimately on the Spirit who bears witness, and it is to be accompanied by that Spirit. It is necessary, therefore, that the conclusion set the writing within the context of the witnessing. That is what the gospel does: by giving a three-part conclusion, it sets the writing within the larger process of witnessing.

In 20:31 the unexpected address in the second person (". . . that you may believe . . .") constitutes a feature which, in a significant number of literary compositions, indicates a conclusion (Uspensky, 1973, 147). But the same feature is found in 19:35 (". . . that you also may believe"). And a further conclusion-indicating feature—the unexpected introduction of a first person narrator—is found in 21:25 (Uspensky, ibid). The sense of an ending, therefore, is spread over all three texts.

The Culmination of the Gospel

Under a Caring Providence the Church
Works in the Marketplace

Objections to the Originality of Chapter 21

Chapter 21 is distinctive and has something of the character of an epilogue. In fact, despite some dissenting voices (e.g., Lagrange, 520–21; Hoskyns, 550; Smalley, 1974, 275–88, Minear, 1983, 85–98), it is usually regarded as an addition or appendix, something which did not belong to the original plan of the gospel (e.g., cf. Westcott, 299; Bernard, 685, 687; Bultmann, 700–706; Dodd, 1953, 290; Barrett, 576–77; Lindars, 618–19; Brown, 1078–80; Schnackenburg, 3:341–44; Becker, 634–35). For this view, the following reasons are proposed:

1. In 20:30–31 there is a conclusion to the gospel. Consequently, anything which follows it is secondary, added.

2. Chapter 20 pronounces a climactic blessing on those who have not seen (20:29). The author who did that is unlikely to have then gone on to tell of those who did see.

3. The sequence between chaps. 20 (in Jerusalem) and 21 (in Galilee) is awkward. In particular, it is unlikely that the disciples would go from the climactic experience of seeing Jesus and receiving a Spirit-filled commission to the prosaic business of fishing.

4. Chapter 21 has an extraordinary diversity of elements and consequently is sometimes seen as lacking unity. Such diversity may seem to suggest a different author: "This noteworthy interweaving of different threads is not otherwise the evangelist's way" (Schnackenburg, 3:342).

These reasons, however, have severe limitations—briefly,

1. The final verses of chap. 20 (20:30–31) do help to conclude the gospel, but on their own they do not constitute the gospel's conclusion. Rather, they are part of a larger pattern consisting of 19:35–37, 20:30–31, and 21:24–25 and, as the comments on these three texts indicate, it is in the larger pattern, rather than in a single text, that the gospel's conclusion is to be found. (This is the possibility broached by Kysar [309] when he speaks of "the larger conclusion.") The essence of the larger pattern is that it is concerned not only with the gospel's destination (the purpose of writing, 20:30–31) but also with its origin (the reliability of

the underlying witness, 19:35). Both elements are necessary, and they are synthesized in the final verses (21:24–25).

2. Chapter 21, though it does indeed tell of Jesus' close interaction with the disciples, never says that they saw him. Verbs of seeing are absent. In dealing with him, they hear and know and speak; and they see each other, but not Jesus. This complete absence of verbs of seeing indicates that even though at one level he is visible, and they are dealing with him in a real-life situation, at another level he is not. Chapter 21, therefore, is not a contradiction of the not-seeing motif in 20:29. On the contrary, precisely by avoiding verbs of seeing it fulfills it; it tells of a time when interaction with Jesus will occur at another level.

3. The sequence between chaps. 20 and 21 is indeed surprising, but that does not mean that the surprising element was a later addition. To call the transition "awkward" tends to prejudge the issue. Much depends on how one regards the fishing. Obviously if it is seen as aimless, or as a return to an earlier stage of life, then it does go against the forward-looking implications of chap. 20. But within John's gospel it does not constitute a return or regression. Since the disciples had never before been spoken of as fishermen, it represents rather some form of advance. And it is far from aimless; it involves the crucial business of providing food, and it acquires overtones of a far-reaching ministry.

   A significantly similar sequence occurs between chapters 5 and 6, between discussing faith in Jerusalem and embarking on a broad new stage in Galilee. There is also some similarity with the sequence between chapters 9 and 10: a climactic statement of individual faith (by the formerly blind man, cf. Thomas) is followed by a picture of community (the flock and the shepherd; cf. Peter, the boat, and the flock). Thus the transition between chaps. 20 and 21 synthesizes other significant transitions (chaps. 5 and 6 are the culminating chapters of Part 2 of the gospel, and chaps. 9 and 10 are at the gospel's center).

4. Schnackenburg (3:342) is correct in noting that chap. 21 involves a unique "interweaving of different threads." But again that does not mean that the chapter is an addition. On the contrary, it shows that it serves admirably as an appropriate conclusion, as a culmination which synthesizes the gospel's many strands. In T. S. Eliot's *Four Quartets,* for example, "the last lines of the last Quartet take up themes from all the preceding ones, thus linking the four together" (Bodelsen, 32). Something similar was found in chap. 6: as the concluding and culminating chapter of the gospel's second part, it wove together, in a way that was new, a wide diversity of threads from the chapters which preceded. The same phenomenon occurs in chap. 21, but in a more intense form.

Towards Restoring Chapter 21 to Its Full Role

The thesis here is that chap. 21, far from being secondary, is central to the gospel. It is secondary only in the sense that, within a marriage, daily companionship is secondary to the wedding. For the marriage is measured not by the wedding's possible sparkle and fireworks but by the gentler flame of daily life.

Chapter 21 is daily life; it is the Word made flesh to the full. It shows the disciples, reborn through the divine Spirit, as embarking on a sea expedition which evokes both ordinary work and the larger mystery which surrounds such work. This chapter highlights crucial details—such as having a bite to eat—yet it also suggests a broad new horizon which, like a new shore, calls one to break free of constriction (especially sins of the past, fear of the future, and communal narrowness). The shore means a new awareness, especially of universalism and of a mind-surpassing love.

The importance of chap. 21 is emphasized by the fact that its dramatic effect is somewhat similar to that of one of the most famous episodes in Greek literature: Xenophon's account of how the Greek expedition to Persia, having journeyed through many difficulties, finally arrived at its source of security and freedom— the sea (Xenophon, *Anabasis,* Bk. 4, esp. chaps. 7–8). There, too, there was initial confusion, a cry of recognition, a rush forward, a reunion near the sea, and a great reminder or symbol of the larger experience. But in John these elements are more domesticated, closer to daily life. The deeper drama is not on the battlefield but in the heart.

Structure

It is generally agreed that chap. 21 consists of two main parts—the narrative concerning both the sea and the meal (vv 1–14) and the subsequent discussion involving Peter and the beloved disciple (vv 15–23).

The initial part (vv 1–14) falls fairly easily into three sections: the catching of the fish (vv 1–6); the reactions, including Peter's throwing of himself into the sea (vv 7–8); and the meal (vv 9–14).

It would seem that within each section there are three subsections:

The catching of the fish (vv 1–6)

- not catching anything (1–3)
- not having anything to eat (4–5)
- having too much to draw in (6)

The reactions (vv 7–8)

- of the beloved disciple (7a)
- of Peter (7b)
- of the disciples (8)

The meal (vv 9–14)

- an initial description of the food and fish (9–11)

- an invitation to eat (12)
- the actual meal (13–14)

The concluding verse (14) closes not only the meal but also the passage as a whole.

The subsequent discussion involving Peter and the beloved disciple is divided by most analysts into two main sections: Jesus' challenging address to Peter (vv 15–19) and Peter's wondering about the beloved disciple (vv 20–23) (cf. UBSGNT, RSV, JB, NAB; Lagrange, 532–33; Hoskyns, 551–52; Schulz, 252–53; Marsh, 667–74; Becker, 644; Gnilka, 159–60; Schnackenburg, 3:360–67; Kysar, 317–19).

However, as is indicated in various ways by some other writers, most clearly perhaps by the NEB, each of these final sections is divided into two subsections. Thus Jesus' address to Peter consists both of a threefold questioning (vv 15–17) and of a pronouncement about Peter's death (vv 18–19). And the account of Peter's wondering about the beloved disciple involves not only Peter's own seeing of the disciple (vv 20–22), but also a summary of a subsequent misunderstanding (v 23).

The final two verses (24–25) are part of the larger pattern of the gospel's threefold conclusion, and to some degree these verses are distinct from the chapter's basic structure.

Repetition and Variation: Chapter 21 as a Culminating Interweaving of Leading Texts

Schnackenburg's comment (3:342) that chap. 21 involves a noteworthy interweaving of different threads provides a valuable clue to one of the chapter's important features: it contains a fusion of some of the gospel's key passages. Even the apparently new elements are not novel; to a large extent they involve continuity with earlier passages.

This does not mean that chap. 21 does not have its own distinct sources. It simply emphasizes that the phenomenon of continuity and repetition, something found throughout the gospel, here reaches a climactic intensity.

Of the many texts which have been reflected and woven together, the four most basic appear to be 1:1–34; chap. 6, esp. 6:1–21; chaps. 13, and 17. By their position, all four are important. Two have opening roles (1:1–34, chap. 13); they inaugurate the gospel as a whole and the last discourse. And two are conclusions or parts of conclusions: chap. 6, as represented in 6:1–21, brings to an end the gospel's second part; and chap. 17 concludes the last discourse. By integrating all four, chap. 21 brings together, as it were, the main streams of the gospel, and it raises the entire work to a new level of synthesis and unity.

Of these four texts (1:1–34, 6:1–21, chaps. 13 and 17) the most foundational in constructing chap. 21 appears to be 1:1–34. Its opening part, the prologue, provides a certain precedent and balance for the epilogue nature of chap. 21. The further episodes of 1:1–34, those describing the initial trial and the initial vision (1:19–28 and 1:29–34), maintain something of the prologue's preliminary character—they deal with a time before Jesus actually walks, in human fashion, on the stage—and as such they too provide a balance for the epilogue nature of chap. 21. Thus, both by its general structure (a three-part text followed by two two-part episodes) and by its role as preliminary, 1:1–34 prepares the way for the gospel's final section.

Then comes the role of chap. 13. Building on the broad structure provided by 1:1–34, it adds precision to that structure, and it supplies a precedent for some of the final chapter's key elements. In particular, the washing of the feet, including those of Peter, supplies the background for understanding the puzzling account of Peter's throwing himself in the sea (21:7b). And the two final passages of chap. 13, passages which, among other things, deal first with *the beloved and Peter* (13:21–30) and then with *Peter* (13:31–38), these supply background and elements for the two final passages in chap. 21—concerning *Peter* (21:15–19) and concerning *Peter and the beloved* (21:20–23).

Next comes the role of 6:1–21. Unlike 1:1–34 and chapter 13—texts which supply a precedent mainly for the final chapter's starting points (especially for its structure and characters)—6:1–21 gives a precedent for something more central, namely for the actual action. In itself 6:1–21 is both a story and a synthesis—it contains within itself a digest of the meaning of chapter 6—and, as such, it provides the background for much of the story and meaning of chap. 21. Some idea of the relationship of the texts may be seen in the following simplified outline:

6:1–21	*21:1–14*
The (eucharistic) meal (vv 1–13)	The event at sea (1–6)
The reaction (superficial, 14–15)	The reaction (insightful, 7–8)
The appearance at sea (16–21)	The (eucharistic) meal (9–14)

The basic order is complementary rather than parallel, and the relationship of one reaction to the other is minimal; the description of the dramatic reaction of Peter owes more to chap. 13 than to 6:14–15.

Yet there is a wide variety of shared elements, most obviously,

- the Galilean setting (6:1; 21:1–2)
- the presence of the disciples (6:3; 21:1–2)
- a food crisis (6:5–7; 21:5)
- the gift of an overflowing meal (6:8–10, 12–13; 21:9–11)
- Jesus' sharing of the food (6:11; 21:13)
- the (diverse) reactions (6:14–15; 21:7–8)
- going to sea and feeling helpless (6:16–18; 21:3)
- the mysterious appearance of Jesus (6:19; 21:4)
- the identification and (implied) acceptance of Jesus (6:20–21; 21:12)

Finally there is the role of chap. 17. However much it belongs to the last discourse, it still stands apart from it, especially in its structure and in the explicitness of its concern for the future church. In so doing it supplies a precedent for chap. 21, for within the resurrection narratives, the structure of chap. 21 also breaks new ground. In addition, like chap. 17, in its concern for the future church it stands out (cf. Minear, 1983, 94).

Thus in ways which are diverse but complementary, chap. 21 brings together some of the gospel's leading texts and builds on them. Its relationship to other passages, particularly the good shepherd text (10:1–21), is also significant. But its primary continuity is with the four texts which, in various ways, are either leading or concluding.

Central Themes of Chapter 21: Providence and Daily Self-Giving, Especially in the Church

Given that chapter 21 involves a developing of several key texts, it is not surprising that it is rich in content.

One of its most basic motifs is that of food and the providing of food. The opening section (vv 1–6) tells of the search for fish, then of having no food at all, and finally of having fish in abundance. The scene on landing (vv 9–14) tells of finding a meal being prepared, of an invitation to eat, and then of the actual meal. Later, in Jesus' address to Peter, there is a repeated commission to provide food ("Feed my lambs. . . . Feed my little sheep" vv 15, 17). And finally, as Peter sees the beloved disciple (v 20), there is an explicit allusion to reclining in love "at . . . supper."

The basic idea conveyed by this repeated food motif is that of providence. It makes sense, therefore, that Brown (1063) should entitle the entire chapter as "an . . . account . . . which . . . show[s] how Jesus provided for the needs of the Church." This helps explain the affinity with chap. 6, for there, too, the providing of food (bread—"the bread of life") was used to convey the idea of providence.

There is, however, one major difference between 6:1–21 and chap. 21. The emphasis in chap. 6 is on providence during life; and the idea of death, through important, is not explicit. But in chap. 21, even though there is no neglect of the reality of providence in daily life, the emphasis on death is far clearer. As will be seen in examining the text, something of death is intimated in Peter's plunge into the sea, and in the subsequent discussion with Jesus (vv 18–19) the idea of death becomes explicit: ". . . But when you are old. . . ."

It is partly because of this difference of emphasis that 21:1–14 reorders the elements found in 6:1–21. The central element, that of the reaction to the miracle (21:7–8, plunging into the sea), instead of being political (6:14–15), contains the intimation of death. And the providing of food, while mentioned at the beginning (21:1–6)—as it is also at the beginning of 6:1–21 (6:1–13)—finds its greatest emphasis in the scene which follows that intimation of death, namely in the meal (21:9–14). In other words, the placing of the providential meal at the end of the narrative, rather than at its beginning, helps to indicate that providence applies not only to the early stages of life, but also to its end. In the subsequent episodes this idea finds enigmatic confirmation: the reference to Peter's death is followed by the picture—puzzlingly unnecessary—of a supper.

Thus the most basic theme of chapter 21 is that of providence, providence even unto death.

Within this framework of divine care the chapter portrays human responsive- ness, both individual and communitarian. It is not clear how this response should be described—probably as love leading to knowing (cf. vv 7, 12, 15–17, 24). It is better in any case not to classify it casually as faith or believing. Chapter 21 refers neither to "seeing" Jesus, nor to "signs," nor to "believing." The sur- prising obedience of the fishermen to the unrecognized Jesus indicates that believ- ing is presupposed.

The portrayal of responsiveness is seen particularly in Peter. On the one hand, he is an individual, a man going to work. Furthermore, the theme of divine self- giving, which is so central to the gospel—especially in the prologue and chap. 13—finds in him its continuation: by subtle touches the text portrays a descent— from his role as clear leader (vv 2–3); to following someone else's insight and throwing himself into the sea (v 7); to being the one who, servantlike, obeys the general command to bring the fish (vv 10, 11a). Thus, Jesus may have ascended, but in his followers, the self-giving goes on.

On the other hand, Peter is also communitarian; his responsiveness is linked to that of others, and it is inseparable from the involvement of the church. Follow- ing the providential catch of fish, there is within the text a kind of chain reaction —from the beloved's recognizing, through Peter's acceptance of that recognition and through the response of "the other disciples," to the point where they all "know" (vv 7–9, 12). And, following the providential meal, there is, in the account of the subsequent episodes, a further chain reaction—from Peter's love- based following of Jesus; through the beloved's following, abiding, and testi- mony; to the final "we know" (v 24).

Thus the practical outcome of provident care and human responsiveness is community, church. And in chap. 21, as in chap. 17, the emphasis on commu- nity, on togetherness and relationships, is unusually strong. Furthermore, it is strengthened by the highlighting of Peter and of the ideas of mission and the eucharist.

It is because of its emphasis on the down-to-earth reality of the church that chap. 21 has been described as being, above all else, "ecclesiastical" (Bultmann, 701–2; Brown, 1081–82; Schnackenburg, 3:343–44). This characterization high- lights a central truth, but it tends to separate it from its context: it does not do justice to the way in which the church is portrayed as being based on self-giving —on the giving of the provident God and on the responsive self-giving which flows through Peter. It also tends to separate the picture of the church from the context of the preceding chapters—as though it were something alien. It is indeed different. As Bultmann (701) emphasizes, in comparison with the church-related questions which are found in 19:16b–chap. 20—questions which are founda- tional, related to the community's existence—the concerns of chapter 21 are much more tangible; they deal with particular people, relationships, authorities. But that does not mean that they are alien. They fit the pattern of other texts within the gospel. Part 2 of the gospel concludes with the confession of Peter (6:67–69). The last discourse concludes with a chapter (17) which is church-related. Against such a background the final emphasis on Peter and the church is thoroughly appropriate.

As well as being ecclesiastical, chap. 21 is eminently human, evocative of profound beauty. It speaks of some of the most basic elements of life—going to work, companionship, fishing, dark emptiness, hunger, dawn, a stranger, surprise, the sharing of insight, the plunge into the sea, the boat journey towards welcome land, morning on the shore, the sight of fire and food, someone waiting, the domesticity of breakfast (no need to dress up), the rich silence; then the talk, breaking through shades of past failures to speak of life—of love, work, sadness, youth, old age, and death. And finally, surprisingly, the sight of someone following and the recollection of someone resting in love. At the end, the failure of talk (the breakdown of language and grammer), and the need, with a vision of love in mind, to keep on.

Thus the ecclesiastical dimension, though present, is but part of a larger picture, one which is simultaneously thoroughly divine and thoroughly human. The conversation with Peter, for instance (21:15–19), does indeed allude to his special position in the church, but it refers first of all to what Peter shares with every disciple and, in one sense, with every human being—the call to true love, to appropriate care for others, and the embracing of the path which eventually leads through death.

Chapter 21 as an Appropriate Culmination

There are several positive indications that chap. 21 is the integral conclusion to the gospel. It is chap. 21, with its reference to Galilee and the coming of Jesus (21:2,22–23), which provides a completion for the gospel's basic time-space structure (see introduction, chap. 4).

It is chap. 21 which completes the story of Peter and the beloved disciple. Without this chapter the account of Peter would be particularly incomplete since, unlike the other gospels, all of which show Peter as crying repentantly (Matt 26:75, Mark 14:72, Luke 22:62), this gospel would otherwise lack a picture of Peter's repentance or rehabilitation. Minear (1983, 91–95, esp. 91) is emphatic: "I am convinced that only in chapter 21 do we discover an adequate end to the story of . . . Peter and the beloved disciple." Duke (1985, 98) is not directly concerned about the matter but, indirectly, comes to a similar conclusion: "Chapter 21 is . . . fitting . . . even . . . necessary . . . to the total portrayal of Simon Peter."

The theme of providence, as found in chap. 21, complements and completes the preceding narratives' idea of a new creation (cf. Brown, 1035, 1037; Mateos and Barreto, 839, 844). A precedent for this creation-providence complementarity is found in the relationships between chaps. 5 and 6 and between chaps. 9 and 10.

The emphasis on loving and knowing complements the tendency of chap. 20 to stress seeing and believing. A somewhat similar shift of emphasis is found between 16:4b–33 (esp. vv 16–24) and chap. 17.

The down-to-earthness of chap. 21 completes and complements the preceding impression, given especially in chap. 20, of being within a place which is some-how sacred, but enclosed (cf. esp. 20:19–28). Here (in chap. 21) life becomes practical: people go to work, and the church takes a form that is tangible. The mystic has come down from the mountain, and the church has entered the com-plexity of life. In a gospel where, beginning with the prologue, so many texts spiral downwards, a gospel in which the Word becomes flesh and belief leads to community, nothing could be more appropriate.

Thus, as already partly indicated, chap. 21 is like chap. 17: it fits the mold of the preceding chapters, yet it also breaks that mold. It completes aspects of the gospel's story and themes, yet in many ways it belongs to another world. At one level of chap. 17 Jesus is on earth, yet more and more he is breaking the barriers of space and entering heaven. In chap. 21 comes the complementary event: the Jesus who has ascended to heaven is now present on earth. In chap. 17, as he ascended in prayer, he had asked for unity. Now ascended, he works in the church —with Peter, the beloved, and the disciples—to effect that unity. And the ulti-mate purpose, in both chaps. 17 and 21, is universal—that the world may believe; that all may be gathered, unbroken, into one.

[21:1–6] The disciples at work in the world—their passage from compounded emptiness to humbling fullness.   The scene at the sea of Tiberias suggests a new beginning. The repetitiveness of v 1 ("revealed . . . revealed as follows") helps to build a tone of simple inaugural solemnity—a down-to-earth echo of the imposing inaugural simplicity of 13:1. The references to "Tiberias" and "Gali-lee" evoke the world at large (cf. comment on 6:1). And the picture of the seven disciples has a certain universality: seven represents completeness; they echo those disciples who, within the gospel, were mentioned first and last (the disciples of 1:35–51, esp. 1:35; cf. Brown, 1096; and Thomas, 20:24–29); and, despite being only seven, one of the impressions they convey is of the kind that one receives when dealing with an indefinite number: one knows some, most obviously Simon Peter, the person who is mentioned first; but, as one looks further, the sense of knowing people gives way gradually to an awareness of those who are known only indirectly or not at all: "Thomas called the Twin, Nathanael from Cana of Galilee [cf. 1:45–51], the sons of Zebedee [never before mentioned in John], and two others of the disciples." Whatever the details, the essential picture is clear: with light touches, the evangelist evokes a new reality—that of the disciples abroad in the world.

When Peter says, "I am going away fishing," his words may indeed sound banal, but so does much of daily life: "I'm going to work"; "I'm going to get some food." This, however, makes sense. It was primarily towards ordinary liv-ing that the Spirit was directed. As Schnackenburg (3:324) commented about the sending of the disciples (20:21–23): "The missionary accent in a narrower sense (the winning of people for the gospel) seems to be missing." Jesus sent people first of all to *live,* to be human beings. Furthermore, this emphasis on human living corresponds with the emphasis of John's gospel as a whole. The Word became ordinary flesh, and Jesus, particularly at the beginning of the gospel, is pictured not so much as preaching the kingdom and going about doing good, but simply as living in God's Spirit and responding generously to those whom he encountered. As time goes on Jesus takes the initiative more frequently, and Peter likewise will assume a missionary role in the narrower sense. Indeed, insofar as the boat suggests the church (following the symbolism of chap. 6), his role in the fishing evokes his church leadership. But the primary emphasis for the moment is on the broader experience of ordinary daily work.

Like much work it is not easy: "In that night they caught nothing." The reference to night is rather jolting. There had been no indication at the beginning of the narrative of impending night, and, though night-fishing was common, the symbolism of the gospel is such that the reference has the effect of setting the disciples and their boat in an atmosphere of alien darkness. The fact that they catch nothing intensifies that effect. Life is not only dark, it is dark and empty.

But when it was morning Jesus stood on the shore. This is a surprise indeed, accentuated by the close juxtapositioning of "night" and "morning." Equally remarkable is the quality of the surprise, its evocation of life and beauty—the sudden presence of Jesus, the suggestion of the beauty of the morning and of standing on the shore.

But the disciples "did not know" that it was Jesus. It is as though, because of this experience of darkness and emptiness, they are unaware of life and beauty.

The whole scene—morning, vitality, not knowing—has echoes of the saddened blindness of Mary Magdalene in the garden (20:1, 14–15). But unlike Mary they do not regress.

In the garden Jesus had said "Woman." Now he says *paidia*, the plural of *paidion*, itself the diminutive form of *pais* "child." It can be translated into a fairly casual expression such as "Lads," and at one level that meaning is valid. But in the context of John's gospel, *paidia* cannot but suggest what it most immediately means—"little children." As such it calls to the disciples' hearts, to that part of them which, whatever their independence and competence, is a small child, ultimately a child of God (cf. 13:33). This reflects a central truth, one which is touched on by writers as diverse as St. Paul (Rom 8:21) and Hegel (*Logic*, 2:24, p. 55: "The harmoniousness of childhood is a gift from the hand of nature; the second harmony must spring from the labour and culture of the spirit. And so the words of Christ . . . [about *becoming* little children] are very far from telling us that we must always remain children").

"Little children, do you have any *prosfagion?*"—another diminutive, one which apparently refers to a side dish or relish, often of fish, rather than to a main dish. Hence Schnackenburg (3:354) translates it as "trimmings" or "fish trimmings." The only comparable element in earlier chapters is the morsel (13:26, 27, 30). In other words, he asks them, as little children, if they have anything at all. And their total response is a simple two-letter *Ou*, "No."

Thus the sense of nothingness, which was first expressed by the nightlong failure to achieve anything, is now compounded by the fact that they are like little children who have not a bite.

Yet it is from this nothingness that their situation improves. Jesus' advice to put the net over the right side leads to an abundance of fish. The right side may have been regarded as lucky but that is not the cause of the change; "the success

. . . is due entirely to . . . obedience to Jesus' word'' (Lindars, 627). The fact that the obedience of Peter and the disciples to the word should be linked to the right side makes sense: in the gospel's only other reference to the "right," the cutting off of what was right (the right ear, 18:10) reflected Peter's failure to hear the word. In other words, within the gospel the right side is connected with hearing; cutting it indicates a failure of hearing; using it shows a return to hearing.

The new-found abundance, however wonderful, is humbling: they "could not draw" them in. It is God and the glorified Jesus who draw people (6:44, 12:32). John's only other usage of "draw" outside of this chapter is in 18:10—Peter's drawing of the sword. Peter, on the basis of his own power, could draw a sword and do damage; but he cannot draw the fish. In other words, despite his might, the swordsman does not draw. The power which comes out of the barrel of a gun is very limited. Even amid their startling fishing success the Peter-led disciples are reminded that they are dealing with a power greater than themselves.

[21:7–8] Recognition and response.   The catch of fish evokes a process of recognition and response that is threefold—that of the beloved disciple (v 7a), that of Peter (v 7b), and that of "the other disciples" (v 8).

The beloved disciple is first and, as with the tomb scene (20:1–10), no explanation is given for his faster reactions except the implication of his love. The catch of fish is not the basis for his believing; the disciples' obedience to the word implies that they believed beforehand. The catch seems rather to be a sign which confirms faith and which sparks it into a fresh degree of life: "It is the Lord." The disciples had, of course, already "seen" the Lord (20:20,25), but this recognition is something more. The nature of this something more is suggested by the fact that the disciple is termed "that (*ekeinos*) disciple. . . ." It is a usage which, when combined with the idea of knowing, recalls 19:35, "and he (*ekeinos*) knows . . ."—a text which suggests the presence of the Spirit. The implication is that the beloved disciple's "It is the Lord" comes from the Spirit.

Once again, therefore, the beloved disciple takes priority over Peter. But again there is no suggestion of antagonism. In fact, it is to Peter that he expresses his recognition. And Peter, apparently with complete simplicity, accepts it and acts on it.

Peter's response is striking: "Hearing that it was the Lord, (he) girded his apron about him, for he was stripped down, and threw (*ballō*, "throw/put") himself into the sea." This has led to a considerable discussion about Peter's clothing and action, for it can suggest "the absurdity of adding clothes before swimming" (Brown, 1072). As with some other texts which are superficially perplexing, the answer seems to lie in theological symbolism, in this case one which is a variation on the death-related symbolism of Jesus taking off clothes and girding himself in order to put (*ballō*) water in a basin and wash the disciples' feet—a washing which would mean that they were clean all over (13:4–11). Peter's passage through the sea reflects the death-related washing and it is also an introduction to the impending theme of Peter's own death (21:18–19). The "girding" implies preparing or bracing himself for the ordeal. "Stripped down" or "naked" is evocative of losing everything, of dying. And "threw himself into the sea" suggests the actual taking of the plunge, the going down into death in order to be with the Lord.

Previously, when Peter was faced with the idea of death, there had been great variety in his reactions: clear acceptance, at least theoretically (6:53,68); glib self-assured acceptance (13:37); violent resistance (18:10); and self-destructive fear (18:17,25–27). Later however, at the tomb, he had come to share something of the faith of the beloved disciple (20:8–10). And now, the Spirit of love, communicated through the beloved disciple, finally enables him, with his mind set on the Lord, symbolically to embrace death.

Then came the other disciples, in the boat, dragging the net. This seems extremely understandable—a simple process of coming ashore—but it is interrupted by the information that they were "not far" (*ou makran*) from the land, about 200 cubits (= 100 yards) a piece of information which is peculiarly placed. It "would come more naturally at the end of v 7" (Brown, 1073). The RSV, in fact, relocates it to the end of the verse. This intrusive peculiarity, as well as the other details of coming ashore, appear to have a further meaning—a suggestion that Peter's plunge had opened the way for the others, had made the land more accessible. In 6:20–21 the land to which the disciples were going was the God-like Jesus, and for that reason it was startlingly accessible ("immediately the boat was" there); the journey was spiritual. Here too, Jesus as Lord is the land to which the disciples are boating, and the peculiar phrasing of the distance is an indication that, at one level of reading, the distance is spiritual. But Peter has helped to close that distance. By accepting so fully that Jesus is Lord, even to the point of self-giving, he helps to bring them to land. And they in turn pull everybody else (the net of fish).

[21:9–16] The meal which reflects providential salvation. As noted in discussing structure, the meal scene has three phrases—the presentation of the food (vv 9–11), the invitation to eat (vv 12), and the actual sharing of the food (vv 13–14). But the meal is not the only factor. Interwoven with it are scenes which reflect salvation from sin and death. The charcoal fire covered with eucharist-related symbols recalls Peter's sin (18:17–18, 25), but it sets that sin in a context which is positive, one in which it ultimately leads to eucharist, thanksgiving. This combination—of treacherous fire with eucharistic fish—is somewhat similar in effect to the final line of T. S. Eliot's *Four Quartet:* "And the fire and the rose are one." In both Eliot and the evangelist there are symbolic indications, as their works come to a close, that, at some ultimate level, opposites merge, dualism is resolved, and the divisiveness of evil is incorporated into a greater positive unity.

The next image confirms this sense of a greater mystery-filled unity: the bringing to land of the unbroken net of large fish is "parabolic of the universal mission of the Church" (Marsh, 665). In other words, the salvation, which is first found in Peter, extends to all. Then, through the reactions of the disciples and the final comment of the narrator, the source of this salvation is brought into focus—Jesus who is "Lord . . . raised from the dead." The implication, given the fact that he shares the bread with them, is that, with him, they too rise from the dead.

Thus the entire transition from night and nothingness (vv 1–5) to abundance and care (the warm breakfast) evokes the providence which leads to salvation. And, as in the providence-related bread-of-life discourse (6:22–59), the text, particularly in its final section, reflects the attitude and practice of *eucharistia*.

One of the peculiarities of the text is that in this third scene of coming to land (vv 9–14) the figure of Peter is curiously downplayed. This is all the more striking because he is so prominent in scene 1 (cf. vv 2–3) and because his throwing of himself into the sea could be seen as implying that his coming to land would involve a dramatic encounter with Jesus. But there is no such drama, and so the narrative may seem defective.

But the apparent deficiency has its purpose. It is part of the larger process, alluded to earlier, of depicting Peter as going through stages of self-emptying. First he was the clear leader (vv 2–3), then the one who followed the insight of the beloved and threw himself into the sea (v 7), and now finally, the one who, instead of occupying center stage, plays a role like that of a servant: when Jesus gives a general command to bring the fish, it is Peter who goes up and drags the net to land. In his self-emptying he had, as it were, gone down, but at this stage, as he embraces the role of servant he "goes up" and—unlike the initial scene when the disciples could not draw the net (v 6)—he now drags it ashore. He can do so at this point because in the meantime he has learned at great cost to embrace the word. In various ways his sins are recalled—his drawing of the sword, his denial at the fire—but he has gone through a purifying process, and now the fire and the drawing are part of the path to a greater salvation.

The fact that Peter has a prominent role in this portrayal of salvation indicates that, while providence is universal, it works in a special way through Peter. And that, in turn, implies a special role and responsibility for the church. A similar message was found in chap. 6. It is the task of the church to reach out to all.

Note. The 153 fish. Concerning the symbolism of the 153 large fish in the unbroken net it is generally agreed that, even though by some fishing standards the number is not overwhelming, in the context it is meant to indicate the magnitude or fullness of the disciples' mission and of salvation; "the figure must represent totality in some way because the catch prefigures the ultimate universal salvation through the church's mission (cf. 11:52)" (Lindars, 629).

Why 153? The number is puzzling—so much so that, even to writers as different as Brown (1075–76) and Staley (1988, 113), it does not seem possible to give it a meaning. Traditionally, there have been three main interpretations (for details, see Lindars, 629–30; Brown, 1074–75; Schnackenburg, 3:357).

1. *Allegory.* Cyril of Alexandria, for instance, sees 153 as comprising 100 (the fullness of the Gentiles), plus 50 (the remnant of Israel), plus 3 (the Trinity).

2. *Gematria.* Since in Hebrew and Greek each letter of the alphabet is associated with a specific number, a large number like 153 can represent the sum of several letters and thus can represent a word or phrase. There are, in fact, several words or combinations of words which give a total of 153: in Hebrew, for instance, *ha-ôlam hab-ba'* ("Age to

Come") or *qhl h'hbh* ("The Church of Love"); or, in Greek, *Simon* (= 76) plus *ichthus* ("fish," = 77).

3. *A mathematical symbol.* The essence of this view, founded on Augustine and developed particularly in Hoskyns (553), is that 153 forms a perfect triangle. In other words, it is one of those numbers which are the sum of all the numbers from 1 to something higher—with the result that they can be arranged in a perfect (equilateral) triangle. Thus, 6 for instance, since it is the sum of all the numbers from 1 to 3, can be arranged in this way:

So can 10, 15, 21, 28, and so on—through 136 (the sum of all the numbers from 1 to 16), 153 (1 to 17), 171 (1 to 18), and further.

This mathematical approach does not exclude the presence of some form of gematria (nor even some element of allegory), but it demands explanation and support: Why a perfect triangle? And why base it on 17? And is there support, in the gospel or outside of it, for the use of such numbers?

Part of the answer may be dealt with quickly: "Triangular numbers were of interest both to Greek mathematicians and to biblical authors" (Brown, 1074).

Furthermore, given the context of the gospel—the fact that so much of its structure is in some way threefold, and that chap. 21 has elements of culminating finality and universalism—there is great appropriateness to a perfect triangle. Its three-sided perfection suggests bringing everything together into a unity.

There is equal appropriateness to 17; each of its most obvious components (10 and 7) symbolize perfection and in their own right were "important in contemporary Jewish thought" (Brown, 1074).

More decisive, however, than this general background and appropriateness, is the fact that within John's gospel there is significant use of the components of 17 (of 10 and 7, and of 12 and 5). Further, this use occurs in contexts which in diverse ways are linked to the culminating catch of fish.

The gospel's first use of 10 is associated with both the coming to Jesus of disciples and with the idea of perfection (see comment on 1:39, ". . . the hour was about ten"). So in a different way is its first use of 7: the reference to the seventh hour ("yesterday at the seventh hour," 4:52) has a certain fullness insofar as it comes at the end of chap. 4 and, building climactically on the Samaritan-related reference to the sixth hour (4:6), it indicates the moment when the Gentile official comes to believe. In other words, within the present gospel, 10 and 7 are first used in contexts which suggest both a certain perfection or fullness, contexts which are also indicators of the coming of diverse believers to Jesus. As such they prepare the way for the use of 17 to express the complete fullness of the spreading of discipleship. In chap. 4 the work of the disciples is expressed through the food-related image of a harvest (4:31–38); in chap. 21, through the meal-related image of a catch of fish. In chaps. 1–4 the images are spread out over several episodes —the 10, the harvest, the 7; in chap. 21, however, since it is the culminating chapter, the corresponding elements are synthesized into a dense unity: 153 great fish.

The 17 finds further backing in the closely related meal account of 6:1–13. The crucial clue is provided by Lindars (630–31): in 6:13, "12 baskets were filled with the fragments of the 5 loaves, omitting all mention of the 2 fish. The sum of 12 and 5 is 17. Just as the leavings typify the universal feeding of the future, so the catch of fish typifies the universal population which is to be fed." Lindars makes this proposal very tentatively, and even backs away from it, but a closer look at the texts shows that it is a trail worth pursuing. The idea that the numbers in 6:1–13 might be connected to those in 21:1–14 finds confirmation in the fact that in these texts, and these texts only, John used the number 200 (6:7; 21:8). More decisive, however, than this enigmatic link is the relationship between the verses in question. The bringing in of the (153) fish (21:10–11) has essentially the same function as the gathering up of the fragments (6:12–13). Both are extraneous to the basic account of the meal: the gathering of the fragments comes after it; the bringing of the fish interrupts it. Both suggest fullness, and both are inaugurated by a command of Jesus: "Gather. . . ."; "Bring. . . ." In the case of the fragments, nothing is lost; and, as regards the fish, the net is not broken.

Thus the idea that the 153 is to be interpreted through its relationship to 17 not only makes sense in itself, it also finds significant support from the context of the gospel as a whole. It is obscure, but that is appropriate; so is the mystery which it represents.

All this does not mean that the symbolism of the net of fish is lost on the person who does not see the connection with 17 and with its delicately complex suggestions of universalism. If the reader cannot figure out the 153, the text still has meaning. In its striking mixture of clarity and obscurity—one knows the externals (the external number), but without understanding fully—it is a symbol of God's activity in gathering in humankind. The reader can make peace with that, trusting—as the whole gospel has challenged to trust—that, as God's work, which surpasses understanding, it has its own coherence. And if the reader finds an explanation that makes sense, then so much the better; it is a sign which confirms the trust.

[21:15–23] Starting over: an introduction to 21:15–23.

Having given a general picture of the providence which works through the church and Peter (21:1–14), chapter 21 now goes on to indicate how, especially in Peter, that providence works out in practice. The text is particularly concerned with love and work and death, and it consists of two episodes—one in which Peter is questioned, rehabilitated, and commissioned (vv 15–19), and a second in which, as he goes along his way, he sees the beloved disciple and thereby catches an enigmatic glimpse of a love transcending death (vv 20–23).

This pattern—a general picture followed by two episodes which comprise practical effects—is essentially the same as that found in chap. 13. Furthermore, as mentioned in discussing the relationship of chap. 21 to earlier chapters, the final episodes of chaps. 13 and 21 are closely related in their content—the first

(21:15–19) with the second (13:31–38), and the second (21:20–23) with the first (13:21–30).

But while content of these episodes reflects chap. 13 (and other texts), their form goes back to 1:1–34, to the two initiatory type-scenes which follow the prologue—the initial trial (1:19–28) and the initial vision (1:29–34). The triple questioning of Peter ("Do you love me?" 21:15–17) involves a variation on the form of the triple questioning of John the Baptist ("Who are you?" 1:19–23). And Peter's enigmatic seeing of the beloved who abides until Jesus comes (21:20–23) entails a variation on how John sees the coming of Jesus (1:29–34).

The details of course are complex. The triple questioning is accompanied in both instances by a summary of the task of those questioned (John as preparatory preacher, crying, "Make straight the way"; and Peter as follow-up pastor, tending the flock). It is also accompanied by the idea of their encountering God in a new way (in Jesus' coming, in death), and by complementary images of their human limitations (John is unworthy to loose the sandal thong, 1:24–28; Peter is unable to fasten his belt, 21:18–19). But the relationship between the questions and the task-summary varies from one text to another. In the case of John the questions and task-summary are distinct: first the questions ("Who are you? . . ."), and then the task summary ("I am the voice . . ."). In the case of Peter they are interspersed, synthesized; each question is followed by a task or commission ("Simon, son of John, do you love me? . . . Feed my lambs").

Similarly with regard to the down-to-earth visions: there is continuity but there is also variation. John's initial vision (1:29–34) was seen earlier to contain two parts, one referring to a preliminary stage (baptism in water, corresponding to the OT period) and the other referring to the more advanced spiritual stage (baptism in the Spirit to be inaugurated by Jesus). The text in chap. 21 contains two corresponding parts, one underdeveloped and the other spiritual, but, since Jesus has already come, the spiritual is put first, and the underdeveloped or preliminary part becomes a stage of misunderstanding. In simplified outline:

1:29–34	*21:20–23*
Preliminary understanding (water/the OT)	
Jesus brings abiding union (the Spirit)	Jesus brings abiding union
	Misunderstanding (the [Jewish] brothers)

The verse, 21:23, reads "the brothers" rather than "the Jews," but the implication—given other uses of "the brothers" (2:12; 7:3,5,10; 20:17)—is of a reference to the Jews.

Note: "Brothers" = Jews. The disbelief of the Jews in chapters 7 and 8 is introduced in the preliminary episode, 7:1–9, by the disbelief of the brothers. Thus in 7:1–9, the brothers, in effect, stand for the unbelieving Jews. This brothers-Jews phenomenon is first found, faintly, in 2:12–22: the distinction between *brothers* and *disciples* introduces the distinct reactions of *Jews* and *disciples*, 2:12,17,18,22. And as indicated in discussing the representative role of Mary Magdalene, 20:11–18, she is identified with one aspect of the death-oriented Jews, with those who have failed to grasp Jesus' message, especially the message of his resurrection. And, therefore, the "brothers" to whom she is sent are likewise to be interpreted as Jews, as those who have missed or misunderstood the message. Consequently, in John 1–20 there is no use of "brothers" that is not associated somehow with the Jews. Thus the meaning of "brothers" in the fourth gospel is not that found in 1 John 3 (where it refers to fellow Christians) but that of Rom 9:3 (where it means Jews).

Returning to the outline (of 1:29–34 and 21:20–23) the *preliminary under-standing* that preceded Jesus is balanced by a *flawed understanding* (misunder-standing) which followed him. "Abiding," of course, may refer to the simple fact of physically remaining, of staying somewhere, but as Schnackenburg (3:370–71) notes concerning 21:22–23, "abiding" is the key word in the misunderstanding, and it apparently refers to abiding in some other way. The other way is the abiding that is spiritual, the abiding which refers to spiritual union.

What is essential is that, once allowance is made for variations—and the vary-ing of type-scenes is a standard procedure (see the betrothal scene in 4:1–42; cf. Alter, 1981, 47–62)—the two episodes of 21:15–23 may be seen to consist, to a significant extent, of an initial trial (vv 15–19) and an initial vision (vv 20–23).

At first sight, such a conclusion is strange. This is the end of the gospel. And it refers to the death of Peter and the beloved disciple. Can an ending be a begin-ning? It would seem that it can. Peter's rehabilitation, however much it is a con-clusion to the account of his fall, is the occasion for his being commissioned and, therefore, for a new undertaking. And the journey on which he then embarks, even though it leads to death, involves also a perception, a supremely down-to-earth vision, of love which, even beyond death, abides.

[21:15–19] The questioning of Peter as a rehabilitation and a commission-ing. In these final episodes the first name in the Greek text, and one that is set almost at the beginning of the text, is that of Peter, initially in the passive, dative, case ("to Simon Peter," v 15), and finally in the leading, nominative, case ("Pe-ter turned, . . ." v 20). It is the kind of prominence he has not enjoyed before, except in the incidents of the sword and the denials (18:10,25). The denying was triple, and so is the questioning and affirming. Thus Peter is rehabilitated. But this scene, though it takes care of the past, does not dwell on it. The primary emphasis is on a testing of character which looks to the future.

The tension between past and future, failure and fidelity, is heightened by the fact that Peter is addressed repeatedly as "Simon, son of John." "Simon" is the name he shared with Judas. "John," on the other hand, he shares with the bap-tizer. (For many readers "John" also suggests the beloved.) The double name evokes the fact that Peter bears within himself the capacity for different roles, for both violent treachery and for selfless service. It also suggests the bringing to-gether of alien elements and, thus, a process of integration.

Amid the difficulty of the trial, the presence of a caring providence is not forgotten. The explicit reference to the breakfast (v 15) evokes it, and the thrice-repeated formula of question, answer, and commission has the basic effect of clarifying the fact that Peter is grounded in the love of the provident down-to-earth God, and that it is that love which acts as the basis for his tending to others.

One of the most puzzling aspects of the scene is its variations in wording:

Do you love (*agapaō*) me more than these?	Yes, Lord, You know (*oida*) that I love (*phileō*) you.	Feed my lambs.
Do you love (*agapaō*) me?	Yes, Lord, You know (*oida*) that I love (*phileō*) you.	Shepherd my sheep.
Do you love (*phileō*) me? Peter became sad because he said. . . . Do you love (*phileō*) me?	Lord, You know (*oida*) all, You know (*ginōskō*) that I love (*phileō*) you.	Feed my little sheep.

It has often been said that the variations are meaningless, and it is true that the efforts to give the variations meaning have not been very successful (cf. Brown, 1102–6). But the lack of success does not necessarily mean the effort should be abandoned, and there are, in fact, indications that the variations are meaningful:

- A do-you-love-me situation is not the time for meaningless variations. In such a discussion every syllable tends to be important. The fact that commentators have not been able clearly to distinguish variations of meanings in John's other uses of *agapaō* and *phileō* (in other passages) proves nothing; these other usages are simply another part of the same problem. (The appeal to a putative Semitic original merely confuses the issue.)

- In the related text, concerning the questioning of John (1:19–21), the minor variations in John's answers are not meaningless (their shrinking quantity intimates his decrease).

- In this text (21:15–17) at least one set of variations is in fact meaningful: the sequence "Feed my lambs. . . . Shepherd my sheep. . . . Feed my little sheep" corresponds to looking after people in the three main stages of life—when people are young (lambs) and need to be fed; when people are adult (sheep) and need shepherding; and when people are old, yet in some ways are once more like children (little sheep) and once again need to be fed. This meaning finds support from the fact that the text which immediately follows implies three basic ages ("When you were young . . .").

The final verses (18–19) summarize basic aspects of the transition from youth to old age. The stretching out of the hands "has been understood both as a posture of prayer and as a reference to crucifixion" (Kysar, 318). The notion of crucifixion is applicable not only to the specific tradition that Peter was crucified, but also to the general idea that, like every disciple, Peter had to take up his cross and follow Jesus. Yet, as with Jesus, this way of the cross leads, not to a sense of absurdity but to a manifesting (literally, glorifying) of God.

Peter's sadness (v 17) stems partly from the fact that the third round of questioning is a reflection of the third phase of life, and since that phase involves aging, it inevitably brings some sadness. So much is over—strengths and joys which can never be recovered; and ahead lies death. It is a variation on the death-related sadness of parting which is emphasized in 16:6,20–22. However, as in that earlier text, this death-related sadness does not take over. Rather it is placed in the context of the sensitivity of Jesus, someone who—in contrast to human confusion and uncertainty—knows everything, particularly every inner feeling (16:16–19, esp. v 19; 21:17). Thus there is sadness, but it is not solitary. It is known by a Jesus-like God who not only is aware of all its aspects but who also has a much larger picture and who can see death in a positive way. Thus in 16:20–22 the death-related sadness is seen as part of a process of birth, and in the case of Peter, his sadness acts as a prelude to the death-related glorifying of God. The end result of this process is a surprising joy—the joy which is spoken of clearly in the account of the seeing of Jesus (16:22) and the joy which, for Peter, will be implied in the final enigmatic vision concerning the beloved.

[21:20–23] Peter's vision—the beloved abiding, regardless of death, until Jesus comes.   Last scene of all is of Peter following, even to his death, and, as he goes, of his seeing the beloved. It has two parts, the first centered on Jesus' enigmatic but crucial statement concerning the beloved abiding (vv 20–22); the second, on a misunderstanding of Jesus' statement by "the brothers" (v 23).

In previous texts "the brothers" was an allusion to the unbelieving Jews (cf. balance between 2:12 and 2:18; 7:3,5,10; see comment on 20:17), and there is no evident reason for interpreting it otherwise here. Thus there is, on the one hand, a statement to Peter, the shepherd of the flock, and, on the other, a misunderstanding of that statement by the unbelieving Jews. Since the statement and the misunderstanding have to do with a question of life and death, it is evident that the misunderstanding is profound. The implication is that, in contrast to Peter and the disciples ("we," v 24), the Jews have seriously misunderstood Jesus' final message.

As already mentioned, the episode as a whole echoes aspects of the scene in which the beloved disciple first appears (13:21–30), a scene which also involves Peter, Judas, and treachery. Without attempting a detailed comparison of the two texts, it may be said that in both cases the beloved has a special closeness to Jesus, particularly with regard to a question of life and death, and that Peter tries to inquire about the elusive truth.

A major clue to the nature of the text is the rather long description of the beloved as the one who had lain on Jesus' bosom. Many commentators have wondered why, if the beloved needed description, it was not given when he was first mentioned (in the boat, 21:7). And some, particularly Bultmann (714), regard the description as a secondary interpolation.

But the text makes sense. As already indicated, the passage as a whole is understandable once it is seen as a particularly down-to-earth form of an initiatory vision, in other words, as a variation on the kind of type-scene vision beheld by John (1:29–34). In the final scene of 1:1–34 the baptizer saw a vision of Jesus coming and of the Spirit abiding on him. Now, at the end of chap. 21, Peter sees the beloved and receives an enigmatic message about abiding and coming.

The first hint that Peter is rising above earthly levels of perception is provided by the scene's opening word—"turning" (*epistrapheis*, from *epi-strephō*, a variant of *strephō*). It is a word which, in John's other uses of it, reflects a decision or change. It is used to describe Jesus' initial move towards the disciples (1:38), the Jews' possible turn towards conversion (12:40, quoting Isa 6:10), and Mary Magdalene's two turns, one negative (she turned backwards) and the other positive (20:14,16). The implication is that, whatever may be involved in the challenge to follow, Peter manages, in a way that he had not done before, to face in a new direction. This is particularly important since he was last seen as giving way to sadness and as facing the prospect of old age and death. Thus, like the recognition scene at sea (21:4–7), Peter's turning has echoes of Mary Magdalene and her sadness.

A Vision of Abiding Love, Even beyond Death

As a result of this turning, the final picture is not of Peter facing a hard truth about growing old and following to death, but, having done that, of his glimpsing a picture of intimate love and of his realizing, however unclearly, that this love transcends death.

The transcending of death is implied in the fact that, even if the disciple dies, the abiding is to continue until Jesus comes. Thus the abiding, the spiritual union, lasts through death and beyond.

It is not clear from the text whether one is to understand that the beloved disciple has, in fact, died, and scholarly opinion on the matter is divided (cf. Brown, 1118–20; Schnackenburg, 3:368–71). The idea that the beloved had already died is to some degree implied, and since there were people who misunderstood Jesus to say that the disciple would not die, it makes sense, particularly if he had actually died, to emphasize that they had misunderstood.

But even if he were alive, it would still make sense to counter the misunderstanding. The countering of misunderstanding is one of the basic processes in the gospel. Furthermore, by alluding to a mistaken idea, common apparently in the early church, of staying alive until the Parousia, it manages to integrate and correct that idea. (It does not exclude a future coming, but it gives it time and integrates it with Jesus' realized presence.) And the simple fact of referring to the death of the beloved disciple—whether or not it had happened—has an immense appropriateness: it helps to bring the story to a fitting close. There was ample motivation, therefore, even if the beloved was still alive, for speaking of his death. And so it is not possible to conclude whether he had actually died.

As with many ambiguities in John's text, it seems best not to insist on an either/or approach. It is true, of course, that once one tries to reconstruct a historical background, then one must indeed try to decide whether the beloved disciple was dead. But the ambiguity may have a positive purpose. It is precisely because the text fails to answer the question satisfactorily that it succeeds in doing something else: it causes the puzzled reader to move over and back between regarding the disciple as alive and regarding him as dead, in other words between visualizing a situation before death and visualizing one after death. Thus at one level— that of the object of mental concentration—it causes a movement and continuity between pre-death and post-death. And this inner movement of the object of the human mind or spirit provides a form of intimation that the Spirit itself also can bridge the divide between life and death.

A Promise Which is Unspeakable

Peter's question concerning the beloved evokes from Jesus a counterquestion concerning Peter himself:

Peter: "Lord, *for him what?*"
Jesus: "If I will that he abide . . . *what to you?* You follow me."

At one level Peter is encountering a form of refusal; he is being told that he should forget the figure of abiding love and should concentrate rather on the task at hand. But at another level, Peter receives a veiled promise. Jesus' reply, even in refusing, maintains continuity with Peter's question (". . . for him what?" "What to you?"), and its "what to you" suggests, at one level, that the "what" is for Peter, that what he associates with the beloved is not to be forgotten. The effect is heightened by the fact that on the only other occasion in John when Jesus gave such a reply (2:4, literally, ". . . what to me and to you?") his apparent refusal was followed, when the time came, with a gift of abundant wedding wine. The two images—of wedding wine and of the beloved reclining—complement each other, and together they develop the gospel's initial picture of the only begotten who is in the Father's bosom (1:18). Thus, despite the sense of refusal, of having to wait, Peter's situation suggests a promise of further union.

But this further dimension is not easy to grasp, and it is significant that the final verse of the scene (v 23) is surrounded by misunderstanding and a further straining of language. The misunderstanding of language is found in the brothers who take Jesus' promise in a material sense. The straining of language is found in the repeated phrase, "If I will that he abide until I come [what (is that) to you?]" Most manuscripts include the "what to you?" (*ti pros se*), but some do not, and it is this shorter reading which, because it is more difficult, seems more probable. Thus Jesus' final words are brief and enigmatic: "If I will that he abide until I come."

Incidentally, this shorter version gives a dovetailing of final syllables—the *mai* of *erchomai* ("come," v 23) with *moi* ("me," v 19)—a detail which seems significant in view of the dovetailing of final syllables which is found in vv 1–14 (*ichthu-ōn, ichthu-ōn, nekr-ōn*, vv 6, 8, 14).

In any case, the shorter version, despite its difficulty, has meaning. The "I will" (*thelō*), repeated from v 22, balances the "where you do not will," which applied to Peter's old age (v 18), and it echoes the climactic and sovereign "I will,'' which concludes the last discourse (17:24, "Father . . . I will that where I am . . .''). Thus it shows Jesus as speaking with full divine authority, and it absorbs Peter's reluctance, his will, into the design of a will which is greater. What Jesus speaks of is an abiding which is indefinite. This abiding "until I come'' stretches into the future and thus it balances, in various ways, the union which existed in the beginning (1:1). If this scene, concerning abiding union, is mind-bending, that is appropriate; so was the original promise of an (eternal) abode (14:1–3). And if it begins with a glaringly unfulfilled "if" ("If I will . . .'') that too is appropriate: it shows that, in wrestling with this grammar-breaking phrase, the expectation of the reader, like that of Peter, has to surrender to a design which surpasses human thought.

[21:24–25] Witnessing and writing as sources of faith-related knowledge. To some degree these closing verses are a repetition and synthesis of the earlier conclusions—particularly of the emphasis on witness in 19:35 and of the emphasis on writing and signs in 20:30–31. (They also reflect 1:34.) As such they summarize the evidence (witness, including writing, and signs) which support the gospel message, and they form an appropriate conclusion both of chap. 21 and of the gospel as a whole.

But they also break new ground. In a variation on the technique of the movie camera which, at the end, withdraws and allows the viewer to see a much larger scene (cf. 20:18), the person who wrote the gospel now provides a view of how the gospel originated, how it was received, and how it was recorded.

The fact that this view is provided does not necessarily mean that it is historical. That is a distinct issue and an important one, but it is one which, on the basis of this text alone, is impossible to answer, and its introduction here tends to obscure the one thing that is reasonably clear—the given view of the gospel's origin.

According to this view the real inspiration behind the gospel is the beloved disciple; it is from him that the witness and the writing come. This need not mean that he physically wrote the gospel. The implication, rather, is that his witness and influence led someone else to write it—as Pilate apparently had others scourge Jesus (19:1) and had others write the inscription (19:19) (cf. Beasley-Murray, 415). There seems to be uncertainty as to how to describe his role—whether as implied author (Culpepper, 1983, 47) or as narrator (Staley, 1988, 115)—but the basic idea is clear: he is the one who was close to the action, who understood it better than anyone else, and who then bore witness to it and saw that it was brought into writing.

In doing this, the beloved was not alone. As Culpepper indicates (1975, 266–70; 1983, 122–23), and as an analysis of 19:35 suggests, the role of the beloved disciple reflects the presence of the Spirit. Even in the scene involving the first unnamed disciples (1:35–39)—the scene in which some see the first appearance of the beloved disciple—there is an implied presence of the Spirit (see comment on 1:35–39). Hence ultimately the book goes back to the Spirit.

This concluding view also provides a glimpse of those who received the gospel —the ''we'' who know that the witness is true. ''True'' here is used ''to designate the content of the revelation in Christ'' (Kysar, 321). The ''we'' balances the ''us'' and ''we'' of the prologue (1:14, 16), and it suggests the entire body of the believers, all those who have come to know the deep truth of the beloved's message.

Finally, there is the ''I suppose'' (v 25)—a detail that gives the impression of an individual who did the actual writing. The implication is that this writer, having both received the inspiration of the beloved disciple and having shared fully in the experience and knowledge of the believers, then set the message in writing.

Such is the picture of the gospel's origin—an inspired witness, a receptive audience, and an unpretentious writer. It is a unified picture and does not require the intervention of an editor, not even for the last verse. The last verse is necessary to chapter 21, for it is through the introduction of the character of the individual writer that the text maintains the ambiguity about whether the beloved disciple has died. Furthermore, from a literary point of view, the introduction of this new character is quite appropriate. In the words of Uspensky (1973, 147): ''It is typical for some narratives that a first-person narrator who did not appear earlier in the story suddenly appears at the end.''

Thus from first verse to last, the gospel may be seen as the unified work of a single writer. And this unity is strengthened by the concluding detail—by the idea that if Jesus' deeds were written down the world could not contain all the books. It is in some ways a strange detail, a variation apparently on the ancient literary custom of hyperbole. But even here the evangelist uses literary convention for his own purposes. The world-surpassing nature of Jesus' works complements the mind-surpassing nature of Jesus' final promise to Peter (21:20–23), and insofar as it speaks of books gathered into one, into a unity which surpasses the world, it provides a balance to the world-surpassing Word with which the gospel began (1:1–3).

Abbreviations

AB	*Anchor Bible*
AbBib	*Analecta Biblica*
ACNT	*Augsburg Commentary on the New Testament*
ANRW	*Aufstieg und Niedergang der Römischen Welt*
BETL	*Bibliotheca ephemeridum theologicarum lovaniensium*
Bib	*Biblica*
BKNT	*Biblischer Komkmentar: Neues Testament*
BTB	*Biblical Theology Bulletin*
BZ	*Biblische Zeitschrift*
BZNW	*Beilhefte zur Zeitschrift für die neutestamentliche Wissenschaft*
CBA	*Catholic Biblical Association*
CBQ	*Catholic Biblical Quarterly*
De Jonge	M. de Jonge, éd. *L'évangile de Jean: Sources, rédaction, théologie.* BETL 44. Leuven: Leuven University, 1977.
EBib	*Enchiridion Biblicum*
EH	*Exegetisches Handbuch*
HUCA	*Hebrew Union College Annual*
ICC	*International Critical Commentary*
IDB	*Interpreter's Dictionary of the Bible*
Int	*Interpretation*
JB	Jerusalem Bible
JBC	Ed. by R. E. Brown *et al.* Englewood Cliffs, N.J.: Prentice Hall, 1968. *The Jerome Biblical Commentary.*
JBL	*Journal of Biblical Literature*
JSNT	*Journal for the Study of the New Testament*
KJV	King James Version
LavTheolPhil	*Laval Théologique et Philosophique*
LumVie	*Lumière et Vie*
LXX	The Greek Old Testament (''the Septuagint'').
MelSciRel	*Mélanges de science religieuse*
NAB	New American Bible
NEB	New English Bible
NCeB	New Century Bible

NDT	*Das Neue Testament Deutsch*
NJBC	*New Jerome Biblical Commentary.* Ed. by R. E. Brown *et al.* Englewood Cliffs, N.J.: Prentice Hall, 1990.
NovT	*Novum Testamentum*
NovTSup	*Novum Testamentum, Supplements*
NTAbh	*Neutestamentliche Abhandlungen*
NTS	*New Testament Studies*
ÖTKNT	*Ökumenischer Taschenbuch Kommentar zum Neuen Testament*
PMLA	*Publications of the Modern Language Association of America*
RA	*Religions in Antiquity.* J. Neusner, ed. *See* Neusner (in bibliography)
RAC	*Reallexicon für Antike und Christentum*
RB	*Revue Biblique*
RevExp	*Review and Expositor*
RHPR	*Revue d'histoire et de philosophie réligieuse*
RNT	*Regensburger Neues Testament*
RSV	Revised Standard Version
SBLASP	*Society of Biblical Literature Abstracts and Seminar Papers*
SBLDS	*Society of Biblical Literature Disseration Series*
ScEs	*Science et esprit*
SE	*Studia Evangelica*
StrB	[H. Strack and] P. Billerbeck, *Kommentar zum Neuen Testament aus Talmud und Midrasch*
SUNT	*Studien zur Umwelt des Neuen Testament*
SvenskExegArs	Svensk Exegetisk Arsbok
TR	*Theologische Rundschau*
TS	*Theological Studies*
UBSGNT	United Bible Societies *Greek New Testament*
WMANT	*Wissenschaftliche Monographien zum Alten und Neuen Testment*
WUNT	*Wissenschaftliche Untersuchungen zum Neuen Testament*
ZAW	*Zeitschrift für die alttestamentliche Wissenschaft*
ZNW	*Zeitschrift fur die neutestamentliche Wissenschaft*

Bibliography

Commentaries (Cited by Author Only)

Barrett, C. K. *The Gospel According to St. John.* 2d ed. Philadelphia: Westminster, 1978.

Bauer, W. *Das Johannesevangelium.* 2d ed. Tübingen: Mohr (Siebeck), 1925.

Beasley-Murray, G. R. *John.* Word Biblical Commentary 36. Waco, Tex: Word Books, 1987.

Becker, J. *Das Evangelium nach Johannes.* ÖTKNT 4. 2 vols. Würzburg: Echter, 1979, 1981.

Belser, J. E. *Das Evangelium des Heiligen Johannes.* Freiburg: Herder, 1905.

Bernard, J. H. *A Critical and Exegetical Commentary on the Gospel According to St. John.* ICC. 2 vols. Edinburgh: T. & T. Clark, 1928.

Blank, J. *Das Evangelium nach Johannes.* Geistliche Schriftlesung. 4 vols. Düsseldorf: Patmos, 1977–81.

Brown, R. E. *The Gospel According to John.* AB. 2 vols. Garden City, N.Y.: Doubleday, 1966–71.

Bruce, F. F. *The Gospel of John.* Grand Rapids, Mich.: Eerdmans, 1983.

Bultmann, R. *The Gospel of John. A Commentary.* Philadelphia: Westminster, 1971. (German ed., 1941.)

Gnilka, J. *Johannesevangelium.* Neue Echter Bibel. Würzburg: Echter, 1983.

Haenchen, E. *A Commentary on the Gospel of John.* Hermeneia. 2 vols. Philadelphia: Fortress, 1984. (German ed., 1980.)

Hendriksen, W. *Exposition of the Gospel According to John.* 2 vols. Grand Rapids, Mich.: Baker, 1954.

Hoskyns, E. C. *The Fourth Gospel.* Ed. F. N. Davey. 2d ed. London: Faber and Faber, 1947.

Kysar, R. *John.* ACNT. Minneapolis, Minn.: Augsburg, 1986.

Lagrange, M.-J. *L'Evangile selon Saint Jean.* Paris: Gabalda, 1948.

Lightfoot, R. H. *St. John's Gospel.* Oxford: Clarendon, 1956.

Lindars, B. *The Gospel of John.* NCeB. Grand Rapids, Mich.: Eerdmans, 1972.

Loisy, A. *Le Quatrième Evangile.* 2d ed. Paris: E. Nourry, 1921.

Maier G. *Johannes-Evangelicum.* BKNT 6. Neuhausen-Stuttgart: Hänssler, 1984.

Marsh, J. *Saint John.* Baltimore, Md.: Penguin, 1968.

Mateos, J. and Barreto, J. *El Evangelio de Juan.* 2d ed. Madrid: Christiandad, 1982.

Morris, L. *The Gospel According to St. John.* Grand Rapids, Mich.: Eerdmans, 1971.

Porsch, F. *Johannes-Evangelium.* Stuttgarter Kleiner Kommentar—NT 4. Stuttgart: Katholisches Bibelwerk, 1988.

Sanders, J. N. *The Gospel According to Saint John.* Ed. B. A. Mastin. New York: Harper & Row, 1968.

Schnackenburg, R. *The Gospel According to St. John.* 3 vols. New York: Crossroads, 1968–82. (German ed., 1965–75.)

Schneider, J. *Das Evangelium nach Johannes.* NTD 4. Göttingen: Vandenhoeck & Ruprecht, 1972.

Schulz, S. *Das Evangelium nach Johannes.* Göttingen: Vandenhoeck & Ruprecht, 1972.

Strathmann, H. *Das Evangelium nach Johannes.* Göttingen: Vandenhoeck & Ruprecht, 1968.

Tillmann, F. *Das Johannesevangelium.* Bonn: Hanstein, 1931.

Wellhausen, J. *Das Evangelium Johannis.* Berlin: Reimer, 1908.

Westcott, B. F. *The Gospel According to St. John.* London: John Murray, 1882.

Wikenhauser, A. *Das Evangelium nach Johannes.* RNT. Regensburg: Pustet, 1961.

Zahn, T. *Das Evangelium des Johannes ausgelegt.* Leipzig: Deichert, 1921.

Bibliographies

Malatesta, E. 1967. *St. John's Gospel 1920–1965. A Cumulative and Classified Bibliography of Books and Periodical Literature on the Fourth Gospel.* Rome: Biblical Institute.

Van Belle, G. 1988. *Johannine Bibliography 1966–1985. A Cumulative Bibliography on the Fourth Gospel.* Leuven: Leuven University and Peeters.

Wagner, G. 1987. *An Exegetical Bibliography of the New Testament. John and 1, 2, 3 John.* Macon, Ga.: Mercer University.

Other Works

Alter, R. 1981. *The Art of Biblical Narrative.* New York: Basic Books.

—. 1984. "The Decline and Fall of Literary Criticism." *Commentary* 77:50–56.

—. 1985. *The Art of Biblical Poetry.* New York: Basic Books.

—. 1986. "Sodom as Nexus: The Web of Design in Biblical Narrative." *Tikkun* 1:30–38.

Anderson, B. W. 1982. "The Problem and Promise of Commentary." *Int* 36:341–55.

Aquinas, Thomas. 1980. *Commentary on the Gospel of Saint John. Part 1.* Trans. J. A. Weisheipl. Albany, N.Y.: Magi.

Armstrong, P. B. 1983. "The Conflict of Interpretations and the Limits of Pluralism." *PMLA* 98: 341–52.

Ashton, J. 1985. "The Identity and Function of the *Ioudaioi* in the Fourth Gospel." *NovT* 27:40–75.

Beardslee, W. A. 1970. *Literary Criticism of the New Testament.* Philadelphia: Fortress.

Becker, J. 1969. "Aufbau, Schichtung und theologiegeschichtliche Stellung des Gebetes in Johannes 17." *ZNW* 60:56–82.

—. 1970. "Die Abschiedsreden Jesu im Johannesevangelium." *ZNW* 61:215–46.

—. 1986. "Das Johannesevangelium im Streit der Methoden (1980–1984)." *TR* 51:1–78.

Becker, U. 1963. *Jesus und die Ehebrecherin. Untersuchungen zur Text- und Überlieferungsgeschichte von Joh 7:53–8:11.* BZNW 28. Berlin: Töpelmann.

Behler, G. M. 1960. *Les Paroles d'Adieux du Seigneur.* Paris: Cerf.

Bernard, J. 1979. "Témoignage pour Jesus-Christ. Jean 5:31–47." *MelSciRel* 36:3–55.

Betz, H. D. 1979. *Galatians: A Commentary on Paul's Letter to the Churches in Galatia.* Hermeneia. Philadelphia: Fortress.

Billerbeck. *See* Strack H. and Billerbeck.

Bodelsen, C. A. 1966. *T. S. Eliot's Four Quartets. A Commentary.* 2d ed. Copenhagen: Rosenkilde & Bagger.

Bohlman, R. A. 1968. *Principles of Biblical Interpretation in the Lutheran Confessions.* St. Louis, Mo. and London: Concordia.

Boismard, M. E. 1956. *Du Baptême à Cana (Jean 1.19–2.11).* Paris: Cerf.

—. 1961. "L'Evolution du thème eschatologique dans les traditions johanniques." *RB* 68:507–24.

—. 1962. "Saint Luc et la rédaction du quatrième evangile (Jn, IV, 46–54)." *RB* 69:185–211.

—. 1988. *Moïse ou Jésus. Essai de christologie johannique.* BETL 84. Leuven: Leuven University and Peeters.

Boismard, M. E. and Lamouille A. 1977. *L'Evangile de Jean. Synopse des quatre évangiles.* Vol. 3. Paris: Cerf.

Booth, W. C. 1983. *The Rhetoric of Fiction.* 2d ed. Chicago and London: University of Chicago.

Borgen, P. 1965. *Bread From Heaven. NovTSup* 10. Leiden: Brill.

Borig, R. 1967. *Das Wahre Weinstock. Untersuchungen zu Joh 15, 1–10.* SUNT 16. München: Kosel.

Bornkamm, G. 1956. "Die eucharistische Rede im Johannes-Evangelium." *ZNW* 47:161–69.

Braun, F. M. 1955. "Hermetisme et Johannisme." *RevThom* 55:22–42, 259–299.

—. 1964. *Jean le théologien.* Paris: Gabalda.

Brodie, T. L. 1993. *The Quest for the Origin of John's Gospel. A Source-Oriented Approach.* New York and Oxford: Oxford University.

Brooks, C. 1974. "New Criticism." *Princeton Encyclopedia of Poetry and Poetics.* Ed. A. Preminger. Princeton: Princeton University, 567–68.

Brown, R. E. 1977. *The Birth of the Messiah. A Commentary on the Infancy Narratives in Matthew and Luke.* Garden City, N.Y.: Doubleday.

—. 1979. *The Community of the Beloved Disciple.* New York: Paulist.

—. 1990. "Hermeneutics." *NJBC* 71.

Bühner, J.-H. 1977. *Der Gesandte und sein Weg im 4. Evangelium.* WUNT 2/2. Tübingen: Mohr.

Bultmann, R. 1955. *Theology of the New Testament.* Vol. 2. London: SCM.

—. 1957. *Die Geschichte der synoptischen Tradition.* Göttingen: Vandenhoeck & Ruprecht.

—. 1963. *History of the Synoptic Tradition.* New York: Harper & Row.

Burkitt, F. C. 1928. "The Mandaeans." *JTS* 29:225–237.

Cahill, P. J. 1983. Review of Y. Simoens, *La Gloire d'aimer. CBQ* 45:709–11.

Chatman, S. 1978. *Story and Discourse. Narrative Structure in Fiction and Film.* Ithaca, N.Y. and London: Cornell University.

Childs, B. S. 1974. *The Book of Exodus. A Critical Theological Commentary.* Philadelphia: Westminster.

—. 1979. *Introduction to the Old Testament as Scripture.* Philadelphia: Fortress.

—. 1985. *The New Testament as Canon.* Philadelphia: Fortress.

Chouraqui, A. 1975. "Une traduction de la Bible." *Etudes* 343:447–62.

Clavier, H. 1959. "L'ironie dans le quatrieme evangile." *SE* 1:261–76.

Clines, D. J. A. 1980. "Story and Poem: The Old Testament as Literature and as Scripture." *Int* 34:115–27.

Collingwood, R. G. 1946. *The Idea of History.* New York: Oxford University.

Conzelmann, H. 1960. *The Theology of St. Luke.* New York: Harper & Row.

Cortès, E. 1976. *Los discursos de adiós de Gn 49 a Jn 13–17: Pistas para la historia de un génera literario en la antigua literatura judía.* Colectanea San Paciano 23. Barcelona: Herder.

Countryman, L. W. 1987. *The Mystical Way in the Fourth Gospel. Crossing over into God.* Philadelphia: Fortress.

Crossan, J. D. 1983. "It is Written: A Structuralist Analysis of John 6." *Semeia* 26:3–21.

Culbertson, D. 1983. "Dante, the Yahwist, and the Sins of Sodom." *Italian Culture* 4:11–23.

—. 1989a. *The Poetics of Revelation. Recognition and the Narrative Tradition.* Studies in American Biblical Hermeneutics 4. Macon, Ga.: Mercer University.

—. 1989b. "Are You Also Deceived? Reforming the Reader in John 7." *Proceedings. Eastern Great Lakes and Midwest Biblical Societies* 9:148–60.

Culler, J. D. 1975. *Structuralist Poetics: Structuralism, Linguistics and the Study of Literature.* Ithaca, N.Y.: Cornell University.

Cullmann, O. 1953. *Early Christian Worship.* SBT 10. London: SCM.

Culpepper, R. A. 1975. *The Johannine School: An Evaluation of the Johannine-School Hypothesis Based on an Investigation of the Nature of Ancient Schools.* SBLDS 26, Missoula, MT: Scholars.

—. 1981. "The Pivot of John's Prologue." *NTS* 27:1–31.

—. 1983. *Anatomy of the Fourth Gospel.* Philadelphia: Fortress.

—. 1988. "The Theology of the Gospel of John." *RevExp* 85:417–32.

Dahl, N. 1975. "The Neglected Factor in New Testament Theology." *Reflection* 73:5–8.

Daube, D. 1956. *The New Testament and Rabbinic Judaism.* London: Athlone.

Dauer, A. 1972. *Die Passionsgeschichte im Johannesevangelium. Eine traditionsgeschichtliche und theologische Untersuchung zu Joh 18:1–19:30.* München: Kösel.

De Guilbert, J. 1954. *The Theology of the Spiritual Life.* New York and London: Sheed & Ward.

De Jonge, M., ed. 1977. *L'Evangile de Jean. Sources, rédaction, théologie.* BETL 44. Leuven: Leuven University, and Gembloux: J. Duculot.

De la Potterie, I. 1977. *La Vérite dans Saint Jean* AnBib 73. 2 vols. Rome: Biblical Institute.

—. 1984. "Structure du Prologue de Saint Jean." *NTS* 30: 354–81.

—. 1986. *La passion de Jésus selon l'évangile de Jean. Texte et Esprit.* Lire la Bible 73. Paris: Cerf.

De Vaux, R. 1965 *Ancient Israel. Its Life and Institutions.* 2d ed. London: Darton, Longman & Todd.

Dodd, C. H. 1953. *The Interpretation of the Fourth Gospel.* Cambridge: Cambridge University.

—. 1957. "A l'arrière-plan d'un dialogue Johannique." *RHPR* 37:5–17.

—. 1963. *Historical Tradition in the Fourth Gospel.* Cambridge: Cambridge University.

Duke, P. D. 1985. *Irony in the Fourth Gospel.* Atlanta, Ga.: John Knox Press.

Eckhart, Meister. 1981. *Meister Eckhart. The Essential Sermons, Commentaries, Treatises and Defense.* Trans. E. Colledge and B. McGinn. New York, Ramsey, N.J., and Toronto: Paulist.

Eliade, M. 1959. *The Sacred and the Profane. The Nature of Religion.* New York: Harcourt, Brace & World.

Eliot, T. S. 1957. *On Poetry and Poets.* London and Boston: Faber and Faber.

Ellis, P. F. 1974. *Matthew: His Mind and His Message.* Collegeville, Minn.: Liturgical.

—. 1984. *The Genius of John. A Compositional-Critical Commentary on the Fourth Gospel.* Collegeville, MN: Liturgical.

Eriugena. *See* O'Meara

Farley, M. 1986. *Personal Commitments*. New York: Harper & Row.

Feeder, L. 1955. "Marlow's Descent Into Hell." *Nineteenth-Century Fiction* 9:280–92. (Reprinted in R. Kimbrough, ed. *Joseph Conrad. Heart of Darkness*. New York: Norton, 1963, 1981–88.)

Festugière, A. J. 1974. *Observations Stylistiques sur L'Evangile de S. Jean*. Etudes et Commentaires 84. Paris: Klincksieck.

Fischel, H. A. 1973. "The Uses of Sorites (*Climax, Gradatio*) in the Tannaitic Period." *HUCA* 44:119–51.

Fischer, G. 1973. *Die himmlischen Wohnungen Untersuchungen zu Joh 14, 2f*. EH 23/38. Bern: Lang.

Fishbane, M. 1985. *Biblical Interpretation in Ancient Israel*. New York and Oxford: Oxford University.

Fitzmyer, J. A. 1981. *The Gospel According to Luke I–IX*. AB 28. Garden City, N.Y.: Doubleday.

Forestell, J. T. 1974. *The Word of the Cross. Salvation as Revelation in the Fourth Gospel*. AnBib 57. Rome: Biblical Institute.

Fortna, R. T. 1988. *The Fourth Gospel and its Predecessor. From Narrative Source to Present Gospel*. Philadelphia: Fortress.

Frei, H. W. 1974. *The Eclipse of Biblical Narrative. A Study in Eighteenth- and Nineteenth-Century Hermeneutics*. New Haven, Conn. and London: Yale University.

Freund, E. 1987. *The Return of the Reader*. London and New York: Methuen.

Froehlich, K., ed. 1985. *Biblical Interpretation in the Early Church*. Sources of Early Christian Thought. Philadelphia: Fortress.

Frye, N. 1971. *Anatomy of Criticism. Four Essays*. Princeton: Princeton University.

—. 1981. *The Great Code. The Bible and Literature*. New York and London: Harcourt Brace Jovanovich.

Gardiner, P. J. 1959. *Theories of History*. New York: Macmillan.

Giblet, J. 1977. "Dévelopements dans la théologie johannique. In De Jonge, 1977, 45–72.

Giblin, C. H. 1984. "Confrontations in John 18,1–27." *Bib* 65: 210–32.

—. 1985. "Two Complementary Literary Structures in John 1:1–18" *JBL* 104:87–103.

—. 1986. "John's Narration of the Hearing Before Pilate (John 18:28–19:16a)." *Bib* 67:221–39.

—. 1990. "The Tripartite Literary Structure of John's Gospel.: Paper read at CBA annual meeting, Notre Dame, Ind., Aug. 1990.

Goulder, M. 1985. "A House Built on Sand." *Alternative Approaches to NT Study*. Ed. A. E. Harvey. London: SPCK, 1–24.

Granskou, D. 1985. *Irony* (unpub.).

Grant, R. M. 1963. *A Short History of the Interpretation of the Bible*. Rev. ed. New York: Macmillan.

Gros Louis, K. R. R. 1982. *Literary Interpretations of Biblical Narratives II*. Nashville, Tenn.: Abingdon.

Grossouw, W. 1966. "A Note on John XIII 1–3." *NT* 8:124–31.

Guerard, A. J. 1950. "Introduction" to *Heart of Darkness and The Secret Sharer. Two Novellas by Joseph Conrad*. New York: New American Library and Doubleday, 7–15.

Habel, N. 1965. "The Form and Significance of the Call Narrative." *ZAW* 77:297–323.

Harrington, D. J. 1980. "Sociological Concepts and the Early Church: A Decade of Research," *TS* 41:181–90.

—. 1990. *John's Thought and Theology. An Introduction*. Wilmington, Del.: Glazier.

Hegel. *See* Wallace.

Hengel, M. 1974. *Judaism and Hellenism.* Philadelphia: Fortress.

Henry, P. 1979. *New Directions in New Testament Study.* Philadelphia: Westminster.

Hirsch, E. 1936. *Das vierte Evangelium.* Tübingen: Mohr-Siebeck.

Holleran, J. W. 1990. "Seeing the Light. A Narrative Reading of John 9." Paper read at the CBA annual meeting, Notre Dame, Ind., Aug. 1990.

Holmberg, B. 1990. *Sociology and the New Testament. An Appraisal.* Philadelphia: Fortress.

Holzmeister U. 1940. "Nathanael Fuitne idem ac S. Bartholomaeus Apostolus?" *Bib* 21:28–39.

Howard, W. F. 1955. *The Fourth Gospel in Recent Criticism and Interpretation.* London: Epworth.

Iser, W. 1974. *The Implied Reader: Patterns of Communication in Prose Fiction from Bunyan to Beckett.* Baltimore, Md.: Johns Hopkins University.

—. 1978. *The Act of Reading. A Theory of Aesthetic Response.* Baltimore, Md.: Johns Hopkins University.

Jefferson, A. 1982. "Russian Formalism." *Modern Literary Theory. A Comparative Introduction.* Eds. A. Jefferson and D. Robey. Totowa, N.J.: Barnes & Noble, 16–37.

Johnson, E. C. 1983. *In Search of God in the Sexual Underworld. A Mystical Journey.* New York: Quill.

Johnston, R. E. C. 1977. *From an Author-Oriented to a Text-Oriented Hermeneutic: Implications of Paul Ricoeur's Hermenentical Theory for the Interpretation of the New Testament.* Leuven: Leuven University, dissertation.

Johnston, W. 1974. *Silent Music. The Science of Meditation.* London: Collins.

—. 1978. *The Inner Eye of Love. Mysticism and Transformation.* London: Collins.

—. 1981. *The Mirror Mind. Spirituality and Transformation.* London: Collins.

—. 1984. *The Wounded Stag.* London: Collins.

Käsemann, E. 1968. *The Last Testament of Jesus.* Philadelphia: Fortress.

Kawin, B. F. 1972. *Telling It Again and Again; Repetition in Literature and Film.* Ithaca, N.Y.: Cornell University.

Kee, H. C. 1989. *Knowing the Truth. A Sociological Approach to New Testament Interpretation.* Minneapolis, Minn.: Fortress.

Keegan, T. J. 1982. "Introductory Formulae for Matthean Discourses." *CBQ* 44:415–30.

Kelber, W. 1974. *The Kingdom in Mark. A New Place and a New Time.* Philadelphia: Fortress.

—. 1983. *The Oral and Written Gospel. The Hermenentics of Speaking and Writing in the Synoptic Tradition, Mark, Paul and Q.* Philadelphia: Fortress.

Kennedy, G. A. 1984. *New Testament Interpretation through Rhetorical Criticism.* Chapel Hill, N.C. and London: University of North Carolina.

Kermode, F. 1979. *The Genesis of Secrecy. On the Interpretation of Narrative.* Cambridge, MA. and London: Harvard University.

Kieffer, R. 1984. "Rum och tid; johannesevengeliets theologiska struktur [Space and Time in the Theological Structure of the Gospel of John]." *SvenskExegArs* 49:109–125. (French trans. in *NTS* 31(1985): 393–409.)

Kikawada, I. M. 1985. *Before Abraham Was. The Unity of Genesis 1–11.* Nashville, Tenn.: Abingdon.

Kimbrough, R., (ed.) 1971, *Joseph Conrad. Heart of Darkness.* Revised ed. New York: Norton.

Krentz, E. 1975. *The Historical-Critical Method.* Philadelphia: Fortress.

Krieger, M. 1964. *A Window to Criticism.* Princeton: Princeton University.

Kurz, W. 1980. "Hellenistic Rhetoric in the Christological Proof of Luke-Acts." *CBQ* 42:171–95.

Kysar, R. 1984. *John's Story of Jesus*. Philadelphia: Fortress.

—. 1985. "The Fourth Gospel. A Report on Recent Research." *ANRW* 2 (25.3): 2391–480.

Lacan, M.-Fr. 1957. "Le Prologue de saint Jean. Ses thèmes, sa structure, son movement." *LumVie* 33:91–110.

Lacomara, A. 1974. "Deuteronomy and the Farewell Discourse." *CBQ* 36:65–84.

Lamouille, A. 1982. Review of Y. Simoens, *La Gloire d'aimer*. *RB* 89:627–29.

Laurentin, R. 1957 *Structure et Théologie de Luc I-II*. EBib. Paris: Gabalda.

Leitch, V. 1983. *Deconstructive Criticism. An Advanced Introduction*. New York: Columbia University.

Lenglet, A. 1985. "Jésus de passage parmi les Samaritains. Jn 4,4–42." *Bib* 66:493–503.

L'Heureux, C. E. 1986. *Life Journey and the Old Testament*. New York and Mahwah, N.J.: Paulist.

McGann, D. 1988. *Journeying within Transcendence. The Gospel of John through a Jungian Perspective*. New York and Mahwah, N.J.: Paulist.

McKenzie, J. L. 1968. *Dictionary of the Bible*. London: Chapman.

McKenzie, R. A. F. 1968. "Job," *JBC* 31.

MacRae, G. W. 1970. "The Fourth Gospel and Religionsgeschichte." *CBQ* 32:17–24.

—. 1973. "Theology and Irony in the Fourth Gospel." *The Word in the World: Essays in Honor of Frederick L. Moriarty*. Eds. R. J. Clifford and G. W. MacRae. Cambridge, Mass.: Weston College, 83–96.

Malina, B. J. 1981. *The New Testament World. Insights from Cultural Anthropology*. Atlanta, Ga.: John Knox Press.

Manuel, F. E. 1965. *Shapes of Philosophical History*. Stanford, Calif.: Stanford University.

Martyn. J. L. 1968. *History and Theology in the Fourth Gospel*. Nashville, Tenn.: Abingdon. (2nd ed. 1979).

—. 1978. *The Gospel of John in Christian History*. New York, Ramsey, N.J., and Toronto: Paulist.

May, G. 1977. *Simply Sane*. New York: Paulist.

Mayo, S. M. 1982. *The Relevance of the Old Testament for the Christian Faith*. Lanham, Md., New York, and London: University Press of America.

Meeks, W. 1966. "Galilee and Judea in the Fourth Gospel." *JBL* 85:159–69.

—. 1972. "The Man from Heaven in Johannine Sectarianism." *JBL* 91:44–72.

Miles, J. A. 1981. "Radical Editing . . . and . . . Willed Confusion," *Traditions in Transformation*. Ed. B. Halpern and J. D. Levenson. Winona Lake, Ind.: Eisenbrauns, 9–31.

Minear, P. S. 1976. *To Heal and to Reveal. The Prophetic Vocation According to Luke*. New York: Seabury.

—. 1983. "The Original Function of John 21." *JBL* 102:85–98.

Mitchell, W. J. T., ed. 1985. *Against Theory. Literary Studies and the New Pragmatism*. Chicago and London: University of Chicago.

Mlakuzhyil, G. 1987. *The Christocentric Literary Structure of the Fourth Gospel*. AnBib 117. Rome: Biblical Institute.

Mollat, D. 1960. *L'Evangile et les Epitres de Saint Jean*. 2d ed. La Sainte Bible. Paris: Cerf.

Moore, S. D. 1988. "Stories of Reading: Doing Gospel Criticism As/With a Reader." *SBLASP* 27. Ed. D. J. Lull. Atlanta, Ga.: Scholars, 141–59.

—. 1989. *Literary Criticism and the Gospels. The Theoretical Challenge.* New Haven, Conn. and London: Yale University.

Murray, P. 1991a. *The Absent Fountain.* Dublin: Dedalus.

—. 1991b. *T. S. Eliot and Mysticism. The Secret History of Four Quartets.* London: Macmillan.

Neyrey, J. 1988. *An Ideology of Revolt. John's Christology in Social Science Perspective.* Philadelphia: Fortress.

Nicholson, G. C. 1983. *Death as Departure. The Johannine Descent-Asecnt Schema.* SLBDS 63. Chico, Calif.: Scholars.

Noack, B. 1954. *Zur johanneischen Tradition. Beiträge zur Kritik an der Literarkritischen Analyse des vierten Evangeliums.* Copenhagen: Rosenkilde.

Norris, C. 1982. *Deconstruction: Theory and Practice.* London and New York: Methuen.

O'Day, G. R. 1986. *Revelation in the Fourth Gospel. Narrative Mode and Theological Claim.* Philadelphia: Fortress.

O'Donoghue, N. D. 1986. "The Celebration of Death". *Furrow* 37:358–70.

Okure, T. 1988. *The Johannine Approach to Mission. A Contextual Study of John 4:1–42.* WUNT 2,31. Tübingen: J. C. B. Mohr.

O'Meara, J. J. 1988. *Eriugena.* New York and Oxford: Oxford University.

Ong, W. J. 1971. *Rhetoric, Romance and Technology.* Ithaca, N.Y. and London: Cornell University.

—. 1977. *Interfaces of the Word. Studies in the Evolution of Consciousness and Culture.* Ithaca, N.Y.: Cornell University.

Osiek, C. 1984. *What Are They Saying about the Social Setting of the New Testament?* New York and Ramsey, N.J.: Paulist.

—. 1989. "The New Handmaid: The Bible and the Social Sciences." *TS* 50:260–78.

Painter, J. 1975. *John: Witness and Theologian.* London: SPCK.

Pazden, M. M. 1991. *The Son of Man: A Metaphor for Jesus in the Fourth Gospel.* Collegeville, Minn.: Liturgical.

Peck, M. S. 1978. *The Road Less Travelled.* New York: Simon & Schuster.

—. 1983. *People of the Lie: The Hope for Healing Human Evil.* New York and London: Simon & Schuster.

Peterson, N. R. 1978. *Literary Criticism for New Testament Critics.* Philadelphia: Fortress.

Quintilian *Institutio Oratoria.* Loeb, with trans. by H. E. Butler. Cambridge, MA: Harvard, 1960.

Ramaroson, L. 1976. "La structure du prologue de Jean." *ScEs* 28:281–96.

Ransom, J. C. 1941. *The New Criticism.* Norfolk, Conn.: New Directions.

Reese, J. M. 1983. *The Book of Wisdom, Song of Songs.* Wilmington, Del.: Glazier.

Rendtorff, R. 1985. *The Old Testament. An Introduction.* Philadelphia: Fortress.

Rensberger, D. 1988. *Johannine Faith and Liberating Community.* Philadelphia: Westminster.

Resseguie, J. L. 1982. "John 9: A Literary-Critical Analysis." *Literary Interpretations of Biblical Narratives II.* Ed. K. R. R. Gros Louis. Nashville, Tenn.: Abingdon, 295–320.

Richter, G. 1967. *Die Fusswaschung im Johannesevangelium. Geschichte ihrer Deutung.* Biblische Untersuchungen 1. Regensburg: Pustet.

—. 1975. "Präsentische und futurische Eschatologie im 4. Evangelium." *Gegenwart und Kommendes Reich.* Eds. P. Fiedler and D. Zeller. Stuttgart: Katholisches Bibelwerk, 117–52.

Rissi, M. 1983. "Der Aufbau des vierten Evangeliums." *NTS* 29:48–54.

Roberge, M. 1984. "La Composition de Jean 6,22–59 dans l'exégèse récente." *Lav-TheolPhil* 40:91–123.

Rosenblatt, M. E. 1988. "The Voice of the One Who Prays in John 17." *Scripture and Prayer*. Eds. C. Osiek and D. Senior. Wilmington, Del.: Glazier, 131–44.

Said, E. W. 1978. *Orientalism*. New York: Pantheon.

Sanders, J. 1984. *Canon and Community*. Guides to Biblical Scholarship. Philadelphia: Fortress.

Sarason, R. S. 1981. "Towards a New Agendum for the Study of Rabbinic Midrashic Literature." *Studies in Aggadah, Targum and Jewish Liturgy in Memory of Joseph Heinemann*. Eds. E. Fleischer and J. J. Peuchowski. Jerusalem: Magnes Press, 55–73.

Schnackenburg, R. 1973. "Strukturanalyse von Joh 17." *BZ* 17:67–78, 196–202.

—. 1977. "Johanneische forschung seit 1955." *L'Evangile de Jean. Sources rédaction, théologie*. In De Jonge, 1977, 19–44.

Schneiders, S. 1975. *The Johannine Resurrection Narrative. An Exegetical and Theological Study of John 20 as a Synthesis of Johannine Spirituality*. Rome: Gregorian University, dissertation.

—. 1981. "The Footwashing. An Experiment in Hermeneutics." *CBQ*. 43:76–92.

—. 1983. "The Face Veil: A Johannine Sign." *BTB* 13:94–97.

—. 1987. "Death in the Community of Eternal Life. History, Theology and Spirituality in John 11." *Int* 41:44–56.

Segovia, F. F. 1982. *Love Relationships in the Johannine Tradition*. SBLDS 58. Chico, Calif.: Scholars.

—. 1985. "The Structure, *Tendenz*, and *Sitz im Leben* of John 13:31–14:31." *JBL* 104:471–93.

Senior, D. 1984. "The Struggle to be Universal." *CBQ* 46:63–81.

Simoens, Y. 1981. *La Gloire d'aimer. Structures stylistiques et intérpretative dans la Discourse de la Cène (Jn 13–17)*. AnBib 90. Rome: Biblical Institute.

Smalley, B. 1964. *The Study of the Bible in the Middle Ages*. Notre Dame, Ind.: University of Notre Dame.

Smalley, S. S. 1974. "The Sign in John XXI." *NTS* 20:275–88.

Smith, D. M. 1982. "John and the Synoptics". *Bib* 63:102–113.

Spicq, C. 1957. *L'Epitre aux Hebreux*. 2d ed. Paris: Cerf.

Spong (Bishop), J. S. 1988. "Open letter to the Bishop of London." *The Independent*. London. July 26, 1988.

Staley, J. L. 1986 "The Structure of John's Prologue: Its Implications for the Gospel's Narrative Structure." *CBQ* 48:241–64.

—. 1988. *The Print's First Kiss: A Rhetorical Investigation of the Implied Reader in the Fourth Gospel*. SBLDS 82. Atlanta, Ga.: Scholars.

Standaert, B. H. M. 1978. *L'Evengile selon Marc. Composition et Genre Littéraire*. Brugge: Sint-Andreisabdij.

Stauffer, E. 1950. "Abschiedsreden." *RAC* 1:29–35.

Steiner, G. 1975. *After Babel: Aspects of Language and Translation*. New York and London: Oxford University.

—. 1989. *Real Presences*. Chicago: University of Chicago.

Sternberg, M. 1985. *The Poetics of Biblical Narrative. Ideological Literature and the Drama of Reading*. Bloomington, Ind.: Indiana University.

Stock, A. 1982. *Call to Discipleship. A Literary Study of Mark's Gospel*. Wilmington: Glazier.

Strack, H. and Billerbeck, P. 1922–61. *Kommentar zum Neuen Testament aus Talmud und Midrash.* 6 vols. Munich: Becksche.

Stuhlmueller, C. 1968. "The Gospel According to Luke." *JBC* 44

Swank, B. 1965. "Vom Werden der Kirche. Evangelium: Jo 13,1–15." *Donnerstag des Herrenmahles. Gründonnerstag.* Ed. Odo Haggenmuller. Stuttgart: Katholisches Bibelwerk, 38–48.

—. 1977. "Ephraim in Joh 11,54." In De Jonge, 1977, 377–83.

Tannehill, R. C. 1984. "The Composition of Acts 3–5: Narrative Development and Echo Effect." *Seminar Papers.* Ed. K. H. Richards. SBLASP 23. Chico, Calif.: Scholars, 217–40.

Teresa of Avila. 1961. *Interior Castle.* Ed. E. A. Peers. New York: Doubleday.

Thompson, M. 1988. *The Humanity of Jesus in the Fourth Gospel.* Philadelphia: Fortress.

Thüsing, W. 1960. *Die Erhöhung and Verherrlichung Jesu in Johannesevangelium.* NTAbh, 21/1–2. Münster: Aschendorff.

Thyen, H. 1971. "Johannes 13 und die 'kirchliche Redaktion' des vierten Evangeliums." *Tradition und Glaube.* Ed. G. Jeremias et al. Göttingen: Vandenhoeck & Ruprecht. 343–56.

Tompkins, J. P. 1980. "The Reader in History: The Changing Shape of Literary Response." *Reader-Response Criticism. From Formalism to Post-Structuralism.* Ed. J. P. Tompkins. Baltimore, Md. and London: Johns Hopkins University, 201–32.

Trever, J. C. 1962. "Palm Tree." *IDB* 3:646.

Trible, P. 1978. *God and the Rhetoric of Sexuality.* Philadelphia: Fortress.

Tucker, G. M. 1985. "Prophecy and the Prophetic Literature." *The Hebrew Bible and Its Modern Interpreters.* Ed. D. A. Knight and G. M. Tucker. Philadelphia: Fortress; and Chico, Calif.: Scholars, 325–68.

Uspensky, B. 1973. *A Poetics of Composition. The Structure of the Artistic Text and Typology of a Compositional Form.* Berkeley and Los Angeles: Univ. of California.

Van den Bussche, H. 1959. *Le Discours d'adieu de Jésus.* Tournai: Casterman.

Von Rad, G. 1972. *Wisdom in Israel.* London: SCM.

Von Wahlde, U. C. 1983. "*Wiederaufnahme* as a Marker of Redaction in Jn 6,51–58." *Bib* 64:542–94.

—. 1989. *The Earliest Version of John's Gospel. Recovering the Gospel of Signs.* Wilmington, Delaware: Michael Glazier.

Wallace, W. 1892. (translator) *The Logic of Hegel.* Translated from *The Encyclopedia of the Philosophical Sciences.* 2d ed. London: Oxford University.

Wead, D. W. 1974. "Johannine Irony as a Key to the Author-Audience Relationship in John's Gospel." *American Academy of Religion. Section on Biblical Literature: 1974.* Ed. Fred O. Francis. Missoula, Mont.: Scholars, 33–50.

Wellek, R. and Warren, A. 1977. *Theory of Literature.* 3d ed. New York and London: Harcourt Brace Jovanovich.

Westermann, C. 1984. *Genesis 1–11. A Commentary.* Minneapolis, Minn.: Augsburg.

Wiesel, E. 1987. "Why Should People Care?" *Explorations* 1(2):1,4.

Wilcox, S. C. 1960. "Conrad's 'Complicated Presentations' of Symbolic Imagery." *Philological Quarterly* 39:1–17. (Reprinted in R. Kimbrough, ed. *Joseph Conrad. Heart of Darkness.* New York: Norton, 1963, 189–95.)

Wilkens, W. 1958. *Die Entstehungsgeschichte des vierten Evangeliums.* Zollikon: Evangelischer.

William of St. Thierry. 1970. *Exposition on the Song of Songs.* In *The Works of William of St. Thierry.* Vol. 2. Cistercian Fathers 6. Spencer, Mass.: Cistercian.

Wilson, R. R. 1984. *Sochiological Approaches to the Old Testament*. Philadelphia: Fortress.

Wilson, J. 1981. ''The Integrity of John 3:22–36.'' *JSNT* 10:34–41.

Wink, W. 1973. *The Bible in Human Transformation: Toward a New Paradigm for Biblical Study*. Philadelphia: Fortress.

Woll, D. B. 1981 *Johannine Christianity in Conflict*. SBLDS 60. Chico, Calif.: Scholars.

Xenophon *Anabasis*. Leob, with trans. by C.L. Brownson. Cambridge, MA: Harvard, 1922.

Yee, G. 1989. *Jewish Feasts and the Gospel of John*. Wilmington, Delaware: Michael Glazier.

Index to Modern Authors

Subject Index